REFERENCE

Encyclopedia of Sleep and Dreams

Encyclopedia of Sleep and Dreams

THE EVOLUTION, FUNCTION, NATURE, AND MYSTERIES OF SLUMBER

VOLUME 2: M–Y

Deirdre Barrett and Patrick McNamara, Editors

GREENWOOD

AN IMPRINT OF ABC-CLIO, LLC
Santa Barbara, California • Denver, Colorado • Oxford, England

Library of Congress Cataloging-in-Publication Data

Encyclopedia of sleep and dreams : the evolution, function, nature, and mysteries of slumber / Deirdre Barrett and Patrick McNamara, editors.

   2 v.
  Includes bibliographical references and index.
  ISBN 978-0-313-38664-0 (alk. paper) — ISBN 978-0-313-38665-7 (e-ISBN)
  I. Barrett, Deirdre. II. McNamara, Patrick, 1956–
  [DNLM: 1. Sleep—Encyclopedias—English. 2. Dreams—Encyclopedias—English.
3. Sleep Disorders—Encyclopedias—English. WL 13]
  616.8'498003—dc23   2011045470

ISBN: 978-0-313-38664-0
EISBN: 978-0-313-38665-7

16 15 14 13 12   1 2 3 4 5

This book is also available on the World Wide Web as an eBook.
Visit www.abc-clio.com for details.

Greenwood
An Imprint of ABC-CLIO, LLC
ABC-CLIO, LLC
130 Cremona Drive, P.O. Box 1911
Santa Barbara, California 93116-1911

This book is printed on acid-free paper ∞

Manufactured in the United States of America

To Ina Livia McNamara on her fourth birthday

Contents

List of Entries

Guide to Related Topics

Many of the cross references that appear after the entries refer to the following topics and their related entries. For example, after the "Achuar" entry: **See also**: entries related to Cross-Cultural Dreams.

Animal Sleep

Comparative Sleep Regulation
Sleep and Bird Songs
Sleep in Aquatic Mammals
Sleep in Insects

Brain Stimulation

External Sensory Stimulation as a
    Technique to Study Dreaming
Use of Noninvasive Techniques in the
    Study of Dreaming

Comparative Sleep Databases

Comparative Sleep Databases
Phylogeny of Sleep Database

Consciousness and Dreams

Cognitive Expertise and Dreams
Consciousness in Dreams
Self-Consciousness and Dreaming

Cross-Cultural Dreams

Aboriginal Australia: Dreams and "the
    Dreaming"
Achuar
African American Dream Beliefs and
    Practices
Ancient Egypt and Dreams
Anthropology and Dreams
Asian Americans and Dreamwork
Bedouin Dream Traditions
Conceptions of Dreaming in the Western
    Desert of Australia
Co-Sleeping
Cross-Cultural Approaches to Dreams
Cultural Diversity and Dreaming
Native American Dreams
Quaker Culture and Dreams
Shamanism and Dreams
Significance of Dreams in Western
    Australian Desert Aboriginal
    Worldview
Traditional Korean Dreams

Dream Content

Animal Figures in Dreams
Central Image (of the Dream)
Characters in Dreams
Color in Dreams
Content Analysis of Dreams: Basic
    Principles
Counterfactuals in Dreams
Delusions and the Classification of
    Typical Dreams
Depictions of Dreams

Disconnection from the External Environment during Dreaming
REM Sleep across the Lifespan
Serotonin in the Regulation of REM Sleep
Sleep Intensity and the Homeostatic Regulation of Sleep

Sleep-Wake Continuum

Bizarre Imagery and Thought in Sleep and Waking
Logical Structure of Dreams and Their Relation to Reality
Subjective Experience across States of Sleep and Wakefulness

Social Psychology of Dreams

Church Dream Groups
Group Work with Dreams
Journaling of Dreams
Leading Dream Groups
Safety in Dream Groups
Social Network Analysis of Dream Content
Teaching Courses on Dreams
Television Consumption and Dreaming

Theories of Sleep

Activation Synthesis Hypothesis of Dreaming
Reverse Learning Theory

Meaning of Dreams via Dream Interpretation

One of the most practical, important, and valuable aspects of dreams is that people can draw meaning from their dreams via dream interpretation. It has been found that dream interpretation can aid in the process of insight (Pesant & Zadra, 2004), can provide a means to explore emotions (Goelitz, 2001), can help decrease psychological distress (Crook & Hill, 2003; Pesant & Zadra, 2004), help with feelings of isolation, lack of support, life transition issues, and provide effective coping strategies (De-Cicco, 2007a, 2007b, 2009; DeCicco & Higgins, 2009). Meaning and insights are gained with a variety of methods, which generally fall into one of two categories: (1) therapist-assisted methods of interpretation and (2) self-guided techniques.

Therapist-assisted techniques are used in therapy sessions or in groups with a therapist who guides or directs the technique. One such technique is a cognitive–experiential method designed by Dr. Clara Hill (Hill, 2003; Hill & O'Brien, 1999). The method is therapist assisted with three stages of interpretation: the exploration, insight, and action stages. A second very successful and widely used method is the Ullman method (Ullman & Zimmerman, 1979), which employs the use of a group setting to create safety while leading dreamers to discovery or insight.

This method has been found to be effective (DeCicco, 2007a) and leads dreamers to discovery through group work that could be otherwise difficult to establish on their own (Wolman & Ullman, 1986). A third example is the Gestalt method, which is one where dreamers are guided to fully integrate the dream material via engaging in the bodily feelings and actions of the dream (Pesant & Zadra, 2004). There are many therapist-assisted techniques for dream interpretation that are widely used around the world and have merit in various situations and environments.

Self-guided techniques (DeCicco, 2009) are first taught by a therapist or workshop leader with detailed instructions and are then carried out by dreamers on their own. Examples of these techniques are the storytelling method (TSM) of dream interpretation (DeCicco, 2007b, 2009), the dream interview method (DIM; Delaney, 1993), and meditative dream reentry (MDR; DeCicco, 2009). TSM provides dreamers with a worksheet that guides them from the dream, through associations, story-making, and finally, to the insight relating to waking life. The DIM is a contemporary method developed by Delaney (1993) and involves the dreamer as the interpreter and has been shown to be successful in practice (Flowers & Zweben, 1996). The third example, MDR, is one that combines relaxation training, guided imagery, and drawing therapy to aid in tapping into the deepest level of meaning of dreams—long-forgotten memories and emotional shifting. The method has been proven to be successful and is especially applicable for dreams with negative imagery or emotions (DeCicco, 2009). Self-guided dream-interpretation techniques are generally user friendly, practical, and scientifically proven to lead dreamers to insight or discovery. Furthermore, they can be used in a formal therapy environment along with other therapeutic techniques (e.g., cognitive-behavioral therapy).

Dream interpretation has been proven to be beneficial and effective in past research for those recovering from trauma, for nightmare treatment, for patients with depression and anxiety, for coping with cancer, for treating patients with addictions, with neurogenic communication disorders, issues of family attachment, and fear and loss (see, e.g., DeCicco, 2007a; Eigen, 2004; Mellman, David, Bustamante, Torres, & Fins, 2001). Various techniques have also been found useful for those caring for the dying, coping with stressful life events, and for aiding in the developmental process of fully becoming one's self (Wadensten, 2009). Lastly, dream interpretation has been found to be applicable for groups, couples, children, and adults. Current research continues to explore the value of finding meaning in dreams with various methods. This is an important component of dream interpretation as it ensures that the methods are reliable and valid. Furthermore, dream-interpretation methods are being translated and tested in various languages other than English to make them widely accessible around the world (e.g., TSM—Italian version, TSM—Spanish version).

Teresa L. DeCicco

References

Crook, R.E., & Hill, C.E. (2003). Working with dreams in psychotherapy: The therapists' perspective. *Dreaming, 13*(2), 83–96.

DeCicco, T.L. (2007a). Dreams of female university students: Content analysis and relationship to discovery via the Ullman method. *Dreaming, 17*(2), 98–112.

DeCicco, T.L. (2007b). What is the story telling? Examining discovery with the storytelling method (TSM) and testing with a control group. *Dreaming, 17,* 227–237.

DeCicco, T.L. (2009). *The giant compass: Navigating your life with your dreams.* North Carolina: Malito Press.

DeCicco, T.L., & Higgins, H. (2009). The dreams of recovering alcoholics: Mood, dream content, discovery, and the storytelling method of dream interpretation. *International Journal of Dream Research, 2*(2), 45–51.

Delaney, G. (1993). The dream interview. In G. Delaney (Ed.), *New directions in dream interpretation* (pp. 195–240). Albany: State University of New York Press.

Eigen, M. (2004). Alone with God. *Journal of Religion and Health*, 43(3), 185–200.

Flowers, L.K., & Zweben, J.E. (1996). The changing role of "using" dreams in addiction recovery. *Journal of Substance Abuse Treatment, 15,* 193–200.

Goelitz, A. (2001). Nurturing life with dreams: Therapeutic dream work with cancer patients. *Clinical Social Work Journal, 29*(4), 375–388.

Hill, C.E. (2003). *Working with dreams: Facilitating exploration, insight, and action.* Washington, DC: American Psychological Association.

Hill, C.E., & O'Brien, K. (1999). *Working with dreams in psychotherapy.* New York: Guilford Press.

Mellman, T.A., David, D., Bustamante, V., Torres, J., & Fins, A. (2001). Dreams in the acute aftermath of trauma and their relationship to PTSD. *International Society for Traumatic Stress Studies, 14*(1), 241–253.

Pesant, N., & Zadra, A. (2004). Working with dreams in therapy: What do we know and what should we do? *Clinical Psychology Review, 24,* 489–512.

Ullman, M., & Zimmerman, N. (1979). *Working with dreams.* New York: Dellacorte Press.

Wadensten, B. (2009). Older people's experience of dream coaching. *Journal of Holistic Nursing, 27*(4), 266–275.

Wolman, B., & Ullman, M. (1986). *Handbook of states of consciousness.* New York: Van Nostrand Reinhold Company.

Media Use and Nightmares

The greatest concern about the potential impact of the media on sleep is whether media use displaces sleep. Television viewing, computer game play, or listening to music—to name just those—are so appealing that they vie for young people's attention at the detriment of sleep time.

Even after the use of the media is abandoned and sleep finally prevails, the impact of the media on sleep does not end. Media use may affect sleep quality as media content may invade dreams.

Even though little research has been done about this subject, a number of conclusions can be drawn from existing studies. In one study, school children were exposed to television, to computer games, or to a movie shortly before bedtime. Even though a two- to three-hour cooling-off period was included, sleep was disturbed in the children who had been exposed to the media compared to a control group that had not been exposed (Dworak, Schierl, Bruns, & Strüder, 2007). This exposure experiment was very modest as the average young person is exposed to much more on a daily basis, often without any cooling-off period. The true impact of the excitement caused by media content in natural settings may therefore be much bigger.

Children are, however, not only exposed to average media content. Research by Joanne Cantor (1998) has shown that exposure to scary films and TV content may lead to enduring fright reactions, even for decades after exposure. The news, too, is a source of scary images. The events of September 11, 2001, for instance, have been shown to lead to posttraumatic stress disorders and to recurring nightmares in children exposed to news about the events (Propper, Stickgold, Keeley, & Christman, 2007).

A cross-sectional study of 2,500 Flemish children (Van den Bulck, 2004) showed that 33 percent of them had frequent nightmares about TV content. Nightmares about computer games were reported by 10 percent of the boys and 5 percent of the girls. These findings were not limited to the heavy users of the media—they occurred at all levels of media use.

Future research should study media-induced nightmares with more valid instruments than self-reports, which are prone to over- and underreporting. Charting of nightmares may reveal which types of content are most likely to lead to such reactions. Because some images produce trauma-like responses, it may be important to examine whether media nightmares need to be countered in a particular way.

Finally, it is important to note that the study of Flemish children quoted previously

(Van den Bulck, 2004) also showed that more than half of the children reported pleasant dreams induced by the various media. Coupled with research on the mood-enhancing properties of the media, this suggests that it is worth examining whether the processes leading to nightmares may also be employed to improve sleep.

Jan Van den Bulck

See also: Nightmares

References

Cantor, J. (1998). *"Mommy I'm scared": How TV and movies frighten children and what we can do to protect them.* San Diego, CA: Harcourt Brace & Company.

Dworak, M., Schierl, T., Bruns, T., & Strüder, H. K. (2007). Impact of singular excessive computer game and television exposure on sleep patterns and memory performance of school-aged children. *Pediatrics, 120,* 978–985.

Propper, R. E., Stickgold, R., Keeley, R., & Christman, S. D. (2007). Is television traumatic? Dreams, stress, and media exposure in the aftermath of September 11, 2001. *Psychological Science, 18,* 334–340.

Van den Bulck, J. (2004). Media use and dreaming: The relationship among television viewing, computer game play, and nightmares and pleasant dreams. *Dreaming, 14,* 43–49.

Media Use and Sleep in Children and Adolescents

During recent decades, accumulating researches reveal the importance of sleep on human-health being. In children and adolescents, sleep is considered particularly crucial for learning and memory, as well as having implications for physical growth, behavioral development, and emotional regulation. Specifically, insufficient sleep and poor sleep quality can result in a profound negative consequence in children and adolescents: first and above all, decreased concentration, impaired memory performance, and therefore poor academic performance, followed by increased aggression and behavioral problems, decreased reaction time and increased vulnerability to injury, and, according to more recent research, disordered energy regulation, and increased obesity.

While the evidence for the importance of sleep and an association between poor sleep and their negative consequences are becoming quite impressive, it is demonstrated that sleep duration among children and adolescents has decreased by approximately 1 hour over the past 10 years and 1.5 to 2 hours over the past 50 years. These findings trigger the heightened concern on the impacts of rapid social development and technology evolution on children's and adolescents' sleep behaviors.

According to the National Sleep Foundation's *2006 Sleep in America Poll* (2006), the majority of American school-aged children and almost all adolescents had at least one electronic media device, such as bedroom television, videogames, mobile telephone, computer, Internet access, and music player. Even in developing countries, with the ongoing economic development, media devices have become commonplace for children and adolescents in urban areas. An increasing number of studies consistently demonstrate that media use has become an influential factor in children's and adolescents' sleep. Among all of the previously mentioned media devices, television is the most popular and widely used. Therefore, our discussion will begin with television.

Television Viewing and Sleep

It was reported that 98 to 100 percent of children and adolescents watch television in developed countries, with the average viewing time ranging from 6.3 to 15.4 hours per week by different cultural backgrounds and different age groups.

There is a general and clear recognition that television viewing has a negative impact on children's and adolescents' sleep, although little consensus regarding which aspects of sleep may be related to television viewing has been achieved. The most consistent results seem to be shorter sleep duration, prolonged sleep-onset latency, and delayed bedtime. In addition, there is growing evidence that sleep disorders involving bedtime resistance, sleep anxiety, parasomnia, and less often sleep-disordered breathing are also related to television viewing. Interestingly, a study found that, similar to television viewing, passive television exposure during waking hours also had negative impacts on children's sleep, including decreased sleep duration and difficulties in initiating and maintaining sleep. In terms of television viewing during daytime, in the evening, or at bedtime, we must emphasize the hazards of television viewing in the evening, especially at bedtime.

Taken together, television viewing among children and adolescents should be restricted, especially at bedtime. In 2001, the American Academy of Pediatrics recommended that children watch no more than one to two hours of quality programming per day. Furthermore, consistent with common bedtime hygiene recommendations, television sets should be removed from children's bedrooms.

Video/Computer Game Playing and Sleep

Regarding video/computer game playing, their rapid popularity took place during the past two decades in line with the innovation and improvement of gaming technology. According to the National Sleep Foundation's *2006 Sleep in America Poll,* approximately half and one third of adolescents had their own videogames and computer/Internet access, respectively.

Similar to television viewing, video/computer game playing has been associated with later bedtime, longer sleep-onset latency, and shorter sleep duration. Moreover, experimental research demonstrated that exposure to videogames for two to three hours prior to bedtime could change sleep architecture, with less time spent in slow-wave sleep, consequently resulting in poor sleep quality and daytime sleepiness. With respect to sleep disorders, a few studies showed that video/computer game playing was linked to sleep latency and subjective insomnia (see Figure 15).

Mobile Telephone Use and Sleep

With the rapid improvement in technology, mobile telephone usage increasingly extends its functioning from the simple, such as for making and receiving calls and text messaging, to the varied, such as for entertainment, including playing

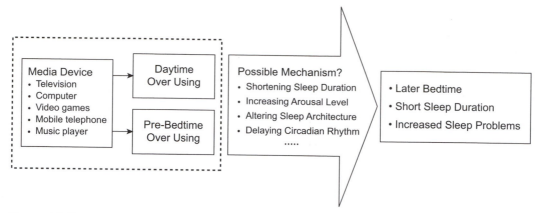

Figure 15: The Potential Impact of Media Using on Sleep. Courtesy Shenghui Li.

games, listening to music, and accessing the Internet. In line with the functioning development and widespread use, mobile phones have been considered a risk factor in children's and adolescents' sleep. Although far from clear and without definite results, several studies provided preliminary evidence that mobile phone use was associated with delayed sleep–wake cycle and disrupted sleep. Moreover, a recent study in Sweden found a borderline significant relationship between daytime tiredness and mobile phone use. Given the wide-ranging functioning and its portability, mobile phones could become the most frequently used media device. More and further research is needed to specifically and accurately clarify the impact of mobile phone usage on sleep.

Apart from television, video/computer games, and mobile phones, music players also have been widely used. Surprisingly, the effect of music on the sleep of children and adolescents has rarely been studied. To the best of our knowledge, only two studies explored the effectiveness of music as

a sleep aid among children and adolescents. More research is needed to assess the positive and negative effects of music on sleep—and the effects of different types of music on sleep.

Potential Mechanism

There are several hypotheses that have been proposed regarding the potential mechanisms of association between media use and sleep. First, media use as a form of unstructured activity, which usually lacks a clear beginning and end, is likely to be easily extended, leading to sacrifice of sleep time, thus shortening sleep duration. Second, exposure to the bright light of the viewing screen before sleep may affect the sleep/wake cycle through suppression of the nocturnal salivary secretion of melatonin and consequently delay the circadian rhythm. Third, media use may increase the activity level of the nervous system and result in heightened alertness, physiological arousal, and difficulty in falling asleep. It has been reported that there is a dose–

response relationship between light intensity and human alertness. Finally, media use as a form of sedentary activity also may alter sleep architecture and lead to poor-quality sleep.

Conclusions

It appears that the use of electronic media by children and adolescents does have a negative impact on their sleep, although the precise effects and mechanisms remain unclear. Based on the previous clarification, use of media devices, especially at bedtime, should be restricted. Particularly, and most importantly, guidelines concerning the hygiene of electronic media use at bedtime should be developed and tailored for specific age groups of children and adolescents.

Shenghui Li

See also: Increasing Sleep Complaints

Reference
National Sleep Foundation. (2006). *2006 Sleep in America poll*. Washington, DC: Author.

Medications Altering Dreaming

A wide variety of prescriptive and supplementary medications are reported to affect dreaming and/or induce nightmares. Until recently, studies addressing medication effects on dreaming focused on those neurochemicals known to affect REM sleep based on the belief that these medications would also affect dreaming. This approach of studying REM sleep as

dreaming had significant research advantages since dreaming/REM sleep could be studied in animal models so that the REM sleep–dreaming correlate became the routine approach utilized in studying dreaming in both animal models as well as in human subjects. REM sleep is controlled based on the interplay between two major neuromodulator systems (aminergic and cholinergic) in the brainstem. More recent versions of this once-simple system, now called AIM (activation, input, modulation), have become increasingly complex as other neurotransmitters and neuromodulators, including GABA, glutamate, and glycine, histamine, nitric oxide, adenosine, dopamine, and other less well-described neuropeptides have been shown to affect REM-sleep generation (Hobson, Pace-Schott, & Stickgold, 2003, pp. 1–50).

More recently, studies utilized data as to the reported effects of medications on dreaming derived from the clinical trials required for the use and release of new agents, as well as physician reports of adverse medication side effects. These studies were carried out in human beings, the only species that can currently report both the content and an experience of whether a dream has occurred. These data indicate that the medications that alter dreaming differ from those known to affect REM sleep with REM-sleep-suppressant medications inducing disturbed dreaming and nightmares, and medications affecting the primary REM-sleep neuromodulator, acetylcholine, having minimal effects on dreaming. The group of pharmacological preparations reported to alter sleep and dreaming is diverse and extensive. Almost all of the agents exerting neurochemical effects on dopamine, nicotine, histamine, GABA, serotonin, and norepinephrine will alter sleep and dreaming for some patients (Pagel, 2006, pp. 225–240; Pagel & Helfer, 2003, pp. 59–67).

Disordered dreaming and nightmares are also commonly reported during the withdrawal from addictive medications and drugs of abuse. This finding has been postulated to be secondary to the occurrence of REM-sleep rebound during withdrawal from REM-sleep-suppressant medication. However, nightmares and disordered dreaming are often reported as part of the withdrawal syndrome from addictive medications not known to affect REM sleep, such as cannabis, cocaine, and opiates. Disturbed dreaming and nightmares may be an intrinsic part of the process of withdrawal from addictive agents (Pagel, 2006, pp. 225–240). Some antibiotics, antivirals, and immunosuppressant drugs can induce complaints of sedation, insomnia, and nightmares. A clear, but poorly defined, relationship exists between host defense and infectious disease, and sleep/dreaming. Some of the agents reported to cause altered dreaming are induction anesthetics utilized in surgery, agents that can also induce waking hallucinations and confusion. This association suggests that agents which alter an individual's conscious relationship to the external environment can alter dream and nightmare occurrence.

The fact that a wide spectrum of pharmacological agents is reported to affect dreaming suggests that the biochemical basis for dreaming is more complex and less understood than is generally suggested. The medications most commonly reported to alter dreaming are widely used across-the-counter preparations, including the sedating antihistamines commonly used to treat allergies and induce sleep, and nicotine-replacement agents utilized in helping individuals to stop smoking. Among prescription medications in clinical use, antihypertensive beta-blockers affecting norepinephrine neuroreceptors are the agents most likely to result in patient complaints of disturbed dreaming. The strongest clinical evidence for a drug to induce disordered dreaming or nightmares is for the selective serotonin-reuptake inhibitor, paroxetine—a medication known to suppress REM sleep.

Based on its neurochemistry, dreaming does not appear to be a simple or derivative state of REM sleep. Medications that induce effects and/or side effects of arousal (insomnia) and/or sedation are those that most commonly were reported to alter dreaming and nightmare frequency. Dream frequency and content is most likely to be altered by medications inducing the effects and/or side effects of insomnia or daytime sleepiness and altering our alertness and cognitive interaction with the world.

James F. Pagel

References

Hobson, J., Pace-Schott, E., & Stickgold, R. (2003). Dreaming and the brain: Toward a cognitive neuroscience of conscious states in sleep and dreaming. In E. Pace-Schott, M. Solms, M. Blagrove, & S. Harnad (Eds.), *Sleep and dreaming: Scientific advances and reconsiderations* (pp. 1–50). Cambridge: Cambridge University Press.

Pagel, J. F. (2006). The neuropharmacology of nightmares. In S. R. Pandi-Perumal, D. P. Cardinali, & M. Lander (Eds.), *Sleep and sleep disorders: Neuropsychopharmacologic approach* (pp. 225–240). Georgetown, TX: Landes Bioscience.

Pagel, J.F., & Helfer, P. (2003). Drug induced nightmares—An etiology based review. *Human Psychopharmacology: Clinical and Experimental, 18,* 59–67.

Medieval Hagiography and Dreams

The great theologian Thomas Aquinas (1225–1274) described four causes of dreams: "two inward ones, arising from daytime preoccupations and from physical humors, and two outward ones, arising from physical sources (temperature or astrological forces) and from God or demons" (Van de Castle, 1994, p. 81). Another late medieval theologian, Bonaventure (ca. 1221–1274), discerned five causes of dreaming: a disposition of the body; an anxiety of the mind; diabolic illusion; angelic revelation; and divine visitation (Kruger, 1992, p. 190). Many more classifications regarding cause and nature of dreams can be found in medieval thought, which inherited important classical categories and schemes of dreams and dreamlike experiences, or created new ones in the same epistemic tradition (Dinzelbacher, 1981). In general, medieval dream theory shows the ambiguous quality of dreams and similar visionary phenomena: they are either important or unimportant, either psychological or spiritual, either legal or illegal, either malevolent or benevolent. Dreams can be an illusion as much as they can be a revelation (Kruger, 1992, p. 74). Furthermore, they are never described in *sec* psychological or physiological terms, but always presented as a multifaceted phenomenon involving the body, the mind, and the senses.

In medieval saints' lives (*vitae;* hagiography), dreams appear during crucial stages in which the saint gains clarity of his life and grows spiritually. The conversion of the saint to a life in the footsteps of Jesus Christ and according to the teachings of the Gospel is a gradual process from a narrow orientation on worldly things to an open attitude toward supernatural signs and admonitions. In this process, the saint is continuously led by images in the form of visions, dreams, apparitions, or revelations; terms that are not well defined and not strictly demarcated from each other in medieval hagiography. As topology dictates, their meaning is not clear to him from the beginning and he fails to interpret them correctly. But with the help of God he gradually experiences the true meaning of the images that are revealed to him, and learns to act on them effectively. He acquires the habit of true interpretation: they are all crucial signposts on his way to God. The dreams and visions therefore function as a *means* for spiritual progress.

But they are also a *measure* for it: dreams and visions signal important spiritual stages that the saint goes through. The saint's biographer uses them as important elements of a literary program, employing the rhetoric of hagiography. He writes a biography within a biography: the course of events in the saint's earthly life parallels the development of his spiritual life. Obviously, all natural facts and events take place under a supernatural direction. Dreams and visions are exemplary for this, as they reveal the presence of the supernatural in everyday circumstances and, at the same time, place natural images in a supernatural context. The dreams of the saint are a most effective instrument in the hands of the medieval hagiographer, who wishes to demonstrate to his faithful public the divine origin of the saint's actions and the imitable aspects of his holiness.

Medieval hagiographical dreams can therefore be said to be symbolic in content as well as in function. The dreams of the man or woman of God are never considered to be a normal, daily, anthropological phenomenon. As the materials of the account of a spiritual journey, they are symbolic in *content,* marking the most important stages on the saint's way to sanctity (Frugoni, 1989, p. 73). They initiate new stages or conclude previous ones, as can be seen in the gradual conversion process of such great saints as Francis of Assisi (Pansters, 2009). The saint's dreams are furthermore symbolic in *function.* They are portrayed as stemming from God, who leads the saint on his spiritual path, whereas in fact the biographer guides the saint's admirer, the story's reader or listener, on his path. If the saint really had dreams revealing that the will of God must remain unclear, the function of the biographical account is not the narration of the saint's holiness in itself. *Vitae* are concerned with the exemplary illustration and divine legitimization of the holiness of the saint as well as with the religious incitement to holiness of its admirers. Both of these aims are reflected in the typical and topological nature of the medieval biographical account. The dreams described are exemplary and *paraenetic* in character: they report miracles in order to create them and virtues in order to induce them. They are more concerned with the dream-reading collective than with the

dreaming individual itself (Frugoni, 1989, p. 76). Both the reception of hagiographical dreams by the medieval public and its effects on medieval spirituality therefore need much further investigation.

Krijn Pansters

See also: entries related to History of Dreams/ Sleep

References

Dinzelbacher, P. (1981). *Vision und Visionsliteratur im Mittelalter.* [*Vision and vision literature during the Middle Ages.*] Monographien zur Geschichte des Mittelalters [Monographs on the history of the Middle Ages] 23. Stuttgart: Hiersemann.

Frugoni, C. (1989). Die Träume in der Legende der drei Gefährten. [Dreams in the legend of the three companions.] In A. Paravicini Bagliani & G. Stabile (Eds.), *Träume im Mittelalter. Ikonologische Studien* [*Dreams in the Middle Ages: Iconological studies*] (pp. 73–90). Stuttgart: Belser.

Kruger, S. F. (1992). *Dreaming in the Middle Ages.* Cambridge Studies in Medieval Literature 14. Cambridge: Cambridge University Press.

Pansters, K. (2009). Dreams in medieval saints' lives: Saint Francis of Assisi. *Dreaming, 19,* 55–63.

Van de Castle, R. L. (1994). *Our dreaming mind: A sweeping exploration of the role that dreams have played in politics, art, religion, and psychology, from ancient civilizations to the present day.* New York: Ballantine Books.

Melatonin Therapy for the Sleep Disorders of Children

Melatonin research in sleep medicine has been very active during the last 20 years. Since there are a huge number of publications on this topic, the readers are referred only to a couple of articles written by our team (Carr et al., 2007; Jan & O'Donnell, 1996; Jan et al., 2007; Wasdell et al., 2008).

Melatonin (N-acetyl-5-ethoxytryptamine) is secreted by the pineal gland, usually throughout the night because healthy sleep habits and darkness promote its production; however, unhealthy sleep habits and light inhibit it. It is also produced in minute amounts by most tissues. Melatonin is a small lipid and water-soluble molecule that readily enters the bloodstream, the spinal fluid, all body compartments, and cells. It has many important functions, such as sleep regulation, brain development, protection against toxins; it has anticonvulsant and anticancer properties; and it is also beneficial in treating many diseases. This molecule is the most powerful antioxidant known and is also a synchronizer of metabolic activities in the body.

For the purpose of sleep promotion, melatonin is synthesized commercially and is sold as an over-the-counter medication in the United States and Canada. In contrast, in Europe it is a prescription drug. Melatonin has very different properties from regular hypnotics and although it has hypnotic properties, it is not considered to be a sleeping pill. The fast-acting formulations, such as sublingual tablets, capsules, and liquid begin to promote sleep within 30 minutes after swallowing them, but their effects only last for four to five hours. They are most useful for those individuals who have difficulty falling asleep. Most slow or controlled release tablets release some melatonin quickly and some slowly; therefore, depending on their makeup they promote sleep for six to eight hours. They are more beneficial for individuals who have prolonged awakenings during the night, with or without difficulty falling asleep.

Melatonin is remarkably free from side effects, even with high doses. It is not addictive and tolerance does not develop after prolonged use. In numerous animal studies, melatonin during pregnancy has not caused any abnormalities in fetuses. It is also safe when taken during puberty, and in humans it does not appear to affect its onset. Melatonin therapy does not cause seizures, as once was thought; in fact it has anticonvulsant properties. It can be taken with most other medications and it even appears to reduce their side effects. One of the observations of some people who are on melatonin therapy is that their dreams are more vivid but it is rarely disturbing enough to prevent treatment. This curious effect of melatonin has not been studied and the neurophysiological reasons for it are not understood. However, melatonin is known to influence both NREM- and REM-sleep stages, and during REM sleep dreaming is the most intense. With prolonged melatonin treatment, dreams tend to become less vivid.

Melatonin therapy is recommended by the American Association for Sleep Medicine for circadian rhythm sleep disorders (CRSD), which include persistent difficulty falling asleep, prolonged awakenings during the night, regular early morning awakenings, and jet lag. There are also other, less common forms of CRSD. These circadian sleep disorders are characterized by dissociations between sleep–wake behaviors and the environment and are associated with abnormally timed or impaired pineal melatonin production. This is why melatonin-replacement therapy is so beneficial for CRSD. Since the brain is closely involved in pineal melatonin production, these sleep disorders are common in children with various neurodevelopmental disabilities, especially with intellectual deficits.

A medical evaluation prior to melatonin therapy is beneficial, because this treatment is mainly effective for CRSD, and sleep difficulties could be caused by more than the 100 sleep disorders that are known to occur in children. Prior to treatment, attempts should be made to establish healthy sleep habits, since milder sleep disturbances may respond to these measures alone.

The oral dose of melatonin should be taken about 30 minutes prior to the desired bedtime. Some physicians also prescribe a smaller dose a few hours before bedtime, but we do not find this practice useful. There is no dose formula to fit everyone, because the type and severity of sleep difficulties markedly vary. Starting with one to three milligrams is best, with small increases every couple of days, until the lowest and most effective dose is reached. Delayed sleep onset can usually be treated with smaller doses, in contrast to sleep-maintenance difficulties. From time to time, when a person is more alert, another dose of melatonin may be taken at bedtime, or a couple of hours later, but repeating the dose toward the morning is rarely helpful. Once the therapeutic threshold has been reached, additional melatonin does not result in deeper sleep. Depending on the type of sleep disturbance, the treatment may be required for only a short time, or for years.

It can be stopped abruptly without ill effects. It is recommended that the treatment should be stopped every 6 to 12 months to see whether it is still necessary.

James E. Jan

See also: entries related to Sleep Disorders

References

Carr, R., Wasdell, M. B., Hamilton, D., Weiss, M. D., Freeman, R. D., Tai, J., . . . Jan, J. E. (2007). Long-term effectiveness outcome of melatonin therapy in children with treatment-resistant circadian rhythm sleep disorders. *Journal of Pineal Research, 43,* 351–359.

Jan, J. E., & O'Donnell, M. E. (1966). Use of melatonin in the treatment of paediatric sleep disorders. *Journal of Pineal Research, 21,* 193–199.

Jan, J. E., Wasdell, M. B., Reiter, R. J., Weiss, M. D., Johnson, K. P., Ivanenko, A., & Freeman, R. D. (2007). Melatonin therapy of pediatric sleep disorders: Recent advances, why it works, who are the candidates and how to treat. *Current Pediatric Reviews, 3,* 214–224.

Wasdell, M. B., Jan, J. E., Bomben, M. M., Freeman, R. D., Rietveld, W. J., Tai, J., . . . Weiss, M. D. (2008). A randomized, placebo-controlled trial of controlled release melatonin treatment of delayed sleep phase syndrome and impaired sleep maintenance in children with neurodevelopmental disabilities. *Journal of Pineal Research, 44,* 54–64.

Methodological Challenges in the Scientific Study of Dreams

The interdisciplinary field of dream studies is rife with questions regarding how, what, and why we dream. How are dreams constructed? Why are dreams often difficult to remember? Are most dreams bizarre?

What are the predictors of dream recall? What is the connection between waking experience and dreaming? Does dreaming serve a developmental function? Does dreaming assist with information processing and memory formation? Can working with dreams bring about personal transformation?

Many methods are used to investigate dreaming, including phenomenology, ethnography, longitudinal case studies, and literary analysis. Each method has its own approach to the question of what constitutes evidence for a truth claim. This entry focuses on the use of scientific method in dream studies. The application of the scientific method entails formulating testable hypotheses to assess the accuracy (validity) of theoretical claims and identifying the range of circumstances (boundary conditions) under which these claims hold true. Dream scientists face numerous methodological challenges in these efforts including how to maximize a study's *construct validity* (e.g., how are dreams defined, measured, sampled?), *internal validity* (e.g., are we studying dreaming as a type of subjective experience or as an instance of autobiographical recall?), and *external validity* (e.g., to whom do our findings apply?).

The first methodological challenge concerns the question of *what* we are studying. Definitions of dreams vary from a detailed narrative account of experiences recalled upon awakening from sleep to any experience specific to the sleep state. Often, dream is used to refer to the verbal report of an experience occurring in sleep and dreaming is used to refer to the processes involved in generating the experience—but even

this distinction is not uniformly agreed upon by dream investigators (Pagel, 2008). Minimally, in any study of dreaming, the abstract concepts of dream and dreaming must be translated into operational definitions that specify, in precise behavioral terms, exactly how a dream or dreaming will be measured.

The second methodological challenge concerns *how* we study dreams and dreaming; that is, how do we obtain evidence of dreaming? Questions associated with this challenge include: What is the measure of dreaming? When and where are these measures obtained? Whose dreams are sampled? We will consider each of these questions in turn.

What is the measure of dreaming? An intractable fact in dream studies is that any measure of dreaming is necessarily indirect: the dream as told is not the dream as experienced. Verbal reports of dreaming are the typical index of dreaming. The reliance on verbal reports poses several challenges to the accuracy of claims made about the features of dreams and about the dream-generation process. Because the narrative report is a verbal representation of a multimodal experience that may be more or less difficult to describe in words, the report is typically guided by a narrative schema that emphasizes the dream story (who/what/when/where) over qualitative aspects such as the perceptual, cognitive, or affective features of the dream experience (Kahan, 1994). In short, certain features of subjective experience are more likely than others to be included in the verbal report.

Other measures of dream recall include questionnaire measures, diary reports,

Internet-based surveys, and the use of targeted probes to assess specific qualities of the dream experience. The recall of dreams is sometimes compared with the recall of waking experiences. Investigators disagree as to the best choice of waking-state comparison: some argue that reports of dreaming experience should be compared with reports of waking experience; others argue for comparing the qualities of dreams with the qualities of waking fantasy. The choice of waking-state comparison is, in important ways, influenced by one's theoretical perspective on the relationship between dreaming and waking. Investigators should take steps to minimize the demand characteristics in their studies and strive to obtain samples of dreaming and waking that are as comparable as possible (Kahan & LaBerge, 2011).

When are measures of dreaming obtained? A study of dreaming is, essentially, a study of autobiographical memory (Horton & Conway, 2009). As the delay between a dream experience and the report of that experience increases, the more the verbal report reflects autobiographical memory and its attendant constructive and reconstructive processing. For example, one recalls less of their dream experience when a demanding cognitive task intervenes between the dream experience and the dream report (Parke & Horton, 2009). A researcher's concern with memory influences on dream reporting will vary with the research question. Dream researchers who are interested in the cognitive or affective processes involved in dream generation should be especially attentive to the influence of memory processes, as well as to the potential limits of verbal report data.

Where (under what conditions) are measures of dreaming obtained? Dream researchers disagree on whether dream experiences are best sampled in the home setting or in the sleep laboratory. Laboratory awakenings allow investigators to control the conditions under which dream reports are obtained. They also minimize the influence of memory factors such as the salience or emotional intensity of the experience on dream recall. Sampling dreams from laboratory awakenings allows researchers to test hypotheses concerning the relationship between the qualities of reported dreams and factors such as sleep stage, time of night, and method of awakening. On the other hand, laboratory-based studies are expensive and time consuming for both participants and investigators. Some researchers have argued that dreams sampled in the sleep lab are less vivid and detailed than those sampled in the home setting; however, carefully conducted studies comparing lab- and home-based dream recall have found few reliable differences (Strauch & Meier, 1996). Recent technological developments in home-sleep recording systems offer a hybrid approach to those investigators interested in acquiring both sleep and dreaming data in the more naturalistic, home environment.

Whose dreams are investigated? The frequency, characteristics, and content of dreams are related to numerous individual difference factors. These include gender, cognitive style, memory abilities, attention skills, attitude toward dreams, and cultural or religious orientation, to name but a few. Ultimately, the questions about dreams/ dreaming that can be investigated scientifically depend on the participants' level of dream recall, verbal expertise, and skill in self-observation. For example, investigators interested in comparing the qualities of dreaming versus waking experience are concerned with obtaining reports of subjective experience that are as accurate as possible. In this regard, participants need excellent source-monitoring skills, notably, the ability to distinguish between the characteristics of what they experienced prior to awakening (e.g., the dream experience) and what they are inclined to add to the experience in the course of recall (e.g., commentary on connection to waking life). A high level of dream recall also may be needed to study particular qualities of dreams, such as perceptual detail, bizarreness, emotion, cognitions, or self-reflective processes. Individual difference factors which may be correlated with dream recall, dream reporting, or dream qualities may be controlled or their influence measured. Of course, the generalizability of the study's findings must be qualified accordingly. Finally, in view of the wide variation in dream recall and skill in dream reporting, dream researchers should be careful to include sample sizes large enough to detect small, yet meaningful, differences.

Researchers who endeavor to apply the scientific method to the study of dreams and dreaming are encouraged to wrestle—creatively, publicly, and persistently—with the substantial methodological challenges inherent in dream science. Such efforts enhance the quality of the empirical evidence obtained and the accuracy of claims made concerning what, how, and why we dream. Finally, these efforts help extend the reach of dream research to the fields of sleep science, cognitive neuroscience, cognitive psychology, anthropology, and sociology.

Tracey Lea Kahan and
Caroline L. Horton

References

Horton, C.L., & Conway, M.A. (2009). The memory experiences and dreams questionnaire: A validated measure of dream remembering. *Imagination, Cognition and Personality, 29*(1), 3–29.

Kahan, T.L. (1994). Measuring dream self-reflectiveness: A comparison of two approaches. *Dreaming, 4*(3), 329–344.

Kahan, T.L., & LaBerge, S. (2011). Dreaming and waking: Similarities and differences revisited. *Consciousness & Cognition, 20*, 494–519.

Pagel, J.F. (2008). *The limits of dream: A scientific exploration of the mind/brain interface.* New York: Academic Press.

Parke, A.R., & Horton, C.L. (2009). A re-examination of the interference hypothesis of dream recall and salience. *The International Journal of Dream Research, 2*(2), 60–69.

Strauch, I., & Meier, B. (1996). *In search of dreams: Results of experimental dream research.* Albany: State University of New York Press.

Middle Ages and Dreams

During the Middle Ages, discussions of dreams and dream interpretation appeared in poetry, philosophy, theology, autobiography, religious writings, and in other areas of thought. For example, three popular types of interpretive manuals survive: the dream alphabet, the dream lunar, and the dream book proper, otherwise known as the *Somniale Danielis*, which was a key to dream imagery supposedly written by the prophet Daniel. All these interpretive systems share the feature of not leaving much room for either God's or human will, according to Steven Kruger, who writes that, additionally, for more sophisticated medieval authors, there was "a remarkable unity of opinion about the essential, fundamentally complex and ambiguous, nature of the dream" (Kruger, 1992, p. 6). This entry will focus on the impact of dreaming on three fields: philosophy, religion, and literature.

In addition to the influential Aristotle (*Parva Naturalia: De Somno et Vigilia, De Insomniis* [*Little Nature: On the Sleep of Vigilance, on Insomnia*] and *De Divinatione per Somnum* [*On Divination in Sleep*]), on the one hand, and Augustine (*Confessions*), on the other, Macrobius (*Commentary on the Dream of Scipio*) and Calcidius (*Commentary on Plato's Timaeus*), two late antique writers, are important to medieval theories of dreaming with their hierarchy of types of dreams, from the mundane to the visionary. Artemidorus's *Oneirocritica* also is referred to in the Middle Ages, particularly in Arabic-language texts. His most influential idea is that the dream interpreter must know about the personality, career, age, and other information about the dreamer. For Aristotle, dreams are merely physical, though he, like Artemidorus, admits that: "the most skilled interpreter of dreams is one who can observe resemblances" (Aristotle, 1996, p. 115); he is also sympathetic to the idea of prophecy, but not to a large degree. Aristotle, who focused on physical ailments that dreams can signal, was by far the most popular writer on dreams. Like the medical writings on dreams by Hippocrates and Galen, Aristotle's naturalistic philosophy of oneirocriticism entered medieval culture through numerous Arabic translations and commentaries, whose influence permeated medical works in England and the continent. Physicians used these texts as keys to reliable diagnoses of patients' illnesses and built on their assertions, such as those about the center of sense perception and the causes of sleep, with new discoveries.

Macrobius divides dreams into five kinds, three of which are true or revelatory (oraculum, visio, and somnium) and two of which are false (insomnium and visum). In doing so, he successfully brings together various ancient theories, from the notion that dreams can be divine to the idea that they are negligible because they result from bad digestion. The genre of the somnium, or enigmatic dream, is the category of dream experience that is probably closest to the literary dream. The enigmatic dream has five types (personal, alien, social, public, and universal), and it "stands between, and in some sense unites, the opposed realms of truth and falsehood" (Kruger, 1992, p. 23). For Macrobius, Cicero's "Dream of Scipio," which appears at the end of *De Re Publica,* contains elements of the first three types, and he brings to bear wider topics such as mathematics, astronomy, morality, geography, and religion. He is the most influential of the allegorists who, as Patricia Cox Miller claims, "operated out of an expectation of textual polysemy and so delighted in the convergence of infinite relationships that oneiric images set in motion" (Miller, 1998, p. 97). Interpreting a dream was like interpreting a poem in full detail, with each image and action worthy of paragraphs of explication.

Augustine's ideas about dreams appear in *Confessions* and *De Continentia (On Continence),* where he holds that dreams can be compelling as well as prophetic, but also that at times another force takes over one's body and creates the conditions in which sexual excitement is possible and is not considered sinful. The *Confessions* contain an observation about the reliability of dreams: "Food pictured in dreams is extremely like food received in the waking state; yet sleepers receive no nourishment, they are simply sleeping. But those fantasies had not the least resemblance to you as you have now told me, because they were physical images, fictional bodily shapes. . . . And yet again the pictures of these realities which our imagination forms are more reliable than the mythological pictures of vast and unlimited entities" (Augustine, 1991, p. 41). His interest in prophetic dreams is demonstrated through an account of a dream of his mother, in which she was encouraged to allow him to live with her, and to sit at the same table in the house together. She cries, and when a young man asks why, she says she mourns her son's perdition (he has taken up with the wrong crowd). He tells her not to worry and then she sees Augustine on same rule as this young man: "By the dream the joy of this devout woman, to be fulfilled much later, was predicted many years in advance to give consolation at this time in her anxiety" (Augustine, 1991, p. 49). In *De Continentia,* Augustine addresses the issue of sexual continence; he had already done so in the famous Chapter 10 of the *Confessions,* where the wet dream is a problematic source of bodily knowledge for him. Augustine shows that when one is responsible for one's sins, one's interiority needs to be disciplined, and that virtue is defined as the struggle to achieve this control.

Religious writers during the Middle Ages were preoccupied with dreams in Islamic, Jewish, and Christian contexts. Medieval Islamic writers, including some Sufis, were influenced by Artemidorus's *Oneirocritica* (second century AD), by Aristotle, and by the Bible.[1] They tended to concentrate on the role of the imagination in creating dreams; al-Ghazali (d. 1111) and Ibn al-'Arabi (d. 1240) are examples of authors with such a preoccupation. Other influential Muslim philosophers who discussed dreams are al-Farabi (d. 950) and Ibn Sina (d. 1037). "It was universally accepted that those who had cultivated their inner faculties and insights could decipher the encoded messages of their own dreams as well as those of others" (Sviri, 1999, p. 252). Sufis recorded their dreams as well as those of others.

In medieval Judaism, Isaac Israeli (10th century) wrote that dream imagery for common people and in prophets' revelations make "dreams a part of prophecy" (Sviri, 1999, p. 255). Moses ibn Ezra, a poet, wrote that dreams derive either from within or from celestial sources, and the latter are the only veridical ones. One minor type of dreaming was the astral dream, considered "the intersection between the astral order and private life, a moment of insight, either a gift from above or a result of human initiative, enabling a person to peer into the future by means of a mantic relationship to the celestial forces that shape that future" (Idel, 1999, p. 236). More common were Kabbalistic dreams that were "a linguistic kind of magic directed at angels"

(Idel, 1999, p. 238), although instructions exist for being the recipient of a dream after standing under the stars. In the 12th century, Abraham ibn Ezra wrote on Daniel, both that naturalistic causes for dreams exist and that dreams could also be interpreted based on what hour a dream occurred and the stars' configuration at that time. His perspective on astral dreams appears in the following century in an anonymous treatise. Maimonides was against this practice, but a letter is attributed to him that condones it and also uses a method of purification, special language including anagrams, and the appearance within the dream of Mercury (Hermes) to foster the dreamer's "magical powers" (Idel, 1999, p. 244) and greater understanding of the Torah. A treatise spuriously attributed to ibn Ezra also contains an "astral-magic vision of drawing down the emanation from above by ritual means" (Idel, 1999, p. 246).

Christian authors were alternately fascinated by and hesitant about dreams. Many mystical writings, such as those by Julian of Norwich, Gertrude of Helfta, Guibert de Nogent, Hermann of Cologne, and *The Book of Margery Kempe* display an affinity for visions and often dedicate their lives to religious pursuits in accordance with their dictates. On an institutional level, however, dreams indicate "the basic limits of ecclesiastical power, showing it incapable of controlling all the arcane of individual religious experience, even if clerics assumed the essential role of saving the dream narratives from oblivion by recording, classifying, and judging them" (Schmitt, 1998, p. 275). As much as authorities in the church wanted to limit individual believers' engagement with dreams, they faced an uphill battle because of the increasing popularity of dream books and other popular interpretive traditions.

Medieval literature contains several famous instances of dreaming, from the framing of the poems *Pearl* and *Piers Plowman* to the work of Chaucer, who includes dreams in several ways in his work. The Nun's Priest's Tale in *The Canterbury Tales* contains the story of a dream and its interpretation by the husband of the dreamer (both characters are birds), and his narrative poems "The Book of the Duchess," "The House of Fame," and "The Parliament of Fowls" all contain dream frames. A. C. Spearing, the most prolific of a group of contemporary scholars of medieval dreaming, writes that "What especially interested Chaucer about the dream poem as a genre, I suggest, were two things—on the one hand, the dream as one of the most intriguing kinds of natural experience we have, and, on the other, the possibility of constructing poems that reproduce certain aspects of that experience as literary form" (Spearing, 2010, p. 167). The aspects of dreaming that Chaucer seemed most eager to represent include careful attention on the part of dreamers and interpreters alike to details of language and dialogue, descriptions of landscapes that place the dreamer in realistic but also imaginative surroundings, and a general tone of nostalgia as the dream is recalled. Literary writers, philosophers, and religious writers alike found in dreams intensely provocative and intensely illuminating material with which to ponder the epistemological status of mental activity when it occurs in the absence of waking life's stimuli.

Jenn Lewin

Note

1. A new English translation of Artemidorus's *Oneirocritica* will appear in October 2012, with slightly revised Greek text and extensive introduction and commentary, written by Daniel E. Harris-McCoy, *Artemidorus' Oneirocritica: Text, Translation, and Commentary* (New York: Oxford University Press, 2012).

References

Aristotle. (1996). *Aristotle on sleep and dreams: A text and translation* (Trans. David Gallup). Warminster, UK: Aris & Philips.

Augustine. (1991). *Confessions* (Trans. Henry Chadwick). Oxford: Oxford University Press.

Barr, J. (2010). *Willing to know God: Dreamers and visionaries in the later Middle Ages.* Columbus: Ohio State University Press.

Edwards, R. (1991). *The dream of Chaucer: Representation and reflection in the early narratives.* Durham, NC: Duke University Press.

Idel, M. (1999). Astral dreams in Judaism: Twelfth to fourteenth centuries. In D.D. Shulman & G.G. Stroumsa (Eds.), *Dream cultures: Explorations in the comparative history of dreaming* (pp. 235–251). New York: Oxford University Press.

Kruger, S.F. (1992). *Dreaming in the Middle Ages.* Cambridge: Cambridge University Press.

Lynch, K.L. (1988). *The high medieval dream vision: Poetry, philosophy, and literary form.* Stanford, CA: Stanford University Press.

Lynch, K.L. (Ed.). (2007). *Geoffrey Chaucer, dream visions and other poems.* New York: W.W. Norton.

Miller, P.C. (1998). *Dreams in late antiquity: Studies in imagination of a culture.* Princeton, NJ: Princeton University Press.

Newman, F.X. (1963). *Somnium: Medieval theories of dreaming and the form of vision poetry* (Doctoral dissertation, Princeton University).

Phillips, H., & Havely, N. (Eds.). (1997). *Chaucer's dream poetry.* London: Longman.

Russell, J.S. (1988). *The English dream-vision: Anatomy of a form.* Columbus: Ohio State University Press.

Schmitt, J.-C. (1998). *Ghosts in the Middle Ages: The living and the dead in Medieval society* (Trans. Teresa Lavender Fagan). Chicago: University of Chicago Press.

Shulman, D., & Strousma, G.G. (1999). *Dream cultures: Explorations in the comparative history of dreaming.* Oxford: Oxford University Press.

Spearing, A.C. (2010). Dream poems. In S.G Fein & R. Raybin (Eds.), *Chaucer: Contemporary approaches* (pp.159–178). University Park: Pennsylvania State University Press.

Sviri, S. (1999). Dreaming analyzed and recorded: Dreams in the world of medieval Islam. In D.D. Shulman & G.G. Stroumsa (Eds.), *Dream cultures: Explorations in the comparative history of dreaming* (pp. 252–273). New York: Oxford University Press.

Windeatt, B.A. (Ed.). (1982). *Chaucer's dream poetry: Sources and analogues.* Cambridge: D.S. Brewer.

Mugwort: A Dream-Stimulating Herb

Oneirogens are plants or other substances that enhance dreaming (Toro & Thomas, 2007). One of the most widely used plants associated with stimulating vivid dreams is mugwort. Its common name originates from its extensive use in brewing beer prior to the introduction of hops. *Wort* is an old English term for herb as many Harry Potter fans have learned. Mugwort's genus name is *Artemisia*, which is linked to the Greek goddess Artemis, who was associated with healing women's diseases and helping with childbirth along with connections to wilderness, wild animals, and hunting (Silverman, 1997). The strong fragrance, the variations in the leaf shape and the unique two colored leaves with silvery fibers on the bottom are probably what drew people to explore the uses of the plant in ancient times.

Mugwort is in the aster family (*Asteraceae*), which has also been known as the daisy or sunflower family. The genus *Artemisia* is commonly found in North and South America, Europe, Africa, and Asia (see the Viable Herbal Solutions website at http://www.viable-herbal.com/singles/herbs/s138.htm). One species of mugwort, *Artemisia vulgaris,* is so common in the eastern United States and Europe that it often appears as a weed (*Artemisia vulgaris,* n.d.). Very similar in appearance and usage is *Artemisia douglasiana,* which is common on the West Coast of the United States in forests and undisturbed areas (Hickman, 1993). Mugwort is a highly aromatic plant that varies in height from one to five feet tall with divided or lobed leaves that are a darker olive green on top and more of a silvery green color with white downy hairs on the bottom. The leaves are polymorphic, meaning that individual leaf shapes may vary with most leaves having three to five lobes or divisions that are mitten like (Foster & Hobbs, 2002). It is easy to cultivate and can become naturalized in a garden. It can be used fresh or dried and the procedures for gathering, drying, and storing mugwort are similar to those used for other herbs, spices, and botanicals.

The dream-inducing properties of mugwort are generally accessed by making a dream pillow with dried mugwort leaves, often mixed with other herbs such as lavender, which is reported to be soothing. Pillows with mugwort can be purchased or made using cotton or other soft fabrics. Users who enjoy crafts may want to design and decorate their own dream pillow with inspiring symbols or with images from their own dreams. Fresh leaves on your pillow are the easiest way to experiment. A tea is another way to try out the oneirogenic effects of mugwort. However, the taste is bitter and those who want to ingest the herb may prefer to purchase or make a capsule with dried or powdered mugwort.

The study of ethnobotany focuses on humans relationships with plants (Veilleux & King, n.d.). Agriculture- and plant-based medicines developed as a result of centuries of trial-and-error experimentation. Many crucial advances in medicine have come from plants and one of the many rationales for preserving the earth's rain forests is the likelihood that crucial medicinal and nutritional plants exist there that have yet to be studied or even discovered. Botanists have identified the chemical properties of oneirogenic herbs that may eventually be linked to influencing dreams or other medicinal benefits. Along with other avenues of dream research, learning more about these plants may contribute to understanding the nature of dreaming and its use in healing and awareness.

Popular interest in dreams, natural healing, and cross-cultural spiritual and medicinal practices burgeoned in the late 20th century. This led to increased interest in oneirogens such as mugwort to enhance dream recall, stimulate vivid dreams, and to cultivate lucid dreams that occur when the dreamer is aware they are dreaming. Despite increased interest and abundant anecdotal reports, research on the possible benefits of oneirogenic plants and other substances is proceeding slowly due to lack of funding. Most of the reported oneirogenic benefits of mugwort and other herbs and substances have not been scientifically confirmed. Therefore, it is important to keep in mind that the information in this article should be taken as educational only and not as a medical recommendation or a substitute for any necessary treatments that are evidence based or approved by the FDA or other governmental entities. In addition, two important cautions to be considered are that some people are allergic to the pollen from mugwort flowers, and that any wild plant should be definitively identified before using it to prevent inadvertent exposure to a harmful plant such as poison oak or ivy, hemlock, or stinging nettles. In addition, thujone, a compound found in varying degrees in mugwort, can have neurotoxic and mutagenic side effects when used in excess, and pregnant women should avoid or use medical advice before ingesting mugwort preparations (*Artemisia vulgaris*, n.d.). In general, if a tea or extract is used, it is best to use water rather than oil to extract the medicinal effects because the resulting tea or tincture will be milder when steeped in water (Foster & Hobbs, 2002). In addition, some people are allergic to the pollen from mugwort flowers. Cooking may reduce or eliminate the risk to those who are allergic. Finally, consider growing your own mugwort and if you do harvest the plant be careful not to disturb

habitats or damage other plants that may be less common.

While research on the oneirogenic plants may proceed slowly, we know that there are a number of potential therapeutic benefits common to all medicinal treatments. The first is the placebo effect that has a powerful therapeutic impact and can enhance traditional and alternative medicine. The patient's expectation of healing can influence the success of any treatment with traditional or alternative medicine. Also, the relationship with the physician, psychotherapist, healer, or shaman can have a positive influence. In addition, using oneirogens or other medical therapies in the context of strongly held cultural religious beliefs and ritual may have an impact that is synergistic, by combining the placebo effect, positive expectations, and culturally sanctioned results along with potential medicinal or psychoactive influences of mugwort or other oneirogens being used.

Plant-based oneirogens have been used in two general ways. They are taken before sleep in various forms to stimulate dreaming and they are used to induce a dreamlike state that closely parallels the sensory and mental experience of a vivid dream. Some of the best known plant oneirogens combine both effects. A good example of an herbal oneirogen used to induce both dreamlike states and powerful dreams is ayahuasca (*Banisteriopsis caapi*), which is used by tribes in the Amazon rainforest region and is referred to as vine of the soul in the Quechua language. In addition to many medicinal properties, it has hallucinogenic effects and is used in religious rituals by many tribes and sometimes combined with other herbs. The Achuar of

Peru use ayahuasca to stimulate dreaming as an integral part of shaman-guided dream healing rituals that are central to the cultural and spiritual practices of the tribe (Parry, 2008). Researchers (Arehart-Treichel, 2011) and journalists (Isaacson, 2010) have reported profound dreams following the ayahuasca ceremonies as well as intense dreamlike experiences during the rituals. Another well-known mind-altering oneirogen is Ubulawu, also known as African Dream Root (*Silene capensis*). The root is used by shamans in southern Africa. Its root contains triterpenoid saponins, which in even small doses are said to induce remarkably prophetic vivid and very colorful dreams that often allow tribe member to contact their ancestors (Toro & Thomas, 2007).

Examples of oneirogenic plants that do not radically affect waking consciousness but significantly alter dreaming include Dream Herb or Bitter Grass the Leaf of God (*Calea ternifolia*), which is used by the Chontal people of Oaxaca, Mexico, for oneiromancy or predicting future events or receiving divine guidance in a dream (Toro & Thomas, 2007). Scientific studies have confirmed that the plant increases dream recall (Olin & Schneider, 2001). Another oneirogen, Red Spider Lily, has an alkaloid, galantamine, which reportedly enhances the experience of dreaming (Yuschak, 2006). Although its oneirogenic effects have not yet been scientifically confirmed, a synthetic extract of galantamine has shown success in treating symptoms of Alzheimer's disease (Olin & Schneider, 2001).

The origins of human fascination with mugwort stretch back across millennia.

Mugwort has been revered over the centuries for its magical, mystical, and spiritual uses especially for warding off evil spirits or enemies and for clairvoyance and promoting romantic success. A 3,600-year-old Egyptian papyrus described the plant in detail (see the Viable Herbal Solutions website at http://www.viable-herbal.com/singles/herbs/s138.htm). In art, Venus, the Roman goddess of love, is sometimes depicted holding a spray of mugwort in her hand (*Artemisia vulgaris,* n.d.). In the first century AD, the Roman writer Pliny the Elder extolled the virtues of mugwort for combating fatigue and stated that, "The wayfaring man that hath the herb tied about him feeleth no weariness at all and he can never be hurt by any poisonous medicine, by any wild beast, neither yet by the sun itself" (Silverman, 1997).

Mugwort is one of the nine magical herbs of the Druidic and Anglo-Saxon tribes and was associated with protection of travelers and fertility rites (*Artemisia vulgaris,* n.d.). In the Middle Ages, mugwort was worn in mid-summer on St. John's Eve to gain security against threats of evil possession. Medieval legends held that a dream pillow of mugwort would allow people to see their entire future in their dreams (Callegari & Durand, 1977). Native Americans rubbed the leaves on their body to prevent dreaming of the dead and to ward off ghosts, and they smoked, drank, and burned the herb for ritual purification (Foster & Hobbs, 2002). In the 21st century, mugwort is used for inducing lucid dreams and for stimulating vivid dreams.

Most of the known oneirogen plants have other reported medicinal uses, often involving mental functioning or the nervous

system. Mugwort has been utilized for centuries in conjunction with acupuncture. The white downy fuzz on the underside of mugwort's leaves is removed and fashioned into cubes that are burned as moxa by acupuncturists The smoking moxa cubes are placed over specific energetic meridians either directly or indirectly to amplify the effects of the treatment. Called moxibustion, this ancient treatment is still widely used in Chinese medicine in the 21st century and has shown promise with difficulties in labor in conjunction with acupuncture (*Artemisia vulgaris,* n.d.).

Mugwort has traditionally been used in herbal medicine for soothing anxiety and for calming people who have suffered a seizure or drug overdose. Wormwood is in the same genus (*Artemisia*) and closely related to mugwort. It was used to prepare Absinthe, a powerful alcoholic drink with psychoactive properties. It was popular in the late 1880s and early 1900s with artists and writers, such as Baudelaire, Edgar Allan Poe, and Van Gogh. In that era, it was linked to brain damage and banned probably due to toxic copper salts used to brew it. Absinthe has become popular again in the 21st century with nontoxic brewing procedures (*Artemisia vulgaris,* n.d.).

Mugwort has many other reported medicinal uses not related to mental functioning, including beneficial effects for menstrual difficulties and labor pains, and for treating fungal and bacterial infections. It is beneficial as an insect repellent and helpful against moths and other insects that invade gardens. It is considered a topical treatment when a person is exposed to poison oak or poison ivy. Mugwort is considered to be a bitter herb that is beneficial in aiding digestion. Wormwood has been used for centuries to treat intestinal worms, hence the common name for the plant. As early as the 10th century, medicinal treatises touted *Artemisia*'s use in repelling worms and other pests. In addition to its ancient use for brewing, it is still used for flavoring beer, especially in Great Britain, and some microbreweries are bringing back mugwort beers. Finally, mugwort seeds have been used for baking and for flavoring in many foods. It is used in Korea as a common ingredient in rice cakes, teas, soups, and pancakes, and mugwort rice cakes, or kusa mochi, are used for Japanese sweets called Daifuku (which means great luck) (*Artemisia vulgaris,* n.d.).

In addition to whatever medicinal, psychological, or spiritual benefits that plant oneirogens, such as mugwort, may prove to have, they are an enjoyable way to focus on remembering and exploring dreams, can lead to a more active connection with dreams, and increase interest in cross-cultural dream healing practices. In addition, learning about plant oneirogens make us more sensitive and aware of our connection with nature and promotes interest in ethnobotany. Finally, the exploration of plant oneirogens and medicinal and nutritional uses of wild plants heightens public awareness about the preservation of native plant species, which could help to slow the accelerating decimation of plant communities that may be crucial to human survival.

Alan Siegel

References

Arehart-Treichel, J. (2011, March 4). Amazon people's dreams hold lessons for psychotherapy. *Psychiatric News, 46*(5), 9.

Artemisia vulgaris. (n.d.). *Wikipedia*. Retrieved from http://en.wikipedia.org/wiki/Artemisia_vulgaris.

Callegari, J., & Durand, K. (1977). *Wild edible and medicinal plants of California*. El Cerrito: Callegari and Durand.

Foster, S., & Hobbs, C. (2002). *Western medicinal plants and herbs*. New York: Houghton Mifflin.

Hanrahan, C. (2011). Mugwort. *Encyclopedia of alternative medicine*. Retrieved from http://findarticles.com/p/articles/mi_g2603/is_0005/ai_2603000533/

Hickman, J. (1993). *The Jepson manual: Higher plants of California*. Berkeley: University of California Press.

Hurd, R. (2009). *Enhance your dreamlife*. Philadelphia: dreamstudies.org.

Isaacson, A. (2010, October 13). Amazon awakening. *New York Times*.

Olin, J., & Schneider, L. (2001). Galantamine for Alzheimer's disease (Cochrane Review). Adult and Geriatric Treatment and Preventative Interventions Branch, National Institute of Mental Health (Cochrane Database Syst Rev 2001;4: CD 001747).

Parry, B. (2008, June 10). *Peruvian jungle*. Retrieved from the BBC website: http://www.bbc.co.uk/amazon/sites/peruvianjungle/pages/content.shtml

Silverman, M. (1997). *A city herbal: Lore, legend and use of weeds*. Woodstock, NY: Ashtree Press.

Toro, G., & Thomas, B. (2007). *Drugs of the dreaming: Oneirogens: Salvia divinorum and other dream-enhancing plants*. Rochester, VT: Park Street Press.

Veilleux, C., & King, S. (n.d.). *An introduction to ethnobotany* (Ed. L. Morganstein). Retrieved from http://www.accessexcellence.org/RC/Ethnobotany/page2.php

Yuschak, T. (2006). *Advanced lucid dreaming: The power of supplements*. Lexington, KY: Lulu Press.

Music and Dreams

Anecdotal reports of music occurring in dreams can be found in a variety of places ranging from concert halls to Internet chat rooms to the field notes of anthropologists. While it is likely easiest to find high occurrences of musical dreams among musicians and among shamans, anyone can dream of music. Popular interest in the topic is evidenced by the many questions related to dreaming of music that have been posted on the interactive website Yahoo! Answers (http://answers.yahoo.com). Visitors to the site can provide responses from their own experience to questions such as "What does it mean when you dream about music?" "Is it possible to dream of music you've never heard before?" and "Strange music in dreams?"

Down through history, in indigenous cultures where shamanism is practiced, it is common for practitioners to be given sacred songs in dreams. Receiving such a dream song is often a confirmation of the shaman's calling, and these songs are used in healing rituals and as a way to connect with the spirit world. One major study of these practices is documented in the book *Healing Sounds from the Malaysian Rainforest* by musicologist and anthropologist Marina Roseman (1993). Roseman spent two years living with the Temiar, collecting stories about the songs that came from dreams. Her collection includes 50 such stories which detail the events of the day leading up to the dream in which the song was received (Roseman, 1993, p. 58).

Although a large-scale study of how common musical dreams are in the general

population has yet to be undertaken, a 30-day study by Valeria Uga et al. (2006) specifically designed to collect musical dreams found music occurring in approximately 20 percent of nonmusicians' dreams (*n* = 30) and in approximately 40 percent of musicians' dreams (n = 35). Among other things, the study reported on three ways music appeared in dreams reported by the musician group: music dreamed exactly as it is known in waking life (55%), music known but dreamed in an unusual version (17%), and an entirely unknown piece of music appearing in a dream (28%) (Uga, Lemut, Zampi, Zilli, & Salzarulo, 2006).

Dreams have provided inspiration to both classical and popular musicians. Beethoven's canon "O Tobias," Igor Stravinsky's "Rite of Spring," Tartini's "The Devil's Trill Sonata," and Wagner's "Tristan and Isolde" are among the classical works that owe their existence to dreams (Barrett, 2001). Irving Massey (2006) cites additional examples in "The Musical Dream Revisited."

The Beatles ballad "Yesterday" is likely the most famous and commercially successful song to have come from a dream. Paul McCartney dreamed the melody, and at first was certain he must have heard it before, feeling skeptical that such a lovely tune had truly originated in a dream. But after playing it for many people he became convinced it was a true dream composition, at which point he wrote the song's hauntingly beautiful lyrics, which have stood the test of time (Barrett, 2001; Grace, 2001).

Other contemporary musicians who have dream-inspired songs to their credit include Sting, Johnny Cash, Patti Smith, Billy Joel, Shawn Colvin, Rodney Crowell, Bruce Cockburn, Rory Block, David Bowie, Brooks Williams, jazz musicians Patti Cathcart and Chick Corea, and the South African a cappella group Ladysmith Black Mambazo (Barrett, 2001; Grace, 2001). In most of the previously mentioned cases, dreams have inspired the lyrics of part or all of a song, rather than the music. Examples include Johnny Cash's "When the Man Comes Around," Shawn Colvin's "Polaroids," Sting's "The Lazarus Heart," and Bruce Cockburn's "Wondering Where the Lions Are." The Internet site Songfacts.com lists 51 popular songs inspired by dreams (Songs Inspired by Dreams, n.d.). No doubt a complete list would run into the hundreds, if not thousands.

It is interesting to consider what it means that we dream of music at all, when dreams are predominantly made up of pictorial images. Stefano Carta addresses this question from the perspective of analytical psychology, in which dreams are viewed as self-representations. He argues that sound and music correspond to a more archaic level of psychological functioning than imagery, and therefore music in dreams underlies visual imagery, and may be the purest expression of the emerging self. When music shows up in a dream, the acoustic emotional qualities contained in the music can provide a foundation through which to interpret the dream's visual imagery (Carta, 2009).

In conclusion, it must be noted that only a small amount of research has been done to date on the prevalence, meanings, implications, and applications of music in dreams. This area of study is still in its in-

fancy, offering many paths to explore and much more to be discovered.

Nancy Grace

References

Barrett, D. (2001). The devil plays the violin: Dreams and music. In *The committee of sleep: How artists, scientists, and athletes use their dreams for creative problem-solving—and how you can too* (pp. 66–81). New York: Crown Publishing.

Carta, S. (2009). Music in dreams and the emergence of the self. *Journal of Analytical Psychology, 54,* 85–102.

Grace, N. (2001). Making dreams into music: Contemporary songwriters carry on an age-old dreaming tradition. In K. Bulkeley (Ed.), *Dreams: A reader on the religious, cultural and psychological dimensions of dreaming* (pp. 167–172). New York: Palgrave.

Massey, I. J. (2006). The musical dream revisited: Music and language in dreams. *Psychology of Aesthetics, Creativity, and the Arts, S*(1), 42–50.

Roseman, M. (1993). *Healing sounds from the Malaysian rainforest: Temiar music and medicine.* Berkeley: University of California Press.

Songs inspired by dreams. (n.d.). Retrieved from the Song Facts website: http://www.songfacts.com/category:songs_inspired_by_dreams.php

Uga, V., Lemut, M. C., Zampi, C., Zilli, I., & Salzarulo, P. (2006). Music in dreams. *Consciousness and Cognition, 5,* 351–357.

N

Naps

Naps can be defined as short periods of sleep that can be taken at any time of the 24 hours.

Interestingly, there is no consensus yet on the maximum length for a sleep episode to be defined a nap. In 1987, Dinges and colleagues proposed that a nap is shorter than half the habitual nocturnal sleep, but almost all of the scientific literature puts the upper limit at two hours, or even one hour, given the little feasibility of longer naps in most of the settings.

At variance with the vast majority of mammals, who are polyphasic sleepers (i.e., they have more than one sleep episode, all over the 24 hours), humans tend to be monophasic in most cases, meaning that they concentrate waking time during the daytime/light hours and have only one major sleep period, usually placed at nighttime/dark hours.

However, there are exceptions to this general rule, and taking naps is a habit of several individuals. This habit can be more or less frequent, and it can depend on a number of different reasons, including: (1) *recuperative* need, when the sleepy and fatigued subject has to recover from a previous sleep deprivation/restriction; (2) *prophylactic* strategies, which are aimed at counteracting an expected sleep deprivation and to maintain performance in particular contexts such as shift work or sustained operations; (3) pure *appetitive* drive, linked to sociocultural and individual characteristics. It is quite evident that napping may be often considered a pleasant activity, and many people report a psychological benefit for napping apparently independent from its physiological effects; (4) *age-related polyphasic sleep–wake rhythms,* which occur in both infant and, to a lesser extent, elderly subjects.

How Frequent Are Naps?

An overview of the most recent scientific literature shows that the overall prevalence of napping ranges from approximately 10 to 65 percent. This large variance obviously depends, on one hand, on the different instruments adopted (interviews, diaries, objective measures) and, on the other hand, on demographic characteristics of the population studied (age, nationality, sociocultural background).

According to the 2005 National Sleep Foundation poll on adults' sleep habits, 55 percent of the general population in United States take a nap at least once a week, and more than 10 percent at least four times a week.

Within the United States, African Americans report more frequent napping than Caucasian individuals. The diffusion of napping behavior in the African culture is supported by a very recent study finding high frequencies of habitual napping in a sample of 276 Nigerian undergraduates, age range 19 to 35: 68.1 percent take one to three naps per week, 14.2 percent take four to seven naps per week, with the mean duration of afternoon naps being 70 minutes for males and 90 minutes for females.

Independent from geographical origin, prevalence studies also suggest that habitual nappers are more likely to be males, with higher educational levels than nonnappers. Napping tends to be a very common phenomenon in children, as well. For example, in Saudi Arabia daytime naps were reported in 40.8 percent of the children aged 5 to 13, and a recent study found that among a group of 27 children, whose sleep was accurately controlled through actigraphy, 32 percent reported daytime naps, a prevalence increasing up to almost 50 percent in those children affected by asthma.

Finally, concerning older subjects, napping appears to be a quite common practice in community-dwelling older adults, not necessarily detracting from nighttime sleep duration or quality. At least one nap per week was reported by 67.2 percent of Chinese people aged more than 50, more commonly in the males (76.4%) than the females (63.6%). Among these, 59.4 percent practiced daily. Similar prevalences have been obtained in elderly populations of other geographical regions. This increase of napping behavior across aging is likely the result of increases in nighttime sleep disturbances, phase advance of circadian rhythms, comorbid medical and psychiatric illnesses, and poor sleep habits, raising the question of how naps are related to subjects' health conditions.

Naps and Health

Notwithstanding the widespread diffusion of napping, data on its impact on health are surprisingly scarce and generally limited to elderly subjects. In elderly people, napping has been reported to be associated with increased risk of mortality, diabetes, falls, and hip fracture. Furthermore, a relationship between napping and cardiovascular disease risk has often been highlighted, though it remains unclear, with several studies reporting an association, but not all, and a few studies even reporting that napping may decrease coronary heart disease risk, depending on nap duration and health status. Napping may also be associated with increased risk of cognitive impairment, particularly with compromised executive function in older women. This last observation would seem at odds with what will be said in a following section of this entry, which will highlight the positive impact of napping on cognition, especially memory. However, it is important to distinguish the potential beneficial effect of experimentally imposed naps on memory from the cognitive impairment associated with the frequent napping of older adults in natural contexts. This contrast, along with the conflicting findings mentioned previously, clearly illustrates the complexity of the interrelationships among napping, health, and cognition, which have yet to be fully delineated. A further difficulty is that no specific causal relation can be inferred from the whole bulk of data. Even where clear associations emerge, it is impossible to determine their direction. On one hand, as far as cardiovascular risk is concerned, recent data show that heart rate and blood pressure significantly increase after awakenings, both from nocturnal and daytime sleep, which would lead to an interpretation of naps as protective against morbidity risk. However, it is more likely that an increase in spontaneous napping, as generally observed with aging, represents a consequence of lifestyle changes (above all, an increase of sedentariness), which in turn depend on health worsening. Indeed it would probably be more useful to distinguish frequent, unplanned, longer naps, with a potential to negatively impact nighttime sleep quality and morbidity risk, from brief planned naps, which could instead be of benefit to the function of older adults.

Naps, Vigilance, and Performance

It is commonly accepted that sleep is necessary for effective daytime functioning, especially in terms of vigilance and neurocognitive performance. Actually, in contrast to the largely negative associations just described between habitual napping and general health, short-term laboratory studies generally report very beneficial effects of a nap on these functions. Therefore, as mentioned in the previous section "Naps and Health," one common application of naps would be to counteract vigilance reduction in the work environment, when prolonged operations (and thus, sleep deprivations) are required.

First of all, there have been intriguing laboratory studies trying to clarify whether a given amount of sleep can provide the same beneficial effects for vigilance and performance when split into two or more shorter episodes (split-sleep regimens). Results were encouraging, in that mens). Results were encouraging, in that performance was shown to be a function of total daily time in bed independent of whether sleep was consolidated or split into two parts. An important practical consequence is that correctly timed split sleep, shown to have positive effects, or at least no negative consequences on neurobehavioral performance, might be used for sleep–wake schedules in work environments that involve restricted nocturnal sleep due to critical task scheduling.

Another major source of data is the on-field studies on shift workers, clearly showing that the alertness- and performance-enhancing effects of naps during both night and afternoon shifts can be quite dramatic. It appears that a daytime nap as short as 10 minutes can improve alertness and performance of sleep-deprived subjects by about 2.5 hours and that short naps may even be beneficial in absence of sleep loss for those with moderately disturbed sleep and possibly for normal sleepers.

To adequately adopt napping strategies as a part of programs aiming to improve safety and health in the work place, some crucial aspects remain to be fully understood: (1) what is the best nap duration to achieve the most effective alerting effects: it has been suggested that naps longer than 45 minutes could be detrimental because they would be frequently associated with awakenings from deep sleep, which in turn result in a higher degree of sleep inertia (i.e., experience of drowsiness and worsening of cognitive performance occurring at awakening); (2) the possible combination with other behavioral or pharmacological strategies (such as caffeine), to maximize alertness at crucial time points as a countermeasure to sleepiness in operational shift work; (3) how neurocognitive effects of naps may be modulated by individual variables (i.e., chronotypologies) and as a function of their circadian placement: for example, taking a nap too late in the day might deeply affect night-sleep continuity and make it difficult to fall asleep at habitual bedtime, whereas taking it in the morning hours could be hampered by the low circadian sleep propensity (i.e., the rising curve of body temperature would result in a short, fragmented and possibly ineffective nap); finally, (4) whether and how different cognitive functions (attention, working memory, higher cognitive functions such as decision making and planning) are differentially influenced by napping.

Naps, Memory, and Dreams

According to studies carried out in the last 10 years, the facilitating role of sleep for memory consolidation of what is learnt before sleep (the so-called sleep effect) would be observed even for the short sleep episodes. Quite surprisingly, and differently from what has been reported for the night-sleep effect, a beneficial nap effect was consistently found for any kind of memory (i.e., both procedural and declarative tasks). However, the effect strength ranges from quite dramatic changes, even including the actual improvement of memory performance at awakening, to less relevant modifications, usually limited to a reduction of the forgetting/deterioration rate, which seemingly depends on numerous factors, either related to sleep or memory. Although there is not yet a clear knowledge of what sleep features are crucial for the nap effect on memory consolidation, more robust effects seem to be given by slightly longer naps, about 60 to 90 minutes, likely due to the buildup of both short-wave sleep and REM sleep. The possible roles of sleep-states amount, sleep continuity, and organization remain to be verified, as well the hypothesis that a memory-enhancing process is triggered by sleep onset per se.

The purported beneficial impact of naps on memory should deserve special attention at early ages, because this might be of interest with respect to learning processes and school performance. A final statement could be made on oneiric activity during naps. Occasionally, the presence of dream recall has been found after all awakenings from nap, with longer recalls after REM awakenings than after NREM awakenings. However, it is still unknown how the contents of dream during naps may differ from those of night-sleep dreams.

Gianluca Ficca

See also: entries related to Sleep and Development; entries related to Sleep Assessment

References

Dhand, R., & Sohal, H. (2006). Good sleep, bad sleep! The role of daytime naps in healthy adults. *Current Opinion in Pulmonary Medicine, 12,* 379–382.

Dinges, D. F., Orne, M. T., Whitehouse, W. G., & Orne, E. C. (1987). Temporal placement of a nap for alertness: contributions of circadian phase and prior wakefulness. *Sleep, 10*(4), 313–329.

Ficca, G., Axelsson, J., Mollicone, D. J., Muto, V., & Vitiello, M. V. (2010). Naps, cognition and performance. *Sleep Medicine Reviews, 14,* 249–258.

National Sleep Foundation (NSF). (2005). Adult sleep habit: 2005 poll. Retrieved from http://www.sleepfoundation.org/

Picarsic, J.L., Glynn, N.W., Taylor, C.A., Katula, J.A., Goldman, S.E., Studenski, S.A., & Newman, A.B. (2008). Self-eported napping, sleep duration and quality in the Lifestyle Interventions and Independence for Elders Pilot (LIFEP) Study. *Journal of the American Geriatric Society, 56,* 1674–1680.

Takahashi, M. (2003). The role of prescribed napping in sleep medicine. *Sleep Medicine Reviews, 7,* 227–235.

Narcolepsy and Dreaming

Narcolepsy is a neurological illness occurring secondary to damage to central nervous system (CNS) cells utilizing oxexin as their primary neurotransmitter. Narcolepsy patients present with symptoms of extreme daytime sleepiness usually develop these symptoms during the psychologically and sexually stormy years of adolescence. Most narcoleptics are intense dreamers who often experience dreamlike epiphenomena, including hypnogogic hallucinations and sleep paralysis. In 50 percent of narcoleptics, REM-sleep intrusion into wakefulness results in symptoms of cataplexy—abrupt episodes of motor weakness occurring with emotion.

Narcolepsy was first described as a diagnosis during a period when diseases such as narcolepsy and epilepsy, now known to have clear neurological basis, were classified among the psychoses and neurosis. Freud's first book on dreaming, published in 1900, led to a psychoanalytic fascination with the dreamlike epiphenomena of narcolepsy. It is not surprising that psychoanalysis was used to treat narcolepsy, particularly during an era in which alternative treatment modalities for narcolepsy included electroshock therapy and psychosurgery. Before the use activating medications for narcolepsy became accepted in the 1930s, many narcoleptics underwent extensive psychoanalysis. Freud postulated that dreams were protectors of sleep, with sleep viewed as a temporary escape from harsh reality into a memory of protected intrauterine nirvana. Psychodynamically, narcolepsy became viewed as a disease of psychological regression. Theoretic constructs based on repression, abuse, mythology, and transference served as a basis for attempts at intense interpersonal therapy for patients with the diagnosis. However, there is little evidence, even based on anecdotal case studies, that psychoanalysis led to an improvement in patient symptoms or affected the course of the illness for individual patients in a positive fashion (Pagel & Scrima, 2010, pp. 129–134). Community and medical conceptions of narcolepsy continue to be affected by this psychogenic history with the diagnosis viewed as one based on suppressed, guilt-ridden, sexual drives. This conceptual association may contribute to social and medical handicaps for some narcolepsy patients with physicians and cohorts demonstrating a lack of understanding and on occasions taking a moral stance in labeling them as "lazy, unable to work, or unable to face the vicissitudes" (Zarcone, 1973, pp. 1156–1168).

In the current era, narcolepsy is clearly a neurological illness with a well-defined genetic and neurotransmitter basis. Psychoanalysis-based therapy is rarely used in its treatment; however, this history continues to affect social and medical attitudes toward patients. While psychoanalysis has failed as a treatment and psycho-pathogenesis as a model when applied to the clinical diagnosis of narcolepsy; the psychoanalytic theory of narcolepsy, as well as the association of narcolepsy with REM-sleep epiphenomena, has been integrated and applied in forming the conceptual framework for some of the most widely accepted neuroscientific theories of consciousness. Narcolepsy epiphenomena were postulated to be related to normal dreaming since they were associated with REM sleep, a state that theoretically came to be equated with the presence of dreaming. This association between REM sleep, narcolepsy, and dreaming forced psychoanalysts to stretch the definition of dreaming to include the REM sleep associated with bizarre, hallucinatory mental activity of narcolepsy that could occur in both sleep and wake states. This definition, "bizarre mental activity occurring in either sleep or wake," is currently the generally accepted psychoanalytic definition of dreaming (Pagel et al., 2001, pp. 195–202). This postulate, that dreams are bizarre, hallucinatory mental activity, has been extended into the theory that dreams are a form of visual hallucination and a valid model for psychosis. Dreaming viewed as perceptual hallucination can be considered as a simple meaningless, perceptual state based on primitive brain-stem activity (REM sleep of the self-referenced mind utilized by the CNS during sleep to detoxify the system of unwanted memories of potentially pathological nature such as obsessions, hallucinations, and delusions [Crick & Mitchinson, 1983, pp. 111–114]). The conception of REM dreaming as bizarre and REM sleep as a psychodynamically primitive state of CNS activation parodying the psychoanalytic id persists in modern versions of activation–synthesis theory, including the activation, input, modulation model (Hobson, 1999, pp. 188–215). While today, psychoanalysis is only rarely utilized in the clinical treatment of narcolepsy, psychoanalytic perspectives of the dreamlike epiphenomena of narcolepsy continue to be incorporated into popular and theoretical conceptions of dreaming, sleep, and consciousness.

James F. Pagel

See also: entries related to Sleep Disorders

References

Crick, F., & Mitchinson, G. (1983). The function of dream sleep. *Nature, 304,* 111–114.

Hobson, J. A. (1999). *Abnormal states of consciousness: AIM as a diagnostic tool in consciousness.* New York: Scientific American Library.

Pagel, J. F., Blagrove, M., Levin, R., et. al. (2001). Defining dreaming—A paradigm for comparing disciplinary specific definitions of dream. *Dreaming, 11*(4), 195–202.

Pagel, J. F., & Scrima, L. (2010). In M. Goswami, S.R. Pandi-Perumal, & M. Thorpy (Ed.). *Psychoanalysis and narcolepsyin narcolepsy—A clinical guide* (pp. 129–134). New York: Springer/Humana Press.

Zarcone, V. (1973.) Narcolepsy. *New England Journal of Medicine, 288,* 1156–1168.

Narcolepsy and Sleep Paralysis, Hypnopompic/Hypnagogic Hallucinations

Narcolepsy is a rare and chronic sleep disorder affecting approximately 0.04 percent of the population. Narcoleptic patients experience excessive daytime sleepiness, cataplexy, and manifestations related to rapid eye movement (REM) sleep, such as sleep paralysis and hypnopompic/hypnagogic hallucinations. The loss of a central nervous system peptide called hypocretin is the reason for the development of narcolepsy. Hypocretin has important functions in promoting wakefulness. Excessive daytime sleepiness, sleep paralysis, and hypnopompic/hypnagogic hallucinations can also occur in individuals who are severely sleep deprived; only cataplexy is unique to narcolepsy.

Sleep–wake-cycle instability is an important hallmark of narcolepsy, specifically between REM sleep and wake states. Sleep paralysis and hypnopompic/hypnagogic hallucinations are a consequence of REM sleep–wake-cycle instability. In REM sleep, the body loses muscle tone and dreaming occurs. During this physiologically normal process, essentially all muscles of the body are paralyzed with the exception of the diaphragm, the primary muscle of breathing. In narcoleptic patients, REM sleep is considered to be unstable because it inappropriately intrudes into their waking states. In other words, REM sleep seems to be inappropriately jumping into wakefulness, causing the individual to be paralyzed while awake. Narcoleptic patients experience some aspects of REM sleep during wakefulness (such as loss of muscle tone as seen in cataplexy) or during transitions from sleep to wake states (sleep paralysis).

Sleep paralysis is the inability to purposefully move one's muscles at sleep onset or upon awakening. In sleep paralysis, components of REM sleep occur inappropriately as the individual falls asleep or awakens. Individuals with sleep paralysis experience a brief loss of voluntary muscle control with an inability to move or speak; however, awareness is preserved. Unlike cataplexy, these episodes are not provoked by intense emotional states. It can be a frightening experience because the individual attempts to, but is unable to move, open eyes, or even speak, and is very aware of this occurrence. Sleep paralysis is often associated with very frightening hypnopompic/hypnagogic hallucinations. The episodes are brief lasting several seconds to minutes, and with time, the experience becomes less frightening.

Hypnopompic/hypnagogic hallucinations are intense dreamlike states that occur at sleep onset (hypnagogic) or more commonly upon awakening (hypnopompic). Like normal dreams, hallucinations are visual in nature, but unlike normal dreams, they are vivid, frightening, or disturbing to the individual. They may involve other senses such as hearing or smell. Visual hallucinations consist of simple forms and shapes to very intricate images including animals or people. Auditory hallucinations may be threatening, leaving the individual upset or terrified. Individuals may report hallucinations such as body floating in air, falling from air, or out-of-body experiences. The exact boundary between hypnopompic/hypnagogic hallucinations and dreams is not a clear one.

Treatment of narcolepsy includes medications that suppress REM-sleep instability and prevent daytime sleepiness. These medications will also treat sleep paralysis and hypnopompic/hypnagogic hallucinations in the same manner by stabilizing REM sleep. One category of antidepressants known as selective norepinephrine/

serotoninergic reuptake inhibitors is used to treat narcolepsy with cataplexy and is effective for sleep paralysis and hypnopompic/hypnagogic hallucinations. The most commonly used drug of this class is venlafaxine, a potent inhibitor of two wake-promoting chemicals in the brain: serotonin and norepinephrine. New treatment options are under investigation for the treatment of narcolepsy including hypocretin replacement therapy, gene therapy, and stem-cell transplantation.

It is important to remember that sleep paralysis and hypnopompic/hypnagogic hallucinations are present in other sleep-related disorders, including any condition that causes severe sleep deprivation. The two phenomena also commonly occur in the general population. Medications used for narcolepsy will also treat sleep paralysis and hypnopompic/hypnagogic hallucinations; however, they are not recommended as treatment for isolated sleep paralysis and/or hypnopompic/hypnagogic hallucinations. If an individual experiences recurrent episodes of sleep paralysis and/or hypnopompic/hypnagogic hallucinations, it is recommended that he or she be evaluated for the presence of an undiagnosed sleep-related disorder, such as obstructive sleep apnea or narcolepsy.

Michelle Cao

See also: entries related to Sleep and Health; entries related to Sleep Physiology

References

Cao, M. (2010). Advances in narcolepsy. *Medical Clinics of North America, 94*(3), 541–555.

Dauviliers, Y., Arnulf, I., & Mignot, E. (2007). Narcolepsy with cataplexy. *Lancet, 369,* 499–511.

Nishino, S., Okuro, M., Kotorii, N., et al. (2010). Hypocretin/orexin and narcolepsy: New basic and clinical insights. *Acta Physiologica, 198,* 209–222.

Ohayon, M. M., Priest, R. G., Caucet, M., et al. (1996). Hypnagogic and hypnopompic hallucinations: Pathological phenomenon? *British Journal of Psychiatry, 169,* 459–467.

Rechtschaffen, A., Wolpert, E., Dement, W. C., et al. (1963). Nocturnal sleep of narcoleptics. *Electroencephalography and Clinical Neurophysiology, 15,* 599–609.

Takahashi, Y., & Jimbo, M. (1963). Polygraphic study of narcoleptic syndrome with special reference to hypnagogic hallucinations and cataplexy. *Folia Psychiatrica Neurologica Japan, 7*(Suppl), 343–347.

Narcolepsy Symptoms, Abnormal REM Sleep, and Hypocretin Deficiency

Narcolepsy, a condition affecting about 1 in 2,000 individuals, is caused by the autoimmune destruction of ~70,000 hypothalamic neurons producing the neuropeptide hypocretin/orexin, a neurobiological system involved in sleep regulation. Since its description, the disorder has fascinated researchers and clinicians, notably because patients experience not only sleepiness and disturbed sleep but also unusual symptoms such as cataplexy, sleep paralysis, REM sleep behavior disorder (RBD), and hypnagogic hallucinations, symptoms that are best explained by a blurring of wakefulness with rapid eye movement (REM) sleep. In sleep paralysis and cataplexy, monosynaptic reflexes are abolished, as they are during REM sleep, suggesting the engagement similar final common neuroanatomical pathways. Similarly, RBD, vivid dreaming, and hallucinations are commonly referred as dissociated REM-sleep events, in which the cardinal features of REM-sleep atonia, vivid dreaming, and loss of awareness are uncoordinated with each other. Narcolepsy is thus an experiment of nature, in which unique subfeatures of REM sleep can be isolated and subjected to investigation.

Part of the narcolepsy phenotype is directly caused by the removal of the effects of hypocretin/orexin on REM sleep and wake propensity. Indeed, pharmaceutical studies using antagonists or agonists support this concept, as does the common observation of reduced REM-sleep latency and the presence of sleepiness in narcolepsy. Importantly, however, the phenotype of narcolepsy cannot be recapitulated by REM sleep or total sleep deprivation alone. Shortened REM sleep, sudden dreaming, hypnagogic hallucinations, or sleep paralysis may occur following sleep deprivation or sleep fragmentation; in contrast, cataplexy has never been reported under these conditions. This suggests that cataplexy is somewhat uniquely different from REM-sleep atonia, a concept also supported by differential neurochemical control in pharmacological studies.

Much has also been learned from recent observations on the natural history of the disease. Following the development of hypocretin deficiency in narcolepsy, sleepiness and abnormal dreaming are usually first to appear, followed by cataplexy and a distressing inability to maintain sleep. Excessive sleep is also common shortly after onset, subsequently replaced by an inability to stay awake and asleep for long periods of time. Sleep paralysis is less-commonly reported prior to puberty, a finding that may reflect a maturational effect or could

be due to the difficulty of identifying this symptom in young children.

It is also notable that around the onset of narcolepsy, spontaneous muscle weakness episodes affecting the jaw or head, or a generalized feeling of weakness with an unstable gait are commonly reported rather than typical cataplexy. Often, several months are required before cataplexy becomes stereotyped and triggered by usual emotions—laughing or humor. These successive changes suggest that cataplexy is the result of network remodeling, perhaps to compensate for what was initially a more-generalized muscle weakness. Similarly, whereas abnormal dreaming in recent onset narcolepsy immediately impairs sleep, the occurrence of prolonged nighttime awakenings often occurs later once the full syndrome is established. This may be explained by the delayed engagement of compensatory wake-promoting systems that could be equally functioning at night and during the day.

As noted by many authors, the projections of the hypocretin system are anatomically widespread, providing the anatomical basis for independent effects on selected REM sleep and non-REM sleep correlates. For example, hypocretin projections to the sublaterodorsal tegmental nucleus (an REM sleep-on region of the brain stem), the locus coeruleus, or even the spinal cord could all be involved in the regulation of REM-sleep atonia, whereas projection to the basal forebrain may be more important for forebrain activation. It is not unreasonable to postulate that differential redundancy (and thus variable compensation after depletion) occurs for hypocretin projections regulating individual REM-sleep features. This compensation is also likely more effective depending on the state of engagement of these systems in other tasks. For example, the reversal of atonia may be most difficult in wakefulness and during sleep–wake transitions, explaining sleep paralysis. Similarly, a pathway compensating for atonia may also be uniquely challenged when laughing, an act reportedly associated with a brief suppression of the spinal monosynaptic H reflex. One of the candidates for this last pathway could involve adrenergic activation, as adrenergic uptake inhibitors (i.e., some antidepressants) are profoundly anticataplectic agents. Further, stimulation of the locus coeruleus seems to gate some of the hypocretin effects following optogenetic stimulation, in particular muscle atonia.

As illustrated previously, narcolepsy is a unique experiment of nature that has yet to reveal its full potential as a tool to understanding various aspects of REM-sleep circuitry and its plasticity in response to hypocretin depletion. Imaging studies in dissociated states, may, for example, provide us with a better understanding one day of how the brain is or is not aware during REM sleep, and why the experience of dreaming is normally so rapidly forgotten (or in abnormal instances pathologically retained). Similarly, optogenic or localized genetic rescue experiments in receptor knockout narcoleptic animals will likely improve our understanding of REM-sleep-regulating networks.

Emmanuel Mignot

See also: entries related to Hormones in Sleep

References

Bassetti, C., Billiard, M., & Mignot, E. (2007). *Narcolepsy and hypersomnia.* New York: Informa Healthcare.

Serra, L., Montagna, P., Mignot, E., Lugaresi, E., & Plazzi, G. (2008). Cataplexy features in childhood narcolepsy. *Movement Disorders, 23*(6), 858–865.

Native American Dreams

Among indigenous peoples, dreams and dreaming are highly valued and often incorporated into ritual practices. Dreams are a primary source for cultural innovation, ritual renewal, communal activities, and personal guidance. With more than 140 recognized Native American communities, each speaking a diverse language, dream categorization and theory is complex and irreducible to any single metatheory or specific cosmology. Overall, the emphasis tends to be on the value of the dream as empowering actions that serve the needs of the community. In many communities, dreams are indexed typologically in terms of the degree of power transmitted to the dreamer. For example, among the Apsarokee dreams are analyzed into four primary categories (Irwin, 2005a, 2005b): no account (most dreams), wish fulfilling (compensatory dreams), medicine dreams (power is given to the dreamer), and what is truly seen (dreams of knowledge often linked to a variety of psychic abilities, including clairvoyance and controlled out-of-body projection). Medicine dreams are rare and given utmost attention as a source of success in life; what is truly seen dreams usually occur to only developed shaman dreamers.

Medicine dreams that confer some degree of power or ability are attained in three ways: spontaneously and unsought, spontaneously in times of crisis linked to prayer and petition to the spirit world, and sought dreams or visions through intense ritual practices. The source of the dream is usually mapped to the cosmological and spiritual world of the seeker in which causal agents are identified as giving a dream of power as a gift from the spirit world. The appropriate attitude of the dreamer in seeking a dream is humility, clear intention, and thankfulness; dreams are sought by shedding tears (occasionally blood, e.g., cutting a finger) and praying intensely without food or water over many days while often confined within a 12-foot fasting circle. The seeker walks toward each of the four directions, with small steps, holding a pipe and praying with each step. Vision-dreams may come while the faster is asleep or wide awake. Other traditions involve confinement in a fasting hut (often for women), in a tree, or while wandering without eating in the forest. The seeker is usually observed by an experienced elder dreamer who can assess the state and well-being of the faster. The ritual fast is normally preceded by a sweat lodge before and after the fast; in the final sweat, dreams are shared and interpreted by elders in utmost privacy. Generally, a dreamer does not discuss a dream with others except with dream experts or with members of a dream society based on those having similar dreams (Irwin, 1994).

The proof of the dream is in the enactment. As dreams are considered sources of sacred power, the successful dreamer must be able to give a public demonstration of that power. Failure to heal after dreams of healing signals a discontinuity between the dreamer and the causal agency of the dream; repeated failure means the dream was not understood. Native dream theory incorporates some degree of variability of success based on the match between the communal need and the specific ability of the dreamer. Someone with a specific illness may not be healed because the gift of healing is meant only for certain types of illness; or, a dreamer is given diagnostic power in the dream but may not be able to diagnose correctly if an illness exceeds the knowledge given in the dream. Dreamers may fast for additional dream powers and those who failed in a dream quest may try again. Dream powers given may include hunting ability, success in warfare, psychic abilities, herbal knowledge, ritual directions and songs, as well as various types of ambiguous power that might harm others. Another major dream category is prophetic dreams, which are the source of many native religious movements based on instructions received in big dreams meant to reconstruct native religious practices and beliefs in the face of colonialism, missionization, and aggressive assault by church and government (Irwin, 2008). More research is needed in the area of specific dream practices in contemporary native urban life and in prisons.

Lee Irwin

See also: entries related to Cross-Cultural Dreams

References

Irwin, L. (1994). *The dream seekers: Native American visionary traditions of the Great Plains*. Norman: University of Oklahoma Press.

Irwin, L. (2005a). Dreams and visions. In S. Crawford & D Kelly (Eds.), *Encyclopedia of American Indian religions* (Vol. 1, pp. 240–249). Santa Barbara, CA: ABC-CLIO.

Irwin, L. (2005b). Vision quest rites. In S. Crawford & D Kelly (Eds.), *Encyclopedia of American Indian religions* (Vol. 3, pp. 1127–1134). Santa Barbara, CA: ABC-CLIO.

Irwin, L. (2008). *Coming down from above: Prophecy, renewal and resistance in Native American religions*. Norman: University of Oklahoma Press.

Neural Metaphor and Dreams

In the three decades since the discovery that ordinary thought is largely metaphorical, metaphor researchers have come to understand that, like all other concepts, conceptual metaphors are physical circuits in the brain. Primary metaphors are acquired by the hundreds in childhood, often prior to language, just by living in the everyday world, where different kinds of experiences often come together.

Every time a child is held affectionately by a parent, the child experiences affection and warmth together, and he or she activates different brain regions. Every time a child sees more water or milk poured into a glass and sees the level rise, distinct brain regions for quantity and verticality are activated. When two brain regions are activated repeatedly, their synapses strengthen, activation spreads over existing pathways, with synapses strengthening every time the two regions are activated together. Eventually, the shortest pathway is found, and a circuit is formed. That circuit is a metaphor physically in the brain. That is how primary metaphors such as *affection is warmth* and *more is up* are formed.

Hundreds of primary metaphors are learned in this way. Because 98 percent of thought is unconscious, the use of such metaphors usually goes unnoticed. The primary metaphors neurally bind with each other and other concepts to form many thousands of conceptual metaphors, all physically in the brain, all mapping inferences from source to target domains, and all fixed and ready to be unconsciously activated whether you are awake or dreaming.

Primary metaphors are embodied in three ways: they arise from bodily experiences, they are physically in the brain, and they give rise to physical behavior, as recent experiments on embodied cognition have shown. Subjects at Yale University were given either warm or cold coffee and then asked to describe someone they imagined just meeting. Those who had the warm coffee imagined meeting friendly, affectionate people. *Affection is warmth* was activated by the warm coffee. Subjects who were asked to say nasty lies about other people chose to either wash their hands or use cleansing wipes afterward. The *morality is purity* metaphor was at work. And so on for dozens of experiments.

In dreams, concerns and experiences of the day tend to activate preexisting metaphor circuitry to produce dreams of relevance to the concerns most active in one's brain during the day.

A woman dreamt that she was walking on a dirt road that became narrower and narrower, then became an uphill trail through dense brush. She climbed to the top of the hill where she saw an anthropology professor of her acquaintance coming out of Trader Joe's. "Don't bother," he said. "The anthropologists have cleaned out the place."

She had, after years of motherhood, got a PhD in anthropology, but could not get a regular job, only teaching a class here and there. She was about to give up and go into another profession. Trader Joe's is the place where the local academics buy party goods. The dream activated widespread conceptual metaphors: *a career is a journey upward* (climbing the ladder of success); *difficulties are impediments to motion* (roadblocks, glass ceilings); *achieving as purpose is getting a desired object,* typically food (as in the fruits of one's labor). In the dream, her career path was long and difficult, it narrowed, the uphill climb was difficult. An academic job in anthropology would have been the fruit of her labor, but the fruit was all taken.

A friend was distraught after splitting up with his lover. He dreamed that night that they had started driving north on a local freeway. As they reached the freeway bridge, a storm blew up and the bridge was blown into the bay.

The widespread metaphors here are *love is a journey*—in which difficulties are an impediment to motion—and *emotional states are weather states*. The lovers start out on their journey, emotional storms arise, and the bridge blown out makes the journey of life impossible.

Much of child rearing is based on metaphors of morality that shape family life. The two most prominent are *morality is obedience,* giving rise to a strict father family, and *morality is nurturance,* giving rise to a nurturant parent family. The *obedience* metaphor makes the strict father the moral authority in the family whose word is law and who has to physically punish all of children's wrongdoings. Therapists have reported to me that bad dreams and corresponding neuroses result, especially where there is a conflict between the metaphors for strictness versus nurturance.

George Lakoff

See also: entries related to Dream Content

References

Lakoff, G. (1993, June). How metaphor structures dreams: The theory of conceptual metaphor applied to dream analysis, *Dreaming.*

Lakoff, G. (1996). *Moral politics.* Chicago: University of Chicago Press.

Lakoff, G. (1997). How unconscious metaphorical thought shapes dreams. In D. J. Stein (Ed.), *Cognitive science and the Unconscious.* American Psychiatric Press.

Lakoff, G., & Johnson, M. (1980). *Metaphors we live by.* Chicago: University of Chicago Press.

Lakoff, G., & Johnson, M. (1999). *Philosophy in the flesh: The embodied mind and its challenge to Western thought.* New York: Basic Books.

Neuroanatomical Correlates of Dream Censorship

The term censor was coined by Sigmund Freud to denote the critical and prohibiting agency in the mind. Since the establishment of the structural model of personality, Freud gradually replaced this term with the term superego to reify the roles of this prominent entity of the mind in both nocturnal and daytime psychic life. The censor or superego is acquired largely from experiences and interactions with significant others. It begins to develop in the oedipal phase (around three years of age) when the ego learns to master the instinctual impulses arising from the id in a bid to preserve the object relation via the mechanisms of identification and reaction formation. The primary purpose of the censorship is to screen out disagreeable ideas, memories, and motives before they enter into the conscious or preconscious system. During sleep, however, this censorship function becomes weaker, thus allowing material from the id to surface in the form of dreams.

The censorship or moral function is an intricate process in both the psychodynamic and the neurodynamic senses. It is the amalgam of primitive inclination and adaptation and of acquired self-monitoring and moral reasoning. Nevertheless, the most basic form of the censor or superego can be conceived as a mental agency that inherits basic sensitivity to emotions; in particular, to anxiety (1). Therefore, it is capable of detecting error, danger, or punishment (2), and is able to develop and learn through behavioral and social conditioning (3). As such, it can make decisions as to whether or not to inhibit directly (4) or it can trigger other mechanisms to defend against dangerous or punishable immediate satisfaction (5), to avoid the negative consequence resulting from doing so (6). In this sense, the censor may influence the process of dream formation but is not necessarily the agency that carries out the dream formation or distortion.

According to Yu (2003, 2006), all foregoing six functional features of the censor can be localized in the orbitofrontal cortex. It has been known that lesions in this region of the brain lead to a group of disorders related to moral and affective functioning, including poor judgment, moral confusion, misinterpretation of the moods and feelings of others, empathic changes and apathy, and sociopathic behaviors. It has also been observed that people with antisocial disorders or moral dysfunctions show neurological symptoms of autonomic and emotional underarousal, and lower fearfulness, poor fear conditioning, and poor avoidance learning. Accordingly, it may be the case that emotional and autonomic arousal constitutes the structural bedrock for conditioning, which is critical for the development and maintenance of moral and inhibitory functions. The orbitofrontal cortex clearly functions for primitive inhibition and morality, not necessarily sustained by logical scaffoldings; instead, under the predisposition of genetic programming and alterations, it is modulated and maintained through social affective interactions and stimulus-response learning. This primitive inhibitory and moral function, which can transpire unconsciously, is a pivotal part of the censor.

The prefrontal convexity—including the orbitofrontal cortex—is deactivated throughout the sleep cycle, while the mesial frontal region—the neural substrate for the instinctual reservoir—are highly active (for details see Yu, 2001, 2003, 2007). This neuropsychological manifestation is reminiscent of Freud's description that the censor is crippled during dreaming sleep and thus its governance over the id energies is loosened. It should be noted, however, that although the prefrontal cortex is significantly deactivated, activity is still present—in other words, it remains operative. On the strength of the neuroimaging findings, Braun et al. (1997) hypothesized that REM episodes occurring later in the sleep period would be characterized by increasing coherence of prefrontal, dorsomedial thalamic, and striatal activity, which could in turn correlate with the time-of-night-dependent changes in the length and complexity of REM-sleep dream reports. Indeed, the level of activation or deactivation of the prefrontal cortex may change across different REM episodes within one sleep epoch and gradually recover its normal activity from its lowest point in the first REM episode, via progressive activation in the intermediate REM episodes, to its full convalescence in postsleep waking. By implication, not only is this vigilant agency never totally quiescent during all REM episodes, it also gradually recuperates from deep relaxation and becomes highly alert toward the end of sleep.

Contemporary brain-imaging research has resulted in a consistent picture of the neural network of dreaming. While the most robust activity in the mesial frontal region is observed in dreaming sleep and the most precipitous decreases are found in the prefrontal cortex, the most tranquil moment of the mesial frontal region occurs in presleep wakefulness, while at the same time the prefrontal cortex is most activated. These oscillatory neurodynamics between the prefrontal and subcortical activities seem to mirror the psychodynamics between the censor and the id.

Calvin Kai-Ching Yu

References

Braun, A.R., Balkin, T.J., Wesensten, N.J., Carson, R.E., Varga, M., Baldwin, P., . . . Herscovitch, P. (1997). Regional cerebral blood flow throughout the sleep-wake cycle. *Brain, 120,* 1173–1197.

Yu, C.K.-C. (2001). Neuroanatomical correlates of dreaming, II: The ventromesial frontal region controversy (dream instigation). *Neuro-Psychoanalysis, 3,* 193–201.

Yu, C.K.-C. (2003). Neuroanatomical correlates of dreaming, III: The frontal-lobe controversy (dream censorship). *Neuro-Psychoanalysis, 5,* 159–169.

Yu, C.K.-C. (2006). Commentary on Simon Boag's "Freudian dream theory, dream bizarreness, and the disguise-censor controversy." *Neuro-Psychoanalysis, 8,* 53–59.

Yu, C.K.-C. (2007). Cessation of dreaming and ventromesial frontal-region infarcts. *Neuro-Psychoanalysis, 9,* 85–92.

Neuroanatomical Correlates of Dreamwork

Sigmund Freud (1900) believed that the manifest content of dreams was not necessarily the direct representation of the dreamers' thoughts and motives. He delineated some dreamwork processes through which the latent dream thoughts are transformed into the manifest content. The most prominent of these distortion processes are regression, condensation, displacement, and symbolism. On the strength of neuroanatomical evidence, some researchers (Solms, 1997; Yu, 2001, 2006) postulate that dreamwork is orchestrated by the neural network made up of the prefrontal cortex, the supramarginal gyrus in the inferior parietal lobule, and the inferior mesial temporal lobe.

The growth of the prefrontal cortex, which continues after birth and does not end until late adolescence, is susceptible to environmental modifications. As the prefrontal cortex develops, a child's behavior begins to become subordinated to logical reasoning, complex programs, and evaluation and correction of errors. Brain-imaging studies have repeatedly found that the prefrontal convexity is substantially deactivated during dreaming when the subcortical regions are highly active. According to Yu (2003, 2007), these findings provide evidence for the mechanism of *temporal regression* that through dreaming, mental activity regresses developmentally from the experience-dependent adult cortex back to the instinctual and motivational system of the brain that dominates in infancy and childhood; mature logical reasoning and modes of thinking are temporarily suspended in the service of illogical, narcissistic, childish ones.

The dorsolateral frontal cortex is one of the major divisions of the prefrontal convexity. Its primary function is to convert thoughts into action by programming motor sequences. The inferior parietal lobule, and in particular the supramarginal gyrus, participates in the highest levels of perceptual information processing, including symbolic operations. This function is required for the conversion of concrete perception into abstract thinking, and for the retention of organized experience. The dorsolateral frontal cortex is deactivated during dreaming, suggesting that the motor gateway from motives to actions is blocked (see Yu [2003] for a review of neurological evidence). By contrast, the posterior brain plays an active part in dream formation (Yu, 2001, 2006), and lesions in the supramarginal gyrus result in global cessation of dreaming (Solms, 1997). Accordingly, the focal point of mentation activity shifts from the dorsolateral frontal region, the executive end of the motor system in waking life, toward the perceptual system,

via the retrograde pathway provided by the inferior parietal lobule. This is exactly what Freud meant by *topographical regression*—the most essential part of the process whereby dreams are formed. Because of this topographical regressive process, away from the motor system and toward the perceptual system, dreamers do not actually engage in motivated activity during sleep but imagine they are doing so.

From an anatomical perspective, there are probably multiple pathways for connecting the subcortical motivational system and the visual cortex. The inferior mesial temporal lobe has been identified as one of the crucial pathways, in addition to the supramarginal gyrus, for the generation of dreams (Yu, 2001). The inferotemporal cortex has intense afferent and efferent connections to both the visual representation cortex and the subcortical motivational system. It is well known that abnormal excitation of the temporal lobe alone during an epileptic attack or exploratory electrical stimulation during surgery can lead to experiential hallucinations and perceptual illusions that bear a resemblance to a dreaming state. The experiential hallucinations caused by excitations to the temporal cortex are often reported to be unfamiliar, strange, and senseless, but after exploration can be broken up into shorter or longer sequences of earlier experiences. This is similar to what Freud referred to as *condensation*. The perceptual illusions triggered by the stimulation of the temporal cortex involve a sudden change in the perceived appearance of an object or in the subjective feeling toward an object, including, for example, things suddenly becoming familiar or appearing to be strange, becoming larger or smaller, and coming closer or going farther away. From the Freudian perspective, any event of incoherent, accentuated, or diminished intensity occurring in dreams is ascribed to the effect of displacement.

The inferior temporal cortex is functionally specialized for object representations. This area of the brain is driven by complexity rather than specificity. The activation of the inferior temporal cortex provides relatively coarse and imprecise representations of visual objects. Additionally, the inferior temporal cortex is centrally engaged in classifying visual stimuli into certain behaviorally meaningful categories, and therefore, forging connections between visual experiences, complex or sequential behavioral patterns, and temporal emotional experiences. This capacity of the inferior temporal cortex is essential for symbolism to take place. Therefore, as with condensation and displacement, the dreamwork mechanism of symbolism most probably transpires in the inferior temporal lobe. Taken together, dreamwork or dream formation may not only be facilitated by the pervasive deactivation of the dorsolateral prefrontal cortex but also positively caused by the activation of the posterior brain and inferior temporal structures.

Calvin Kai-Ching Yu

References

Freud, S. (1900). The interpretation of dreams. In J. Strachey (Ed. & Trans.), *The standard edition of the complete works of Sigmund Freud* (Vols. 4–5). London: Hogarth Press.

Solms, M. (1997). *The neuropsychology of dreams: A clinico-anatomical study*. Hillsdale, NJ: Erlbaum.

Yu, C.K.-C. (2001). Neuroanatomical correlates of dreaming: The supramarginal gyrus controversy (dream work). *Neuro-Psychoanalysis, 3*, 47–59.

Yu, C.K.-C. (2003). Neuroanatomical correlates of dreaming, III: The frontal-lobe controversy (dream censorship). *Neuro-Psychoanalysis, 5*, 159–169.

Yu, C.K.-C. (2006). Memory loss is not equal to loss of dream experience: A clinico-anatomical study of dreaming in patients with posterior brain lesions. *Neuro-Psychoanalysis, 8*, 191–198.

Yu, C.K.-C. (2007). Cessation of dreaming and ventromesial frontal-region infarcts. *Neuro-Psychoanalysis, 9*, 85–92.

Neuroanatomy of Dreams

Dreaming is a complex neurophysiological process that requires the correct state and intact neuroanatomy. Although it can emerge from any sleep stage, rapid eye movement (REM) sleep is the most common stage for dreaming. Because the act of dreaming involves visual imagery, somesthetic perception, memory, emotion, and perhaps the subconscious mind, almost any region of the brain may be involved. For these reasons, accurate assessment of the neuroanatomy of dreaming is challenging and best achieved by dividing the phenomenon into two constituent parts; the neuroanatomy of REM sleep and the neuroanatomy of the dreaming process.

REM sleep is an ultradian physiological state that occupies approximately 20 percent of a healthy adult's night sleep and is characterized by REMs, muscle atonia, and a low-voltage, fast electroencephalogram (EEG). REM-sleep episodes become progressively longer as the sleep period progresses, with the longest

REM episodes occurring in the morning before arising. REM sleep is driven by a mutually inhibitory flip-flop switch in the mesopontine tegmentum consisting of REM-off (e.g., ventrolateral periaqueductal gray and lateral pontine tegmentum) and REM-on (e.g., sublaterodorsal nucleus and precoeruleus) areas. Each area contains γ-aminobutyric acid (GABA-ergic) neurons that heavily innervate and inhibit the opposing area. The REM-on area also contains glutaminergic neurons located in two areas, with one regulating the REM EEG through projections to the basal forebrain, and the other regulating REM atonia through projections to the medulla and spinal cord (Lu et al., 2006). Other important brain regions include the pedunculopontine, laterodorsal tegmental, and extended ventrolateral preoptic nuclei, all of which inhibit REM-off neurons, and the dorsal raphe, locus coeruleus, and orexin (hypocretin) producing neurons, all of which excite REM-off neurons. The orexin (hypocretin) neurons stabilize the REM-sleep flip-flop switch and prevent unwanted switching of the sleep/wake state or intrusion of REM phenomenon (such as atonia during cataplexy, or dreams during hypnagogic hallucinations) into wakefulness (Lu et al., 2006).

Much has been learned regarding functional human neuroanatomy by studying loss of function following neurological insult. Cessation of dreaming following neurological damage was first observed by Jean-Martin Charcot in 1883, followed by Hermann Wilbrand in 1887, resulting in the term CWS (Charcot–Wilbrand syndrome) to describe this phenomenon (Charcot, 1883; Wilbrand, 1887). Recently, sleep and dream researcher J. Allan Hobson (2002) provided a first-person account of sleep and dream loss and peduncular hallucinosis following an acute ischemic lateral medullary cerebrovascular accident. Although these and other cases have been reported, detailed neuroimaging, polysomnography, and neuropsychological testing have been lacking, throwing into question whether the neurological insult actually eliminated dreaming, or just compromised the ability to generate REM sleep or report dream content (e.g., visual nonremembrance).

More recently Bischof and Bassetti reported the case of a 73-year-old female with acute total dream loss following bilateral posterior cerebral artery infarction. Polysomnography demonstrated intact REM sleep, but dreams were not recalled, even following multiple awakenings from polysomnographically determined REM sleep. Neuropsychological testing was unremarkable and primary sleep disorders were absent. Detailed neuroimaging revealed infarction of the bilateral occipital lobes, including the visual cortices as well as the right inferior lingual gyrus and right posterolateral thalamus (Bischof & Bassetti, 2004). This important case demonstrates that dreaming and REM sleep are dissociable states. REM sleep alone is not sufficient for the generation of dreaming, but rather other processes, particularly those emanating from the occipital lobes and the inferior lingual gyrus (a brain region involved with the processing of emotions and visual memories) appear to be crucial to the dreaming process.

In conclusion, dreaming is a complex neurophysiological process with REM sleep playing a crucial role. Although many neuroanatomical regions have been implicated, it appears that the occipital lobes, and perhaps the inferior lingual gyrus, are key components of the dreaming mechanism. The complexities of dreaming make creation of an animal model to study the phenomenon unrealistic. Therefore, future studies focusing on loss of function following neurological insult are likely to provide the best insights into this fascinating phenomenon going forward.

Nathaniel F. Watson

See also: entries related to Sleep and the Brain

References

Bischof, M., & Bassetti, C.L. (2004). Total dream loss: A distinct neuropsychological dysfunction after bilateral PCA stroke. *Annals of Neurology, 56*(4), 583–586.

Charcot, M. (1883). Un cas de suppression brusque et isole´e de la vision mentale des signes et des objets (formes et couleurs). *Progressive Medicine, 2,* 568–571.

Hobson, J. A. (2002). Sleep and dream suppression following a lateral medullary infarct: A first-person account. *Consciousness and Cognition, 11,* 377–390.

Lu, J., Sherman, D., et al. (2006). A putative flip-flop switch for control of REM sleep. *Nature, 441*(7093), 589–594.

Wilbrand, H. (1887). Ein Fall von Seelenblindheit und Hemianopsie mit Sectionsbefund. *Dtsch Z Nervenheilkd, 2,* 361–387.

Neuroanatomy of REM Sleep and Depression

One of the best-documented relationships between mood disorders and sleep is the relationship between depression and REM sleep. The basic finding is that depressed people go into REM too quickly and some may stay in REM too long. Now NREM sleep is affected in depression as well, and things get quite complex once you start asking questions such as are the REM changes characteristic of all forms of depression? (No) or do they occur in all demographic groups? (No) and so forth. Nevertheless, there does seem to be a deep relationship between REM sleep per se and depression. The definitive evidence for this comes from neuroanatomy and from the fact that REM deprivation temporarily reverses the depression, at least in most people with major depression. Most investigators suspect that the reason for the deep relation between REM and major depressive disorder (MDD) may lie in the neuroanatomy of both states. So it is worth reviewing the neuroanatomy of REM sleep and of depression to see how they overlap and causally interact.

MDD (American Psychiatric Association, 2000) is associated with a range of symptom clusters, including the hallmark persistent sad, anxious, or empty feelings. Cognitive distortions of depression feature a barrage of negative self-appraisals that lead to feelings of hopelessness and/or pessimism, guilt, worthlessness, and/or thoughts of suicide, or even suicide attempts. Memory too is affected with negative and painful memories favored in recall and in acquisition and consolidation processes. Dreams become intensely unpleasant experiences with elevated levels of what used to be called masochistic content or scenes of aggression by unknown strangers against the dreamer/self. Nightmares become more frequent occurrences in the dream life of the depressed individual.

Although REM sleep has long been known to be altered in depression, its role in production of symptomology of depression has never been adequately clarified (for reviews see Armitage, 2007; Nutt, Wilson, & Paterson, 2008; Tsuno, Besset, & Ritchie, 2005). The repeatedly confirmed fact that both selective REM and total sleep deprivation provides dramatic and immediate (though temporary) relief for some people with depression (Vogel, 1975) supports the claim that REM does indeed play some role in production of at least some depressive symptoms in some people with MDD.

Mayberg (1997) presented a limbic–prefrontal interactional model of the neuroanatomy of depression that consists of three neurofunctional compartments that account for differing clusters of depressive systems. Cognitive disturbances of depression are related to dysfunction in the dorsal compartment of the model, which includes the dorsolateral prefrontal cortex and dorsal anterior cingulate, and posterior cingulate. Emotional, vegetative, and somatic symptoms of depression (affect sleep and appetite) are associated with disturbances of the ventral compartment, which consists of orbitofrontal, paralimbic cortical, subcortical, and brainstem regions. The rostral compartment (the rostral anterior cingulate cortex, corresponding to Brodmann area 24a) has connections to both the dorsal and ventral compartments and may serve an important regulatory role in the overall network. I will focus here on interactions between the dorsal and ventral components of the model as these seem most relevant to sleep in depression.

To understand interactions of dorsal versus ventral components in sleep we have to assume that they operate in mutual inhibitory balance with the dorsal system playing the leading role. Its job you might say is to regulate arousal levels in the ventral system. If the dorsal system is damaged or inhibited by any physiological dysfunction then the ventral system would be released from regulatory constraints and would exhibit chronic overactivation.

Consistent with the regulatory role of the dorsal system over paralimbic and other preterontal circuits and functions; and consistent with Mayberg's limbic–cortical model of depression, resting-state PET and single-photon emission computed tomography studies in patients with unipolar depression have most consistently found *decreased* function in the dorsolateral prefrontal (e.g., Mayberg, Lewis, Regenold, & Wagner, 1994) and *increased* activation in ventral system structures (Liotta et al., 2000). Once the dorsal system is impaired, the systems it regulates are released from top–down inhibitory control and you get *increases* in activation of ventral system structures in depressed patients. Such increases in activity in depressed patients have been documented via rCMRglc (regional cerebral metabolic glucose) and rCBF (regional cerebral blood flow) studies in ventrolateral, ventromedial, and orbitofrontal cortex and subgenual prefrontal cortex, amygdala, and insular cortex (Liotta et al., 2000).

Consistent with an etiological role of these overactivated brain systems in production of depressive symptomology, pretreatment abnormalities found in prefrontal, and limbic–paralimbic areas in depressed patients appear to normalize with recovery from depression (Drevets et al., 2002;).

Now we know from neuroimaging studies of REM sleep in healthy people that REM is associated with downregulation of the dorsal system and upregulation of the ventral system during each episode of REM. REM normally activates the ventral system and deactivates the dorsal system in healthy people, thus reproducing the depressive state. Brain-activation patterns in REM demonstrate high activation levels in limbic/amygdaloid sites and portions of medial prefrontal cortex but *hypoactivation* of dorsolateral prefrontal cortex sites (Pace-Schott, 2005). Thus, it appears that each REM episode is associated with a reproduction of key aspects of the neuroanatomy of depression, and it is therefore not unreasonable to ask if REM can negatively impact dorsal and ventral systems in such a way as to be depressogenic.

If it is true that REM reproduces the neuroanatomy of depression during each REM episode then how does that manifest in people with depression to begin with? We would predict that REM measures would be enhanced in people with depression; that is, if we could dampen down or suppress those REM phenomena, the depression would be relieved. It is well known that certain REM-sleep indices are enhanced in depression. Reduced REM-sleep latency and increased REM density and REM time are commonly observed in depressed patients (Tsuno et al., 2005). REM-sleep deprivation can temporarily alleviate depressive symptoms (Vogel, Thurmond, Gibbons, Sloan, & Walker, 1975). Most antidepressant drugs suppress some aspect of REM sleep and degree of REM suppression is correlated with degree of symptomatic relief in responders (Vogel et al., 1975).

Thus, attention to the overlap of the neuroanatomy of REM sleep and of depression yields insights into treatment options. What remains unanswered, however, is why REM sleep would reproduce the anatomy of depression in the first place? Why would Mother Nature create a physiological system that each night periodically activates the ventral system and activates it in such a way as to enhance negative affect (after all, most dreams contain significant amounts of negative affect)?

Patrick McNamara

See also: entries related to Sleep and the Brain

References

American Psychiatric Association. (2000). *Diagnostic and statistical manual of mental disorders* (4th ed.). Washington, DC: Author.

Armitage, R. (2007). Sleep and circadian rhythms in mood disorders. *Acta Psychiatrica Scandinavica, 115*(S433), 104–115.

Drevets, W. C., Price, J. L., Bardgett, M. E., Reich, T., Todd, R. D., & Raichle, M. E. (2002). Glucose metabolism in the amygdala in depression: Relationship to diagnostic subtype and plasma cortisol levels. *Pharmacology Biology & Behavior, 71,* 431–447.

Liotta, M., Mayberg, H. S., Brannan, S. K., McGinnis, S., Jerabek, P., & Fox, P. T. (2000). Differentials corticolimbic correlates of sadness and anxiety in healthy subjects: Implications for affective disorders. *Biological Psychiatry, 48,* 30–42.

Mayberg, H. S. (1997). Limbic-cortical dysregulation: A proposed model of depression. *Journal of Neuropsychiatry and Clinical Neurosciences, 9,* 471–481.

Mayberg, H. S., Lewis, P. J., Regenold, W., & Wagner, H. N. (1994). Paralimbic hypoperfusion in unipolar depression. *Journal of Nuclear Medicine, 35,* 929–934.

Nutt, D.J., Wilson, S.J., & Paterson, L.M. (2008). Sleep disorders as core symptoms of depression. *Dialogues in Clinical Neuroscience, 10*(3), 329–335.

Pace-Schott, E.F. (2005). The neurobiology of dreaming. In M.H. Kryger, T. Roth, & W.C. Dement (Eds.), *Principles and practice of sleep medicine* (4th ed., pp. 551–572). Philadelphia: Elsevier.

Tsuno, N., Besset, A., & Ritchie, K. (2005). Sleep and depression. *Journal of Clinical Psychiatry, 66,* 1254–1269.

Vogel, G.W. (1975). A review of REM sleep deprivation. *Archives of General Psychiatry, 32,* 749–761.

Vogel, G.W., Thurmond, A., Gibbons, P., Sloan, K., & Walker, M. (1975). REM sleep reduction effects on depression syndromes. *Archives of General Psychiatry, 32,* 765–777.

Neurobiology of Psychoanalysis in Wake and REM Sleep

Sigmund Freud (1917) wrote that "we must recollect that all of our provisional ideas in psychology will presumably one day be based on an organic substructure." To what extent has his prediction been confirmed?

Freud's basic theory was that a form of unconscious censorship blocks access to consciousness of memories, drives, wishes, and feelings because they would induce behavioral disturbances (anxiety) due to their emotional or ethical unacceptability. However, the intrusion of such unconscious events can be incidentally observed through parapraxes (slips of the tongue, of the pen, forgetting, misreading, mislaying). Further, during dreaming, as developed in his *The Interpretation of Dreams* (1900), the efficiency of censorship is decreased, allowing latent thought content to enter the dreamer's consciousness under the figurative form of manifest content, produced by dreamwork involving condensation and displacement. When this happens, the elaborated processes that regulate waking-mind function and follow the reality principle would give way to the primary process which follows the pleasure principle, leading to disguised phantasmatic satisfaction of unconscious wishes.

Today, several experimental psychology studies have confirmed that there are indeed active processes that suppress (repress) unwanted memories from entering consciousness during waking, with neuroimaging studies even suggesting the primary involvement of the prefrontal cortex in their generation. Indeed, the more this brain level is activated—as memory-controlling structures (hippocampus) are deactivated—the more effective the repression of memories is. This repression ability is favored by sleep and decreases with advancing age.

In contrast, it is difficult to find any neurobiological support for an organized dreamwork that would produce meaningful symbolic content during the REM dreaming sleep stage, since dream mentation only shows psychotic-like properties. Indeed, electroencephalographic studies of gamma rhythm and central responsiveness (evoked potential findings) clearly show disconnections between forebrain structures, as is seen in schizophrenia, and also show disinhibitory processes, which is an index of deficits in central control processes. Neuroimaging results also mainly indicate deactivation of the dorsolateral prefrontal cortex, which is activated during waking, emphasizing the loss of brain-control processes during REM sleep. Moreover, it has long been established by pharmacological research that dopamine receptor blockers, which suppress psychotic symptoms, tend to decrease dreaming; also, new neuroleptics used in the treatment of schizophrenia increase noradrenergic and serotonergic function, and both of these neuromodulators are nearly entirely absent during REM sleep. Finally, neurochemical results have shown that dopamine levels are reduced in the prefrontal cortex during REM sleep while glutamate levels remain unchanged, in both cases similar to what is observed in schizophrenia. Further, there is a maximal release of dopamine and a decrease in glutamate in the nucleus accumbens during REM sleep, again as is seen in schizophrenia. These results underline the conclusion that increases in central dopamine and decreases in glutamate induce both psychotic symptoms and vivid dreaming.

In view of the previous results, it is improbable that, in the context of such disorganized brain function and in the presence of such psychological abnormalities, there is an organized censorship that acts during REM sleep to modify mental content and make it acceptable to an unconscious.

Finally, another significant assertion of Freud now encounters difficulties in view of modern neurobiological knowledge: "The forgetting of dreams remains inexplicable unless the power of the psychical censorship is taken into account." It has been established that there is, generally, evanescence of dreams upon awakening. However, several known physiological processes are better able than Freud's theory to explain this forgetting in such a neurobiologically disturbed brain. First, cortisol, which inhibits memorization, is released by the suprarenals in the early morning. Also, in the seconds preceding behavioral arousal, waking function reappears in the brain with the release of noradrenaline; this could favor a break with previously present psychological processes. Recent research has also indicated that endogenous increases in Ca^{2+}/calmodulin-dependent protein kinases II (CaMKII) upon arousal, or a transient decrease in the sensitivity of β-noradrenergic receptors could explain the nonrecording of dreams in the waking memory. Finally, it has been established that the specific dorsolateral prefrontal cortex, which is involved in memory processes, recovers its waking properties with a longer delay than do all other forebrain structures. This could also contribute to the obliteration of dreams.

Consequently, today's neurobiological knowledge tends to support the psychoanalytic theory of unconscious processes with respect to the repression of access of mental content to the waking consciousness. In contrast, because of the major disturbances that occur in brain function during REM sleep, sooner or later in dreams there is usually a disintegration, a loss of coherence, an appearance of a psychotic-like kind of mentation that is incompatible with Freud's postulated lucid yet unconscious censorship that would transform unacceptable mental content to render it acceptable. Finally, with respect to dream recall, there is often some rebuilding of content upon arousal (Gottesmann, 2010).

Claude Gottesmann

See also: entries related to Sleep and the Brain

References

Freud, S. (1900). *The interpretation of dreams*. London: The Hogart Press.

Freud, S. (1917). The history of the psychoanalytic movement (Trans. A. A. Brill). In *Nervous and mental disease monograph series, no. 25*. (Original work published 1914.)

Gottesmann, C. (2010). To what extent do neurobiological sleep-waking processes support psychoanalysis. *International Review of Neurobiology, 92*, 233–290.

Neurofeedback for Sleep Problems

Neurofeedback is a sophisticated type of biofeedback, which basically refers to an operant-conditioning paradigm. Participants are instructed to learn to self regulate distinct parameters of their cortical activity as assessed by the means of electroencephalography (EEG). The aim of neurofeedback is to teach individuals what specific states of cortical arousal feel like and how to activate such states voluntarily. During neurofeedback EEG is recorded and the relevant components are extracted and fed back to the individual using an online feedback loop (audio, visual, or audiovisual). The individual's task may then be to increase/decrease the respective cortical parameter. When the correct EEG pattern is produced, the subject receives a positive response or reward by the computer. There is a growing body of evidence (for review, see Hoedlmoser, Dang-Vu Thien, Desseilles, & Schabus, 2010) suggesting that it is feasible to learn to regulate specific brain oscillations by neurofeedback. Thereby it becomes possible to directly counteract the maladaptive brain activity, which is associated with various disorders such as epilepsy, attention deficit hyperactivity disorder, or sleep disorders.

Unfortunately, much of the previous research concerning neurofeedback has suffered from a lack of standardized measures of target symptoms, neglected the assessment of actual training-related EEG changes, and conducted studies with inappropriate control groups or insufficient sample sizes. Additional, well-controlled empirical studies are thus recommended before neurofeedback can be considered a reliable nonpharmacological treatment. Concerning sleep and sleep problems we recently focused our research on the sensorimotor cortex, which shows a very distinct oscillatory pattern in a frequency range between 12 and 15 Hz, also termed sensorimotor rhythm (SMR). SMR appears to (1) be dominant during quiet but alert wakefulness, and (2) synchronizes by the inhibition of motor behavior. Furthermore, this frequency range is known to be abundant during light nonrapid eye movement (NREM) sleep, and is overlapping with the sleep spindle frequency band. Sterman, Howe, and MacDonald (1970) were the first to demonstrate that operant conditioning of SMR during wakefulness can influence subsequent sleep. Hauri and colleagues (1981) then applied neurofeedback of various EEG parameters to disordered sleep. These early results revealed that patients benefit from that kind of SMR training; then, surprisingly, research on that topic faded away. Currently we intend to clarify the nature of these effects in healthy controls as well as insomnia patients.

In the first study (Hoedlmoser et al., 2008) healthy subjects who were randomly assigned to either a SMR-conditioning protocol or to a randomized-frequency-conditioning protocol were studied. Results confirmed the increase of 12 to 15 Hz activity over the course of 10 training sessions in the experimental group. Interestingly, the increased SMR activity (1) was also expressed during subsequent sleep by eliciting positive changes in various sleep parameters such as sleep spindle number or sleep onset latency and (2) was associated with the enhancement of declarative memory performance. As these fascinating results pointed to the possibility that people suffering from insomnia could likewise benefit from these protocols, we conducted a second study with subjects suffering from primary insomnia. Results indicate an increase of 12 to 15 Hz activity over the course of 10 SMR neurofeedback sessions. Furthermore, the change in SMR activity tends to be correlated with a reduction in the number of awakenings from pre- to post-SMR training. Interestingly, subjective sleep quality was also enhanced over the course of neurofeedback and furthermore sleep onset latency was tendentiously reduced after SMR but not after randomized training. Last but not least slow sleep spindles during deep NREM sleep were found to be exclusively enhanced after SMR training. In summarizing, results indicate that healthy individuals as well as people suffering from primary insomnia can experience subjective as well as objective benefits from SMR conditioning. Further refining and empirically assessing respective protocols for clinical use appears worthwhile as instrumental conditioning of EEG can directly target clinically altered brain activity.

Kerstin Hoedlmoser

See also: entries related to Dreams and Therapy

References

Hauri, P. (1981). Treating psychophysiologic insomnia with biofeedback. *Archives of General Psychiatry, 38,* 752–758.

Hoedlmoser, K., Dang-Vu Thien, T., Desseilles, M., & Schabus, M. (2010). Non-pharmacological alternatives for the treatment of insomnia. In Y. E. Soriento (Ed.), *Melatonin, sleep and insomnia* (pp. 69–101). New York: Nova Science Publishers.

Hoedlmoser, K., Pecherstorfer, T., Gruber, G., Anderer, P., Doppelmayr, M., Klimesch, W., & Schabus, M. (2008). Instrumental conditioning of human sensorimotor rhythm (12–15 Hz) and its impact on sleep as well as declarative learning. *Sleep, 31,* 1401–1408.

Sterman, M. B., Howe, R. C., & MacDonald, L. R. (1970). Facilitation of spindle-burst sleep by conditioning of electroencephalographic activity while awake. *Science, 167,* 1146–1148.

Neuropsychology of Lost Dream Recall

There are two core issues in the neuropsychology of dream recall, and they are linked. The first is that dreams are notoriously difficult to remember. The second is that some people recall no dreams upon waking and claim on this basis that they do not dream at all. Among the latter group particular interest attaches to those who claim to have *lost* the ability to dream following focal brain damage. This is because the site of the damage could identify parts of the brain that are pivotal for dreaming.

This in turn may yield new insights into the function of dreams.

The first systematic study of this (Solms, 1997) revealed two significant facts. The first was that reported cessation of dreaming was indeed associated with damage to a specific part of the brain (in fact to two specific parts of the brain). The second was that it was *not* associated with damage to the part of the brain that generates REM sleep—which had hitherto been assumed to also generate dreams. Surprisingly, nobody had ever determined whether damage to the cholinergic pontine brainstem causes loss of dreaming. This is a minimum requirement for any structural–functional correlation in neuropsychology: if a particular structure performs a particular function then loss of the first must cause loss of the second. If not, then the structure does not perform the function at issue. Solms (1997, 2000) therefore concluded that dreams are not generated in the pontine brainstem.

Loss of dreaming turned out to be associated with damage in higher structures: (1) ventromesial frontal lobe white matter and (2) occipito–temporal cortex. (Solms initially thought the critical region was the so-called overlap zone between occipital, temporal, and parietal cortex but subsequent research narrowed the focus to Brodmann areas 19 and 37 [Bischof & Bassetti, 2004; Poza & Martí Massó, 2006; Yu, 2001].) What are the functions of these two parts of the brain and what do they reveal about dreaming? The occipito–temporal region is implicated in visual short-term memory and therefore in the capacity to generate visuospatial mental imagery. It is not surprising that loss of this capacity

undermines dreaming; this does not provide much insight into the function of dreams. It merely confirms that they are a primarily visual form of hallucination. The situation is different when it comes to ventromesial frontal white matter. Recent research has narrowed the focus to the dopaminergic part of the ventromesial frontal white matter (Dahan et al., 2007; Lena et al., 2005; Solms, 2001)—which is implicated in appetitive reward-seeking behavior (Panksepp, 1998). This suggests that dreams are generated by (or) responses to instinctual urges (Solms, 2011). This has major theoretical significance (cf. Freud, 1900).

Unsurprisingly, these conclusions led many commentators (e.g., Hobson & Pace-Schott, 1999) to question their methodological basis. How do we know whether patients who report loss of dreaming following brain damage are really not dreaming; is it not possible that they are merely *forgetting* their dreams? This brings us back to the unreliability of dream recall, which is presumably exacerbated by brain damage.

This challenge can be met in three ways. First, the memory functions of dreaming and nondreaming patients with similar lesions can be compared. In doing so, Solms (1997) found differences in visual short term but not visual or verbal long-term memory. This confirms the conclusion reached previously: dreaming is contingent on intact visual working memory. The fact that long-term memory is completely preserved in nondreaming patients, however, suggests that these patients would encode new long-term memories of dream episodes if they occurred. A second approach is to examine the dream-recall capacities of patients with confirmed inability to encode episodic memories. This has not been systematically investigated but anecdotal reports exist, which confirm that densely amnesic patients—such as the famous case of HM (S. Corkin, personal communication, 2009)—do indeed report dreams immediately upon awakening from REM sleep. This is because visual working memory is preserved in such patients (Moscovitch et al., 2005). A third approach is to subject nondreaming patients to REM awakening, thereby ensuring maximal temporal proximity to dream episodes. All such studies to date of nondreaming neurological patients confirm the absence of dream reports upon REM awakening (Bischof & Bassetti, 2004; Michel & Sieroff, 1981; Poza & Martí Massó, 2006; Schanfald, Pearlman, & Greenberg, 1985).

In short, notwithstanding the methodological challenges of *all* dream research, the available evidence strongly supports the view that acquired loss of dreaming (so-called Charcot–Wilbrand syndrome) does indeed occur.

Mark Solms

References

Bischof, M., & Bassetti, C.L. (2004). Total dream loss: A distinct neuropsychological dysfunction after bilateral PCA stroke. *Annals of Neurology, 56,* 583–586.

Dahan, L., Astier, B., Vautrelle, N., Urbain, N., Kocsis, B., & Chouvet, G. (2007). Prominent burst firing of dopaminergic neurons in the ventral tegmental area during paradoxical sleep. *Neuropsychopharmacology, 32,* 1232–1241.

Freud, S. (100/2001). *The interpretation of dreams.* Empire Books, NY.

Hobson, J. A., & Pace-Schott, E. (1999) Response to commentaries. *Neuropsychoanalysis, 1,* 206–224.

Lena, I., Parrot, S., Deschaux, O., Muffat-Joly, S., Sauvinet, V., Renaud, B., et al. (2005). Variations in extracellular levels of dopamine, noradrenaline, glutamate, and aspartate across the sleep—wake cycle in the medial prefrontal cortex and nucleus accumbens of freely moving rats. *Journal of Neuroscience Research, 81*(6), 891–899.

Michel, F., & Sieroff, E. (1981). Une approche anatomo-clinique des deficits de l'imagerie oneirique, est-elle possible? In *Sleep: Proceedings of an international colloquium.* Milan: Carlo Erba Formitala.

Moscovitch, M., Rosenbaum, R., Gilboa, A., Addis, D., Westmacott, R., Grady, C., . . . Nadel, L. (2005). Functional neuroanatomy of remote episodic, semantic and spatial memory: A unified account based on multiple trace theory. *Journal of Anatomy, 207,* 35–66.

Panksepp, J. (1998). *Affective neuroscience: The foundations of human and animal emotions.* New York: Oxford University Press.

Poza, J., & Martí Massó, J. (2006). Total dream loss secondary to left temporo-occipital brain injury. *Neurologia, 21,* 152–154.

Schanfald, D., Pearlman, C., & Greenberg, R. (1985). The capacity of stroke patients to report dreams. *Cortex, 21,* 237–247.

Solms, M. (1997). *The neuropsychology of dreams: A clinico-anatomical study.* Mahwah, NJ: Erlbaum.

Solms, M. (2000). Dreaming and REM sleep are controlled by different brain mechanisms. *Behavioral and Brain Sciences, 23,* 843–850.

Solms, M. (2001). The neurochemistry of dreaming: Cholinergic and dopaminergic hypotheses. In E. Perry, H. Ashton, & A. Young (Eds.), *The neurochemistry of consciousness* (pp. 123–131). John Benjamin's Publishing Co.

Solms, M. (2011). Neurobiology and the neurological basis of dreaming. In P. Montagna & S. Chokroverty (Eds.), *Handbook of clinical neurology, 98: Sleep disorders—Part 1* (3rd series, pp. 519–544). New York: Elsevier.

Yu, C. (2001). Neuroanatomical correlates of dreaming: The supramarginal gyrus controversy (dream work). *Neuropsychoanalysis, 30,* 47–59.

Nightly Sleep Duration and Mortality: The Story of a U-Shaped Relationship

Shorter nightly sleep duration is a hallmark of modern Western society, thought to be due, in part, to longer work schedules and a greater allotment of time to leisure activities such as television and the Internet. This trend is troublesome, as, overwhelmingly, the epidemiological evidence indicates that short sleep is related to a higher risk of overall, as well as cardiovascular, mortality (Cappuccio, D'Elia, Strazzullo, & Miller, 2010; Gallicchio & Kalesan, 2009). In a meta-analysis of 25 cohorts from 15 studies, Cappuccio et al. (2010) showed that short sleepers, defined generally as individuals reporting less than seven hours per night, had a statistically significant 12 percent increased risk of death compared to normal sleepers (generally defined as those sleeping seven to eight hours per night). This increase in risk associated with short sleep appears to be consistent among men and women, across age groups, and by country (Cappuccio et al., 2010).

Similarly, the epidemiological literature indicates that longer sleep duration is also related to an increased risk of death (Cappuccio et al., 2010; Gallicchio & Kalesan, 2009). Based on data from 27 cohorts from 16 studies, Cappuccio et al. (2010) estimated that long sleepers, generally defined as individuals reporting nine or more hours of sleep per night, were 30 percent more likely to die than normal sleepers. This increased risk associated with long sleep appears to be stronger among older compared to younger individuals (46% vs. 22% increase in the risk of mortality), but does not differ by sex. There is also some evidence to suggest a stronger relationship between long sleep and mortality among studies conducted in East Asia compared to studies conducted in Europe and the United States (48% vs. 25% increase in the risk of mortality). Cappuccio et al. (2010) hypothesized that this may be due to a longer life expectancy in Asian countries such as Japan and that, in general, the studies conducted in Asia were composed of older individuals.

Despite the consistency of the relationships between sleep duration and mortality, there is some debate in the literature as to whether the increases in mortality risk associated with both short and long sleep are real or whether they are due to other (confounding) variables (Cappuccio et al., 2010; Gallicchio & Kalesan, 2009). Numerous factors are related to both sleep duration and mortality that could serve as potential confounders, including age, education, marital status, health behaviors (e.g., smoking), and the presence of health conditions such as hypertension and depression (Grandner, Hale, Moore, & Patel, 2010). While most of the epidemiological literature examining sleep duration and mortality from which the Cappuccio et al. (2010) results were derived took into account these potential confounding factors, there remains the potential for bias due to unmeasured confounding (i.e., other important confounding factors that have not been identified or were not measured or considered in the analyses) or residual confounding by factors that have been included in the published studies.

Yet, despite the debate, the results reported in the epidemiological literature are generally consistent, suggesting that the associations are real. However, the specific mechanisms underlying the associations between sleep duration and mortality are poorly understood. Short-term forced sleep deprivation has been shown in experimental studies to cause adverse endocrinologic, immunologic, and metabolic effects (Spiegel, Leproult, & Van Cauter, 2005), but it is unknown whether these studies are applicable to chronic sleep deprivation. Interestingly, it may be that short sleep elevates stress levels, leading to disease, neuronal damage, and earlier aging (Grandner et al., 2010). Even less is known about potential mechanisms underlying the association between long sleep and mortality. Among the postulated mechanisms are an increased amount of sleep fragmentation among long sleepers compared to normal sleepers, adverse changes in cytokine levels associated with long sleep, and lack of physiological challenge such that long sleepers are not exposed to potentially beneficial mild stressors (Grandner & Drummond, 2007).

The state of the research on sleep duration indicates that sleep duration is a risk marker for mortality; it is yet unknown as to whether interventions aimed at modifying sleep behaviors would serve to decrease morbidity and overall mortality in the general population. Indeed, if, in particular, short sleep duration is a true risk factor for mortality, with the increasing number of individuals reporting shorter sleep times, such an intervention would have a large public health impact. Research in this area is needed, as well as in the area of mechanisms by which shorter and longer sleep may lead to an increased risk of death.

Lisa Gallicchio

See also: entries related to Sleep and Development; entries related to Sleep Disorders

References

Cappuccio, F. P., D'Elia, L., Strazzullo, P., & Miller, M. A. (2010). Sleep duration and all-cause mortality: A systematic review and meta-analysis of prospective studies. *Sleep, 33,* 585–592.

Gallicchio, L., & Kalesan, B. (2009). Sleep duration and mortality: A systematic review and meta-analysis. *Journal of Sleep Research, 18,* 148–158.

Grandner, M. A., & Drummond, S. P. (2007). Who are the long sleepers? Towards an understanding of the mortality relationship. *Sleep Medicine Reviews, 11,* 341–360.

Grandner, M. A., Hale, L., Moore, M., & Patel, N. P. (2010). Mortality associated with short sleep duration: The evidence, the possible mechanisms, and the future. *Sleep Medicine Reviews, 14,* 191–203.

Spiegel, K., Leproult, R., & Van Cauter, E. (2005). Metabolic and endocrine changes. In C. Kushida (Ed.), *Sleep deprivation: Basic science, physiology, and behavior* (pp. 293–317). New York: Marcel Dekker.

Nightmare Content in Adults

Nightmares are defined as disturbing mental experiences that generally occur during REM sleep and often result in awakening

(ICSD-2 [International Classification of Sleep Disorders-2]). Whereas nightmare frequency in different populations have been studied extensively—see, for example, the meta-analysis by Schredl and Reinhard (2011), research regarding nightmare content is rather scarce, especially in adults.

Garfield (1984) analyzed 158 nightmares in children, who reported that the most common themes were: being chased (49%), sensing something scary (18%), injury/death (17%), losing something (5%), and falling (3%). In another content analytic study (N = 381 dreams), Schredl and Pallmer (1998) obtained comparable results: being chased (42%), sensing something scary (20%), deaths/injuries of significant others (20%), and falling (11%). Other topics such as examinations (3%), natural disasters (4%), or war (5%) occurred less often.

For adults, three studies (Dunn & Barrett, 1988; Hearne, 1991; Kales et al., 1980) elicited nightmare content in small clinical samples (sample sizes varied from 30 to 38, the mean ages of the samples were about 35 years). The four most prominent themes in the Kales et al. (1980) study were fear of attack (73%), fear of falling (73%), fear of death (60%), and choking/suffocation (30%). The nightmare topics in the sample of Dunn and Barrett (1988) were distributed as follows: being chased (72%), deaths of family/friends (64%), falling (53%), own death (39%), threatening animals/monsters (33%), and violent destruction scenes such as war and natural disasters (24%). The nightmare sufferers in the Hearne (1991) study reported other themes to be most prominent in their nightmares: witnessing horror/violence (32%), experiencing attack/danger (29%), flight (13%), sinister presence (13%), being late (5%), suffocation (3%), hallucinated creatures (3%), and being paralyzed (3%). The most detailed study was carried out by Zadra, Duval, Begin, and Pilon (2004) analyzing 125 nightmares reported by 125 women (mean age: 32 years) who kept a dream diary, one dream per participant. The thematic analyses yielded the following distribution of nightmare topics: physical aggression (26%), ominous mood (12%), failure/helplessness (10%), interpersonal conflicts (9%), and being ignored or rejected (6%). Other themes occurring 5 percent or less included being chased but not caught, presence of demons, frightening insects or spiders, health problems or concerns, being stuck or trapped, and accidents. The present study investigated nightmare frequency and the frequency of various topics in them. The five most common nightmare topics in a representative German sample (N = 1,022) were falling, being chased, paralyzed, being late, and the deaths of close persons (Schredl, 2010).

Summarizing the results while keeping in mind that the methodological approaches and samples have been very different, the main topics seem to be being chased, injury/death of others, falling, and witnessing violence. Even though several topics can be explained by the continuity hypothesis of dreaming (e.g., the higher occurrence of examination dreams in persons with high educational levels; Schredl, 2010), further research is needed to investigate the possibly metaphoric relationship between nightmare topics such as falling or being chased and waking-life stressors.

Michael Schredl

See also: entries related to Dream Content

References

Dunn, K. K., & Barrett, D. (1988). Characteristics of nightmare subjects and their nightmares. *Psychiatric Journal of the University of Ottawa, 13,* 91–93.

Garfield, P. L. (1984). *Your child's dreams.* New York: Ballentine.

Hearne, K.M.T. (1991). A questionnaire and personality study of nightmare sufferers. *Journal of Mental Imagery, 15*(3–4), 55–64.

Kales, A., Soldatos, C. R., Caldwell, A., Charney, D., Kales, J.D., Markel, D., et al. (1980). Nightmares: Clinical characteristics and personality pattern. *American Journal of Psychiatry, 137,* 1197–1201.

Schredl, M. (2010). Nightmare frequency and nightmare topics in a representative German sample. *European Archives of Psychiatry and Clinical Neuroscience, 260,* 565–570.

Schredl, M., & Pallmer, R. (1998). Geschlechtsunterschiede in Angstträumen von SchülerInnen. *Praxis der Kinderpsychologie und Kinderpsychiatrie, 47,* 463–476.

Schredl, M., & Reinhard, I. (2011). Gender differences in nightmare frequency: A meta-analysis. *Sleep Medicine Reviews, 15,* 115–121.

Zadra, A., Duval, M., Begin, E., & Pilon, M. (2004). Content analysis of nightmares. *Sleep Supplement, 27,* A64.

Nightmares

Nightmares are repeated occurrences of dreams that are extremely dysphoric, extended in time and well remembered upon awakening; they usually involve active efforts to avoid apparent threats to one's survival, security, or physical integrity. Nightmare episodes generally occur during the second half of the sleep period. On waking up, the nightmare experience, or the sleep disturbance that it produces, usually leads to a degree of clinically significant distress or impairment. A DSM-IV (Diagnostic and Statistical Manual of Mental Disorders-IV) diagnosis of *nightmare disorder* is made when the frequency and severity of nightmares result in significant distress or impairment—usually considered to be at least one such nightmare per week. Although nightmares may occur in the course of a general medical condition or as a result of using, abusing, or withdrawing from medications or other drugs, the DSM-IV considers them in such cases to be only secondary to a *nightmare disorder* diagnosis, and a diagnosis of *nightmares due to a general medical condition* or *substance-induced nightmare disorder* would be applied instead.

Nightmares may also occur in the course of several other mental disorders such as *generalized anxiety disorder, social anxiety disorder, panic disorder, schizophrenia, mood disorders, adjustment disorders,* and *personality disorders.* And they frequently occur in the course of normal and atypical bereavement during which grief figures as the predominant dysphoric dream emotion; these may form a distinct subtype of dreams (Kuiken, Lee, Eng, & Singh, 2006). It is important to distinguish *nightmare disorder* from posttraumatic nightmares, which are more severe, more disturbing, and often, but not necessarily, associated with *acute stress disorder* or *posttraumatic stress disorder* (PTSD). Both *nightmare disorder* and PTSD nightmares are distinguished from *sleep terrors,* which also involve fear-based arousals but which typically arise from non-REM sleep, are not accompanied by such vivid and elaborate dreams, and do not result in awakenings from which recall of the experience is as clear and detailed.

Nightmares typically occur in a lengthy and elaborate dream sequences that seem real while they occur and cause anxiety, fear, terror, or some other dysphoric emotion such as anger or disgust. The content of the nightmares usually focuses on the individual's attempts to avoid or cope with imminent physical danger such as being pursued, attacked, or injured, but it may also involve themes that evoke anger, revulsion, and other negative emotions.

Because dreaming is usually longer and more intense in the second half of the night, nightmares are also more likely to occur later in the night. However, any factor that increases dream intensity earlier in the night (e.g., sleep fragmentation or deprivation, jet lag, REM-sensitive medications) might also lead to nightmares at this time. Some nightmares may not induce an awakening and only be recalled in the morning or later in the day, possibly because their associated dysphoric emotions are less intense; some refer to these as bad dreams (Zadra, Pilon, & Donderi, 2006).

Body movements and vocalizations are not characteristic of *nightmare disorder* because of the loss of skeletal muscle tone that normally occurs during REM sleep, but they may occur under situations of emotional stress or sleep fragmentation (e.g., pregnancy, postpartum state). Some parents (1.3% to 3.9%) report that their preschool children have nightmares often or always. The prevalence of nightmares increases from ages 10 to 13 for both males and females but thereafter continues to increase to ages 20 to 29 for females but decrease variably for males. Adult females report having nightmares more often than do men, with ratios ranging from approximately 2:1 to 4:1. The gender difference continues in adulthood even though nightmare prevalence decreases steadily with age for both sexes. Among adults, prevalence is 2 to 5 percent for nightmares often or always and 8 to 30 percent for nightmares one or more per month. Prevalence for adult/elderly samples is only 1 to 2 percent for nightmares often or always.

Twin studies have identified genetic effects on the disposition to nightmares and on the co-occurrence of nightmares and other parasomnias such as somniloquy.

PTSD nightmares are unique in that they replicate, in whole or in part, the terrifying and often-excruciating experiential details of the trauma (Mellman & Pigeon, 2005). About 50 percent of patients report such replicative nightmares (Wittmann, Schredl, & Kramer, 2007). PTSD nightmares also depict modified replays that change details of the trauma but preserve or amplify associated emotions (Hartmann, Zborowski, Rosen, & Grace, 2001; Mellman & Pigeon, 2005). So although 50 percent of combat veterans with PTSD report dreams containing explicit combat details (Esposito, Benitez, Barza, & Mellman, 1999), a much greater proportion (83%) report dreams containing threats (Esposito et al., 1999) compared with non-PTSD combat controls (46%) (Hall & van de Castle, 1966). PTSD nightmares may also contain elements of much earlier traumatic and adverse events, or repetitious but nontraumatic elements (Wittmann et al., 2007). To illustrate, survivors of Hurricane Iniki reported dreams about general stressors (74% vs. 48% for controls) and about especially stressful life experiences

(67% vs. 37%), but only rarely about the hurricane itself (13%) (Pagel, Vann, & Altomare, 1995).

Theoretical and empirical work on nightmares from Freud to the present day converges on, and to some extent supports, the notions that (1) emotion regulation is a normal function of dreaming and (2) nightmares are either exemplary expressions or psychopathological disturbances of this function (Nielsen & Lara-Carrasco, 2007). The work has produced several possible mechanisms that may be central to emotion regulation during dreaming, including desomatization, contextualization, progressive emotional problem solving, and fear-memory extinction. It provides suggestive evidence that some aspects of dream content (e.g., self-character interactions, emotions), and not simply the physiological state of REM sleep per se, are implicated in the emotion regulation function.

There are several recent comprehensive reviews of nightmares available (Levin & Nielsen, 2007; Nielsen, 2010; Nielsen & Zadra, 2010; Phelps, Forbes, & Creamer, 2008; Spoormaker, Schredl, & Bout, 2005).

Tore Nielsen

See also: Lucid Dreaming Therapy for Nightmares

References

Esposito, K., Benitez, A., Barza, L., & Mellman, T. (1999). Evaluation of dream content in combat-related PTSD. *Journal of Traumatic Stress, 12,* 681–687.

Hall, C., & van de Castle, R.I. (1966). *The content analysis of dreams.* New York: Appleton-Century-Crofts.

Hartmann, E., Zborowski, M., Rosen, R., & Grace, N. (2001). Contextualizing images in dreams: More intense after abuse and trauma. *Dreaming, 11,* 115–126.

Kuiken, D., Lee, M.-N., Eng, T., & Singh, T. (2006). The influence of impactful dreams on self-perceptual depth and spiritual transformation. *Dreaming, 16,* 258–279.

Levin, R., & Nielsen, T.A. (2007). Disturbed dreaming, posttraumatic stress disorder, and affect distress: A review and neurocognitive model. *Psychological Bulletin, 133,* 482–528.

Mellman, T.A., & Pigeon, W.R. (2005). Dreams and nightmares in posttraumatic stress disorder. In M.H. Kryger, T. Roth, & W.C. Dement (Eds.), *Principles and practice of sleep medicine* (4th ed., pp. 573–578). Philadelphia: Elsevier Saunders.

Nielsen, T.A. (2010). Disturbed dreaming as a factor in medical conditions. In M. Kryger, T. Roth, & W.C. Dement (Eds.), *Principles and practice of sleep medicine* (5th ed., pp. 1116–1127). New York: Elsevier.

Nielsen, T.A., & Lara-Carrasco, J. (2007). Nightmares, dreaming and emotion regulation: A review. In D. Barrett & P. McNamara (Eds.), *The new science of dreams* (pp. 253–284). Westport, CT: Praeger Greenwood.

Nielsen, T.A., & Zadra, A. (2010). Idiopathic nightmares and dream disturbances associated with sleep-wake transitions. In M. Kryger, T. Roth, & W.C. Dement (Eds.), *Principles and practice of sleep medicine* (5th ed., pp. 1106–1115). New York: Elsevier.

Pagel, J.F., Vann, B.H., & Altomare, C.A. (1995). Reported association of stress and dreaming—Community background levels and changes with disaster (Hurricane Iniki). *Dreaming, 5,* 43–50.

Phelps, A.J., Forbes, D., & Creamer, M. (2008). Understanding posttraumatic nightmares: An empirical and conceptual review. *Clinical Psychology Review, 28*(2), 338–355.

Spoormaker, V.I., Schredl, M., & Bout, J.V. (2005). Nightmares: From anxiety symptom to sleep disorder. *Sleep Medicine Reviews, 10,* 19–31.

Wittmann, L., Schredl, M., & Kramer, M. (2007). Dreaming in posttraumatic stress disorder: A critical review of phenomenology, psychophysiology and treatment. *Psychotherapy and Psychosomatics, 76,* 25–39.

Zadra, A., Pilon, M., & Donderi, D.C. (2006). Variety and intensity of emotions in nightmares and bad dreams. *Journal of Nervous and Mental Disease, 194,* 249–254.

Objective and Subjective Dreams

In popular culture, it is commonly assumed that dreams pertain primarily, if not solely, to the personality of the individual dreamer. This attribution, which corresponds to the ethos of separatism that characterizes American society, is not found in dreaming cultures. In most indigenous traditions, it is recognized that there are little dreams pertaining to the daily life of the dreamer and big dreams pertaining to the ongoing life of the tribe.

In his first essay on dreams, written in 1917, C.G. Jung made a distinction between subjective dreams, which refer to the dreamer and their worldview, and objective dreams, which refer to the larger world around. He recognized that these adjectives were value laden, with objectivity being privileged over subjectivity (Jung, 1966, para. 130). Since the dreaming mind is capable of distinguishing between inside and outside, self and other, we might think instead of dreams being inward facing and outward facing (Sabini, 2008). Dreams themselves often indicate which direction they face: we dream of being inside our childhood home or outside on a city street, of repairing the interior of our home or changing the outgoing message on our voicemail.

Dreams that refer to a person known to us do not necessarily imply that they pertain to that person in actuality. The dream may be showing our subjective picture of that person or it may be using that figure to signify an aspect of ourselves. To understand the direction a dream faces, a process of discernment needs to be undertaken; this will counteract any tendency to take the dream superficially at face value.

From a collection of dreams made over a 10-year period, those determined to be outward facing rather than subjective showed certain specific characteristics: (1) Their imagery is very plain, without fantastical or dreamlike elements; (2) the action is much as it would be in waking life; (3) there is little or no emotion on the dreamer's part; (4) the dreamer often has few if any associations to the dream, and meaning can be made of it only when it is considered to be outward facing (Sabini, 2006).

Western psychology has contributed to an understanding of projection, the subliminal process by which we give over to others a tendency or quality that belong to ourselves. The opposite process, absorbing into ourselves a quality or tendency that belongs to others, has received much less attention. This distinction between the subjective and objective dimensions of dreams, by which their contents face inward or outward, provides an important template for discerning the purpose or function a dream may have. It is a heuristically important template with many possible applications for both dream research and dreamwork.

Meredith Sabini

References

Jung, C. G. (1966). *Two essays on analytical psychology*. Princeton, NJ: Princeton University Press.

Sabini, M. (2006). Dreams about others: How can we recognize them? *DreamTime, 23*(2), 32–33.

Sabini, M. (2008). Encountering the primordial self. *Jung Journal: Culture & Psyche, 2*(4), 34–69.

Obstructive Sleep Apnoea, Metabolism, and Hormones

Obstructive sleep apnoea (OSA) is a common condition that is increasing in prevalence in parallel with obesity and type-2 diabetes mellitus. While obesity is a key factor in the development of OSA, only up to 50 percent of OSA is due to obesity. With obesity being a key player in OSA, any independent impact of OSA on circulating metabolic hormones and/or metabolism is difficult to confirm definitively. Nevertheless, accumulating evidence points toward important interactions among OSA, hormones, and metabolism. These interactions can be through hormone-related conditions (e.g., obesity, hypothyroidism) predisposing to or aggravating OSA, and/or OSA (through mechanisms such as intermittent hypoxia and increased sympathetic nervous system activity) predisposing or aggravating hormone-related conditions such as diabetes mellitus, hypertension, and the metabolic syndrome. A number of associated features of OSA suggest that sleep apnoea belongs to the metabolic syndrome cluster—the association with visceral obesity, male gender preponderance, postmenopausal increase of its prevalence, and systemic effects, for example, hypertension and diabetes. OSA is also more common in ethnic minorities (African Americans and Hispanics) who are at increased risk of the metabolic syndrome and diabetes.

OSA, Diabetes, and Metabolic Syndrome

There is a high prevalence of OSA in obese individuals and a high prevalence of obesity in patients with OSA (Svatikova et al., 2005). The impact of obesity on OSA includes impact on upper airway anatomy, ventilatory control, and pharyngeal airway tone. Leptin resistance in obesity may also have an impact on ventilatory control. OSA may perpetuate obesity through effects on sleep fragmentation and loss. Visceral obesity is a major driver for type-2 diabetes mellitus and the metabolic syndrome. Diabetes is more prevalent in patients with sleep-disordered breathing (SDB, which includes OSA) and this relationship appears to be independent of other risk factors. However, it is not clear whether SDB is causal in the development of diabetes. A study examining the potential association of OSA with the metabolic syndrome found that OSA was independently associated with increased systolic and diastolic blood pressure, higher fasting insulin and triglyceride levels, decreased HDL cholesterol, increased cholesterol:HDL ratio, and a trend toward higher homeostatic model assessment (a measure of insulin resistance) values. They also found that metabolic syndrome was 9.1 times (95% confidence interval 2.6, 31.2: $p < .0001$) more likely to be present in patients with OSA (Coughlin, Mawdsley, Mugarza, Calverley, & Wilding, 2004).

The prevalence of OSA in patients with type-2 mellitus ranges from 20 percent to as high as 80 percent depending on the population studied and the study setting (Foster et al., 2009). The association between OSA and glucose metabolism is complex (Wolk & Somers, 2007). A common confounder in the studies is visceral obesity. Data from animal models of hypoxia show that intermittent hypoxia can induce insulin resistance. Insulin resistance is also observed in physiological hypoxia in humans such as at high altitude and in pathological conditions associated with hypoxia such as chronic obstructive pulmonary disease. Apart from hypoxia, human laboratory sleep-deprivation studies show that sleep loss is associated with insulin resistance. Sleep loss and fragmentation can enhance levels of insulin counter-regulatory hormones such as cortisol. OSA is also characterized by a pro-inflammatory state and elevated cytokine levels (e.g., tumor necrosis factor-α), which may lead to insulin resistance (Ciftci, Kokturi, Bukan, & Bilgihan, 2004).

If OSA has an independent relationship with insulin resistance, then treatment with continuous positive airway pressure (CPAP) should improve insulin sensitivity. Studies on the effect of CPAP have, however, reported conflicting results. The reasons for conflicting findings include patient selection, initial diabetes control, diabetes duration, control treatments, and duration of CPAP treatment. Ongoing and future studies should clarify whether CPAP improves diabetes control and prevents or delays diabetes complications.

Hypothyroidism and Acromegaly

Hypothyroidism is a common condition (more common in women) associated with weight gain and dyslipidemia. It can predispose to obstructive sleep apnea through not only weight gain but also through mucopolyscacharide and protein deposition in the pharynx. Testing for hypothyroidism is thus important in patients presenting with OSA, although in the majority of cases, the two conditions are coincidental. Acromegaly is a rare disease that affects both sexes equally and has a prevalence rate between 38 and 60 cases out of 1,000,000 population. Acromegaly is the result of excess growth-hormone secretion usually caused by a pituitary tumor. This excess of growth hormone leads to an insidious development of coarse facial features, bone growth, and soft tissue swelling. A large number of publications have described the association between sleep apnoea and acromegaly. A correlation has been established between craniofacial changes and the presence and severity of apnoeas. Other mechanisms for sleep apnea in acromegaly include pharyngeal edema, alterations in ventilatory control, and obesity. Treatment of acromegaly improves OSA. Some have suggested that growth-hormone deficiency, as occurs commonly in patients treated for pituitary disorders, may also be associated with OSA; further studies are required to investigate this potential association.

Sex Hormones and Polycystic Ovarian Syndrome (PCOS)

Decreased libido is frequently reported in male patients with OSA. Reduced libido has also been observed in women with OSA. Few studies have examined the impact of CPAP treatment on sexual dysfunction. OSA is associated with decreased pituitary–gonadal function; low luteinizing hormone and testosterone levels are observed suggesting a central problem (central hypogonadism). While these alterations may be related to obesity, some may be secondary to sleep deprivation and/or intermittent hypoxia (Grunstein et al., 1989). Androgens may have an influence on ventilatory control. Androgen replacement may exacerbate preexisting OSA, although evidence for this is weak.

PCOS is defined as oligoovulation or anovulation, hyperandrogenemia or clinical manifestations of androgen excess, and polycystic ovaries as demonstrated by ultrasonography. It is the most common endocrine-related condition of reproductive-aged women, affecting nearly four million women in the United States alone. Obesity is seen in many of these women and is frequently central in nature (increased waist-to-hip ratio). Women with PCOS have an increased prevalence of type-2 diabetes and lipid abnormalities. Insulin resistance, hyperinsulinemia, and beta-cell dysfunction are common in PCOS (Diamati-Kandarakis, 2006). Women with PCOS are up to 30 times more at risk of OSA compared to women without PCOS. Also, women with PCOS and OSA are more likely to be insulin resistant. Whether the association between PCOS and OSA is independent of visceral adiposity is unclear. OSA treatment with CPAP in women with PCOS has been shown to improve insulin sensitivity and reduce blood pressure. These responses are, however, dependent on associated degree of obesity and CPAP usage duration.

Conclusions

The metabolic syndrome represents a constellation of cardiovascular risk factors and is developing into a major public health problem. The increased prevalence of the metabolic syndrome is linked to the epidemic of obesity, which is also accompanied by an increasing prevalence of OSA. OSA and the metabolic syndrome show many common features, and in fact, may often coexist. The coexistence of OSA with the metabolic syndrome may contribute to the clustering of abnormalities defined as the metabolic syndrome and may have widespread implications for cardiovascular morbidity and mortality. Whether the association of OSA with the metabolic syndrome and diabetes is independent of visceral adiposity is debatable. Nevertheless, OSA may independently contribute to morbidity and mortality in patients with the metabolic syndrome and diabetes mellitus. OSA is associated with several hormone abnormalities and endocrine disorders. Clinical vigilance is necessary to recognize these associations so that appropriate treatment can be instituted. Understanding the associations of hormones with OSA will increase our understanding of the potential role of various hormones in ventilatory control and pharyngeal anatomy, and the roles of sleep fragmentation, short sleep duration, and intermittent hypoxia on endocrine function.

Marzieh Hosseini Araghi
and Shahrad Taheri

See also: entries related to Hormones in Sleep; entries related to Sleep and Development

Note

Both Dr. Shahrad Taheri and Dr. Marzieh Hosseini Araghi are funded by the National Institute for Health Research (NIHR) through the Collaborations for Leadership in Applied Health Research and Care for Birmingham and Black Country (CLAHRC-BBC) program. The views expressed in this publication are not necessarily those of the NIHR, the Department of Health, NHS South Birmingham, University of Birmingham, or the CLAHRC-BBC Theme 8 Management/Steering Group.

References

Babu, A. R., Herdegen, J., Fogelfeld, L., Shott, S., & Mazzone, T. (2005). Type 2 diabetes, glycemic control, and continuous positive airway pressure in obstructive sleep apnea. *Archives of Internal Medicine, 165,* 447–452.

Blanco, P., Blanco-Ramos, J. J., Zamarron Sanz, M. A., Souto Fernandez, C., Mato Mato, A., & Lamela Lopez, J. (2004). Acromegaly and sleep apnea. *Archivos de Bronconeumología, 40,* 355–359.

Ciftci, T. U., Kokturi, O., Bukan, N., & Bilgihan, A. (2004). The relationship between serum cytokine levels with obesity and obstructive sleep apnea syndrome. *Cytokine, 28,* 87–91.

Coughlin, S. R., Mawdsley, L., Mugarza, J. A., Calverley, P. M., & Wilding, J. P. (2004, May). Obstructive sleep apnoea is independently associated with an increased prevalence of metabolic syndrome. *European Heart Journal, 25*(9), 735–741.

Diamati-Kandarakis, E. (2006). Insulin resistance in PCOS. *Endocrine, 30,* 13–17.

Foster, G. D., Sanders, M. H., Millman, R., Zammit, G., Borradaile, K. E., Newman, A. B., . . . Sleep AHEAD Research Group. (2009). Obstructive sleep apnea among obese patients with type 2 diabetes. *Diabetes Care, 32*(6), 1017–1019.

Grunstein, R. R., Handlesman, D. J., Lawrence, S. J., Blackwell, C., Caterson, I. D., & Sullivan, C. E. (1989). Neuroendocrine dysfunction in sleep apnea: Reversal by continuous positive airways pressure therapy. *Journal of Clinical Endocrinology and Metabolism, 68,* 352–358.

Punjabi, N. M. (2008). The epidemiology of adult obstructive sleep apnea. *Proceedings of the American Thoracic Society, 5,* 136–143.

Svatikova, A., Wolk, R., Gami, A. S., Pohanka, M. & Somers, V. K. (2005). Interactions between obstructive sleep apnea and the metabolic syndrome. *Current Diabetes Report, 5,* 53–58.

Svatikova, A., Wolk, R., Lerman, L. O., Juncos, L. A., Greene, E. L., McConnell, J. P. & Somers, V. K. (2005). Oxidative stress in obstructive sleep apnoea. *European Heart Journal, 26,* 2435–2439.

Tasali, E., & Ip, M. S. (2008). Obstructive sleep apnea and metabolic syndrome: Alterations in glucose metabolism and inflammation. *Proceedings of the American Thoracic Society, 5,* 207–217.

Wolk, R., & Somers, V. K. (2007). Sleep and the metabolic syndrome. *Experimental Physiology, 92,* 67–78.

Olfactory Stimuli and Dreams

Whether and how external stimuli are processed during sleep has been studied mainly by two different paradigms: event-related potentials and incorporation into dream content. Using olfactory stimuli is of interest because of several reasons.

First, Stuck et al. (2007) showed that ol-factory stimuli without trigeminal components such as hydrogen sulfide do not cause arousals even in high concentrations. On the other hand, Stuck, Weitz, Hörmann, Maurer, and Hummel (2006) found that olfactory event-related potentials can be measured during sleep indicating that chemosensory stimuli are processed by the sleeping brain. Secondly, olfactory stimuli were processed differently within the brain compared to auditory stimuli: This includes the predominantly ipsilateral processing of the olfactory stimuli, and the almost direct projection from the olfactory bulb to the amygdala (areas for the processing of memories and emotions) and the association to the hippocampus via the transitional entorhinal cortex. The fact that olfactory information processing largely bypasses the spinal cord, the brain stem, and the thalamus—in contrast to all other sensory systems—explains the small number of arousals after stimulation because thalamic reticular nuclei are involved in arousal generation (Stuck et al., 2007).

Two sleep laboratory studies have been conducted in this area so far. Trotter, Dallas, and Verdone (1988) carried out a small pilot study with five participants to study the effect of olfactory stimuli on dream content. The incorporation rate was 19 percent (79 successful trials in 22 nights). The following example was reported by a participant after presentation of a freshly cut lemon:

> I dreamed I was in Golden Gate Park. I was walking by some gardenias. They were just opening. All of a sudden, I could smell the gardenias, but they

smelled like lemons instead of gardenias. (Trotter et al., 1988, p. 95)

No effect of the pleasantness of the stimuli (pleasant stimuli: coffee, peanut butter, roses, cinnamon, chocolate, lemon; unpleasant stimuli: wood alcohol, dirty ashtray, match smoke, mold, dog feces, onion) on dream emotions was reported (Trotter et al., 1988). Several methodological issues, such as lack of control condition and presentation technique (inducing arousals), however, limit the generalizability of this findings. The second study (Schredl et al., 2009) used a sophisticated stimulation methodology (stimulation without disturbing the sleeper, no odor present at the moment of awakening, control condition) and did not find any explicit incorporation of olfactory stimuli in the dream reports ($N = 15$ participants). In accordance with the specific processing of olfactory stimuli within the brain, the emotional quality of the olfactory stimuli using H_2S (smell of rotten eggs) and phenyl ethyl alcohol (PEA) (smell of roses) affected the emotional content of dreams: the positively toned stimulus yielded more positively toned dreams, whereas the negative stimulus was followed by more negatively toned dreams.

The findings indicate that olfactory stimuli are processed by the sleeping brain; it would be interesting to carry out learning experiments (associating specific odors with declarative material) to study whether this declarative material is incorporated into subsequent dreams if the corresponding odor cue is presented during sleep—as olfactory stimuli might enhance sleep-related memory consolidation

(Rasch, Buchel, Gais, & Born, 2007). It would also be interesting to study the effect of positively toned olfactory stimuli on nightmares.

Michael Schredl

See also: entries related to Dream Content

References

Rasch, B., Buchel, C., Gais, S., & Born, J. (2007). Odor cues during slow-wave sleep prompt declarative memory consolidation. *Science, 315*(5817), 1426–1429.

Schredl, M., Atanasova, D., Hörmann, K., Maurer, J.T., Hummel, T., & Stuck, B.A. (2009). Information processing during sleep: The effect of olfactory stimuli on dream content and dream emotions. *Journal of Sleep Research, 18,* 285–290.

Stuck, B.A., Stieber, K., Frey, S., Freiburg, C., Hörmann, K., Maurer, J.T., et al. (2007). Arousal responses to olfactory or trigeminal stimulation during sleep. *Sleep, 30,* 506–510.

Stuck, B.A., Weitz, H., Hörmann, K., Maurer, J.T., & Hummel, T. (2006). Chemosensory event-related potentials during sleep— A pilot study. *Neuroscience Letters, 406,* 222–226.

Trotter, K., Dallas, K., & Verdone, P. (1988). Olfactory stimuli and their effects on REM dreams. *Psychiatric Journal of the University of Ottawa, 13,* 94–96.

Overgeneral Memories

Autobiographical memory is the aspect of memory that is concerned with the recollection of personally experienced past events. It is of fundamental significance to an individual's sense of self, and thus, is related to other aspects of human functioning such as goal pursuit, problem-solving abilities, and mood regulation. Overgenerality refers to a lack of specificity when recalling a certain event. Unlike *specific memories,* which have taken place in less than one day and are linked with a particular place and time, *overgeneral memories* usually take place over a range of time. Because that period of time may be definite (i.e., have an explicit beginning and ending) or be less distinct, overgeneral memories tend to be more variable than specific memories.

For example, literature has defined three subtypes of overgeneral memories: *categoric, extended,* and *lifetime period. Categoric* memories refer to a series of repeated events or a single event that occurs multiple times (e.g., *brushing my teeth every morning*; *visiting my grandmother's house every year for Christmas dinner*). *Extended* nonspecific memories are memories that have continued for more than one day, but still have a distinct beginning and end (e.g., *being sick with pneumonia, taking a semester of calculus, traveling to Niagara Falls on vacation*). *Lifetime-period* memories (Conway & Pleydell-Pearce, 2000) usually have a less clear beginning and end, but demonstrate basic thematic knowledge about general locations, activities, plans, behaviors, etc., that are characteristic of a certain period of time (e.g., *when I was young I used to be afraid of the dark*; *when I was dating my high school boyfriend I wanted to become a chef*).

As "mental constructions generated from an underlying knowledge base" (Conway & Pleydell-Pearce, 2000, p. 261), autobiographical memories are sensitive to cues. Most studies investigating autobiographical memory use a cuing methodology referred to as the autobio-graphical memory test (AMT). During the AMT, both positively (e.g., happy, ex-cited, proud) and negatively (e.g., scared, angry, disappointed) valenced cue words are presented to participants. Participants are prompted to recall if a specific event reminds them of that word. In response to cues, executive control processes often reshape or recall autobiographical knowl-edge that is salient to a person's working sense of self. In accordance with this no-tion, several studies have demonstrated that not only do suicidally depressed pa-tients usually respond more slowly to pos-itively valenced cues, but they reported more overgeneral memories than healthy control participants. Perhaps more inter-estingly, several studies have replicated the finding that group differences between suicidal patients and controls are due to in-creased retrieval of categorical memories, with no such differences in numbers of ex-tended memories (Williams et al., 2007).

Williams and colleagues reviewed re-search examining the specificity of mem-ory in people suffering from affective disorders (e.g., major depressive disor-der [MDD], posttraumatic stress disorder [PTSD], etc.). Overall, emotionally dis-turbed patients tend to summarize catego-ries of events rather than retrieving a single episode when asked to recall autobiograph-ical experiences (Williams et al., 2007). Such findings may suggest that overgen-eral memories serve to protect against re-call of painful personal events.

A closer look at patients with MDD explains the far-reaching effects of over-general memory recollection. In MDD, patients experience emotional changes (feelings of extreme sadness and hopeless-ness), cognitive changes (low self-esteem, guilt, memory and concentration difficul-ties), changes in behavior and motivation (feeling agitated or slowed down, reduced interest in social or recreational activi-ties), and changes in bodily functioning (sleep, appetite, energy). Thus, it is not surprising that numerous studies of over-generality in autobiographical memory is correlated with poor problem-solving per-formance (Goddard, Dritschel, & Burton, 1996) and the prediction of persistence of depression (Dalgleish, Spinks, Yiend, & Kuyken, 2001).

In addition, observing overgenerality holds significance because memory re-mains nonspecific in people with a history of emotional disorder, even if not currently in an episode. The fact that overgenerality can be seen without needing to be activated by low mood indicates that overgenerality in autobiographical memory may act as a between-episode marker of future vulner-ability to depression. Thus, not only may nonspecific memory assessed when one is not depressed predict later mood dis-turbance, but overgenerality appears to be more of a trait marker that causes a vul-nerability to depression, rather than a state marker of depression (Brittlebank, Scott, Williams, & Ferrier, 1993).

Because self-concept and autobiograph-ical memories are so intimately related, the level of specificity when recalling a certain event has obvious implications for one's sense of self. Discrepancies between re-called memories and one's perceived self may produce feelings of internal inconsis-tency. When memories are specific, self-discrepancies usually provide the type of psychological tension necessary to motivate a person to set personal goals and generate plans to attain those goals—demonstrating how memory affects motivation and goal pursuit. In turn, emotions are often impacted by goal pursuit and goal attainment, evidencing autobiographical memories' ultimate role in mood regulation. Both a top–down and bottom–up process, "autobiographical knowledge can . . . constrain the goal structure of the working self, but it is also evident that the working self may determine what autobiographical knowledge can be accessed and how that is to be constructed into a memory" (Conway & Pleydell-Pearce, 2000, p. 272). In fact, very vivid and specific memories often arise in response to experiences in which the self and goals are highly integrated (e.g., experiences of goal attainment or progress toward attainment) or markedly inharmonious (e.g., plan failure) (Conway & Pleydell-Pearce, 2000).

In particular, Beike and Landoll (2000) investigated how several types of cognitive reactions to personally discordant recalled events could resolve feelings of internal inconsistency. Providing justifications for the inconsistency, recruiting additional specific events that oppose those recalled, and putting the event behind oneself (closure) were three cognitive reactions found to moderate the relationship between inconsistent recall and well-being. While overgeneral memories may promote the perpetuation of depression and other affective disorders, gaining control of memory, particularly memory specificity may have far-reaching implications for mental health.

While the role of memory specificity and sleep is less obviously related, research supports the correlation between sleep dysfunction and mood dysregulation. With the negatively valenced mnemonic content of REM sleep, and REM's role in distorted memory functions in both PTSD and depression (McNamara, Auerbach, Johnson, Harris, & Doros, 2010), it would not be far-fetched to consider a correlation between REM sleep and overgeneral memories.

A pilot study investigating how sleep facilitates the production and recall of overgeneral memories was conducted in 2009 with 50 healthy, college-aged participants. Participants slept in the sleep lab for two consecutive nights. While the first night was a habituation night, the second night participants underwent an overnight polysomnography in which electroencephalography activity was monitored as each participant was awoken twice by a sleep technician (once in REM sleep and once in NREM sleep).

All subjects performed a series of cognitive tasks four times throughout the night: once before going to bed, once after being awoken from REM sleep, once after being awoken from NREM sleep, and once in the morning. The tasks were both written and spoken, taking about 15 minutes to complete each time. Some of these tasks required participants to recall a dream or dreams they might have had prior to awakening. Another task was similar to the AMT, where participants were presented with positively (e.g., happy), negatively (e.g., lonely), and neutrally (e.g., apathetic) valenced cue words during each condition. They then were asked to recall a personal memory in response to each word, recording the memory and providing its approximate date on audio tape. Each cued memory was later transcribed verbatim and blindly scored for specificity.

Excluding memories that were recalled after positive and negative cue words (because such emotionally valenced words are more likely to elicit specific responses), overgeneral memories were more frequent after REM sleep than after NREM-sleep awakenings. In REM sleep, 38.6 percent of memories were overgeneral while only 27.9 percent of NREM-sleep memories were overgeneral ($\chi^2(1, N = 87) = 0.02$, $p < .05$) (Abrams & McNamara, 2009). Findings suggest that REM sleep may help to modulate memories via generation of nonspecific memories.

In addition, findings support the possibility that REM sleep is depressogenic, implying that REM sleep may help to create nonspecific memories that contribute to negative ruminations central to depression. Following is an example of an overgeneral memory protecting from a painful past event:

Negative REM Dream

- *"I dreamt about my friend . . . me and my roommate stopped being friends . . . a month ago. So, I think I dreamt about her. And . . . we were at Thanksgiving together and it was just really awkward. And it ended up that our families were actually friends together."*

Neutral Memory Recalled after that REM Awakening

- *"I was really apathetic about a month ago when one of my best friends got . . . really wrapped up in college and with her new friends. And she was just . . . saying how her new college friends were her new best friends. And I was just really apathetic towards the whole situation, even though I should have really cared about it, just because that's how she's kind of always been. She's always been really easily influenced. So . . . I just really didn't care about it. It wasn't anything new to me."*

This participant reported an unrelated overgeneral memory in response to the neutral cue word (apathetic) presented after her REM awakening. The dream that she recalled after her REM awakening appears negative, as she accounts the recent end of a friendship and the awkwardness she felt at an imaginary Thanksgiving dinner when she realized their families were still friends. In the previous case, one could argue that REM sleep may have contributed to the production of an overgeneral memory as if to protect the participant from a painful past event (i.e., the loss of a friendship). Although dreams are not always based on reality, they often do play a role in memory consolidation and the processing of information collected during the day. In the previous case, the dream recalled after awakening from REM was triggered by a recent event in her life, and her tendency toward overgenerality may have guarded the participant from having to process the painful specifics surrounding the event.

Although the pilot study had several limitations such as a small sample size ($N = 50$), a lack of diversity in the sample (predominantly college aged, American, Caucasian, and middle class), and the use of only self-reported measures of wellbeing, the study highlights the potential role of REM sleep in overgeneral memory production. Thus, findings further support the relationship between mood dysregulation and sleep dysfunction.

Overall, the widely replicated finding that overgeneral memories are more frequently recalled in patients with affective disorders than healthy controls suggests a strong relationship between overgeneral autobiographical memories and self-concept. Whether overgeneral memories cause, are caused, or just contribute to mood dysregulation is less obvious. However, because autobiographical memories either reflect or project an individual's self-concept, autobiographical memories and the degree of specificity in which they are recalled will either reflect or project onto other aspects of their functioning.

Emily Abrams

References

Abrams, E., & McNamara, P. (2009, October 16). Overgeneral memories are more frequent after REM than NREM sleep awakenings. Poster presented at the UROP Symposium at Boston University, Boston, MA.

Beike, D. R., & Landoll, S. L. (2000). Striving for a consistent life story: Cognitive reactions to autobiographical memories. *Social Cognition, 18,* 292–318.

Brittlebank, A. D., Scott, J., Williams, M. G., & Ferrier, I. N. (1993). Autobiographical memory in depression: State or trait marker? *British Journal of Psychiatry, 162,* 118–121.

Conway, M. A., & Pleydell-Pearce, C. W. (2000). The construction of autobiographical memories in the self-memory system. *Psychological Review, 107,* 261–288.

Dalgleish, T., Spinks, H., Yiend, J., & Kuyken, W. (2001). Autobiographical memory style in seasonal affective disorder and its relationship to future symptom remission. *Journal of Abnormal Psychology, 110,* 335–340.

Goddard, L., Dritschel, B., & Burton, A. (1996). Role of autobiographical memory in social problem solving and depression. *Journal of Abnormal Psychology, 105,* 609–616.

McNamara, P., Auerbach, S., Johnson, P., Harris, E., & Doros, G. (2010). Impact of REM sleep on distortions of self concept, mood and memory in depressed/anxious participants. *Journal of Affective Disorders, 122,* 198–207.

Williams, J., Thorsten Barnhofer, M. G., Crane, C., Hermans, D., Raes, F., Watkins, E., & Dalgleish, T. (2007). Autobiographical memory specificity and emotional disorder. *Psychological Bulletin, 133,* 122–148.

P

Parapsychology and Dreams

Parapsychology can be defined as disciplined inquiry into reported experiences and behaviors that seem to defy mainstream science's concepts of space, time, and energy. Several parapsychologists (most of them psychologists or psychiatrists) have studied dream reports in which these effects are alleged to have occurred. These unusual dreams have been a topic of fascination throughout the millennia and were usually attributed to supernatural forces, finding their way into the mythologies and sacred writings of various faiths. However, the first attempt to study them experimentally was published in 1895 by G. Ermacora, who worked with an Italian claimant medium who attempted to influence the dreams of a child, a phenomenon referred to as telepathy by parapsychologists. In 1966 L. Rhine and colleagues surveyed some 7,000 anecdotal reports of interest to parapsychologists, noting that nearly two thirds reputedly occurred in dreams (Rhine, Pratt, Stuart, Smith, & Greenwood, 1966).

In 1966 M. Ullman and colleagues initiated a decade-long experimental study in a medical center sleep laboratory; a protocol was devised in which a telepathic transmitter would interact with a research participant who would then enter a sound-proof sleep room for the night, with electrodes attached so that periods of rapid eye movement (REM) sleep could be monitored (Ullman, Krippner, & Vaughan, 1973). The transmitter was given a randomly selected envelope and retired to a distant room; the envelope contained an art print (the target). The transmitter would open the envelope, view the target, and attempt to send its images to the participant, who, in turn, had been told to attempt incorporating the images into his/her dreams. Experimenters awakened the participant during REM sleep, tape recording all dream reports, which were later transcribed. Upon the completion of the experimental series (typically 8 to 10 nights), outside judges worked blind and independently with these transcripts and copies of the art prints, assigning numerical scores to each transcript–target combination. These scores were analyzed statistically to determine if the correct transcript–target matches differed from the incorrect matches. This occurred often enough to confirm the telepathy hypothesis; indeed, a meta-analysis of some 450 nighttime dream sessions at Ullman's laboratory produced odds of 75 million to 1 against achieving such results by chance. Notably, five professional magicians visited the laboratory and examined the research protocol, concluding that it was too tight to permit unconscious cueing or conscious deceit on the night of the experiment, the only possibilities for chicanery being on the part of staff members who could have altered the transcripts before sending them to the judges or on the part of those statisticians who analyzed the data. As a result, the transcribers were advised to keep duplicate copies of the transcripts should an investigation be called for, and the analysis was assigned to outside statisticians who were not members of the laboratory staff.

Several attempted replications were carried out by investigators in other laboratories. Many well-known dream researchers initiated these studies, including I. Strauch and D. Foulkes, who obtained negative results; C. Hall, who reported positive results (but with data too sparse to permit statistical analysis); and G. Globus, who reported ambiguous results. After examining the

Moonchild by Dierdre Luzwick symbolizes what parapsychologists suspect is the hidden telepathic entanglement of people who, on the surface, seem to be cut off from others. (Reproduced from the original art of Dierdre Luzwick)

Ullman experiments and those done elsewhere (principally in British university settings with participants who stayed at home and were awakened at random intervals by telephone) C. Roe and S. Sherwood (2009) concluded that "combined effect size estimates for both sets of studies suggest that judges could correctly identify target materials more often than would be expected by chance, using dream reports" (p. 211). They also reported a significant difference between the two datasets; the results favoring those carried out at Ullman's laboratory.

One psychic claimant participated in two eight-night studies in which he attempted to dream about a target that would be randomly selected once he awoke; a phenomenon referred to as precognition by parapsychologists; both studies produced significant results but no attempt was made to repeat them in other laboratories.

Critics of this body of work cite the lack of replicability. However, S. Krippner (2007) and his associates conducted retrospective studies indicating a correspondence between putative telepathic and precognitive dream reports and geomagnetic activity, specifically low sunspot activity and electrical storms while participants were dreaming. Hence, if future studies yield greater replicability, and if they are executed under conditions that rule out coincidence, sensory cueing, statistical artifacts, and fraud, these data suggest that there are biological capacities for unusual behaviors that may be sensitive to geomagnetic activity, bringing these parapsychology-derived data closer to similar environment–brain interactions already reported in mainstream science.

Stanley C. Krippner

References

Friedman, H. L., & Krippner, S. (2010). Editors' epilogue: Is it time for a détente? In S. Krippner & H. L. Friedman (Eds.), *Debating psychic experience: Human potential or human illusion?* (pp. 195–204). Santa Barbara, CA: Praeger.

Krippner, S. (2007). Anomalous experiences and dreams. In D. Barrett & P. McNamara (Eds.), *The new science of dreaming* (Vol. 2, pp. 285–306). Westport, CT: Praeger.

Rhine, J. B., Pratt, J. G., Stuart, C. E., Smith, B. M., & Greenwood, J. A. (1966). *Extrasensory perception after sixty years.* Boston: Bruce Humphries.

Roe, C. A., & Sherwood, S. J. (2009). Evidence for extra-sensory perception in dream content: A review of experimental studies. In S. Krippner & D. J. Ellis (Eds.), *Perchance to dream: The frontiers of dream psychology* (pp. 211–238). New York: Nova Science.

Ullman, M., Krippner, S., & Vaughan, A. (1973). *Dream telepathy.* London: Turnstone Books.

Parasomnias and Nocturnal Frontal Lobe Epilepsy

Parasomnias are defined as "clinical disorders that are not abnormalities of the processes responsible for sleep and awake states per se but are undesirable physical phenomena that occur predominantly during sleep" (American Academy of Sleep Medicine, 2005). Parasomnias, comprising a dozen clinical features, are divided into three groups (see Table 3). With the exception of REM behavior disorder, parasomnias usually occur during childhood, more often with episodic recurrence, but onset or persistence during adulthood is not rare. The prevalence in the population (always or often) is 1 to 11 percent. The aetiopathogenesis remains unknown, but an underlying impairment of arousal mechanisms triggering dissociation between the motor component of the awake state and EEG electrical activity (i.e., dissociated state) has been postulated (Mahowald & Schenck, 2005).

Nocturnal frontal lobe epilepsy (NFLE) is a partial epilepsy in which seizures, characterized by complex, often bizarre, motor behavior or sustained dystonic posture, occur almost exclusively during sleep (non-REM sleep in 97% of cases). The clinical spectrum of nocturnal frontal lobe seizures (NFLS) comprises distinct paroxysmal sleep-related attacks of variable semiology, intensity, and duration, representing different aspects of the same epileptic condition (Tinuper & Lugaresi, 2002) (see Table 4). Seizures have a remarkable interindividual stereotyped semiology. Due to the rarity of this condition, epidemiological data are lacking. Onset is

Table 3: Parasomnias According to ICSD-2

Arousal disorders

    Confusional arousals

    Sleep terrors

    Sleepwalking

Parasomnias usually associated with REM sleep

    Nightmares

    REM behavior disorder

    Sleep paralysis

Other parasomnias

    Sleep enuresis

Source: Adapted from ASDA & American Academy of Sleep Medicine (2005).

mainly during adolescence and males are more frequently affected. Neurological and neuropsychological examinations and neuroradiological findings are normal in 86 percent of cases and interictal and even ictal EEG fails to disclose epileptiform abnormalities in half of the patients. Carbamazepine completely abolishes NFLS or gives remarkable relief in two thirds of patients, whereas the seizures prove resistant to any antiepileptic drug treatment in the remainder (Provini et al., 1999).

NFLE is a syndromic entity that includes both sporadic and familial cases. In familial cases, NFLS recur in an autosomal dominant manner and this condition is named autosomal dominant NFLE. Mutations in genes coding for the alfa4, alfa2, and beta2 subunits of the neuronal nicotinic acetylcholine receptor have been identified, confirming genetic heterogeneity (Marini & Guerrini, 2007).

Since the first description in 1981, the problem of the differential diagnosis between NFLS, parasomnias, and pseudoseizures has been debated (see Table 5). The difficulty in differential diagnosis between NFLE and parasomnias is hampered by the possible coexistence in NFLE patients or their relatives of nocturnal parasomnic attacks. We recently documented by a large case–control study a higher frequency of

Table 4: Clinical Features of Nocturnal frontal Lobe Seizures (NFLS) and The Most Common Parasomnias

Hypermotor seizures

Body movements that can start in the limbs, head, or trunk

Complex, often violent behavior

Often with a dystonic–dyskinetic component

Sometimes with cycling or rocking or repetitive body movements

Prevalent in the trunk or legs

The patient may vocalize, scream, or swear

Fear is a frequent expression

Asymmetric, bilateral tonic seizures

Sustained non-customary forced position

Paroxysmal arousals

Bilateral and axial involvement resembling a sudden arousal

Opening of the eyes

Sitting up in bed

Sometimes frightened expression

Epileptic wanderings

Same beginning as above

Semi-purposeful ambulatory behavior

Mimicking sleepwalking

Source: Tinuper et al. (2007).

arousal parasomnias not only in patients with NFLE but also in their relatives, suggesting an abnormal, possibly cholinergic, arousal system as the common physiopathological substrate (Bisulli et al., 2010). A complex genetic component may be shared by parasomnias and NFLE causing an impairment in the pathway controlling physiological arousal. Prospective studies on children with parasomnias are needed to

Table 5: Clinical Features of Nocturnal frontal Lobe Seizures (NFLS) and The Most Common Parasomnias

	Disorders of arousal	Nightmares	RBD	NFLS
Age at onset (years)	3–8	Usually 3–6	After 50	Any age
Gender	Either	Either	Male predominance	Male predominance
Family history of parasomnias	+	+	−	+
Spontaneous evolution	Tend to disappear	Tend to disappear	Rare spontaneous remission	Increased frequency?
Episodes / month	Sporadic	Sporadic	Almost every night	Almost every night
Occurrence during the night	First third	Last third	At least 90 minutes after sleep onset	Any time
Sleep stage onset of episodes	NREM sleep (st. 3–4)	REM sleep	REM sleep	NREM (mainly st. 2)
Triggering factors	++ (sleep deprivation, febrile illness)	++ (stress, traumatic events)	−	+/−
Episodes / night	Usually one	Usually one	From one to several	Several
Episodes duration	1–10 minutes	3–30 minutes	1–2 minutes	seconds to 3 minutes
Stereotypic motor pattern	−	−	−	+
Autonomic discharge	+++	+	−	++(+)
Consciousness if awakened	Impaired	Normal	Normal	Normal
Recall of the episode on awakening	No	Yes	Yes	Inconstant

Source: Tinuper et al. (2007).

clarify the long-term evolution of these sleep disturbances and verify the percentage of subjects subsequently developing NFLE.

Another crucial clinical point is the semeiological overlap between NFLS and parasomnias. Whereas some ictal features of NFLS seem to be typical of the mesial frontal epileptic zones (asymmetric tonic posturing), others are hard to confine to a specific cortical frontal area and are quite similar to parasomnic behavior. Furthermore, dystonic–dyskinetic elements suggest an ictal involvement of subcortical structures. Therefore the ictal cortical discharges may not be confined to the orbitofrontal regions but disinhibit other cortical (deep temporal) or subcortical structures and provoke primitive behaviors (Tassinari, Gardella, Meletti, and Rubboli, 2003). Irrespective of the nature of the causal trigger the complex motor semiology characterizing NFLS and some parasomnias is the same and consists in the activation of repetitive motor patterns related to the activation of central pattern generators. Invasive studies using deep implanted electrodes in drug-resistant NFLE patients could clarify this point.

Even though many aspects of parasomnias and NFLE have been clarified in the last two decades, the problem of differential diagnosis remains a challenge for clinicians. The difficulties in distinguishing nocturnal epileptic seizures from parasomnias reflect just one aspect of the intriguing issue of the pathophysiological relationships between all types of paroxysmal motor behaviors during sleep.

Francesca Bisulli and Paolo Tinuper

See also: entries related to Sleep Disorders

References

American Academy of Sleep Medicine. (2005). *The international classification of sleep disorders: Diagnostic and coding manual* (2nd ed., Ed. ASDA). Westchester, IL: American Academy of Sleep Medicine.

Bisulli, F., Vignatelli, L., Naldi, I., Licchetta, L., Provini, F., Plazzi, G., . . . Tinuper, P. (2010, April). Increased frequency of arousal parasomnias in families with nocturnal frontal lobe epilepsy: A common mechanism? *Epilepsia, 51*(9), 1852–1860.

Mahowald, M. W., & Schenck, C. H. (2005). Insights from studying human sleep disorders. *Nature, 43,* 1279–1285.

Marini, C., & Guerrini, R. (2007). The role of the nicotinic acetylcholine receptors in sleep-related epilepsy. *Biochemical Pharmacology, 74,* 1308–1314.

Provini, F., Plazzi, G., Tinuper, P., Vandi, S., Lugaresi, E., & Montagna, P. (1999). Nocturnal frontal lobe epilepsy: A clinical and polygraphic overview of 100 consecutive cases. *Brain, 122,* 1017–1031.

Scheffer, I. E., Bhatia, K. P., Lopes-Cendes, I., Fish, D. R., Marsden, C. D., Andermann, F., Andermann, E., et al. (1994, February 26). Autosomal dominant frontal epilepsy misdiagnosed as sleep disorder (Review). *Lancet, 343*(8896), 515–517.

Tassinari, C. A., Gardella, E., Meletti, S., & Rubboli, G. (2003). The neuroethological interpretation of motor behaviours in "nocturnal-hyperkynetic-frontal-seizures": Emergence of "innate" motor behaviours and role of central pattern generators. In A. Beaumanoir, F. Andermann, P. Chauvel, L. Mira, & B. Zifkin (Eds.), *Frontal lobe seizures and epilepsies in children* (pp. 43–45). New Barnet, UK: B. John Libbey.

Tinuper, P., & Lugaresi, E. (2002). The concept of paroxysmal nocturnal dystonia. In C. W. Bazil, B. A. Malow, & M. R. Sammaritano (Eds.), *Sleep and epilepsy: The clinical spectrum* (pp. 277–282). New York: Elsevier Science.

Tinuper, P., et al. (2007). Disorders in sleep: Guidelines for differentiating epileptic from non-epileptic motor phenomena arising from sleep. *Sleep Medicine Reviews, 11*, 255–267.

Tinuper, P., et al. (2010). Familial frontal lobe epilepsy and its relationship with other nocturnal paroxysmal events. *Epilepsia, 51*(Suppl. 1), 51–53.

Partial Sleep Deprivation

Sleep deprivation refers to having wakefulness that is extended beyond the 16 hours that is considered a normal day. Acute sleep deprivation refers to a single episode of reduced sleep (see the entry "Acute Sleep Deprivation"). Partial sleep deprivation refers to a reduction in total sleep rather than complete deprivation of sleep. The amount of partial sleep loss can vary from just getting up an hour earlier than normal to many nights with total sleep reduced to four hours or less. Most research with partial sleep deprivation has examined changes in function after one or two nights with total sleep reduced to four or six hours. Understanding partial sleep loss is important because questionnaires have suggested that 15 percent of normal adults sleep less than six hours per night on weekday nights and therefore suffer from some amount of partial sleep deprivation on a weekly basis.

Behavioral Effects

The general effects of partial sleep deprivation are similar to those seen after acute sleep deprivation (see the entry "Acute Sleep Deprivation") except that they are generally milder when the partial sleep loss is for only one to two nights. However, chronic partial sleep deprivation that allowed four hours of sleep per night for two weeks resulted in cognitive deficits that were of the same magnitude as those seen after one to two nights of total sleep deprivation. Data also suggest that chronic partial sleep deprivation can have cumulative or stress-related effects that can differ from findings after a short period of total sleep deprivation.

Studies have shown that adults are significantly more sleepy, as measured by falling asleep more rapidly in naps, after only one night with time in bed reduced from eight to six hours. Sleepiness on the following day increases as time in bed decreases. Sleepiness also becomes more apparent as consecutive nights of reduced sleep increase. One large study found that performance on a reaction time task, a memory task, and a math task was consistently decreased after sleep had been restricted to four or six hours for several nights. Both time to react and the number of very slow or absent responses (called lapses in attention) were increased. Such data suggest some overall cognitive slowing and increases in microsleeps, .5- to 10-second periods of loss of attention where external awareness is briefly lost. These cognitive and response speed changes suggest that partial sleep deprivation could also have a negative impact on driving. A study has shown that there is an increased incidence of sleep-related motor vehicle crashes in drivers sleeping less than seven hours per night. Empirical studies have shown decreased driving ability in driving simulators after one night of sleep reduced to two hours or with sleep chronically reduced to four or six hours.

Physiological Effects of Partial Sleep Deprivation

A number of physiological changes become apparent during partial sleep deprivation. For example, subjects allowed three or five hours in bed for seven nights had more slow eye movements (consistent with early signs of sleep onset) and an increased latency to pupil constriction. An increase in slow EEG frequencies, often associated with sleep onset or sleep, and a decrease in higher EEG frequency alpha activity, associated with wakefulness, was also found in subjects with sleep reduced to four or six hours per night for several nights.

Studies of partial sleep deprivation have suggested that sleep restriction to four hours per night for six nights may result in increased sympathetic activation, decreased glucose tolerance, and increased risk of inflammation (as measured by C-reactive protein). Other studies of immune function have shown some decrease in immune function. One study showed that the antibody response to an influenza vaccination was decreased by more than 50 percent 10 days after a vaccination that followed six nights of sleep restricted to four hours per night. Responses were the same three to four weeks later, but the results imply that partial sleep deprivation could alter acute immune responses.

A number of studies have shown negative health consequences associated with short habitual sleep durations, although it is not always clear that short sleep durations reflect chronic partial sleep deprivation rather than a short sleep requirement. However, studies have shown that there is an increased mortality risk for individuals reporting less than six hours of sleep per night. Similarly, an increased risk of coronary events was found in women sleeping seven hours per night or less in one study and with individuals sleeping less than five hours per night in another study. Sleeping less than five hours per night has also been associated with an increased risk of hypertension.

Individual Differences

It is known that some individuals are consistently more sensitive to the loss of even small amounts of sleep while others are not impaired by greater loss of sleep. However, these differences are not always apparent to the individual and have not been related to other variables at this time.

Recovery

Sleep is all that is needed to reverse the negative effects of partial sleep deprivation in humans. Partial sleep deprivation typically results in a disproportionate reduction in REM sleep because individuals typically have much more REM sleep near the end of their sleep period (which is cut off during partial sleep deprivation). As a result, recovery sleep after partial sleep deprivation is typically characterized by an increase in total sleep time with a particular increase in REM sleep called REM rebound.

Michael H. Bonnet

See also: Acute Sleep Deprivation; entries related to Sleep Physiology

References

Ayas, N.T., White, D.P., Manson, J.E., Stampfer, M.J., Speizer, F.E., Malhotra, A., & Hu, F.B. (2003). A prospective study of sleep duration and coronary heart disease in women. *Archives of Internal Medicine, 163*(2), 205–209.

Banks, S., & Dinges, D.F. (2010). Chronic sleep deprivation. In M. Kryger, T. Roth, & W.C. Dement (Eds.), *Principles and practice of sleep medicine*. Philadelphia, PA: Saunders.

Gangwisch, J.E., Heymsfield, S.B., Boden-Albala, B., Buijs, R.M., Kreier, F., Opler, M.G., . . . Malaspina, D. (2008). Sleep duration associated with mortality in elderly, but not middle-aged, adults in a large US sample. *Sleep, 31,* 1087–1096.

Philip, P., Sagaspe, P., Taillard, J., Valtat, C., Moore, N., Akerstedt, T., . . . Bioulac, B. (2005). Fatigue, sleepiness, and performance in simulated versus real driving conditions. *Sleep, 28*(12), 1511–1516.

Rosenthal, L., Roehrs, T.A., Rosen, A., & Roth, T. (1993). Level of sleepiness and total sleep time following various time in bed conditions. *Sleep, 16,* 226–232.

Spiegel, K., Sheridan, J.F., & Van Cauter, E. (2002). Effect of sleep deprivation on response to immunization. *Journal of the American Medical Association, 288,* 1471–1472.

Van Dongen, H.P.A., Maislin, G., Mullington, J.M., & Dinges, D.F. (2003). The cumulative cost of additional wakefulness: Dose-response effects on neurobehavioral functions and sleep physiology from chronic sleep restriction and total sleep deprivation. *Sleep, 26,* 117–126.

Vgontzas, A.N., Liao, D., Bixler, E.O., Chrousos, G.P., & Vela-Bueno, A. (2009). Insomnia with objective short sleep duration is associated with a high risk for hypertension. *Sleep, 32,* 491–497.

Phasic Ponto–Geniculo–Occipital/Pontine Wave (PGO/P-Wave)

Prominent phasic events of REM sleep are field potentials in the pontine tegmentum, which begin just prior to the onset of REM sleep and continue through its duration (Datta, 1997, 2010). These field potentials have been recorded in both the lateral geniculate body (LGB) and the occipital cortex of the cat. Since, in the cat, these field potentials originate in the pons (P) and then propagate to the geniculate (G) and occipital cortex (O), they are called PGO waves. PGO waves in the cat could also be recorded at points throughout the extent of the thalamus and cortex. However, such PGO waves reach their highest amplitude in the LGB, primary visual cortex, and association visual cortex. In addition to the pons, thalamus, and cortex, phasic potentials have been recorded in both the oculomotor nuclei and the cerebellum of the cat. Phasic potentials of pontine origin have also been recorded in the amygdala, cingulate gyrus, and hippocampus, suggesting that PGO waves also occur in the limbic system. More importantly, mapping techniques have demonstrated that (for the cat at least) the pons is the primary site of origin for PGO-wave activity. PGO waves have also been documented and studied in other mammalian species, including non-human primates, humans, and rodents. In nonhuman primates, PGO-wave-like phasic field potentials have been recorded from the LGB and pons of macaques and in the LGB of baboons. In humans, phasic potentials have been recorded in the striate cortex during REM sleep. Such striate field potentials are probably cortical components of state-specific phasic potentials of pontine origin. PGO waves have also been recorded in the human pons during and immediately before REM sleep. In rats, initial attempts to record potentials in the LGB, based on PGO-wave recordings in the cat, were unsuccessful. Subsequent studies have recorded PGO-like waves in the pons of the rat that are equivalent to those in the pons of the cat. The initial failures indicated that state-specific pontine phasic waves in rats do not excite LGB neurons in a way that could produce geniculate components of PGO waves. More recently, the absence of PGO-wave-like activity in the rat LGB has shown to be due to the lack of afferent inputs from P-wave-generating cells to the LGB (Datta, Siwek, Patterson, & Cipolloni, 1998). This field potential in the rat is therefore called a P-wave, since it does not activate the geniculate nucleus.

The waveform, amplitude, and frequency characteristics of PGO waves recorded from the pons, geniculate, and occipital cortex have been most intensively examined in the cat (Datta, 1997; Datta & MacLean, 2007). PGO waves are biphasic in shape with a duration of 60 to 120 milliseconds and an amplitude between 200 and 300 microvolts. The P-wave in the rat is equivalent to the pontine component of the PGO wave in the cat, with similar duration (75–100 milliseconds) and amplitude (100–150 microvolts). PGO/P-waves during REM sleep can occur as a singlet or as clusters containing a variable number of waves (three to five waves per burst) at a density range of 30 to 60 spikes/minute. Singlet PGO/P-waves, known as Type I waves, occur commonly in non-REM

sleep and are independent of eye movement; conversely, clusters of PGO waves (Type II waves) are associated with eye-movement bursts and are typically indicative of REM sleep. Type II PGO-wave activity accounts for 55 to 65 percent of the total number of PGO waves recorded during REM sleep (Datta & Patterson, 2003).

Since PGO/P-wave activity always precedes REM sleep, several investigators have proposed that PGO/P-wave mechanisms are causally linked to the cellular and molecular mechanisms for both the triggering and regulation of the total amount of REM sleep. In addition to REM-sleep induction, PGO/P-waves have also been implicated in several other important brain functions such as sensorimotor integration, learning and memory, dreaming, self-organization, development of the visual system, and startle responses (Datta, 1997, 2010; Morrison & Bowker, 1975). Although several functional roles for PGO/P-wave activity have been proposed, other than memory consolidation these functions remain mostly correlative.

Utilizing chemical microstimulation, cell-specific lesions, and single-cell recording techniques, the PGO/P-wave generator in the cat was localized within the caudolateral-peribrachial (C-PBL) area (Datta, 1997; Datta & MacLean, 2007). Subsequently, using similar experimental techniques to those used in the cat, the P-wave generator in the rat was localized within the dorsal part of the subcoeruleus nucleus (Datta, 2006; Datta & Patterson, 2003). In humans, as in the cat, the PGO/P-wave generator is located in the C-PBL area. Immunohistochemical identification of cholinergic and glutamatergic cell types in the brainstem indicates that PGO/P-wave-generating cells in the cat are capable of synthesizing both acetyl-choline and glutamate, and thus these cells could be labeled as both cholinergic and glutamatergic; whereas in the rat, P-wave-generating cells have been identi-fied by specific monoclonal antibodies as glutamatergic, but not cholinergic (Datta, 2006). These P-wave-generating neurons project to the hippocampus, amygdala, en-torhinal cortex, and many other regions of the brain known to be involved in cogni-tive processing. The PGO/P-wave genera-tor in both the cat and rat receives afferent projections from the raphe nucleus and nu-cleus locus coeruleus (LC). These P-wave-generating glutamatergic neurons remain silent during wakefulness and slow-wave sleep (SWS), but during the transition from SWS to REM sleep and throughout REM sleep these neurons discharge high-frequency spike bursts in the background of tonically increased firing rates (Datta, 2006; Datta & Hobson, 1994).

Since the P-wave generator is also in-volved in sensorimotor integration, the differences in the anatomical location and neurotransmitter identity of the P-wave generator between the rat and cat may pro-vide a species-specific advantage (Datta, 2006). Specifically, in prey animals (i.e., the rat), the P-wave generator is anatom-ically closer to the LC. This shorter dis-tance is advantageous during REM sleep (when animals are naturally paralyzed due to muscle atonia) because it permits quick communication with the LC for flight re-sponse, and facilitates escape from preda-tors. This rapid flight response is vital for the survival of prey animals. In contrast,

the predatory mammalian (such as the cat and human) PGO-wave generator is farther from the LC and instead close to the PPT. Since predators rarely face the threat of predation, there is no advantage to having a quick arousal response to any nonthreat-ening type of noise during REM sleep. Furthermore, frequent interruptions could actually harm a predatory animal by pre-venting the necessary regenerative func-tions of REM sleep. Thus, for these types of noises, the P-wave generator signals the cholinergic PPT to intensify REM sleep rather than wake the animal up by activat-ing the LC.

It has been demonstrated that choliner-gic activation of the PGO/P-wave genera-tor increases glutamate release in the dorsal hippocampus (DH). In addition, P-wave activity has been shown to have a positive influence on hippocampal theta-wave ac-tivity in the DH. Most recently, it has been demonstrated that the activation of these P-wave-generating neurons increases glu-tamate release and activates postsynaptic N-Methyl-D-aspartate (NMDA) receptors in the DH. Activation of P-wave-generat-ing neurons increases phosphorylation of the transcription factor cAMP response el-ement binding protein (CREB) in the DH and amygdala by activating intracellular protein kinase A (PKA). The P-wave-generating neurons activation-dependent PKA-CREB phosphorylation increases the expression of activity-regulated cyto-skeletal-associated protein (Arc), brain-derived nerve growth factor (BDNF), and early growth response-1 (Egr-1) genes in the DH and amygdala. The P-wave genera-tor activation-induced increased activation of PKA and expression of pCREB, Arc,

BDNF, and Egr-1 in the DH are shown to be necessary for REM-sleep-dependent memory processing (Datta, Li, & Auerbach, 2008). These findings are significant because they provide the most direct evidence to substantiate the idea that P-wave generator activation during post-training REM sleep is critical for REM-sleep-dependent memory processing. Although the functions of PGO/P-waves remain a mystery in neuroscience, ongoing research on their generation and functions is very promising. Hopefully in the near future, a complete and detailed mechanism for the regulation of PGO/P-wave generator activity will be discovered, which will then be vital to unraveling the functions of PGO/P-wave activity.

Subimal Datta

See also: entries related to Sleep Physiology

Note

This work is supported by the U.S. National Institutes of Health Research grants NS34004 and MH59839.

References

Datta, S. (1997). Cellular basis of pontine ponto-geniculo-occipital wave generation and modulation. *Cellular and Molecular Neurobiology, 17,* 341–365.

Datta, S. (2006). Activation of phasic pontine-wave generator: A mechanism for sleep-dependent memory processing. *Sleep and Biological Rhythms, 4,* 16–26.

Datta, S. (2010). Sleep: Learning and memory. G. F. Koob, M. Le Moal, & R. F. Thompson (Eds.), *Encyclopedia of behavioral neuroscience* (Vol. 3, pp. 218–226). Oxford: Academic Press.

Datta, S., & Hobson, J. A. (1994). Neuronal activity in the caudo-lateral peribrachial pons: Relationship to PGO waves and rapid eye movements. *Journal of Neurophysiology, 71,* 95–109.

Datta, S., Li, G., & Auerbach, S. (2008). Activation of phasic pontine-wave generator in the rat: A mechanism for expression of plasticity-related genes and proteins in the dorsal hippocampus and amygdala. *European Journal of Neuroscience, 27,* 1876–1892.

Datta, S., & MacLean, R. R. (2007). Neurobiological mechanisms for the regulation of mammalian sleep-wake behavior: Reinterpretation of historical evidence and inclusion of contemporary cellular and molecular evidence. *Neuroscience and Biobehavioural Reviews, 31,* 775–824.

Datta, S., & Patterson, E. H. (2003). Activation of phasic pontine wave (P-wave): A mechanism of learning and memory processing. In J. Maquet, R. Stickgold, & C. Smith (Eds.), *Sleep and brain plasticity* (pp. 135–156). Oxford: Oxford University Press.

Datta, S., Siwek, D. F., Patterson, E. H., & Cipolloni, P. B. (1998). Localization of pontine PGO wave generation sites and their anatomical projections in the rat. *Synapse, 30,* 409–423.

Morrison, A. R., & Bowker, R. M. (1975). The biological significance of PGO spikes in the sleeping cat. *Acta Neurobiologiae Experimentalis, 35,* 821–840.

Philosophy of Mind and Dream Characters

How should we regard the characters that appear in dreams? Are they mere inventions of the mind of the dreamer? Or are they something more than that? To what extent do they exhibit full-fledged criteria of mind and agency? If they do satisfy criteria of the mental, do they then deserve some sort of moral status as well? To what extent can we accord them the status of the real? Perhaps they are best treated as we do characters in a novel or a movie. Are they simply creatures of the imagination? We will see that this option is not open for characters in dreams and thus their ontological status remains undecided.

Philosophers claim that a *person* is defined as a being who is capable of reasoning, who displays intentionality and emotion, who is self-conscious, and who has an identity that persists through time. Surprisingly, there is evidence that either the dreamer (dream ego) or other dream characters display these criteria for mentality.

Besides the dreamer himself, dream characters appear in more than 95 percent of adult reports of dreams (Hall & Van de Castle, 1966). In children, dream characters involve people, animals, and unusual beings like monsters and spirits. In adults, the same range of characters appear but with a reduction in the frequency with which animals appear. For most adults, the average number of characters in every dream in addition to the dream ego is between three and four (Hall, 1951; Kahn, Stickgold, Pace-Schott, & Hobson, 2000). Male characters slightly predominate in women's dreams and definitely predominate in men's dreams. Belying the common conception of dreams as bizarre, dream characters are only very rarely (only 14% of all instances) depicted in any kind of a bizarre manner. Dream characters also show staying power across dream episodes (Foulkes & Schmidt, 1983)—they are not fleeting inventions of the mind. They change and grow in ways appropriate to the narrative of the dream series they are appearing in. Dream characters can reappear in recurring dream series and in dream series that occur across a single night when they appear to remember previous interactions with the dreamer and adjust their behavior accordingly. Characters can either be depicted quite realistically or they can simply just be known to be present. This feature of dream characters indicates that the dream ego is using theory of mind skills to cognize the presence and intentions of other dream characters.

A substantial proportion (between 25% and 48% depending on definitions) of male characters is unknown or unfamiliar to the dreamer (Hall & Van de Castle, 1966; Kahn, Pace-Schott, & Hobson, 2002). In an early study of more than 1,000 dreams, Hall (1963) reported (1) that strangers in dreams were most often males; (2) that aggressive encounters were more likely to occur in interaction with an unknown male than with an unknown female or a familiar male or female; and (3) that unknown males appeared more frequently in dreams of males than of females. Using the Hall–Van de Castle system, Domhoff (1996) looked at the role of enemies in dreams. Enemies were defined as those dream characters who typically interacted (greater than 60% of the cases) with the dreamer in an aggressive manner. Those enemies turned out to be male strangers and animals. Interactions with female strangers are predominantly friendly in the dreams of both males and females. Domhoff (2003) more recently has shown that when male strangers appear in a dream, the likelihood that physical aggression will occur in that dream far exceeds what would be expected on the basis of chance. In short, male strangers signal physical aggression. This is an extremely important result of research on dream content, as it suggests that dream characters may encode selected emotional signals in rule-governed ways, thus pointing to a mental operation whereby characters embody intense emotional charge.

While menacing strangers are certainly emotionally compelling, other dream characters that are not strangers can be as well. We have all experienced the reappearance of a loved one in a dream. Whether the loved one was lost simply due to breakup or separation or via death, the reappearance in the dream can be startlingly real. In the case of bereavement, vivid images of the deceased may persist for years in dreams (Cookson, 1990). When the loved one appears in dreams, there is a tendency to want to stay in the dream world and not wake up. These sorts of dreams feel like visitations more than fleeting impressions. They are experienced as communications from the loved one. In this case, the dream character comes alive and temporarily revives the emotional life of the bereaved—such is the power of dream characters.

What do characters (other than the dreamer himself) do in dreams? Generally speaking, they engage in social interactions of various kinds. About 68.2 percent of aggressive actions and 52 percent of friendly interactions are initiated by other characters. When the dreamer is the initiator of an interaction, most aggressive interactions occur in REM dreams and friendly interactions occur in NREM dreams (McNamara, McLaren, Smith, Brown, & Stickgold, 2005; McNamara et al., 2010). Interactions between the dreamer and another character very often involve conversation or thought exchanges. These verbal exchanges have repeatedly been demonstrated to be syntactically well-formed utterances that were entirely appropriate to the dream context.

In summary, dream characters seem to be fully imagined or fully realized persons. They have minds, intentions, desires, and emotions that operate independently of the will of the dreamer. They may even have memories. To underline the autonomous character of dream characters consider the fact that dream characters not only think in ways that are totally independent of the will of the dream ego or dreamer, but they also act in ways that are totally independent of the will of the dreamer. As mentioned previously, dream characters appear to initiate emotional encounters with the dream ego, whether the dream ego likes it or not. Indeed, some dream characters will touch, push, or attack the dreamer—in ways the dreamer dislikes, fears, or hates—events that the dreamer clearly does not want to happen. When the dreamer is under attack from some other character, the dreamer never wishes it were so. Instead, the dreamer does everything he or she can to flee the aggression. Aggression against the dreamer is also quite common, at least in dreams that come from the REM sleep state. If we take a very common dream theme such as the dreamer being chased by a male stranger who intends to hurt the dreamer, we will see that attribution of intentional states and other mental states to the dream character does occur as a normal part of the dreaming process. Fifty-nine percent of the time the intention of the attacker is known to the dreamer, and 75 percent of the time the dream ego does nothing to cause or incite the attack (Hall, 1955). The character who is chasing the dreamer clearly satisfies criteria for possessing mind or consciousness. He can manipulate his attention. Indeed, he keeps his eye on the dreamer and can adjust his chase route to catch the dreamer as she attempts to lose him. The stranger also evidences will and volition when he intends his target and adjusts his actions to get his target. The stranger also evidences awareness of subjective experiences when his rage levels change as a function of the chase. His mood changes from menacing and hate-filled rage to malicious delight and satisfaction when the target is about to be caught. Now all of these considerations concerning the mental status of the stranger character in a dream also apply, except more strongly to the case of the dreamer herself. The dreamer is a character in the dream too. She intends to escape. She plans and adjusts her behavior accordingly. She has internal subjective experiences of fear, terror, relief, or despair, depending on the outcome of the chase. In addition, she can also access memories that attest to her persisting identity across time periods and beyond the current dream episode. In lucid dreams, where the dreamer is aware that she is dreaming, other characters in the dream demonstrate a striking independence of mind and feeling, as well as separate perspectives and knowledge not available to the dreamer (Tholey, 1989).

In short, dream characters, both the dreamer and other characters within a dream, appear to satisfy some of the most stringent criteria philosophers have produced for mind, agency, or personhood. Dream characters act as independent agents in dreams. They are sometimes emotionally compelling in ways that characters we meet in waking life are not. Whatever the philosophical status of dream characters as full-fledged mental agents, our ancestors certainly treated them as such. It may even be said that dream characters were just as important emotionally to persons in those days as were other waking characters.

Patrick McNamara

References

Cookson, K. (1990). Dreams and death: An exploration of the literature. *Omega Journal of Death and Dying, 21*, 259–281.

Domhoff, G. W. (1996). *Finding meaning in dreams: A quantitative approach.* New York: Plenum.

Domhoff, G. W. (2003). *The scientific study of dreams: Neural networks, cognitive development, and content analysis.* Washington, DC: American Psychological Association.

Foulkes, D., & Schmidt, M. (1983). Temporal sequence and unit composition in dream reports from different stages of sleep. *Sleep, 6*, 265–280.

Hall, C. (1963). Strangers in dreams: An empirical confirmation of the Oedipus complex. *Journal of Personality, 31*, 336–345.

Hall, C., & Van de Castle, R. I. (1966). *The content analysis of dreams.* New York: Appleton-Century-Crofts.

Hall, C. S. (1951). What people dream about. *Scientific American, 184*, 60–63.

Hall, C. S. (1955). The significance of the dream of being attacked. *Journal of Personality, 24*, 168–180.

Kahn, D., Pace-Schott, E., & Hobson, J. A. (2002). Emotion and cognition: Feeling and character identification in dreaming. *Consciousness and Cognition, 11*, 34–50.

Kahn, D., Stickgold, R., Pace-Schott, E. F., & Hobson, J. A. (2000). Dreaming and waking consciousness: A character recognition study. *Journal of Sleep Research, 9,* 317–325.

McNamara, P., Andresen, J., Clark, J., Zborowski, M., & Duffy, C. A. (2001). Impact of attachment styles on dream recall and dream content: A test of the attachment hypothesis of REM sleep. *Journal of Sleep Research, 10,* 117–127.

McNamara, P., Johnson, P., McLaren, D., Harris, E., Beauharnais, C., & Auerbach, S. (2010). REM and NREM sleep mentation. *International Review of Neurobiology, 92,* 69–86.

McNamara, P., McLaren, D., Smith, D., Brown, A., & Stickgold, R. (2005). A "Jekyll and Hyde" within: Aggressive versus friendly interactions in REM and non-REM dreams. *Psychological Science, 16,* 130–136.

Merritt, J.M., Stickgold, R., Pace-Schott, E., Williams, J., & Hobson, J. A. (1994). Emotion profiles in the dreams of men and women. *Consciousness and Cognition, 3,* 46–60.

Tholey, P. (1989). Consciousness and abilities of dream characters observed during lucid dreaming. *Perceptual and Motor Skills, 68,* 567–578.

Photography and Dreams

The use of photography as a medium for dream imagery seems paradoxical. Photography is a recording medium; the photographic image captures patterns of light reflected off objects in the physical world. The dream is a subjective experience. Since dreaming is not an experience of the physical world, it would seem an unlikely, if not impossible, subject matter for photography. Yet artists working in this medium argue that it is precisely the implied verity of the photograph that gives photographic dream images their power.

From the beginning, an expressive approach to image making has woven through the history of photography as an alternative to documentary photography, and this has included dream imagery. In the 1930s, the surrealists in Paris developed a style of street photography that reflected their interest in dreams and synchronistic experiences. In 1941, Bill Brandt, a British documentary photographer who had briefly been an assistant to Man Ray, published a dream sequence, "Nightwalk: A Dream Phantasy in Photographs," in *Coronet*. In the 1950s and 1960s, Minor White, an influential teacher and founder of the journal *Aperture* developed an approach to photography as spiritual practice that emphasized exploring inner states by capturing their equivalents in the physical world. But it was in the 1960s and 1970s that dream imagery became an explicit genre in photography, through the work of early pioneers such as Jerry Uelsmann (who studied with White), Ralph Gibson, and Arthur Tress. Uelsmann's (1982) work was seminal; although not about dreams, his use of multiple enlargers to create complex, dreamlike montages offered an alternative to documentary photography by showing that powerful photographic images could be created in the darkroom.

Photographers have developed different strategies for working with dream imagery. Ralph Gibson shoots straight photography, but the dreamy quality of his work is enhanced in the darkroom through a grainy, high contrast look. At the other end of the spectrum, Uelsmann's complex method of creating montages in the darkroom has been succeeded by the digital composite, a form being explored by many contemporary photographers, including his wife, Maggie Taylor. In the 1970s, Ralph Eugene Meatyard and Les Krims staged dreamlike tableaus which they then photographed, an approach later used by Anders Aabel to create images from his own dreams. Arthur Tress, and later Wendy Ewald, interviewed children about their dreams and enlisted their help in staging and photographing their dream images. Duane Michals stages scenes and then creates narrative sequences of photographic images that tell dreamlike stories.

Richard A. Russo

References

Aabel, A., & Knarvik, J. C. (2002). *Somnia: En bok om drommer.* Oslo: Schibsted.

Ewald, W. (2000). *Secret games: Collaborative works with children 1969–1999.* Zurich: Scalo Publishers.

Gibson, R. (1970). *The Somnambulist.* New York: Lustrum Press.

Meatyard, R. E. (1974). *Ralph Eugene Meatyard* (Ed. with text by J. B. Hall). Millerton, NY: Aperture.

Michals, D. (1984). *Sleep and dream.* New York: Lustrum Press.

Tress, A. (1972). *The dream collector.* New York: Avon Books.

Uelsmann, J. (1982). *Jerry N. Uelsmann: Twenty-five years a retrospective* (Ed. J. L. Enyeart). New York: Little, Brown.

Phylogenetic Comparative Methods and Sleep

Sleep in mammals and birds occurs in two physiologically distinct states: active sleep involves desynchronized brain states and rapid eye movements (REM sleep), while quiet sleep involves synchronized brainwaves known as slow-wave activity (non-REM or NREM sleep). To obtain data on sleep in different species, researchers typically take an experimental approach in which they use electroencephalograms to quantify the relative amounts of REM and NREM sleep. From these studies, we have learned much about individual differences in sleep; the cyclicity of sleep between these two states; and sleep in relation to disease, life history events, and external stimuli.

Imagine that we take the data from many different studies of REM and NREM, aggregate the data into means for the different species, and systematically examine variation in sleep characteristics across species (Allison & Cicchetti, 1976; Zepelin & Rechtschaffen, 1974). From such a *comparative approach,* we gain new insights to the evolution of sleep that are not possible with studies of individual species. The comparative approach has long been the cornerstone of efforts to understand biological diversity because comparison provides a way to understand general evolutionary patterns and to test specific hypotheses.

More recently, biologists have developed statistically rigorous ways to investigate the evolution of traits on evolutionary trees (Harvey & Pagel, 1991; Martins, 1996; Nunn, 2011). These *phylogenetic comparative methods* have revolutionized our understanding of evolution and greatly expanded the questions that can be addressed. With these methods, for example, researchers can investigate how two traits covary through evolutionary time (correlated evolution), they can make inferences about the evolutionary history of a trait (reconstruct ancestral states), and they can examine how the evolution of a trait has influenced subsequent patterns of speciation and extinction (diversification analysis). To appreciate these methods, it is important to understand that the history of life on earth can be represented as an evolutionary tree, or *phylogeny,* where the branches represent lineages of organisms through time, and the nodes represent speciation events in which a lineage is separated into two or more descendent lineages. Two species that share a more recent common ancestor are more closely related. More closely related species also tend to have more similar trait values, that is, the traits show *phylogenetic signal* (Blomberg & Garland, 2002). Such effects can be seen on a phylogeny, with more closely related species having more similar sleep characteristics (see Capellini, Barton, McNamara, Preston, & Nunn, 2008; Preston, Capelleni, McNamara, Barton, & Nunn, 2009).

Researchers interested in sleep have used phylogenetic methods to investigate correlated evolution and ancestral sleep states in mammals, birds, and other animals (Lesku, Roth, Rattenborg, Amlaner, & Lima, 2009; McNamara, Barton, & Nunn, 2010). In studies of correlated evolution, the methods overcome an important statistical issue—the nonindependence of data points—and provide a way to estimate the degree of phylogenetic signal in the data. When phylogenetic signal exists, it indicates that different lineages have evolved independently yet still retain some variation through common ancestry. This pattern also means that it is important to take phylogenetic history into account when analyzing comparative data. Studies that used phylogeny-based methods have

demonstrated several interesting patterns in mammals, including that basal metabolic rate and predation risk at the sleep site correlate negatively with sleep quotas (Capellini et al., 2008; Lesku, Roth, Amlaner, & Lima, 2006), and white blood cell counts and sleep quotas show a positive association (Preston et al., 2009). Results involving brain size have produced mixed results (Capellini et al., 2008; Capellini, McNamara, Preston, Nunn, & Barton, 2009; Lesku et al., 2006), suggesting that cognitive factors are not a primary driver of variation in sleep architecture. In birds, greater exposure to predation was shown to reduce slow-wave sleep durations (Roth, Lesku, Amlaner, & Lima, 2006).

In terms of reconstructing ancestral states, the methods again make use of phylogenetic signal, and a critical issue involves quantifying the statistical confidence we can place in particular reconstructions. For example, instead of simply putting a value at an internal node on the tree, recent methods allow evolutionary biologists to assess the probability of a particular character state (such as presence of REM sleep), or to put a 95 percent confidence interval on a quantitative measure of sleep (such as the duration of REM sleep). Reconstruction methods have been used less commonly to study sleep. In one recent example, Nunn et al. (2010) used Bayesian methods to estimate that the ancestral primate slept for 11.3 hours per night, with a 95 percent confidence interval ranging from 9.4 to 13.4 hours. In this context, it is interesting that the typical human sleep duration of around 8.5 hours lies outside this confidence interval. In the future, ancestral state reconstructions could be used to investigate broader evolutionary patterns of sleep characteristics, including a formal test for the independent evolution of REM sleep in mammals and birds (Rattenborg & Amlaner, 2010).

Charles Nunn

References

Allison, T., & Cicchetti, D. V. (1976). Sleep in mammals—Ecological and constitutional correlates. *Science, 194,* 732–734.

Blomberg, S. P., & Garland, T. (2002). Tempo and mode in evolution: Phylogenetic inertia, adaptation and comparative methods. *Journal of Evolutionary Biology, 15,* 899–910.

Capellini, I., Barton, R. A., McNamara, P., Preston, B., & Nunn, C. L. (2008). Ecology and evolution of mammalian sleep. *Evolution, 62,* 1764–1776.

Capellini, I., McNamara, P., Preston, B., Nunn, C., & Barton, R. (2009). Does sleep play a role in memory consolidation? A comparative test. *PLoS ONE, 4.*

Harvey, P. H., & Pagel, M. D. (1991). *The comparative method in evolutionary biology.* Oxford: Oxford University Press.

Lesku, J., Roth, T., Rattenborg, N., Amlaner, C., & Lima, S. (2009). History and future of comparative analyses in sleep research. *Neuroscience and Biobehavioral Reviews, 33,* 1024–1036.

Lesku, J. A., Roth II, T. C., Amlaner, C. J., & Lima, S. L. (2006). A phylogenetic analysis of sleep architecture in mammals: The intergration of anatomy, physiology, and ecology. *The American Naturalist, 168,* 1–13.

Martins, E. P. (Ed.). (1996). *Phylogenies and the comparative method in animal behavior.* New York: Oxford University Press.

McNamara, P., Barton, R., & Nunn, C. (2010). *Evolution of sleep: Phylogenetic and functional perspectives.* Cambridge: Cambridge University Press.

Nunn, C. L. (2011). *The comparative approach in evolutionary anthropology and biology.* Chicago: University of Chicago Press.

Nunn, C., McNamara, P., Capellini, I., & Barton, R. (2010). Primate sleep in comparative perspective. In C. Nunn, P. McNamara, & R. Barton (Eds.), *Evolutionary and phylogenetic perspectives on sleep* (pp. 123–144). Cambridge: Cambridge University press.

Preston, B. T., Capelleni, I., McNamara, P., Barton, R. A., & Nunn, C. L. (2009). Parasite resistance and the adaptive significance of sleep. *BMC Evolutionary Biology, 9.*

Rattenborg, N. C., & Amlaner, C. J. (2010). A bird's-eye view of the function of sleep. In P. McNamara, R. Barton, & C. Nunn (Eds.), *Evolution of sleep: Phylogenetic and functional perspectives.* Cambridge: Cambridge University Press.

Roth, T. C., Lesku, J. A., Amlaner, C. J., & Lima, S. L. (2006). A phylogenetic analysis of the correlates of sleep in birds. *Journal of Sleep Research, 15,* 395–402.

Zepelin, H., & Rechtschaffen, A. (1974). Mammalian sleep, longevity, and energy metabolism. *Brain Behavior and Evolution, 10,* 425–470.

Phylogeny of Sleep

Sleep and sleep-like rest have been described in several vertebrates and invertebrates (Cirelli & Tononi, 2008; McNamara, Barton, & Nunn, 2010; Siegel, 2008). The evolution of sleep, however, has been studied mostly in mammals where data for several species are available. In placental and marsupial mammals and in birds sleep is composed by two distinct neurophysiological states, a rapid eye movement (REM) sleep, and a non-REM (NREM) sleep. During a sleep cycle, episodes of NREM sleep are followed by episodes of REM sleep, and several REM–NREM sleep cycles are repeated throughout a bout of sleep. Monotremes—echidna

(*Tachyglossus aculeatus*) and platypus (*Ornithorhynchus anatinus*)—have NREM sleep and some signs of REM sleep, while there is currently no convincing evidence of REM-like sleep in reptiles (McNamara, Nunn, Barton, Harris, & Capellini, 2007). Therefore it is still unclear whether REM sleep evolved from a mixed REM–NREM sleep state of early reptiles or it evolved independently in mammals and birds. Aquatic mammals and birds can also sleep unihemispherically, with unihemispheric NREM sleep being obligatory only in cetaceans (Rattenborg, Amlaner, & Lima, 2000).

Mammals and birds exhibit great variation in sleep patterns. This includes differences among species in the daily REM- and NREM-sleep durations, REM–NREM sleep-cycle length, and in how sleep is accommodated in the 24 hours (e.g., the number and duration of daily sleep bouts, the phasing of sleep). Mammalian total daily sleep time, as sum of REM- and NREM-sleep durations, varies between 3 to 4 hours in ungulates and 20 hours in armadillos (*Chaetophractus villosus*), with an REM–NREM sleep cycle ranging from 6 minutes in the chinchilla (*Chinchilla laniger*) to 90 minutes in humans and chimpanzees (*Pan troglodytes*) (Capellini, Preston, McNamara, Barton, & Nunn, 2010; McNamara, et al. 2008). Unlike mammals, birds have very short episodes of REM sleep, generally lasting less than 10 seconds (Rattenborg & Amlaner, 2010). The phasing of sleep can be monophasic when all sleep is consolidated into one daily bout, or biphasic or polyphasic when two or more sleep bouts are alternated with bouts of activity (Capellini et al., 2010; McNamara et al., 2008).

This diversity in mammalian sleep patterns is not randomly distributed with respect to phylogeny. Conversely, closely related species sharing recent common ancestors exhibit strong similarities in sleep times (Capellini, Barton, McNamara, Preston, & Nunn, 2008a; see Figure 16).

Thus, like all biological traits, mammalian sleep patterns are shaped by the evolutionary history of the species—with closely related species being more similar to one another than expected by chance—and natural selection. Natural selection promotes sleep because of its adaptive benefits but constrains time for sleep because of its ecological costs (Capellini et al., 2010). Ultimately, natural selection leads to divergence in sleep patterns between species when these are under different selective pressures, but also determines convergence when analogous selective pressures act on different species, leading to similar sleep patterns to evolve independently in distantly related species.

Hypotheses on the benefits of sleep for the brain are abundant, such as consolidating memories, promoting brain development, maintenance, or repair, but support for these ideas is mixed (Siegel, 2001, 2005; Stickgold, 2005; Zepelin, Siegel, & Tobler, 2005). Contrary to suggestions that a major function of NREM sleep in mammals and birds is energy conservation, because of their great energetic expenditure to maintain a high metabolic rate and body

Male ibex (*Capra ibex*) sleeping in Gran Paradiso National Park (Italy). Artiodactyls, like the ibex, sleep the least among all mammals. (Roberta Pedrotti)

temperature (Berger & Phillips, 1995), recent studies have found that species with higher energy requirements have the shortest—not the longest—sleep durations (Capellini et al., 2008a; Lesku, Roth, Amlaner, & Lima, 2006). Indeed the amount of energy saved during sleep appears to be negligible (Stahel, Megirian, & Nicol, 1984). There is instead growing evidence that sleep promotes immunocompetence. Not only does sleep facilitate an immune response in individuals challenged by parasitic infections (Bryant, Trinder, & Curtis, 2004), but also mammals that evolved longer sleep times have higher immunity levels and lower infection levels (Preston, Capellini, McNamara, Barton, & Nunn, 2009).

Beyond parasites, other ecological factors influence sleep evolution. Sleeping individuals are more vulnerable to predation because sleep is accompanied by reduced responsiveness to external stimuli (Lima, Rattenborg, Lesku, & Amlaner, 2005). High predation risk promotes the evolution of short sleep durations in mammals and birds; thus species that sleep in

Figure 16: Closely related species sharing a more recent common ancestor exhibit more similar sleep times than more distantly related species. Thus, sleep durations are not randomly distributed with respect to phylogeny. For example, all macaques (genus Macaca) sleep for about 8 to 9 hours a day, with approximately 1 hour REM sleep, while more distantly related primates, such as lemurs, sleep 10 to 15 hours a day (From McNamara et al. [2010]. Reprinted with permission.)

Red panda (*Ailurus fulgens*) sleeping on a bamboo roof in a Paris zoo. Red pandas are solitary and are active during the night, dawn, and dusk. Their sleep pattern has not been studied yet. (Isabella Capellini)

exposed sites, such as the ground in open grassland, sleep less than species that sleep in protected sites, such as tree holes or dens (Capellini et al., 2008a; Lesku et al., 2006; Roth, Lesku, Amlaner, & Lima, 2006). However, predation risk does not explain species differences in phasing of sleep and REM–NREM sleep-cycle length (Capellini, Nunn, McNamara, Preston, & Barton, 2008b). Because time for sleep is detracted to other important activities, such as rearing offspring, sleep should be associated with opportunity costs. Mammals that need to spend much time foraging, such as those with high energetic requirements or herbivorous diet, or social species that need time for social interactions, sleep less (Capellini et al., 2008a). The necessity to forage frequently in small mammals, characterized by relatively high energetic requirements for their size and limited fat reserves, might also be responsible for the evolution of polyphasic sleep and short REM–NREM sleep cycles in these species (Capellini et al., 2008b). Therefore polyphasic sleep is mostly found in small mammals, while monophasic sleep evolved in association with a medium to large body size (see Figure 17; Capellini et al., 2008b). Body size is instead unrelated to sleep durations in both mammals and birds (Capellini et al., 2008a; Lesku et al., 2006; Roth et al., 2006). Finally, the distribution of resources in the environment can potentially influence the evolution of sleep. For example, when food resources and sleeping sites are distant from one another, monophasic sleep and shorter sleep durations should evolve to save time for traveling between sites (Acerbi, McNamara, & Nunn, 2008).

Whether shorter sleep times are evolutionary compensated by increases in sleep intensity is still an open question. However, monophasic sleep, characterized by longer sleep cycles, might deliver the benefits of sleep more efficiently than polyphasic sleep with its shorter sleep cycles (Capellini et al., 2008b). Longer sleep cycles probably reduce the total daily sleep time because they limit the total time in transitional sleep stages needed to enter deep NREM sleep (see Figure 18). Indeed, monophasic sleep, which evolved from polyphasic sleep (see Figure 17), is associated with shorter sleep durations, and might represent an evolutionary advantage of larger-bodied species (Capellini et al., 2008b).

Isabella Capellini

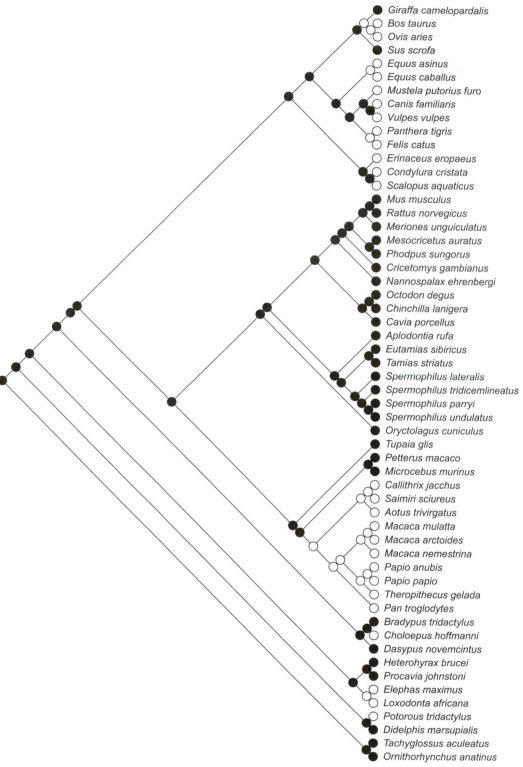

Figure 17: Evolutionary History of Phasing of Sleep (Maximum Likelihood Reconstruction). Polyphasic sleep (black) is strongly supported as the ancestral character state in mammals, while monophasic sleep (white) has independently evolved multiple times in medium- and large-bodied mammals. (From McNamara et al. [2010]. Reprinted with permission.)

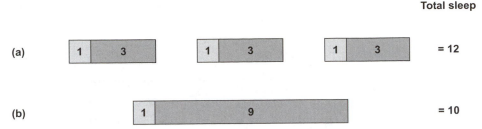

Figure 18: Longer Sleep Cycles Require Less Time in Transitional Sleep Stages, Ultimately Leading to a Reduction in Total Daily Sleep Time. In (a) a hypothetical species sleeping nine units of time in deep sleep (darker shade), needs 3 units of time in transitional sleep (one per unit of deep sleep; lighter shade) when the total deep sleep is partitioned in three blocks; this leads to a total of 12 units of sleep. Conversely, in (b) only 1 unit of time in transitional sleep is needed if all the deep sleep is consolidated into one block, leading to a total of 10 units of sleep. Thus monophasic sleep, that is associated with longer sleep cycles and shorter daily sleep time, might deliver the benefits of sleep more efficiently than polyphasic sleep. (Redrawn from Capellini et al. [2010]. Reprinted with permission.)

References

Acerbi, A., McNamara, P., & Nunn, C.L. (2008). To sleep or not to sleep: The ecology of sleep in artificial organisms. *BMC Evolutionary Biology, 8,* 10.

Berger, R.J., & Phillips, N.H. (1995). Energy conservation and sleep. *Behavioral Brain Research, 69,* 65–73.

Bryant, P.A., Trinder, J., & Curtis, N. (2004). Sick and tired: Does sleep have a vital role in the immune system? *Nature Reviews Immunology, 4,* 457–467.

Capellini, I., Barton, R.A., McNamara, P., Preston, B.T., & Nunn, C.L. (2008a). Phylogenetic analysis of the ecology and evolution of mammalian sleep. *Evolution, 62,* 1764–1776.

Capellini, I., Nunn, C.L., McNamara, P., Preston, B.T., & Barton, R.A. (2008b). Energetic constraints, not predation, influence the evolution of sleep patterning in mammals. *Functional Ecology, 22,* 847–853.

Capellini, I., Preston, B.T., McNamara, P., Barton, R.A., & Nunn, C.L. (2010). Ecological constraints on mammalian sleep architecture. In P. McNamara, R.A. Barton, & C.L. Nunn (Eds.), *Phylogeny of sleep* (pp. 12–33). Cambridge: Cambridge University Press.

Cirelli, C., & Tononi, G. (2008). Is sleep essential? *PLoS Biology, 6,* 1605–1611.

Lesku, J.A., Roth, T.C., Amlaner, C.J., & Lima, S.L. (2006). A phylogenetic analysis of sleep architecture in mammals: The integration of anatomy, physiology and ecology. *American Naturalist, 168,* 441–453.

Lima, S.L., Rattenborg, N.C., Lesku, J.A., & Amlaner, C.J. (2005). Sleeping under the risk of predation. *Animal Behaviour, 70,* 723–736.

McNamara, P., Barton, R.A., & Nunn, C.L. (Eds). (2010). *Evolution of sleep.* Cambridge: Cambridge University Press.

McNamara, P., Capellini, I., Harris, E., Nunn, C.L., Barton, R.A., & Preston, B. (2008). The phylogeny of sleep database: A new resource for sleep scientists. *The Open Sleep Journal, 1,* 11–14.

McNamara, P., Nunn, C.L., Barton, R.A., Harris, E., & Capellini, I. (2007). Phylogeny of sleep and dreams. In D. Barrett & P. McNamara (Eds.), *The new science of dreaming: Biological aspects* (pp. 12–22). Westport, CT: Praeger.

Preston, B.T., Capellini, I., McNamara, P., Barton, R. A, & Nunn, C.L. (2009). Parasite resistance and the adaptive significance of sleep. *BMC Evolutionary Biology, 9,* 7.

Rattenborg, C.N., & Amlaner, C.J. (2010). A bird's-eye view of the function of sleep. In P. McNamara, R.A. Barton, & C.L. Nunn (Eds.), *Phylogeny of sleep* (pp. 145–171). Cambridge: Cambridge University Press.

Rattenborg, C.N., Amlaner, C.J., & Lima, S.L. (2000). Behavioral, neurophysiological and evolutionary perspectives on unihemispheric sleep. *Neuroscience and Biobehavioral Reviews, 24,* 817–842.

Roth, T.C., Lesku, J.A., Amlaner, C.J., & Lima, S.L. (2006). A phylogenetic analysis of the correlates of sleep in birds. *Journal of Sleep Research, 15,* 395–402.

Siegel, J.M. (2001). The REM-sleep memory-consolidation hypothesis. *Science, 294,* 1058–1063.

Siegel, J.M. (2005). Clues to the function of mammalian sleep. *Nature, 437,* 1264–1271.

Siegel, J.M. (2008). Do all animals sleep? *Trends in neuroscience, 31,* 208–213.

Stahel, C.D., Megirian, D., & Nicol, S.C. (1984). Sleep and metabolic rate in the little penguin (*Eudyptula minor*). *Journal of Comparative Physiology B: Biochemical, Systemic and Environmental Physiology, 154,* 487–494.

Stickgold, R. (2005). Sleep-dependent memory consolidation. *Nature, 437,* 1272–1278.

Zepelin, H., Siegel, J.M., & Tobler, I. (2005). Mammalian sleep. In M.H. Kryger, T. Roth, & W.C. Dement (Eds.), *Principles and practices of sleep medicine*. New York: Saunders.

Phylogeny of Sleep Database

One way to study potential functions of sleep as well as the evolutionary history of sleep is to construct databases that contain data on sleep expression in as many species as possible. Early comparative databases on sleep durations in mammals contained only about 40 or so species and the quality of some of the data points was questionable. The largest database on comparative sleep patterns constructed to date is probably the database housed at Boston University and known as "The phylogeny of sleep" database. It is accessible online at www.bu.edu/phylogeny. This Web site provides background on the database itself, hypotheses regarding the evolution of sleep expression and functions, details on how the database was constructed, and a portal to search the latest version of the database. If the database is ever transferred from Boston University to some other location, forwarding links and information will be provided.

The current version of the Phylogeny of Sleep database was constructed with support from the National Institute of Mental health and contains sleep quotas retrieved from 178 separate literature references representing 130 different mammalian species in 50 families and 17 orders. Sleep quotas refer to sleep durations of the two major phases of mammalian sleep: rapid eye movement or REM sleep and non-REM sleep.

In addition to containing data on sleep for the largest number of species ever assembled the data in the database are also scored for quality. Previous comparative datasets did not score their data for quality indices, such as whether the data were collected from restrained animals, the duration of recording, or the availability of food and water during observations. These experimental procedures likely impact the estimates of REM- and NREM-sleep durations as studies of selected species' sleep in the wild versus in the lab have shown. Luckily most studies of sleep expression in animals published since 1953—the year REM was discovered—did in fact provide detailed descriptions of the methods under which sleep data were gathered.

Data for the Phylogeny of Sleep database were obtained from previous data compilations, as well as an exhaustive literature search dating back to 1953, to gather new data. Key terms used in literature searches were REM, NREM, sleep architecture, EEG, and total sleep time. Searches were conducted within bibliographic databases that cover publications in English, French, Russian, German, and Spanish. Whenever possible, investigators recorded the sex and age of the individual animals whose sleep was measured, breaking down male and female values when possible.

Although data on sleep of aquatic mammals are included in the database, extreme caution should be used when analyzing this data until a consensus emerges among experts on sleep in these animals as to how best to summarize sleep expression in these animals. Members of three different orders that contain aquatic mammals—cetaceans (dolphins, porpoises, and whales), carnivores (seals, sea lions, and otters), and sirenians (manatees) typically engage in *unihemispheric* sleep. Cetaceans exhibit a clear form of unihemispheric slow-wave sleep (SWS). EEG signs of REM are absent, but cetaceans show other behavioral signs of REM, including rapid eye movements, penile erections and muscle twitching. The two main families of Pinnipeds, Otariidae (sea lions and fur seals) and Phocidae (true seals), show both unihemispheric and bihemispheric forms of sleep. Phocids sleep *under* water (obviously holding their breath), and both hemispheres exhibit either REM or SWS. Amazonian Manatees (*Trichechus inunguis*) also sleep while under water exhibiting three sleep states: bihemispheric REM, bihemispheric SWS, and unihemispheric SWS. Both hemispheres awaken to surface and breathe. A further complication of sleep expression in these animals is that some facultatively adjust their sleep patterns when sleeping on land. Thus to fully capture daily sleep quotas in these animals one would want to record sleep times for both REM and NREM in both the right and left hemispheres on land and in the water.

With respect to assessing and improving data quality in the Phylogeny of Sleep database, information was extracted on the following laboratory conditions and experimental procedures from the original sources:

- Recording method (EEG). Whether sleep duration estimates were based on EEG recordings or not.
- Telemetry (yes or no). Whether sleep duration estimates were based on telemetric recordings in the wild.
- Recording time as reported in hours (categorical three-state variable). Studies were assigned to one of three categories: <12 hours recording time, between 12 and <24 hours, and recording time equal to or longer than 24 hours.
- Diet (yes or no). Whether experimental animals were fed *ad libitum* or not.
- Photoperiod (yes or no). If subjects were maintained under a natural light condition of 12 hours light and 12 hours dark, or not (24 hours light or reversed light conditions).

- Ambient temperature (yes or no). Whether subjects were tested in an environment with temperatures within the natural range for the species under study.
- Adaptation (habituation; yes or no). Whether studies allowed the experimental animals to habituate to recording and laboratory conditions before data were collected.
- Restraint (yes or no). Whether or not subjects were restrained during sleep-recording sessions.
- Behavioral observations (yes or no). Whether any sleep-related behavioral observations were noted in the species under study. This could include any mention of sleep posture, eyes opening and closing, tail jerking, penile erection during REM, neck paralysis during REM, and so on.

The addition of these data-quality scores on each study contained in the database allows researchers to select those studies/species for which we have the best data and then conduct analyses on this high quality dataset.

Preliminary analyses suggest that recording times under 12 hours systemically underestimate the true values for total sleep, REM-, and NREM-sleep durations across species relative to longer recording times. Ideally only data obtained from animals who received 24 hours of EEG recordings should be used in analyses. But this condition obviously lowers the N in analyses.

A search application at the Web site has been developed that allows users to search the core Phylogeny of Sleep database. A glossary of search terms is provided to assist users visiting the Web site. Once the user performs the search of the sleep dataset according to his or her specified criteria, an annotated reference and selected search information will be displayed. If the user wants more detail, he or she can click on the reference, and the full reference and record for that species for that particular paper will be displayed. The user can save this search as a .csv file. Additionally, in the upper right-hand corner of each page, there is a *contact* tab that will allow the user to send questions and comments about the database. References in the database are formatted in a common style and thus are suitable for generating bibliographies for manuscripts that use the data.

The value of this database can be further enhanced by (1) adding a series of measures of sleep intensity for each of the species represented in the dataset, (2) building a comparable database on avian sleep, (3) expanding data collection on ecological variables for the species in the dataset, and (4) updating all of these databases as new information becomes available.

In summary, the Phylogeny of Sleep database/Web site constitutes an important resource for sleep scientists as it contains data that is representative of as many mammalian orders as possible and it uses data collected under reasonably standardized conditions to ensure data quality and comparability.

Patrick McNamara

See also: entries related to Evolution of Sleep

Reference

McNamara, P., Capellini, I., Harris, E., Nunn, C. L., Barton, R. A., & Preston, B. (2008). The phylogeny of sleep database: A new resource for sleep scientists. *The Open Sleep Journal, 1,* 11–14.

Pittsburgh Sleep Quality Index

The Pittsburgh Sleep Quality Index (PSQI; Buysse, Reynolds, Monk, Berman, & Kupfer, 1989) is a commonly used index of sleep quality based on self-report across several domains of sleep functioning during a time period of one month. The PSQI simultaneously assesses seven clinically relevant components of sleep quality (subjective sleep quality, sleep latency, duration, efficiency, disturbances, use of sleep medication, and daytime dysfunction) in the preceding month. Acceptable internal consistency (Cronbach's alpha = .83), test–retest reliability ($r = 85$), and validity of the PSQI have been demonstrated in sleep-disordered, psychiatric, and medical samples. In Buysee et al.'s original study a global PSQI score greater than 5 yielded a diagnostic sensitivity of 89.6 percent and specificity of 86.5 percent in distinguishing good and poor sleepers. PSQI scores have been shown to correlate with prospective sleep dairy data and polysomnographic measures of sleep quality.

Patrick McNamara

See also: Basics of Sleep Recordings

Reference

Buysse, D.J., Reynolds III, C.F., Monk, T.H., Berman, S.R., & Kupfer, D.J. (1989). The Pittsburgh Sleep Quality Index: A new instrument for psychiatric practice and research. *Psychiatry Research, 28*(2), 193–213.

Play and the Dream

Many people consider their dreams to be nightly forms of entertainment. They experience their dreams as play. They remember frolicking, experimenting, and adventuring in their dreams. While most people do not play every night in their dreams, most of us have had fun adventures in our dreams. Thus, some dream theorists have suggested that dreaming springs from the same biological sources that promote play in juveniles of all mammalian species. Both play and dreams involve a stance of pretend or simulations of actions, interactions of worlds, energetic displays of seemingly useless simulations for their own sake, creativity, strong emotions, and so forth. Thus, it seems reasonable to pursue the question of potential interrelations between play and dreaming.

In animals, three types of play have been noted: locomotor, object, and social play. Locomotor play involves energetic displays of motor abilities and can occur in either a solitary or social arena; object play involves a focus on an object or objects that are manipulated in endless ways; and social play involves social interactions with a conspecific. Each of these three forms of play may have different causal bases, ontogenies, phylogenies, and functions, but may nevertheless occur together in a single bout of play.

But there are dissimilarities between play and dreams as well. While play is typically associated with pleasurable affect, dreams are not. Play utilizes special signaling procedures (e.g., the bow stance in canids) to convey to a conspecific that this is pretend, not an attack, and so on. No such signals have yet been identified in dreams, though it must be admitted that dreams have not yet been analyzed for their signaling properties. Finally, play is most frequently observed among juveniles, while dreaming is a lifelong process.

Jean Piaget was one of the first psychologists to study the dream as play. According to Piaget, it is as if each night we return to preoperational forms of cognition in our dreams and then, when we remember a dream, we try to translate this form of cognition into an adult language. Piaget emphasizes the role of the image in dreams as a first-draft form of imitation and of accommodation and adaptation to the external world. Once the child acquires the capacity to form images, these images begin to form a system of meanings and symbolic thought capable of representing some aspects of the child's world. Since imitative images develop in the context of the child's affective life, the system of meanings is bound up with the affective life. Affect-laden imitative imagery supports preoperational thought in the child and is never abandoned as the child develops and grows into the capacity to utilize operational and abstract forms of thought. The affect-laden system of imitative images also grows and can be used in various forms of activity, from dreams to play to art and imagination. Thus, dream thought should not be seen as regression away from more advanced forms of waking thought (though some of Piaget's writings seem to suggest just this); rather, dream thought is a living system supporting all these extra-rational, symbolic forms of cognition.

Patrick McNamara

Poetry and Dreams

Dreams have figured in Western poetry from the beginning. The ancient Mesopotamian epic *Gilgamesh,* one of the earliest known works of Western literature, contains several dream accounts, notably Enkidu's dream foretelling his own fate. Dreams appear in most of the major literary works of the ancients, from Homer's long poem, *The Odyssey* (e.g., Penelope's dream of the eagle killing 20 geese in Book 19), to the many dream texts in the Bible (e.g., Jacob's dream of the ladder, Gen. 28:10–17; Joseph's dream telling him to flee to Egypt with Jesus and Mary, Matt. 2:13). In this early literature, dreams are generally depicted as premonitory or as messages from the gods, reflecting the beliefs of the times.

In the seventh century, an illiterate herdsman named Caedmon had a dream in which a voice commanded him to create and sing verses in praise of God. The poem that came to him in the dream was a nine-line song of praise, now known as "Caedmon's Hymn," his only surviving work. Caedmon was the first poet on record to compose in Old English; thus a dream stands at the beginning of English poetry. The "Dream Vision," which can be traced back to early works like Cicero's *Dream of Scipio,* became an important form in medieval literature, although these poems, rather than drawing on night dreams, used the dream as a frame within which to present allegorical compositions. Noteworthy examples include Chaucer's *Book of the Duchess* and *Parliament of Fowls.* The plays of William Shakespeare (1564–1616) include many dreams, as well as memorable verses about dreaming, like Prospero's observation in Act IV of *The Tempest*: "We are such stuff / As dreams are made on, and our little life / Is rounded with a sleep."

It was not until the beginnings of modernity in the 19th century that dream poetry as we know it today, that is, poetry inspired by or based on actual dreams, began to be written. The Romantic poets shifted the focus of poetry to inner states and feelings, including dreams and visions. Samuel Taylor Coleridge explored his own dream life in poems like "The Pains of Sleep." Coleridge also wrote what is probably the best-known dream poem, "Kubla Khan," which purportedly came to him full blown in a dream (and most of which was lost when he was interrupted by "the man from Porlock" while writing it down).

Freud's (1955) *The Interpretation of Dreams* identified the unconscious as the source of creative inspiration, and had a profound impact on all the arts in the 20th century. Freud distinguished between primary and secondary processes. Primary process thinking is emotional, associative, and irrational (the realm of the id); secondary process thinking is verbal, rational, and organized (the ego). Material rising from the unconscious (primary process) is repressed by the conscious mind (secondary process) but finds expression in dreams and art. In psychoanalysis, Freud laid the foundation for dreams as both source and subject matter in modern poetry The first great art movement built on Freud's ideas was surrealism. Although surrealist poets like Breton and Éluard wrote some poems based on dreams, they were more interested in capturing—in their work and in daily life—a wild, associative flow of ideas and images akin to that experienced in dreaming.

Jung (1966), in his essay "On the Relation of Analytical Psychology to Poetry," expanded on Freud's ideas. Jung distinguished two kinds of poetry, one a product of the conscious mind, shaped and designed to have the effect intended, the other arising from the unconscious and thus forced on the author and exhibiting a strangeness of form and content filled with symbolic meaning that can only be understood intuitively. While also locating the source of creativity in the unconscious, Jung expanded our understanding beyond Freud's personal unconscious by exploring collective levels of the unconscious.

Rycroft (1979) challenged the Freudian dichotomy between primary and secondary processes (somewhat echoed by Jung), arguing that the creative process is an ongoing interaction between the two modes, which cannot be separated. A review of how poets actually work (Booth, 1987; Levertov, 1981; Townley, 1998) supports this view, showing that writing poetry is an ongoing dynamic interaction between unconscious inspiration and conscious craft. For this reason, Russo (2003) objected to Rycroft's characterization of dreams as involuntary poetry (a view repeated in many popular writings on dreams). For him, the view that we are all poets in our dreams is false; dreams are not poems because they do not involve the conscious application of craft. Russo also argued that writing dream poems, in one aspect, may be viewed as a type of dreamwork.

Other movements in 20th-century poetry that drew inspiration from dreams include the Beatniks, especially Jack Kerouac and Allen Ginsberg, who tried to capture the actual flow of consciousness in their writing, and the so-called "Deep Image" poets, notably Robert Bly, who might be considered the heirs to surrealism, in that they sought to go below the waking rational mind to the deep source of poetry.

Other contemporary poets whose work includes significant dream-related material include Elizabeth Alexander, Margaret Atwood, Frank Bidart, Louise Glück, Maxine Kumin, and Denise Levertov.

Richard A. Russo

References

Booth, P. (1987). Poems after dreams. In R. A. Russo (Ed.), *Dreams are wiser than men* (pp. 79–85). Berkeley, CA: North Atlantic Books.

Freud, S. (1955). *The interpretation of dreams* (Trans. and Ed. J. Strachey). New York: Basic Books. (Original work published in 1900)

Hollander, J. (1997). Dreaming poetry. In J. Hollander (Ed.), *The work of poetry*. New York: Columbia University Press.

Jung, C. G. (1966). On the relation of analytical psychology to poetry. In *The spirit in man, art, and literature* (CW 15, Trans. G. Adler & R.F.C. Hull). Princeton, NJ: Princeton University Press. (Original work published in 1922)

Levertov, D. (1981). Interweavings: Reflections on the role of dream in the making of poems. In D. Levertov (Ed.), *Light up the cave*. New York: New Directions.

Russo, R. A. (1987). *Dreams are wiser than men*. Berkeley, CA: North Atlantic Books.

Russo, R. A. (2003). Dream poetry as dream work. *Dreaming, 13*(1), 13–28.

Rycroft, C. (1979). *The innocence of dreams*. New York: Pantheon.

States, B. O. (1997). Involuntary poetry. In B. O. States (Ed.), *Seeing in the dark*. New Haven, CT: Yale University Press.

Townley, R. (Ed.). (1998). *Night errands: How poets use dreams*. Pittsburgh, PA: University of Pittsburgh Press.

Portable Monitoring of Sleep

Monitoring and measuring sleep variables can be an expensive process given that the individual needs to come into a sleep lab, be fitted with EEG and other monitoring devices, and then be observed and attended by a sleep tech during the night. Sleeping in a scientific lab with people watching you all night is known to substantially affect sleep patterns as well. That is why many investigators do not even bother to collect sleep data on the first night of the visit to the sleep lab. The data from a first night in the sleep lab does not accurately reflect sleep physiology. It is only after the person gains some familiarity with the sleep lab that the data become more trustworthy. Measurement of sleep in the sleep lab is also expensive and time consuming for all concerned.

For some people, sleeping in a sleep lab actually improves their sleep relative to baseline home conditions. This improvement in sleep quality may be due to reduced anxiety levels. Many traumatized individuals feel safer when sleeping in the lab environment and this feeling may translate into better sleep. When people believe they are being monitored by experts they apparently feel safer. Take, for example, the case of people with posttraumatic stress disorder (PTSD). Polysomnographic (PSG) studies of sleep architecture in PTSD when assessed in the sleep lab yield an inconsistent picture. To understand the contribution of nightmares, in particular, to PTSD symptomology, it is extremely important to study them in the home environment. Nightmare frequencies in the sleep lab are typically below 10 percent (of nights). Nightmares must be considered to be a key cognitive abnormality of PTSD. When nightmares are targeted for treatment, distress associated with PTSD can be significantly reduced. Assessing nightmare frequency, content, and distress are therefore key to treating PTSD effectively, but this assessment process is best done in the home.

We would therefore like to have a way to measure important aspects of sleep without having to bring the individual into a sleep lab, where a sleep tech has to attend them all night long and where they need to be hooked up to all kinds of expensive equipment. Home monitoring is also more convenient for those being tested, including patients with medical disorders. Portable polysomnographs have been developed in recent years so that sleep can be measured in the home environment while using fewer monitor leads with no one attending them thus drastically reducing costs of the sleep measurement/assessment process.

The first practice standards concerning portable sleep monitoring were enunciated by the American Academy of Sleep Medicine in 1994. The core ideas in that paper still apply to practice 15 years later. The original standard of practice defined four different types of portable sleep assessments, depending on the number of measurements captured by the monitors utilized. Three of the four assessment techniques are compared against the gold standard (Type I) sleep lab full PSG assessment with sleep tech for both cardiorespiratory and sleep-stage measures. Type II assessment is a form of portable polysomnography in the home that includes sleep-stage/neurophysiological assessment. Type III has at least four recorded parameters, including air flow and two respiratory-effort channels. Type IV requires only two parameters, one of which must be air flow or chest wall movement measurement.

While Types II–IV portable polysomnographs allow some measurement of the severity of breathing disturbances, these measures cannot be used to diagnose sleep apnea. Thus when dealing with medical disorders of any kind, home polysomnography should be done only in conjunction with a comprehensive sleep lab (Type I) evaluation. Even though the overnight assessment need not be attended by a sleep tech, the overall process must be supervised by a certified or eligible sleep-medicine specialist. Home polysomnography is not recommended for patients with comorbidities such as moderate-to-severe chronic obstructive pulmonary disease; neuromuscular disease; congestive heart failure; or other sleep disorders (e.g., central sleep apnea, insomnia, parasomnia, chronic renal disease, or narcolepsy).

Another problem with home polysomnography is the risk of data loss. If the equipment fails no immediate repair will be possible. In addition, patients or participants may simply remove the equipment without warning. Participants or patients need to be instructed on how to move about while wearing the monitor so that no electrode connections are lost.

Patrick McNamara

See also: Basics of Sleep Recordings

Precognitive Dreaming

A precognitive dream is defined as a dream that seemingly includes knowledge about the future which cannot be inferred from actually available information (Stowell, 1995). Precognitive dreams have been reported throughout history; famous examples are the pharaoh's dream of seven fat and seven thin cows and Bishop Lanyi's dream of the assassination of Archduke Franz Ferdinand at the beginning of World War I. Although the phenomenon is often considered paranormal, it occurs quite frequently: 17.8 to 38 percent persons of large samples of individuals reported that they experienced at least one precognitive dream, and in student samples, the prevalence rates are even higher: 51.3 to 64.9 percent (Schredl, 2009). Most studies indicate that women report more precognitive dreams than men, while the frequency of precognitive dreaming declines with age.

Although large surveys of spontaneous cases, diary studies, and laboratory studies have been carried out to study precognitive dreaming, research in factors that might be associated with reporting of these types of dreams, such as personality dimensions or psychopathology, is rather scarce. That the occurrence of precognitive dreams is correlated with dream-recall frequency in general seems plausible since a person who hardly recalls any dream will not be able to experience a precognitive dream (Schredl, 2009). In a student sample ($N = 444$), the personality dimensions absorption, thin boundaries, and somatization were related to the frequency of precognitive dreams even when dream-recall

frequency was statistically controlled. The findings support the idea that specific personality characteristics might predispose for precognitive dreaming.

The most extensive studies were carried out by the research group at the Maimonides hospital in New York (Ullman, Krippner, & Vaughan, 1989). The participant in both studies was Malcolm Bessent, an English, and sensitive with a history of reported spontaneous precognitive dreams. After eight sleep laboratory nights with REM awakenings for dream collection, a word from the dream element list of a dream content analytic book was chosen at random. An experimenter created a multisensory environment around this word, using items that were directed to visual, auditory, gustatory, olfactory, and tactile–kinesthetic inputs to which the subject was exposed. Three independent judges rated each of the eight dream protocols against the eight words/descriptions of the multisensory experience. Both studies yielded five hits; each finding highly significant (Ullman et al., 1989). Because of the expenditure necessary for sleep laboratory studies and the problems inherent in single-case diary studies (e.g., in estimating the chance likelihood of observed coincidences), Jackson (1967) suggested a two-group design using dream diaries, in which Group A keeps a dream diary over a one-week period and is then exposed to a special waking experience (one that would be unusual for all participants) and subsequently records another week of their dreams. Members of Group B also keep dream diaries over two weeks, but they are not exposed to the special waking experience. The advantage of this controlled design is the possibility to estimate the effect of the unusual experience on subsequent dreams, using the contents of the dreams of Group B as a base rate. The precognitive effect can be tested by comparing the dreams of Groups A and B recorded before being exposed to the special waking experience. Despite the conflicting results of previous diary studies, a pilot study (Schredl, Götz, & Ehrhardt-Knudsen, 2010) was able to apply this design and demonstrated a precognitive effect.

To summarize, precognitive dreams were often reported by persons, and future studies should pursue the experimental research in this area to gather more evidence for the phenomenon. In addition, the effect of precognitive dreams on the person should be studied since case reports indicate that some dreamers develop severe worries around this topic.

Michael Schredl

References

Jackson, M.P. (1967). Suggestions for a controlled experiment to test precognition in dreams. *Journal of the American Society for Psychical Research, 61,* 346–353.

Schredl, M. (2009). Frequency of precognitive dreams: Association with dream recall and personality variables. *Journal of the Society for Psychical Research, 73,* 81–90.

Schredl, M., Götz, S., & Ehrhardt-Knudsen, S. (2010). Precognitive dreams: A pilot diary study. *Journal of the Society for Psychical Research, 74*(900), 168–175.

Stowell, M.S. (1995). Researching precognitive dreams: A review of past methods, emerging scientific paradigms, and future approaches. *Journal of the American Society for Psychical Research, 89,* 117–151.

Ullman, M., Krippner, S., & Vaughan, A. (1989). *Dream telepathy: Experiments in nocturnal ESP* (2nd ed.). Jefferson, NC: McFarland & Co.

Prefrontal Cortex in Dreaming

In dreaming, the relative importance of the different domains of conscious experience become altered relative to waking. For example, in the perceptual domain, the visual modality predominates awareness during dreaming, whereas awareness of the different sensory modalities is more balanced in waking (Hobson, Pace-Schott, & Stickgold, 2000). This experiential difference may result from a changed distribution of activity among different brain regions as seen in positron emission tomographic (PET) functional neuroimaging of the brain during sleep compared to waking. Using PET, relative activity of different brain regions can be estimated by relative cerebral blood flow. In the case of the perceptual domain, among primary and association sensory cortices that occupy more posterior portions of the brain, there is relative activation in the ventral stream visual association cortex during REM despite continued sleep-associated deactivation of other posterior cortical regions (Braun et al., 1997).

This reallocation of brain activity in REM sleep compared to waking is even more prominent in regions of the prefrontal cortex (PFC). The PFC, along with most other cortical and subcortical areas, becomes less active following sleep onset with activity further lessening relative to waking as NREM sleep deepens through Stage 2 into slow-wave sleep (Kaufmann et al., 2006). However, with the onset of REM sleep, midline limbic regions of the frontal cortex, including the anterior cingulate (ACC) and medial prefrontal cortex (mPFC) reactivate to levels equaling and sometimes exceeding those of waking while lateral PFC areas remain in a NREM-like deactivated state (Braun et al., 1997) (reviewed in Maquet et al., 2005; Pace-Schott, 2011).

Before proceeding, however, it must be noted that although REM-sleep dreams are more visually vivid, animated, emotional, and bizarre, NREM dreaming is also common (Nielsen, 2000) and, therefore, REM physiology can be considered the optimal but not the exclusive substrate of dreams (Hobson et al., 2000). Given this caveat, what is it about this pattern of frontal brain activity in REM that might account for some of the distinctive experiential features of dreams?

First and foremost is the lack of insight in dreams, described by Alan Rechtschaffen as the "Single-Mindedness and Isolation of Dreams" (Rechtschaffen, 1978). Specifically, insight is lacking as to the fact that one is dreaming and that there are other possible states of consciousness (i.e., being awake). The rare exception is the state of lucid dreaming in which one becomes aware that one is dreaming (LaBerge, 2007). It has long been speculated that the relative inactivity of lateral portions of PFC during REM might account for loss of insight and that transient restoration of such activity during REM might lead to lucidity (Hobson et al., 2000). Compelling evidence that this is indeed the case has come from a recent quantitative EEG study that showed lucid dreaming

to be characterized by frontal gamma frequency (30 to 80 Hz) activity more like that of waking than of nonlucid REM dreaming (Voss, Holzmann, Tuin, & Hobson, 2009).

During nonlucid REM dreaming, diminished working memory, a cognitive function subserved in part by the lateral PFC, may contribute to this lack of awareness of one's mental state by allowing access to the here and now but not to what recently happened (Pace-Schott, 2011). Hence, although dreams may have an internally coherent plot arising from progressing associations to here and now dream percepts and events, this plot can easily tangent in illogical directions due to an inability to reflect on (or attend to) the recent past. Lateral PFC inactivity, coupled with inactivity of parietal multimodal association cortices, may more generally produce executive function deficits in dreaming such as impaired physical logic, disorientation to time and place, uncritical acceptance of bizarreness, and an inability to perform strategic memory retrieval (Hobson et al., 2000; Maquet et al., 2005; Pace-Schott, 2011). Prominent examples of dream illogic are the ad hoc explanations devised by the dreamer to explain bizarre occurrences (Hobson et al., 2000). Similarly, extraordinary abilities such as flying are not questioned by the nonlucid dreamer nor are appearances by personages long deceased.

Associated with lateral prefrontal deactivation in REM, the neurochemical milieu of REM sleep is radically altered from that of waking. Activation of the forebrain originates largely from cholinergic activation of the diencephalon and basal forebrain and lacks the noradrenergic, serotonergic, and histaminergic influences present in waking (Hobson et al., 2000). Norepinephrine is known to be crucial for attention and working memory functions of the PFC (Arnsten & Li, 2005), although recent evidence suggests that influence of another catecholamine, dopamine, may not similarly diminish during REM (Dahan et al., 2007) and may even contribute to the psychosis-like psychotomimetic aspects of dreams (Gottesmann, 2002).

Of equal or more interest than cognitive deficits associated with dreams and their putative neuroanatomy are the similarly REM-associated activations of limbic PFC areas whose activity may provide the content and form of dream consciousness. Eric Nofzinger and colleagues (Nofzinger et al., 2004) have identified an anterior paralimbic REM activation area, a group of anterior midline structures that consistently activate with the onset of REM following NREM. This region contains key cortical and subcortical components of the emotional and social brain, including subcortical structures that subserve fear and defensive behavior (amygdala, hypothalamus, periaqueductal gray), instinctual behaviors (hypothalamus), reward-seeking behavior (ventral tegmental area, ventral striatum), and the memory of such experience (amygdala, hippocampal formation) (Braun et al., 1997). An additional crucial component of all of these circuits is the midline cortical limbic structures that are implicated in the identification, regulation, conscious experience, and memory of emotional experiences. These include the insular cortex, subgenual and rostral ACC (sgACC and rACC), medial orbital PFC (mOPFC), anterior mPFC, and, more

posteriorly, parahippocampal, entorhinal, and related cortices (Braun et al., 1997; for reviews see Maquet et al., 2005; Pace-Schott, 2011).

What might these midline frontal structures contribute to the experience of dreaming?

First is the ubiquity of personally salient emotion in dreams. The experiential output of fear, defensive, and reward systems can all be easily identified in dreams and may be selectively overexpressed in psychopathologies such as the re-experiencing of trauma in PTSD or drug dreams in abstinent addicts. The ventral portions of the mPFC (vmPFC) that include the sgACC, rACC, and mOPFC, are believed to be involved in the regulation of such emotional systems (Milad, Rauch, Pitman, & Quirk, 2006) and, in dreaming, feelings associated with conscious attempts to regulate emotional behavior (e.g., shame and guilt, embarrassment) are also ubiquitous.

Other functions ascribed to mPFC regions include social cognition, self-referential cognition, and emotionally guided decision making. Dreaming is often a highly social experience populated by known and unknown characters with whom the dreamer has personally salient interactions. Similarly, common are thoughts surmising these characters' feelings, thoughts, and intentions. This social cognitive function, often termed theory of mind (ToM), has been quantitatively shown to be ubiquitous in dreams (Kahn & Hobson, 2005). Neuroimaging studies using tasks that recruit ToM have consistently shown activation of both ventral and dorsal regions of the mPFC (Amodio

& Frith, 2006). Therefore it is not surprising that, despite the attenuation of some executive skills consequent to low lateral PFC activity, higher-level social cognition persists in dreams.

Both ventral and dorsal portions of the mPFC have been identified as anterior components of the brain's default network, originally identified by Marcus Raichle and colleagues (Raichle et al., 2001) as a densely interconnected group of primarily midline cortical areas that consistently deactivate in response to effortful or exteroceptive tasks. The anterior portions of the default network have been further fractionated by hypotheses that vmPFC subserves self-centric cognition, whereas the dorsal mPFC subserves ToM and behavioral rehearsal for social interactions (Gusnard, Raichle, & Raichle, 2001). Further neuroimaging studies of this network have associated these anterior portions of the default network with the prospective simulation of future reality (Buckner, Andrews-Hanna, & Schacter, 2008). Other functions ascribed to vmPFC include guidance of decision making by emotional memories of responses to past experiences termed somatic markers by Antonio Damasio and colleagues (Bechara, Damasio, & Damasio, 2000).

Peculiarities of dream memory may also be explicable by differential activation of medial and lateral PFC. The mPFC has been associated with early verification of material retrieved from memory (feeling of rightness), whereas lateral frontopolar regions have been associated with more exacting cognitive monitoring and verification (Moscovitch & Winocur, 2002). Similarly, the vmPFC is activated

in association with the sense that an item in memory is accessible (whether or not it in fact is) sometimes termed feeling of knowing (Schnyer, Nicholls, & Verfaellie, 2005). Bizarre certainty as well as bizarre uncertainty is common in dreaming (Hobson, 1988). For example, in a study of how dream characters were recognized, a large proportion was identified on the basis of just knowing (Kahn, Stickgold, Pace-Schott, & Hobson, 2000). Therefore, high medial and low lateral PFC activity in REM may bias dream mentation toward uncritical credulity and acceptance of even bizarre elements as being accurately retrieved from memory without more rigorous verification.

Lastly, there are both normal and pathological forms of created memory that involve regions of the mPFC. Neuroimaging studies have shown the mPFC to be involved in normal processes of narrative generation (Mar, 2004). Moreover, disruption of the vmPFC, for example, by hemorrhage of the anterior communicating artery, can lead to spontaneous confabulation in which entire false narratives are created and experienced as veridical memory (Schnider, 2003).

In conclusion, the pattern of activity in the PFC during REM, in combination with activation of subcortical limbic structures, predisposes the REM-sleep dreaming brain to generate and uncritically accept cognition with a narrative structure that is biased toward emotionally salient, self-relevant, and socially interactive scenarios. Future studies in which dreamers undergo functional imaging during REM and are then awoken to give dream reports could provide more direct information on brain activity during dreaming and link specific aspects of dream experience to regional brain activity.

Edward Pace-Schott

References

Amodio, D. M., & Frith, C. D. (2006). Meeting of minds: The medial frontal cortex and social cognition. *Nature Reviews, 7*, 268–277.

Arnsten, A. F., & Li, B. M. (2005). Neurobiology of executive functions: Catecholamine influences on prefrontal cortical functions. *Biological Psychiatry, 57*, 1377–1384.

Bechara, A., Damasio, H., & Damasio, A. R. (2000). Emotion, decision making and the orbitofrontal cortex. *Cerebral Cortex, 10*, 295–307.

Braun, A. R., Balkin, T. J., Wesenten, N. J., Carson, R. E., Varga, M., Baldwin, P., . . . Herscovitch, P. (1997). Regional cerebral blood flow throughout the sleep-wake cycle. An H2(15)O PET study. *Brain, 120*(Pt 7), 1173–1197.

Buckner, R. L., Andrews-Hanna, J. R., & Schacter, D. L. (2008). The brain's default network: Anatomy, function, and relevance to disease. *Annals of the New York Academy of Science, 1124*, 1–38.

Dahan, L., Astier, B., Vautrelle, N., Urbain, N., Kocsis, B., & Chouvet, G. (2007). Prominent burst firing of dopaminergic neurons in the ventral tegmental area during paradoxical sleep. *Neuropsychopharmacology, 32*, 1232–1241.

Gottesmann, C. (2002). The neurochemistry of waking and sleeping mental activity: The disinhibition-dopamine hypothesis. *Psychiatry and Clinical Neurosciences, 56*, 345–354.

Gusnard, D. A., Raichle, M. E., & Raichle, M. E. (2001). Searching for a baseline: Functional imaging and the resting human brain. *Nature Reviews, 2*, 685–694.

Hobson, J. A. (1988). *The dreaming brain.* New York: Basic Books.

Hobson, J. A., Pace-Schott, E. F., & Stickgold, R. (2000). Dreaming and the brain: Toward a cognitive neuroscience of conscious states. *Behavioral and Brain Sciences, 23*, 793–842.

Kahn, D., & Hobson, J. A. (2005). Theory of mind in dreaming: Awareness of feelings and thoughts of others in dreams. *Dreaming, 15*, 48–57.

Kahn, D., Stickgold, R., Pace-Schott, E. F., & Hobson, J. A. (2000). Dreaming and waking consciousness: A character recognition study. *Journal of Sleep Research, 9*, 317–325.

Kaufmann, C., Wehrle, R., Wetter, T. C., Holsboer, F., Auer, D. P., Pollmacher, T., & Czisch, M. (2006). Brain activation and hypothalamic functional connectivity during human non-rapid eye movement sleep: An EEG/fMRI study. *Brain, 129*, 655–667.

LaBerge, S. (2007). Lucid dreaming. In D. Barrett & P. McNamara (Eds.), *The new science of dreaming: Content, recall, and personality correlates* (Vol. 2, pp. 307–328). Westport, CT: Praeger, Greenwood Press.

Maquet, P., Ruby, P., Maudoux, A., et al. (2005). Human cognition during REM sleep and the activity profile within frontal and parietal cortices: A reappraisal of functional neuroimaging data. *Progress in Brain Research, 150*, 219–227.

Mar, R. A. (2004). The neuropsychology of narrative: Story comprehension, story production and their interrelation. *Neuropsychologia, 42*, 1414–1434.

Milad, M. R., Rauch, S. L., Pitman, R. K. & Quirk, G. J. (2006). Fear extinction in rats: Implications for human brain imaging and anxiety disorders. *Biological Psychology, 73*, 61–71.

Moscovitch, M., & Winocur, G. (2002). The frontal cortex and working with memory. In D. T. Stuss & R. T. Knight (Eds.), *Principles of frontal lobe function* (pp. 392–407). New York: Oxford University Press.

Nielsen, T. A. (2000). A review of mentation in REM and NREM sleep: "Covert" REM sleep as a possible reconciliation of two opposing models. *Behavioral and Brain Sciences, 23,* 851–866.

Nofzinger, E. A., Buysse, D. J., Germain, A., Carter, C., Luna, B., Price, J. C., . . . Kupfer, D. J. (2004). Increased activation of anterior paralimbic and executive cortex from waking to rapid eye movement sleep in depression. *Archives of General Psychiatry, 61,* 695–702.

Pace-Schott, E. F. (2011). The neurobiology of dreaming. In M. H. Kryger, T. Roth, & W. C. Dement (Eds.), *Principles and practice of sleep medicine* (5th ed.). Philadelphia: Elsevier.

Raichle, M. E., Macleod, A. M., Snyder, A. Z., Powers, W. J., Gusnard, D. A., & Shulman, G. L. (2001). A default mode of brain function. *Proceedings of the National Academy of Sciences, 98,* 676–682.

Rechtschaffen, A. (1978). The single-mindedness and isolation of dreams. *Sleep, 1,* 97–109.

Schnider, A. (2003). Spontaneous confabulation and the adaptation of thought to ongoing reality. *Nature Reviews, 4,* 662–671.

Schnyer, D. M., Nicholls, L., & Verfaellie, M. (2005). The role of VMPC in metamemorial judgments of content retrievability. *Journal of Cognitive Neuroscience, 17,* 832–846.

Voss, U., Holzmann, R., Tuin, I., & Hobson, J. A. (2009). Lucid dreaming: A state of consciousness with features of both waking and non-lucid dreaming. *Sleep, 32,* 1191–1200.

Pregnancy Dreams

The dreaming mind is very active during pregnancy. Pregnant women tend to have vivid and upsetting dreams, at times nightmares. This may give them an opportunity to be interested in dreams. There are certain types of dreams that are commonly found during pregnancy: water dreams; animal dreams; dreams that deal with psychological, physical, and relational changes; dreams that identify with the process that the baby is going through; and so on. Architectural dreams, dreams about the unborn baby, and themes of dependency–independence are also common.

Water seems everywhere in pregnancy, from the embryo starting its life floating in the amniotic fluid up to the moment when the full-term baby is pushed out of the mother's body with a large amount of water. The anatomical structures of the female body and the process of pregnancy, labor, and delivery are depicted by such bodies of water as canals, water passages, swimming pool, oceans, waves, tidal waves, and so on, in dreams.

Animal dreams are very common during pregnancy. Furry mammals, fish, amphibians, and farm animals are popular. Some women have dreams that trace the evolutionary process, while other women dream of animals that hold personal meanings to them.

Dreams reflect rapidly changing phases during pregnancy: in the beginning of pregnancy, some women may have conception dreams that deal with joy and anxiety of being pregnant. When their bodily changes are noticeable, bodily concerns may be addressed in dreams. Themes of bodily and sexual unattractiveness are dreamed. And as women approach the due date, dreams dealing with anxiety about labor and delivery become more prominent.

And not to mention, they dream of their unborn baby. Although emotional bonding already starts in the womb, expecting parents cannot see the baby's face until birth, except vague images from the ultrasound. They may see the baby's face, body, and so on. Besides hopeful dreams it is common to have anxiety dreams: the baby is deformed, of unusual size, or has unusual abilities. In most cases these are not true dreams but just reflect anxiety of the dreamer.

Having anxiety dreams is in fact a good sign. Research found that women who did not have such dreams during pregnancy were more prone to postpartum depression. Like other dreams, pregnancy dreams facilitate huge adaptation that pregnant women and their partners go through during the nine months. This includes bodily and physiological changes, changes in the sense of self, relationships and social roles, emotional instability, among other things.

In a therapeutic sense pregnancy dreams may be avenues to self-growth by offering women the opportunity to regress and reexamine their sense of self and relationships. Jungians have said that pregnant women tend to have more archetypal dreams that are more common during major life transitions.

Also in the transpersonal realm some have said that the unborn child communicates various things to his mother via dreams: for example, his past lives, his personality, and so forth. In some cultures dreams are used in a particular way: among Ese Eja people in Peru, babies are named after the dreams that their mother or father had in the beginning of pregnancy. In various cultures, different signs (such as food craving) have been seen as indications for the sex of the baby.

Dreams are not only concerning ongoing pregnancy: women may dream of future pregnancy, or past, terminated pregnancy. Some women have conception dreams where they know their pregnancy before any medical examination. Any forms of terminated pregnancy may leave scars in their mind; for the grieving woman, dreams can offer inner safety to heal their injuries. Dreams may also remind both women and men of their past experiences of a birth, typically of their siblings during their childhood.

Expecting fathers do not have direct physical experiences that their pregnant wives have, but still share many emotional, sexual, and relational aspects of pregnancy. They may even develop the couvade syndrome, which mimics pregnant women's physical and psychological changes.

Pregnancy dreams of those who are not pregnant or not the partner of a pregnant woman can be interpreted more symbolically: being pregnant with ideas, plans, or projects; a termination of pregnancy as abortion of a project, and so on.

Dreams have particular significance in the context of pregnancy, which is physical and emotional by nature and still holds many mysteries even in the age of advanced science. Pregnancy dreams offer good examples of the dreaming mind knowing more than what we believe we know.

Misa Tsuruta

References

Kron, T., & Brosh, A. (2003). Can dreams during pregnancy predict postpartum depression? *Dreaming, 13,* 67–81.

Siegel, A. B. (2002). *Dream wisdom: Uncovering life's answers in your dreams.* Berkeley, CA: Celestial Arts.

Primary Disorders of Hypersomnolence and Dreams

Hypersomnias of central origin include narcolepsy, idiopathic hypersomnia (IH), recurrent hypersomnias, and various secondary hypersomnias (American Academy of Sleep Medicine, 2005). Perhaps the most well-known primary disorder of hypersomnolence, narcolepsy, has been recognized since the 19th century, and has an estimated prevalence ranging from 1 in 2,000 individuals in the United States to about 1 in 600 people in Japan. The classic tetrad of symptoms includes excessive daytime sleepiness (100%), cataplexy (60–70%), sleep paralysis (25–50%), and hypnagogic hallucinations (20–40%), but the tetrad is present together in only 10 to 15 percent of cases. Narcolepsy is subcategorized into three forms based on whether or not cataplexy or an underlying disorder is present: narcolepsy with cataplexy, narcolepsy without cataplexy, and secondary narcolepsy (American Academy of Sleep Medicine, 2005). There is very little studied regarding dreaming and recurrent or secondary narcolepsy.

Cataplexy is characterized by sudden loss of bilateral muscle tone commenced by experiencing strong emotions, usually positive in nature, such as laughter, but negative emotions, such as anger, can provoke it as well. Sleep paralysis is a particularly frightening, transient, generalized inability to move or to speak during the transition between sleep and wakefulness. Generally, the symptoms resolve within several minutes. Lastly, hypnagogic hallucinations are vivid perceptual experiences typically occurring at sleep onset, often with realistic awareness of the presence of someone or something, and include visual, tactile, kinetic, and auditory phenomena. Each of these symptoms is thought to reflect inappropriate intrusion of REM into wakefulness, and may be associated with dreamlike content. Interestingly, though common in narcolepsy with cataplexy, these symptoms are not specific and can occur in normal people and in other sleep disorders, including IH and sleep apnea. Other features seen frequently in narcolepsy include fragmented sleep (70–80%), and automatic behavior characterized by repeated performance of stereotypic functions, such as writing, speaking, ambulating, or even driving without purpose or true awareness (20–40%).

Less common, and less well-studied than narcolepsy, IH is characterized by a history of excessive daytime sleepiness, a tendency toward long unrefreshing naps, and an extreme difficulty with arousal and subsequent alertness termed sleep drunkenness. Further subcategorization of IH separates the condition into two forms based on whether or not long sleep time, greater than 10 hours, is described (American Academy of Sleep Medicine, 2005).

In both conditions, diagnosis typically rests on an appropriate history and confirmation of hypersomnia by performing nocturnal polysonography followed by a multiple sleep latency test (MSLT). In both narcolepsy and IH, a mean sleep latency of less than 8 minutes is expected, where normal sleep latencies typically exceed 10 minutes. Narcolepsy (both with and without cataplexy) characteristically will show evidence of REM intrusion early (less than 15 minutes) into sleep during nocturnal sleep and during the MSLT naps. Two or more sleep onset REM periods (SOREMPs) in an appropriate setting is a fairly specific finding for narcolepsy. In IH, fewer than two SOREMPs are expected (American Academy of Sleep Medicine, 2005).

Dreaming and Narcolepsy

Symptoms characteristic of narcolepsy, including cataplexy, sleep paralysis, and hypnagogic hallucinations, are due to an unusual propensity to transition rapidly from wakefulness into REM sleep and to experience dissociated REM-sleep events. Reports for nocturnal dream-recall frequency are mixed, but tend to suggest that narcoleptic patients have increased recall for nocturnal dreams, and especially following dreaming during the naps of the MSLT (Fosse, 2000; Fosse, Stickgold, & Hobson, 2002; Mazzetti et al., 2010; Schredl, 1998). Compared with controls, narcolepsy patients show more reflective awareness of dreaming. The dream content of patients with narcolepsy may contain more negative and bizarre elements, increased awareness of paralysis, increased intensity of anxiety, fear, joy, and elation, but decreased anger or surprise than controls (Cipolli et al., 2008; Fosse, 2000; Mazzetti et al., 2010; Roth & Brůhova, 1969; Schredl, 1998). Moreover, REM sleep behavior disorder is observed at greater than expected frequency in patients with narcolepsy with cataplexy (Knudsen, Gammeltoft, & Jennum, 2010).

Dreaming and Idiopathic Hypersomnia

Dreaming in IH has not been extensively studied. Compared to narcolepsy, patients with IH are significantly less likely to report vivid dreams (Anderson, Pilsworth, Sharples, Smith, & Shneerson, 2007). Preliminary reports suggest that patients with IH show no increase in dream recall compared with healthy controls, but may have higher negativity and aggressive behaviors and feelings associated with their dreams (Schredl, 2010).

Thus, in summary, there is a wide range of symptomatology within the primary disorders of hypersomnolence related to dreams. In narcolepsy with cataplexy, many of the defining symptoms occur as a result of an unusual propensity to transition rapidly from wakefulness into REM (or dreaming) sleep as well as patients subjectively noting more vivid, disturbing dreams. Conversely, in IH, although prone to increased amounts of sleep, difficulties awaking, and subsequent lack of alertness, they are less likely to have increased dream recall or more vivid dreams. Though these distinctions have been made, there remains overlap between syndromes and research is ongoing to further define these conditions and their characteristics.

Kristin Chase Spoon
and Timothy Morgenthaler

See also: entries related to Sleep Disorders

References

American Academy of Sleep Medicine. (2005). *International classification of sleep disorders: Diagnostic and coding manual* (2nd ed.) Westchester, IL: American Academy of Sleep Medicine.

Anderson, K. N., Pilsworth, S., Sharples, L. D., Smith, I. E., & Shneerson, J. M. (2007). Idiopathic hypersomnia: A study of 77 cases. *Sleep, 30*(10), 1274–1281.

Cipolli, C., Bellucci, C., Mattarozzi, K., Mazzetti, M., Tuozzi, G., & Plazzi, G. (2008). Story-like organization of REM-dreams in patients with narcolepsy-cataplexy. *Brain Research Bulletin, 77*(4), 206–213.

Fosse, R. (2000). REM mentation in narcoleptics and normals: An empirical test of two neurocognitive theories. *Consciousness and Cognition, 9*(4), 488–509.

Fosse, R., Stickgold, R., & Hobson, J. A. (2002). Emotional experience during rapid-eye-movement sleep in narcolepsy. *Sleep, 25*(7), 724–732.

Knudsen, S., Gammeltoft, S., & Jennum, P. J. (2010). Rapid eye movement sleep behaviour disorder in patients with narcolepsy is associated with hypocretin-1 deficiency. *Brain, 133*(2), 568–579.

Mazzetti, M., Bellucci, C., Mattarozzi, K., Plazzi, G., Tuozzi, G., & Cipolli, C. (2010). REM-dreams recall in patients with narcolepsy-cataplexy. *Brain Research Bulletin, 81*(1), 133–140.

Roth, B., & Brůhova, S. (1969). Dreams in narcolepsy, hypersomnia and dissociated sleep disorders. *Experimental Medicine and Surgery, 27*(1–2), 187–209.

Schredl, M. (1998). Dream content in patients with narcolepsy: Preliminary findings. *Dreaming, 8*(2), 103–107.

Schredl, M. (2010). Do sleep disorders affect the dreaming process? Dream recall and dream content in patients with sleep disorders. *Sleep Medicine Clinics, 5*(2), 193–202.

Psychiatric Diagnosis and Dreams

The civic origins of Western medicine and philosophy can be historically traced back to ancient Greece. Temples were dedicated to the Greek god of medicine Asklepius, whose rod, the snake entwined staff, remains a medical symbol to this day. These sanctuaries were designed to induce dream states that were hoped to provide medical prescriptions, healing, and prognostications. Heraclitus was the first known Greek philosopher to assert that dreams were not of supernatural origin. Instead, he promoted the view that dreams functioned as the individual's retreat into a private communicational world which was continuous with the phenomena of the waking world.

Hippocrates, considered by many as the father of Western scientific medicine, believed that accurate clinical observation of signs and symptoms provided the foundation for the physician's ability to diagnose illness. The original form of the Hippocratic Oath invoked the name of Asklepius. In the ancient world, the physician's use of dreams as a medical tool was widely open to debate. Some believed that dreams could be used as a diagnostic and therapeutic tool; others rejected this idea. The ancient Roman physician Galen saw dreams as playing an active medical role in diagnosis and treatment. Galen reported that as a young man he was visited by a subdiaphragmatic abscess that may have proven fatal if not properly treated. Galen tells us that in a dream, he encountered the god Asklepius who proceeded to instruct him "to open an artery in his hand between the thumb and the first finger and to let it bleed spontaneously" (Oberhelman, 1983). The dream's prescribed surgical procedure worked.

While the Western civic debate about the nature and meaning of dreams continued on, the medical interest in the dream historically waxed and waned over the millennia. The history, tradition, and scientific evolution of psychodynamic psychiatry witnessed a metamorphosis from primitive forms of healing to magnetism and hypnotism and on to the psychiatric psychoanalytic movement. Beginning with the epochal groundbreaking medical work of Sigmund Freud at the beginning of the 20th century, the dream found a central place in the psychoanalytic treatment of psychiatric disorders. Freud's talking cure relied on dreams to reveal unconscious repressed conflicts and tensions, making them conscious and working them through. Dissatisfied with what many saw as Freud's reductionistic method, other physicians and philosophers developed different interpretative diagnostic and therapeutic frameworks to understand the psychodynamics of the dream, conscious behavior, and psychopathology. A methodological pluralism of psychiatric and philosophical schools of thought about the meaning of dreams was developed, such as the Jungian, Adlerian, existentialism, phenomenalism, and cognitive approaches.

The pioneering scientific work of the sleep and dream researcher William C. Dement, who was interested in psychiatric applications of dreams, helped to medically explore the relationship between rapid eye movement and dreaming. Dement himself reportedly had a dream that he had lung cancer. Dement who was a two pack a day smoker, quit. Milton Kramer tells his readers; "It is essential in a psychiatrist's work with patients that he understand as much of their inner life as possible. The dream is one vehicle to facilitate the rapid entry into a person's life" (Kramer, 1966). In a different voice, Sally Mitchison in 1999 provided a medical commentary about the state of the art and science of the psychiatric use of dreams: "I suggest that ignoring

dreams impoverishes our understanding of patients. It also closes off areas of personal enquiries and exploration that are potentially fruitful and enabling for patients." By the end of the 20th century, the medical and professional use of dreams as a valued psychiatric diagnostic tool had become an endangered species (Mitchison, 2009).

In 2001, in his seminal article, Morton F. Reisser asked: "Does the dream have a place in contemporary psychiatry?" Reisser tells us:

> Now the availability of new brain imaging techniques, along with the increasing sophistication and sensitivity of cognitive psychological techniques, make the dream an ideal subject for experimental exploration of the relationship between mind and brain, which has always been an issue of central importance in psychiatry. And, as we become increasingly appreciative of the dream as an integrated product of adaptive mind/brain functions, the therapeutic potential for working with the dream clinically should become increasingly clear. (Reisser, 2001)

In recent news, therapeutic excitement in the psychiatric and dream research fields was created when the European Science Foundation announced that there appeared to be a psychodynamic connection between the brain activity of lucid dreaming and psychosis. The news release suggests that dream therapy could be used as a treatment modality for psychiatric use (European Science Foundation, 2009).

The question remains: can we pragmatically use the dream as a medical tool to arrive at a psychiatric diagnosis? Indeed, physicians both ancient and modern have affirmed the clinical use of the dream as a diagnostic tool. Learning to observe the differential signs and symptoms of psychopathology is pragmatically crucial in making a skilled and accurate diagnostic medical determination. The medical professional field has created a number of clinical conceptual systems to evaluate health-related problems. The World Health Organization's *International Statistical Classification of Diseases and Related Health Problems* has provided physicians worldwide with a clinical diagnostic classification system. *The Diagnostic and Statistical Manual of Mental Disorders* (DSM-IV) has similar classification criteria that assists in understanding mental health issues. As a relatively recent psychological addition to the field, *The Psychodynamic Diagnostic Manual* provides a diagnostic system similar to the ICD and the DSM-IV; however, it devotes itself to the clinical psychodynamic perspective. Numerous medical professionals such as Rudolf Dreikurs (1963) and Glen O. Gabbard (2005) have written about psychodynamic psychiatry.

Joseph Natterson, editor of *The Dream in Clinical Practice* (1993), provides an anthology of writings both by physicians and philosophers who subscribe to the instrumental use of the dream as an important source of medical information for mental health professionals. The dream presents differential diagnostic information about the dynamic workings of psychopathology found in such cases as schizophrenia, manic-depressive disorder, phobias, and personality disorders. Especially in cases where a patient has little or no conscious insight into the causes of their chief symptom or complaint, dreams can contribute invaluable clues for the clinical examination and diagnostic investigation. The medical concept of trauma was radically changed by Freud's investigation of dreams, which revealed that it was not only the body that could be injured, but also the mind. Patients who have some insight may have chosen to repress and forget a past history marked by traumas. In the clinical setting, these traumas and psychological injuries are found to have gone unresolved and untreated. Deirdre Barrett, editor of *Trauma and Dreams* (1996), gives voice to such posttraumatic memories and nightmares of war, the Holocaust, rape, and incest survivors. From a clinical Gestalt psychology perspective, each of us carries a certain amount of psychological traumatic baggage and unfinished business from our past.

As Milton Kramer explains, the dream offers the psychiatrist an invaluable entrance into a person's personal dynamic inner life. From this psychiatric perspective, the dream allows the professional to observe the patient's psychodynamic vital signs and symptoms. This clinical symptom reading of the vital signs of the dream can uncover the buried phenomenological traumas, conflicts, and problems that exist in a person's *Lebenswelt* (lifeworld). The philosophical concept of the lifeworld was coined by the philosopher Edmund Husserl (1970) who believed that the developmental process of consciousness in individuals is deeply rooted in a world of social meanings that is prestructured and constituted by historical and cultural influences. In this sense, the dream permits the professional to perceptually enter into a person's conscious and unconscious lifeworld. Observing the often uncensored and raw phenomenological causes of psychopathological symptoms at work is paramount to creating a detailed medical case history.

By exploring a patient's dreams, a clinician can compile an etiological record, providing the clinical foundation for an accurate in-depth understanding of the patient's medical casc history. In most cases, the dream functions as a vital phenomenological source of both anamnestic and etiological information. This information would otherwise be medically unavailable because of the patient's lack of conscious recall. Dreams serve to help medical professionals to chart and fill in the conscious gaps of the patient's developmental inner lifeworld. This in-depth medical case history information can then help the physician in the construction of a precise differential diagnostic determination and in the creation of a well-structured treatment plan while at the same time ensuring medical continuity of care. In securing this clinical record information, the dream also becomes a medical source and vital sign of the prognostic indicators of psychotherapeutic progress.

Certainly, the dream has proven to be an invaluable diagnostic and psychotherapeutic tool in many medical clinical practices. Echoing Sally Mitchison's earlier commentary, it is surprising how many times patients are referred to clinicians that have already been seen by other medical professionals, yet these professionals did not ask the client about their dreams. Invariably, the causes of the health troubles that the patients were *still* suffering

from were readily made evident by the medically unheard and disregarded language of their dreams and nightmares. As a professional the costs of taking the time to listen to a person's dreams is small. The medical upside of the psychodynamic approach is that if we do take the time to hear the vital wisdom of the dream, the health benefits for the patient can be substantial. What remains certain is that dreaming will continue to happen for those of us living, as will the civic and medical speculation about the nature of the dream. As Morton Reisser suggests, the future clinical prospects are exciting. With medical technology improving, people will hopefully soon discover clear scientific answers to the question of the role that dreams play in the mind, the brain and the lifeworld each of us lives in.

Mark Hagen

See also: entries related to Sleep and Health

References

Barrett, D. (Ed.). (1996). *Trauma and dreams*. Cambridge, MA: Harvard University Press.

Dreikurs, R. (1963). Psychodynamic diagnosis in psychiatry. *American Journal of Psychiatry, 119,* 1045–1048.

European Science Foundation. (2009, May). *The dreaming mind-brain, consciousness and psychosis: Bridging the gap from the phenomenology of mentation to neurons.* European Science Foundation workshop held in Challand Saint Anselme (Aosta), Italy.

Gabbard, G. O. (2005), *Psychodynamic psychiatry in clinical practice* (4th ed.). Arlington, VA: American Psychiatric Publishing.

Husserl, E. (1970). *Crisis of European sciences and transcendental phenomenology.*

Evanston, IL: Northwestern University Press.

Kramer, M. (1966, May). Psychiatric transactions and the use of the experimental dream. *Journal of the National Medical Association, 58,* 185–190.

Mitchison, S. (1999). The value of eliciting dreams in general psychiatry. *Advances in Psychiatric Treatment, 5,* 296–302.

Natterson, J. (Ed.). (1993). *The dream in clinical practice.* New York: Jason Aronson.

Oberhelman, S. (1983). Galen, *On Diagnosis from Dreams. Journal of the History of Medicine and the Allied Sciences, 38,* 36–47.

Reisser, M. (2001). The dream in contemporary psychiatry. *American Journal of Psychiatry, 158,* 351–359.

Quaker Culture and Dreams

Since their emergence in the mid-1600s, the Protestant religious group known as Quakers, or the Society of Friends, has looked to their dreams for spiritual inspiration. Quakers founded their church on the belief that everyone held the seed of truth and could access the inner light. As a general rule, Quakers do not hire ministers and hold silent meetings, although anyone who feels the call to speak can do so. Friends often share dreams and visions during meetings, print them in publications, and copy them into commonplace books. Unlike some other religious groups who thought that God stopped sending prophetic messages after Biblical times, Quakers hold that God continues transmitting direct communications, including prophetic dreams.

The quintessential Quaker understanding of dreams can be found in the works of George Fox. Fox identified three kinds of dreams. First, a multitude of business sometimes caused dreams. Second, there were whisperings of Satan in the night-season. Third, and most important, one could sometimes hear speakings of God to man in dreams. The record is replete with Fox's own dreams and visions, as when he gathered a flock on a hill, released people from the underworld, made time slow down, killed a fierce bull, and saw friends in a damp valley. Sometimes Fox offered very specific interpretations for these experiences. A dream about slaughtering a bull, for example, proved that God supported more formal meetings. At other times Fox remained elusive. Thus it would be up to the right eye and reader to see and read the mystery behind the vision about time. Above all, Fox believed that people should cautiously discern dreams, and in 1647 he told a group of seekers that they relied too much on dreams, warning them that if they could not "distinguish between dream and dream, they would mash or confound all together"(Gerona, 2004, p. 34).

Quakers thus competed with other seekers and radical Protestants who promoted dreams and visions on the streets of England and in sectarian publications during and after the 17th-century English Civil Wars. In *Visionary Women,* historian Phyllis Mack (1992) argues that this period opened new spaces for women to advance their visionary ideas, and many of these women became Quakers. This was also the moment when different factions wrangled over the basic features of Quakerism and Quaker organization, in part by promoting particular dreams. Thus William Rogers charged Fox with appealing to ignorant people by publishing his "Imaginations under the Notion of Night-Visions." While another Fox opponent, Thomas Crispe, published Edward Burrough's 1661 vision, because it had been "plainly fulfilled, and proved a true Vision" (Gerona, 2004, pp. 60–63). Fox won the larger battle to develop a more bureaucratic meeting structure, including women's meetings. Although these meetings discouraged the more anarchic (or antinomian) members and their dreams, meetings continued to value select dreams and oversaw their interpretation and dissemination. Because Friends believed in the visionary nature of some dreams, they often conflated the terms dream and vision.

By the 18th century the practice of dream interpretation became ensconced in a more corporate structure. Meetings recognized public ministers (though they remained unpaid), and many of them became preachers or had life-changing experiences following a dream. Equally important, Quaker leaders often shared reform-minded dreams to sway others. When Robert Pyle dreamed that he could not carry a black pot up a ladder in 1698, he interpreted this to mean that he should not buy a slave and Quakers should turn away from slavery. About 60 years later, renowned Quaker minister John Woolman also recorded several dreams that criticized slavery. In *Teach Me Dreams,* historian Mechal Sobel (2000) argues that dreams allowed Woolman to develop his abolitionist position as he formulated a more modern view of his own self and others. Different Quaker ideas that received support in dreams included: religious reform, temperance, anticonsumption, Indian relations, and pacifism. Wars brought an upsurge in dreams, as when Minister Ann Moore shared her visionary nightmare to dissuade troops from fighting during the Seven Years' War. The circulation of Quaker dreams also rose during the revolutionary period.

By the 19th century, increasing numbers of Friends recorded personal dreams in private diaries and journals, and began to pay more attention to distinctions between dreams, visions, and other altered states. Some continued to publicize momentous dreams such as Joseph Hoag and Daniel Barker, who predicted the 19th-century Quaker schisms and the Civil War. Friend and theologian Howard Brinton (1972) first wrote about early Quaker dreamers in *Quaker Journals,* and today many Friends still look to their dreams for inspiration.

Carla Gerona

See also: entries related to Cross-Cultural Dreams

References

Brinton, H. (1972). *Quaker journals: Varieties of religious experience among friends.* Wallingford, PA: Pendle Hill Publications.

Gerona, C. (2000, Fall). Mapping Ann Moore's secrets: Dream production in late-eighteenth century Quaker culture. *Journal of Feminist Studies in Religion, 16,* 43–70.

Gerona, C. (2004). *Night journeys: The power of dreams in transatlantic Quaker culture.* Charlottesville: University of Virginia Press.

Mack, P. (1992). *Visionary women: Ecstatic prophecy in seventeenth-century England.* Berkeley: University of California Press.

Sobel, M. (2000). *Teach me dreams: The search for self in the Revolutionary era.* Princeton, NJ: Princeton University Press.

Quality of Life and Sleep Disorders in Chronic Kidney Disease

Although significant advancements have been achieved in treating end-stage renal disease (ESRD), their effects on health-related quality of life (HRQOL) are dismal. In fact HRQOL, which measures patient's functioning, well-being, and general health perception in the physical, psychological, and social domain, is reduced in adults and children treated with hemodialysis (HD) or peritoneal dialysis (PD) and in chronic kidney disease (CKD). Low HRQOL scores are associated with depression, sleep disorders, pain, morbidity, poor nutrition, perceived social support, and lead to increased mortality and hospitalization (Kimmel et al., 1995; Mapes et al., 2003; Valdebarrano, Jofre, & Lòpez-Gòmez, 2001). The effects of HRQOL on mortality are frequently observed in older patients across all continents.

Patients on dialysis undergo many losses, including the role in the family, the job, the self image, the strength, the libido, the social relations, the possibility of holding on to a demanding job, to practice a sport, or to have a choice with regard to food and beverages. Even traveling, and the selection of a place for vacation, is limited. Furthermore, losses are associated with an impending, perpetual fear of death. Kidney Disease Loss Scales indicate that patients on dialysis, because of their losses, fall into depression. The latter, in association with a positive affect (coping), causes poor quality of life. These findings disclose a potential for diagnosis and therapy, because providing psychosocial support to patients, targeting losses, might prove beneficial (Kimmel et al., 1995).

HRQOL declines over time in patients with CKD, on HD, or PD, and is influenced by severity of CKD, age, gender, anemia, pain, diabetes, cardiovascular comorbidities, use of beta-blockers, obesity, and unemployment. Low scores for HRQOL correlate with depression, poor sleep, alexithymia, social support, and illness perception and may also depend on the patients'

level of education and physician–patient communication. Low scores for HRQOL may affect the relation of patients with family (dyadic conflicts) and health caregivers, and the attendance and compliance with the dialysis regimen (Kimmel et al., 1995). Short daily HD and daily nocturnal HD improve HRQOL scores as indicated by reduced symptoms, post-dialysis fatigue, and thirst. In addition, improvements in eating, sexual function, mental health, overall health, social functioning, and physical and household management are improved within a short period of time. An effect of the greater enthusiasm of a dialysis team, the greater attention they give patients, their more frequent interactions with patients, and the increased frequency of controls might have a salutary role per se.

Renal transplantation (TX) results in a quality of life superior to that of patients on HD or PD, and in some cases it is comparable to that in the general population, as it emerged in a study of more than 6,000 TX patients followed in 66 studies. TX produced significant improvement of the physical component in 78 percent of patients, of the psychosocial aspects in 70 percent, and of global health perception in 100 percent. Anxiety, however, was not reduced following TX, thus pointing to a switch from a dialysis-driven anxiety to an anxiety driven by fear of graft loss (Dew et al., 1997; Valdebarrano et al., 2001). The improvements in HRQOL following TX observed in cross-sectional studies were confirmed in longitudinal studies.

These findings indicate that the effects of therapy in ESRD should be evaluated not only in terms of survival but also according to HRQOL. Since low HRQOL scores disclose adverse effects, they should be evaluated continuously throughout all stages of the natural history of kidney disease, irrespective of the modality of treatment.

Rosa Maria De Santo

See also: entries related to Sleep Disorders

References

Chan, R., Brooks, R., Erlich, J., Chow, J., & Suranyi, M. (2009). The effects of kidney-disease-related loss on long-term dialysis patients' depression and 1uality of life: Positive affect as a mediator. *Clinical Journal of the American Society of Nephrology, 4,* 160–167.

Dew, M. A., Switzer, G. E., Goychoolea, J. M., Allen, A. S., Di Martini, A., Kormos, R. L., & Griffith, B. P. (1997). Does transplantation produce quality of life benefits? *Transplantation, 64,* 1261–1273.

Kimmel, P. L., Peterson, R. A., Weihs, K. L., Simmens, J. S., Boyle, D.-H., Cruz, I., . . . Veis, J. H. (1995). Aspects of quality of life in hemodialysis patients. *Journal of the American Society of Nephrology, 6,* 1418–1426.

Mapes, D. L., Lopes A. A., Sathayathum, S., Mc Cullough, K. P., Goodkin, D. A., Locatelli, F., . . . Port, F. K. (2003). Health-related quality of life as a preditor of mortality and hospitalization: The Dialysis Outcomes and Practice Patterns Study (DOPPS). *Kidney International, 64,* 339–349.

Valdebarrano, F., Jofre, R., & Lòpez-Gòmez, J. M. (2001). Quality of life in end-stage renal disease patients. *American Journal of Kidney Diseases, 38,* 443–464.

Qur'an and Dreams

Twenty-four verses of the Holy Qur'an discuss dreams in five chapters: Joseph, Yunus, The Spoils, The Victory, and The Ranks (Saheeh International Group, 1997).

Joseph

In his childhood "Joseph said to his father: O my father! indeed, I saw (in a dream) eleven stars and the sun and the moon; I saw them prostrating to me" (4).

He said, "O my son, do not relate your vision to your brothers or they will contrive against you a plan. Indeed Satan, to man, is a manifest enemy!" (5). "Thus will your Lord choose you and teach you the interpretation of dreams and complete His favour upon you and on the offspring of Jacob, as He completed it upon your fathers before, Abraham and Isaac! Indeed, your Lord is Knowing and Wise" (6).

His ability to interpret dreams was manifest, and when Joseph was unjustly imprisoned in Egypt: "There entered the prison with him two young men. One of them said: 'Indeed, I see myself (in a dream) pressing wine'. The other said: 'Indeed, I see myself (in a dream) carrying upon my head bread from which, the birds were eating. Inform us of its interpretation. Indeed, we see you to be of those who do good'" (36).

Joseph tells the first man that he will be released and serve the king wine, while the second man will be crucified, and the birds will eat from his head.

Joseph's skill as a dream interpreter comes to the attention of Egypt's king, who was concerned by two dreams of his own:

"And the king (of Egypt) said: 'Verily, I see (in a dream) seven fat cows, being eaten by seven lean ones—and seven spikes [of grain] and others [that were] dry. O notables! Explain to me my dream, if you should interpret visions'" (43). They said, "It is but a mixture of false dreams that cannot be interpreted" (44).

Joseph was able to interpret the dreams correctly as of seven years of abundance will be followed by seven years of famine.

Yunus

Good dreams are glad tidings for believers: "For them [the allies of Allah] are good tidings in the worldly life and in the hereafter" (64). The good news in this world is the good dream that a servant may see, or it is seen about him (Ibn Kathir, 2000).

The Spoils

Muhammad (PBUH) saw a dream the night before the battle of "Bader":

> Allah showed them to you in your dream as few; and if He had shown them to you as many, you [believers] would have lost courage and would have disputed in the matter [of whether to fight], but Allah saved [you from that]. Indeed, He is Knowing your inmost thoughts. (43)

The value of the dream is clearly not in the accuracy of its representation of physical reality, but rather in its emotional effect (Bulkeley, 2002).

The Victory

The dream in this chapter foretold the conquering of Makkah two years earlier (Ishaq, 2002):

Certainly has Allah showed to His Messenger the vision in truth. You will surely enter al-Masjid al-Haram, when Allah wills, in safety, with your heads shaved and [hair] shortened, not fearing [anyone]. He knew what you did not know and has arranged before that a conquest near [at hand]. (27)

The Ranks

In the dream of this chapter, God commands Abraham to sacrifice his son: "We [Allah] gave him good tidings of a forbearing boy" (101). "And when he reached with him [the age of] exertion, he said, 'O my son, indeed I have seen in a dream that I sacrifice you, so see what you think'. He said, 'O my father, do as you are commanded. You will find me, if Allah wills, of the steadfast'" (102).

The dream led Abraham and his son to surrender themselves to Allah's will: "And when they had both submitted (to Allah) and he put him down upon his forehead (103), We called to him, 'O Abraham, (104), You have fulfilled the vision'." Indeed, "We thus reward the doers of good" (105). Indeed, "this was the clear trial" (106).

Mohamed Omar Salem

References

Bulkeley, K. (2002). Reflections on the dream traditions of Islam. *Sleep and Hypnosis, 4*(1), 4–14.

Ibn Kathir. (2000). *Tafsir Ibn Kathir*. Houston: Dar-us-Salam Publications.

Ishaq. (2002). *The life of Muhammad* (Trans. A. Guillaume). Oxford: Oxford University Press.

Saheeh International Group. (1997). *The Qur-'an; Arabic text with corresponding English meanings*. Jeddah: Abul Qasim Publishing House.

R

Rapid Eye Movement Sleep in Critically Ill Patients

Intensive care unit (ICU) environment is not propitious for restoring sleep (Drouot, Cabello, d'Ortho, & Brochard, 2008). Alterations in sleep have potential detrimental consequences. Accurate sleep analysis requires full polysomnography, but polysomnographic patterns of normal sleep are frequently lacking in these patients and conventional scoring rules may be inadequate. Patients experience severe alterations of sleep with sleep loss, sleep fragmentation, and sleep–wake cycle disorganization, and many factors may contribute to these abnormalities, including patient-related factors (e.g., disease severity) and environmental factors (e.g., continuous exposure to light and noise, around-the-clock care, and medications). Health-support techniques such as mechanical ventilation and sedation may also contribute to sleep disruption. The impact of sleep disturbances on morbidity and mortality in ICU patients remains unknown but a recent study suggests a possible neuropsychological dysfunction that could hamper clinical outcome.

Normal human sleep cycles between two states, non-REM sleep and rapid eye movement (REM) sleep, at approximately 90-minute intervals. Non-REM sleep has three distinct EEG stages, with higher-amplitude, lower-frequency rhythms. Energy reconstitution and recovery from previous wake occur during NREM-sleep episodes. REM sleep is characterized by REMs, dreaming, and skeletal-muscle hypotonia. In REM sleep, the EEG shows active high-frequency, low-amplitude rhythms.

In this entry, we will focus on the causes and consequences of REM-sleep alterations in critically ill patients.

Methods and Difficulties for Sleep Study in ICU

Although time consuming and uncomfortable for critically ill patients, full polysomnography is the only reliable tool for measuring and scoring sleep, especially in patients with marked sleep disturbances (Bourne, Minelli, Mills, & Kandler, 2007). Accurate sleep scoring requires the recording of at least three EEG signals (preferentially F4-A1, C4-A1, O2-A1), two electrooculography signals, and a submental electromyography signal. Additional signals are usually recorded, such as airflow, thoracic and abdominal movements, electrocardiogram, and pulse oximetry. Sound and light levels have to be monitored regarding their potential role in sleep disruption (Gabor, Cooper, & Hanly, 2001).

The Problem of Scoring Sleep in ICU Patients

Sleep scoring using either the standard of Rechtschaffen and Kales (1968) or the recently modified rules (Silber et al., 2007), poses a specific problem in critical-care patients (Ambrogio, Koebnick, Quan, Ranieri, & Parthasarathy, 2008; Watson, 2007; Watson, Ely, Malow, & Pandhari-pande, 2006). Indisputably, a variable portion of critically ill patients does not have the usual polysomnographic (PSG) patterns and markers of NREM sleep (Bourne et al., 2007; Roche-Campo et al., 2010; Watson, 2007). The presence of theta and delta EEG activities during wakefulness, rapid fluctuation between EEG features of wake and NREM sleep, REMs during stage 2 sleep, low-amplitude fast frequencies due to sedation, and delta burst arousal pattern are often observed (Watson et al., 2006). Such abnormal EEG patterns are important to identify since they are associated with poor outcome (Roche-Campo et al., 2010).

REM-sleep scoring can be difficult when submental muscle atonia, a hallmark of REM sleep, is lacking. REM sleep without atonia seems uncommon in ICU patients (Schenck & Mahowald, 1991). Whether loss of muscle atonia is related to preexisting disease, medications, or the ICU environment remains to be established (Schenck & Mahowald, 1991). A study of ICU patients with Guillain-Barre syndrome showed a higher incidence of REM-sleep abnormalities (including loss of atonia, short REM latency, and daytime REM-sleep episodes) compared to ICU patients with paraplegia (Cochen et al., 2005). However, experienced scorers could identify REM sleep even when sleep is hardly disrupted (Ambrogio et al., 2008; Roche-Campo et al., 2010).

Sleep Disruptions in ICU

Severe sleep–wake disorganization is a major characteristic of sleep in ICU patients. Studies using long-time recordings consistently showed abnormal sleep distribution over the 24-hour cycle, with as much as 50 percent of sleep occurring during the day including REM-sleep episodes (Gabor et al., 2003; Hardin, Seyal, Stewart, & Bonekat, 2006). Studies in ICU patients have shown decreased total sleep time, and altered sleep quality with marked fragmentation (Cabello et al., 2008; Gabor et al., 2003; Roche-Campo et al., 2010).

Sleep-stage distribution is substantially altered in ICU patients. Marked deficits in slow-wave sleep (sleep stages 3 and 4) were documented in medical ICU patients and postsurgical patients (Gabor et al., 2003; Knill, Moote, Skinner, & Rose, 1990; Orr & Stahl, 1977). REM sleep is often reduced or abolished (Broughton & Baron, 1978; Gabor et al., 2003), especially during the first night following surgery (Knill et al., 1990; Orr & Stahl, 1977).

Sleep studies conducted in surgical ICU patients have underlined that the time point of sleep recording may contribute to interindividual variability of sleep parameters, especially for REM sleep. The results showed marked reduction or elimination of REM sleep (and slow-wave sleep) during the first two postoperative nights, with a significant rebound of REM sleep in the third or fourth postoperative night (Johns, Large, Masterton, & Dudley, 1974; Knill et al., 1990; Orr & Stahl, 1977), contrasting with little (Knill et al., 1990) or no (Orr & Stahl, 1977) rebound of slow-wave sleep.

Causes of REM-Sleep Disruptions

The high level of noise, alarms ringing, continuous lighting, and 24-hour patient care make sleep difficult. In studies using polysomnography and synchronized recordings of environment, noise and patient-care activities explained only 30 percent of all arousals and awakenings (Gabor et al., 2003). Although sensibility to auditory stimulations is higher during REM sleep from NREM sleep (Bastuji, Perrin, & Garcia-Larrea, 2002), no studies have questioned the arousability to noise during REM sleep in ICU patients.

REM sleep is usually associated with decreased ventilatory responses to hypercapnia and to hypoxia (Kryger, 2000). Whether these respiratory responses have consequences on the frequency of arousals and awakenings are not known. However, experiments in rodents showed that hypercapnia increased the amount of REM sleep (Ioffe, Jansen, & Chernick, 1984), suggesting that hypercapnia may not be a major disrupting factor for REM sleep.

In recent years, a REM-related sleep-disordered breathing (SDB) has been introduced by sleep researchers to refer to a specific SDB characterized by daytime sleepiness and respiratory disturbances confined to REM sleep (Haba-Rubio, Janssens, Rochat, & Sforza, 2005). Similarly, patients with obesity-hypoventilation syndrome frequently display hypoventilation during REM-sleep periods (Chouri-Pontarollo et al., 2007) that could specifically cause REM-sleep alteration. However, the prevalence and impact on health of these REM-sleep respiratory disorders in ICU patients are unknown.

Consequences of REM-Sleep Disruptions

In rats, total or REM-sleep deprivation can cause death (Rechtschaffen, Bergmann, Everson, Kushida, & Gilliland, 1989) and in healthy humans sleep deprivation or sleep fragmentation alters both neurobehavioral function (Banks & Dinges, 2007) and the immune responses (Bryant, Trinder, & Curtis, 2004). In ambulatory patients, the adverse effects of sleep disruption include cognitive deficiencies, daytime sleepiness, adrenergic hyperactivity, and an increased risk of cardiovascular events. Sleep alterations in critically ill patients are considerably more severe than in ambulatory patients and may adversely affect patient outcomes.

Recently, we recorded sleep at the third or fourth day after admission in 27 conscious nonsedated patients suffering from acute respiratory failure, requiring noninvasive ventilation. We showed that a significant reduction of REM sleep was associated with a poor outcome of noninvasive ventilation (Roche-Campo et al., 2010). Furthermore, in this prospective study, patients with low percentage of REM sleep in the first days following admission were at high risk of delirium during the ICU stay (Roche-Campo et al., 2010). ICU delirium is a common syndrome in critically ill patients that seriously increases mortality (Ely et al., 2004).

Conclusion

ICU patients experience severe sleep alterations with reductions in non-REM- and REM-sleep stages, marked sleep fragmentation, circadian-rhythm disorganization, and daytime sleepiness. The sources of these sleep alterations are numerous and include endogenous factors such as disease severity and exogenous factors such as environmental conditions. The impact of these acute sleep alterations of ICU patients may be serious in terms of morbidity but also in terms of mortality. A crucial issue is to identify which patients are at risk to display severe consequences of sleep disruption.

Xavier Drouot

See also: entries related to Sleep Physiology

References

Ambrogio, C., Koebnick, J., Quan, S.F., Ranieri, M., & Parthasarathy, S. (2008). Assessment of sleep in ventilator-supported critically Ill patients. *Sleep, 31,* 1559–1568.

Banks, S., & Dinges, D.F. (2007). Behavioral and physiological consequences of sleep restriction. *Journal of Clinical Sleep Medicine, 3,* 519–528.

Bastuji, H., Perrin, F., & Garcia-Larrea, L. (2002). Semantic analysis of auditory input during sleep: Studies with event related potentials. *International Journal of Psychophysiology, 46,* 243–255.

Bourne, R.S., Minelli, C., Mills, G.H., & Kandler, R. (2007). Clinical review: Sleep measurement in critical care patients: Research and clinical implications. *Critical Care, 11,* 226.

Broughton, R., & Baron, R. (1978). Sleep patterns in the intensive care unit and on the ward after acute myocardial infarction. *Electroencephalography and Clinical Neurophysiology, 45,* 348–360.

Bryant, P.A., Trinder, J., & Curtis, N. (2004). Sick and tired: Does sleep have a vital role in the immune system? *Nature Reviews Immunology, 4,* 457–467.

Cabello, B., Thille, A.W., Drouot, X., Galia, F., Mancebo, J., d'Ortho, M.P., et al. (2008). Sleep quality in mechanically ventilated patients: Comparison of three ventilatory modes. *Critical Care Medicine, 36,* 1749–1755.

Chouri-Pontarollo, N., Borel, J.C., Tamisier, R., Wuyam, B., Levy, P., & Pepin, J.L. (2007). Impaired objective daytime vigilance in obesity-hypoventilation syndrome: Impact of noninvasive ventilation. *Chest, 131,* 148–155.

Cochen, V., Arnulf, I., Demeret, S., Neulat, M.L., Gourlet, V., Drouot, X, et al. (2005). Vivid dreams, hallucinations, psychosis and REM sleep in Guillain-Barre syndrome. *Brain, 128,* 2535–2545.

Drouot, X., Cabello, B., d'Ortho, M.P., & Brochard, L. (2008). Sleep in intensive care unit. *Sleep Medicine Reviews, 12,* 636–641.

Ely, E.W., Shintani, A., Truman, B., Speroff, T., Gordon, S.M., Harrell, F.E., Jr., et al. (2004). Delirium as a predictor of mortality in mechanically ventilated patients in the intensive care unit. *Jama, 291,* 1753–1762.

Gabor, J.Y., Cooper, A.B., Crombach, S.A., Lee, B., Kadikar, N., Bettger, H.E., et al. (2003). Contribution of the intensive care unit environment to sleep disruption in mechanically ventilated patients and healthy subjects. *American Journal of Respiratory and Critical Care Medicine, 167,* 708–715.

Gabor, J.Y., Cooper, A.B., & Hanly, P.J. (2001). Sleep disruption in the intensive care unit. *Current Opinion in Critical Care, 7,* 21–27.

Haba-Rubio, J., Janssens, J.P., Rochat, T., & Sforza, E. (2005). Rapid eye movement-related disordered breathing: Clinical and polysomnographic features. *Chest, 128,* 3350–3357.

Hardin, K.A., Seyal, M., Stewart, T., & Bonekat, H.W. (2006). Sleep in critically ill chemically paralyzed patients requiring mechanical ventilation. *Chest, 129,* 1468–1477.

Ioffe, S., Jansen, A.H., & Chernick, V. (1984). Hypercapnia alters sleep state pattern. *Sleep, 7,* 219–222.

Johns, M.W., Large, A.A., Masterton, J.P., & Dudley, H.A. (1974). Sleep and delirium after open heart surgery. *British Journal of Surgery, 61,* 377–381.

Knill, R.L., Moote, C.A., Skinner, M.I., & Rose, E.A. (1990). Anesthesia with abdominal surgery leads to intense REM sleep during the first postoperative week. *Anesthesiology, 73,* 52–61.

Kryger, M.H. (2000). Respiratory physiology: Breathing in normal subjects. In M.H. Kryger, T. Roth, & W.C. Dement (Eds.), *Principles and practice of sleep medicine* (pp. 229–253). Philadelphia: W.B. Saunders Company.

Orr, W.C., & Stahl, M.L. (1977). Sleep disturbances after open heart surgery. *American Journal of Cardiology, 39,* 196–201.

Rechtschaffen, A., Bergmann, B.M., Everson, C.A., Kushida, C.A., & Gilliland, M.A. (1989). Sleep deprivation in the rat: X. Integration and discussion of the findings. *Sleep, 12,* 68–87.

Rechtschaffen, A., & Kales, A. (1968). *A manual for Standardized Terminology, Techniques and Scoring System for Sleep Stages of Human Subjects* (pp. 1–12). Washington, DC: Public Health Service, U.S. Government Printing Office.

Roche-Campo, F., Drouot, X., Thille, A.W., Galia, F., Cabello, B., d'Ortho, M.P., et al. (2010). Sleep quality for predicting noninvasive ventilation outcome in patients with acute hypercapnic respiratory failure. *Critical Care Medicine, 38,* 705–706.

Schenck, C.H., & Mahowald, M.W. (1991). Injurious sleep behavior disorders (parasomnias) affecting patients on intensive care units. *Intensive Care Medicine, 17,* 219–224.

Silber, M.H., Ancoli-Israel, S., Bonnet, M.H., Chokroverty, S., Grigg-Damberger, M., Hirshkowitz, M, et al. (2007). The visual scoring of sleep in adults. *Journal of Clinical Sleep Medicine, 3*(2), 121–131.

Watson, P.L. (2007). Measuring sleep in critically ill patients: Beware the pitfalls. *Crit Care, 11,* 159.

Watson, P.L., Ely, E.W., Malow, B., & Pandharipande, P. (2006). Scoring sleep in critically ill patients: Limitations in standard methodology and the need for revised criteria [abstract]. *Critical Care Medicine, 34,* A83.

Recall of Dreams

Recalling dreams upon awakening is the prerequisite of all dream research and clinical work with dreams because it is the only way to know what the person has dreamed—with dreaming defined as subjective experience during sleep. Despite the widely held assumption that the brain and the consciousness never sleep, that is, some form of experiencing is always present (Wittmann & Schredl, 2004), dream-recall frequency varies considerably within and between subjects.

As the measurement technique strongly affects the findings of a dream-recall study, the pros and cons of the three major approaches (questionnaire, diary, laboratory awakenings) will be briefly discussed. Eliciting dream-recall frequency by a questionnaire scale does not affect the person because of its retrospective nature; though recall might be biased. Schredl (2004), however, was able to construct a scale with high retest reliability. Dream diaries minimize recall bias because dream recall is elicited upon awakening, but keeping a dream diary can enhance dream-recall frequency dramatically, especially in low dream recallers (Schredl, 2002). REM awakenings and NREM awakenings produce very high recall rates, about 50 to 90 percent (Schredl, 2007), which is much higher than dream recall in the home setting. On the other hand, these three types of measures correlate with each other moderately.

The factors that might affect dream recall have been divided into trait and state factors (Schredl, 2007). Whereas personality traits like repression and extraversion or general intelligence did not correlate with dream-recall frequency in most studies, personality dimensions like boundary thinness, openness to experience, and creativity were correlated (small effect sizes) with dream recall. The most important state factors are frequency of nocturnal awakenings (frequency awakenings increase the chance to recall a dream), participating in a dream study and starting psychotherapy with emphasis on dreams (increases dream frequency), and drugs or presence of a mental disorder like depression indicating that brain activation during the night might also affect dream recall. The interaction between dream-recall frequency and attitude toward dreams is bidirectional, as interest in dreams might increase dream recall by focusing on dreams whereas high dream recall might stimulate the person's interest in his or her dreams. Using attitude scales that are not confounded with dream-recall frequency, however, showed relatively small correlations between the two parameters (Schredl, 2007). Overall, a comprehensive study (Schredl, Wittmann, Ciric, & Götz, 2003), including several areas of factors (creativity, personality, sleep, visual memory, attitude toward dreams), revealed that the explained variance for interindividual differences in home dream-recall frequency is less than 10 percent. Although the findings are best explained by the arousal–retrieval model formulated by Koulack and Goodenough (1976), many questions in this field are unanswered. For example, it would be very interesting to study whether differences in sleep inertia (impairment of cognitive functioning directly after waking up) are related to differences in dream-recall frequency. A second interesting question is whether it is possible to increase NREM dream recall by training to 100 percent—like the recall rates obtained after REM awakenings—in order to have substantial corroboration of the claim that the consciousness (and the brain) never sleeps.

Michael Schredl

See also: entries related to Sleep and the Brain; entries related to Sleep Assessment

References

Koulack, D., & Goodenough, D. R. (1976). Dream recall and dream recall failure: An arousal–retrievel model. *Psychological Bulletin, 83,* 975–984.

Schredl, M. (2002). Questionnaire and diaries as research instruments in dream research: Methodological issues. *Dreaming, 12,* 17–26.

Schredl, M. (2004). Reliability and stability of a dream recall frequency scale. *Perceptual and Motor Skills, 98,* 1422–1426.

Schredl, M. (2007). Dream recall: Models and empirical data. In D. Barrett & P. McNamara (Eds.), *The new science of dreaming—Volume 2: Content, recall, and personality correlates* (pp. 79–114). Westport, CT: Praeger.

Schredl, M., Wittmann, L., Ciric, P., & Götz, S. (2003). Factors of home dream recall:

A structural equation model. *Journal of Sleep Research, 12,* 133–141.

Wittmann, L., & Schredl, M. (2004). Does the mind sleep? An answer to "What is a dream generator?" *Sleep and Hypnosis, 6,* 177–178.

Regulation of Sleep and Wake Systems

Sleep is an active process that results from the interplay between wake- and sleep-promoting centers in the brain. The wake and sleep systems not only inhibit the activity of each other but each also reinforces its own stability, much akin to a flip-flop switch. Such a system is inherently stable and is designed to avoid intermediate states. This section will first describe the wake and sleep systems on a biochemical level followed by a discussion of the current model of sleep and wake regulation.

The classically described wake-promoting systems consist of cholinergic and monoaminergic nuclei that send projections indirectly to the cerebral cortex to maintain wakefulness. The ascending reticular activating system, as they are commonly known, carries fibers that use cholinergic (acetylcholine) and monoaminergic (histamine, serotonin, dopamine, and norepinephrine) neurotransmitters and are highly active during wake. A more recently discovered wake-promoting system is the orexin system that contains neurons origination predominantly in the hypothalamus. These orexinergic neurons maintain wakefulness by projecting to the cerebral cortex and providing excitatory input to the cholinergic and monoaminergic arousal nuclei. The orexin system is thought to have the most potent effect on maintaining wakefulness and a defective orexin system will result in narcolepsy, a disorder characterized by excessive sleepiness.

Sleep is broadly divided into two types: rapid eye movement (REM) and nonrapid eye movement (NREM) sleep. NREM is regulated by the ventrolateral preoptic nucleus and the median preoptic nucleus, both of which act to inhibit the activity of all of the wake-promoting nuclei mentioned earlier. Animal models suggest that the median preoptic nucleus is primarily responsible for the transition from wake to NREM sleep and the ventrolateral preoptic nucleus maintains sleep. The transition from NREM sleep to REM sleep has been postulated to be controlled by the interaction between a REM-on region and a REM-off region. These two regions are also mutually inhibitive, and at the same time each reinforces its own activity, to stabilize the sleep state. Interestingly, the cholinergic and monoaminergic wake systems may play roles as REM modulators as cholinergic neurons are active during REM sleep and directly excite the REM-on region. Similarly, monoaminergic neurons show low activity during NREM sleep and may excite REM-off cells to prevent sudden, unexpected transitions into REM sleep.

Our current model of sleep regulation stems from Borbély's (1982) work, which was later expanded on by Edgar, Dement, and Fuller (1993). The two-process model of sleep regulation is composed of a homeostatic (Process S) and a circadian (Process C) process that work together to control the timing and duration of sleep. Process S, or sleep propensity, increases during wake state and is dissipated by sleep. It is that feeling of increasing sleepiness experienced by an individual who stays up past bedtime. In fact, the longer an individual is awake, the higher the sleep propensity, which will require extra sleep to dissipate. While electroencephalographically measured slow-wave activity is the surrogate often used to quantify Process S, brain adenosine level is the proposed molecular equivalent based on animal studies. Indeed, basal forebrain adenosine concentration increases with sleep deprivation and decreases during sleep.

Process C, the circadian rhythm of alertness, opposes Process S by promoting and maintaining wakefulness during the day. Circadian rhythms are near 24-hour cycles that exist in all organisms. In mammals, circadian rhythm is generated by the master clock in the suprachiasmatic nucleus, which regulates not only sleep but many other physiological rhythms, such as temperature and hormone secretion rhythms. There is actually a biphasic circadian rhythm to alertness, with a decrease in alertness approximately six to eight hours after waking (corresponding to the early afternoon sleepiness that often follows lunch), followed by a decrease in sleep tendency and increase in alertness through the early evening hours. The suprachiasmatic nucleus actually has indirect projections to both the wake-promoting orexin neurons and the sleep-related ventrolateral preoptic nucleus, thus providing an anatomic basis for circadian regulation of the sleep–wake cycle.

Significant progress has been made in our understanding of sleep and wake regulation but our knowledge is far from complete. Future research will undoubtedly elucidate novel pathways important in sleep and sleep disorders, and provide new targets for therapy.

Brandon S. Lu

See also: entries related to Sleep Physiology

References

Borbély, A. A. (1982). A two process model of sleep regulation. *Human Neurobiology, 1,* 195–204.

Edgar, D. M., Dement, W. C., & Fuller, C. A. (1993). Effect of SCN lesions on sleep in squirrel monkeys: Evidence for opponent processes in sleep-wake regulation. *Journal of Neuroscience, 13,* 1065–1079.

Lu, B. S., & Zee, P. C. (2010). Neurobiology of sleep. *Clinics in Chest Medicine, 31*(2), 309–318.

Lu, J., Sherman, D., Devor, M., & Saper, C. B. (2006). A putative flip-flop switch for control of REM sleep. *Nature, 441,* 589–594.

Saper, C. B., Chou, T. C., & Scammell, T. E. (2001). The sleep switch: Hypothalamic control of sleep and wakefulness. *Trends Neuroscience, 24,* 726–731.

Religion and Dreams

Religion is a highly contested word that some scholars say should be abandoned entirely because of its Christian bias and universalist assumptions. Most scholars today recognize these concerns but still use the term to refer to an awareness of powers that transcend human control or understanding and yet have a formative influence on, and active presence within, human life. Dreams have played a variety of roles in virtually every religious tradition throughout history. The cross-cultural and historical evidence suggests that dreaming may function as a kind of primal psychic wellspring of religious experience.

The earliest texts of Hindu culture, the *Vedas,* contain several spells and incantations to ward off bad dreams and elicit good ones. The *Upanishads,* ancient mystical texts focusing on discovering the self's identity with ultimate reality, speak of dreams as the creations of the dreamer's own mind that can be transcended by an enlightened mind. The Buddha himself, whose teachings originated in India and later spread throughout Asia, was conceived in a dream, according to a widely known story about his mother, Queen Maya. Buddhist practitioners, especially in the Tibetan tradition, developed sophisticated methods of altering their conscious functioning within the dream state, using these experiences to take further steps along the path toward Enlightenment. The Chinese tradition of nature mysticism known as Daoism regarded dreaming as an authentic mode of existence, neither more nor less real than the waking world. The Daoist sage Zhuangzi told of his dream of being a butterfly, then waking up and wondering if he was a sage who dreamed about a butterfly, or a butterfly who was dreaming of being a sage.

In the ancient cultures of Mesopotamia, religious revelations in dreams were frequently reported by kings, priests, and military leaders to signify the strength of their relationships with the gods. The Sumerian epic of Gilgamesh was unusual in portraying the nightmares of a warrior king who confronts the painful limits of his power and divine favor. The Hebrew Bible is filled with dramatic dream revelations, particularly in the Book of Genesis. The patriarchs Abraham, Jacob, and Joseph all looked to dreams as sources of direct connection with God, particularly in times of doubt and despair. Some of the Hebrew prophets such as Jeremiah cautioned against too much attention to dreams, but later texts such as the Babylonian Talmud showed a continuing Jewish interest in the study of dreams and dream interpretation.

The Christian New Testament's Book of Matthew presents the story of Jesus' birth, a harrowing narrative directly shaped by several heaven-sent dreams warning his parents of threats against them and the life of their newborn child. Dreams served as a source of divine guidance in the missionary work of Paul, directing him to visit certain regions, warning him of potential dangers, and reassuring him in times of anxiety. Some early Christian theologians and martyrs were deeply influenced by their dreams, but the monastic emphasis on celibacy led Augustine and other church authorities to warn people against the seductive temptations that appear in dreams. This basic theological tension—between a respect for the divine power of dreams and a fear of being deceived or misled by them—has pervaded the Christian tradition right into the present day.

In Islam's foundational text, the *Qur'an,* dreams serve as a medium by which God communicates with humans, offering divine guidance and comfort, warnings of impending danger, and prophetic glimpses of the future. Muhammad describes several of his own dreams in the *Qur'an* and in the *hadiths* (the collected sayings of the Prophet). Inspired by these teachings, Muslim philosophers and theologians over the centuries developed new techniques of dream interpretation. The most famous of these was Ibn Sirin, whose name was reverently attached to dream-interpretation manuals long after his death. Ibn Sirin emphasized that the same dream image could have different meanings for different people, and he drew on passages from the *Qur'an* for linguistic and thematic analogies to help understand specific dream images. Muslims today, particularly those in Sufi mystical traditions, continue to practice the dream incubation ritual known as *istikhara,* seeking God's help by praying about a concern or problem before going to sleep and then awaiting a possible blessing in the form of a favorable dream (or, perhaps, a warning in the form of an unfavorable dream).

Evidence from anthropology suggests that many of the indigenous cultures of the world—in Australia, Africa, the Americas, and elsewhere—were even more actively engaged with their dreams than the major religious traditions just mentioned. Virtually all these cultures had individuals who were specialists in shamanic (another contested word) practices of healing, prophecy, ritual, and dreaming. The impact of modernization has been devastating on indigenous cultures, but in a few cases their shamanic practices and dream traditions have survived, and new dreams have become the basis for spiritual renewal and adaptive community building.

Kelly Bulkeley

See also: Islam and Dreams; Qur'an and Dreams

References

Bulkeley, K. (2008). *Dreaming in the world's religions: A comparative history.* New York: New York University Press.

Irwin, L. (1994). *The dream seekers: Native American visionary traditions of the Great Plains.* Norman: University of Oklahoma Press.

Jedrej, M.C., & Shaw, R. (Eds.). (1992). *Dreaming, religion, and society in Africa.* Leiden: E.J. Brill.

Shulman, D., & Stroumsa, D. (Eds.). (1999). *Dream cultures: Explorations in the comparative history of dreaming.* New York: Oxford University Press.

Von Grunebaum, G.E., & Callois, R. (Eds.). (1966). *The dream and human societies.* Berkeley: University of California Press.

Young, S. (1999). *Dreaming in the Lotus: Buddhist dream narrative, imagery, and practice.* Boston: Wisdom Publications.

REM–NREM Dream Content Specializations

There are two major phases of sleep in mammalian species: an active and a quiet phase. In most mammals, these two phases of sleep can be characterized as REM and NREM, respectively, with REM or rapid eye movement sleep being the more active phase. In humans, when subjects are awakened from REM sleep they generally report a dream—a narrative involving the dreamer who interacts with others in ordinary or extraordinary ways in both familiar and strange settings. That is less often the case when subjects are awakened from NREM sleep. Although dream-recall rates are reduced in NREM relative to REM awakenings, there is no question that dreaming occurs in NREM-sleep states. The purpose of this entry is to briefly explore dream content differences of REM and NREM dreams.

When people are awakened from REM sleep they generally report dreams with lots of emotion, lots of social interactions, and a fair number of bizarre and improbable elements. When someone is awakened from Stage II NREM sleep in the sleep laboratory, however, bizarre elements and unpleasant emotions are less likely to appear in the dream. Some authors also believe that one or the other dream state exhibits greater narrative structure. Most authors claim that REM dreams are more story-like than their NREM counterparts.

Such is the typical, though by no means consensus, view of the content differences in dreams associated with REM- and NREM-sleep states. Many investigators, however, dispute the claim that there are such clear-cut content differences between the two sleep states, or, if differences are admitted, they are dismissed as one of degree or intensity. For these latter investigators, there is but one dream generator in the brain, and that is REM sleep—all sleep mentation derives its fuel and phenomenology from that generator. Our own position is that sleep mentation is colored by the tone of the prevailing sleep stage—it varies over the course of a sleep episode as a function of brain-activation patterns.

When one looks at content differences taken from reports emerging from REM versus NREM sleep, one finds very dramatic differences for a small but extremely significant set of content indicators—namely, social interactions. It appears then for this small set of content indicators that there may be two dream generators: one for REM and one for NREM sleep, each with specialized functions. McNamara, McLaren, Smith, Brown, and Stickgold (2005) studied 100 REM sleep reports, 100

NREM sleep reports, and 100 wake reports (equated in length) that had been collected in the home from eight men and seven women using the nightcap sleep/wake mentation monitoring system. They scored the dreams for number and variety of social interactions. The dreams and wake reports had been collected via use of the nightcap monitoring system. The nightcap (Mamelak & Hobson, 1989) consists of a 25-mm × 8-mm piezoelectric eyelid-movement sensor and a cylindrical, multipole mercury switch that detects head movements (Ajilore, Stickgold, Rittenhouse, & Hobson, 1995). The nightcap counts eyelid and head movements in intervals of 250 milliseconds, identifying an eyelid-movement interval whenever a voltage in excess of 10 mV is detected within an interval. The sensor and associated circuitry are sensitive to REMs and twitches of the levator palpebrae and orbicularis oculi (eyelid muscles), but not to the slow eye movements characteristic of other sleep states. After scoring the reports with standardized techniques for scoring dream content, McNamara et al. found dramatic differences in the types of social interactions depicted in the two dream states:

- Social interactions were more likely to be depicted in dream than in wake reports. There were 56 social interactions in the 100 REM reports; 34 in the 100 NREM reports, and 26 in the 100 wake reports. The REM versus NREM and the REM versus wake differences were statistically reliable (both $p < .001$).

- Aggressive social interactions were more characteristic of REM sleep than NREM sleep or wake reports. Sixty-five percent of the REM reports contained an aggressive social interaction while one third of the NREM reports, and 23 percent of wake reports contained an aggressive interaction. The REM versus NREM and REM versus wake differences were statistically significant (p's < .01). Twenty-five percent of the aggressions in REM dreams were physical aggressions while there were no physical aggressions recounted in wake reports. Eighteen percent of NREM reports contained physical aggressions. The dreamer was the aggressor in 52 percent of REM reports (with aggressions), 0 percent of NREM reports with aggressions, and 100 percent of the few wake reports that contained an aggression.

- Dreamer-initiated friendliness was more characteristic of NREM than REM sleep. It is important to note that dreamer-initiated aggressive interactions were reduced to zero in NREM-sleep dreams, while dreamer-initiated friendly interactions were twice as common in NREM as in REM sleep (90% vs. 54%, respectively, $p < .05$).

Note that these data were gathered using the nightcap technology. The nightcap can only identify REM- and NREM-sleep states and it cannot differentiate sleep states within NREM sleep. So, for example, we do not know if all dreams in the NREM-sleep category came from Stage II or some other NREM-sleep stage. One needs standard EEG technology to identify sleep states within NREM sleep. McNamara et al. (2010), therefore, conducted a second set of studies to replicate this set of findings using standard EEG technology. They found that when you look only at those dreams where the dreamer was directly involved in (e.g., initiating) a social interaction, then clear differences emerge between REM- and NREM-sleep dreams. As in the previous study with the nightcap technology, they found (using standard EEG methods) that

in dreamer-involved friendly interactions, the dreamer was the befriender in only 42 percent in REM-sleep dreams but was the befriender in 71 percent in NREM-sleep dreams. In dreamer-involved aggressive interactions, the dreamer was the aggressor in 58 percent in REM-sleep dreams and only 29 percent in NREM-sleep dreams. REM and NREM dreams appear to exhibit clear differences in the types of social interactions they simulate.

Why should this be so? Brain-activation patterns are significantly different for REM and NREM, with REM demonstrating high activation levels in limbic/amygdaloid sites and deactivation of dorsolateral prefrontal cortex sites, and NREM/slow-wave sleep associated with deactivation of thalamic functions and emergence of synchronized wave activity throughout neocortical sites. Stage II NREM, however, involves higher activation levels in the cortex than Stage IV, and it is Stage II NREM dreams that were likely captured in McNamara et al.'s studies.

The differences in the types of social interactions handled by REM vs. NREM may also influence differences in emotional content of the two sleep/dream states. If aggressive social interactions are more frequent in REM than in NREM then one would expect more emotions that are appropriate to the aggression in REM. If the dreamer is the aggressor, then the emotions might be rage but also power and agency. If the dreamer is the victim then of course the emotions would be fear, anguish, and the like. Spontaneously recalled dreams are typically filled with emotion. Between 75 percent and 95 percent of spontaneously recalled dreams (likely REM dreams) contain at least one emotion. Other investigators have found three to four emotions per dream. Most authors report that negative emotions are significantly more intense in REM than NREM, whereas positive emotions were not.

Do the REM-NREM differences in simulation of social interactions relate at all to putative memory processing differences associated with REM and NREM sleep states? Many authors have suggested various ways in which NREM interacts with REM in processing of memories. Some authors have suggested that NREM is associated with consolidation of memories of life episodes while REM sleep is associated with processing of semantic and procedural aspects of memories. Thus at present there is no clear connection to REM–NREM dream content differences with memory processing functions of these sleep states.

Do REM or NREM dream content variables influence daytime behavior? If you are more aggressive in your REM dreams are you more aggressive during the daytime? Or perhaps high aggression in dreams allows you to be less aggressive during the daytime? There are as yet no data that speak directly to the issue. Kramer (1993) reported that selected emotional content variables showed statistically significant change across the night's REM dreams and were predictive of mood improvement in the morning. These content variables involved change in the *number and variety of characters* in dreams across a single night of dreaming. Self-reported mood upon awakening in the morning was related to the increase in number of characters in dreams across the night.

From the earlier summary of REM–NREM dream content studies it is reasonable to conclude that (1) sleep mentation may exhibit striking processing specializations; (2) that these specializations include number and variety of social interactions; and (3) specific dream content variables (including number and variety of dream characters) may predict mood states during the following morning.

Identification of reliable REM/NREM content and processing specializations, around emotion, memory, personality, and social cognition will carry significant implications for clinical research and treatment of disorders involving these basic functions. If it is found, for example, that REM dreams specialize in simulations of aggressive and unpleasant social interactions, then we would want to know what the level of this content indicator is in various disorders of mood and personality. Do depressives, or criminal offenders, or personality-disordered individuals exhibit especially high levels of aggression in REM versus NREM dreams? Is severity of the disorder linked to frequency of the relevant content indicators? Is the subjective quality of sleep correlated with dream content? If dream content influences sleep quality, might it also influence daytime functioning? Can manipulation of the relevant content indicators ameliorate or treat symptoms of both sleep and other types of sleep-related disorders? To underline the potential importance of this question consider recent reports citing REM and nightmare content indicators as significant predictors of suicidal ideation in depressed individuals (Agargun & Cartwright, 2003; Agargun et al., 1998). If a clinician monitored such dream content indicators in individuals at risk for suicide attempts he or she could potentially identify early warning signs of new ideation around suicide and could therefore act to prevent a new suicide attempt.

Patrick McNamara

See also: entries related to Dream Content

References

Agargun, M. Y., & Cartwright, R. (2003). REM sleep, dream variables and suicidality in depressed patients. *Psychiatry Research, 119*(1–2), 33–39.

Agargun, M. Y., Cilli, A. S., Kara, H., Tarhan, N., Kincir, F., & Oz, H. (1998). Repetitive frightening dreams and suicidal behavior in patients with major depression. *Comprehensive Psychiatry, 39,* 198–202.

Ajilore, O. A., Stickgold, R., Rittenhouse, C., & Hobson, J. A. (1995). Nightcap: Laboratory and home-based evaluation of a portable sleep monitor. *Psychophysiology, 32,* 92–98.

Hobson, J. A., & Pace-Schott, E. F. (2002). The cognitive neuroscience of sleep: Neuronal systems, consciousness and learning. *Nature Reviews Neuroscience 3*(9), 679–693.

Hobson, J. A., Stickgold, R., & Pace-Schott, E. F. (1998). The neuropsychology of REM sleep dreaming. *Neuroreport, 9*(3), R1–R14.

Kramer, M. (1993). The selective mood regulatory function of dreaming: An update and revision. In A. Moffit, M. Kramer, & R. Hoffman (Eds.), *The functions of dreaming* (pp. 139–145). Albany: State University of New York Press.

Mamelak, A. N., & Hobson, J. A. (1989). Nightcap: A home-based sleep monitoring system. *Sleep, 12,* 157–166.

McNamara, P., Johnson, P., McLaren, D., Harris, E., Beauharnais, C., & Auerbach, S. (2010). REM and NREM sleep mentation. *International Review of Neurobiology, 92,* 69–86.

McNamara, P., McLaren, D., Smith, D., Brown, A., & Stickgold, R. (2005). A "Jekyll and Hyde" within: Aggressive versus friendly social interactions in REM and NREM dreams. *Psychological Science, 16*(2), 130–136.

Smith, M. R., Antrobus, J. S., Gordon, E., Tucker, M. A., Hirota, Y., Wamsley, E. J., . . . Emery, R. N. (2004). Motivation and affect in REM sleep and the mentation reporting process. *Consciousness and Cognition, 13,* 501–511.

REM Sleep across the Lifespan

The discovery of rapid eye movement (REM) sleep and its association with dreaming in the mid-20th century stimulated research about sleep architecture and increased researchers' attention to REM sleep. Thus, whether REM sleep amounts decline as a percentage of sleep over the lifespan of healthy adults emerged as a research question in the mid-1990s.

The answer has been controversial because studies supporting apparent age-related changes in sleep architecture were not carefully controlled. For instance, many research subjects considered healthy were not screened for depression, sleep apnea, and other possible pathologies known to affect sleep architecture. Nevertheless, after much scrutiny of existing studies, narrative summations generally report that REM minutes decline a small amount as a percentage of sleep from young adulthood through old age. The decline is generally described as small (i.e., from two to three percentage points).

Despite consensus among narrative reviewers, conflicting reports about the linear and nonlinear nature of adults' decline in REM sleep continue to exist in quantitative literature reviews. Reported differences likely result from the application of traditional meta-analytic methods designed to compare group differences to a question better addressed by exploration of nonlinear correlation.

Ideally, the natural history of sleep-architecture changes over the lifespan would be studied using a very large, century-long cohort study and prospective measurements of sleep stages taken annually in the same controlled setting with the same cutting-edge polysomnography technology and adoption of a standard study protocol. Realistically, research reviewers interested in age-related sleep architecture changes will have only diverse study findings that can be meta-analyzed or otherwise evaluated and summarized.

Fortunately, the number of primary studies reporting information about REM sleep at different ages is extensive, thus making various approaches to quantitative research synthesis feasible. Thus, sleep scientists have used several of the best meta-analytic techniques available to examine how sleep stages, including REM, change over the adult lifespan.

The first meta-analysis to be completed that addressed developmental changes in sleep architecture (Floyd, 1995–1999) focused on testing several hypotheses including: REM sleep declines linearly in healthy adults over the lifespan. This claim was tested against the alternate hypothesis that the apparent decline in REM percentage reported in several studies, but not found in several other studies, could be accounted for by failure to screen subjects carefully for several factors associated with age including mental

and physical health status. This first meta-analysis used results from 44 samples representing 1,388 male and female subjects. Studies were completed and presented in print between 1960 and 1999. Because a potentially linear relationship was under exploration, the r-family of meta-analytic effect–size indicators was used rather than the d-family, which is commonly used as effect–size indicators in the analysis of group differences. A medium-sized mean-weighted correlation between age and REM percentage was found, $r = -36$ $(-.41; -.31)$. Too few studies reported separate results for women to compare the magnitude of correlations between age and REM percentage for men versus women. When samples that failed to carefully control subjects for pathology (i.e., samples may have included subjects who use drugs or alcohol or have mental disorders, organic diseases, obstructive sleep apnea, or other sleep disorders) were excluded from the meta-analysis, the correlation between age and REM percentage remained significantly different from zero. The moderator that most influenced the correlation between age and REM percentage was failure to control for sleep apnea and other sleep disorders. Although these meta-analytic results were the first to support the existence of an age-related decline in REM percentage that could not be accounted for by health status or variation in study methods, examination of REM percentage values for samples with different mean ages suggested another intriguing question: Is there significant nonlinearity in the rates of change in REM percentage and other sleep architecture stages over the adult lifespan?

Two comprehensive meta-analyses have been reported that explored the apparent nonlinearity in how sleep-stage percentages change in healthy subjects from young adulthood to old age. Both examined studies completed and presented between 1960 and 2004. Both included results for REM percentage.

One approach used was to partition studies into those that compared different combinations of young adult, middle-aged, and elderly samples (Ohayon, Carskadon, Guilleminault, & Vitiello, 2004). Cutoffs for distinguishing young and middle-aged adults were not explicated, but studies of the elderly were those with subjects 60 years of age or older. In addition, mean values of REM percentage were plotted as a function of mean age for each sample and least-squares analysis was used to estimate the linear component of change. The earlier meta-analytic findings of a negative correlation between age and REM percentage after controlling for health status were replicated, $r = -.34$. Also replicated were previously reported findings for sleep and aging research including: (1) primary researchers' failure to control of sleep apnea and other sleep disorders is a major threat to validity of early studies of sleep and normal aging and (2) primary researchers' failure to report findings separately by gender precludes thorough examination of gender differences. With regard to nonlinear change for REM percentage, this team of meta-analysts reported inconsistent findings regarding possible ages along the adult lifespan when changes in REM percentage may speed up or slow down with regard to decline and depicted the decline in REM percentage as essentially linear through age 90.

As a method for detecting nonlinearity, the use of the d-family of effect–size indicators to contrast within-group correlations for all possible combinations of age groups (e.g., young adults vs. middle-aged adults, middle-aged adults vs. elderly adults, etc.) has several limitations including restriction of range for age when calculating the correlations for age and REM percentage for young, middle-aged, and elderly subgroupings. Visual examination of sample means for samples of increasing age without attention to sample size and sample variance can also distort meta-analytic results.

To overcome these limitations, another approach to meta-analysis of primary study findings was chosen to facilitate exploration of nonlinearity in REM percentage changes over the adult lifespan. The chosen approach was a research synthesis method specifically designed to detect nonlinear sleep change (Floyd, 2000–2004; Floyd, Janisse, Medler, & Ager, 2000). Another advantage of the method is that it increases the number of studies in the meta-analysis by making use of one-group study designs, as well as designs comparing several age groups. Thus, 382 English-language research reports were located that provided REM percentage values for 4,171 adult subjects aged 18 to 92 (Floyd, Janisse, Jenuwine, & Ager, 2007). Using these newer synthesis methods, the correlation between age and REM percentage was estimated to be in the small range, $r = -.168$ $(-.193; -.142)$. Because these newer methods make use of raw score units rather than mean-weighted effect sizes, it was also possible to report that REM percentage declined 2.9 percent from ages 18 to 75, but from ages 76 to 85 approximately 1.6 percent of the decline in REM percentage was recovered. Although very sparse data exist for subjects more than 85, the little data that exist support a small continuing increase in REM percentage.

The methods employed for this latest research synthesis generated findings considered more definitive than previous meta-analyses of aging-related sleep change because of their ability to identify a specific age within an age group at which the rates of linear decline reach zero and reverse direction; that is, 75.59 years of age in the more-than-age-60 samples available for this latest meta-analysis. These newer methods also provided slopes as needed to identify rates of change in percentage of REM sleep per time period. Once again the effects of primary researchers' failure to use strict criteria to eliminate from their sample subjects with sleep apnea was evident as was the paucity of study results regarding women's sleep values. However, more recently published reports were found to: (1) be better controlled for health status of subjects, (2) include higher percentages of women, and (3) report sample statistics separately for both men and women.

All approaches to research synthesis are limited by the types of primary studies completed and available for further analysis. For instance, it is not possible to explore gender differences when sleep researchers, who included both men and women in their studies, report data for the combined sample only.

There is another limitation affecting all meta-analyses of aging-related sleep change: The sleep findings for older samples reported by primary researchers may

be an artifact of sampling, a factor also outside the control of the meta-analyst. Specifically for the most recent meta-analysis, subjects aged 75 to 92 who were available for primary sleep laboratory studies may not be from the same population as those subjects available at younger ages. It is impossible to know if younger subjects will mature into subjects like the already-studied old-old subjects. And vice versa, it is impossible to know that those subjects aged 75 to 92 had REM percentage values like younger samples when they were younger. Thus, the meta-analyst's desire for a large prospective cohort study of sleep stages from birth to old age can be appreciated. Although the wish for such a study is unrealistic, smaller cohort studies including polysomnography data from both men and women who are followed over several years are needed to fully answer questions about intra-individual sleep architecture changes over the adult lifespan.

In summary, the fact is: Changes in REM percentage, which can be detected when using existing samples of subjects who are healthy for their ages, are very small. Nevertheless, the percentage of sleep time spent in REM remains substantial at roughly 20 percent of total sleep time over the entire adult lifespan. Thus, the functions served by REM sleep in adults, including dreaming, appear available from young adulthood through old age. Understanding sleep architecture including the placement and amounts of REM sleep continues to fascinate sleep researchers. As several neurocognitive theories emerge to explain why we dream, interest remains high as sleep researchers wonder: Will an understanding of the purpose of dreaming ultimately shed light on why the healthiest seniors more than age 75 (who are able to undergo polysomnography) have slightly higher REM percentage than their apparent counterparts between ages 60 and 75?

Judith Ann Floyd

See also: entries related to Sleep and Development

References

Floyd, J. A. (1995–1999). R01 NR 003880: Aging-related sleep changes: A meta-analysis 1995–1999.

Floyd, J. A. (2000–2004). R01 NR 003880: Aging-related sleep changes: A meta-analysis 2000–2004.

Floyd, J. A., Janisse, J. J., Jenuwine, E. S., & Ager, J. A. (2007). Changes in REM-sleep percentage over the adult lifespan. *Sleep, 30,* 829–836.

Floyd, J. A., Janisse, J. J., Medler, S. M., & Ager, J. A. (2000). Non-linear components of age-related change in sleep initiation. *Nursing Research, 49,* 290–294.

Ohayon, M. M., Carskadon, M. A., Guilleminault, C., & Vitiello, M. V. (2004). Meta-analysis of quantitative sleep parameters from childhood to old age in healthy individuals: Developing normative sleep values across the human lifespan. *Sleep, 27,* 1255–1273.

REM Sleep Behavior Disorder

REM sleep behavior disorder (RBD) is a parasomnia (viz., behavioral, experiential, autonomic nervous system disorder of sleep) (American Academy of Sleep Medicine [AASM], 2005) that was formally identified and named in 1986–1987 (Schenck & Mahowald, 2002), and which has an experimental animal model involving brainstem lesions in cats that was first reported in 1965 (Schenck & Mahowald, 2002). (RBD has also been reported to occur naturally in dogs and cats [Schenck & Mahowald, 2002].) RBD is included within the International Classification of Sleep Disorders (2nd ed.; ICSD-2), with established diagnostic criteria, and is the only 1 of 12 primary parasomnias in the ICSD-2 that is required to have video-polysomnographic confirmation for its diagnosis (AASM, 2005). RBD is a multifaceted motor, behavioral, and dream disorder of REM sleep in which the affected person will simultaneously act out abnormal dreams that cause injury or sleep disruption to self or bed partner from the complex, vigorous, and violent behaviors that are often accompanied by talking, shouting, and swearing (AASM, 2005; Mahowald & Schenck, 2010; Schenck & Mahowald, 2002). The dreamer has his eyes closed (in contrast to a sleepwalker) while attending to the dream action, and is oblivious to the bedside surroundings, thus posing an ongoing risk of injury when the acting-out behavior—for example, kicking, punching, jumping out of bed, running—collides with the bedroom furniture, floor, walls, or the bed partner. The typical patient with RBD is a middle-aged or older male, a prominent finding in the world literature that remains enigmatic. However, it is possible that as many females of similar age also act out their dreams, but usually without sufficient vigor or aggression to cause harm, and thus medical attention is rarely sought. Only large-scale studies using video-polysomnographic monitoring can definitively answer this intriguing question. RBD can emerge in early childhood (usually with narcolepsy or brainstem tumor), and the oldest reported case was 88 years old. RBD can be idiopathic, symptomatic of a neurological disorder, or be induced by medications (particularly antidepressants). These topics will be discussed further.

The abnormal dreams begin concurrently with the emergence of dream enactment, or else begin shortly, by weeks or months, before the onset of dream enactment. There is usually a close correspondence, or isomorphism, between the dreamed action and the observed/videotaped behavior of the person who is dreaming. Thus, the dream changes and the acting out of these altered dreams presumably share a common pathophysiology, particularly since both abnormalities are controlled with the same pharmacotherapy, to be described further on. The activation–synthesis model of dream generation (updated by Hobson and colleagues to become the activation–input–modulation model) may be particularly suitable for explaining this aspect of RBD, since it focuses on the brainstem as the site for generating motor-behavioral patterns that then, through ascending neural pathways, stimulate the cerebral cortex to synthesize dreams based on these motor system patterns. (With RBD, the brainstem is the presumed site of pathology, as will be elucidated.) Patients report increased vividness, emotional intensity, and unpleasantness during action-packed dreams that often feature confrontation, aggression, and violence with unfamiliar people or animals, or insects. The dreamer is rarely the primary aggressor, and must suddenly defend himself or his wife from an assault. Not uncommonly, a wife will be awakened by her husband's blows and yell at him to stop his assault, and after coming to wake state he will explain that he was actually defending his wife in his dream. However, a controlled study has shown that men with RBD do not demonstrate any daytime tendency for increased aggressiveness despite increased aggressiveness in their dreams, indicating that it is a disturbed physiology of REM sleep that is responsible for sleep aggression in RBD rather than a nocturnal, sleep- and dream-related extension of daytime irritability, anger, or temper outbursts. In a minority of cases, sports-related dreams are reported (with or without aggression), along with a broad range of nonviolent, elaborate behaviors emerging with dream enactment, such as laughing, singing, whistling, gesturing, clapping, arm flailing, sitting up, crawling, dancing, engaging in work-related activities, fictive eating and drinking; and even masturbation-like behaviors and repetitive pelvic thrusting mimicking coitus.

The vigorous and violent behaviors of RBD commonly result in injury (ecchymoses, fractures, lacerations—including arteries and tendons), which at times can be severe and even life threatening to self and bed partner, with forensic implications (Schenck, Lee, Cramer Bornemann & Mahowald, 2009). Not surprisingly, patients often have to resort to a variety, and at times extreme, home remedies for self-protection until they can be properly diagnosed and effectively treated (Schenck & Mahowald, 2002). Some of the reported measures include tethering oneself to a bedpost with a belt and rope; tying oneself up in bed with dog leashes; or sleeping in a padded bed or waterbed, or on a mattress placed on the floor in a room

A 70-year-old RBD patient with recurrent injuries from dream-enactment demonstrates tethering himself to bed to keep safe while asleep (prior to diagnosis and successful pharmacotherapy). He nearly strangled his wife to death one night when he dreamt that he had shot a deer, but when it was still alive and "blathering" he decided to "finish it off by snapping its neck," which is when his wife's screaming awakened him to find his hands wrapped around her neck while attempting to strangle her. This story was also described by the patient in *Sleep Runners: The Stories Behind Everyday Parasomnias,* Slow-Wave Films, LLC, 2004. (Photo reprinted from *Paradox Lost: Midnight in the Battleground of Sleep and Dreams,* 2005, by Carlos H. Schenck, MD, page 64, www.parasomnias-rbd.com, with permission of the publisher, Extreme-Nights, LLC)

devoid of furniture. Men with RBD can be falsely accused of intentional spousal abuse by family, friends, and health care providers. In fact, men with RBD are typically considered to be kind and gentle people. Not one case of marital separation or divorce has been reported on account of RBD, with one exception in a recently married couple.

REM sleep across mammals is characterized by an adaptive, physiological, generalized paralysis of the skeletal muscles, called REM atonia, which is briefly interrupted by brief, inconsequential phasic muscle twitches (Mahowald & Schenck, 2010; Schenck & Mahowald, 2002). (The ocular muscles that produce REMs; the middle ear muscle; and the diaphragm that is essential for breathing, are all spared the muscle paralysis of REM sleep.) The core electromyographic (EMG) abnormalities of RBD consist of continual or intermittent loss of REM atonia, allowing for increased muscle tone, and/or excessive phasic muscle twitching of the chin and limbs during REM sleep (AASM, 2005; Mahowald & Schenck, 2010; Schenck & Mahowald, 2002). Periodic limb movements during both REM and NREM sleep are common, indicating generalized REM-/NREM-sleep motor dyscontrol in RBD (Mahowald & Schenck, 2010; Schenck & Mahowald, 2002).

There is a close correspondence between the categories of behaviors released during REM sleep in the experimental cat model of RBD and in human RBD (regardless of whether the human case is idiopathic, symptomatic of a neurologic disorder, or medication induced): minimal limb twitching and jerking; orientation; exploration—locomotion; attack behavior, including running and jumping (Schenck & Mahowald, 2002). Also, the categories of behaviors not found in the animal model of RBD are not found or are very rarely found in human RBD: sexual, feeding, or grooming behaviors, along with micturition, defacation. Apart from the prominent tonic and phasic EMG and behavioral abnormalities during REM sleep, all other features of REM sleep remain intact in RBD, such as latency to REM sleep, REM sleep percentage of total sleep time, number of REM-sleep periods, and the customary REM sleep/NREM sleep cycling (Schenck & Mahowald, 2002).

RBD can be an acute or chronic disorder (AASM, 2005; Mahowald & Schenck, 2010; Schenck & Mahowald, 2002). Acute RBD is primarily found in drug withdrawal or drug intoxication states, and other toxic-metabolic states, and is generally a reversible condition (Mahowald & Schenck, 2010; Schenck & Mahowald, 2002). Chronic RBD can be an idiopathic or symptomatic disorder that generally persists without eventual remission, and therefore requires ongoing pharmacotherapy. In four large series of RBD involving 52, 91, 93, and 231 patients, respectively, idiopathic RBD was the initial diagnosis after clinical and PSG evaluations in 25, 42, 43, and 44 percent, respectively, with central nervous system (CNS) disorders being causally linked to RBD onset in the preponderance of cases (Boeve, 2010; Schenck & Mahowald, 2002). RBD has been linked with most categories of CNS disorders (Mahowald & Schenck, 2010; Schenck & Mahowald, 2002), indicating that the neuronal centers and pathways located in the brainstem that subserve REM atonia and also that normally inhibit behavioral release in REM sleep (as identified in the animal model) can be anatomically compromised by the gamut of neurologic disorders. Narcolepsy, a CNS disorder of excessive sleepiness, REM-sleep attacks, cataplexy, sleep paralysis, and hypnagogic hallucinations, is strongly linked with RBD (Mahowald & Schenck, 2010; Schenck & Mahowald, 2002). RBD and narcolepsy epitomize dissociated states in which admixtures of REM sleep and wakefulness manifest with pathological behaviors and experiences. It is important to note that most or all of the neurological disorders that can induce RBD can also manifest as subclinical RBD, in which the PSG markers of RBD are present, but without any clinical parasomnia behaviors. Thus, there must be disinhibition of brainstem motor-behavioral pattern generators during REM sleep, besides a compromise of REM atonia, to result in clinical RBD (Schenck & Mahowald, 2002). Additionally, reports of medication-induced RBD (Mahowald & Schenck, 2010; Schenck & Mahowald, 2002), principally involving antidepressants (SSRIs, venlafaxine, mirtazapine, tricyclic antidepressants—but not buproprion, a dopaminergic/noradrenergic agent), and also beta-blockers, selegiline, and so on, indicate how there can be pharmacologic interference of CNS serotonergic, monoaminergic, and cholinergic neurotransmission resulting in RBD. Also, caffeine excess, including chocolate excess, can cause or aggravate RBD (Mahowald & Schenck, 2010). Certain CNS autoimmune disorders, such as limbic encephalitis and Guillain-Barre syndrome, can trigger RBD, thus revealing autoimmune mechanisms in RBD genesis in some cases (Mahowald & Schenck, 2010).

A major frontier in clinical medicine and RBD research involves the strong link between RBD and the neurodegenerative Parkinsonian disorders (Parkinson's disease [PD], multiple system atrophy [MSA], dementia with Lewy bodies [DLB], and pure autonomic failure) (Boeve, 2010; Mahowald & Schenck, 2010; Schenck & Mahowald, 2002). These disorders share similar α-synuclein positive intracellular inclusions, and so they are now considered collectively as the α-synucleinopathies. There is growing evidence that RBD may be a sensitive and specific clinical marker for the synucleinopathies. In middle-aged and older patients initially diagnosed with idiopathic RBD, more than two thirds will eventually develop a Parkinsonian disorder, on average in 11 to 14 years (Boeve, 2010; Mahowald & Schenck, 2010)—but the range can extend up to 50 years (Boeve, 2010). Conversely, RBD is present in >90 percent of MSA patients, in about 70 percent of DLB patients, and in about 50 percent of PD patients (Boeve, 2010). Also, in the setting of dementia, the presence of RBD almost always indicates the presence of DLB (Boeve, 2010), rather than Alzheimer's disease (AD), a tauopathy, or some other form of dementia. (Nevertheless, cases of RBD with tauopathies, such as AD, progressive supranuclear palsy, etc., have been reported.) Various studies have found that the presence of RBD in PD generally confers increased morbidity of PD across several dimensions, such as degree of PD motor impairment, dementia, psychosis, and visual hallucinations.

There are major clinical and research implications related to these striking findings, which are beyond the scope of this chapter. For example, middle-aged and older patients diagnosed with idiopathic REM Behavior Disorder (iRBD) most likely need to be forewarned, along with their spouses, about the increased risk of eventual Parkinsonism. Also, patients with iRBD provide an ideal research group for testing potential neuroprotective agents that can hopefully delay or even prevent the progression to Parkinsonism (Boeve, 2010). To date, only two postmortem brain studies have been conducted on patients clinically diagnosed with iRBD until their death, and in both cases brainstem Lewy body pathology was found, thus indicating these patients had subclinical Parkinsonism with the only clinical manifestation being RBD (Boeve, 2010). The strong link between RBD and Parkinsonism is neuroanatomically and neurophysiologically understandable, since there are strong reciprocal connections between the brainstem motor nuclei involved in REM sleep and the brainstem extrapyramidal nuclei affected by Parkinsonism (Boeve, 2010; Schenck & Mahowald, 2002). The clinical consequences of this set of pathological links spans across wakefulness and REM sleep. One glimpse of the fascinating research findings in this area consists of the normalization of behavior (in more than one dimension; for example, faster, stronger, smoother movements; normalized facial expressions; louder, more intelligible speech) during REM sleep compared to wakefulness in RBD in all 53 patients with PD in one study (Boeve, 2010). Thus, during REM sleep in RBD, the brainstem extrapyramidal system that is compromised by PD is somehow bypassed, allowing for normalized behavior—within the pathological state of RBD.

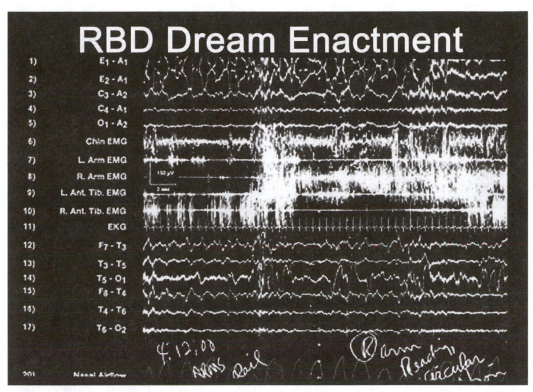

Polysomnographic correlates of nocturnal dream-enacting behavior. REM sleep contains dense, high-voltage REM activity (1–2) and an activated EEG (3–5, 12–17). The EKG (11) has a constant rate of 64 per minute, despite vigorous limb movements, which is typical of RBD. Chin (submental) EMG tone is augmented with phasic accentuations (6). Arms (7–8) and legs (9–10) show nonperiodic bursts of intense EMG twitching, which accompany gross behavior noted by the technician. This sequence culminates in a spontaneous awakening, when the man reports a dream containing behaviors that closely match his behavior in the sleep lab noted by the technologist: "4:12:00 Arms flail . . . R arm reaching in circular motion." (Carlos Schenck)

Brain-imaging studies in iRBD using PET and SPECT have found a decreased striatal dopaminergic innervation and a reduced presynaptic striatal dopamine transporter binding in RBD, similar to what has been found with early PD (Boeve, 2010). Additionally, there is a long and growing list of CNS impairments in iRBD that mimic those impairments found in PD, DLB, and related disorders (Boeve, 2010), including (but not limited to) profound impairment of olfactory function; color vision discrimination dysfunction; neuropsychological dysfunction (especially visuospatial construction and memory); whole brain perfusion abnormalities; decreased frontal cortex/pons blood flow; and reduced cardiac ^{123}I-MIBG uptake (indicating loss of cardiac sympathetic terminals). There are similarities between the topographic distribution of the EEG slowing in patients with iRBD and the pattern of perfusional and metabolic impairment observed in DLB and PD. Furthermore, EEG slowing documented during wakefulness in nondemented patients with PD is strongly related to the presence of RBD (Boeve, 2010). These findings lend support to a common etiopathogenesis between these conditions. The iRBD brain appears very similar to a Parkinsonian brain in its range of dysfunction, and so it is not surprising that iRBD is a strong risk factor for future Parkinsonism.

RBD has two recognized variants (AASM, 2005), including the parasomnia overlap disorder (RBD combined with sleepwalking and sleep terrors—disorders of arousal from NREM sleep), and status dissociatus (a parasomnia with obliteration of the boundaries across sleep stages and wakefulness).

The differential diagnosis of RBD includes several disorders in adults that can also present with dream-enacting behaviors (Mahowald & Schenck, 2010; Schenck & Mahowald, 2002), including: NREM parasomnias (sleepwalking, sleep terrors); nocturnal seizures (viz., temporal lobe, or complex partial seizures); and obstructive sleep apnea pseudo-RBD, in which recurrent sleep apnea events trigger immediate postarousal vigorous and violent dream-enacting behaviors. However, up to 35 percent of reported RBD patients (usually with neurodegenerative disorders) are not aware of dream-enacting behaviors, which is why dream enactment is not a required diagnostic criterion for RBD (AASM, 2005).

The therapy of RBD is especially gratifying, as an extensive world literature has reported successful control in >80 percent of treated patients, usually with the bedtime administration of the benzodiazepine clonazepam, which appears to suppress phasic motor overactivity and behavioral release (Mahowald & Schenck, 2010; Schenck & Mahowald, 2002). There is no evidence suggesting that long-term clonazepam therapy of RBD increases the risk of future Parkinsonism. Second-line or co-first-line therapy consists of melatonin, which appears to partially or substantially restore REM atonia (Mahowald & Schenck, 2010). However, a double-blind, placebo-controlled study of RBD therapy has not been conducted. There is a long list of alternative therapies that may need to be considered in treatment-resistant cases (Mahowald & Schenck, 2010). Maximizing the safety of the bedside environment should always be advised, such as moving the bed away from the window and removing hard objects from the bedside.

In conclusion, RBD represents a fascinating experiment of nature that is strategically situated at an important crossroads of the neurosciences and clinical (sleep) medicine (Schenck & Mahowald, 2002).

Carlos Schenck

References

American Academy of Sleep Medicine (AASM). (2005). *International classification of sleep disorders: Diagnostic and coding manual* (2nd ed.). Westchester, IL: American Academy of Sleep Medicine.

Boeve, B. F. (2010). REM sleep behavior disorder: Updated review of the core features, the RBD-neurodegenerative disease association, evolving concepts, controversies, and future directions. *Annals of the New York Academy of Science, 1184,* 15–54.

Mahowald, M. W., & Schenck, C. H. (2010). REM sleep parasomnias. In M. H. Kryger, T. Roth, & W. C. Dement (Eds.), *Principles and practice of sleep medicine* (5th ed., pp. 1083–1097). Philadelphia, PA: Elsevier Saunders.

Schenck, C. H., Lee, S. A., Cramer Bornemann, M. A., & Mahowald, M. W. (2009). Potentially lethal behaviors associated with rapid eye movement sleep behavior disorder (RBD): Review of the literature and forensic implications. *Journal of Forensic Sciences, 54*(6), 1475–1484.

Schenck, C. H., & Mahowald, M. W. (2002). REM sleep behavior disorder: Clinical, developmental, and neuroscience perspectives 16 years after its formal identification in SLEEP. *Sleep, 25,* 120–138.

REM Sleep Properties

Mammalian sleep comes in two general forms or phases called REM and non-REM sleep. Rapid eye movement (REM) sleep accounts for about 22 percent of total sleep time in humans. The proportion of REM to total sleep is high in marsupials but quite low in some great apes. For decades it was believed that REM amounts varied with altriciality status or the extent to which species could fend for themselves at birth. But now it appears that REM durations track more closely evolutionary increases in the size of the amygdala and related brain components. Whatever the causes of REM variation across mammalian species REMs in most or all of these species displays some very peculiar biological properties. The phasic aspects of REM in particular are peculiar. These characteristics include intermittent muscle twitching, autonomic nervous system (ANS) discharges, rapid eye movements, bursts of pontine–geniculo–occipital waves, and elaborate mental simulations of possible worlds (dreams). We know that virtually all mammals express REM, but of course it is difficult to tell if all these animals dream. When the normal REM-associated motor inhibition is abolished surgically or pharmacologically we see animals in the REM state apparently hallucinating and behaving as if they are acting out their dreams. Most of us have had the experience of witnessing our cats or dogs crying out and moving their paws during sleep such that it seems certain that they are dreaming. I personally think it is prudent to assume that all mammals experience some sort of mental simulations during REM.

Mammals (with the possible exception of humans) also exhibit a theta rhythm in the hippocampal formation during REM. This theta rhythm appears to be associated with memory consolidation processes. The ANS instabilities that occur as part of REM are more difficult to explain. They become more extreme as duration of REM episodes increases across the night. During the early morning hours when REM intensity is at its peak, the ANS instabilities may even contribute to cardiac arrhythmias and heart attacks. What could possibly be the function of these ANS storms? To my knowledge no one has proposed any functional account for ANS storms. Instead they are considered to be side effects of intense activation of core brain regions such as the amygdale. Another peculiar property of REM is that too much or too little REM is associated with deleterious effects. In short, there is an optimal amount of REM that a person must have to function optimally. Like non-REM (NREM) sleep, REM deprivation results in a rebound phenomenon confirming that a certain amount of REM is required and must be made up if lost. Interestingly, after total sleep deprivation, NREM sleep is made up before REM.

Thus, REM's phasic characteristics include bursts of rapid eye movements under the closed eyelids; myoclonic twitches of the facial and limb muscle groups; increased variability in heart rate, respiration, and blood pressure; ANS discharges; and of course dreaming. Besides these phasic properties REM is also associated with tonic phenomena that are equally puzzling. Tonic REM characteristics include a desynchronized electroencephalogram, penile erections, and atonia of the antigravity muscles. Other correlates of REM include effects on release of selected hormones—especially growth factors. No one to my knowledge has yet provided an adequate theory as to why REM is associated with penile erections or paralysis of the antigravity muscles. Surely the animal is more vulnerable to predation if it is asleep and paralyzed. Whatever function REM is performing must override the powerful need to protect against vulnerability to predation. Penile erections are also a mystery. Are they just side effects to the high activation levels in brainstem and limbic regions or is there some functional purpose involved? We simply do not know the answers to these questions. REM's properties constitute one of the great unsolved mysteries of biology. Why do they co-occur or occur in sequence roughly every 90 minutes during the sleep cycle? Why would Mother Nature want to paralyze you, activate your limbic system, deactivate your dorsal prefrontal cortex, put you through ANS intense storms, activate your sexual system, and then force you to watch these things we call dreams?

Patrick McNamara

See also: entries related to Sleep Physiology

REM Sleep Properties as Neurobiological Endophenotypes of Schizophrenia

For centuries, the similarities between dreaming and psychiatric mentation have been underlined by philosophers, writers, and neuropsychiatrists. Today, numerous neurobiological findings support the closeness of the brain states found during REM sleep and schizophrenia. (1) During REM sleep there is no alpha rhythm, and in schizophrenia there is a strong alpha rhythm deficit during waking. In a sound-proof relaxing room, the schizophrenic patient shows nearly no alpha rhythm, in contrast to nonschizophrenic individuals. There is thus a decrease in habituation processes related to a central inhibition deficit. (2) Gate control is disturbed during REM sleep, and the recovery cycle of the auditory N_{100} component of the evoked potential is disinhibited, as is seen in schizophrenia during waking. The same forebrain abnormality is thus present in both states. This cortical disinhibition during REM sleep had earlier been shown in cats through pyramidal neuron discharges and the recovery cycle of evoked potentials. (3) The gamma rhythm centered around 40 Hz (hertz) becomes uncoupled in the cortical areas, between the hippocampus and the cortex, and the intrahippocampal gamma coherence is decreased. This intracerebral disconnection is one of the main hypotheses to explain schizophrenia. (4) There is no resetting of the gamma rhythm by sensory stimulation during REM sleep. This is also a characteristic of sensory deafferentation, which favors (similar to the lowering of gate control) the appearance of schizophrenic hallucinations. (5) The dorsolateral prefrontal cortex is deactivated during REM sleep, as it is in schizophrenia, particularly when cognitive functions are impaired. (6) There is one situation in which the dorsolateral prefrontal cortex and the posterior cingulate cortex are together deactivated, as there are during REM sleep and in schizophrenia; this is when pianists are so involved in their playing that they lose contact with the environment. (7) The deactivation of the primary visual cortex during REM sleep is now open to discussion. However, the disconnection from sensory inputs, which favors hallucinations, is reinforced by thalamic presynaptic inhibition during the REM-sleep eye movements. (8) This functional deafferentation that occurs during REM sleep could also explain the increased pain threshold that is observed during acute schizophrenic episodes. (9) On emerging from dreaming there is a lack of differentiation between self- and hetero-sensory stimulation (tickle), as is the case in the schizophrenia waking state. (10) Noradrenergic and serotonergic neurons become silent during REM sleep, and there is a deficit of both of these neuromodulators in schizophrenia. (11) Prefrontal dopamine concentrations are lower during REM sleep than in the waking state, whereas glutamate is unchanged; both of these are also observed in schizophrenia. (12) In rats, the level of dopamine in the nucleus accumbens is maximal while glutamate is minimal, also as in schizophrenia. (13) Central pharmacological increases in dopamine and decreases in glutamate induce both psychotic symptoms and vivid dreaming. (14) Cortical acetylcholine concentrations in cats are lower during REM sleep than with active waking. Such decreases promote hallucinations and cognitive deficits, both of which are observed in schizophrenia.

Today, we can also anticipate an additional similarity between REM sleep and schizophrenia. It concerns the central level of inhibitory gamma-aminobutyric acid (GABA). In schizophrenia, it has already been established that there is a forebrain deficit in GABAergic function. Several arguments suggest that a similar deficit is present during REM sleep as well. (1) GABAergic interneurons, mainly situated in cortical layers 3 and 5, impinge the pyramidal neurons, which are highly activated during REM sleep. (2) The stimulation of dopaminergic neurons activates GABAergic interneurons and inhibits the majority of pyramidal cells, and, once again, dopamine release is lower during REM sleep than during waking (see earlier). (3) Dopamine promotes GABA release in the prefrontal cortex. (4) Amphetamines induce c-Fos-mediated activation of prefrontal cortex interneurons. All of these results strongly suggest that there should be a decrease in GABA levels during REM sleep. Moreover, it has been shown that, in addition to a direct inhibition of pyramidal cells through 5-HT$_{1A}$ receptor activation, serotonin activates cortical GABAergic interneurons through 5-HT$_2$ receptors, which in turn inhibit pyramidal neurons.

The silencing of serotonergic neurons during REM sleep should thus induce an accordingly lower level of GABAergic activity.

All of the previously mentioned neurobiological properties of REM sleep are similar to features of schizophrenia and represent probable endophenotypes of this psychiatric disease. The identification of the genetic basis of these neurobiological characteristics of REM sleep could thus provide crucial information that might help in the prevention or cure of schizophrenia symptoms, at first through the help of pharmacology (Gottesmann, 2005; Gottesmann and Gottesman, 2007).

Claude Gottesmann

See also: entries related to Sleep Physiology

References

Gottesmann, C. (2005). Dreaming and schizophrenia. A common neurobiological background. *Sleep and Biological Rhythms, 3,* 64–74.

Gottesmann, C., & Gottesman, I. (2007). The neurobiological characteristics of the rapid eye movement (REM) dreaming sleep stage are candidate endophenotypes of depression, schizophrenia, mental retardation and dementia. *Progress in Neurobiology, 81,* 237–250.

REM Sleep-Related Motor Paralysis

One of the most paradoxical features of REM sleep is that phasic eye movements and muscle twitches occur on a background of paralysis in the antigravity musculature, including the jaw, neck, and limbs. As far as we can tell this REM sleep-related paralysis occurs in all mammals who have REM sleep—though not all such animals have yet been studied. In any case REM sleep-related paralysis is ubiquitous in mammals. But why? Given that even a temporary paralysis can make an animal extremely vulnerable to predation why does it occur? It must be part of an extremely important system or else natural selection would have long eliminated paralysis from sleep. What benefit could possibly outweigh the risks associated with paralysis-related vulnerability to predation? No one yet knows. Presumably, the benefits must have something to do with REM sleep as paralysis is unique to REM sleep. The standard belief concerning the functional benefits of paralysis is that it prevents animals from acting out their dreams while otherwise asleep. But this account of paralysis seems odd unless one believes that dreams of animals (assuming that they do dream) somehow involve dangerous activities. Other theories of REM sleep paralysis suggest that it forces the animal to conserve energy, but calculations concerning energy savings due to immobility suggest that any savings that occur would be minimal and these savings would accrue in any case without the need for paralysis if the animal just stayed still but alert. Thus, REM sleep-related paralysis remains a mystery. Whatever its functions it is clear that it can be used in useful ways for clinical purposes. Absence of REM sleep-related muscle atonia is partially diagnostic of REM sleep behavior disorder, for example. Two major pathways seem to be involved in REM sleep-associated muscle atonia. The first includes the pontine cholinergic neurons that activate glutaminergic neurons in the medullary reticular formation. These in turn activate glycinergic neurons that inhibit motor neurons. In the second pathway, GABAergic neurons inhibit serotonin and noradrenergic neurons that normally maintain excitatory drive on motor neurons.

Patrick McNamara

See also: entries related to Sleep Physiology

Reverse Learning Theory

In a controversial article published in *Nature* in 1983, Francis Crick and Graeme Mitchison proposed that rather than dreams being a source of new knowledge, their function is to cleanse the brain of unwanted or dysfunctional knowledge. They call this process unlearning or reverse learning.

Their basic argument is that some patterns of thinking and behavior learned during the day are not only less beneficial than others, but may even be potentially harmful. The sleeping brain's job each night is to perform internal housekeeping, weeding out negative information and patterns of thought and discarding them, while saving only the good. This cleaning process is what we remember as dreams.

This view disturbed many dreamworkers, because it implies that, far from being a source of wisdom and knowledge, dreams are composed of useless information. Crick and Mitchison went so far as to suggest that keeping dream journals and interpreting dreams might inadvertently be counteracting the healthy functioning of REM sleep (REMS), by salvaging material the dreaming brain was trying to throw out. "We dream to forget," they wrote. "Attempting

to remember one's dreams should perhaps not be encouraged, because such remembering may help to retain patterns of thought which are better forgotten."

To support their theory, Crick and Mitchison cited two salient facts about dreaming: infants spend much more time in REMS than adults, and most dreams are forgotten. In their view, infants need to dream more because their brains are developing rapidly and there is consequently more housecleaning to do. Forgetting dreams would be a sign of a healthy brain; naturally we would forget most dreams, since that is precisely what the brain is trying to do. In addition, they argued that the relatively large brains of monotremes and the two species of dolphin that do not have REMS suggests that reverse learning during REMS may allow the brain in other mammals to be smaller.

Critics replied that there are other, perhaps better, ways to account for these facts. Recent research suggests that dreaming has something to do with memory consolidation—the opposite of forgetting. If dreaming is related to memory storage, or to creating neural networks, we would expect to see more active dreaming in infants. The fact that we do not remember most dreams only implies that whatever their function may be, it does not require conscious memory and processing.

Furthermore, the theory fails to address other well-documented aspects of dreaming. For example, dreams tend to be coherent narratives, which would be unnecessary if the brain was simply discarding information; and though the reverse learning theory makes a certain superficial sense if we consider only incoherent and bizarre dreams, it fails to explain dreams that *successfully solve* waking-life problems—not to mention big dreams that bring healing or spiritual guidance.

In light of these criticisms, and since Crick and Mitchison simply posited the existence of a special mechanism that operates during REMS but offered no specific account of what they believed happens in the brain during dreaming, the reverse learning theory is generally considered speculative and unconvincing.

Richard A. Russo

References

Crick, F., & Mitchison, G. (1983). The function of dream sleep. *Nature, 304,* 111–114.

Crick, F., & Mitchison, G. (1986). REM sleep and neural nets. *Journal of Mind and Behavior, 7,* 229–250.

Role of Subcortical Structures in Dreaming

The specific function of brain structures involved in the processing of dream experiences is still partly unknown, although the development and application of brain-imaging techniques has provided a new body of findings concerning the functioning of selective regional brain-activation pattern in REM sleep (REMS) and nonrapid eye movement sleep (NREMS), aiming to relate dream phenomenology to underlying brain activity. The metabolic decline during NREM sleep on central core structures (i.e., brain stem and thalamus), which are known to play a role in the generation of the <1 Hz slow oscillations, and the increased limbic and paralimbic activation during REM sleep may explain the observed phenomenological differences in dream recall (Maquet, 2000). This is theoretically relevant since memories may be instrumental in the formation of dreams and that their emotionally relevant characteristics may strengthen and consolidate these memory elements. Recent studies have outlined a fairly coherent picture of how two deep gray matter (GM) structures, the hippocampus and the amygdala, play an important role in the processing of mnestic and emotional sources of dream contents, respectively, and interact in dreaming both during REMS and NREMS. According to this view, the role of the hippocampus during sleep should mediate the partial reproduction of memories of events that occurred during wakefulness into dream contents. Intracranial recordings in epileptic patients provided evidence that rhinal–hippocampal connectivity mediates memory formation in the waking state, and a successful dream recall upon awakening from a period of REM sleep shows a close association with an enhancement in rhinal–hippocampal and intrahippocampal EEG connectivity during such period (Jacobs and Kahana, 2010). This suggests that the ability to memorize dreams may be related to a coordinated activity between cortex and hippocampus.

With regard to the amygdala, it is involved in both control of the encoding and retrieval of emotional memories and the physical expression of emotions during wakefulness.

Therefore, this structure may be also involved in the processing of emotionally significant memories during sleep, and the emotional load in dreams might be related to its high activation. Empirically, it has been observed that amygdalar activity is higher during REM and NREM sleep compared to wakefulness and a bilateral amygdalar activation in subjects capable to report a dream upon awakening from REMS (Maquet, 2000).Several recent findings converge to indicate that also *structural* characteristics of hippocampus and amygdala are associated with cognitive and emotional processing in waking tasks, suggesting that the individual morphoanatomy of these two structures, which is stable over time, may be related to similarly stable (i.e., *trait-like*) individual features of dream experience. This prediction has been confirmed by microstructural analyses of magnetic resonance (MR) brain scans and of diffusion tensor imaging analysis of MR images of the hippocampus and the amygdala. These images allow measuring the volume of GM and microstructural alterations of GM as expressed by reduced cellular barriers that restrict the free diffusion of water molecules in tissues. These measures of interindividual differences in the brain tissue of the hippocampus–amygdala complex are directly related to specific qualitative (mainly, emotions and bizarreness) features of dreaming (De Gennaro et al., 2011). Contrarily, the quantitative measures (the mean number of dreams recalled) did not show any significant relationship with these neuroanatomical measures.

Memory and emotional sources seem to be a key to dream formation and therefore further investigation of amygdalar processes in relation to the hippocampus might help to clarify the involvement of subcortical structures and functional networks underlying dream organization during sleep, to obtain a more comprehensive view of the neural correlates of dreaming in humans.

Cristina Marzano and
Luigi De Gennaro

See also: entries related to Sleep and the Brain

References

De Gennaro, L., Cipolli, C., Cherubini, A., Assogna, F., Cacciari, C., Marzano, C., . . . Spalletta, G. (2011). Amygdala and hippocampus volumetry and diffusivity in relation to dreaming. *Human Brain Mapping, 32*(9), 1458–1470.

Jacobs, J., & Kahana, M. J. Direct brain recordings fuel advances in cognitive electrophysiology. (2010). *Trends in Cognitive Sciences, 14,* 162–171.

Maquet, P. (2000). Functional neuroimaging of normal human sleep by positron emission tomography. *Journal of Sleep Research, 9,* 207–231.

S

Safety in Dream Groups

Dreams are a very personal experience and any work with or sharing of dreams incurs some emotional risk to the dreamers involved. The environment where dreams are shared needs to include elements of emotional, psychological, and spiritual safety, to help the dreamer feel safe in sharing his/her dreams. One of the leading associations for dream study, the International Association for the Study of Dreams (IASD), makes reference to this issue in its dreamwork ethics statement (International Association for the Study of Dreams, n.d.). The fact that the IASD developed an ethical statement in its early days is evidence of the need for such guidelines. Many dreamworkers and dream-group leaders include certain safety mechanisms so that the person sharing their dream will feel safe in the process.

One model from outside the dreamwork world that can be very helpful as background material is the model of the Quaker Clearness Committee, developed in the 1660s, by the early Quakers as a tool to help determine if marriage was a calling for them (Palmer, 1988). They were rediscovered in the 1960s among young Friends (Quakers) who used the clearness committee to help them discern leadings and other questions of spiritual import in individual lives. Clearness committees offer guidelines for emotional safety in any group process, including dream groups (see Palmer, n.d.).

One of the more popular methods of dreamwork involves group members using the phrase "If it were my dream. . ." in commenting on dreams presented to the group. By using this phrase the person commenting on the dream takes responsibility for their comments, understanding that their comments reflect their approaching the dream as if it happened to them. The group member is not trying to get inside the dreamer's life, but to find parallel emotions and associations in their own life, so that they can make the dream their own.

The clearness committee is a tool used to help with the process of discernment, an ancient practice of seeking the call of God in the midst of decisions in one's life. This is a religious use, but the practice can be equally used among nonreligious people who are seeking the best decisions for themselves. The clearness committee is based in part on the idea that the individual seeking discernment has inner wisdom that will guide them along in life, if they can simply focus on that inner wisdom and hear it clearly. The clearness committee is designed to help the individual hear clearly that voice of inner wisdom, or the voice of God, depending on the life or faith perspective of the person seeking guidance.

Palmer indicates the following guidelines for a clearness committee:

The function of the clearness committee is not to give advice or alter and "fix" people but to help people remove obstacles and discover the divine assistance that is within. (Palmer, n.d.)

This applies to dreamwork, following the IASD ethics guidelines, in that those working with the dream are not trying to force their interpretation on the dreamer. The dreamer is always given the freedom to accept or reject the interpretation offered, when it is given with the words "If it were my dream . . ."

The committee members speak, governed by a simple but difficult and demanding rule: Members must limit themselves to asking the focus person questions—honest, caring questions. This means no advice, no "why don't you . . .?" no "My uncle had the same problem and he . . ." no "I know a good book/diet/therapist/technique that would help you a lot." (Palmer, n.d.)

Ethical dreamwork may not literally follow this guideline, but the similarities of atmosphere setting are great. Ethical dreamwork believes that the dreamer will know the meaning of the dream and will know whether the advice given by someone else in the group will be meaningful or helpful or not.

The beauty of the clearness committee is its ability to guard the individual's own values and understandings of life. The dream group is not trying to heal the dreamer, or fix the dreamer's attitude toward life, but to help the dreamer better understand his or her own values and clarify those values as they are portrayed in the dream. The group may also help the dreamer understand new directions or options in their life, by allowing the dreamer to see more clearly the possible meanings of images and symbols that appear in their dream. The goal of the clearness committee, and of dreamwork that respects the integrity of the dreamer, is to allow the maximum freedom and individuality of the dreamer. This brings the clearness committee and the ethics statement of the IASD close together, providing maximum safety for dreamers, dreamworkers, and group members.

Geoff Nelson

References

International Association for the Study of Dreams. (n.d.). *About IASD*. Retrieved from http://www.asdreams.org/idxaboutus.htm

Palmer, P.J. (n.d.). *The clearness committee: A communal approach to discernment*. Center for Courage and Renewal. Retrieved from http://www.couragerenewal.org/parker/writings/clearness-committee

Palmer, P. (1988, July/August). The learness committee: A way of discernment. *Weavings*.

School of Metaphysics Approaches to Dream Incubation

Dream incubation is the process of consciously invoking a specific dream or asking a dream to provide an answer to a specific problem or question. Dream incubation is an ancient practice that became prominent in the classical period when dreams were incubated for healing.

In physical science, incubation refers to providing the proper conditions for growth and development; for example, incubating a virus in the body or incubating a chick in a special device that keeps the egg warm. As applied to the creative process, incubation may be considered as a time of subconscious reflection. An idea can incubate in the subconscious mind after putting aside the conscious mind research, letting go of preconceived ideas, and letting the brain and conscious mind rest so that the subconscious mind can crystallize or bring together in new ways the insight needed.

Incubating a dream involves a conscious decision to ask for a specific kind of dream (such as a flying dream, or a lucid dream) or asking for a solution to a problem (solving a brainteaser or more serious questions such as career choices or scientific formulas).

Scholars note that written records of incubating dreams can be traced back to the third millennium BCE. Dream incubation became well known in the temples of the Greek god Asclepius. In ancient Greece, dreams were considered to be divine transmissions; thus, dreams were incubated to receive healing from the god Asclepius. In some cases, the dreamer received healing in the dream and awakened cured. In other cases, Asclepius diagnosed and prescribed treatments in the dream that were administered to the dreamer upon awakening.

Dream incubation is reported as a custom in many societies and cultures, including in ancient Egypt, Assyria and Mesopotamia, China, and in American Indian tribes including the Ojibwa, and in the Islamic tradition. In modern times, incubation is used for guidance and problem solving. Modern dream researchers and psychologists report the effectiveness of dream incubation.

Both ancient and modern-day incubators report specific steps that are necessary for the incubation process. Metaphysical research on visualization describes how the conscious mind communicates with the subconscious mind to incubate a dream. The conscious mind produces a seed idea or intention, then shines mind light on it by writing, drawing, and preparing with sacred ritual. Relaxing the mind and body enables the dreamer to release the seed idea from the conscious mind so that it can develop, or incubate, in the subconscious mind.

The School of Metaphysics, a not-for-profit educational organization headquartered at Windyville, Missouri, teaches a practical science of mind/body/spirit integration. Students of metaphysics practice daily exercises to develop skills in concentration, meditation, and visualization. These practices are effective for dreamers who want to consciously incept an idea in their own subconscious mind.

Metaphysics defines mind as a whole system that includes the spirit and what some people describe as soul, or inner self. This is understood as separate from the brain and physical neuropathways. Incubation begins with the dreamer's conscious imaging. The dreamer formulates a clear idea or question that he or she wants answered from a dream, or an experience that he or she wants to have in the dream state. This idea or question must be pictured, or imaged. The School of Metaphysics describes the language of the mind as one of images or pictures.

To effectively plant this idea in the subconscious mind, the dreamer concentrates on the image through practices such as drawing and writing. Keeping a dream journal by the bed, and writing the next morning's date, demonstrates an expectation that the dreamer will receive the desired answer or dream experience. The proper mental conditions and the ideal physical conditions, along with a clear expectation of receiving the desired dream answer, are all requirements for successful dream incubation.

These steps combine ancient knowledge with modern practice:

1. *Prepare for sleep mindfully.* It is also helpful to remove any distractions from the sleeping place and to withdraw the attention from any kind of stimulation such as television or loud music or literature with graphic and strong emotional content. Other suggestions are to refrain from eating after dark and to eliminate stimulants such as caffeine or mood-altering drugs or alcohol.

2. *Prepare the sleeping place.* The sacred temples of Asclepius were used only for dream incubation. Most modern dreamers do not have the luxury of a place used only for that purpose, but some construct a special tent or wear special pajamas, or place objects by the bedside that are infused with special meaning. Some dreamers choose a particular dreaming stone to hold in their hand as they fall asleep, to concentrate on the desired dream.

3. *Clear the mind.* A concentration exercise is beneficial, such as gazing at the tip of a finger or a candle flame. Writing down or speaking out loud about any unfinished business or worries can also help clear the mind to prepare for incubating the dream. It is suggested to review the day backward, drawing out of the memory images such as snapshots of the day's events, starting with the most recent and going backward to the morning. This is like putting files away in their proper places so that the desk is clear for the work at hand.

4. *Set a clear intention for the dream incubation.* Formulate this as a specific desire. State the intention in a well-defined sentence. Form a *clear mental image* of the desired dream or outcome.

It is especially helpful to ask an *open-ended question* rather than expecting the subconscious mind to make a decision. The School of Metaphysics understands the conscious mind to hold the decision-making faculty. The subconscious mind can provide understanding and insight. So, for example, if a dreamer wants to incubate a question about moving to a new location, it is better to ask a question like, "What opportunity exists for me in California?" or "What understanding can I gain from moving?" rather than, "Should I move to California?"

5. Do a *stream of consciousness writing* exercise, writing nonstop for 10 to 20 minutes about the desired topic, to clear the brain of any preconceived ideas. This writing often develops insight, allowing the dreamer to draw forth perceptions that he or she may not have consciously recognized.

6. *Draw a picture* of the dream desire or dream-incubation topic. The purpose of writing and drawing about the topic is to engage both left and right brain, or conscious and subconscious minds.

7. *Relax the body.* Deep, rhythmic breathing with muscle relaxation is helpful. Relaxing the body aids the dreamer to remove the attention from the body to go into a deep sleep. It is helpful to lie on one's back, inhale deeply through the nose, hold the breath, and then exhale completely through the mouth. Gently tensing the muscles while holding the breath, and then relaxing the muscles on exhalation helps to remove bodily tension. Some practitioners progressively tense and relax the muscles of each major muscle group, starting with the feet and going up the body to the top of the head. This provides a complete and deep relaxation.

8. *Write down the question or desire for the dream incubation* in a dream notebook. Place the notebook with a pen or pencil by the side of the bed. Date the notebook for the following morning (if the sleep period is at night) or for that day (if the dreamer is taking a daytime nap).

9. Silently or out loud, repeat the dream question over and over, like a *chant* or mantra. This is most effective when done in the drowsy state just prior to falling asleep.

10. *Expect to receive a dream* with the answer to the incubated question, or the kind of dream desired.

11. *Record the dream* in a dream notebook.

12. *Heed the message* by acting on the answer in waking life.

The final step of dream incubation is the one most open to debate among modern dream researchers. In ancient times, dream interpretation was a separate function from dream incubation. It was believed that the incubated dream was literal, either with an explicit message or a direct healing. Many modern dream researchers use methods of interpretation to interpret dreams symbolically.

The School of Metaphysics teaches a method of interpreting dreams symbolically with the Universal Language of Mind™. When a dreamer incubates a dream, the dream answer is interpreted symbolically as a message providing guidance from the inner self for the dreamer's soul progression. Additionally, in some cases, the incubation response may be a literal answer. For example, dreamers have received book titles in words, have seen images of projects they needed to do, or seen images of places they subsequently visited. The metaphysical viewpoint is that dreams may be interpreted multidimensionally; in other words, both with a symbolic message and with literal instruction.

Whether they are revealed in direct or symbolic messages, dreams may give us answers to many of life's mysteries. Healing, guidance, prophecy, creative solutions, entrepreneurial discoveries, scientific innovations, and artistic inspiration are just some of the uses of dream incubation.

Laurel Clark

References

Barrett, D. (2001). *The committee of sleep.* New York: Crown Publishing Group.

Clark, L. (2007). *The law of attraction and other secrets of visualization.* Windyville, MO: SOM Publishing.

Clark, L. (2009, June). *The law of attraction: The art and science of dream incubation.* Presented at International Association for the Study of Dreams Annual Conference, Chicago, IL.

Dreamschool.org. (n.d.). Retrieved from www.som.org

Garfield, P. (1974). *Creative dreaming.* New York: Simon and Schuster.

Meier, C. A. (1989). *Healing dream and ritual: Ancient incubation and modern psychotherapy.* Basel, Switzerland: Daimon Verlag. (Originally published in German, 1949, and translated into English under the title *Ancient incubation and modern psychotherapy,* 1967.)

Reed, H. (1976). Dream incubation: A reconstruction of a ritual in contemporary form. *Journal of Humanistic Psychology, 16*(4), 53–69.

Seasonal Affective Disorder in Sleep

Seasonality is a term that refers to changes in mood and depression that vary with changes of the seasons. These may vary in terms of type and severity. Seasonal affective disorder (SAD) is a more specific term used to describe affective disorders with a clear history of seasonal fluctuations. According to the *Diagnostic and Statistical Manual of Mental Disorders* (text revision; DSM-IV-TR) (American Psychiatric Association [APA], 2000), a seasonal pattern specifier can be applied to a pattern of major depressive episodes in bipolar disorders (Bipolar I or Bipolar II) or in recurrent major depressions. More specifically, in the case of winter depressions, a seasonal pattern with onset in the fall and winter and either a full remission or switch to mania/ hypomania in the spring for the previous two years. In the case of seasonal depressions, seasonal episodes must outnumber nonseasonal episodes and the SAD must be independent of other stressors that may contribute to depression. Others may also specify that the diagnosis requires the absence of other major psychiatric diagnoses (Rosenthal et al., 1984). Some may experience seasonal depressive symptoms that do not meet clear criteria for the definition of SAD. These subsyndromal forms (S-SAD) affect more people but are less disruptive of mood, activity, or productivity. Light therapy, which is effective in reversing SAD symptoms, has been reported to be beneficial as well in treating S-SAD (Lam & Levitt, 1999).

Care must also be taken to distinguish these patients from those with a bipolar disorder. As evidence from multiple studies has accumulated, however, the reported proportion of SAD sufferers with diagnosed bipolar disorders is between 11 and 50 percent (Sohn & Lam, 2004). Most SAD sufferers alternate between a winter symptom cluster and normal good mood and energy. SAD symptoms include a cluster of complaints and symptoms including decreased activity, sadness, anxiety, social withdrawal, increased appetite (especially carbohydrates), weight gain, decreased libido, and hypersomnia. Depressed SAD sufferers sometimes report instead the more typical vegetative symptoms of decreased appetite, weight loss, and insomnia. Other symptoms include cold intolerance and intensified premenstrual mood difficulties in women. A lack of motivation and energy with a desire to stay indoors are common symptoms. Sleep may be longer and daytime sleepiness greater, but sleep itself is likely to be of poorer quality (Rosenthal et al., 1984). These patients may also become symptomatic in response to prolonged dark or cloudy weather in any season (Rosenthal et al., 1984).

Another way to approach this issue is to examine the impact of depression on sleep physiology. In particular, one may see a shift in the timing of the sleep period with other characteristic changes in both REM and NREM sleep. In REM, it is not uncommon to encounter a shortening of the onset latency and a shifting of the distribution so that earlier cycles have REM periods of longer duration in contrast to the more typical shift toward later times in the sleep period (Benca, Obermeyer, Thisted & Gillin, 1992). N3 or slow-wave sleep, on the other hand, may demonstrate a reduction in total duration and a delay in onset (Kupfer, Reynolds, Ulrich, & Grochocinski, 1986). Such findings also seem to suggest a disruption in normal circadian physiology and a clue to the relationship between SAD and sleep physiology.

Initially, the photoperiod hypothesis was used to understand the underling pathophysiology of SAD (Rosenthal et al., 1984). Emphasis was placed on photoperiod (number of hours between sunrise and sunset), hours of daily sunshine, and mean daily temperature. Light therapy was utilized to extend the total amount of daylight exposure. Animal models of hibernation emphasized the total length of the dark period as the major factor in altering behavior (Arendt, 1998). The emphasis on photoperiod duration was attractive and predictive. There appeared to be a strong correlation between photoperiod and risk of SAD (Young, Meaden, Fogg, Cherin, & Eastman, 1997).

Alternative considerations include a phase-shift hypothesis based on a presumed mismatch between the sleep–wake cycle and other circadian rhythms and a melatonin-based hypothesis based on presumed differences in melatonin levels. Melatonin is of interest because of the relation between bright-light exposure in darkness and melatonin production (Lockley, Brainard & Czeisler, 2003). Furthermore, administrations of both exogenous melatonin and bright-light exposure have been used in the management of circadian-rhythm sleep–wake disorders (Lewy, Lefler, Emens, & Bauer, 2006).

Another attractive feature of the phase-shift model is that SAD patients have a greater tendency to be phase delayed and early-morning light exposure may be more effective than evening-light exposure (Lewy et al., 1998; Terman & Terman, 2005). It may be that some of the variability in these studies can be attributed to the fact that a subset of SAD patients may be advanced. It may be that response to antidepressant treatment may correlate with the degree of melatonin phase shift and that this shift may be a delay in some or an advance in others (Doghramji, Gaddy, Stewart, Rosenthal, & Brainard, 1990). On the other hand, there are still some studies that suggest that phase shift may not be critical in SAD. Similar issues are present when one looks at the impact of exogenous melatonin. Although the benefits of melatonin in SAD have not been consistent, there may be some benefit in subjects who were most phase delayed (Lewy et al., 2003).

The dual-vulnerability hypothesis is another alternative that may account for some of this variability. In brief, this approach considers the two factors: seasonality and depression. It is the seasonality factor that is most responsive to the phase-shift effect. As a consequence, S-SAD, as compared to SAD subjects, will be much more responsive to light treatment (Lam, Tam, Yatham, Shiah, & Zis, 2001; Young, Watel, Lahmeyer, & Eastman, 1991).

Sanford Auerbach

See also: Chronotype

References

American Psychiatric Association (APA). 2000. *Diagnostic and statistical manual of mental disorders* (text rev., 4th ed.). Washington, DC: Author.

Arendt, J. (1998). Melatonin and the pineal gland: Influence on mammalian seasonal and circadian physiology. *Reviews of Reproduction, 3*(1), 13–22.

Benca, R. M., Obermeyer, W. H., Thisted, R. A., & Gillin, J. C. (1992). Sleep and psychiatric disorders: A meta-analysis. *Archives of General Psychiatry, 49*(8), 651–668.

Doghramji, K., Gaddy, J. R., Stewart, K. T., Rosenthal, N. E., & Brainard, G. C. (1990). 2-versus 4-hour evening phototherapy of seasonal affective disorder. *Journal of Nervous and Mental Disease, 178*(4), 257–260.

Kupfer, D. J., Reynolds, C. F., III, Ulrich, R. F., & Grochocinski, V. J. (1986). Comparison of automated REM and slow-wave sleep analysis in young and middle-aged depressed subjects. *Biological Psychiatry, 21*(2), 189–200.

Lam, R. W., & Levitt, A. J. (Eds.). (1999). *Canadian consensus guidelines for the treatment of seasonal affective disorder.* Vancouver, BC, Canada: Clinical and Academic Publishing.

Lam, R. W., Tam, E. M., Yatham, L. N., Shiah, I. S., & Zis, A. P. (2001). Seasonal depression: The dual vulnerability hypothesis revisited. *Journal of Affective Disorders, 63*(1–3), 123–132.

Lewy, A. J., Bauer, V. K., Cutler, N. L., Sack, R. L., Ahmed, S., Thomas, K. H., . . . Jackson, J. M. (1998). Morning vs evening light treatment of patients with winter depression. *Archives of General Psychiatry, 55*(10), 890–896.

Lewy, A. J., Lefler, B. J., Emens, J. S., & Bauer, V. K. (2006). The circadian basis of winter depression. *Proceedings of the National Academy of Sciences of the United States of America, 103*(19), 7414–7419.

Lewy, A. J., Lefler, B. J., Hasler, B. P., Bauer, V. K., Bernert, R. A., & Emens, J. S. (2003). Plasma DLMO10 zeitgeber time 14: The therapeutic window for phase-delayed winter depressives treated with melatonin. *Chronobiology International, 20*(6), 1215–1217.

Lockley, S. W., Brainard, G. C., & Czeisler, C. A. (2003). High sensitivity of the human circadian melatonin rhythm to resetting by short wavelength light. *Journal of Clinical Endocrinology and Metabolism, 88*(9), 4502–4505.

Rosenthal, N. E., Sack, D. A., Gillin, J. C., Lewy, A. J., Goodwin, F. K., Davenport, Y., . . . Wehr, T. A. (1984). Seasonal affective disorder: A description of the syndrome and preliminary findings with light therapy. *Archives of General Psychiatry, 41*(1), 72–80.

Sohn, C. H., & Lam, R. W. (2004). Treatment of seasonal affective disorder: Unipolar versus bipolar differences. *Current Psychiatry Reports, 6*(6), 478–485.

Terman, M., & Terman, J. S. (2005). Light therapy for seasonal and nonseasonal depression: Efficacy, protocol, safety, and side effects. *CNS Spectrums, 10*(8), 647–663.

Young, M. A., Meaden, P. M., Fogg, L. F., Cherin, E. A., & Eastman, C. I. (1997). Which environmental variables are related to the onset of seasonal affective disorder? *Journal of Abnormal Psychology, 106*(4), 554–562.

Young, M. A., Watel, L. G., Lahmeyer, H. W., & Eastman, C. I. (1991). The temporal onset of individual symptoms in winter depression: Differentiating underlying mechanisms. *Journal of Affective Disorders, 22*(4), 191–197.

Self-Assessment Tools of Circadian Typology in Children, Adolescents, and Adults

Circadian typology is one of the most robust individual differences in circadian rhythms, which is described by a continuum between two extremes (Natale & Cicogna, 2002, p. 809): morning types (occasionally labeled larks) go to bed and awake early; evening types (at times labeled owls) have later bedtime and wake-up time and are tired when waking up. Intermediate types or neither type represent the larger part of the population (around 60% to 70%) and demonstrate patterns of behavior being a part of an intermediate area between the two extreme types of this continuum. Chronotypes mainly differ in their circadian phase, which is delayed more often in evening than in morning types.

The importance of a valid and reliable assessment of circadian preference has been recently remarked by the observed relationships between circadian typology on one hand and some psychiatric pathologies, such as bipolar disorder, depression, drug addiction, and seasonal depression, on the other. Several self-assessment tools have been proposed to determine circadian preference in adult populations over the years. The first one was the Morningness-Eveningness Questionnaire (MEQ) (Horne & Östberg, 1976, p. 97). The MEQ is a 19-item mixed-format scale in which the subject is requested to indicate his/her own life rhythms and habits as far as going to sleep and waking up are concerned, and to supply further useful information to find the most suitable rhythm. Questions are multiple choice or open, where the subjects can fill out their own preferred time for going to bed and getting up, without being forced to choose from a series of set times. They are laid out in an ordinal scale, with each answer being assigned a value. The MEQ scores range between 16 and 86 and the following cutoff criteria have been put forward: 16 to 30, extremely evening type; 31 to 41, moderately evening type; 42 to 58, neither or intermediate type; 59 to 69, moderately morning type; 70 to 86, extremely morning type.

Although many instruments have been developed between 1979 and 2003, the MEQ represents the most used method in chronopsychological research, even if there is still no unanimous agreement on which questionnaire is the best suited to assess circadian preference. However, the instruments put forward after the MEQ did not lead to a significant improvement. Indeed the Cronbach's alphas of those tools are not significantly higher than those of the MEQ; some of them do not collect information about the preferred sleep–wake cycle timing and finally several do not have cutoff criteria to assign each subject to the appropriate category of circadian typology.

Regarding the children–adolescents populations, the MEQ has been adapted to those populations, leading to the Morningness-Eveningness Questionnaire for Children and Adolescents (MEQ-CA) (Ishihara, Honma, & Miyake, 1990, p. 1353). The MEQ-CA differs from MEQ quite simply in item formulation, with items specifically referring to scholastic rather than working activities. The number of items does not change and so the total score range is the same of the MEQ for adults, as well as the cutoff criteria. Thus contrary to other self-assessment tools for children–adolescents that have a different number of items from the versions for adults, the MEQ-CA is a suitable tool for cross-sectional and longitudinal studies.

This last consideration adds more value to the MEQ as the most appropriate tool to assess circadian preference both in children–adolescents and adults.

Lorenzo Tonetti

See also: Chronotype

References

Horne, J. A., & Östberg, O. (1976). A self-assessment questionnaire to determine morningness–eveningness in human circadian rhythms. *International Journal of Chronobiology, 4,* 97–110.

Ishihara, K., Honma, Y., & Miyake, S. (1990). Investigation of the children's version of the morningness-eveningness questionnaire with primary and junior high school pupils in Japan. *Perceptual and Motor Skills, 71,* 1353–1354.

Natale, V., & Cicogna, P. (2002). Morningness-eveningness dimension: Is it really a continuum? *Personality and Individual Differences, 32,* 809–816.

Self-Consciousness and Dreaming

The position that dreams are conscious, but not self-conscious, is rooted in Gottfried Leibniz's challenge to the Cartesian definition of mind as an immaterial *subject* that is simultaneously *conscious of* internal objects and *conscious of* itself. Laying the foundations for modern psychology, Leibniz reconceived the mind as a bundle of sensations that is capable of being introspected, is paralleled by brain events, and is sometimes, but not always, accompanied by self-consciousness. Turning Leibniz's conceptualization into psychological science, the father of experimental psychology Gustav Fechner demonstrated the existence of subliminal sensations: conscious sensations below the absolute threshold, or *limen,* for self-consciousness. And subsequently, clarifying the conceptual foundations of this new science, the founder of American psychology William James distinguished self-consciousness—the sense of self as *subject of consciousness*—from self-concept—the sense of self as *object of consciousness*—and

from self-determination—the sense of self as *agent behind conscious thought and action*. In applying these scientific concepts, the father of clinical psychology Sigmund Freund interpreted both the dream and the psychotic hallucination as conscious sensations that emerge during the attenuation of self-consciousness. And more recently, focusing on the theoretical and empirical differences between the dream image and the wakeful image, Rechtschaffen (1978) and Kunzendorf (1987–1988, 2000) have noted that—whereas wakefully imaged sensations are tacitly accompanied by self-consciousness *that one is imaging sensations (rather than perceiving them)* and, generically, by self-consciousness *that one is having sensations*—dreamed sensations are accompanied by neither.

In this theoretical context, Kahan and LaBerge (1994) have called attention to lucid dreams and have argued that their existence undermines the historic conceptualization of dreams as accompanied neither by self-consciousness *that one is having them* nor by self-consciousness *that one is imaging them*. In response, Kunzendorf et al. (2006–2007) have countered that the lucid dream is, essentially, a pseudohallucination: a hallucinatory image that is inferred to be imaginary on account of its implausible contents, but that is still hallucinatory because it is not being monitored as centrally innervated by the brain and is not being paralleled by any self-consciousness *that one is imaging it*. Consistent with this counterargument, over one third of the lucid dreamers studied by Kunzendorf et al. (2006–2007) confirmed that, during at least one lucid dream, "I have heard a real noise (an alarm clock, e.g.)

and have believed the noise to be part of my lucid dream, or have believed it to be some other noise within my lucid dream, without any immediate self-awareness that I was actually perceiving the noise" (p. 314). Accordingly, lucid dreamers are not self-consciously monitoring the actual source of their sensations, as they do during wakefulness; rather, they are inferring, correctly, that their dreamed sensations are imaginary and, incorrectly, that their perceived sensations are imaginary.

The fact that lucid dreaming is unaccompanied by self-consciousness, however, does not imply that it is unaccompanied by the sense of self as *agent*. The 93 lucid dreamers studied by Kunzendorf et al. (2006–2007, p. 200) confirmed that, in over one quarter of their lucid dreams, "other people simply do whatever I want them to do" (p. 319). Given such concordance between their dreams' contents and their wishes, then, these lucid dreamers also confirmed that, during at least one lucid dream, they experienced the sense of *self as agent* and were "able to control what was happening in the dream" (p. 316). Thus, the self-determinative sense of self as *agent* not only is conceptually differentiable from the self-conscious sense of self as *subject,* in accordance with the insights of William James, but also is psychologically independent of self-conscious in the case of lucid dreaming.

Robert G. Kunzendorf

References

Kahan, T.L., & LaBerge, S. (1994). Lucid dreaming as metacognition: Implications for cognitive science. *Consciousness and Cognition, 3*, 246–264.

Kunzendorf, R.G. (1987–1988). Self-consciousness as the monitoring of cognitive states: A theoretical perspective. *Imagination, Cognition, and Personality, 7*, 3–22.

Kunzendorf, R.G. (2000). Individual differences in self-conscious source monitoring: Theoretical, experimental, and clinical considerations. In R.G. Kunzendorf & B. Wallace (Eds.), *Individual differences in conscious experience* (pp. 375–390). Amsterdam: John Benjamins.

Kunzendorf, R.G., Treantafel, N., Taing, B., Flete, A., Savoie, S., Agersea, S., & Williams, R. (2006–2007). The sense of self in lucid dreams: "Self as subject" vs. "self as agent" vs. "self as Object." *Imagination, Cognition, and Personality, 26*, 303–323.

Peters, R.S. (Ed.). (1965). *Brett's history of psychology.* Cambridge, MA: MIT Press.

Rechtschaffen, A. (1978). The single-mindedness and isolation of creams. *Sleep, 1,* 97–109.

Self in Dreams, The

Most contemporary philosophers and empirical researchers working on dreams agree that dreams are conscious experiences, because they are phenomenal states: There is *something it is like* to dream. This has important consequences for epistemology and for philosophy of mind. For instance, the potential of dreams to replicate waking experience leads to Descartes's famous exposition of dream skepticism in the *Meditations,* where he realizes that he can never be sure that he is awake rather than dreaming. It also suggests that the same type of consciousness as experienced in wakefulness can arise under drastically different neurofunctional conditions: most dreams occur during REM sleep, during which sensory input and motor output are blocked. Dreams seem to demonstrate that the content of phenomenal consciousness, whether we are dreaming or waking, is a virtual reality created by the brain.

A more fine-grained analysis of self-experience in dreams, however, reveals systematic differences between dreaming and wakefulness. A phenomenal self is present in a majority of dreams, but typically lacks important phenomenal and functional properties standardly associated with waking self-consciousness (Metzinger, 2003, 2009; Windt & Metzinger, 2007). Dreamers typically lack control over volition and attention and cannot remember important facts about their waking lives. They rarely think about events occurring in the dream, and when they do, their reasoning tends to be confabulatory. Because of their inability to think about their current relation to the dreamworld, they entertain delusional beliefs about the ongoing dream, confusing it with reality, and lack insight into their current cognitive deficits. Dreamers are not *rational* subjects, and they cannot be considered as *behavioral or cognitive agents* in the sense of deliberately controlling their actions or even their own thought processes. This suggests that phenomenologically, dreams can only be considered as subjective experiences in a weaker sense than waking experiences. Lucid dreams are an important counterexample: realizing that one is dreaming requires a stable first-person perspective, enabling one to form a conscious model of one's relation to the currently experienced dreamworld. This is why lucid dreamers cannot only think about the dreamlike nature of their ongoing dream, but also control both

their own behavior and the dream itself. In terms of being cognitive and even rational subjects and in terms of agency, lucid dreamers more closely resemble waking self-experience than nonlucid ones.

Another point that makes dreams interesting for self-consciousness has to do with the bodily self. REM-sleep dreams arise in a state of near-complete functional disembodiment, because the sleeping body is both paralyzed and deafferented during REM sleep. An interesting question is whether dreams nonetheless give rise to the experience of having a body. Movement sensations are frequent in the dream state, but touch, pain, olfactory, and thermal sensations are extremely rare (Hobson, Pace-Schott, & Stickgold, 2000). The general conclusion is that the dream self is not only *functionally* disembodied with relation to the physical body, but also *phenomenally* embodied only in a weak sense. Dreams are constituted by immersive spatiotemporal hallucinations: the experience of self-location in a spatiotemporal reference frame is both necessary and sufficient for dreaming, but dreams do not necessarily involve the experience of having a bodily self (Windt, 2010).

For any general theory of consciousness, dreams are relevant, because they provide a global contrast condition for standard waking consciousness. Dreams show that the subjective experience of being a self can be dissociated from the experience of being a cognitive or even a bodily self, and that the first-person perspective comes in different strengths. Alongside other altered states, such as out-of-body experiences, they can help us understand the minimal conditions for phenomenal selfhood (Blanke & Metzinger, 2009).

Jennifer M. Windt and
Thomas Metzinger

References

Blanke, O., & Metzinger, T. (2009). Full-body illusions and minimal phenomenal selfhood. *Trends in Cognitive Sciences, 13*(1), 7–13.

Hobson, J. A., Pace-Schott, E. F., & Stickgold, R. (2000). Dreaming and the brain: Toward a cognitive neuroscience of conscious states. *Behavioral and Brain Sciences, 23,* 793–842.

Metzinger, T. (2003). *Being no one: The self-model theory of subjectivity*. Cambridge, MA: MIT Press.

Metzinger, T. (2009). *The ego tunnel: The science of the mind and the myth of the self.* New York: Basic Books.

Windt, J. M. (2010). The immersive spatiotemporal hallucination model of dreaming. *Phenomenology and the Cognitive Sciences, 9,* 295–316.

Windt, J. M., & Metzinger, T. (2007). The philosophy of dreaming and self-consciousness: What happens to the experiential subject during the dream state? In D. Barrett & P. McNamara (Eds.), *The new science of dreaming* (Vol. 3, pp. 193–247). Westport, CT: Praeger Perspectives/Greenwood Press.

Self-Organization from Chaos in Dreams

Dreams have seemingly conflicting attributes; on the one hand they often seem chaotic while at the same time they display an order and complete narrative structure. They seem chaotic in that the dream often confounds time, place, and age. People in dreams may have an age that differs from their actual age, where they may be younger or older in the dream. Places in dreams may feel the same but look very different than in the physical space of wake life. Dreams display a chaotic behavior when scenes seem to change abruptly and shifts in plot line come without warning. On the other hand the dream does not consist of random words or images that have no relation to each other. On the contrary, the dream is a well-ordered story with precise images that are an integral part of the story, and which makes sense to the dreamer while dreaming. The dreamer, not recognizing anything particularly bizarre, often reacts to the actions of people and events in the dream, as he would when awake. The chaotic nature of dreams goes undetected by the dreamer within the dream but becomes obvious upon awakening.

Can one reconcile the chaotic nature of the dream with its nonrandom cognitive and emotional story-like structure? How could the evident order of dreams arise from the chaos of rapid and nonrapid eye movement sleep neurophysiology? An answer to this question has been suggested by Hobson, Pace-Schott, and Stickgold (2000): the brain is doing the best job it can to make sense of random neuronal firing, or as Payne (2010) puts it, the brain attempts to impose meaning on fragmented memory traces. There is an underlying process to this. This underlying process is self-organization (Nicolis & Prigogine, 1977). Self-organization is a process by which order emerges from chaos. Or, more generally, a process by which a more (or differently) organized structure emerges from one that is less (or differently) structured. Phrases, sentences, and paragraphs emerge as the cognitive correlates of an interactive neural dialogue within selective cortical and subcortical regions by a process of self-organization. When awake, our attentive processes superimpose a top–down organization on our thoughts. The effect of this top–down control is to weed out illogical, irrelevant, and incomplete thoughts and images that may emerge. When awake, self-organization takes place in a balanced cholinergic and aminergic neuromodulatory environment, the aminergic bathing of the cortex and other forebrain areas confers the ability to attend to a task, to think about it, and to direct appropriate action (Flicker, McCarley, & Hobson, 1981; Servan-Schreiber, Printz, & Cohen, 1990), whereas when dreaming the serotonin and norepinephrine parts of the aminergic system shut down and cortisol levels peak during REM periods (Payne, 2010). Since these neuromodulators affect cognitive function, mood, the ability to retrieve memories, and the ability to pay attention, self-organizing processes will be different in dreaming than in waking. The aminergically demodulated dreaming brain is only minimally capable of attending to a task or to direct action. The dream narrative thus unfolds with essentially no direct overt action possible by the dreamer as he might take when awake (or, to some extent when lucid). Thoughts, words, images, and feelings that emerge by means of self-organizing processes in the dreaming brain will still share similarities with those in the wake brain. This is because many of the same regions of the brain are active in both waking and in dreaming; but different because of the changed neuromodulatory environment of the dreaming brain and the deactivation of the dorsal lateral prefrontal cortex and the precuneus (Braun et al., 1997; Maquet et al., 1996), and because the ability to make reality checks is absent while dreaming. Any unusual scene and plot changes are recognized as such only upon awakening. Dreams provide entirely new creations woven together by self-organizing processes in which elements of a story interact and affect what comes next. (Kahn & Hobson, 1993; Kahn, Krippner, & Combs, 2000). The dream, in a sense, has a mind of its own.

David Kahn

See also: entries related to Dream Theories

References

Braun, A. R., Balkin, T. J., Wesensten, N. J., Carson, R. E., Varga, M., Baldwin, P., . . . Herscovitch, P. (1997). Regional cerebral blood flow throughout the sleep–wake cycle. *Brain, 120,* 1173–1197.

Flicker, C., McCarley, R. W., & Hobson, J. A. (1981). Aminergic neurons: State control and plasticity in three model systems. *Cellular and Molecular Neurobiology, 1,* 123–166.

Hobson, J. A. (1988). *The dreaming brain.* New York: Basic Books.

Hobson, J. A., Pace-Schott, E. F., & Stickgold, R. (2000). Dreaming and the brain: Toward a cognitive neuroscience of conscious states. *Behavioral and Brain Sciences, 23*(6), 793–842.

Kahn, D., & Hobson, J. A. (1993). Self-organization theory of dreaming. *Dreaming, 3,* 151–178.

Kahn, D., Krippner, S., & Combs, A. (2000). Dreaming and the self-organizing brain. *Journal of Consciousness Studies, 7,* 4–11.

Maquet, P., Peteres, J. M., Aerts, J., Delfiore, G., Degueldre, C., Luxen, A., & Franck, G. (1996). Functional neuroanatomy of human rapid-eye-movement sleep and dreaming. *Nature, 383,* 163.

Nicolis, G., & Prigogine, I. (1977). *Self-organization in non-equilibrium systems.* New York: John Wiley.

Payne, J. D. (2010). Memory consolidation, the diurnal rhythm of coritsol, and the nature of dreams: A new hypothesis. *International Review of Neurobiology, 92,* 103–129.

Servan-Schreiber, D., Printz, H., & Cohen, J. D. (1990). A network model of catcholamine effects gain, signal-to-noise ratio, and behavior. *Science, 249,* 892–895.

Selfscape Dreams

Hollan uses the term selfscape dreams (2003, 2004, 2005, 2009) to refer to emotionally and imaginally vivid, easily remembered dreams that reflect back to the dreamer how his or her current organization of self relates various parts of itself to itself, its body, and to other people and objects in the world. These are the type of dreams that, anywhere in the world, awaken people in the middle of the night and the emotional residues of which carry over into the waking life of the following days, weeks, or years. Cultures that focus attention on dreams, categorize them, and label them, especially those that identify some types of dreams as prophetic, often recognize that these vivid dreams can be related to the fate and well-being of the dreamer.

Selfscape dreams provide the mind with an updated map of the self's contours and affective resonances: its relative vitality or decrepitude, its relative wholeness or division, its relative closeness to or estrangement from others, and its perturbation by conscious and unconscious streams of emotions. Such dreams will be found everywhere in the world because they serve a basic self-orienting function. Their content and imagery, on the other hand, will vary because the relationships of part-self to part-self and of self to world they map and represent vary from culture to culture and from person to person even within the same culture.

The concept of selfscape dreams was originally stimulated by some of the work of the psychoanalysts Heinz Kohut and W.R.D. Fairbairn, both of whom believed that the manifest content of dreams could be related to the dreamer's state of self, not necessarily in a direct or iconic way, but in the way that paintings and other artistic forms use the nonverbal vocabulary of condensation, displacement, contiguity of occurrence in time or place, and perceptual or functional similarity to express relations among people, emotions, objects, and the world. According to Kohut and Fairbairn, the manifest content does not disguise the psychological meaning of dreams, as Freud argued, but helps to reveal it—if one knows enough about the circumstances of the dreamer's life and culture and the vocabulary of nonverbal expression.

But the concept of selfscape dreams also draws on recent work in the neurosciences. Antonio Damasio notes how deeply the mind is rooted in the body and its biological processes, especially its dependence on continuously updated representations of the body as it interacts with the world. He further suggests that neural representations of the self must be continuously updated and modified in a manner similar to that of bodily processes, and he speculates that the earliest representations of the self very likely emerge from or coincide with representations of the body as it interacts with the world. Accordingly, representations of the body, self, and world are inextricably tied together through complex emotional states and processes, all of which must be continuously updated and modified as they stimulate and impinge on one another. Although Damasio only briefly mentions dreams in his own work, dreaming clearly involves many of the emotional processes and representations of the body, self, and world that are his central focus.

Hollan uses the concept of selfscape dreams to integrate some of these ideas about dreams and psychological processes and to highlight both similarities and differences among dream researchers. The term is obviously a play on those used by Kohut and Fairbairn to emphasize how the manifest contents of dreams can be related to self-organization. But along the lines of Dasmasio's work, it also emphasizes how dreams may provide a current map or update of the self's contours and affective resonances relative to its own body, as well as to other objects and people in the world. Self-processes emerge and maintain themselves in the biological and imaginal space between body and world. Selfscape dreams map this terrain.

Douglas Hollan

See also: entries related to Dream Content

References

Hollan, D. (2003). Selfscape dreams. In J. M. Mageo (Ed.), *Dreaming and the self: New perspectives on subjectivity, identity, and emotion*. Albany: State University of New York Press.

Hollan, D. (2004). The anthropology of dreaming: Selfscape dreams. *Dreaming, 14,* 170–182.

Hollan, D. (2005). Dreaming in a global world. In C. Casey & R. B. Edgerton (Eds.), *A companion to psychological anthropology: Modernity and psychocultural change*. Malden, MA: Blackwell Publishers.

Hollan, D. (2009). The influence of culture on the experience and interpretation of disturbing dreams. *Culture, Medicine, and Psychiatry, 33,* 313–322.

Serotonin in the Regulation of REM Sleep

Based on electrophysiological, neurochemical, neuropharmacological, and genetic approaches, it is currently accepted that serotonin (5-HT) functions to promote wakefulness (W) and to inhibit REM sleep (REMS). The reciprocal interaction hypothesis of REMS generation identifies cholinergic neurons of the laterodorsal and pedunculopontine tegmental nuclei (LDT/PPT) as promoting REMS and posits the inhibition of these neurons by, among others, serotonergic afferents from the dorsal raphe nucleus (DRN). The REMS-induction region of the medial pontine reticular formation, one of the neuroanatomical structures proposed to be responsible for REMS generation, includes predominantly glutamatergic neurons, which are in turn activated by efferent connections of the LDT/PPT.

Mutant mice that do not express 5-HT_{1A} or 5-HT_{1B} receptor exhibit greater amounts of REMS than their wild-type counterparts, which could be related to the absence of a postsynaptic 5-HT_{1A} and 5-HT_{1B} inhibitory effect on the cholinergic neurons of the LDT/PPT. In contrast, 5-HT$_7$ receptor knockout mice spend less time in REMS than their wild-type counterparts, mainly during the light period.

The infusion of a 5-HT$_{1A}$ receptor agonist (8-OH-DPAT, flesinoxan) into the DRN increases REMS in the rat. The effect has been ascribed to the selective activation of the somatodendritic 5-HT$_{1A}$ receptor. In contrast, local microinjection of 5-HT$_{1B}$ (CP-94253), 5-HT$_{2A/2C}$ (DOI), 5-HT$_3$ (m-chlorophenylbiguanide), or 5-HT$_7$ (LP-44) receptor agonists into the DRN selectively suppresses REMS in the rat. Activation of the 5-HT$_{1B}$ receptor in the DRN has been shown to inhibit the release of gamma-aminobutyric acid (GABA). Thus, the decrease of GABA-inhibitory tone on 5-HT neurons would result in an increment of 5-HT release at postsynaptic sites and the suppression of REMS. The activation of long projection GABAergic interneurons that express 5-HT$_{2A/2C}$ or 5-HT$_7$ receptor could be responsible for the inhibition of cholinergic cells in the LDT/PPT and the suppression of REMS. On the other hand, the reduction of REMS observed after the local microinjection of a 5-HT$_3$ receptor agonist depends on the activation of glutamatergic interneurons and the increased release of 5-HT.

Systemic injection of flesinoxan reduces REMS in laboratory animals. Similar effects have been observed following the administration of 8-OH-DPAT to vehicle-treated and serotonin-depleted animals. The reduction of REMS after systemic flesinoxan or 8-OH-DPAT administration would be related to the activation of postsynaptic 5-HT$_{1A}$ receptors on REM-on neurons of the LDT/PPT, similar to the physiological effect of 5-HT.

Systemic administration of the selective 5-HT$_{1B}$ receptor agonists CGS 12066B and CP-94253 reduces REMS in the rat. On the other hand, acute pharmacological blockade of the 5-HT$_{1B}$ receptor with GR 125939 produces an increase of REMS in wild-type mice.

Intraperitoneal injection of the nonselective 5-HT$_{2A/2C}$ receptor agonists DOI and DOM or the selective 5-HT$_{2C}$ agonist RO 60–0175 reduces REMS in rodents. Indirect evidence tends to indicate that GABA is involved in the DOI-induced suppression of REMS. Interestingly, the administration of nonselective and selective 5-HT$_{2A}$ antagonists or a 5-HT$_{2A}$ receptor inverse agonist also reduces REMS.

m-Chlorophenylbiguanide injected into the left lateral ventricle increased REMS latency, whereas REMS and the number of REM periods were reduced in the rat. Pretreatment with the 5-HT$_3$ receptor antagonist MDL-72222 prevented the reduction of REMS. On the basis of a series of neuropharmacological studies it has been proposed that the m-chlorophenylbiguanide-induced reduction of REMS is related to the increased availability of monoamines at central sites.

Intraperitoneal administration of the 5-HT$_7$ receptor agonist LP-211 during the light phase has been shown to reduce REMS in laboratory animals. Pretreatment with the selective 5-HT$_7$ antagonist SB-269970 prevented the action of LP-211 on REMS.

Attempts to characterize the role of serotonin receptors on REMS have been limited to the 5-HT$_{1A}$, 5-HT$_{1B}$, 5-HT2$_{A/2C}$,

5-HT$_3$, and 5-HT$_7$ receptors. Activation of the postsynaptic 5-HT$_{1A}$ and 5-HT$_{1B}$ receptors induces the hyperpolarization of target neurons in the LDT/PPT. On the other hand, activation of 5-HT$_{2A}$, 5-HT$_{2C}$, and 5-HT$_7$ receptors leads to the depolarization of GABAergic cells that innervate the structures involved in the promotion of REMS. The behavioral state is suppressed during both instances.

The 5-HT$_3$ receptor is well known for stimulating the release of monoamines and GABA in the brain stem, which could tentatively explain its disruption of REMS.

Jaime M. Monti

References

Monti, J. M., & Jantos, H. (2009). The roles of dopamine and serotonin, and of their receptors, in regulating sleep and waking. In G. Di Giovanni, V. Di Matteo, & E. Esposito (Eds.), *Progress in Brain Research, 172,* 625–646.

Monti, J. M., Jantos, H., & Monti, D. (2008). In J. M. Monti, S. R. Pandi-Perumal, & C. M. Sinton (Eds.), *Serotonin and sleep-wake regulation: Neurochemistry of sleep and wakefulness.* Cambridge: Cambridge University Press.

Sexual Dreams: Meaning and Practical Insight

In an all-too-rare study of 109 women and 64 men, about 8 percent of their dreams contained obviously sexual content (Zadra, 2007). While it is difficult to know how often the broad population of a given nation or culture dreams of sexual images and concerns at different periods in a lifetime, it is clear that many people count sexual dreams as among their most delightful and/or their most unpleasant dream experiences. While research on the topic of the meaning of sexual dreams is difficult to fund and conduct, curiosity runs high.

In 35 years of teaching dream interpretation using the dream interview method, an existential (Boss, 1977), client-metaphor-based approach, I have worked with many dreams with no apparent sexual content that bring to the dreamer's mind sexual matters—and, with many dreams laden with sexual imagery that the dreamer relates to nonsexual, work, or relationship issues. And of course, sometimes a penis really is a penis. To grasp the meaning of any dream it is important to follow the dream, and not a dream theory or metapsychology that presupposes the structure of the psyche or the meaning of a given image.

If the interpreter/interviewer, played by the therapist or the practiced dreamer, elicits experience–near-verbal descriptions of the dream imagery and feelings without interjecting his or her own associations, intuitions, or interpretations, the dreamer will usually be able to find the metaphoric bridge from the descriptions to waking-life concerns (Delaney, 1994).

Consider the surprising example of this dream of a 24-year-old man:

> I see my wife having sex with my father. They orgasm, and my father leaves the bedroom. My wife says, "Can't you be better than your father?"

Asked, "What is your father like," the dreamer said he was honest, fun, a good guy, but he just could not make it monetarily. Asked how he felt in the dream, he said he was shocked, and felt his wife was daring him. He concluded that the dream was focusing his attention on how much he was like his father, a good guy who was failing at making a living. He felt that his wife was daring him to break through his hitherto unrecognized fear of outdoing his beloved father.

The major categories of the functions of sexual dreams in my practice include those in which the dreamer reexamines sexual inhibitions, reassesses his or her sexual skills and styles, discovers conflicts and sexual potentials in an ongoing relationship, discovers patterns of relationship in past and current sexual relationships, explores less-conflicted sexual experiences, explores early sexual conflicts and trauma, and considers the desirability of potential long-, or short-term sexual partners or mates.

The major categories of the imagery of dreams that treat these sexual and relationship issues are many. Following are the most common in my experience. (1) Having sex with an unexpected partner, a coworker, a celebrity, a past lover, a family member, a person of a different sexual orientation. (2) Kissing, being naked with, wishing to have sex with someone in a dream. (3) Seeing others have sex in a dream, sometimes with your partner. (4) Feeling coerced to show your body or have sexual interactions with others (Delaney, 1997). This dream is so common among those who have been sexually abused in childhood, that it is wise to work on the dream, very gingerly, and only in the context of a solid psychotherapeutic relationship.

Many women dream of making love to President Obama. Some might assume different things about the meaning of such a dream. Is Obama a representation of the dreamer's father? Is he a positive or negative figure? To find out, it serves to have the interviewer say, "Pretend I come from another planet and do not know this guy. Who is he and what is he like?" Then to ask, "What is he like in your dream?" Feed back the description and ask if the description reminds the dreamer of anyone or anything in her life. Now ask how the love-making went and if that action and those feelings remind her of anything in her life. By asking focused, nonleading questions, rather than offering interpretive guesses, you have a good chance of discovering what the dream is about!

Gayle M. V. Delaney

References

Boss, M. (1977). *I dreamt last night*. New York: Gardner Press.

Delaney, G. (1994). *Sensual dreaming*. New York: Ballantine Books.

Delaney, G. (1997). *In your dreams*. San Francisco: HarperSanFrancisco.

Zadra, A. (2007). 1093: Sex dreams: What do men and women dream about? *Sleep, 30*(Abstract Suppl.), A376.

Shakespeare and Dreams

To enter Shakespeare via dreams uniquely deepens our understanding of both. William Shakespeare (1564–1616) wove dreaming through all genres of his drama: histories, tragedies, comedies, and romances. Dreams figure in political intrigue, fatally betray lovers, allow communication with the dead, and enable visitations from the gods. Rather than solely presenting dreams as remembered and reported experiences of the sleeping mind, Shakespeare experimented with multiple variants of the dreaming process, including its correlation with sleep and death. The grieving Hamlet exclaims, "ay there's the rub;/ For in that sleep of death what dreams may come" (III.i.). Macbeth calls sleep "death's counterfeit" and Lady Macbeth's collusion in their multiple murders leads to her sleepwalking (somnambulism) and sleep-talking (somniloquy) (V.i.).

The view that dreams, like poems, contain symbolically significant images, have a metaphorical tenor, and require interpretation underlies all Shakespearean oneirics (dream content). In the plays, dreams serve many conventional literary functions such as revealing character, advancing plot, and producing dramatic irony, but they do so in a special way. In addition, Shakespeare uses dreams to expose cultural beliefs shared by both characters and readers, beliefs that have ramifications for societies as a whole. His inventiveness also displays dreaming's affinities with theatrical illusion and with the workings of the creative imagination in all the arts as in *A Winter's Tale.*

Shakespeare draws dream material from his Greco-Roman, Arabic, English, Italian, and other sources, but goes beyond them to anticipate ideas that only gain credence centuries later. He repeatedly depicts the continuity hypothesis that dreams are integrally related to the dreamer's waking life, involving fears and desires as well as practical aspects of that life: the merchant Shylock dreams of money bags (*Merchant of Venice* II.v); the anxious lover dreams of betrayal (*A Midsummer Night's Dream* II.ii). In addition, dreaming wives accurately foresee the death of their husbands (Calpurnia in *Julius Caesar* and Andromache in *Troilus and Cressida*). Shakespeare exploits this foreshadowing—Carl Jung called such dreams "prospective"—to intensify dramatic suspense.

Further, Shakespeare inherited and transformed ideas, later investigated in modern sleep laboratory research, that dreaming moves through regular phases during the night's sleep. In 2 *Henry VI,* the treasonous duchess dreams (in the morning hours) of becoming queen, but ends in humiliation and banishment. She also incorrectly interprets the loyal duke's dream as positive. He, who dreams in the night hours, however, correctly understands the broken shaft image in his dream to represent his coming fall from power. Moral character as well as somatic processes is held to cause differences between the content and meaning of dreams that occurred before midnight and those from the predawn hours.

While the word nightmare occurs only once (*King Lear* III.iv, referring to a nocturnal demon) in the 37 plays attributed wholly or partly to Shakespeare, bad dreams predominate; they are labeled troublous, timorous, tormenting, terrible, hideous, fearful, and ominous. Dreamers and interpreters can be found throughout Shakespeare's diverse population: men and women, kings and courtiers, lovers and warriors, victims and murderers, and even one island monster, Caliban (*The Tempest*).

Shakespeare also presents a whole spectrum of attitudes toward dreams drawn from folklore and popular culture. These attitudes coexist with more learned or expert views and often alternate within one character. Believers and dismissers abound: Mercutio calls dreams "children of an idle brain" (*Romeo and Juliet* I.iv). Other characters group dreaming with the irrational, madness, drunkenness, superstition, and the nonsense of boys and women. Shakespeare challenges any character who tries to make a strict differentiation between waking reality and the dream world. He mocks humans' certainty about their own perceptions and exposes the dangerous, often fateful misinterpretations they unwittingly make. Going further, Shakespeare includes dream reports that appear to be manipulative fabrications. In *Othello* (III.iii), Iago claims to have observed Cassio dreaming and talking in his sleep about Othello's wife Desdemona, proving her infidelity to her husband. By depicting such uses and abuses of dreams and interpretations, Shakespeare extends the range of dream representation in literary texts.

The full scope of Shakespearean oneirics remains to be explored. Readers will want to counteract a centuries-old tendency to focus primarily on *A Midsummer Night's Dream*. Such focus has led to neglect of plays like the histories and tragedies based on Roman and British chronicles, which themselves contain dreaming as a significant feature. The accumulated dream material in Shakespeare's *Complete Works* leads to no simple resolution but captures dreaming's inexhaustible range as a subject and its fundamental alliance with literature. (See the entry "Literature and Dreams.") Shakespeare problematizes all schemes of oneiric and literary interpretation and all theoretical tenets whether related to remembering, reporting, or interpreting. One theme proves constant, however: dreaming is a powerful, dynamic, ubiquitous force in the lives of individuals, families, and whole societies.

Carol S. Rupprecht

References

Bulkeley, K. (1998). Penelope as dreamer: A reading of Book 19 of *The Odyssey*. *Dreaming, 8,* 229–242.

Rupprecht, C. S. (Ed.). (1993a). *The dream and the text: Essays on literature and language.* Albany: State University of New York Press.

Rupprecht, C. S. (1993b). The nightmares of history: Shakespeare's use of dreams in the *Henry VI* tetralogy. *Dreaming, 3,* 211–227.

Shamanism and Dreams

Shamans are community-sanctioned spiritual practitioners who obtain valuable information from unusual sources, including dreams, using this information for the benefit of their community, often in healing sessions, initiation rituals, and conflict resolution. For example, the *naachin* (dreaming shamans) among the Dunne-za people in Canada claim to experience communication with spirits and travel to upper and lower worlds in their dreams, obtaining songs that can assist both the living and the dead.

The importance of dreams for Native Americans was noted in 1923 by R. Benedict, who identified their use as the most basic expression of their spirituality. Several decades later, other anthropologists stressed the importance of learning about indigenous peoples' dreams if their cultures were to be adequately fathomed, noting, for example, that societies using dreams to seek and control supernatural powers were more likely to live by hunting, gathering, and fishing activities than by agriculture and animal husbandry. The *bare* shamans of Brazil's hunting and gathering Bororo tribe are called to their profession by spirits who appear in their dreams and, later, in waking visions. Among the Temiar people in the forests of Malaysia, spirit helpers appear in dreams where they suggest foods, dances, and melodies that will enhance a shaman's power. Some shamans enter into a marriage with their tutelary spirits in their dreams; both male and female shamans among the Saora people of India could have both spirit and human spouses, and raise children from both types of union.

Although denigrated by European colonists, Western religious authorities, and several 20th-century psychiatrists, shamanic dream systems have gradually attained the interest and respect of social scientists as well as significant numbers of the general population. Indeed, some pop psychologists have appropriated Native American spiritual practices, including dreamwork, and passed them off as authentic, often charging considerable amounts of money in the process. Even when financial gain does not seem to be a motive, enthusiasm has far outstripped the knowledge and ability of many non-native people who involve themselves in and even lead shamanic dream ceremonies.

In an attempt to preserve what is known about shamanic dream systems and to present this knowledge to the academic community, S. Krippner and A. Thompson (1996) described 16 systems (from the United States and Canada) using a 10-facet model. A close examination of these (and

The Hunt by Dierdre Luzwick contrasts the world of the shaman with contemporary society, a contrast often apparent in shamans' dreams. (Reproduced from the original art of Dierdre Luzwick)

other) shamanic dream systems reveals a remarkable complexity and erudition that exceeded the simplistic dream systems brought to the Americas, Africa, and Asia by the European conquerors. European dreamers were urged to ignore their dreams as the dreamer would not know which were divinely inspired and which were demonic. Shamans, on the other hand, had no such dilemma as they had centuries of traditional dreamwork to fall back on, allowing them to determine the nature of a dream report.

In many of these dream systems, individuals and family members were encouraged to work with their own dreams, only bringing them to shamans if their meaning could not be fathomed. This practice was attributed to the Southeast Asian Senoi people by an amateur anthropologist who described the Senoi as a dream culture. His work is controversial, in part because it did not conform to the anthropological standards for fieldwork developed later in the 20th century. However, there are several examples of indigenous groups that might be referred to as dream cultures. For example, the Guarani Indians in southeastern Brazil also have a venerable dream tradition. Tribal legends hold that in primordial times native people divided themselves into three groups: the People of the Sun, the People of the Moon, and the People of Dreams. The Xavante and the Guarani are members of this latter group; some of their communities hold dream circles, or morning dream–sharing sessions. Often, a dream is shared that begins to give direction to the daily life of the village and it is not necessarily the dream of a *pajé* or shaman. Indeed, a child can have a dream that indicates a new direction for a community.

The Xavante Indians of central Brazil live in a mosaic of ecosystems, sharing the land with jaguar, puma, anteaters, termites, parrots, and a variety of other wildlife. The dream world is an essential element of Xavante life because dreams allow them to maintain contact with their animal helpers as well as their ancestors. When Xavante shamans and other elders dream about the immortals, they share the dream with the entire village, which begins preparing a reenactment of the dream with the elders playing the roles of the ancestors. These dream ceremonies help to align the present with the past, providing cultural continuity. On other occasions, tribal members will sing and dance each other's dreams, thus developing a sense of trust among tribal members.

Cultural myths often come to life in a dream as sources of support or as sources of anxiety, depending on the underlying nature of a conflict that existed at the time of the dream. In the case of the Northern Iroquois, for example, several centuries before Sigmund Freud, this society understood that dreams revealed the secret wishes of the soul. As an observant Jesuit priest wrote after a visit to the Hurons, these people believe that their souls have desires that are concealed. Accordingly, the priest continued, when these desires are accomplished, it is satisfied; but, on the contrary, if it be not granted what it desires, it becomes angry, and not only does not give its body the good and happiness that it wished to procure for it, but often it also revolts against the body, causing various diseases, and even death. Among the Northern Iroquois, it was felt that dreams often reveal desires that one cannot comprehend during wakefulness, and the shamans often permitted dreamers to act out directly or symbolically these secret wishes in private or in a community setting.

For many of the North American systems surveyed by Krippner and Thompson, dreams do not typically require systematic interpretation; their message is direct and undisguised. For those dreams that require some type of interpretation, the variety of approaches in these models represents the plurality and polymorphic nature of Native American traditions. Some tribal dream-working approaches resemble those used by Western dream specialists, for example, psychodrama, dream sharing, roleplaying. Those native dream systems that posited universal symbols are reminiscent of the Jungian notion of archetypes. For the Jungians as well as for such societies as the Hopi, Kwakiutl, Mojave, and Navajo, individual permutations of the symbol are recognized and taken into account while working with dreams. Admittedly, this approach to Native American dreaming is what anthropologists call *etic*, imposing a Western model on accounts written by Western anthropologists, rather than the *emic* approach in which accounts are given by tribal people themselves.

There are instances of Native American dreamers taking extreme measures to change the outcome of a dream by play-acting the event. A Mohawk warrior who dreamed he was taken captive and tortured by fire insisted that his peers restrain him and burn him with red hot metal to prevent his later capture. During the *Ononharoia,* a sacred midwinter ritual held on some Iroquois reservations, tribal members engage in dream-guessing contests that often turn into dream giveaways. Treasured possessions, husbands, and wives have been known to be given away during an *Ononharoia,* which translates as upturning of minds.

In studies of this sort, there is an equivalence problem, the construction of meaning units that might not be comparable in different cultural settings. It would be a valuable exercise for indigenous dreamworkers to explain their own models of dreaming. B. Tedlock (1991) has suggested that researchers interact within natural contexts and engage in dream sharing. In such contexts, the introduction of the researcher's own dreams would be quite natural, even expected, and might reveal the researcher's unconscious reactions to the peoples they are attempting to study. This participant-observation method would abandon the viewing of native people's dreams as what postmodernists refer to as the other in favor of an interaction in which both the researcher and the research participant comment on each other's dream reports.

Several shamanic dream models distinguish between ordinary dreams and visionary dreams. Some groups treat nightmares differently than dreams in general and some categorize dreams on the basis of their purported origin. Some classify them in terms of various types and degrees of power and knowledge represented (e.g., among the Mojave, there are omen dreams and power dreams). The Ojibwa have at least a dozen categories of dreams, for example, bad, beautiful, impure, ominous, painful, visionary. The Menominee employed a language that was subtle, complex, and radically different from any Western language in its organization of action and object, time, and occurrence. This language permeated Menominee dreams, providing these people with a social map within which all persons could be placed as well as a set of values to live and die by. Hence an intensive study of the complex Menominee myths and rituals on their own terms might be of greater value than a comparison with other worldviews.

Although skepticism and divergent thinking is not unknown in native societies, the power of traditional myths is accepted by most of the dreamers in these cultures. Myths may come to life in the dream as sources of support or as sources of anxiety, depending on the underlying nature of the immediate conflict. For example, the South American Mapuche system includes a variety of ways in which this support or anxiety is handled by community dreamworkers.

There is an urgent need for more information in these areas, and cross-cultural studies can play an important role in this quest. Are there universal human biological processes that are mediated by cultural settings? Or are dreams and similar phenomena basically dependent on time and place? These questions are the focus of much cross-cultural research. However, native cultures are changing in the wake of acculturation; those still retaining their traditional ways of living and dreaming present critically important research opportunities.

Stanley C. Krippner

See also: entries related to Cross-Cultural Dreams

References

Benedict, R. (1923). *The concept of the guardian spirit in North America*. Menasha, WI: American Anthropological Association.

Degarrod, L. N. (2004). Dreams and visions. In M. N. Walter & E. J. N. Fridman (Eds.), *Shamanism: An encyclopedia of world beliefs, practices, and cultures* (pp. 89–95). Santa Barbara, CA: ABC-CLIO.

Krippner, S. (2009). Anyone who dreams partakes in shamanism. *Journal of Shamanic Practice, 2,* 33–40.

Krippner, S., & Thompson, A. (1996). A 10-facet model of dreaming applied to dream practices of sixteen Native American cultural groups. *Dreaming, 6,* 71–96.

Tedlock, B. (1991). The new anthropology of dreaming. *Dreaming, 1,* 161–174.

Short Sleep

Short sleep typically refers to the habitual, voluntary curtailment of sleep opportunity to six hours or fewer. However, a number of other definitions have been used in the scientific literature to describe short sleep, which has made generalization across studies difficult. Nonetheless, there is a sizeable literature that suggests problems associated with short sleep, from studies of experimental sleep restriction (Banks & Dinges, 2007), epidemiological surveys using retrospective self-reports of habitual sleep duration, and a growing number of studies that evaluate individuals whose retrospective self-report of short sleep is supported by objective corroboration (Grandner, Patel, Gehrman, Perlis, & Pack, 2010). Sleep loss due to short sleep represents a major unmet public health problem (Colten & Altevogt, 2006).

Classic polysomnographic studies of individuals whose sleep is curtailed in the laboratory suggest that shortened sleep comprises less REM and Stage 2 sleep, but no difference in slow-wave sleep. More recent studies have found that habitual short sleepers may be better able to tolerate higher homeostatic sleep pressure. Also, they may experience differences in circadian rhythms that indicate a shorter nighttime signal. Subjectively, individuals who report habitual short sleep also report more sleep-related complaints, such as difficulty falling and staying asleep, and daytime sleepiness.

Short sleep is related to a number of functional outcomes (Banks & Dinges, 2007; Grandner et al., 2010). Sleep restriction in the laboratory produces increased subjective and objective sleepiness, as well as marked deficits in performance (e.g., reaction time, vigilance, attention). In addition, other cognitive domains have been shown to be impacted, including working memory and executive function.

Short sleepers may be at greater risk for negative cardiometabolic outcomes (Grandner et al., 2010), including hypertension, myocardial infarction, stroke, sympathetic nervous system changes, glucose intolerance, impaired insulin resistance, type-2 diabetes, and obesity. Regarding obesity, many studies have replicated the finding that less sleep is associated with increased body mass, as well as factors related to weight gain, such as poor diet. Additionally, a number of biomarkers for cardiovascular and metabolic risk may be abnormal in short sleepers, including leptin, ghrelin, and markers of inflammation.

Laboratory sleep restriction studies suggest that short sleepers may demonstrate increased basal activity of neuroendocrine stress systems, altered hypothalamic–pituitary–adrenal axis functioning, and increased stress reactivity, as well as increased pain sensitivity and perception. Additionally, less sleep is associated with impairments in mood regulation, including increased negative and decreased positive effect, as well as increased risk of depression.

Many studies, representing samples from several continents, have documented that sleep duration (short or long) is associated with increased mortality risk (Grandner, Patel, Hale, & Moore, 2010). The cause for this increase in risk is unclear, and is likely multifactorial, representing a combination of the many negative health outcomes mentioned earlier.

Despite these many risks, short sleep is prevalent. As many as 20 percent or more of American adults report six hours of sleep per night or less. It is likely that this group is highly heterogeneous, including individuals who may need less sleep and do not show any impairment, individuals who sleep less because of a sleep disorder (e.g., insomnia), and individuals who, for a number of reasons such as work or family obligations, curtail their sleep.

This heterogeneity, when taken in context with the diversity of negative health outcomes implicated, as well as the various studies that suggest impairment associated with sleep loss and/or insufficient sleep, suggest important future research directions. Short sleepers need to be better characterized, with differentiation among those who are true short sleepers with no impairment, those who suffer from sleep disorders, and those who are impaired due to sleeping six hours or less on average. Then, interventions at the individual and community level can educate the public about the importance of sleep for health and improve outcomes for these individuals through improved sleep.

Michael A. Grandner

See also: entries related to Sleep and Development

References

Banks, S., & Dinges, D. F. (2007). Behavioral and physiological consequences of sleep restriction. *Journal of Clinical Sleep Medicine, 3*(5), 519–528.

Colten, H.R., & Altevogt, B.M. (2006). Institute of Medicine Committee on Sleep Medicine and Research. In *Sleep disorders and sleep deprivation: An unmet public health problem.* Washington, DC: Institute of Medicine, National Academies Press.

Grandner, M.A., Patel, N.P., Gehrman, P.R., Perlis, M.L., & Pack, A.I. (2010). Problems associated with short sleep: Bridging the gap between laboratory and epidemiological studies. *Sleep Medicine Reviews, 14,* 239–247.

Grandner, M.A., Patel, N.P., Hale, L., & Moore, M. (2010). Mortality associated with sleep duration: The evidence, the possible mechanisms, and the future. *Sleep Medicine Reviews, 14,* 191–203.

Knutsonm, K.L., & Van Cauter, E. (2008). Associations between sleep loss and increased risk of obesity and diabetes. *Annals of the New York Academy of Science, 1129,* 287–304.

Significance of Dreams in Western Australian Desert Aboriginal Worldview

Australia was the only continent populated by a people pursuing a single mode of adaptation—that of hunting and gathering—from their arrival some 60,000 years ago into modern times. The Aborigines are a genetically, linguistically, and culturally distinct people, unaffected by outside influences until just a few centuries ago. They are also unique among hunter–gatherers in the great disparity between their sparse material culture and the rich, highly elaborate religious life that pervaded their worldview and culture. In the arid interior, as in most of Aboriginal Australia, two closely interrelated cultural symbols framed everything: the dreaming, or creative era, when mythological beings are said to have placed people, languages, culture, and natural species onto the land as they traveled; and the law, which comprises the moral codes and rules for living also left behind by the founding being. Living humans are multiply connected to the dreaming through totemic associations, rituals, songs, stories, dreams, and a host of landscape features that are imbued with meaning.

The Western Desert covers about one sixth of the arid interior of the continent, yet remained largely undisturbed until well into the 20th century: there are desert Aborigines still alive today who can recount their first contact experiences with whites. Population densities had to be very low and, correspondingly, the ranges over which groups moved during the food quest were huge, yet every small band of wanderers retained a deep-seated attachment to its home territory. The homeland was the source and repository of both the spirit-children from whom its members came and the natural species on which their subsistence depended. Yet no matter how far beyond their core homeland areas people were drawn by drought, insufficient food supplies, or ritual and religious responsibilities, they could easily remain in touch with, visit, look after, and nourish them— thanks to their professed ability to travel in dream-spirit form.

Besides long-established rituals performed throughout the region, many of them associated with male initiation, there was a steady output of more ephemeral local rituals based on dreams. Typically, these were composed by one or more mature adults whose dream spirits traveled far and wide, and sometimes encountered spirit-beings, beautifully decorated humanoids that sometimes revealed new songs and dances to them. Upon awakening from such dream journeys, and usually feeling exhausted from the experience, people related details to others, and soon a theme would emerge; for example, various weather phenomena. Others would then also dream and supply more songs and dances, which were also discussed to arrive at the real meaning of what had been witnessed. These were then added to the corpus of songs, until such time as the group deemed the new ritual ready for public performance. Individuals thus had the task of molding these revealed fragments of song, dance, body designs, and sacred dancing regalia into a coherent ritual whole, which would be shared with others. Although such contemporary rituals were small in scale and generally short lived in terms of performance, many of the songs were remembered and sung around camp fires. These elements stand as proof that the creative powers remain alert to and interested in worldly affairs. The role of the individual, as a receiver and transmitter rather than originator of new knowledge, accords well with the strong egalitarian ethos found in most Australian Aboriginal societies.

Rather than report that, "Last night I dreamt I was at X waterhole," a person would say, "Last night I was at X waterhole" then go on to tell what happened there. The dream spirit (*partunjarri*) is an integral part of a person's being, which is why people should never be suddenly awoken, lest their dream spirit be unable to reenter in time, thus leaving both spirit and body susceptible to sorcery attacks. Newly discovered sacred objects are explained as being revealed or hinted at, during dreams or reveries, through signs that prompt a person to react. The resulting revelation of a find to others, with a description of where and under what circumstances it was located, transfers the event from an individual to a collective concern. Consensus is sought and the true religious meaning of the find is arrived at through protracted discussion, in the light of relevant mythological knowledge of both the location and the object's characteristics, such as shape, size, or color. The act of dreaming and the entry of new knowledge into the human realm were thus inextricably intertwined in Australian Aboriginal societies.

Robert Tonkinson

See also: entries related to Cross-Cultural Dreams

References

Berndt, R.M., & Berndt, C.H. (1988). *The world of the first Australians*. Canberra: Aboriginal Studies Press.

Tonkinson, R. (1970). Aboriginal dream-spirit beliefs in a contact situation: Jigalong, Western Australia. In R.M. Berndt (Ed.), *Australian Aboriginal anthropology* (pp. 277–291). Nedlands: The University of Western Australia Press, for the Australian Institute of Aboriginal Studies.

Tonkinson, R. (1974). *The Jigalong mob: Aboriginal victors of the desert crusade*. Menlo Park, CA: Cummings.

Tonkinson, R. (2002). *The Mardu Aborigines: Living the dream in Australia's desert* (2nd ed.). Fort Worth, TX: Holt, Rinehart and Winston.

Tonkinson, R. (2005). Individual creativity and property-power disjunction in an Australian desert society. In *Property and equality, Vol. 1: Ritualization, sharing, egalitarianism* (pp. 32–46). Oxford, UK: Berghahn.

Sleep and Arthritis

Arthritis is the leading cause of chronic illness in the United States and is characterized by articular as well as extra-articular manifestations that cause substantial disability and decreased quality of life. Almost 45 million adults in the United States (20% of the adult population) have arthritis diagnosed by a doctor. The prevalence of diagnosed arthritis increases to 50 percent in adults aged 65 and older. Data from the 2007 National Health Interview Survey show that insomnia was described by 32.1 percent of persons with arthritis compared to 13.9 percent of persons without arthritis and excessive daytime sleepiness by 17.5 percent with arthritis versus 7.9 percent without arthritis (Louie, Tektonidou, Caban-Martinez, & Ward, 2011). Thus, sleep disorders affect a large number of people with arthritis. In this brief overview, we summarize sleep abnormalities in persons with inflammatory rheumatologic disorders.

Rheumatoid arthritis (RA), an inflammatory arthritis involving the peripheral joints, affects an estimated 1.5 million adults in the United States. Sleep complaints and related daytime symptoms have been reported in 54 to70 percent of adult rheumatoid-arthritis patients. These symptoms include difficulty falling asleep, poor-quality sleep, nonrestorative sleep, nocturnal awakenings, early morning awakening, and daytime fatigue. A study using a Medical Outcome Study sleep questionnaire and visual analogue sleep scale administered to 8,676 patients with RA confirmed that sleep disturbance is increased in these patients and concluded that 25 to 42 percent of this increase can be attributed to RA. Actigraphy in patients with RA has shown a positive correlation between increased nocturnal pain and body movements and a negative correlation between nocturnal pain and sleep efficiency and the duration of the longest sleep period; a greater number of nocturnal awakenings was associated with increased intensity of morning pain. Polysomnographic studies of patients with RA during flares have shown increased sleep fragmentation, frequent nocturnal awakenings, and reduced sleep efficiency compared to nonflare RA patients. During flares, sleep fragmentation correlates positively with fatigue and joint pain. Increased rheumatoid disease activity has been associated with increased time in Stage wake, Stage 1 NREM sleep, and slow-wave sleep (SWS) and decreased time in Stage 2 NREM sleep. Primary sleep disorders associated with RA include sleep apnea, sleep state misperception, restless legs syndrome, and periodic leg movements. Almost 80 percent of RA patients with occipital cervical spine lesions have sleep apnea.

Juvenile idiopathic arthritis (JIA), also known as juvenile RA, includes a heterogeneous group of disorders characterized by chronic inflammatory arthritis affecting children under age 16. It is associated with sleep disruption, excessive daytime sleepiness, and pain. Polysomnographic studies show sleep fragmentation with increased arousals, increased stage shifts, and increased percentage of alpha-delta sleep. Disturbed NREM sleep is evidenced by increased percentage of cyclic alternating pattern (CAP) during SWS stages, increased duration of CAP sequences, and increased CAP A2 subtype (Abad et al., 2008). Retrognathia and posterior rotation of the mandible are relatively common in JIA and may predispose to sleep apnea.

Systemic lupus erythematosus, an autoimmune disorder with diverse clinical manifestations, including polyarthritis clinically similar to RA, is estimated to affect about 1.5 million people in the United States. About 60 percent report sleep disturbances and fatigue. Polysomnographic studies have linked increased disease activity with reduced sleep efficiency, increased Stage 1 sleep, reduced delta sleep, alpha intrusions, increased arousals, and sleep fragmentation. Associated primary sleep disorders include sleep apnea, periodic leg movements, and narcolepsy with cataplexy (Abad et al., 2008).

Spondyloarthropathies are estimated to affect 0.6 to1.9 percent of the U.S. population. These diseases, which include ankylosing spondylitis (AS), typically affect the sacroiliac joints and spine but may also affect the peripheral joints. Patients with AS often experience nocturnal pain and complain of insomnia and fatigue. Polysomnographic studies have found that increased pain is associated with increased Stage 1 sleep, movement time, and SWS. Obstructive sleep apnea has been reported in 40 percent of AS patients aged 35 and older (Solak, 2009). In some patients, hypertrophy and ossification of the cervical anterior longitudinal ligament produces oropharyngeal compression that causes sleep apnea.

Psoriatic arthritis (PsA) occurs in 5 to10 percent of patients with psoriasis and is characterized by inflammation of the peripheral joints and, in about 20 percent of PsA patients, the development of spondylitis. Psoriasis itself may be associated with poor sleep due to pruritus and discomfort from the cutaneous lesions, but the presence of PsA is the most significant predictor of sleep interference in these patients. Polysomnographic data are lacking (Abad et al., 2008).

Osteoarthritis (OA), characterized by loss of articular cartilage with joint space narrowing and osteophyte formation, is the most common type of arthritis, affecting about 20 million people in the United States. Sleep disturbances are common in these patients and are associated with pain, number of arthritic joints, and depression, among other factors. Polysomnography shows increased Stage 1 NREM sleep, reduced Stage 2 NREM sleep, and increased sleep fragmentation. Following total hip arthroplasty, OA patients have reported improved sleep, and actigraphy has shown less sleep fragmentation (Abad et al., 2008).

Cytokines in Sleep and Arthritis

Although the relationship between cytokines and disordered sleep in patients with arthritis is uncertain, it is interesting that cytokines associated with inflammatory arthritis are also important in regulating sleep (Abad et al., 2008; Moldofsky, 2010). RA is associated with increased levels of TNF-α, interleukin-1 (IL-1), and IL-6 in synovium and synovial fluid and in the serum of some patients. TNF-α, IL-1, and

IL-6 induce fatigue and are somnogenic. Abnormal circadian secretion of IL-6 and TNF-α has been postulated to result in difficulty sleeping at night and fatigue in patients with chronic insomnia. Could the increased levels in TNF-α, IL-1, and IL-6 that are present in patients with arthritis partially explain some of the sleep difficulties and reported fatigue in these disorders?

In recent years, monoclonal antibodies (mAb) that target specific cytokines or their receptors have become available for the treatment of inflammatory arthritis (Abad et al., 2008). Do these agents improve the quality of sleep in these patients? Anti-TNF therapy did not lower overall sleep disturbance scale scores or improve daytime somnolence in rheumatoid-arthritis patients in one study. Yet, infusion of the anti-TNF mAb infliximab has been reported to improve sleep in many patients with RA. Administration of etanercept, a fusion protein that binds TNF-α, has been reported to reduce mean apnea hypopnea index and decrease sleepiness, but there was no significant difference in sleep variables (such as sleep latency and total sleep time). RA patients treated with anakinra, a recombinant human IL-1 receptor antagonist, have shown significant improvement in four of the six sections of the Nottingham Health Profile, which includes sleep questions. In patients with AS, golimumab, a human mAb directed against TNF-α, has been shown to significantly reduce sleep disturbance and improve health-related quality of life (Deodhar et al., 2010) Thus, although clinical studies have yielded variable results, most have reported improved sleep after treatment with these agents.

Conclusion

These studies raise several interesting questions. To what extent does arthritis cause or exacerbate sleep disorders, and to what extent do sleep disorders exacerbate the symptoms of arthritis? Is the improved sleep reported by many patients after treatment with cytokine antagonists related to decreased pain or to blocking of cytokines or to possible other factors? What effect does treatment of associated sleep disorders have on the symptoms of arthritis? These important questions are only now starting to be addressed. Clearly, further studies are needed.

An important clinical lesson is that fatigue in patients with arthritis may reflect not only active arthritis but also disordered sleep, including sleep apnea. Optimal treatment of these patients includes not only therapy directed toward their arthritis, but also evaluation for sleep abnormalities that may contribute to their pain and fatigue.

Vivien C. Abad and
Maurice E. Hamilton

See also: entries related to Sleep Disorders; entries related to Sleep Physiology

References

Abad, V. C., Sarinas, P. S. A., & Guilleminault, C. (2008). Sleep and rheumatologic disorders. *Sleep Medicine Reviews, 12,* 211–228.

Deodhar, A., Braun, J., Inman, R. D., Mack, M., Parasuraman, S., Buchanan, J., . . . van der Heijde, D. (2010). Golimumab reduces sleep disturbance in patients with active ankylosing spondylitis: Results from a randomized, placebo-controlled trial. *Arthritis Care & Research, 62,* 1266–1271.

Louie, G. H., Tektonidou, M. G., Caban-Martinez, A. J., & Ward, M. M. (2011).

Sleep disturbances in adults with arthritis: Prevalence, mediators, and subgroups at greatest risk: Data from the 2007 National Health Interview Survey. *Arthritis Care and Research, 63*(2), 247–260.

Moldofsky, H. (2010). Rheumatic manifestations of sleep disorders. *Current Opinion in Rheumatology, 22,* 59–63.

Solak, O. (2009). The prevalence of obstructive sleep apnoea syndrome in ankylosing spondylitis patients. *Rheumatology, 48,* 433–435.

Sleep and Bird Songs

Songbirds are the only terrestrial animals other than humans that learn extensive and complex vocalizations as juveniles. Numerous parallels between vocal learning in songbirds and human infants have led to the use of the songbird as a model system for studying the development and neural basis of vocalization. Songbirds display REM sleep, non-REM intermediate sleep comparable to mammalian Stages 1 and 2, and high-amplitude slow-wave sleep (SWS), also called deep sleep or non-REM Stage 3. Focused research on the relationship between sleep and bird song began in the late 1990s on the zebra finch (*Taeniopygia guttata*), and has led to the first discovery of a connection between sleep and vocal learning.

Research on the interaction between sleep and bird-song learning is a model for integrating behavioral and neurobiological studies. A major result of this research is that juvenile zebra finches appear to replay songs they are learning during sleep, which aids the learning process and may be a mechanism underlying memory consolidation. The behavioral research consistent with this off-line processing hypothesis includes the finding that songs produced after sleep in juvenile zebra finches are different from songs produced the previous afternoon during the period when the birds are undergoing rapid learning, and that the magnitude of this difference predicts the accuracy of the final (crystallized) song. This difference is actually that songs in the morning are more primitive and unstructured; however, this change is not due to a lack of practice overnight, nor is it something that happens in the morning per se (a circadian phenomenon), and adult birds do not exhibit it. The probable reason for the temporary deterioration is that songs are replaying in the bird brain during sleep without the auditory feedback that happens when a bird is awake, so the song has drifted in the same way that the song of a deafened bird does. Nevertheless, this replay during sleep benefits memory formation, and the subsequent plasticity in the morning might provide raw material to then focus the song through daytime singing, facilitating more accurate copying in the end. Thus it is not simply sleep, but the interaction between sleep and subsequent practice, which enhances vocal learning in juvenile birds. A related behavioral finding is that at the very beginning of tutoring the songs of zebra finches do not display learning that same day but rather the next morning, suggesting that neural networks might change overnight in line with the previous day's experiences.

Additional evidence for the function of sleep in bird-song learning comes from neurophysiological studies. During sleep, the neural firing in the HVC nucleus (an important source of singing motor commands) in juveniles is lower than in adults and increases as song structure improves through development. Moreover, gene expression, a marker of neuronal activity, increases during sleep in a region that stores the target song the bird is learning, supporting the idea of off-line processing.

In the robust nucleus of the archistriatum (RA), a target of the HVC, burst patterns during singing are associated with specific elements of a song. Perhaps most importantly for the off-line processing hypothesis, identical burst patterns are found during sleep in the absence of singing, perhaps indicating song replay. RA bursts during sleep emerge only after exposure to a tutor (training) song and are less structured than in sleeping adults. Features of bursting are more similar among juveniles exposed to the same tutor than across different tutors, suggesting that the sleep bursts are specific to the vocalizations currently being learned.

Lastly, both the HVC and RA in juveniles and adults respond preferentially to playback of their own song only during sleep, indicating a special role of sleep in the learning or maintenance of song production.

A role of sleep in perceptual learning has also been shown in the European starling (*Sturnus vulgaris*). A study testing the ability of starlings to distinguish between two novel songs showed that auditory discrimination in starlings was superior immediately after waking and remained stable throughout the day. These results, together with similar results in young chickens with respect to visual images, suggest that the benefit of sleep may not be specific to song

motor learning, but may serve memory consolidation more generally.

David C. Lahti and
Carolyn Pytte

See also: entries related to Evolution of Sleep

References

Brawn, T. P., Nusbaum, H. C., & Margoliash, D. (2010). Sleep-dependent consolidation of auditory discrimination learning in adult starlings. *Journal of Neuroscience, 30,* 609–613.

Derégnaucourt, S., Mitra, P. P., Feher, O., Pytte, C., & Tchernichovski, O. (2005). How sleep affects the developmental learning of bird song. *Nature, 433,* 710–716.

Gobes, S.M.H., Zandbergen, M. A., & Bolhuis, J. J. (2010). Memory in the making: Localized brain activation related to song learning in young songbirds. *Proceedings of the Royal Society B, 277,* 3343–3351.

Margoliash, D., & Schmidt, M. F. (2010). Sleep, off-line processing, and vocal learning. *Brain and Language, 115,* 45–58.

Nick, T. A., & Konishi, M. (2005). Neural song preference during vocal learning in the zebra finch depends on age and state. *Journal of Neurobiology, 62,* 231–242.

Sleep and Brain Networks

About 20 years ago, the first neuroimaging studies of human sleep were published, which used positron emission tomography (PET) or single-photon emission computed tomography to describe localized changes in regional cerebral blood flow during the specific nonrapid eye movement (non-REM) and REM-sleep stages. In brief, these data revealed a reduced metabolism during non-REM sleep as compared with wakefulness, while cerebral activity recovers again to levels close to or even locally exceeding wake-like activation during REM sleep. Later on, with the development of magnetic resonance compatible electroencephalography (EEG) systems and the possibility to exploit the higher temporal resolution of functional magnetic resonance imaging (fMRI) as compared to PET, these findings were not only reproduced but also extended to describe details of neural activation and deactivation associated with sleep stage–specific EEG events such as sleep spindles, K-complexes, and slow waves (see also the entry "Functional Neuroimaging during Human Sleep").

Recently, spontaneous changes in cerebral activation as reflected in ultra-slow blood oxygen level dependent signal fluctuation—being the basis of the fMRI contrast—in the range <0.1 Hz have gained broad interest in the neuroscience community because they occur in functionally related areas. In wakefulness, it has repeatedly been shown that these spontaneous changes in cerebral activity are organized in various resting-state networks (RSNs), including primary sensory networks, for example, sensorimotor, auditory, and visual networks, and in networks related to cognitive capabilities like the dorsal and ventral attention system, the frontoparietal control system, and the so-called default mode network (DMN). The nodes of these networks show synchronized fluctuations in activity even in the absence of any external task. In daytime measurements, the subject is generally only instructed to close his/her eyes, to think of nothing in particular, and to not fall asleep. fMRI is then continuously sampled more

than about 5 to 10 minutes, and data are either analyzed using seed-based correlation or data-driven independent component analysis (ICA). Since physiological noise such as heart beat or respiration may also directly contribute to signal fluctuations in the ultra-slow frequency range or project into this range, one needs to carefully exclude such artifacts. In seed-based analyses, this is regularly achieved by introducing additional nuisance regressors in the general linear model, to account for artifacts introduced by the subject's motion or by unspecific signal fluctuations, which are most strongly represented in white matter (WM) or cerebral spinal fluid (CSF) compartments. Using ICA, physiological noise generally gives rise to additional nuisance components with a typical spatial distribution encompassing WM and CSF regions or at brain borders, also characterized by strong signal contributions in the frequency range above 0.1 Hz. The low experimental demand and the independence of the subject's motivation to cooperate in a cognitive test made RSN measurements extremely appealing for studying psychiatric populations.

The physiological meanings of RSNs have been extensively studied. While the relation of sensory networks to the respective function appears trivial, the meaning of signal fluctuations in more cognitive networks, especially the DMN, is not as clear. In wakefulness, the DMN has been identified to be particularly active when the subject is engaged in introspection; for example, during future envisioning, recalling autobiographical or episodic memories, or mind wandering. Anatomically, the DMN includes the posterior cingulate

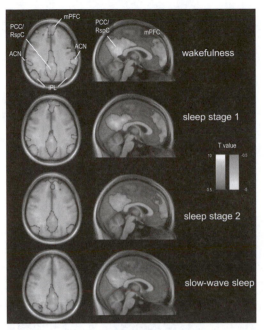

Overview of spatial configuration of the DMN and its anticorrelated network (ACN) ACN in different sleep stages. Group statistical maps (pcluster. FWE < 0.05) are shown along with a color code of T values. While the DMN remained robustly detectable throughout all sleep stages, visual inspection revealed several regional redistributions, such as stepwise decrease of functionally connected mPFC and diminishing ACN activity. Note the stability of the IPL nodes, and the decreased significance for the PCC/RspC. Adapted from (Sämann et al. 2011). (Michael Czisch)

cortex (PCC), retrosplenial cortex (RspC) and precuneus, the medial prefrontal cortex, posterior inferior parietal lobule (IPL) and, less tightly bound, the inferior temporal gyrus and the hippocampal formation (HF). The dorsal and ventral attention systems reveal anticorrelated activity with respect to the DMN, and are especially engaged when attention is directed to external tasks. Responsiveness to external stimuli has been shown to rely on the very activity of the attention system at the moment of stimulus delivery. Nodes of the attention system, anticorrelated in signal fluctuation to the DMN, are the anterior IPL, insula, and the lateral prefrontal cortex.

The PCC is the cerebral region with highest overall metabolic demand. Using PCC seed analysis, the DMN can reliably be identified, showing the strong connection of this major hub to the DMN. The anatomical distribution of the DMN with the inclusion of the PCC, RspC, and precuneus, along with its role in introspection, led to the notion that it may be linked to aspects of conscious awareness. A meta-analysis of radio tracer studies on the influence of various sedative agents identified a common decrease in cerebral activation in the PCC/RspC and precuneus, and the thalamus (Alkire & Miller, 2005). Decreased activation in the PCC/RspC may be regarded as a key feature of reduced consciousness. The DMN, however, has also been identified in anaesthetized monkeys, challenging the view of this network merely reflecting human consciousness. Furthermore, the DMN undergoes developmental changes, being segregated into several independent networks during early childhood (Supekar et al., 2010), showing strongest integrity in adulthood and a disintegration in elderly subjects, while consciousness itself is certainly not similarly dependent on age.

Still, the diametral cognitive features of self-awareness and external awareness, presumably reflected in the activity of the DMN and the attention system, can be assumed to be reduced in states of altered vigilance, for example, sedation, coma, as well as during natural sleep. It was shown that conscious sedation led to reduced functional connectivity of the PCC in the DMN. In locked-in syndrome patients as well as in minimally conscious, vegetative, or comatose patients, connectivity among all DMN areas was found to be negatively correlated with the degree of clinical consciousness impairment (Vanhaudenhuyse et al., 2010). This fostered the hypothesis that in individual subjects, a relative change in the configuration of DMN and of its anticorrelated counterpart should also be detectable during natural human sleep. Today, three studies have targeted possible RSN changes induced by non-REM sleep. Larson-Prior et al. (2009) studied six different RSNs in a small sample ($n = 6$) during wakefulness and light non-REM sleep (three primary sensory RSNs and the DMN as well as the attention and executive RSNs). All reported RSN were maintained in light sleep, and only the dorsal attention system showed slightly increased intranetwork correlations during sleep. No evidence for reduced functional connectivity during sleep was reported for any network. However, two other studies reported disintegration of the DMN and the attention system during deep non-REM sleep: Horovitz et al. (2009) reported that the DMN network components showed altered correlation during deep sleep (comprising sleep Stages 2 to 4), most pronounced as a breakdown of frontal cortical involvement in the DMN. Again, a rather small sample size was studied ($n = 7$). Our own data (Sämann et al., 2011), derived from 25 subjects and containing data of wakefulness, wake–sleep transition (sleep Stage 1), light sleep (Stage 2) as well as deep slow-wave sleep (SWS; Stages 3 and 4) also showed

a strongly reduced intranetwork coupling during light sleep and SWS, as compared to wakefulness, reflected by a breakdown of cortico–cortical coupling particularly between the posterior and anterior midline nodes.

The integration of the PCC/RspC node to the DMN itself was strongly reduced during sleep, starting to fade already at sleep onset, while the IPL nodes did not reveal

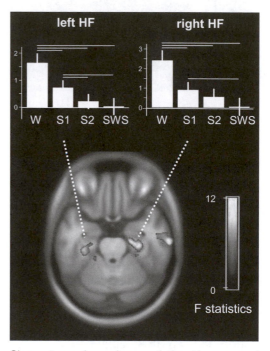

Sleep-stage dependency of the hippocampal contribution to the DMN. Clusters represent areas with significant main effect of sleep stage on focal DMN strength (pcluster.FWE < 0.05). Graph bars represent contrast estimates for each factor level (i.e., wakefulness W; sleep stages S1, S2; and SWS) as extracted from the peak voxels. Horizontal lines indicate significant post hoc comparisons as assessed by T contrasts. Note that HF reduces its contribution to the DMN to insignificance during SWS. Adapted from (Sämann et al. 2011). (Michael Czisch)

any alterations. These findings fit well to the proposed role of the PCC/RspC as a key node of the neural network of conscious-ness, and may explain the loss of conscious perception during sleep. Furthermore, the pronounced dichotomy between the DMN and its anticorrelated attention network as seen in wakefulness was strongly reduced, suggesting a disintegration of the opposing cognitive features. While also the attention network remains detectable throughout all sleep stages, its reduced intranetwork con-nectivity may represent a physiological correlate of diminished, but not abolished responsiveness to external stimuli during sleep. These speculations are in line with experiments employing neurophysiologi-cal recordings, which showed reduced coupling of frontal and parietal activity during sleep.

Two additional studies investigated whether sleep deprivation has an effect on the DMN configuration. It was shown that both the DMN and the anticorrelated net-work reveal reduced functional intranet-work coupling even after a rather mild intervention using partial sleep deprivation with restriction to four hours sleep during a single night (Sämann et al., 2010). These findings render the DMN rather sensitive to changes in vigilance.

Interestingly, the HF is the first structure to reduce its contribution to the DMN.

A stepwise retraction of its involvement can be observed already during transition from wakefulness to sleep, with vanishing contributions in SWS. The HF has been shown to be only moderately linked to the DMN in wakefulness, however, being re-liably co-activated in tasks with involve-ment of memory recollection. Our own

data (unpublished results) suggest that the HF builds up sleep-specific connectivities to neocortical sites, especially enhanced during sleep Stage 2 and during occurrence of sleep spindles. This may reflect an in-creased capacity of information flow from the HF as a short-term memory storage to other brain regions likely involved in long-term memory consolidation. Sleep has been proposed to enhance memory consolida-tion by allowing for an offline reprocess-ing of memory traces. Most studies suggest an important role of SWS in this process; however, our data may hint toward a two-step model with light sleep Stage 2 allowing for most efficient memory transfer, while reprocessing may be optimal during SWS where the cerebral network breaks down into small individual clusters, especially in frontal brain areas, laying the ground for enhanced focal information reprocessing. In this context, the structural integrity of RSNs, network properties, and HF func-tional connectivity also in REM sleep, proposed to subserve procedural learning during sleep, needs to be considered; how-ever, such data are still lacking. The suc-cessive breakdown of HF integration into the DMN during non-REM sleep may also help to explain why episodic memory re-ports are more frequent when the subject is awoken from light sleep than from deep sleep, suggesting that reduced access to ep-isodic memory may represent a behavioral correlate of hippocampal disintegration.

To summarize, the DMN network, de-fined by temporally coherent spontaneous signal fluctuations in fMRI, is not bound to wakefulness, preserved self-awareness, or conscious mental processing. Still, both the DMN and its anticorrelated attention

network undergo changes in correlation with vigilance alterations, be it sedation, natural sleep, or even increased sleep pressure after sleep deprivation. However, it should be noted that DMN integrity must be regarded a relative measure of vigilance only, as its overall integrity is also affected by age-dependent processes, with DMN nodes being less strongly connected during early childhood and in older adults. Relative vigilance dependent changes, on the other hand, need to be carefully considered in clinical or normative DMN studies, as comorbidities such as increased sleep pressure or light sleep during data recording may strongly affect RSN analyses and may be mistakenly interpreted as reflections of an underlying clinical pathology. This argues for a minimal experimental control of the vigilance state, which will affect the appealing simplicity of RSN measurements.

Michael Czisch

See also: Disturbed Sleep and Posttraumatic Stress Disorder

References

Alkire, M. T., & Miller, J. (2005). General anesthesia and the neural correlates of consciousness. *Progress in Brain Research, 150,* 229–244.

Horovitz, S. G., Braun, A. R., Carr, W. S., Picchioni, D., Balkin, T. J., Fukunaga, M., & Duyn, J. H. (2009). Decoupling of the brain's default mode network during deep sleep. *Proceedings of the National Academy of Science, 106,* 11376–11381.

Larson-Prior, L. J., Zempel, J. M., Nolan, T. S., Prior, F. W., Snyder, A. Z., & Raichle, M. E. (2009). Cortical network functional connectivity in the descent to sleep. *Proceedings of the National Academy of Science, 106,* 4489–4494.

Sämann, P. G., Tully, C., Spoormaker, V. I., Wetter, T. C., Holsboer, F., Wehrle, R., & Czisch, M. (2010). Increased sleep pressure reduces resting state functional connectivity. *MAGMA, 23,* 375–389.

Sämann, P. G., Wehrle, R., Hoehn, D., Spoormaker, V. I., Peters, H., Tully, C., . . . Czisch, M. (2011). Development of the brain's default mode network from wakefulness to slow wave sleep. *Cerebral Cortex, 21*(9), 2082–2093.

Supekar, K., Uddin, L. Q., Prater, K., Amin, H., Greicius, M. D., & Menon, V. (2010). Development of functional and structural connectivity within the default mode network in young children. *NeuroImage, 52,* 290–301.

Vanhaudenhuyse, A., Noirhomme, Q., Tshibanda, L. J., Bruno, M. A., Boveroux, P., Schnakers, C., . . . Boly, M. (2010). Default network connectivity reflects the level of consciousness in non-communicative brain-damaged patients. *Brain, 133,* 161–171.

Sleep and Cardiometabolic Risk

Sleep influences metabolic and cardiovascular physiology. *Sleep deficiency* can be defined as the presence of insufficient sleep duration and/or inadequate sleep quality, such as by a sleep disorder. Adequate sleep duration, typically thought to be in the range of seven to nine hours per night for most adults, can be operationalized as a lack of impairment of cognitive functions or other symptoms, or simply the lack of need for an alarm clock. In large epidemiologic studies, seven to eight hours per night of sleep confers the least risk to health. Less than seven hours per night of habitual sleep is associated with a higher risk of chronic diseases, including obesity, type-2 diabetes mellitus, hypertension, cardiovascular

disease, and even early mortality (Buxton & Marcelli, 2010). These chronic conditions represent a large portion of the burden of morbidity and mortality both in the United States and across the world.

Obesity and diabetes have recently become very common, coinciding with shorter sleep durations and sleep disorders in developed countries. The magnitude and duration of sleep restriction are likely to be important factors in determining the speed and extent of any metabolic changes. Weight is influenced by short sleep from hormones, such as leptin and ghrelin, which are released at different levels when people do not get enough sleep, increasing the drive to eat. Sleep loss also reduces insulin sensitivity (Buxton et al., 2010), the pancreatic response to calorie intake, and increases the risk for diabetes via a variety of other putative mechanisms (reviewed in Knutson & Van Cautter, 2008).

Hypertension and cardiovascular disease risks are also closely tied to sleep duration. High blood pressure, as defined by at least 140/90 mmHg, physician diagnosis, or use of antihypertensive medication, is a strong indicator of cardiovascular risk. Since high blood pressure can result from sleep deficiency, then the risk of cardiovascular disease also increases when there is sleep deficiency. Women are especially prone to the harmful effects of reduced sleep duration on cardiovascular function. Women who slept for less than six hours/night had a higher occurrence of hypertension than women who obtained at least six hours/night (Stranges et al., 2010).

Long sleep periods of more than eight hours per night can also be a risk factor for cardiometabolic diseases. In contrast with short sleep duration, which is thought to cause cardiometabolic problems, long sleep duration is more often thought to be an epiphenomenon of other comorbidities, such as sleep disordered breathing or depression. Sleep duration that is less than seven hours per night or greater than nine hours per night has been be described as extremes of sleep duration that amplify cardiometabolic risks. Increasing the proportion of the population achieving seven to eight hours of daily sleep, and treating sleep disorders, may substantially reduce chronic disease risk (Buxton & Marcelli, 2010).

The extent to which sleep deficiency affects cardiometabolic risks is just beginning to be understood and more laboratory studies are needed to provide information about the extent, mechanisms, and dynamics of these changes. Similarly, epidemiological studies are needed to address the socio-ecological framework or context in which sleep deficiency occurs "to the extent there is spatiotemporal and/or social variation in the age-specific patterns of any particular health outcome, it suggests modifiable causes are at play, whose mechanisms could presumably be altered by informed action" (Krieger, 2011, p. 31).

Orfeu Marcello Buxton

See also: entries related to Sleep and Health

References

Buxton, O. M., & Marcelli, E. (2010). Short and long sleep are positively associated with obesity, diabetes, hypertension, and cardiovascular disease among adults in the United States. *Social Science and Medicine, 71*(5), 1027–1036.

Buxton, O. M., Pavlova, M., Reid, E., Wang, W., Simonson, D. C., & Adler, G. K. (2010,

June). Sleep restriction for one week reduces insulin sensitivity in healthy men. *Diabetes, 28.*

Knutson, K. L., & Van Cauter, E. (2008). Associations between sleep loss and increased risk of obesity and diabetes. *Annals of the New York Academy of Science, 1129,* 287–304.

Krieger, N. (2011). *Epidemiology and the people's health: Theory and context.* New York: Oxford University Press.

Stranges, S., Dorn, J. M., Cappuccio, F. P., Donahue, R. P., Rafalson, L. B., Hovey, K. M., . . . Trevisan, M. A. (2010). Population-based study of reduced sleep duration and hypertension: The strongest association may be in premenopausal women. *Journal of Hypertension, 28*(5), 896–902.

Sleep and Culture

Human sleep is a biological developmental process, which is modified and interpreted by culturally based environmental and social norms, values, and beliefs (Jenni & O'Connor, 2009). Understanding the relative contribution of culture and its interaction with biological factors to determine sleep behavior is necessary to appreciate the cultural diversity of sleep practices, as well as the biological boundaries of sleep requisites throughout development.

Cultural norms and beliefs not only shape sleep practices, but also determine the interpretation of normal versus abnormal sleep in different developmental stages. Practices such as co-sleeping, delayed bedtime in adolescence, or daytime napping in adulthood may be considered normal in some cultures, yet abnormal, disruptive, and problematic in others. As a corollary, incompatibility between biological sleep requisites and culturally acceptable sleep practices may lead to disturbances in sleep and development (Jenni & O'Connor, 2009).

While considerable research has focused on the biological mechanisms of sleep, to date, relatively little work has been done on the effects of culture. Cultural investigations of sleep behaviors and disorders are derived from comparisons between groups of nations with common cultural values, lifestyles, and/or social structures (e.g., Western vs. non-Western countries), among different countries within a group of nations (e.g., different Western or European countries) and among ethnic minorities within countries (e.g., African Americans). The terms culture, ethnicity, and race in these studies are often used synonymously.

The vast majority of studies on sleep and culture have focused on infants and young children, in which cultural effects on sleep practices are largely mediated by parents. Sleep position and co-sleeping have received considerable attention in Western countries over the past two decades, in the context of sudden infant death syndrome (SIDS), advocating for placing infants in the supine position and against co-sleeping. In Asian and other non-Western cultures, co-sleeping is highly prevalent, due to different cultural values, different living arrangements, as well as considerably lower rates of SIDS. It has been suggested that while Western culture has generally opposed co-sleeping as part of traditional child-rearing practices aimed to promote independence and individualism, non-Westernized cultures practice

co-sleeping to enhance values emphasizing maternal bonding, breast-feeding, family cohesion, and social relationships (Anuntaseree et al., 2008).

The biological sleep need has been established for different age groups, yet its cultural interpretation differs, as demonstrated by cultural variations in the timing and duration of sleep. School children in North America have shown consistent and earlier bedtimes and longer sleep duration than South American, Asian, and Southern European countries. Whereas academic achievement has been implicated as a cultural value underlying late bedtimes and early rise times in Asian cultures, family and social interaction characterize late and lenient bedtimes in Mediterranean European and South American cultures (Jenni & O'Connor, 2009; Liu, Liu, Owens, & Kaplan, 2005).

Daytime napping has been attributed to a siesta culture, referring to geographical areas with warm climate; however, this concept is gradually disappearing in Westernized countries, and napping is generally considered a cross-cultural phenomenon, although ethnic differences in its prevalence have been demonstrated in different age groups (Valencia-Flores et al., 1998).

Comparative studies have demonstrated that sleep disturbances are universal in children, adolescents, and adults; however, ethno-cultural differences in their prevalence exist, and likely reflect cultural differences in their presentation and etiology (Liu et al., 2005; Roberts, Roberts, & Chen, 2000). In general, cultures that favor more restrictive sleep practices may present with a higher prevalence of sleep disturbances, based on their strict interpretation of what

is considered normal sleep. Racial factors pertaining to genetic and health dispositions also play a role.

To date, most studies investigating cultural differences in sleep practices and disturbances have relied on epidemiological data from which underlying cultural factors have been inferred. Thus, cultural underpinnings are poorly understood. Future studies should use qualitative methodology to directly target cultural values and beliefs to better appreciate the fundamental cultural factors that determine sleep behaviors in different age groups, and to provide the basis for understanding the role of culture in the etiology of sleep disturbances. Distinctions should be made between culture, ethnicity, and race. Investigation of the functional implications of cultural diversity in sleep practices is another important area that has yet to be explored.

Tamar Shochat

See also: Anthropology of Sleep

References

Anuntaseree, W., Mo-Suwan, L., Vasiknanonte, P., Kuasirikul, S., Ma-A-Lee, A., & Choprapawon, C. (2008). Factors associated with bed sharing and sleep position in Thai neonates. *Child: Care, Health and Development, 34*(4), 482–490.

Jenni, O. G., & O'Connor, B. B. (2009). Children's sleep: An interplay between culture and biology. *Pediatrics, 115*(1), 204–216.

Liu, X., Liu, L., Owens, J. A., & Kaplan, D. L. (2005). Sleep patterns and sleep problems among schoolchildren in the United States and China. *Pediatrics, 115*(1 Suppl.), 241–249.

Roberts, R. E., Roberts, C. R., & Chen, I. G. (2000). Ethnocultural differences in sleep complaints among adolescents. *Journal of Nervous and Mental Disease, 188*(4), 222–229.

Valencia-Flores, M., Castaño, V. A., Campos, R. M., Rosenthal, L., Resendiz, M., Vergara, P., . . . Bliwise, D. L. (1998). The siesta culture concept is not supported by the sleep habits of urban Mexican students. *Journal of Sleep Research, 7*(1), 21–29.

Sleep and Dreams in Psychiatric Disorders and Autism

Definition of Psychiatric Disorders

Standard guideline criteria such as the Diagnostic and Statistical Manual of Mental Disorders (DSM) and the International Statistical Classification of Diseases and Related Health Problems are widely accepted in terms of diagnoses of psychiatric (mental health) disorders, but there is no general definition of psychiatric disorders that is universally accepted. A review of various sources nonetheless reveals the following set of key elements: a pattern in which a person's thoughts, emotions, or behavior is severely deviant from accepted norms, associated with distress or disability, and that interferes with the capacity to function in life. More than a third of people report to have suffered from a metal health disorder at some point in their lives. This entry will cover the topic of sleep and dreams in the most common forms of psychiatric disorders: anxiety, depression, and schizophrenia, as well as in autism.

Anxiety

There are many diagnostic subcategories in anxious disorders including, among others: generalized anxiety disorder, panic disorder, social phobia, obsessive-compulsive disorder, and posttraumatic stress disorder (PTSD). Although the severity index may be variable from one diagnosis to another, sleep disorders are present in most—and may be even more so in children and adolescents. Difficulty with sleep initiation and maintenance is a common finding in anxiety disorders, as shown by long sleep latencies and low sleep efficiency caused by long and/or multiple awakenings. The internal structure of sleep itself can also be challenged: low amounts of slow-wave sleep (SWS: non-REM sleep Stages 3 + 4) can be found while REM-sleep abnormalities are more rarely reported, except for decreased REM-sleep-onset latency in obsessive-compulsive disorders. As in other cases of psychiatric disorders, insomnia persists after a treatment for PTSD as up to 50 percent of remitted patients reported residual insomnia.

With a prevalence of around 60 percent, nightmares are a salient feature of PTSD and, in fact, make up a diagnostic element in the DSM algorithm. The content of nightmares in PTSD is most often recurrent and associated to the traumatic event. Imagery rehearsal therapy is known to be an excellent treatment option (Krakow & Zadra, 2006).

Major Depressive Disorder

Sleep in major depressive disorder (MDD), such as anxiety, is most often characterized by difficulties initiating and maintaining sleep. Not only does insomnia appear as a risk factor for new onset and recurrence of MDD, but it may also increase prior to recurrence and, like anxiety, it often remains after successful treatment for MDD. It is occasionally reported that some depressed patients may display hypersomnia instead of insomnia; even though it is a possibility, such cases should first be investigated for comorbid sleep apnea, seasonal variance of symptoms, and other medical conditions causing fatigue or somnolence. Research reports on the structure of sleep in MDD are quite univocal, with low amounts of SWS and a facilitation of REM sleep (short latency, long duration, and high density of rapid eye movements). Short REM-sleep latency is not a marker of depression as it is also present in schizophrenia, borderline personality disorders, eating disorders, and obsessive-compulsive disorders. Still, there are reports of a negative correlation between suicidality scores and REM-sleep latency, and a positive correlation between suicidality and REM-sleep duration leading to the hypothesis that suicidal persons fail to integrate effect into long-term memory during REM-sleep dreaming.

Depressed individuals dream as much as healthy persons. The recent review of De Koninck (in press) reports that while some authors describe the dreams of depressed individuals as dull and bland, others could make detailed content analyses. He argues that divergent findings may rely on a selection bias from one study to another, with mild, moderate, or remitted patients reporting more negative dream elements while more severe patients would generate more neutral dreams. In any case, and even though dream reports of depressed individuals may be shorter, content analyses overall reveal more negative elements, with more failures and misfortunes, but hostility directed toward self and others is not a prominent feature. A recent review of Kramer (2010) reports that patients with more negative elements in dreams from the first half of the night compared to the second half are more likely to be in a better psychological condition after one year.

Schizophrenia

Sleep studies in neuroleptic-free schizophrenia patients have been reviewed by Chouinard, Poulin, Stip, and Godbout (2004). The meta-analysis of 20 studies (321 patients vs. 331 healthy controls) revealed difficulties initiating and maintaining sleep, which were worse in neuroleptic-withdrawn patients than in neuroleptic-naïve patients—although only neuroleptic-naïve patients showed a significantly increased duration of nocturnal awakening time versus controls. There were no significant effect sizes whatsoever on SWS, REM-sleep latency, and REM-sleep duration. Since, for example, 9 of the 20 reviewed studies reported significant differences on REM-sleep latency, Chouinard et al. (2004) suggested that unavailable moderator variables such as chronicity, severity, and diagnosis subtype as well as gender could be responsible for the inconsistent evidence toward the existence of abnormal SWS and REM sleep in schizophrenia. These variables should thus be controlled for in future studies.

With this advisory note in mind, our literature review indicates that dreams of persons with schizophrenia have been reported to be more hostile, bizarre, and populated with strangers in older studies (see Kramer, 2010). More recent studies such as that of Lusignan et al. (2009)

indicate that schizophrenics successfully treated with atypical neuroleptics subjectively report the same rate of dream recall, recurrent dreams, and frequency of emotions in their dreams but a greater number of nightmares, compared to healthy controls. Dream reports collected upon REM-sleep awakenings are shorter, with more unknown characters but without more bizarre elements than controls—which contrasts with questionnaires studies. It has also been reported that dreams of psychotic patients contain more elements of aggression, particularly toward the dreamer, and that more dramatic reports could precede a psychotic relapse. Such cases could explain reports of dreams being close to daytime mentation.

Autism

Sleep in autism is characterized by signs of insomnia, including a longer sleep latency, more frequent nocturnal awakenings, decreased SWS but normal REM-sleep latency and duration compared to controls, and whether participants have a low or a normal IQ.

Studies of dreams in autism are few and most often rely on clinical anecdotes. The most recent report used questionnaires and dream narratives obtained upon REM-sleep awakenings in autistics with a normal IQ. Results indicated a lower dream recall; shorter dreams with less features such as fewer settings, objects, characters, social interactions, activities, and emotions in the clinical group compared to controls (Daoust, Lusignan, Braun, Mottron, & Godbout, 2008). The authors

concluded that these results may reflect the neurocognitive style of autistics.

Conclusion

Difficulties in initiating and maintaining sleep are present in most psychiatric diagnoses reviewed here, as well as in autism. Dream characteristics do not always reflect daytime symptomatology, although uncontrolled variables are part of almost every published report.

Roger Godbout

See also: entries related to Sleep and Development; entries related to Sleep Disorders

References

Chouinard, S., Poulin, J., Stip, E., & Godbout, R. (2004). Sleep in untreated patients with schizophrenia: A meta-analysis. *Schizophrenia Bulletin, 30,* 957–967.

Daoust, A. M., Lusignan, F. A., Braun, C.M.J., Mottron, L., & Godbout, R. (2008). Dream content analysis in persons with an autism spectrum disorder. *Journal of Autism and Developmental Disorders, 38,* 634–643.

De Koninck, J. (in press). Dreams and dreaming. In C. Morin & C. Epsie (Eds.), *Oxford handbook of sleep and sleep disorders.* Oxford: Oxford University Press.

Krakow, B., & Zadra, A. (2006). Clinical management of chronic nightmares: Imagery rehearsal therapy. *Behavioral Sleep Medicine, 4,* 45–70.

Kramer, M. (2010). Dream differences in psychiatric patients. In S. R. Pandi-Perumal & M. Kramer (Eds.), *Sleep and mental illness* (pp. 375–382). Cambridge: Cambridge University Press.

Lusignan, F. A., Zadra, A., Dubuc, M. J., Daoust, A. M., Mottard, J.P., & Godbout, R. (2009). Dream content in chronically-treated persons with schizophrenia. *Schizophrenia Research, 112,* 164–173.

Sleep and Dreams in Western Antiquity

In the Homeric poems (c. 750–723? BCE), the god of sleep is located on the Isle of Lemnos, where even Juno flew to visit the brother of death to induce sleep in Zeus (*Iliad* XIV, 270). According to Hesiod (born, c. 700 BCE), "Nix bore hateful Moros (doom) and black Ker (destiny) and Thanatos (death), she bore Hypnos and the tribe of Oineroi" (*Theogony* 211–212). Caldwell appropriately stresses that the children of night are all connected with her, they are terrible and are the personification of sleep (Hypnos), dream (Oineroi), death (Thanatos), and blame (Momos). Sleep is the devil with a child's body and death is the old man with the white head (Caldwell, 1987, p. 1).

Sleep is significantly associated with the life of Epimenides (660/657–500 BCE), who was born and died in Crete, and is sometimes included in the list of the seven sages of antiquity. He lived for 150 years, sleeping for nearly 60 years. In his work *Longlived,* Flegontes tells that Epimenides lived for 154 years, others for 157 years, and still others for 160 years; those living in Crete say 260 years. Xenophanes of Colophon lived for 154 years (Giannatoni, 2004, p. 2; Reale, 2006a, p. 3). According to *The Presocratics* (41, 42), "this man was sent by his father to look for a sheep . . .; however, having lost his way he fell asleep in a cave where he slept for the subsequent 57 years. When he woke up he continued to look for the sheep, since he was convinced that he had slept just for a few hours."

Epicharmus (c. 525 to c. 450 BCE) was born in an unknown place. Samos, Cadmos, and Megara Iblea have their own rights in claiming to be the place of his birth. Known as the inventor of comedy, he lived in Syracuse at the time of Gelon and Hyeron, and considered dreams as the best method for divination; in this he agreed with Philocorus of Athens: "In fact since we do not have the power to dream, how can a man cause a vision since he is not empowered to dream?"

For Heraclitus of Ephesus (who flourished from 504–501 BCE) "in sleep sense-channels are closed, so that the mind is prevented from growing together with what lies outside." Furthermore, according to Heraclitus "we become intelligent by aspiring the divine logos through respiration and during sleep we forget, when we awake we are again intelligent. In fact, during sleep, sensing pores are closed and the intelligence within us is separated from that which envelopes us, by saving during respiration a contact point, like a root and when we are separated the capability of memory is lost. Upon waking, by looking through pores like through windows, it is possible to reestablish the connection and the capability to reason is restored." For Heraclitus the soul was connected with the heat of fire and "sleep is regarded as due to a reduction of organic heat." In Fragment 21, Clemens Alexandrinus (*Stromata* III21[II 205 7]) reports that "Heraclitus names death the birth when he says 'Death is all that we see when are awake and sleep is all that we see while asleep'."

Euclides of Megara (450–380 BCE) identified sleep as a young devil, and he described death as an old man with white hair. For Diogenes of Apollonia, who flourished from 440 to 430 BCE, "sleep is caused by a moistening of the airsoul." More specifically, it is said to occur when blood fills the veins and drives the air in them to the chest and stomach (Aëtius, 2006, pp. 5.24.3, A29).

For Alcmaeon (510?–440? BCE), who lived in the sixth century BCE (his life overlapped in part with Pythagoras's life span), "all senses are in some way connected to the brain and for this reason they are incapacitated if it is disturbed or shifted, for it obstructs the passages through which the sensation take place" (Theophrastus, *De sensu*). Only humans are capable of making a synthesis of sensations. Animals are incapable of it. The brain is the center of sensations, and the head is the center of psychical life. "Sleep is caused by the confinement of blood to larger blood-vessels, whereas waking is brought about by re-diffusion; death supervenes when it is completely withdrawn" (Vlastos, 1987). For Alcmaeon life is equality between powers, disease is the outcome of prevalence of one power. So good health is achieved when opposites are balanced. Life is motion, death supervenes since men "cannot link the beginning to end," that is, to follow the circular path of motion which is followed by divine stars. According to Philo of Alexandria, God's work connected the end with the beginning and "caused the end to return to the beginnings. Soul, located in the brain, is motion and therefore immortal and animates the cosmos" (Guthrie, 1982).

For Anaxagoras (500/497?–428 BCE) sleep was a process unrelated to the soul and entirely due to the body, and therefore it could be considered as "exhaustion of physical energy."

Empedocles (492–432 BCE)

In Aëtius we read: "Empedocles thinks that sleep depends on a moderate cooling of the warmth in the blood, death, by contrast, is due to a total cooling— Empedocles thinks that death is caused by separation of the element fire, of the element air, of the element water, of the element earth which assembled together give origin to man, therefore death is common to body and soul, sleep depends on the separation of the element fire" (Reale, 2006c). Philiponus reports that "Empedocles discussing differences among dreams affirms that from the activities during the day fancies are generated in the night, those fancies are named thought. Thinking during dreams induces different things" (Reale, 2006d). A lot can be read about vaticinations and oracles in Empedocles's *Purifications,* where he addresses the people of Akragas: "Some of them need vaticinations others affected by terrible pains for a long time ask for responses capable of healing diseases of any kind" (Reale, 2006b). Finally, Parmenides is also aware of the physiological views of the Akragantine philosopher, which are given in a strong synopsis: "In Empedocles's view, sleep resulted from blood cooling, death ensued when heat left it completely."

Antiphontes (Last Part of the Fifth Century BCE)

The most revolutionary of all was Antiphontes, mathematician and philosopher of the last part of the fifth century, who authored four treatises, *On Interpretation of Dreams* (*Peri kriseo s onéion*), which has been lost (Onfray, 2006). As a sophist, he thought that men are equal and that human nature can guarantee happiness. He also wrote on the squaring of the circle. That is, he dealt with very difficult problems, the most difficult a philosopher of his time cared to debate. He was a caustic philosopher, belonging to the category of those who doubted everything and was never prone to be domesticated. Furthermore, he had a natural charisma. His words were penetrating and sharp. At Corinth, a city that during the seventh and the sixth century BCE achieved extraordinary levels of social and economic development, he opened an office in the main square of the city, an arrangement that was very much at variance with those of his contemporary philosophers. "There he used to admit patients and started treating them with a new method based on talks with the patient. He starts by listening to the patient in confidence, a verbal therapy. The content of the conversation aims to annihilate the pain which had driven the patients to Antiphontes's office. The details of this therapy were included in the book *The Art of Escaping Afflictions* which has been lost" (Onfray, 2006). Antiphontes's reputation as a great physician grew and he proved capable of living up to his good name. Antiphontes also took good advantage of his rich clients to advertise his name and fame. He stimulated curiosity around him, due to his unprecedented activity, based on an innovative methodology that was not part of practice during his time. His words were essential, he used polished expressions without giving the impression of looking for refinement; his speech was fluent, clear, and hypnotizing, thus helping patients to get rid of disease or to cope with it and its consequences. He investigated dreams, and about things that happened during night hours, when humans lose contact with the external world. "Antiphontes gave to dreams a cardinal role in the economy of his therapy. He suggested interpreting them. Seven centuries before the publication of *The Key of Dreams* of Artemidorus of Ephesus, he practiced a dream critique based on rational *exegesis* and on the use of pure and simple logic of well interpreted causality. His method refers to the analysis and research of aggravating factors" (3). Antiphontes emerges as being very capable in the art of persuasion. In Fragment (no. 3), he is precise: "in every man the mind directs the body towards health and disease and towards all the remaining aspects of life" (Reale, 2006b; Onfray, 2006). In this respect, Antiphontes opposed Socrates and his practice of teaching virtue, and his very sober conduct; he refused to scorn the money he received from his patients, since it procured him temporary well-being; he was not ashamed of the earnings in exchange for his teachings, which for him were not only legal but also honest. He emerged as an anticipator of the advent of psychoanalysis, or better as the inventor of a therapy that is similar to psychoanalysis and anticipated not only Freud but also Lacan (Onfray, 2006). The dissent between Antiphontes and Socrates can be followed in Xenophon's *memorabilia,* in which Antiphontes concedes that Socrates is a fair man; however, he accuses him (1) of teaching things of no value that are not worthy of payment and for which no payment is requested or given; (2) of living a very modest life, not different from that of a slave, without shoes and tunic, using the same clothes in winter and in summer, and eating and drinking poor food and beverages; (3) of arrogance for teaching politics without being a politician. Socrates answers with his decision for a life oriented toward the divine.

In *The Presocratics* (Giannatoni, 2004; Reale, 2006a), an extensive, appealing chapter deals with Antiphontes. There one reads the following information from Plutarch's *Vitae:* "they say that he composed tragedies on his own and in collaboration with the tyrant Dionysius. While practicing poetry he also composed *'the art of avoiding suffering',* which is a cure similar to what physicians prescribe to patients; having set up a physician's office at Corinth near the main square (agora), and announced that he was able to heal patients by talking to them, and after hearing about the causes of the illness, he used to comfort the diseased."

Subsequently, having judged that the profession was not appropriate for his personality, Antiphontes entered the field of public speaking. For Philostratus (*Vitae sophistarum*), Antiphontes was very able in persuading and was nicknamed Nestor since he was able to convince people to accept his point of view; he used to give lectures on the art of suppressing pain. He used to say that for him there was no pain that could resist his cure (the patient did no longer feel pain whatever the initial grade). Lucianus (*Vera historia*) refers to the Isle of Dreams where Antiphontes the interpreter of dreams presided as the oracle, a role received by Sleep. In *Gnomologium Vindobonense* (50, 14 Wachsmuth), one reads that Antiphontes, when asked to explain the divinatory art, answered that it was the guesses of a thoughtful man. For Antiphontes "the mind directs the body toward health and toward disease and toward any aspect of life" (Giannatoni, 2004; Reale, 2006a).

Sleep and Dreams in Plato (429–347 BCE)

For Plato sleep begins when light is turned off. The dark supervenes. Eyes shut off and keep internally the fire of the light. Light meets with its opposite—darkness. Relations with the external world become minimal, and sensations disappear. The internal fire weakens senses. For Plato, as well as for Eraclitus, the processes that occurred during sleep at night could be compared to the switching on of light in the absence of it. Serafina Rotondaro, who has extensively written with originality, in his PhD thesis at the University of Naples, about sleep and dreams in Plato (15), stresses the fact that "Greek thought utilized dreams as diagnostic tools. From Hippocrates to Galen, dreams were used to trace organic disease. For Plato, sleep softens tiredness." In *Leges* (VII 808b6-c2) Plato points out that "sleep is useful to the body. One should sleep a little, an indispensable minimum. Only those lacking responsibility sleep a lot. The master and the mistress of the house shall sleep a little. A long sleep is not appropriate, neither for law of nature nor for bodies nor to souls, nor to the actions of body and soul." In addition a person "who sleeps is of no value, as a dead body" (*Leges* 808b5–6). Sleep is not conducive to ingenuity, and is a state of torpidity and immobility; the loss of productivity during sleep must be avoided.

Sleep and Dreams in Aristotle (384–322 BCE)

Sleep and dreams are discussed by Aristotle in *Parva naturalia (Small Essays on Philosophy of Nature)*, which include *De Somno et Vigilia (On Sleep and Waking)*, *De Insomniis (On Dreams)*, and *De divinatione per somnum (Divination during Sleep)*. In *De somno et Vigilia*, waking and sleep are described as being opposed to each other. During sleep there is a loss of perception. Sleep is deprivation of waking, and waking a deprivation of sleep.

"Sleep and waking belong to the same part of the animal, since they are antagonists, sleep appears as a lack of waking. In fact in nature as everywhere contraries appear within the same receptor and constitute its affections" (*On Sleep and Waking,* 453 b 25). Sleep is something that affects body and soul and during sleep there is no perception. Plants do not sleep and are different from animals. "They lack the sensitive part" (*On Sleep and Waking* 454a15). Sleep is necessary since waking induces fatigue, which would prevent the exercise of the perception that is necessary for living. One cannot be always sleepy. "The sleep is an affection of the perceptive part, like a kind of enchainment and immobility, so that it is necessary that all that sleeps entails a perceptive part" (*On Sleep and Waking* 454 b 15). Sleep affects both perception and motion and therefore animals are quiet during sleep (but the lack of movements is not absolute). The fact that the principle of perception in animals (456 a 1) depends on the same body site, which regulates the principle of the movement, has been defined elsewhere. Of the three places examined, this site is in the middle, between the head and the lower abdomen. In bloody animals, it is the part surrounding the heart (456 a 1–455 a 5).

Perception begins in the thorax, in the area of the heart. Sleep follows alimentation, which generates blood, which then diffuses in the whole body. Since during the concoction of the food evaporation occurs, blood is cooled and sent to the brain. At this point the head becomes cold and heavy, and the blood comes down to the heart where it pushes the heat typical of that region. At this time the animal sleeps. Sleep has nothing to do with fainting. Therefore the incapability to perceive is due to a process by which the food is turned into blood. This also has beneficial effects in protecting animals from excessive accumulation of heat.

The essay *On Dreams* has been analyzed innovatively by Luciana Repici in six propositions, as follows (Repici, 2003a): Dreaming is an affection of the perceptive part of the soul's imaginative part (1). Images of dream arise during sleep, and leave permanent traces of perceptions during waking (2). During the perceptive processes in waking it is possible to percept quickly even movements due to small differences (3). During perception in waking, deception may occur in cases of passion or disease (4). Images of dreams appear during sleep when the residual movements during daytime are carried by blood to the heart (5). The image of dreams deceives since during sleep there is no true perception and what appears is only similar to the truth (6).

Dreaming belongs to the perceptive part of the soul. It is a perception of images of objects as they present during sleep. Dreaming is related to the part of the soul that is activated during sleep. The images during sleep are residual movements due to perception during waking.

This is explained by using the example of the current of the rivers: "We have to assume that similarly to small whirlpools which take place in rivers, any movement takes place continuously" (*On Dreams* 461a 8). When waters meet obstacles they may fragment and may turn into a vortex. The small movements are induced by blood. Of course the images during sleep may be misleading since no perception occurs during sleep, so what is seen is only similar to the truth. Repici stresses that "sleep deceives not as in the case of something which is considered false taking into account the data of perception, but as something that during waking is seen in a certain way when we are ill or when we are healthy and aware but let ourselves be carried on by appearances" (Repici, 2003b).

For Aristotle "dream is the image generated by movements of the residual effects of perception during sleep, since one sleeps" (*On dreams* 464 b). Concerning the lack of dreams in some persons, and the fact that some of them have dreams during old age, it is to be explained by the changes in the quantity of perspiration. When perspiration is abundant it does not cause dreams; in old people, perspiration is scanty, and could lead to increased dreaming.

"By progressing age it is not absurd that a dream might appear due to age related changes or due to affections" (*On Dreams* 462 b 10).

Divination during sleep is introduced by L. Repici (2003b) through the following propositions: (1) to believe in divinatory sleep one should take for granted that they are sent by gods; (2) dreams do not anticipate future events; (3) dreams are not sent by the divinity, they originate in nature and by nature they are demonic; (4) most dreams do not come into reality since in nature not all happens according to previsions; (5) dreams of extraordinary events or out of the capability of the dreamer are either coincidences or are due to perceptive movements that are perceived only during sleep; (6) predictive dreams do not require extraordinary capabilities; (7) the precise interpretation of dreams can only be done by people who are knowledgeable about it Here Aristotle negates the existence of divinatory dreams. Dreams cannot anticipate the future. If that happens it should be considered a coincidence. Aristotle also underlines the importance of the capability of drawing on similarities, and makes clear that linear, simple dreams are easy to understand, whereas there are difficulties in interpreting broken dreams, which should be compared with images that are reflected on water.

The most technically able interpreter of dreams is he who can observe similarities, since anyone can interpret linear dreams. I refer to similarities since images are sometimes similar to the appearance reflected on water as was said before. In that case if the movement is intense the reflection and the reflected appearances are not similar to true things. Capable of interpreting dreams are those who can discern in one cumulative look reflected, broken and twisted appearances. (*On Dreams* 464 b 515)

Repici (2003b) appropriately compares Aristotle's position *On Dreams* to that taken by Hippocrates in *The Diet* and stresses that Hippocrates asked that the work be done by expert people. For Hippocrates only specialists (diviners) could be allowed to interpret dreams. He too accepted the existence of divinatory sleeps, in which dreams are generated by the soul that, during sleep, has no link with the body and has a great deal of independent activity. Also Democritus had negated divinatory sleeps; dreaming during sleep was, however, a natural possibility.

Rosa Maria De Santo and
Natale Gaspare De Santo

See also: entries related to History of Dreams/Sleep

References

Caldwell, R.R. (1987). *Hesiod's theogony.* Newport, MA: Focus Classical Library.

Giannatoni, P. (2004). *I Presocratici.* Bari: Laterza.

Guthrie, W.K.C. (1982). *A history of Greek philosophy* (Vol. 1). Cambridge: Cambridge University Press.

Onfray, M. (2006). *Les sagesses antiques.* Contre-histoire de la philosophie. Tome I. Paris: Grasset & Fasquelle. (Italian translation.)

Reale, G. (2006a). *I Presocratici.* Milan: Bompiani.

Reale, G. (2006b). *I Presocratici.* Milan: Bompiani, 112.

Reale, G. (2006c). *I Presocratici.* Milan: Bompiani, 85.

Reale, G. (2006d). *I Presocratici.* Milan: Bompiani, 108.

Repici, L. (2003a). *Aristotele.* Il sonno e i sogni. Venezia: Marsilio Editore; note 5, 160.

Repici, L. (2003b). *Aristotele.* Il sonno e i sogni. Venice: Marsilio Editore, 40–47.

Rotondaro S. (1998). *Il sogno in Platone—Fisiologia di una metafora.* Naples: Loffredo.

Vlastos, G. (1987). *Studies in Greek philosophy.* In D.W. Graham (Ed.), *The Presocratics* (Vol. 1, pp. 94–96). Princeton, NJ: Princeton University Press.

Sleep and Evolution of Detailed Focal Vision

Few evolutionists have contributed to the myriad of theories of sleep's origin and functions. Papers of nonevolutionists with the word evolution in their title only draw conclusions based on comparisons between various evolutionary endpoints in extant species.

It is suggested here that the evolutionary progression from restful waking to primitive sleep was initiated when animals evolved the increasingly complex, highly mobile lifestyles supported by detailed focal vision. Such vision requires enormous amounts of neural processing. Thus, almost half the primate's neocortical neurons and brain circuitry are needed to represent the pictorial world. This processing is vastly more complex than for any other sense, probably more so than for all others combined. Information advances from the primary visual cortex along a dorsal *where* pathway and a ventral *what* pathway. Without focusing on anything specific, one becomes aware of the simultaneous presence of almost limitless numbers of objects, of all sizes, shapes, orientations, positions, depths, and colors.

In those past times, as animals acquired detailed focal vision, their lifestyles became markedly altered. With sharper discriminations and engagement in multifarious new activities, including fast, wide-ranging movements, and rapid actions and responses, it would have been crucial to retain vast stores of long-term memories. In these circumstances, the parallel processing capacity of some regions of these animals' brains would have become severely taxed. It would have become increasingly difficult for brain regions with multiple functions to meet requirements associated with crucial, largely unpredictable hazards and routine essential needs, while also meeting needs to acquire and maintain vast stores of memories.

In essence, an adaptation that initially conferred great efficiency of brain operation, before the evolution of detailed focal vision and great mobility, would have become increasingly less efficient as such lifestyles evolved, had not compensating features evolved in parallel—first restful waking and, eventually, primitive sleep. Accordingly, the selective pressure for primitive sleep, that is, sleep's ultimate cause, probably was the need to resolve these developing conflicts. This could have been achieved most readily through development of a period of greater brain unresponsiveness to outside occurrences than exists during restful waking, namely, primitive sleep. By including a portion of the 24-hour life cycle when enormously increased needs for memory processing could be accommodated efficiently, primitive sleep greatly reduced any conflict arising during urgent waking-brain activities, particularly the rapid processing and responding to increasingly complex and varied visual inputs.

It follows from this mode of origin of primitive sleep that sessile and very slowly moving animals would have no need for sleep. It also follows that sleep would be engaged in only during that portion of an animal's existence when danger was at a relative minimum and rapid movements usually were unnecessary; for example, during the night for day-active animals.

Thus, the long-sought ultimate function of sleep appears to be an enabling one. Sleep enables the brain to operate with uniformly high efficiency. This was accomplished by the evolution of a vigilance state to which low-priority waking-brain activities, particularly the enormously increased needs for memory processing, could be deferred. But even this enabling does not prevent the occurrence of illusions in humans, at least, during infrequent periods of overflow of visual information. This scenario for the origin and ultimate function of sleep does not rule out the evolution of secondary (proximate) functions that may have become essential, including rest, rejuvenation, and deep-seated rhythmical changes influencing physiological processes.

Looking beyond superficial appearances, some contradictory occurrences that long contributed to obscuring sleep's ultimate function, find their explanations. These included a continuing need for sleep by blind animals. In these, brain circuitry otherwise normally devoted to vision assumes other essential functions. Another seeming contradiction was the absence of sleep in some fast-swimming fishes with excellent vision but characteristically highly monotonous lifestyles. In these, conflicts between other waking-brain activities and needs for learning are minimal.

Occasionally a natural experiment provides the critical test for a theory. This occurred when sleep was discovered in a jellyfish, a member of a phylum with only two germ layers. *Chironex fleckeri* has 24 eyes (ocelli), 8 of which are of complex camera types, such as the lensed eyes of vertebrates. True to expectations, when acting as fast-moving, voracious predators, these jellyfish sleep 15 hours per day. But their possession of a passive alternate lifestyle was even more revealing. When hunting entirely passively, no sleep is needed. Apparently, sleep only becomes necessary when the needs of the waking brain exceed the brain's waking capacity. Typically, but not always, this boundary is crossed only after the evolution of detailed focal vision.

J. Lee Kavanau

See also: entries related to Evolution of Sleep

Reference

Kavanau, J. L. (2006). Is sleep's "supreme mystery" unraveling? An evolutionary analysis of sleep encounters no mystery; nor does life's earliest sleep, recently discovered in jellyfish. *Medical Hypotheses, 66,* 3–9.

Sleep and Growth Hormone Release

Circulating levels of a number of growth-related hormones appear to both influence, and be influenced, by sleep. Nighttime levels of these hormones typically exceed their daytime levels. Nocturnal growth-hormone (GH) levels, for example, are at least four times the daytime level of GH in young men. The synchronized brain waveforms of NREM slow-wave sleep (SWS) are associated with a major surge in GH release. The surge in GH release in humans is particularly marked in males. Somatostatin (SS) too is influenced by sleep processes, but it inhibits both GH and GH-releasing hormone (GHRH). Levels of GH appear to be regulated via sleep-related stimulation of GHRHergic neurons of the anterior pituitary and the medial preoptic region. As GHRH and GH levels rise with SWS, GH, and insulin-like growth factor, feedback onto GHRH neurons inhibits GH release and regulates GH levels.

Significant reductions in NREM-sleep amounts are found in transgenic mice with GHRH deficiency and in mutant rats with a defect in the GHRH receptor signaling system. In giant transgenic mice with excess GH (100 to 200 times the normal levels of GH), NREM-sleep times were increased moderately, but REM-sleep times were increased substantially during the light period (when rats typically sleep). Systemic injection of the powerful SS analogue octreotide suppresses sleep in normal rats but not in transgenic mice with excess GH levels. In sum, brain activity associated with generation of SWS appears to facilitate a surge in GH activity, especially in young males. The situation, however, is complex, with multiple metabolic inputs and hormonal and neurotransmitter signaling systems contributing to GH release during sleep.

Patrick McNamara

See also: entries related to Genetics of Sleep

Sleep and Mild Cognitive Impairment

Neural mechanisms involved in the control of the sleep–wake cycle are particularly vulnerable to senescence, mainly affecting sleep quality and organization within the circadian period. Sleep fragmentation and deficits of slow-wave sleep (SWS) reported in elderly subjects have been attributed to age-related reductions of the ventrolateral preoptic (VLPO) nucleus (Swaab & Fliers, 1985), an anterior hypothalamic structure critically involved in sleep onset and maintenance. The increased prevalence of sleep disorders in neurodegenerative diseases suggests that sleep disturbances evolve progressively in the years before clinical diagnosis in persons at high risk of developing these prevalent conditions.

Alzheimer's disease (AD) results in a substantial synapses loss and massive cell death caused by the formation of neurofibrillary tangles and senile plaques in regions critical for memory function, which may explain the progressive memory decline in these patients. Underlying neuropathological events develop for several years before diagnosis in a silent but irreversible manner. The cognitive status that fills the gap between normal aging and dementia is known as mild cognitive impairment (MCI). These persons show objective memory deficits and daily functioning as well as a fourfold increased risk for developing AD as compared to neurologically intact elders. Accordingly, between 19 and 50 percent of MCI cases progress to dementia (usually AD) over a period of three years.

Polysomnographic studies have shown that sleep efficiency is significantly reduced in MCI patients as a result of augmented intrasleep wake and SWS fragmentation. The duration of REM sleep is also shortened, especially in those MCI patients who also carry the ε4 allele of the apolipoprotein (*ApoE*) gene, the major genetic risk for AD. Interestingly, only MCI patients, but not cognitively normal elders, show a linear relationship between the amount of phasic REM sleep (presence of oculomotor activity) and performance in immediate memory tests (Cantero, Hita-Yañez, Gil-Neciga, & Atienza, under review). All together, these results suggest that significant sleep disruptions accompany incipient neurodegeneration underlying MCI status, which may have implications for early diagnosis of AD and/or preliminary therapeutic management.

Impaired sleep at early neurodegeneration stages is supported by two different lines of evidence. On the one hand, recent studies have shown that amyloid-beta (Abeta) accumulation is positively correlated with the amount of time spent awake and with the increased levels of orexin (Kang et al., 2009), a neuropeptide synthesized by neurons in the lateral hypothalamic area, which inhibits activity of the VLPO neurons. As a consequence, increased wake time during sleep would activate molecular pathways critically involved in the production of toxic amyloid oligomers, which in turn may trigger the pathogenic cascade of AD several years before clinical diagnosis. On the other hand, *postmortem* studies have shown that molecular mechanisms behind melatonin deficits and disrupted circadian melatonin rhythm are already present in preclinical stages of AD (Wu et al., 2003), likely caused by dysfunctions of the sympathetic regulation of pineal melatonin synthesis by the suprachiasmatic nucleus (SCN). In line with this hypothesis, there is evidence that the SCN is affected by neuronal loss and neurofibrillary tangle formation in late phases of AD (Stopa et al., 1999). Therefore, sleep difficulties shown by MCI persons may potentially result from early structural damage and/or synaptic dysfunctions between circadian structures and sleep-active neurons. Further research is needed to elucidate whether impaired sleep at incipient stages of neurodegeneration correlates with higher conversion rate to AD, and/or with worse AD prognosis in the subsequent years.

Jose L. Cantero, Eva Hita-Yañez,
and Mercedes Atienza

See also: entries related to Sleep Disorders

References

Cantero, J.L., Hita-Yañez, E., Gil-Neciga, E., & Atienza, M. (under review). Sleep patterns in persons at high-risk of developing Alzheimer's disease.

Kang, J.E., Lim, M.M., Bateman, R.J., Lee, J.J., Smyth, L.P., Cirrito, J.R., ... Holtzman, D.M. (2009). Amyloid-beta dynamics are regulated by Orexin and the sleep-wake cycle. *Science, 326,* 1005–1007.

Stopa, E.G., Volicer, L., Kuo-Leblanc, V., Harper, D., Lathi, D., Tate, B., & Satlin, A. (1999). Pathologic evaluation of the human suprachiasmatic nucleus in severe dementia. *Journal of Neuropathology and Experimental Neurology, 58,* 29–39.

Swaab, D.F., & Fliers, E. (1985). A sexually dimorphic nucleus in the human brain. *Science, 228,* 1112–1115.

Wu, Y.H., Feenstra, M.G., Zhou, J.N., Liu, R.Y., Toranõ, J.S., Van Kan, H.J., ... Swaab, D.F. (2003). Molecular changes underlying reduced pineal melatonin levels in Alzheimer disease: Alterations in preclinical and clinical stages. *The Journal of Clinical Endocrinology & Metabolism, 88,* 5898–5906.

Sleep and Obesity

The association between sleep disorders and obesity has been recognized for many years. From the first description of Joe the fat boy who fell asleep in any situation at any time of day (*The Pickwick Papers* by Charles Dickens), to the large sophisticated studies in clinical and general populations, the association of sleep apnea and obesity has proven to be one of the most well-established facts in sleep medicine literature. In 2004–2005, the field was jolted by a series of publications on the association of short sleep duration and obesity. Several epidemiologic studies showed a consistent association between self-reported sleep duration and body mass index (BMI) (Cappuccio et al., 2008), whereas experimental laboratory studies showed that curtailment of sleep in healthy subjects leads to increased appetite and reduction of leptin, a hormone that suppresses appetite (Spiegel, Tasali, Penev, & Van Cauter, 2004). The message from these novel findings was simple and exciting, "sleep more and you will lose weight."

However, most of the population studies were based on self-reported sleep duration. In the Penn State Cohort study (Vgontzas et al. 2008), the shortest sleep duration was reported by obese subjects with insomnia, followed by obese individuals with excessive daytime sleepiness or poor sleep. The effect of chronic emotional stress was stronger than that of BMI on self-reported sleep duration, with a synergistic effect between the two factors. This study concluded that short sleep duration is reported by obese individuals who have sleep complaints and are chronically stressed (Vgontzas et al., 2008). At the same time, other large epidemiologic studies suggested that self-reported short sleep is influenced by social stressors, such as socioeconomic and minority status, and unhealthy behaviors (i.e., cigarette smoking, consuming four or more alcoholic drinks per day, and lack of physical activity). Thus, self-reported short sleep duration seems to be a marker of sleep complaints and chronic psychosocial stress.

Since self-reported sleep duration appears to be influenced by many factors, the interest of several investigators naturally shifted toward examining the association of objective sleep duration and BMI. The first studies found no association or a very weak association between objective sleep duration and BMI, and the two most recent ones using actigraphy reported an association between sleep duration and obesity in elderly community samples; however, the results were weakened after controlling for several confounders. A recent study by Theorell-Haglow and colleagues was the first using full-night polysomnography to demonstrate a significant inverse association between sleep duration and waist circumference, a marker of central obesity, in 400 middle-aged women. There is evidence that objective sleep abnormalities in obese individuals are strongly associated

with emotional stress, whereas, in the absence of sleep complaints or stress, sleep and its structure are not different from those of nonobese subjects.

However, these studies were all cross-sectional, and the direction of the association could not be inferred. A recent study using actigraphy failed to show a prospective association between baseline objective sleep duration and development of obesity after five years (Lauderdale et al., 2009). Clearly, these first findings do not support a simplistic model (i.e., sleep more and you will lose weight).

There is no doubt that sleep and obesity are strongly connected. The nature and the direction of this association requires further studies—longitudinal, interventional, or both—and using measures from multiple domains, including sleep (both objective and subjective), stress (physiological, emotional, and social), and mental and physical health. In the meantime, the sleep field should be comfortable with the suggestion that obesity requires a multidimensional approach, that is, stress management, reduction of risky behaviors, promotion of healthy lifestyle at both an individual and a community level, and, of course, better quality and, in some instances, greater quantity of sleep.

Alexandros N. Vgontzas and Julio Fernández-Mendoza

See also: entries related to Hormones in Sleep; entries related to Sleep Disorders

References

Cappuccio, F. P., Taggart, F. M., Kandala, N. B., Currie, A., Peile, E., Stranges, S., & Miller, M. A. (2008). Meta-analysis of short sleep duration and obesity in children and adults. *Sleep, 31*(5), 619–626.

Lauderdale, D. S., Knutson, K. L., Rathouz, P. J., Yan, L. L., Hulley, S. B., & Liu, K. (2009). Cross-sectional and longitudinal associations between objectively measured sleep duration and body mass index: The CARDIA Sleep Study. *American Journal of Epidemiology, 170,* 805–813.

Spiegel, K., Tasali, E., Penev, P., & Van Cauter, E. (2004). Brief communication: Sleep curtailment in healthy young men is associated with decreased leptin levels, elevated ghrelin levels, and increased hunger and appetite. *Annals of Internal Medicine, 141,* 846–850.

Vgontzas, A. N., Lin, H. M., Papaliaga, M., Calhoun, S., Vela-Bueno, A., Chrousos, G. P., & Bixler, E. O. (2008). Short sleep duration and obesity: The role of emotional stress and sleep disturbances. *International Journal of Obesity, 32,* 801–809.

Vgontzas, A. N., Tan, T. L., Bixler, E. O., Martin, L. F., Shubert, D., & Kales, A. (1994). Sleep apnea and sleep disruption in obese patients. *Archives of Internal Medicine, 154,* 1705–1711.

Sleep and Shift Work

Shift workers perform their work at night and sleep during the daytime. Both activities occur at an unfavorable biological time of day. The circadian pacemaker located in the suprachiasmatic nucleus of the hypothalamus generates a near 24-hour rhythm that affects nearly all aspects of physiology and cognitive functions. These circadian rhythms are primarily synchronized to the environmental light and dark cycle and normally modulate sleep and wake propensity in concert with many other components of physiology. Sleep is generally of higher quality when it occurs during the biological night. A circadian waking drive during the daytime maintains wakefulness.

In controlled laboratory studies, subjects display a circadian variation in short-term memory, cognitive performance, and alertness that is closely and tightly coupled to the timing of the body temperature rhythm. These cognitive functions begin to decline about 16 hours after awakening and reach a low point at a clock time that is one to three hours after the habitual wake time in the absence of sleep (Czeisler & Buxton, 2010).

With shift-work exposure, circadian rhythms are misaligned with respect to the irregular sleep–wake cycle imposed by shift- and night-work demands (Czeisler & Buxton, 2010). After a nighttime work shift, and even with high sleep pressure, sleep is often less consolidated. Disruptive noises and other factors may interfere with sleep. Once awakened, shift workers may not try or be able to sleep further, resulting in a shorter total sleep duration than they might obtain at night.

Full adaptation to a night-work schedule is atypical because robust circadian rhythms change relatively slowly, whereas the sleep–wake and light–dark cycles vary across the workweek. Shift workers may sleep during the day after a night shift, or stay awake during the bright light of daytime for social or other reasons. The circadian pacemaker cannot adapt to such an inconsistent light and dark cycle and maintain the synchronization between circadian physiology and sleep–wake behavior. A nocturnal schedule thus sets up a conflict between circadian physiology and the demands of work and sleep. Getting light only at night and sleeping in darkness during the daytime is insufficient because the synchronizing effects of bright-light exposure during a morning impedes the adaptation of the circadian system to a night-work schedule (Crowley, Lee, Tseng, Fogg, & Eastman, 2003). Extended naps before a night shift, and caffeine during a night shift can reduce overnight sleepiness (Schweitzer, Randazzo, Stone, Erman, & Walsh, 2006).

Despite building sleep pressure and sleepiness because of a short habitual sleep duration during the daytime, some shift workers paradoxically exhibit daytime insomnia presumed to be due to the circadian drive for alerting in the biological daytime, and because of environmental sleep disruptors during the day. In the extreme, shift-work sleep disorder (SWD) is formally characterized by chronic, pathological levels of sleepiness at night during the work periods and commute, and yet insomnia during daytime sleep periods. Approximately 5 to 10 percent of night-shift workers may have SWD, which is associated with disrupted social life, absenteeism, depressive symptoms, and gastrointestinal disorders. During work at night, SWD patients may have increased risk of accidents, particularly while commuting home when circadian-driven alertness is lowest (Drake, Roehrs, Richardson, Walsh, & Roth, 2004). Modafinil administration is an FDA-approved treatment for excessive sleepiness due to SWD (Czeisler et al., 2005). The International Agency for Research on Cancer, an intergovernmental entity of the World Health Organization, considers night work a probable carcinogen via its effect on *circadian disruption* (World Health Organization & The International Agency for Research on Cancer, 2010).

Orfeu Marcello Buxton

See also: Increasing Sleep Complaints

References

Crowley, S. J., Lee, C., Tseng, C. Y., Fogg, L. F., & Eastman, C. I. (2003). Combinations of bright light, scheduled dark, sunglasses, and melatonin to facilitate circadian entrainment to night shift work. *Journal of Biological Rhythms, 18,* 513–523.

Czeisler, C. A., & Buxton, O. M. (2010). The human circadian timing system and sleep-wake regulation. In M. Kryger, T. Roth, & W. Dement (Eds.), *Principles and practices of sleep medicine* (pp. 402–419). Saunders, New York.

Czeisler, C. A., et al. (2005). Modafinil for excessive sleepiness associated with shift work sleep disorder. *New England Journal of Medicine, 353,* 476–486.

Drake, C. L., Roehrs, T., Richardson, G., Walsh, J. K., & Roth, T. (2004). Shift work sleep disorder: Prevalence and consequences beyond that of symptomatic day workers. *Sleep, 27,* 1453–1462.

Schweitzer, P. K., Randazzo, A. C., Stone, K., Erman, M., & Walsh, J. K. (2006). Laboratory and field studies of naps and caffeine as practical countermeasures for sleep-wake problems associated with night work. *Sleep, 29,* 39–50.

World Health Organization & The International Agency for Research on Cancer. (2010). *IARC Monographs on the Evaluation of Carcinogenic Risks to Humans, 98,* 573–574.

Sleep and Suicide

Suicide in the world is one of the most common reasons leading to death. However, some authors tend to think that it is largely preventable. It may be suggested that manipulations of specific behavioral patterns and therapeutic approaches improve cognitive dysfunctions in suicidal individuals and may be preventable for suicidal actions.

Although an association between suicide and insomnia had been proposed approximately a hundred years ago, a strong relationship between sleep and suicide has been suggested scientifically only for the last two decades. This association is quite important because sleep disturbances are seen as one of the preventable reasons of suicidal behavior.

Sleep disturbances may have prognostic significance in predicting suicide among patients with mood disorders. About two decades ago, insomnia was considered to be one of the modifiable risks for suicide. Our group showed that not only insomnia but also hypersomnia is associated with suicidal behavior in patients with major depression. We also demonstrated that there was a significant association between poor sleep quality and suicidal behavior in depression. Only a few electroencephalographic (EEG) sleep studies have examined the relationship between sleep and suicidal behavior in patients with depressive and psychotic disorders. Some researchers compared EEG sleep of major depressives with and without a history of suicidal behavior. They found suicide attempters had longer sleep latency, lower sleep efficiency, and fewer late-night delta wave counts than normal controls. They also demonstrated that nonattempters, compared with attempters, had less REM time and activity in the second REM period, but more delta wave counts in the fourth non-REM period. I and my colleague, Dr. Rosalind Cartwright, in a sleep laboratory–based study, found that suicidal subjects have a shorter mean REM latency, a higher mean REM percentage, and different within-night distribution of dream quality and affect than nonsuicidal depressed subjects. This study also showed a difference in dreamlike quality of the REM-content reports between the first and second halves of the night associated with suicidal tendency.

In addition to these sleep laboratory studies, my team examined the association between repetitive and frightening dreams and suicidal tendency in patients with major depression. They reported that the patients with frequent nightmares, particularly women, had higher suicide scores and were more likely to be classified more suicidal than the others. Is depression an independent predictor of a relationship between sleep disturbances and suicide? After controlling for depressive symptoms, only nightmares demonstrated an association with suicidal ideation. A prospective follow-up study in a sample drawn from the general population also reported that the frequency of nightmares is directly related to the risk of suicide. This is quite important because treatment of nightmares by using drugs or psychotherapeutic techniques may modify suicide risk. Nightmares might reflect a negative dream affect, and terminal insomnia might play a role in preventing depressed morning mood. Feeling worse in the morning rather than later in the day may be related to the intervening dream content and affect. Thus, REM-sleep deprivation that occurs closer to the morning may have a therapeutic effect on mood regulation and diminish negative dream affect and content in depressed subjects with mood dysfunction or diurnal mood symptoms. Nightmares were found to be related to suicide attempts in unipolar depressed patients in terms of melancholic features. Middle and terminal insomnia also are related to suicide attempts in patients with melancholic features. On the contrary, these associations were not found in those without melancholic features. In addition, nightmares are more common among those with suicidal attempt than nonattempters.

The underlying mechanisms of the relationship between sleep disturbances and suicide are controversial. Some authors suggested that physiological sleep fragmentation might contribute to emotional exhaustion in terms of occurrence of suicidal behavior. Serotonin (5-HT) may play a key role in this association. 5-HT is a neurotransmitter that plays a direct or indirect role in sleep regulation.

Findings from the contemporary research suggest that treating sleep disturbances may be a possible means of reducing associated risk of suicidal ideation. Sleep is easily modi?able through the use of medication or behavioral interventions. It may be suggested that appropriate drugs and sleep-related interventions (e.g., sleep hygiene, stimulus control) play a role in reducing the risk of suicidal ideation. I think future research will focus on prevention of suicide by manipulating sleep characteristics. With regard to nightmares and dreaming, therapeutic approaches (e.g., imagery rehearsal therapy) and dreamwork in therapy may be useful.

Mehmed Y. Agargun

See also: entries related to Sleep and Health

Sleep and the Endocrine System

Circulating hormones released by the endocrine system are key regulators of body homeostasis and, in this role, have an important bidirectional relationship with sleep. Two processes regulate sleep: the homeostatic (Process S) and circadian (Process C). These processes are both closely related to the secretion of various hormones, influencing their secretion to various extents. Many hormones show unique 24-hour secretory patterns (diurnal or circadian); for some hormones, the effects of sleep are superimposed on their 24-hour secretory rhythm.

One of the few hormones to vary with the hypnogram sleep-stage cycles is plasma renin activity (PRA; Brandenberger, Follenius, Simon, Ehrhart, & Libert, 1988). The kidneys release PRA to regulate blood pressure through the renin–angiotensin–aldosterone system. PRA levels cycle between slow-wave sleep (SWS) and REM sleep with highest levels during SWS and lowest levels during REM sleep when sympathetic activation is highest. PRA and aldosterone levels are markedly diminished with sleep deprivation confirming the importance of sleep in their secretion. Urine osmolality and urine flow also vary with the hypnogram with urine osmolality being higher and urine flow lower in REM sleep. Urine flow is generally reduced at night demonstrating a diurnal pattern.

The secretion of other hormones is closely related to sleep or circadian rhythms, or both. Hormones affected by sleep can either be stimulated or inhibited by sleep. Experimentally, distinguishing sleep-related and circadian-related hormone release is possible through sleep laboratory studies with frequent blood sampling (Van Cauter, Plat, & Copinschi, 1998). These include studies of sleep deprivation and studies that alter the timing of sleep. Hormones whose secretion are generally circadian, will show little relationship to sleep (i.e., little effect of sleep or sleep deprivation) while hormones whose secretion are related to sleep are mainly released during sleep, independent of its timing.

Hormones that are classically related to sleep with a weak circadian link include growth hormone (GH) and prolactin (PRL) secreted by the anterior pituitary gland (Van Cauter & Copinschi, 2000). These hormones have a very close relationship with SWS. Deprivation of SWS reduces GH release, while increasing SWS with drugs such as gammahydroxybutyrate results in greater GH release. Ageing, which is associated with reduced SWS, is also associated with diminished GH release. Sleep disruption results in reduced GH secretion. GH secretion is regulated by hypothalamic GH-releasing hormone (GHRH), which is stimulatory, and somatostatin, which is inhibitory. GHRH activity is increased in early sleep while somatostatin activity is reduced. Ghrelin is a hormone released by the stomach whose levels are increased by fasting and are higher during sleep. Ghrelin has an important role in appetite stimulation via the hypothalamus, but also has a role as a GH secreatgogue by acting at the GH secreatgogue receptors expressed on somatotrophs in the anterior pituitary. Ghrelin may also have an important role in GH secretion during sleep. A reciprocal relationship appears to exist between sleep and GHRH and ghrelin secretion as both GHRH and ghrelin, whose levels are higher during sleep, also promote SWS. PRL secretion is intimately related to sleep and sleep onset with significant rise in levels during sleep, which are more pronounced in women. This increase is likely to be related to reduced dopaminergic tone, as tubero-infundibular dopamine is the key inhibitory regular of PRL secretion from the anterior pituitary. Like GH, PRL release is associated with SWS. PRL may regulate both REM and SWS. SWS levels are higher in breast-feeding and in patients with PRL secreting pituitary tumors (prolactinomas).

Cortisol is a hormone secreted by the adrenal gland under the influence of pituitary adrenocorticotrophic hormone. Cortisol shows a clear ultradian (short pulses), as well as circadian secretion. Lowest cortisol levels occur in the early hours during sleep, at the same time when GH hormone release is highest, with highest cortisol levels occurring just before awakening. This inhibition of the hypothalamic–pituitary–adrenal activity during early sleep, which occurs during the first few hours after sleep onset, may be important in supporting memory formation (Born & Fehm, 2002). Individuals who experience acute or chronic stress show a significant weakening in the suppression of the hypothalamic–pituitary–adrenal activity, which could consequently result in disturbances in the regular formation of memories during sleep. While the secretion of cortisol is generally circadian, sleep deprivation and sleep disruption have been shown to result in higher cortisol levels suggesting an effect of sleep (Leproult, Copinschi, Buxton, & Van Cauter, 1997; Vgontzas et al., 1999). These observations from experimental studies are confounded by the inability to cater for circadian effects during sleep-deprivation experiments. Higher cortisol levels have also been observed with insomnia and with sleep disruption.

Thyroid-stimulating hormone (TSH) is released by thyrotrophs of the anterior pituitary under stimulatory control of hypothalamic thyroid releasing hormone. TSH levels are highest in the evening, showing a steep rise before sleep onset from 9 P.M., peaking at about 1 to 2 A.M., and then declining through the rest of the 24 hours. While the TSH rise occurring before sleep suggests circadian regulation, TSH levels rise markedly with sleep deprivation suggesting that sleep has an inhibitory effect on TSH secretion. This inhibitory effect appears to be mediated by SWS. During recovery after sleep deprivation, when slow-wave activity is increased, TSH levels are suppressed. The relationships between TSH secretion after sleep deprivation and thyroid hormone release are controversial. TSH levels decrease with prolonged sleep deprivation; an explanation may be increased thyroid hormone levels acting through the negative feedback loop, but stress of sleep deprivation may also play a role. Insulin (released from pancreatic beta cells) levels vary with sleep; both glucose and insulin levels are higher during sleep suggesting that an element of insulin insensitivity occurs during sleep, but also that glucose levels remain higher because of slightly reduced brain glucose utilization and increased secretion of counter-regulatory hormones such as GH that increase glucose mobilization. In experimental studies, sleep deprivation is associated with an insulin-resistant state (Spiegel, Leproult, &Van Cauter, 1999).

Leptin is a hormone released by the adipocyte to signal extent of fat stores to the hypothalamus. Leptin regulates appetite, energy expenditure, and immune and other functions. Leptin levels show a clear 24-hour rhythm that is very similar to TSH with levels rising prior to sleep, reaching a peak at 2 A.M. and then declining to basal levels at the end of sleep. This pattern of secretion is accentuated in obese individuals who have elevated levels of leptin due to leptin resistance. Sleep deprivation in human sleep laboratory studies and short sleep duration in population studies are associated with lower leptin levels. Sleep deprivation and short sleep duration are also associated with elevated ghrelin levels (Taheri, Lin, Austin, Young, & Mignot, 2004). The combination of low leptin and ghrelin levels observed with sleep deprivation and short sleep could explain the relationship between short sleep duration and obesity as low leptin and high ghrelin signal a strong energy deficit resulting in increased food consumption.

Gonadal hormone secretion depends on developmental stage with diurnal rhythms of hormone secretion accentuated during puberty. In adult males, testosterone shows diurnal secretion with low evening levels and a rise in the night with highest levels in the morning. The nocturnal rise in testosterone appears to be related to REM sleep. Plasma testosterone is correlated with total sleep time in older men. The sleep disturbances that occur in the elderly may thus explain the lower testosterone levels in elderly men. The situation regarding gonadal hormone secretion and sleep in women is complex as there are variations with the menstrual cycle and menopausal status.

The intimate relationships among hormone release, sleep, and circadian rhythms reflect close interactions among these physiological systems in the regulation of body homeostasis. While many of the relationships of hormone release with sleep have been examined for classical endocrine hormones, further research is required to examine these interactions for other hormones and also to examine further sleep–endocrine relationships in physiological (e.g., jet lag) and disease states. The sleep–endocrine relationship is likely to make a major contribution to the reported health effects of variations in sleep duration.

Alison Cartwright and Shahrad Taheri

See also: entries related to Sleep Physiology

Note

Both Dr. Shahrad Taheri and Dr. Alison Cartwright are funded by the National Institute for Health Research (NIHR) through the Collaborations for Leadership in Applied Health Research and Care for Birmingham and Black Country (CLAHRC-BBC) programme. The views expressed in this publication are not necessarily those of the NIHR, the Department of Health, NHS South Birmingham, University of Birmingham, or the CLAHRC-BBC Theme 8 Management/Steering Group.

References

Born, J., & Fehm, H.L. (2002). The neuroendocrine recovery function of sleep. *Noise Health, 2,* 25–37.

Brandenberger, G., Follenius, M., Simon, C., Ehrhart, J., & Libert, J.P. (1988). Nocturnal oscillations in plasma renin activity and REM-NREM sleep cycles in humans: A common regulatory mechanism? *Sleep, 11,* 242–250.

Leproult, R., Copinschi, G., Buxton, O., & Van Cauter, E. (1997). Sleep loss results in an elevation of cortisol levels the next evening. *Sleep, 20,* 865–870.

Spiegel, K., Leproult, R., & Van Cauter, E. (1999). The impact of sleep debt on metabolic and endocrine function. *The Lancet, 354,* 1435–1439.

Taheri, S., Lin, L., Austin, D., Young, T., & Mignot, E. (2004). Short sleep duration is associated with reduced leptin, elevated ghrelin, and increased body mass index. *PLoS Medicine, 1*(3), e62.

Van Cauter, E., & Copinschi, G. (2000). Interrelationships between growth hormone and sleep. *Growth Hormone and IGF Research* (Suppl. B), S57–S62.

Van Cauter, E., Plat, L., & Copinschi, G. (1998). Interrelations between sleep and the somatotropic axis. *Sleep, 21,* 553–566.

Vgontzas, A.N., Mastorakos, G., Bixler, E.O., Kales, A., Gold, P.W., & Chrousos, G.P. (1999). Sleep deprivation effects on the activity of the hypothalamic-pituitary-adrenal and growth axes: Potential clinical implications. *Clinical Endocrinology, 51,* 205–215.

Sleep and the Generation of New Nerve Cells in the Adult Brain

It has long been a dogma in neuroscience that the mammalian brain can no longer generate new nerve cells or neurons once it reaches adulthood. However, research over the last few decades has now firmly established that even the adult brain contains undifferentiated stem cells that give rise to new neurons (Gross, 2000). Yet, such adult neurogenesis only occurs in significant amounts in a few areas of the brain, particularly the dentate gyrus of the hippocampal formation and the subventricular zone of the lateral ventricles (Gross, 2000, Abrous, Koehl, & Le Moal, 2005).

While much of our current knowledge on neurogenesis in the adult mammalian brain is based on studies in laboratory rodents, the production of new neurons in adulthood has been confirmed in humans as well. In elderly cancer patients who were treated with bromodeoxyuridine (BrdU), which is incorporated into the DNA of dividing cells, postmortem analysis of brain tissue and immunostainings for BrdU together with specific neuronal markers unequivocally demonstrated the existence of proliferating cells and generation of new neurons in the hippocampus (Eriksson et al., 1998). Although the exact function of adult-born neurons is still a matter of debate, neurogenesis in the hippocampus in particular has received a great deal of attention because this brain region is an important part of the circuitry involved in the regulation of higher cognitive functions. Integration of new cells into the existing circuitry might be involved in memory processes and the regulation of emotionality (Abrous et al., 2005).

Since sleep is considered to be important for cognitive functions and brain plasticity, various studies have examined how the generation and integration of new neurons in the adult brain is affected by sleep and sleep loss (Meerlo, Mistlberger, Jacobs, Heller, & McGinty, 2009). While disruption of sleep for a period shorter than one day appears to have little effect on the basal rate of cell proliferation, prolonged restriction or disruption of sleep may have cumulative effects leading to a major decrease in hippocampal cell proliferation, cell survival, and neurogenesis. Although most experimental methods of sleep deprivation to some degree affect both nonrapid eye movement (NREM) and rapid eye movement (REM) sleep, the available data suggest that decreases in hippocampal cell proliferation are related to a reduction in REM sleep, whereas decreases in the number of cells that subsequently develop into adult neurons may be related to reductions in both NREM and REM sleep (Meerlo et al., 2009). Importantly, while short sleep deprivation may not affect the basal rate of cell proliferation, one study in rats showed that even a fairly mild sleep restriction may prevent the increase in neurogenesis that occurs with hippocampus-dependent learning (Hairston et al., 2005). Since sleep deprivation also disturbs memory formation, this finding suggests that promoting survival, maturation, and integration of new nerve cells may be a previously unknown mechanism by which sleep supports learning and memory processes. The formation and storage of memories in the brain is partly based on structural remodeling and strengthening of connections or synapses between nerve cells. Sleep following learning is thought to contribute to this process by replaying the information and by initiating molecular cascades involved in neuronal plasticity (Stickgold & Walker, 2005). Such sleep-dependent structural plasticity may not only involve existing neurons but could also include the maturation of new neurons and their integration into the network. Further studies are required to confirm this neurogenic link between sleep and learning; yet, the first results open up a new avenue for research on the possible mechanism of sleep-related memory formation.

Studies on the relevance of adult neurogenesis in humans have been limited by

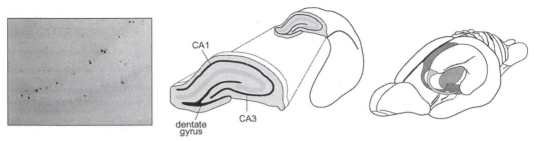

Overview of a rat brain with the hippocampus (right panel) and a cross section with the hippocampal subregions (middle panel). Neurogenesis in the dentate gyrus is often studied by labeling dividing cells with BrdU (photograph on the left). (Peter Meerlo)

lack of methods for *in vivo* measurement of newly generated nerve cells in the brains of healthy, living subjects. Nevertheless, the experiments in laboratory rodents provide a clear framework suggesting that newly generated neurons in adulthood may be involved in hippocampal plasticity. While modest sleep restriction may interfere with enhancement of neurogenesis associated with learning processes, prolonged and more serious sleep disruption may even affect the basal rates of cell proliferation and neurogenesis. The effects of sleep loss may endanger hippocampal integrity and could ultimately lead to cognitive dysfunction and contribute to the development of mood disorders (Meerlo et al., 2009).

Peter Meerlo

References

Abrous, D.N., Koehl, M., & Le Moal, M. (2005). Adult neurogenesis: From precursors to network and physiology. *Physiological Reviews, 85,* 523–569.

Eriksson, P.S., Perfilieva, E., Bjork-Eriksson, T., Alborn, A.M., Nordborg, C., Peterson, D.A., & Gage, F.A. (1998). Neurogenesis in the adult human hippocampus. *Nature Medicine, 4,* 1313–1317.

Gross, C.G. (2000). Neurogenesis in the adult brain: Death of a dogma. *Nature Reviews Neuroscience, 1,* 67–73.

Hairston, H.S., Little, M.T.M., Scanlon, M.D., Barakat, M.T., Palmer, T.D., Sapolsky, R.M., & Heller, H.C. (2005). Sleep restriction suppresses neurogenesis induced by hippocampal learning. *Journal of Neurophysiology, 94,* 4224–4233.

Meerlo P., Mistlberger, R., Jacobs, B.L., Heller, C., & McGinty, D. (2009). New neurons in the adult brain: The role of sleep and consequences of sleep loss. *Sleep Medicine Reviews, 13,* 187–194.

Stickgold, R., & Walker, M.P. (2005). Memory consolidation and reconsolidation: What is the role of sleep? *Trends in Neuroscience, 28,* 408–415.

Sleep and the Metabolic Syndrome

Cardiovascular disease is the most common cause of mortality in the Western world. The metabolic syndrome is a cluster of several interrelated cardiovascular risk factors, including central adiposity, hyperglycemia, dyslipidemia, and hypertension. There are variations in the definition of the metabolic syndrome but two main definitions are usually applied, which are similar with small yet distinct differences.

The National Cholesterol Education Program (NCEP) Adult Treatment Panel (ATP) III requires the presence of at least three of the following components:

1. Central obesity determined by waist circumference of ≥102 cm for males and ≥88 cm for females;
2. Dyslipidemia: classified by triglyceride level of ≥1.7 mmol/L (150 mg/dL);
3. Dyslipidemia: classified by HDL-cholesterol level of <40 mg/dL for males, <50 mg/dL for females;
4. Blood pressure of ≥130/85 mmHg;
5. Fasting plasma glucose level of ≥6.1 mmol/L* (110 mg/dL)

*or ≥5.6 mmol/L (>100 mg/dL) if applying the consensus definition.

The second definition was developed and revised by the International Diabetes Federation (IDF). To qualify for the metabolic syndrome, the definition requires that an individual must have the following:

1. Central obesity (defined by waist circumference according to ethnic-specific values). However, if BMI is >30 kg/m², central obesity is assumed and waist circumference need not be measured.

Plus any *two* of the following components:

2. Raised triglycerides: >150 mg/dL (1.7 mmol/L), or specific treatment for this lipid abnormality;
3. Reduced HDL cholesterol: <40 mg/dL (1.03 mmol/L) for males and <50 mg/dL (1.29 mmol/L) for females, or specific treatment for this lipid abnormality;
4. Raised blood pressure: systolic BP > 130 or diastolic BP > 85 mmHg, or treatment of previously diagnosed hypertension;

5. Raised fasting plasma glucose: >100 mg/dL (5.6 mmol/L), or previously diagnosed type-2 diabetes.

The individual components of the metabolic syndrome, as well as the syndrome itself, have been associated with increased cardiovascular disease risk and it is estimated that around 20 to 25 percent of the world's adult population have the metabolic syndrome. There is evidence that the cardiovascular risk conferred by the metabolic syndrome is greater than the risk of the individual components added together. Although the risks associated with the metabolic syndrome are well characterized, factors contributing to pathogenesis of the syndrome are less well defined. Obesity and insulin resistance are considered key to the syndrome. Other underlying contributory factors remain unclear, although genetics, ageing, hormone alterations and lifestyle behaviors are all thought to have a link with development of the metabolic syndrome.

It is well established that lifestyle behaviors play a major role in the development of type-2 diabetes mellitus and obesity. Physical inactivity and poor diet are unequivocally associated with the two conditions. More recently, it has emerged that another lifestyle behavior is closely linked with obesity, diabetes, and cardiovascular disease development and all-cause mortality—sleep. Currently, the largest population study to identify a relationship between sleep duration and mortality sampled 1.1 million American adults (Kripke, Garfinkel, Wingard, Klauber, & Marler, 2002). The study reported lowest mortality rates in individuals with a nocturnal sleep duration of seven to eight hours. Those who slept for less than 6 hours or more than 8.5 hours were found to be at higher risk for all-cause mortality. Furthermore, the same study found a U-shaped association between sleep duration and body mass index (BMI).

There are abundant research studies that have identified a relationship between sleep duration and the individual components of the metabolic syndrome. Epidemiological and experimental studies have provided strong evidence to suggest a link between short sleep duration and BMI (Taheri, Lin, Austin, Young, & Mignot, 2004). Long sleep duration has also been linked with an increased BMI but is more widely reported in adults and so it is believed that this may be a consequence of other adverse health conditions rather than a direct cause. Similarly, there is substantial evidence suggesting short sleep and poor-quality sleep are linked with insulin resistance, glucose intolerance, and subsequently, the development of type-2 diabetes (Spiegel, Knutson, Leproult, Tasali, & Van, 2005). Epidemiological evidence has also revealed hypertension to be associated with both short and long sleep duration across all age groups. There is a small amount of emerging evidence suggesting that persistent short sleep duration as well as long sleep duration are related to an increased risk of high cholesterol in adolescents and older adults, respectively.

The mechanisms underpinning the observed associations between sleep and metabolic syndrome development are believed to be related to hormone alterations. Short sleep duration has been previously associated with higher levels of the hormone ghrelin and lower levels of the hormone leptin (Taheri et al., 2004). Alterations in these two appetite-regulating hormones can, in part, explain the increased prevalence of obesity, particularly as national polls have indicated a one- to two-hour reduction in sleeping hours in recent decades. Ghrelin is released by the stomach and signals hunger to the hypothalamus. Leptin is released by adipocytes and signals the extent of fat stores. Low leptin levels signal a reduction in fat stores thus stimulating hunger. In relation to the development of type-2 diabetes, evidence exists that short sleep duration and poor sleep quality are associated with insulin resistance through a number of potential mechanisms, including elevated sympathetic nervous system activity, increased growth-hormone secretion, and elevated evening cortisol. Obesity and type-2 diabetes mellitus are not only rising at an uncontrollable rate across the globe but are also believed to be the two main diseases driving the development of the metabolic syndrome.

Based on accumulating evidence concerning sleep-duration quality and its relationship with the individual components of the metabolic syndrome, it is perhaps not surprising that sleep duration has been linked with the syndrome itself. The relationship was first hypothesized in 1999 and, since then, a small number of geographically diverse studies have supported the association between sleep and the metabolic syndrome. In a large majority Caucasian sample conducted in the United States, it was shown that the shortest sleepers, defined as <6 hours, were 83 percent more likely to have the metabolic syndrome than those who slept seven to eight hours (Hall et al., 2008). The same study found similar results in long sleepers, defined as >8 hours, who were 81 percent at more risk of the metabolic syndrome. Both long and shortest sleepers had a significantly higher risk for impaired fasting glucose and the central adiposity component was only significantly higher in the group of shortest sleepers. Sensitivity analysis, which excluded those taking antihypertensive medication, resulted in the relationship becoming nonsignificant in long sleepers but remained in shortest sleepers, although slightly attenuated. The Korean National Health and Nutrition Survey, conducted in 2001 (Choi et al., 2008) revealed that individuals with long sleep durations (8 hours and ≥9 hours) had a significantly higher risk of having the syndrome compared to those sleeping seven hours, after full adjustment. Although the study found a small but increased risk in shorter sleepers (≤5 hours and 6 hours) this relationship was not statistically significant after adjustment. A large sample of Japanese male workers were examined for the presence of metabolic syndrome in relation to sleep duration but this study found no relationship in those sleeping ≥6 hours compared to those who slept <6 hours (Kawada, Okada, & Amezawa, 2008). A European study has also been conducted in Portugal (Santos, Ebrahim, & Barros, 2007). The authors used similar sleep categories as the other two studies but used ≥9 hours as their reference category. All categories of sleep (≤6 hours, 7 hours, and 8 hours) across both genders had a reduced risk of the metabolic syndrome indicating that long sleep durations had a high risk of the metabolic risk. The largest study to

date in older Chinese found long sleep duration (≥8 hours) was associated with a 15 percent increased prevalence of the metabolic syndrome compared to those sleeping seven to eight hours after adjustment for a wide range of confounders (Arora et al., 2010).

Interestingly, none of the studies applied the IDF definition for identification of the syndrome. The Portuguese study was the only one that applied the NCEP ATP III criteria. The U.S., Chinese, and Korean studies used a revised version of the NCEP ATP III, revised by the American Heart Association, which identified the glucose criterion as 5.6 mmol/L rather than 6.1 mmol/L and the Japanese study used country-specific criteria. The findings from the studies are similar but control for different potential confounders, which could explain the small amount of variance. Despite the overwhelming evidence demonstrating that short sleep duration is associated with diabetes and obesity development, the evidence for the metabolic syndrome per se, arguably indicates long sleep duration to be a significant factor. However, it should be noted that the studies that examined the relationship were all cross-sectional and there is no longitudinal evidence to confirm a causal link. Still, the possibility remains that long sleep is a consequence, rather than a cause of the metabolic syndrome. Thus, there is a need for both experimental laboratory and large population studies to examine the relationship between sleep and the metabolic syndrome.

Teresa Arora and Shahrad Taheri

See also: entries related to Sleep Disorders

Note

Dr. Shahrad Taheri is funded by the National Institute for Health Research (NIHR) through the Collaborations for Leadership in Applied Health Research and Care for Birmingham and Black Country (CLAHRC-BBC) programme. The views expressed in this publication are not necessarily those of the NIHR, the Department of Health, NHS South Birmingham, University of Birmingham, or the CLAHRC-BBC Theme 8 Management/Steering Group.

References

Arora, T., Lam, K., Jiang, C., Zhang, W., et al. (2010). Long sleep duration is associated with the metabolic syndrome: The Guangzhou Biobank Cohort Study [abstract]. *Sleep, 33.*

Choi, K. M., Lee, J. S., Park, H. S., Baik, S. H., Choi, D. S., & Kim, S. M. (2008). Relationship between sleep duration and the metabolic syndrome: Korean National Health and Nutrition Survey 2001. *International Jounral of Obesity, 32,* 1091–1097.

Hall, M. H., Muldoon, M. F., Jennings, J. R., Buysse, D. J., Flory, J. D., & Manuck, S. B. (2008). Self-reported sleep duration is associated with the metabolic syndrome in midlife adults. *Sleep, 31,* 635–643.

Kawada, T., Okada, K., & Amezawa, M. (2008). Components of the metabolic syndrome and lifestyle factors in Japanese male workers. *Metabolic Syndrome and Related Disorders, 6,* 263–266.

Kripke, D. F., Garfinkel, L., Wingard, D. L., Klauber, M. R., & Marler, M. R. (2002). Mortality associated with sleep duration and insomnia. *Archives of General Psychiatry, 59,* 131–136.

Santos, A. C., Ebrahim, S., & Barros, H. (2007). Alcohol intake, smoking, sleeping hours, physical activity and the metabolic syndrome. *Preventive Medicine, 44,* 328–334.

Spiegel, K., Knutson, K., Leproult, R., Tasali, E., & Van, C. E. (2005). Sleep loss: A novel risk factor for insulin resistance and type 2 diabetes. *Journal of Applied Physiology, 99,* 2008–2019.

Taheri, S., Lin, L., Austin, D., Young, T., & Mignot, E. (2004). Short sleep duration is associated with reduced leptin, elevated ghrelin, and increased body mass index. *PLoS Medicine, 1,* e62.

Sleep and Thermoregulation

Sleep has thermoregulatory consequences for endotherms. Reduction of body temperature (T_b) and metabolic rate (MR) during sleep conserves energy, and sleep may have evolved to lower the thermoregulatory set point and reduce the energetic demands of endothermy (Berger & Philips, 1995). Many studies support the assumption that sleep, daily torpor, and hibernation are homologous states along a continuum of T_b reduction and energy conservation. Shallow torpor and deep hibernation may have arisen as an extension of sleep to achieve greater energy conservation through more extreme lowering of T_b and MR (Berger, 1984; Heller & Ruby, 2004).

Precision of thermoregulation is reduced during short-wave sleep (SWS), with a 1–2 °C reduction in T_b and a decline in MR of 10 percent below wakeful levels at thermoneutrality, with greater energetic savings at lower ambient temperatures (T_a). Mechanisms include reduction in the hypothalamic set point for thermosensitivity, increased peripheral vasodilation, and increased sweating (Berger & Philips, 1995; Glotzbach & Heller, 1976). During rapid eye movement (REM) sleep, the thermoregulatory system is inactivated, resulting in further reduction of T_b and

MR. Shivering, panting, and sweating are absent during REM sleep and there is an absence of hypothalamic thermosensitivity (Berger & Philips, 1995; Glotzbach & Heller, 1976). Thermoregulatory changes associated with sleep and sleep state result in variation in T_b and MR independent of the circadian rhythm. The length of REM-sleep periods is positively correlated with body mass, reflecting the thermal inertia of larger animals. Many endotherms spend more time in REM sleep near thermoneutrality than at low T_a, where thermoregulation associated with SWS is required to maintain normothermia (Berger & Philips, 1995; Glotzbach & Heller, 1976).

There is much support for the energy-conservation hypothesis for the evolution of sleep. Large birds increase the time spent asleep in response to fasting to conserve energy (Berger & Philips, 1995) and SWS and thermoregulation develop concurrently during ontogenesis of altricial mammals and birds (Berger, 1984; Berger & Philips, 1995). SWS appears universal among mammals and birds (that evolved endothermy independently), but unequivocal evidence of SWS is lacking for ectotherms (Berger, 1984; Berger & Philips, 1995). An endothermic arthropod, the honey bee, undergoes periods of sleep-like behavior associated with reduced neural activity and unresponsiveness (Berger & Philips, 1995). This suggests convergent evolution of sleep and endothermy in at least three evolutionary lineages.

Torpor and hibernation are deeper regulated drops in T_b and MR that conserve energy. Sleep and torpor share many behavioral characteristics: animals retire to a secure retreat, assume a typical posture, remain quiescent, and have increased sensory thresholds. Entry into torpor and hibernation occur during periods of SWS

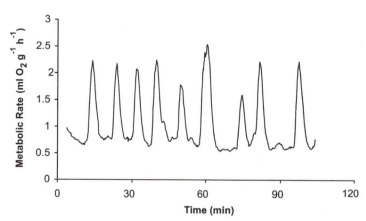

Changes in metabolic rate of the numbat *(Myrmecobius fasciatus)* at an ambient temperature of 20°C are attributed to changes in sleep state. Periods of short-wave sleep are associated with thermoregulation and an increase in metabolic rate, and periods of rapid eye movement sleep with a decrease in metabolic rate as thermoregulation is abandoned. Figure adapted from Cooper and Withers (2002). (Christine Cooper)

(Berger, 1984; Heller & Ruby, 2004). Periods of wakefulness during torpor entry reduce the rate of T_b decline, and prolonged wakefulness restores euthermia. Some hibernators have an endogenous circadian rhythm in T_b during hibernation, providing further evidence that sleep and torpor are homologous (Heller & Ruby, 2004).

During shallow torpor, animals spend the majority of their time in SWS, spending more time in SWS as the depth of torpor increases until REM sleep is entirely absent in deep torpor. SWS during torpor ensures that T_b is regulated continuously. REM sleep is absent during the arousal phase of torpor, with wakeful electroencephalogram patterns until T_b is approximately 33 °C, then SWS dominates the remainder of the arousal (Berger, 1984; Heller & Ruby, 2004).

Most research on sleep has been on endotherms, so work examining sleep in ectotherms, particularly partially endothermic groups such as arthropods and some reptiles, would enhance understanding of the evolutionary derivation and the role of sleep. More studies of a circadian rhythm in hibernators could strengthen the evidence of a link between sleep, torpor, and hibernation. Of particular interest is work examining the role of sleep in periodic arousals from long-term hibernation. Long-term hibernators appear severely sleep deprived following arousal and recovery sleep after arousal reduces this slow-wave activity (SWA), suggesting that arousals during long-term hibernation are necessary for restorative sleep. However, sleep depriving animals after arousal eliminated peaks in SWA, suggesting that posthibernation sleep was not necessary for restorative processes. Therefore further work is required to better understand the relationships among sleep, torpor, and hibernation (Heller & Ruby, 2004).

Christine Elizabeth Cooper

See also: entries related to Evolution of Sleep; entries related to Sleep Physiology

References

Berger, R. J. (1984). Slow wave sleep, shallow torpor and hibernation: Homologous states of diminished metabolism and body temperature. *Biological Psychology, 19,* 305–326.

Berger, R. J., & Philips, N. H. (1995). Energy conservation and sleep. *Behavioural Brain Research, 69,* 65–73.

Cooper, C. E., & Withers, P. C. (2002). Metabolic physiology of the numbat (*Myrmecobius fasciatus*). *Journal of Comparative Physiology B, 172,* 669–675.

Glotzbach, S. F., & Heller, H. C. (1976). Central nervous regulation of body temperature during sleep. *Science, 194,* 537–539.

Heller, H. C., & Ruby, N. R. (2004). Sleep and circadian rhythms in mammalian torpor. *Annual Reviews of Physiology, 66,* 275–289.

Sleep Apnea in Heart Failure

Within Westernized nations, heart failure (HF) is a major public health concern. The burden of the disease continues to increase as the population ages, and the prognosis is grim, with 50 percent of patients dying within five years of diagnosis. Although there are different types of HF, the disease can be broadly defined as the heart's inability to pump sufficient blood supply to meet the body's needs.

It is widely recognized that HF patients have disproportionately high rates of disturbed sleep, a phenomenon that increases with severity of disease. This association first garnered scientific interest in the 1950s, but it was not until relatively recently that sleep disordered breathing (SDB) was acknowledged as a risk factor for incident HF, as well as a predictor of poor prognosis. Unfortunately, assessment and treatment of SDB are still often neglected in the care and management of HF patients.

Sleep apnea syndrome, a specific form of SDB, is common in HF, being found in approximately half of all patients (Naughton & Lorenzi-Filho, 2009). An apneic event in sleep apnea is characterized as the absence of airflow of ≥90 percent for ≥10 seconds. In HF, the presence of sleep apnea has been associated with poor quality of life and increased risk of morbidity and mortality. Sleep apnea syndrome can be classified into two primary categories: central sleep apnea (CSA) and obstructive sleep apnea (OSA). CSA in HF occurs as a result of the slower circulation of blood and a consequent unmasking of the apneic threshold due to the decrease in the partial pressure of carbon dioxide in the blood resulting in cessation of breathing. CSA is characterized by inconsistent breathing patterns, where the breathing repeatedly starts and stops. OSA, on the other hand, is caused by a blockage of the airway, usually when the soft tissue in the rear of the throat collapses and closes during sleep. CSA and OSA should not be seen as completely separate phenomena because many HF patients with CSA also have OSA events, referred to as mixed apnea. CSA may render the upper airway more prone to collapse. HF is the most common cause of CSA, and OSA is a known risk factor for

HF diagnosis. Although there are limited data in HF patients, longitudinal studies indicate that untreated CSA and/or OSA increase risk of mortality.

There is no gold standard for the treatment of sleep apnea in HF. Studies using continuous positive airway pressure (CPAP) or auto-titrating CPAP report improvements in apnea severity in OSA, as well as physical functioning, emotional well-being, and fatigue. CPAP and auto-titrating CPAP have been found to lower morbidity and mortality in HF patients with OSA (Kasai et al., 2008; Smith et al., 2007). However, there is still no direct evidence to suggest that treating OSA will reduce incident HF. The positive effects of CPAP for OSA should not be extrapolated to HF patients with CSA. Randomized control trials of therapy for CSA in HF have not established a significant benefit with respect to hospitalization or mortality and thus, there is no consensus on an optimal treatment strategy. CSA is thought to be a consequence of underlying cardiac dysfunction and thus, optimal treatment of HF using angiotensin-converting enzyme inhibitors, diuretics, and β-blockers have been associated with alleviation of CSA (Somers et al., 2008). Theophylline, nocturnal oxygen supplementation, bi-level positive airway pressure, and automated adaptive servoventilation have all shown promise in reducing CSA.

In summary, the presence of sleep apnea adversely affects quality of life of HF patients, and may increase their risk of further morbidity and of mortality. Considering the high prevalence of sleep apnea syndrome in HF as well as other cardiac conditions, there is burgeoning collaborative effort between cardiology and chronobiology to further understand its role in cardiovascular outcomes, especially in HF.

Jessica Ann Jiménez
and Paul J. Mills

See also: entries related to Sleep Disorders

References

Kasai, T., Narui, K., Dohi, T., Yanagisawa, N., Ishiwata, S., Ohno, M., . . . Momomura, S. (2008). Prognosis of patients with heart failure and obstructive sleep apnea treated with continuous positive airway pressure. *Chest, 133*(3), 690–696.

Naughton, M. T., & Lorenzi-Filho, G. (2009). Sleep in heart failure. *Progress in Cardiovascular Diseases, 51*(4), 339–349.

Shahar, E., Whitney, C. W., Redline, S., Lee, E. T., Newman, A. B., Nieto, F. J., . . . Samet, J. M. (2001). Sleep-disordered breathing and cardiovascular disease: Cross-sectional results of the sleep heart health study. *American Journal of Respiratory Critical Care Medicine, 163*(1), 19–25.

Smith, L. A., Vennelle, M., Gardner, R. S., Mc-Donagh, T. A., Denvir, M. A, Douglas, N. J., & Newby, D. E. (2007). Auto-titrating continuous positive airway pressure therapy in patients with chronic heart failure and obstructive sleep apnoea: A randomized placebo-controlled trial. *European Heart Journal, 28*(10), 1221–1227.

Somers, V. K., White, D. P., Amin, R., Abraham, W. T., Costa, F., Culebras, A., . . . Young, T. (2008). Sleep apnea and cardiovascular disease: An American Heart Association/American College of Cardiology Foundation scientific statement from the American Heart Association Council for High Blood Pressure Research Professional Education Committee, Council on Clinical Cardiology, Stroke Council, and Council on Cardiovascular Nursing In collaboration with the National Heart, Lung, and Blood Institute National Center on Sleep Disorders Research (National Institutes of Health). *Journal of the American College of Cardiology, 52*(8), 686–717.

Sleep as We Age

When we look at both objective and subjective parameters of sleep quality and duration as we age, the news is not good. With increasing age, total sleep time and sleep efficiency decline. Older age is associated with shorter sleep time, diminished sleep efficiency, and more arousals. Sleep in the elderly tends to be shallow, fragmented, and variable in duration. Subjectively, satisfaction with sleep quality is lower (Ohayon, Carskadon, Guilleminault, & Vitiello, 2004). The percentages of sleep spent in deep sleep (Stage 3) and rapid eye movement sleep (REMS) decline significantly. Older adults have less of both REMS and Stage 3, with slow-wave sleep decreasing linearly at 2 percent per decade up to 60 years then remaining fairly constant up to age 95 (Ancoli-Israel, Ayalon, & Salzman, 2008). Changes in sleep quality with age are more likely to affect waking function. Insomnia in the elderly contributes to a decrease in reported quality of life. The only sleep variable that increases with age is WASO—time awake in bed after sleep onset.

So is sleep disturbance inevitable in late life? Most studies suggest that aging itself probably does not result in poor sleep. Although it is widely believed that older adults sleep less than younger adults—survey results ($N = 1,000$) suggest that most older adults (>65 years of age) sleep an average of seven hours per night (Quan et al.,

2005). The increases in sleep disturbances associated with aging are likely secondary to comorbid health conditions, the medications used to treat these disorders, as well as altered circadian rhythms that can be associated with the process of aging.

Sleep apnea, the most physiologically disruptive and dangerous of the sleep-associated diagnoses becomes more common with age. The percentage of individuals with moderately severe apnea (apnea hyponea index [AHI] >15) increases from 10 percent at age 39 to 49 to >20 percent for individuals beyond the age of 60. This apnea is also more physiologically disruptive in the elderly; more likely to be associated with increased blood pressure and cardiovascular disease. More severe apnea (AHI >30) is associated with increased frailty and cognitive impairment in elderly women. Periodic limb movements in sleep increase in frequency and are present in up to 45 percent of older adults.

Psychiatric diagnoses in the elderly often result in sleep disturbance. Anxiety symptoms are associated with poor sleep efficiency and increased sleep fragmentation in older women. The psychiatric and medical disorders known to chronically disturb sleep in >40 percent of affected patients include: depression/mood disorders, chronic pain, anxiety disorders, cardiac and vascular disease, pulmonary disease, rheumatological disorders, gastrointestinal disorders, endocrine disease, renal disease, genitourinary problems, and neurological disorders. Among older adults the incidence of sleep disturbance correlates best with depression, impaired health, and decline in physical functioning (Quan et al., 2005).

Circadian disturbance is common in the elderly, including circadian-rhythm sleep disorder, advanced sleep-phase type, which characterizes up to 60 percent of elderly individuals, and circadian-rhythm sleep disorder, irregular sleep–wake type, most often seen in the institutionalized elderly. The medication types known to cause sleep disruption are commonly used for the treatment of medical and psychiatric disorders in the elderly (Pagel, 2005); see the following list.

Medication Types Known to Cause Insomnia

Adrenocorticotropin (ACTH) and cortisone
Antibiotics—quinalonesAnticonvulsants
Antihypertensives (alpha agonists, beta-blockers, central agents)
Antidepressants (SSRIs)
Antineoplastic agents
Appetite suppressants
Beta agonists
Caffeine
Decongestants
Diuretics
Dopamine agonists
Ephedrine and psuedoephedrine
Ethanol
Ginsing
Lipid and cholesterol lowering agents
Niacin
Oral contraceptives
Psycho-stimulants and amphetamines
Sedative/hypnotics
Theophylline
Thyroid preparations

Dream recall also has been shown to decline in the elderly; however, once again this finding seems more likely to be secondary to increasing incidence of associated disease than the increase in age. Both worsening insomnia and increased levels of obstructive sleep apnea more common with increasing age have been shown to lead to diminished dream recall (Pagel & Shocknasse, 2007; Young et al., 2002).

In sum, it seems apparent that sleep is a marker of health. With good health comes good sleep, but with age, health inevitably declines, as does the quality of sleep.

James F. Pagel

See also: entries related to Sleep and Development

References

Ancoli-Israel, S., Ayalon, L., & Salzman, C. (2008). Sleep in the elderly: Normal variations and common sleep disorders. *Harvard Reviewof Psychiatry, 16*(5), 279–286.

Ohayon, M. M., Carskadon, M. A., Guilleminault, C., & Vitiello, M. V. (2004). Meta-analysis of quantitative sleep parameters from childhood to old age in healthy individuals: Developing normative sleep values across the human lifespan. *Sleep, 27*, 1255–1273.

Pagel, J. F. (2005). Medications and their effects on sleep. *Primary Care, 32*(2), 491–510.

Pagel, J. F., & Shocknasse, S. (2007) Dreaming and insomnia: Polysomnographic correlates of reported dream recall frequency. *Dreaming, 17*(3), 140–151.

Quan, S. F., Katz, R., Olson, J., Bonekat, W., Enright, P. L., Young, T., et al. (2005). Factors associated with the incidence and persistence of symptoms of disturbed sleep in an elderly cohort: The Cardiovascular Health Study. *American Journal of the Medical Sciences, 329*, 163–172.

Young, T., Shahar, E., Nieto, F. J., Redline, S., Newman, A. B., Gottlieb, D. J., et al. (2002). Predictors of sleep-disordered breathing in community-dwelling adults. *Archives of Internal Medicine, 162*(8), 893–900.

Sleep Development in Infancy and Early Childhood

One of the most fascinating aspects of sleep is the dramatic change it undergoes during development. Although the reasons behind the striking shifts that occur in sleep are unclear, these shifts have been widely researched. Across early development, significant changes occur in the timing of sleep, in the amount of sleep, and in the characteristics of sleep itself. As with most phenomena that have been studied across human development, there is a wide range of interindividual variability displayed in sleep characteristics. Little is known regarding the implications of this variability during early development, although there is some indication that short sleep during later childhood is related to impairments in children's neurobehavioral functioning (Sadeh, Gruber, & Raviv, 2003).

Timing of Sleep

Perhaps the most prominent change that occurs in early infancy is the development of the diurnal rhythm of sleep. While newborns spend approximately equal amounts of time awake and asleep across the 24-hour day, by three months of age, sleep has consolidated such that infants are spending a higher proportion of the nighttime hours asleep and a higher proportion of the daytime hours awake (Kleitman & Engelmann, 1953). Infants typically have two to three daytime naps; during the second year of life, most infants give up the morning nap in favor of one afternoon nap. The final daytime nap gets dropped sometime between the ages of three to five years

(Iglowstein, Jenni, Molinari, & Largo, 2003). The dropping of the daytime nap is partly dictated by the sociocultural variable of school schedules. Opportunities for napping in U.S. public schools are not offered by the time a child reaches first grade (around the age of six years). It is also important to note that, while sleep is characterized as consolidated to the nighttime hours, children under the age of 12 months typically experience nighttime awakenings (Burnham, Goodlin-Jones, Gaylor, & Anders, 2002). Thus, nighttime sleep is not continuous, but is typically interrupted by one to two awakenings that may or may not require parental assistance.

Amount of Sleep

Another shift that occurs is in the amount of sleep, regardless of the time of day. Infants—indeed, the young of all species yet studied—spend a higher proportion of time asleep when compared to their adult counterparts. The typical human newborn spends between 16 and 18 hours asleep across the 24-hour day (Kleitman & Engelmann, 1953). While sleep consolidates to the nighttime hours, the total amount of sleep per 24 hours remains remarkably stable at around 12.5 hours through 24 months of age (Montgomery-Downs & Gozal, 2006). During the early childhood years, total amount of sleep declines gradually (Iglowstein et al., 2003). Similar to adults, young children display variability in the amount of nighttime sleep they receive, and appear to need, for optimal functioning. As yet, there is no identified threshold for an optimum amount of sleep for all young children and this is a ripe area

for future research, as is study of the consequences of not obtaining an optimum amount of sleep during this age span.

Characteristics of Sleep

Turning now to sleep itself, it is observed that dramatic shifts occur in the proportion of time that infants spend in active versus quiet periods of sleep. In humans, active sleep is considered a form of, or precursor to, adult rapid eye movement (REM) sleep, although there is some controversy about this in nonhuman mammals (e.g., Frank & Heller, 2003). Likewise, in humans, quiet sleep is considered a form of, or precursor to, what will be called nonrapid eye movement (NREM) sleep. Active and quiet sleep can be characterized by visually observing infant sleep and noting the presence or absence of movements. In fact, behavioral observation is considered as accurate as EEG-recorded human sleep, especially during early development when characteristic brain wave patterns are still emerging (Anders & Sostek, 1976). During the first year of life, active sleep is characterized by regularly occurring large and small muscle movements, REMs, and heart rate and breathing irregularities. Quiet sleep may contain some spontaneous, irregular movements, but is accompanied by regular respiration and heart rates. Across the first year of life, the proportions of active and quiet sleep shift dramatically, with active sleep much more prominent in the early months and quiet sleep becoming more prominent toward the first birthday and beyond (Burnham et al., 2002). In addition, and in contrast to the adult pattern of NREM at sleep onset, young infants typically transition from wakefulness directly into active sleep during the nighttime sleep period.

Melissa M. Burnham

See also: entries related to Fetal Sleep

References

Anders, T. F., & Sostek, A. M. (1976). The use of time-lapse video recording of sleep-wake behavior in human infants. *Psychophysiology, 13,* 155–158.

Burnham, M. M., Goodlin-Jones, B. L., Gaylor, E. E., & Anders, T. F. (2002). Nighttime sleep-wake patterns and self-soothing from birth to one year of age: A longitudinal intervention study. *Journal of Psychology and Psychiatry, 43,* 713–725.

Frank, M. G., & Heller, H. C. (2003). The ontogeny of mammalian sleep: A reappraisal of alternative hypotheses. *Journal of Sleep Research, 12,* 25–34.

Iglowstein, I., Jenni, O. G., Molinari, L., & Largo, R. H. (2003). Sleep duration from infancy to adolescence: Reference values and generational trends. *Pediatrics, 111,* 302–307.

Kleitman, N., & Engelman, T. G. (1953). Sleep characteristics of infants. *Journal of Applied Physiology, 6,* 269–282.

Montgomery-Downs, H. E., & Gozal, D. (2006). Sleep habits and risk factors for sleep-disordered breathing in infants and young toddlers in Louisville, Kentucky. *Sleep Medicine, 7,* 211–219.

Sadeh, A., Gruber, R., & Raviv, A. (2003). The effects of sleep restriction and extension on school-age children: What a difference an hour makes. *Child Development, 74,* 444–455.

Sleep Diaries

A sleep diary is a record of sleep experiences kept by an individual for some period of time. The most widely used sleep diary is the Pittsburgh Sleep Diary (Monk et al., 1994), which reports reasonably stable and high validity/reliability rankings. Clinicians sometimes ask people with sleep complaints to keep a diary of sleep experiences for a few weeks so that the clinician can form an impression of the ways in which the sleep problem manifests. Researchers have also found sleep diaries useful in capturing subjective perceptions of sleep duration and sleep quality, as well as dream reports over long periods of time. Of course like every other method relying on self-report of the individual the data gained from sleep diaries needs to be treated with caution. As long as the investigator remembers that the data tell us about the individual experiences of his sleep, few problems of interpretation arise. But the sleep diary cannot be used as an objective record of sleep patterns or problems. A typical sleep diary contains pages that require the individual to record various kinds of events. Sleep logs, for instance, require the individual to record the times he goes to bed, the times he wakes up, estimates of sleep latency and wake time after sleep onset, and subjective measures of sleep quality. Typically, participants fill out daily sleep-log information for one to three weeks prior to the overnight sleep studies in a clinical sleep lab. Among the information collected in sleep diaries is: subjective daily rankings of sleep quality, bedtime, sleep-onset time, number of awakenings, wake-up time, number of naps, duration of each nap, sleep location, and frequency and content of dreams. Various derivative indexes can be derived from these basic self-report data. For example, an SDI (sleep disturbance index) equals the average frequency of night-wakings per week, plus the average rating on daily sleep quality.

Patrick McNamara

Reference

Monk, T.H., Reynolds, C. F., Kupfer, D.J., Buysse, D.J., Coble, P.A., Hayes, A.J., et al. (1994). The Pittsburgh Sleep Diary. *Journal of Sleep Research, 3*, 111–120.

Sleep Disordered Breathing in Teenagers

Although it is known that adolescents need more than eight hours of sleep per night, they usually obtain less sleep than required. Some studies have shown that social activities and other behavioral patterns shape adolescents' lifestyles toward a predominantly nighttime behavior, while school schedules require them to be fully awake early in the morning. This interaction leads to reduced weekday sleep time and a persistent sleep debt (Carskadon, Acebo, & Jenni, 2004).

Reduction of nighttime sleep due to reduced or altered sleep schedules has been associated with excessive sleepiness and impaired school performance. Several studies have shown increased sleep episodes or changes in sleep patterns following learning tasks (Stickgold, 2005). For example, a positive correlation between the number of non-REM sleep cycles and memorization of word lists exists. Maze learning has been shown to increase Stage 2, non-REM sleep and electroencephalographic (EEG) slow-wave activity. Similar increases in EEG spindles have been reported following memorization of word lists that correlated positively with memory performance (Stickgold, 2005).

Sleep in the early part of the night, dominated by extensive epochs of slow-wave sleep, has been found to enhance declarative memories (episodic and semantic), which rely mainly on the hippocampal memory formation. On the other hand, nondeclarative forms of memory (the procedural memory that refer to sensory motor skills) strongly rely on cortico–striatal circuitry, benefiting more from periods of late nocturnal sleep that are characterized by high levels of REM sleep (Stickgold, 2005).

It is known that during adolescence, circadian phase delays are often out of phase with academic schedules producing an increased risk for sleepiness, reduced academic performance, and other significant morbidity. A very important general principle about the circadian system relevant to learning is that it adapts slowly to changes in sleep/wake schedules. Thus, adolescents who rapidly shift sleep/wake schedules between school nights and weekends or vacations may expect an adverse effect on their circadian rhythms (Carskadon et al., 2004). Another important principle relevant to education is that the circadian system adapts more easily to delays than to advances in the sleep/wake schedule. That is why it is easier to stay up late and sleep in late on weekends and also it is easier to travel; that is, two to three time zones to the west rather than the east (Golombek & Cardinali, 2008). The relevance of these principles to adolescent sleep patterns is paramount. Many adolescents abruptly shift sleep between regular school schedules, requiring early morning awakening, and late bedtimes due to social activities, leisure, etc., causing quick shifts back to late bedtimes and sleeping in on weekends and vacations. For example, a typical Argentine adolescent goes to bed at 3:00 A.M. on weekends and sleeps in until noon. This will cause a phase delay in their circadian system within a few days (Golombek & Cardinali, 2008).

However, shifting to an earlier waking time after a weekend, compatible with going to school early in the morning, will require several days of a stable schedule to shift the temperature and hormone rhythms completely back to a normal phase. Indeed, adolescents are pushed to an awake state during their period of minimum body temperature, when their body is not prepared to be awake and active. Slow, steady, and consistent changes in sleep/wake timing will permit the circadian system to realign to a more appropriate pattern.

In addition to insufficient sleep, sleep disordered breathing (SDB) ranging from primary snoring to obstructive sleep apnea syndrome, affects 10 to 25 percent of children between 3 and 12 years and may also contribute to poor academic performance (Ulualp, 2010). SDB is associated with behavioral dysfunctions including aggression, impulsiveness, and decreased attention. Additionally, children with SDB display lower IQ scores and lower scores on tests of memory and other executive functions. Both reduced sleep and frequent oxygen desaturations likely contribute to these negative outcomes (Ulualp, 2010).

Given the high prevalence and important consequences of sleep loss in adolescents, there is a clear need for readily available and sensitive measures of sleepiness at this age. Specifically, the ability to easily assess the relative degree of sleepiness in this age group may improve the identification of at-risk individuals and help track treatment progress over time. In adolescent research settings, subjective measure of sleepiness may complement objective methods and can provide valuable information when time-consuming objective assessment is not be feasible. Since questionnaires used to evaluate excessive sleepiness associated with sleep disorders and insufficient sleep in adults are inadequate for younger populations, the Pediatric Daytime Sleepiness Scale (PDSS) was introduced as a validated measure for sleepiness in children. Using this scale, daytime sleepiness was found to be related to lower school grades and other negative school-related outcomes (Drake et al., 2003).

We evaluated the sleep habits with PDSS in a Spanish-speaking population of different cities in Argentina (Pérez-Chada et al., 2007). We set out to investigate whether self-reported sleepiness as measured by the PDSS is related to academic performance. The association between SDB and academic performance was also examined. This comprised a sample of 2,210 adolescents from urban areas in Argentina. We enrolled male and female students in their last grades of primary school and first two years of secondary school (between 9 and 17 years old). Forty-nine percent of subjects reported sleeping less than eight hours on weeknights while 83 percent slept less than eight hours per night during weekends. Snoring was reported by 511 subjects (23%). Witnessed apneas were reported in 11 percent of the sample.

Mean PDSS scores were higher for snorers than nonsnorers indicating more sleepiness in this group. Snorers had lower mean grades in mathematics and language. To further explore the relationship between sleepiness and academic results we segregated the sample into quartiles of PDSS values. Average grades for mathematics and language showed significant differences among groups (nonsnorers, occasional, and frequent snorers) in each quartile, especially at the highest ones. PDSS was associated with academic failure in both mathematics and language; that is, each point of increase in the scale was associated with a 5 percent increase in risk for failure. Lack of adequate sleep time was prevalent in our results and insufficient sleep, especially on weekends, was common in this population. Thus a substantial portion of the relationship between sleepiness and academic performance was likely to be due to self-imposed lack of sleep (Pérez-Chada et al., 2007).

Studies on U.S. adolescents show that sleep debt comes from loss of sleep on weeknights, with compensation on weekends (Carskadon et al., 2004). In the Argentine sample, sleep debt was mainly produced on the weekends, probably reflecting a more active nighttime lifestyle in this population and possibly a lower priority for sleep. In this setting sleep debt is likely to be produced by leisure activities, and the direction of causality is likely unidirectional.

In the Argentine sample, 3 percent of adolescents were obese, while 15 percent were overweight (Pérez-Chada, Drake, Pérez Lloret, Videla, & Cardinali, 2009).

Several studies determined that obesity is strongly associated with poor cognitive function (Mietus-Snyder & Lustig, 2008). Magnetic resonance imaging studies of 114 individuals, 40 to 66 years old, showed that both age and body mass index (BMI) were associated with decreased brain volume (Ward, Carlsson, Trivedi, Sager, & Johnson, 2005). In the Argentine sample, those subjects in the higher BMI quintiles had significantly lower mathematics and language marks. A significantly higher proportion of subjects in the fifth quintile failed in mathematics and language as compared to subjects in the first quintile (Pérez-Chada et al., 2009).

Therefore, BMI and sleepiness, as assessed by PDSS, were independent predictors of poor academic performance in the sample of Argentine school students. Therefore, there is a need to increase awareness of this problem in the education and health communities and to translate knowledge already available to strategies to improve the situation.

Daniel Pérez-Chada and
Daniel P. Cardinali

See also: Sleep in Adolescents; entries related to Sleep and Development; entries related to Sleep Disorders

References

Carskadon, M. A., Acebo, C., & Jenni, O. G. (2004). Regulation of adolescent sleep: Implications for behavior. *Annals of the New York Academy of Science, 1021,* 276–291.

Drake, C., Nickel, C., Burduvali, E., Roth, T., Jefferson, C., & Pietro, B. (2003). The pediatric daytime sleepiness scale (PDSS): Sleep habits and school outcomes in middle-school children. *Sleep, 26,* 455–458.

Golombek, D. A., & Cardinali, D. P. (2008). Mind, brain, education, and biological timing. *Mind, Brain and Education, 2,* 1–6.

Mietus-Snyder, M. L., & Lustig, R. H. (2008). Childhood obesity: Adrift in the "limbic triangle." *Annual Review of Medicine, 59,* 147–162.

Pérez-Chada, D., Drake, C. L., Pérez Lloret, S., Videla, A. J., & Cardinali, D. P. (2009). Diurnal rhythms, obesity and educational achievement in South American cultures. *International Journal of Neuroscience, 119,* 1091–1104.

Pérez-Chada, D., Pérez Lloret, S., Videla, A. J., Cardinali, D. P., Bergna, M. A., Fernández-Acquier, M., . . . Drake, C. L. (2007). Sleep disordered breathing and daytime sleepiness are associated with poor academic performance in teenagers: A study using the pediatric daytime sleepiness scale (PDSS). *Sleep, 55,* 219–224.

Stickgold, R. (2005). Sleep-dependent memory consolidation. *Nature, 437,* 1272–1278.

Ulualp, S. O. (2010). Snoring and obstructive sleep apnea. *Medical Clinics of North America, 94,* 1047–1055.

Ward, M. A., Carlsson, C. M., Trivedi, M. A., Sager, M. A., & Johnson, S. C. (2005). The effect of body mass index on global brain volume in middle-aged adults: A cross sectional study. *BMC Neurology, 5,* 23.

Sleep Disorders and Dreaming

This section will focus on several sleep disorders that have been studied in relation to dreaming: insomnia, sleep apnea syndrome, narcolepsy, and restless legs syndrome. For other disorders, like idiopathic hypersomnia, or NREM parasomnias, such as sleep walking or night terrors, systematic dream content analytic studies are lacking. However, extensive reviews are available for nightmares (see this encyclopedia), REM sleep behavior disorder (see this encyclopedia), and dreaming in posttraumatic stress disorder (see this encyclopedia).

Schredl, Schäfer, Weber, and Heuser (1998) found an elevated dream-recall frequency in insomnia patients in contrast to healthy controls, a finding that was no longer significant if number of nocturnal awakenings (self-report measure) was statistically controlled. Percentage of dream recall after REM awakenings carried out in the laboratory did not differ between insomnia patients and controls (Ermann, Peichl, Pohl, Schneider, & Winkelmann, 1993). Schredl et al. (1998) found more negatively toned dreams in patients with insomnia. In addition, nightmare frequency was elevated in patients with insomnia (Schredl, 2009b). The occurrence of problems within the dream was directly correlated with the number of waking-life problems the patients reported in the questionnaire. Therefore, dreams might reflect the topics that are at least partially responsible for the development and maintenance of the primary insomnia.

In sleep apnea, the findings regarding the dream-recall frequency are inconsistent (Schredl, 2009a). In the 19th century, nightmares were thought to be caused by decreased flow of oxygen (e.g., due to pillow blocking of the mouth and nose). However, parameters such as minimal oxygen saturation, nadir, or respiratory disturbance index do not correlate with dream-recall frequency and nightmare frequency in sleep apnea patients (Schredl & Schmitt, 2009; Schredl et al., 2006). Overall, the low incidence of breathing-related dream topics might be explained by adaptation, that is, the increase in number and severity of sleep apneas over months and years might explain why these stimuli are rarely incorporated into dreams, whereas external stimuli are at least sometimes incorporated into dreams (Schredl, 2009a). It would be intriguing to conduct a systematic study where the sleeper wears a mask that would allow transient occlusion of airflow and thus would allow testing whether a novel apnea is more often incorporated into dreams.

Narcolepsy is a sleep disorder characterized by a disinhibition of the REM sleep–regulations systems, and, therefore, the findings of increased dream-recall frequency and higher occurrence of nightmares are not astonishing (Schredl, 2010). In addition, dream content is more bizarre (Schredl, 1998a) and more negatively toned, whereas dream reports of the first REM period were longer in patients compared to healthy controls (Fosse, Stickgold, & Hobson, 2002). Asking for dreams while taking a sleep history of the patient might, in theory, helps to differentiate narcolepsy from other forms of hypersomnia, such as idiopathic hypersomnia.

Lastly, Schredl (2001) found a negative correlation between number of periodic limb movements associated with arousals and dream-recall frequency in a sample of 131 restless legs patients. Taken together that high respiratory disturbance indices are related to less-bizarre dreams in sleep apnea patients (Schredl, Kraft-Schneider, Kröger, & Heuser, 1999), one might hypothesize that frequent micro-arousal might interfere with the dreaming process itself. Systematic studies in this area, however, are lacking.

To summarize, research indicates that altered sleep physiology and waking stressors present in patients with sleep disorders do affect dream recall and dream content in a considerable way. Dreams might be helpful in the diagnosis and treatment of sleep disorders.

Michael Schredl

References

Ermann, M., Peichl, J., Pohl, H., Schneider, M.M., & Winkelmann, Y. (1993). Spontanerwachen und Träume bei Patienten mit psychovegetativen Schlafstörungen. *Psychotherapie, Psychosomatik und Medizinische Psychologie [Psychotherapy, Psychosomatics, and Medical Psychology], 43*, 333–340.

Fosse, R., Stickgold, R., & Hobson, J. A. (2002). Emotional experience during rapid-eye-movement sleep in narcolepsy. *Sleep, 25*, 724–732.

Schredl, M. (1998a). Dream content in patients with narcolepsy: Preliminary findings. *Dreaming, 8*, 103–107.

Schredl, M. (1998b). *Träume und Schlafstörungen: Empirische Studie zur Traumerinnerungshäufigkeit und zum Trauminhalt schlafgestörter PatientInnen. [Dreams and sleep disorders: Empirical study of the frequency of dream recall and dream content in the dreams of sleep disordered patients.]* Marburg: Tectum.

Schredl, M. (2001). Dream recall frequency and sleep quality of patients with restless legs syndrome. *European Journal of Neurology, 8*, 185–189.

Schredl, M. (2009a). Dreams in patients with sleep disorders. *Sleep Medicine Reviews, 13*, 215–221.

Schredl, M. (2009b). Nightmare frequency in patients with primary insomnia. *International Journal of Dream Research, 2*, 85–88.

Schredl, M. (2010). Dreams in patients with narcolepsy. In M. Goswami, S.R.

Pandi-Perumal, & M. J. Thorpy (Eds.), *Narcolepsy: A clinical guide* (pp. 125–127). New York: Springer.

Schredl, M., Kraft-Schneider, B., Kröger, H., & Heuser, I. (1999). Dream content of patients with sleep apnea. *Somnologie, 3,* 319–323.

Schredl, M., Schäfer, G., Weber, B., & Heuser, I. (1998). Dreaming and insomnia: Dream recall and dream content of patients with insomnia. *Journal of Sleep Research, 7,* 191–198.

Schredl, M., & Schmitt, J. (2009). Dream recall frequency and nightmare frequency in patients with sleep disordered breathing. *Somnologie, 13,* 12–17.

Schredl, M., Schmitt, J., Hein, G., Schmoll, T., Eller, S., & Haaf, J. (2006). Nightmares and oxygen desaturations: Is sleep apnea related to heightened nightmare frequency? *Sleep and Breathing, 10,* 203–209.

Sleep Disorders in Patients with Chronic Kidney Disease

Sleep disorders (SD) are very common in chronic kidney disease (CKD) needing dialysis (De Santo, Perna, Di Iorio, & Cirillo, 2010b) and were described for the first time in 1970, a few years after the introduction of hemodialysis (HD). A 41 to 85 percent prevalence of SD has been demonstrated in adult and children on HD and on peritoneal dialysis (PD). The worst sleepers (nearly 100%) are HD patients with secondary hyperparathyroidism that is not adequately controlled by medical therapy (De Santo et al., 2010b).

In the study of Merlino et al. (2004) in HD and PD patients, SD were present as insomnia (69.1%), obstructive sleep apnea syndrome (23.6%), restless legs syndrome (18.4%), nightmares (13.3%), excessive daytime sleepiness (11.8%), rapid eye movement behavior (2.3%), sleep walking (2.1%), and possible narcolepsy (1.4%). SD in HD patients predict quality of life and mortality risk, as it emerged in the Dialysis Outcomes and Practice Patterns Study, in which poor sleepers, in comparison with good sleepers, had a 16 percent higher relative risk of death. The dialysis shift is important. Patients dialyzing in the morning have a heavier SD burden. The worst sleep is recorded during the night of the longest interdialytic interval. Surprisingly, SD are not healed in patients receiving a successful renal transplantation (TX).

Recent studies have focused on SD affecting patients in the early stages of CKD. SD were disclosed a few weeks after patients were diagnosed with a CKD, which later in life might probably lead to HD therapy or less probably to a TX. This was demonstrated throughout CKD Grades 1 to 3—Grade 1: estimated GFR (eGFR) $\geq$90 mL/minute; Grade 2: eGFR $\leq$90 and $\geq$60 mL/minute; and Grade 3: eGFR $\leq$60 and $\geq$30 mL/minute. These findings demonstrate that the intrusion of CKD in life of patients triggers SD, which are a marker of the coping process with a chronic disease (De Santo et al., 2010b).

A three-year longitudinal study of Sabbatini et al. (2008) suggests that progression of renal disease is accompanied by a progressive worsening of SD, but an independent association was not demonstrated. Furthermore a four-year longitudinal study in CKD patients achieving target systolic and diastolic blood pressures, has shown that depression correlates with sleep quality in logistic regression analysis (De Santo et al., 2010a).

A list of nearly 50 putative determinants for SD in CKD needing or not HD therapy have been grouped in: (1) demographic factors, (2) lifestyle-related factors, (3) disease-related factors, (4) psychological factors, (5) treatment-related factors, and (6) socioeconomic factors. Important factors emerged: age in group 1; cigarette smoking and obesity in group 2; GFR, anemia, parathyroid hormone, calcium concentrations, neurotransmitters production, hypertension and antihypertensive drugs and bone pain, hypoxemia and pruritus in group 3; depression, perceived quality of life, and disease intrusiveness in group 4. The dialysis team, the shift, the day of the weekly treatment schedule, albumin and C-reactive protein concentrations, comorbid conditions, losses and dependencies of a dialysis-dependent life emerge in group 5. The lower economic conditions and living in urban environment emerge in the last group (Parker, 2003). Finally, recent studies disclosed a disrupted circadian melatonin rhythm that might be amenable to therapy.

In our laboratory, hypertension was associated with SD in HD and CKD patients. The association disappeared in the four-year longitudinal study where systolic and diastolic blood pressure, under a tight control, fell within target values in CKD patients (De Santo et al., 2010a).

Patients can be studied by a combination of various questionnaires, and through a systematic approach, focusing on narrative, physical examination, interviews, and laboratory tests. A sleep specialist may be needed. Therapy is based on psychological support, use of benzodiazepines, dopaminergic agents, opioids, and anticonvulsants.

Nasal continuous positive airway pressure is the treatment for sleep apnea.

Rosa Maria De Santo

See also: entries related to Sleep Disorders

References

De Santo, R. M., Bilancio, G., Santoro, D., Li Vecchi, M., Perna, A., De Santo, N. G., & Cirillo, M. A. (2010a). A longitudinal study of sleep disorders in early-stage chronic kidney disease. *Journal of Renal Nutrition, 2020,* S59–S63.

De Santo, R. M., Perna, A., Di Iorio, B. R., & Cirillo, M. (2010b). Sleep disorders in kidney disease. *Minerva Urologica e Nefrologica, 62,* 111–128.

Merlino, G., Piani, A., Dolso, P., et al. (2004). Sleep disorders in patients with end-stage renal diseases undergoing dialysis therapy. *Nephrol Dial Transplant, 1919,* 1815–1822.

Parker, K. P. (2003). Sleep disturbances in dialysis patients. *Sleep Medicine Reviews, 2*(2), 131–143.

Sabbatini, M., Pisani, A., Crispo, A., Ragosta, A., Gallo, R., Pota, A., . . . Cianciaruso, B. (2008). Sleep quality with chronic renal failure: A 3-year longitudinal study. *Sleep Medicine, 9,* 240–246.

Sleep Disorders in Patients with Heart Failure

Most individuals who have experienced heart failure (HF) suffer from sleep disordered breathing (SDB), characterized by disrupted sleep, reduced sleep efficiency, and feeling of fatigue, due to an elevation in sympathetic nervous system activity. Cardiovascular manifestations of SDB include atrial fibrillation, congestive heart failure, increased platelet coagulability, ischemic cardio-cerebral event, left ventricular hypertrophy, left ventricular systolic and diastolic dysfunction, nocturnal angina, pulmonary hypertension, systemic hypertension, and sudden cardiac death (Khan, Hazin, & Han, 2010).

SDB, which is associated with excess mortality, may manifest either as obstructive sleep apnea (OSA) or central sleep apnea (CSA), with Cheyne–Stokes respiration (CSR). CSA–CSR, described more 200 years ago, is a form of periodic breathing alternating apneas and hypopneas, with waxing and waning periods of ventilation. Its prevalence in HF ranges from 20 to 60 percent OSA, characterized by partial or complete closure of the upper airways during sleep leading to intervals of disrupted breathing lasting more than 10 seconds, causes hypertension and left ventricular hypertrophy, and has a prevalence in the range of 20 to 40 percent (Khan et al., 2010; Naughton & Lorenzi-Filho, 2009).

Patients with HF are in a state of chronic hyperventilation probably due to pulmonary congestion. CSA and OSA may coexist in the same patient (Khan et al., 2010; Naughton & Lorenzi-Filho, 2009; Valdivia-Arenas, Powers, & Khayat, 2009). CSA and OSA through hypoxia stimulate an increased sympathetic activity leading to vasoconstriction and to increased afterload for the failing heart. OSA, because of its hemodynamic effects, may cause HF decompensation.

CSA is typical of stable HF patients, whereas OSA is typical of decompensated or advanced HF. Typical symptoms of OSA are snoring, tiredness, feeling of fatigue, daytime sleepiness, impaired cognitive function, depression, and disrupted sleep. But they may be unspecific, and due to HF, as well as to SDB. The inspiratory efforts against the occluded pharynx cause an increase of negative intrathoracic pressure, which, in turn, increases the venous return. The latter promotes an increase of the right intraventricular septum and a leftward shift of the ventricle during diastole, thus left ventricular filling is reduced.

The prevalence of SDB in HF is 40 to 70 percent, whereas in the general population it is below 10 percent. In HF, the severity of apnea, independently associated with poor quality of life (reduced physical functioning), is independent of fatigue and depression.

Patients on a heart-transplant waiting list have high prevalence (40–50%) of SDB, more than 80 percent of them have CSA–CSR at the peak of hyperpneic phase, and a minority have OSA. In both CSA and OSA, the most frequent disorder is waking after sleep onset, whereas daytime sleepiness is rare (Lofaso, Verschueren, Dubois Rande, Harf, & Goldemberg, 1994). After heart transplantation CSA–CSR is abolished; however, patients have moderate-to-severe sleep apnea, periodic limb movement, and restless legs syndrome (30–45% of the cases) associated with low quality of life, disrupted sleep, reduced REM sleep, high arousal index, daytime sleepiness, and systolic and diastolic hypertension. The mechanism of restless legs syndrome and periodic limb movement remains to be elucidated. The sleep-apnea/hypopnea syndrome is a potential cause of graft failure, since it can contribute to the atherosclerotic process of coronary graft vasculopathy (Javaheri et al., 2004).

Polysomnography should be used for appropriate diagnosis and follow-up, as well as to evaluate the effects of nasal continuous positive airways pressure, which is the standard treatment. Patients who are obese should lose weight, and all should abstain from alcohol and sedatives, since they are predisposed to pharyngeal collapse during sleep.

Rosa Maria De Santo

See also: entries related to Sleep Disorders

References

Javaheri, S., Abraham, W.T., Brown, C., Nishiyama, H., Giesting, R., & Wagoner, L.E. (2004). Prevalence of obstructive sleep apnea and periodic limb movement in 45 subjects with heart transplantation. *European Heart Journal, 25,* 260–266.

Khan, F., Hazin, R., & Han Y. (2010). Apneic disorders associated with heart failure: Pathophysiology and clinical management. *Southern Medical Journal, 103,* 44–50.

Lofaso, F., Verschueren, P., Dubois Rande, J.L., Harf, A., & Goldemberg, F. (1994). Prevalence of sleep-disordered breathing in patients on a heart transplant waiting list. *Chest, 106,* 1689–1694.

Naughton, M.T., & Lorenzi-Filho, G. (2009). Sleep in heart failure. *Progress in Cardiovascular Diseases, 51,* 339–349.

Valdivia-Arenas, M.A., Powers, M., & Khayat, R.N. (2009). Sleep-disordered breathing in patients with decompensated heart failure. *Heart Failure Reviews, 14,* 183–193.

Sleep Disturbances in Posttraumatic Stress Disorder (PTSD)

PTSD refers to a disorder involving anxiety, hyperarousal, and memory-based reexperiencing of components of past traumatic experiences. Sleep disturbance and nightmares are core DSM-IV-TR (*Diagnostic and Statistical Manual*) symptoms of PTSD falling in the increased-arousal and reexperiencing diagnostic criterion categories, respectively. Sleep problems are commonly reported by individuals with PTSD (Lamarche & De Koninck, 2007). Sleep lab studies confirm significant aberrations in various components of sleep architecture. A recent meta-analysis examined 20 extant polysomnographic studies comparing PTSD to control groups (Kobayashi, Boarts, & Delahanty, 2007). These authors identified increased Stage 1 NREM, decreased slow-wave sleep or SWS (NREM Stages 3 and 4), and increased rapid eye movement density in REM as the most consistent alterations of sleep in PTSD versus control group. Additional abnormalities expressed in subgroups of PTSD patients included shorter total sleep time, increased sleep-onset latency, reduced Stage 2 NREM, and increased percentage REM.

The association of sleep disturbance and PTSD is even more striking when we simply ask people with PTSD what bothers them the most. The most commonly reported complaints by people diagnosed with PTSD are difficulty falling and staying asleep. The sleep problems furthermore very closely track fluctuations in severity of PTSD symptoms. For example, one-month retrospective severity ratings of sleep problems, as measured by the Pittsburgh Sleep Quality Index, increased as people reported that their PTSD symptoms increased from moderate to severe to extremely severe. In short, sleep problems and complaints increase in tandem with severity of overall PTSD symptoms. Persistent trauma-related nightmares are a near-universal symptom of PTSD and their occurrence alone can fulfill the DSM-IV reexperiencing category criterion. Therefore, both objective and subjective sleep disturbance, including nightmares, represent core features of PTSD.

Sleep abnormalities following traumatic experiences may also predict later development of PTSD. For example, people who have been in a motor vehicle accident and then experienced sleep disturbance immediately following their trauma were much more likely to develop PTSD than people in auto accidents who did not experience significant sleep problems after their accident. After any severe trauma if the persons involved experience sleep problems, and especially if they experience nightmares, then they are more likely to develop long-term symptoms of PTSD. Several studies have specifically linked REM abnormalities in the early aftermath of traumatic injury to later development of PTSD. For example, if a shortened duration of REM periods assessed within one month of trauma occurs, then development of PTSD symptoms two months posttrauma appears to be more likely.

These clinical facts are consistent with animal studies that show that high-severity stressors such as electric shock, prolonged immobilization, or fear-conditioning procedures reduce REM sleep in rats. Rats undergo a full panoply of stress reactions when subjected to these kinds of procedures. That stress response includes all of the neurochemical and neuroanatomical changes seen in people under high stress, such as activation of the hypothalamic–pituitary–adrenal axis, increased levels of corticotropin releasing factor, and acti-

vation of aminergic systems. These same physiological factors are implicated in PTSD. For example, it has been suggested that the natural circadian rise of cortisol during late sleep may influence consolidation of emotional memories, and that disturbance of this system may contribute to development of PTSD. Interestingly, the alpha-1 adrenergic receptor antagonist prazosin has proved remarkably effective in ameliorating nightmares and disruptions of sleep continuity in PTSD patients. The drug presumably works by inhibiting the REM-related rise in sympathetic drive and in central adrenergic tone.

While the pathophysiology of PTSD is incompletely understood, sleep disturbance is a near-universal feature of the disorder, and treatment of sleep-related symptoms of PTSD (such as nightmare frequency and distress, insomnia, sleep paralysis, periodic limb movements, etc.) is associated with clinically significant improvements in overall PTSD severity and in daytime functioning. Several lines of evidence point to a particularly important role of REM sleep and its underlying brain activity in the pathogenesis of both the nightmare distress and the daytime cognitive and emotional symptoms of PTSD. Severely distressing and repetitive nightmares, which typically arise from REM sleep, are a hallmark of PTSD. Shorter and more fragmented REM periods and increased REM density have been reliably documented in PTSD, and posttrauma REM abnormalities may predict later development of PTSD. In PTSD, abnormalities in sleep quality, REM sleep, and dreaming may result from excessive activity in central noradrenergic stress circuits that oppose brain stem REM generator mechanisms. This excessive arousal may disrupt activity in the amygdala–prefrontal networks that are normally activated during REM sleep. These networks are known to mediate learned fear and emotion regulation more generally. Their breakdown would render the individual vulnerable to chronic overarousal and sleep and dream disturbances. Modulation of sleep is therefore a potential therapeutic adjunct to psychotherapeutic and pharmacologic treatments for PTSD.

Patrick McNamara

See also: entries related to Sleep Disorders

References

Kobayashi, I., Boarts, J.M., & Delahanty, D.L. (2007). Polysomnographically measured sleep abnormalities in PTSD: A meta-analytic review. *Psychophysiology, 44,* 660–669.

Lamarche, L.J., & De Koninck, J. (2007). Sleep disturbance in adults with posttraumatic stress disorder: A review. *Journal of Clinical Psychiatry, 68,* 1257–1270.

Sleep, Dreams, and Personality

Does sleep affect personality? Do dreams influence personality? It has long been hypothesized that normal sleep plays an emotional regulatory role in healthy humans. Sleep deprivation lowers mood, increases irritability, impairs decision making, and diminishes recognition of emotions. Recently, these sleep-deprivation effects on emotion regulation have been linked with diminished prefrontal regulation of subcortical limbic activity (Yoo, Gujar, Hu, Jolesz, & Walker, 2007). Relative to waking, normal sleep may also serve an emotion regulatory function (Pace-Schott, in press).

However, much less is known about relationships between habitual sleep patterns and stable, trait-like aspects of emotion regulation and self-management. Individual variability in mood-regulatory capacity can exist as a stable aspect of personality (Canli, 2004). Similarly, enduring trait-like differences in sleep architecture have been observed (Buckelmuller, Landolt, Stassen, & Achermann, 2006). Because there is selective activation during REM sleep of the same midline limbic structures (Nofzinger et al., 2004) that have been associated with interindividual differences in personality traits (Canli, 2004), there may be similarities between sleep and waking behaviors that share these brain substrates.

We recently conducted an exploratory study, which was the first to assess relationships between personality traits and objectively quantified linguistic elements of REM and NREM dreams along with PSG measures from the same night. In this study, 64 healthy young adults completed a battery of tests measuring personality and emotion regulation traits and then spent two nights, one habituation and one experimental, in the sleep laboratory with polysomnographic monitoring. Following counterbalanced awakenings from REM and NREM sleep, participants audio-taped any dreams they were having right before being awoken.

Personality and emotion regulatory measures included the *Perspective Taking and Empathic Concern* scales from the Interpersonal Reactivity Index (Davis, 1983), *The Behavioral Inhibition (BIS) Scale and the Behavioral Activation (BAS) Scales* (Carver & White, 1994), and the *Temperament and Character Inventory* (TCI; Cloninger, Przybeck, Svrakic, & Wetzel, 1994). The TCI measures personality traits across four dimensions of temperament (harm avoidance, novelty seeking, reward dependence, and persistence) and character (self-directiveness, cooperativeness, and self-transcendence).

The linguistic contents of REM and NREM dream reports were extracted using an objective computerized word-count procedure, the linguistic inquiry and word count (Pennebaker, Francis, & Booth, 2001). Five linguistic-content predictor variables included total number of words in each report (TWC) as well as words in several target categories, positive emotion words, negative emotion words, words that refer to mental states (cognition), and words referring to social situations (social) all expressed as a percentages of TWC. Although potentially influenced by instrumental awakenings, four sleep architecture variables were also examined as predictors of personality variables. These included NREM Stage 2 (N2 percentage), slow wave (N3 percentage), and REM (REM percentage) as percentages of total sleep time as well as REM latency from sleep onset (REML).

Positive, cognitive, and social words in NREM reports were positively associated with novelty seeking, persistence, and empathic concern, respectively. In contrast, for REM dreams, only a negative relationship between negative words

and self-directiveness was apparent. REM percentage was associated positively with empathic concern and self-directiveness. Behavioral activation was associated negatively and self-transcendence positively with N3 percentage.

The fact that word counts from specific categories in NREM rather than REM dreams positively correlated with adaptive traits in waking was somewhat surprising given the greater frequency and intensity of dreaming in REM as well as our finding that REM, but not NREM, sleep physiology was associated with these same trait measures. However, it is consistent with findings that dreamer-initiated friendliness is more characteristic of NREM than REM dreams, whereas aggressive social interactions were more characteristic of REM (McNamara, Mclaren, Smith, Brown, & Stickgold, 2005). Activation of limbic structures during this state may produce intense emotional responses, including instinctual programs such as aggression (see Pace-Schott, in press), while simultaneously strengthening or maintaining circuits that support emotional regulation in waking.

The percentage of sleep spent in REM was also associated with empathic concern and TCI self-directiveness. REM biology may therefore be associated with both the ability to simulate others' emotions and the ability to self-regulate to pursue personal goals. Functional neuroimaging studies show that evocation of empathy activates limbic cortices such as the anterior insula, anterior cingulate cortex, and orbitofrontal cortex, as well as subcortical limbic structures such as the amygdala, ventral striatum, and cerebellum (see Singer & Lamm, 2009, for a review). Most of these regions fall within what has been termed the anterior paralimbic REM activation area (Nofzinger et al., 2004), a midline region activated in REM and widely speculated to be the substrate of REM's role in emotion regulation and the emotional and social nature of REM dreams (Pace-Schott, in press). The shared network hypothesis suggests that brain circuits that generate the experience of empathy overlap with those that generate an individual's own emotional and somatic experience in similar circumstances (Singer & Lamm, 2009). It is notable that these same anterior limbic regions form an important node in brain networks believed to generate prospective simulation of future circumstances as well as the understanding of mental states of others termed theory of mind or mentalizing (Buckner, Andrews-Hanna, & Schacter, 2008). Therefore, individuals with a greater amount of REM sleep may process or rehearse emotional experiences to a greater extent during sleep, including mentalizing in relation to dream characters. Alternatively, both greater REM percentage and empathic concern may reflect greater structural integrity or functional efficiency of limbic networks subserving empathy and other forms of and social cognition.

Slow-wave sleep is a behaviorally quiescent state associated with increased parasympathetic tone; thus it is not surprising that N3 percentage should be negatively associated with behavioral activation. The positive association of N3 percentage with TCI self-transcendence is more difficult to explain. The reduction in self-consciousness

and behavioral quiescence associated with N3 might, in an indirect manner, be associated with tendencies or abilities to dissociate from egocentric perspectives in waking. Association of REM percentage and emotional engagement with one's self (self-directiveness) and others (empathic concern) may reflect a more general relationship of REM with approach behaviors. In contrast, N3's negative association with behavioral activation (BAS) and positive association with self-dissolution (self-transcendence) suggest a relationship of slow-wave sleep with behavioral withdrawal and restorative processes.

This exploratory study must be followed up with additional hypothesis-driven examination of undisturbed sleep and dream reporting from larger numbers of participants. Nonetheless its findings suggest that stable individual differences in personality and emotion regulation may be associated with stable aspects of sleep physiology and dream content.

Edward Pace-Schott, Patricia Lynn Johnson, and Patrick McNamara

References

Buckelmuller, J., Landolt, H.P., Stassen, H.H., & Achermann, P. (2006). Trait-like individual differences in the human sleep electroencephalogram. *Neuroscience, 138,* 351–356.

Buckner, R.L., Andrews-Hanna, J.R., & Schacter, D.L. (2008). The brain's default network: Anatomy, function, and relevance to disease. *Annals of the New York Academy of Science, 1124,* 1–38.

Canli, T. (2004). Functional brain mapping of extraversion and neuroticism: Learning from individual differences in emotion processing. *Journal of Personality, 72,* 1105–1132.

Carver, C.S., & White, T.L. (1994). Behavioral inhibition, behavioral activation, and affective responses to impending reward and punishment: The BIS/BAS scales. *Journal of Personality and Social Psychology, 67,* 319–333.

Cloninger, C.R., Przybeck, T.R., Svrakic, D.M., & Wetzel, R.D. (1994). *The temperament and character inventory (TCI): A guide to its development and use.* St. Louis, MO: Center for Psychobiology of Personality.

Davis, M.H. (1983). Measuring individual differences in empathy: Evidence for a multidimensional approach. *Journal of Personal Social Psychology, 44,* 113–126.

McNamara, P., Mclaren, D., Smith, D., Brown, A., & Stickgold, R.A. (2005). Jekyll and Hyde within: Aggressive versus friendly interactions in REM and non-REM dreams. *Psychological Science, 16,* 130–136.

Nofzinger, E.A., Buysse, D.J., Germain, A., Carter, C., Luna, B., Price, J.C., . . . Kupfer, D.J. (2004). Increased activation of anterior paralimbic and executive cortex from waking to rapid eye movement sleep in depression. *Archives of General Psychiatry, 61,* 695–702.

Pace-Schott, E.F. (in press). The neurobiology of dreaming. In M.H. Kryger, T. Roth, & W.C. Dement (Eds.), *Principles and practice of sleep medicine* (5th ed.). Philadelphia: Elsevier.

Pennebaker, J.W., Francis, M.E., & Booth, R.J. (2001). *Linguistic inquiry and word count.* Mahwah, NJ: Erlbaum Publishers.

Singer, T., & Lamm, C. (2009). The social neuroscience of empathy. *Annals of the New York Academy of Science, 1156,* 81–96.

Yoo, S.S., Gujar, N., Hu, P., Jolesz, F.A., & Walker, M.P. (2007). The human emotional brain without sleep—A prefrontal amygdala disconnect. *Current Biology, 17,* R877–R878.

Sleep, Dreams, and the Time Sense

Two issues will be discussed in the following: sleep-state misperception and the relation between subjective experience time within in the dream and the duration of REM sleep. Sleep-time misperceptions are common among patients with insomnia; they tend to overestimate their sleep-onset time, their time awake after sleep onset, and, thus, underestimate their total sleep time (Edinger & Fins, 1995). These misperceptions can be of clinical relevance and are included in International Classification of Sleep Disorders nosology as a separate entity termed paradoxical insomnia, comprising about 5 percent of the patients suffering from difficulties of falling and maintaining sleep (American Academy of Sleep Medicine, 2005). Interestingly, these misperceptions—interpreted as symptom of cognitive hyperarousal—decrease during cognitive-behavioral treatment (sleep training).

In dream research, an often-cited dream example reported by the French sleep and dream researcher Alfred Maury raised the question whether the recalled dream is possibly generated like a flash during the process of awakening. Maury reported a long and intense dream about the French revolution, which ended with the dreamer in the guillotine and the sleeper waking up with a piece of his wooden bed top having fallen on his neck. Because of the dream's logic, Maury thought that the dream was generated during the awakening process (see Erlacher & Schredl, 2008).

The first approach to falsify this hypothesis was to correlate the subjectively experienced time in dreams with the actual time spent in REM sleep prior to the awakening. In the study of Dement and Kleitman (1957), the participants were awakened in a random order either after 5 or 15 minutes of REM sleep and asked to estimate whether the elapsed sleep interval was 5 or 15 minutes. From 111 awakenings, 83 percent of the judgments were correct. Furthermore, the elapsed length of the REM period correlated with the length of the dream report. The latter findings were replicated by Hobson and Stickgold (1995).

Another line of research provided evidence for a link between real time and dream time. Roffwarg, Dement, Muzio, and Fisher (1962) obtained in their dream study the following dream example:

> The last thing I remember is looking down at a small piece of paper, held at about chest level, trying slowly and haltingly, dwelling on each word, to translate something that looked like 3 lines of French poetry. It took about 20 or 30 seconds to do it, probably. I don't remember if I looked up at any time from the paper. As I remember, essentially, I kept my eyes on the paper. (p. 240)

The corresponding electrooculogram of the previously cited example showed three small but rapid eye movements to the left (22 seconds, 8 seconds, and 0.5 seconds prior to the awakening) indicating that dream action and actually measured eye movements matched.

For lucid dreaming, LaBerge (1985) showed that time intervals for counting from 1 to 10 in the dream are similar to the time intervals for counting during wakefulness. In these studies dream-time intervals can be compared to real time intervals by analyzing eye signals made by the dreamer (Erlacher & Schredl, 2008). This close relationship was replicated by Erlacher and Schredl (2004) but performing squats (deep knee bends) required 44.5 percent more time in lucid dreams than in the waking state.

To summarize, subjective experience time in dreams match pretty well with real time; the conception that dreams elapse in milliseconds is not supported by empirical evidence.

Michael Schredl

See also: entries related to Dream Content

References

American Academy of Sleep Medicine. (2005). *The international classification of sleep disorders (ICSD-2)*. Westchester, IL: Author.

Dement, W. C., & Kleitman, N. (1957). The relation of eye movements during sleep to dream activity: An objective method for the study of dreaming. *Journal of Experimental Psychology, 53,* 339–346.

Edinger, J. D., & Fins, A. I. (1995). The distribution and clinical significance of sleep time misperceptions among insomniacs. *Sleep, 18,* 232–239.

Erlacher, D., & Schredl, M. (2004). Time required for motor activity in lucid dreams. *Perceptual and Motor Skills, 99,* 1239–1242.

Erlacher, D., & Schredl, M. (2008). Do REM (lucid) dreamed and executed actions share the same neural substrate? *International Journal of Dream Research, 1,* 7–14.

Hobson, J. A., & Stickgold, R. (1995). The conscious state paradigm: A neurocognitive approach to waking, sleeping, and dreaming. In M. S. Gazzaniga (Ed.), *The cognitive neurosciences* (pp. 1373–1388). Cambridge, MA: MIT Press.

LaBerge, S. (1985). *Lucid dreaming*. Los Angeles: Jeremy P. Tarcher.

Roffwarg, H. P., Dement, W. C., Muzio, J. N., & Fisher, C. (1962). Dream imagery: Relationship to rapid eye movements of sleep. *Archives of General Psychiatry, 7*, 235–258.

Sleep EEG across Adolescent Development

Adolescence is a time of immense social, cognitive, and physiological transformation. During this period sleep behavior and biology undergo numerous changes. The gold standard used to quantify cortical activity during sleep is the electroencephalogram (EEG), which can be recorded noninvasively. During adolescence, the sleep EEG undergoes marked changes, which exceed those observed later in life. For one, a number of studies have shown that the amount of slow-wave sleep (SWS; sleep Stages 3 and 4) declines across this period. An early longitudinal study measured SWS in children when they were prepubertal (ages 10 to 12 years) and again when they were postpubertal (ages 14 to 16 years), finding a decline of approximately 40 percent in this measure. The precise age at which this decline begins, the rate of the decline, and the contribution of individual variability remain unknown, as does its mechanism and function. Concurrent to the decline in SWS is a significant, yet less pronounced, increase in Stage 2 sleep. Despite changes in the distribution of sleep stages across adolescence, sleep need remains stable: when given an opportunity postpubertal adolescents will sleep for as long as their prepubertal counterparts. The duration of REM sleep also does not change across adolescence; however, the time to

the first REM episode after sleep onset (called REM latency) is longer in children than in late adolescents. This phenomenon is often called a skipped REM episode and becomes rare in late adolescence.

Another readily observable maturational alteration of the sleep EEG is the substantial decline in the amplitude of the EEG signal during NREM and REM sleep. As with the decline in the amount of SWS, the age at which the EEG amplitude decline begins is unknown. The decline itself, however, is thought to reflect the pruning of synapses that occurs during this developmental period. Because the amplitude of EEG waves is dependent on synchronous synaptic activity, a decrease in the number of synapses would translate into a decline in EEG amplitude.

A more subtle change in the sleep EEG concerns a hallmark of Stage 2 sleep: sleep spindles. Sleep spindles are transient oscillations between 11 and 16 Hz, and are reflected in the sleep EEG spectrum as a peak in this frequency range. The frequency of the spectral peak in the spindle range (11 to 16 Hz) increases across adolescence, suggesting that spindle oscillations become faster with increasing age. Some have postulated that this increase may reflect cortical mylenation (or increased white matter), which is known to occur in this developmental phase.

In summary, adolescence is a time of remarkable cortical growth and restructuring. The sleep EEG reflects a number of these maturational developments, including the decline in the number of synapses and perhaps increased mylenation. The mechanisms and functional significance of the developmental changes to sleep physiology require further elucidation with the ultimate aim of assessing the impact of sleep on mental and physical health during adolescence.

Leila Tarokh

See also: entries related to Sleep and Development; entries related to Sleep Assessment

References

Campbell, I. G., & Feinberg, I. (2009). Longitudinal trajectories of non-rapid eye movement delta and theta EEG as indicators of adolescent brain maturation. *Proceedings of the National Academy of Science, 106*(13), 5177–5180.

Carskadon, M. A. (1982). The second decade. In C. Guilleminault (Ed.), *Sleep and waking disorders: Indications and techniques* (pp. 99–125). Menlo Park, CA: Addison Wesley.

Feinberg, I. (1982). Schizophrenia: Caused by a fault in programmed synaptic elimination during adolescence? *Journal of Psychiatric Research, 17*(4), 319–334.

Tarokh, L., & Carskadon, M. A. (2010). Developmental changes in the human sleep EEG during early adolescence. *Sleep*.

Sleep Fragmentation

Sleep fragmentation refers to alteration of the microstructure of sleep by the frequent appearance of three-second and longer increases in EEG frequency called EEG arousals (Bonnet, 2005). These EEG arousals are also associated with other signs of central nervous system activation including increased heart rate, blood pressure, and metabolic rate. It is normal to have some brief arousals during sleep, but the great majority of these are never remembered. However, in some situations, disruptive repetitive external stimuli or medical conditions may greatly increase the number of these events and produce severely degraded sleep that can become nonrestorative.

Sleep fragmentation is common in patients who have significant sleep disorders such as obstructive sleep apnea (Bennett, Langford, Stradling, & Davies, 1998). These patients typically have EEG arousals as they resume respiration. Research in dogs with a model of sleep apnea has shown that sleep disturbance associated with apnea events and similar sleep fragmentation without the apnea events both produced similar increases in sleepiness (Bowes, Woolf, Sullivan, & Phillipson, 1980). This led to the conclusion that common symptoms found in patients with sleep apnea may be more related to the sleep disturbance than to the respiratory pathology. In these patients, elimination of sleep apnea also corrects the sleep fragmentation, and the patients usually have normalized alertness within a few days.

Many studies in humans have shown that sleep fragmentation produced by frequent periodic auditory stimuli (among others) results in residual daytime sleepiness, poor performance in reaction time and memory tests, and degraded mood similar to that seen after sleep deprivation. The degree of residual sleepiness was related to the frequency of disturbance during a night and continued to increase from night to night when the sleep fragmentation continued. Subjects were as sleepy after two nights of frequently fragmented sleep as they were after two nights with no sleep at all. Sleep and alertness returned to normal when the fragmentation stopped in a manner that is analogous to recovery after sleep deprivation.

Studies have shown that decreases in performance and mood are very similar following fragmented sleep and after sleep deprivation, even though some patients may not be aware that they suffer from significant sleep fragmentation. It has also been found that fragmented sleep is accompanied by increased metabolic rate and decreased respiratory sensitivity.

These research studies suggest that there should be a high correlation between the amount of sleep fragmentation, frequently expressed as an arousal index (number of EEG arousals per hour of sleep), and the amount of sleepiness reported by patients with sleep disorders. Unfortunately, clinical research in this area has typically shown only mild (but usually statistically significant) correlations between level of sleep fragmentation and measures of daytime sleepiness in patients with sleep disorders (Bennett et al., 1998). These correlations may be low because a number of other factors, including weight, presence of depression, use of stimulating or depressing medications, variability in presentation of clinical sleep disorder, and individual differences in nocturnal sleep requirement may also account for a significant amount of the relationship variance.

In recent years, studies in small animals have replicated many of the findings described. However, these studies have also allowed an examination of changes in brain function related to sleep fragmentation. Studies have suggested that sleep fragmentation appears to be related to increases in adenosine, which might help to account for increased sleepiness and impaired ventilation. Other studies have suggested that sleep fragmentation may be associated with impaired hippocampal function (Guzman-Marin, Bashir, Suntsova, Szymusiak, & McGinty, 2007), and this could account for memory deficits seen in association with the sleep disturbance.

Identification of disturbed sleep as a significant factor in sleep restoration has been a relatively recent insight. Much data now suggest that sleep is a time-based process that restores alertness and performance. Additional neurophysiological studies of schedules of sleep fragmentation should be able to describe central nervous system changes controlling this sleep process and increase understanding of the central controllers of sleep and sleepiness.

Michael H. Bonnet

References

Bennett, L. S., Langford, B. A., Stradling, J. R., & Davies, R. J. (1998). Sleep fragmentation indices as predictors of daytime sleepiness and nCPAP response in obstructive sleep apnea. *American Journal of Respiratory and Critical Care Medicine, 158*(3), 778–786.

Bonnet, M. H. (2005). Sleep fragmentation. In C. Kushida (Ed.), *Sleep deprivation: Basic science, physiology, and behavior*. New York: Marcel Dekker.

Bowes, G., Woolf, G. M., Sullivan, C. E., & Phillipson, E. A. (1980). Effect of sleep fragmentation on ventilatory and arousal responses of sleeping dogs to respiratory stimuli. *American Review of Respiratory Disease, 122*(6), 899–908.

Guzman-Marin, R., Bashir, T., Suntsova, N., Szymusiak, R., & McGinty, D. (2007). Hippocampal neurogenesis is reduced by sleep fragmentation in the adult rat. *Neuroscience, 148*(1), 325–333.

Sleep in Adolescents

Sleep is a necessary function for development and behavior throughout the life span. The amount of sleep and its timing for various age groups is determined by biological regulation and by environmental and psychosocial factors. One of the hallmarks of adolescent development is a shift to a later sleep phase, indicated by a preference toward later bedtimes and later wake-up times. This tendency is often accompanied by curtailed sleep during weekdays and by distinct differences between weekday and weekend sleep timing and duration (Crowley, Acebo, & Carskadon, 2007).

During adolescence, both circadian and homeostatic bioregulatory mechanisms change (Taylor, Jenni, Acebo, & Carskadon, 2005). Puberty is characterized by a delay in the circadian timing system, including a delay in the evening onset of melatonin, a hormone indicated in sleep initiation and regulation. Homeostatic sleep pressure, indicating the amount of sleepiness that has accumulated since the last sleep episode, is slower and more resistant in adolescence. Evidence from human and animal studies suggests that changes in circadian and homeostatic mechanisms during puberty may be common phenomena among different cultures and different mammalian species (Hagenauer, Perryman, Lee, & Carskadon, 2009).

In a seminal laboratory investigation of biological sleep need, it has been demonstrated that healthy adolescents require approximately nine hours of sleep per night (Carskadon et al., 1980). While this sleep quota does not change markedly throughout puberty, daytime sleepiness increases, possibly indicating a growing need for sleep in adolescents. However, in their natural environment, adolescents undergo a continuous sleep debt. Ecological studies consistently show that habitual weekday sleep duration is well under the recommended nine hours, and decreases significantly with age (Yang, Kim, Patel, & Lee, 2005).

The gap between sleep need and the actual amount of sleep attained may be explained by a clash between biological and environmental factors underlying adolescent sleep patterns. Environmental factors include early school start times, academic workload, extracurricular and social activities, employment, limited parental supervision, and excessive exposure to electronic media, including television, computer games, and the Internet. In addition, psychosocial factors related to poor sleep in adolescents include stress, anxiety, depressed mood, overweight and obesity, alcohol or caffeine consumption, and smoking (Crowley et al., 2007; Yang et al., 2005).

Consequently, these environmental and psychosocial factors contribute to insufficient sleep, disturbed or mistimed sleep patterns, sleep disorders and subsequent daytime sleepiness, and fatigue. In turn, decreases in health, daytime functioning, academic performance, and quality of life have been implicated as possible consequences of poor and inadequate sleep in adolescents.

In contrast to weekdays, adolescent sleep patterns during weekends and vacations are more in line with biological sleep requisites (Yang et al., 2005). Weekend sleep duration is considerably longer, suggesting that it may reflect the underlying biological sleep need. It has also been suggested that adolescents sleep longer during the weekend to compensate for accumulated sleep debt during the week. Timing of the weekend sleep episode is consistently later than that during the week, reflecting the characteristic delayed sleep phase and the underlying changes in bioregulatory sleep mechanisms described earlier.

In summary, biologically driven changes in the timing of sleep toward an evening phase preference increase gradually from early to late puberty. Superimposed on this delayed sleep tendency are environmental and psychosocial factors, which often interfere with the ability of adolescents to achieve adequate sleep. Consequently, insufficient and erratic sleep patterns are prevalent, and are negatively associated with several areas of health, daytime functioning, and performance.

Future investigations should establish normative sleep quotas for different age groups, as a basis for launching programs for health promotion, aimed at modification of environmental norms that may be amenable to change. Early school start time is considered the most important contributor to weekday sleep deprivation and has been studied most extensively. Interventions such as delaying school start times, increasing parental awareness and involvement in adolescent sleep schedules, and setting structured, limited exposure times to electronic media devices may ameliorate some of the negative consequences of sleep deficits in adolescence.

Tamar Shochat

See also: Sleep as We Age

References

Carskadon, M. A., Harvey, K., Duke, P., Anders, T. F., Litt, I. F., & Dement, W. C. (1980). Pubertal changes in daytime sleepiness. *Sleep, 2*(4), 453–460.

Crowley, S. J., Acebo, C., & Carskadon, M. A. (2007). Sleep, circadian rhythms, and delayed phase in adolescence. *Sleep Medicine, 8*(6), 602–612.

Hagenauer, M. H., Perryman, J. I., Lee, T. M., & Carskadon, M. A. (2009). Adolescent changes in the homeostatic and circadian regulation of sleep. *Developmental Neuroscience, 31*(4), 276–284.

Taylor, D. J., Jenni, O. G., Acebo, C., & Carskadon, M. A. (2005). Sleep tendency during extended wakefulness: Insights into adolescent sleep regulation and behavior. *Journal of Sleep Research, 14*(3), 239–244.

Yang, C. K., Kim, J. K., Patel, S. R., & Lee, J. H. (2005). Age-related changes in sleep/ wake patterns among Korean teenagers. *Pediatrics, 115*(1 Suppl.), 250–256.

Sleep in Aquatic Mammals

Sleep has been extensively studied in aquatic mammals, including fully aquatic cetaceans and semiaquatic pinnipeds. All studied cetaceans (the bottlenose dolphin, harbor porpoise, Amazon river dolphin, and the beluga and the pilot whale) display EEG slow waves in one cerebral hemisphere while the other hemisphere exhibits predominantly low-voltage EEG activity, indicative of waking. This state was defined as unihemispheric slow-wave sleep (USWS) (Mukhametov, Supin, & Polyakova, 1977). USWS is the main sleep state in all studied cetaceans occupying up to 90 percent of the total sleep time with the remaining time being represented by episodes of low-voltage bilateral and asymmetrical slow-wave activity. Episodes of USWS last as long as two hours, alternating between the two hemispheres (reviewed in Lyamin et al., 2008c).

Rapid eye movement (REM) sleep is present in all terrestrial mammals that have been examined. However, a long period of electrophysiological and behavioral studies has not led to a conclusive opinion whether REM sleep is present in cetaceans. Muscle jerks, body twitches, and rapid eye movements (all are features of REM sleep) are often documented in behaviorally resting and sleeping cetaceans but a large portion of those jerks occur parallel with EEG slow waves (either low-voltage and bilateral or unihemispheric), suggesting that this is a state of slow-wave sleep (SWS). Therefore, based on the current data, we cannot exclude that REM sleep (1) is either absent in cetaceans or (2) it occurs in a modified form that escapes detection (Lyamin et al., 2002, 2008c; Mukhametov, 1984).

All cetaceans can sleep while slowly swimming; this is another striking feature of the cetacean sleep when compared to the sleep of terrestrial mammals. It was proposed that the waking hemisphere in dolphins and whales may be engaged in maintenance of motion during USWS but no asymmetry in motor activity is observed in cetaceans at these times (Lyamin et al., 2008c; Lyamin, Mukhametov, & Siegel, 2004; Mukhametov et al., 1977). Almost continuous swimming is characteristic of all small cetaceans (e.g., Commerson's dolphins and harbor porpoises). On the contrary, long periods of immobility while floating at the surface, submerging to depth or even lying on the bottom of the pools are

typical of large cetaceans (e.g., on average 40 to 70 percent of the nighttime in adult belugas and killer whales, Lyamin et al., 2002, 2008c). At the same time, the dolphin and killer whale mothers and their calves also become obligate swimmers for the initial postpartum period displaying only one of the cetacean sleep behaviors (Lyamin et al., 2005, 2007). Continuous swimming appears to be required for thermoregulation, because small cetaceans (both adults and neonates) have larger surface area to volume ratios than adults and their blubber is not specialized to provide enhanced thermal insulation. Both factors result in greater amounts of heat loss to the environment compared to that in larger species (Lyamin et al., 2008c). The essential point is that USWS remains the major sleep state in cetaceans regardless of the sleep behavior displayed.

One would agree that maintaining of visual contact during sleep is of great importance to cetaceans and particularly to mothers and their newborn calves. Ten years before USWS was discovered it had been proposed that dolphins sleep with one eye closed and one eye open at a time to visually monitor the environment (Lilly, 1964). When observing pacific white-sided dolphins it was noted that they often slowly swim and apparently sleep in an echelon formation. At these times one eye was usually open while the other eye was closed in such a way that the open eye was always directed toward their conspecifics (Goley, 1999). Bottlenose dolphin calves when continuously swimming next to their mothers are often seen with one eye open while the other eye remains closed. The

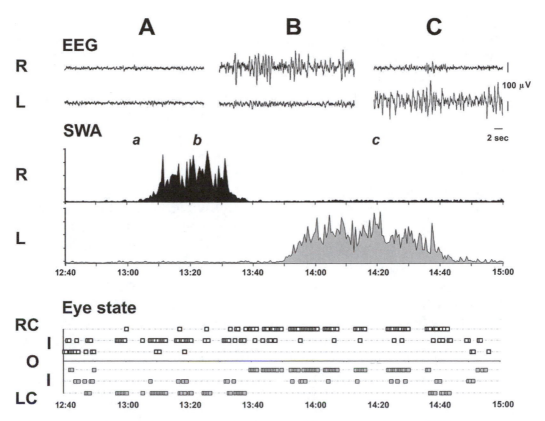

Unihemispheric sleep in a bottlenose dolphin. Top row: Electroencephalogram (EEG) of the right (R) and left (L) cortical hemispheres during waking (A), right (B) and left (L) hemispheric slow-wave sleep. Middle row: Slow-wave activity (SWA, EEG power in the range of 1.2–4.0 Hz, 30 sec epochs) in the two hemispheres recorded over a period of 2 hours and 20 minutes showing episodes of unihemispheric sleep in the right and left hemispheres. EEG power was normalized as a percentage of the maximum power in each hemisphere during this period. Letters a, b, and c mark the time of polygrams expanded in the top row. Bottom row: The state of each dolphin eye (R, right; L, left) over the same period scored in real time (O, open; I, intermediate; or C, closed) and then categorized for 30-second epochs. Each mark represents one epoch. (Oleg Lyamin)

eye directed toward the mother is open more often than the eye directed to the opposite direction, suggesting that calves continue to maintain visual contact with their mothers during sleep (Lyamin et al., 2007). Studies on belugas and bottlenose dolphins revealed that during USWS, the eye contralateral to the waking hemisphere is open or in an intermediate state (95% to 98% of the observation time), while the eye contralateral to the sleeping hemisphere was largely closed (40% to 60%). In contrast to terrestrial mammals, both eyes were rarely noted to be closed in dolphins and belugas (less than 2.0% of the observation time). All these data provide support for the hypothesis that USWS in cetaceans serves a sentinel function, specifically to scan at least half the environment for predators and to maintain coherence of the group while asleep (Lyamin et al., 2004, 2008c).

The need to come to the surface to breathe is an obvious life sustaining requirement for any aquatic mammal. Small-sized cetaceans (e.g., the harbor porpoise) maintain regular breathing when continuously swimming and being asleep with respiratory pauses that rarely exceed 60 seconds in duration. Respiratory acts in dolphins are fully compatible with uninterrupted USWS; that is, they do not necessarily cause arousal and behavioral awakening (Lyamin et al., 2008c). Larger cetaceans (e.g., the beluga) display long apneas (longer than 10 minutes) during sleep while floating at the surface and submerging to depth. It is known that barbiturates induce bilateral high-voltage SWS in dolphins, which immediately caused a cessation of breathing. Diazepam (or valium) depending on the dose induces either USWS or high-voltage bilateral SWS without a cessation of breathing. However, immediately prior to each respiration the EEG amplitude in one or in both hemispheres drops, so that dolphins enter the state of either USWS or waking (Mukhametov & Polyakova, 1981). These data are considered to support the idea that USWS is necessary for autonomic breathing in cetaceans (Mukhametov, 1984).

In contrast to fully aquatic cetaceans, pinnipeds live both on land and water. To date, sleep has been examined in 10 species of pinnipeds: four eared seals (the northern fur seal, Cape fur seal, Steller's sea lion, southern sea lion), five true seals (the gray seal, Caspian seal, harp seal, northern elephant seal, harbor seal), and in the only leaving species of walruses.

Among the eared seals (fur seals and sea lions, the Otariidae family), sleep has been most extensively studied in the northern fur seal (e.g., Lyamin et al., 2008b; Lyamin & Mukhametov, 1998). When on land, fur seals predominately display bilateral SWS and REM sleep in the range of normal variations. Both are typical for all terrestrial mammals. At the same time fur seals exhibit SWS with greatly expressed interhemispheric EEG asymmetry (also called asymmetrical SWS), which resembles USWS in cetaceans. The proportion of asymmetrical SWS while on land is minimal in 10- to 20-day-old fur seal pups (on average 5% of the total SWS time) and maximal in juveniles (45%). The degree of EEG asymmetry in fur seals greatly increases when they sleep in water. At the same time the amount of REM sleep substantially decreases (up to 90% of REM sleep on land) and can be virtually absent for a period of one to two weeks. Another remarkable feature is striking motor asymmetry in fur seals when they are sleeping in water. They sleep at the surface on their sides, paddling with one foreflipper, while holding the three other above the surface. The paddling flipper is always contralateral to the waking hemisphere. This behavior and sleep posture prevents heat loss while fur seals are asleep in water. The last but not the least is that fur seals can sleep with only one eye closed while the other eye briefly opens. Similar to that in dolphins, the open eye is always contralateral to the waking hemisphere while the closed eye is contralateral to the sleeping hemisphere. The association between USWS, motion, and brief opening of one eye suggests that USWS in fur seals serves (1) to maintain vigilance to detect predators and conspecifics as well as (2) to sustain motion and sleep posture to optimize thermoregulation while asleep (Lyamin et al., 2004). As in terrestrial mammals, the breathing pattern of fur seals during SWS is regular. In REM sleep, breathing becomes irregular but apneas rarely last longer than 30 seconds. The studies in other otariids revealed largely a similar sleep pattern and sleep behaviors as described for the northern fur seal (Pryaslova et al., 2009).

Regardless of if true seals (the Phocidae family) sleep on land or in water, SWS in these animals is always bilateral, as in terrestrial mammals. Individual REM-sleep episodes in phocids are shorter then in otariids. They usually occur in series following SWS. In contrary to dolphins and fur seals, there are no reports of asymmetrical eye opening in sleeping true seals. Phocids can hold their breath for dozens of minutes (in some species for one hour) while asleep. During SWS, sleep apneas alternate with periods of fast regular breathing. During REM sleep, breathing becomes sporadic and many episodes occur within a single apnea. The sleep of phocids in water is also accompanied by complete immobility but they usually wake up when surfacing to breathe. Many phocids live in cold freezing seas with limited access to the open water. The ability to sleep during apneas minimizes time spent at the water surface. It is seen as a vital adaptive feature of the phocid sleep (e.g., Castellini et al., 1994;

Lyamin, Oleksenko, & Polyakova, 1993; Mukhametov, Supin, & Polyakova, 1984).

The majority of SWS recorded in the only electrophysiologically examined walrus was scored as bilateral SWS. When in water, sleep occurred while the walrus was floating motionless at the surface or lying on the bottom of the pool. Episodes of asymmetrical SWS were occasionally recorded both on land and in water and correlated with a brief one eye opening as in fur seals (Lyamin et al., 2008a). A behavioral study also revealed that walruses occasionally become almost continuously active (80% to 99% of the time) for a period of three to four days which was followed by extended periods of rest lasting up to 19 hours. The breathing pattern in walruses was regular during quiet wakefulness and SWS while on land as in fur seals and it was interrupted while in water with alternating apneas and ventilations as in eared seals (Pryaslova et al., 2009). Therefore, the pattern of sleep in the walrus appears to be linked to the need to sleep while submerged as it is in phocids.

In conclusion, the need to come to the surface to breathe, more efficient monitoring of the environment, and thermogenesis appear to be the main factors that have led to the evolution of the present sleep phenomenology in aquatic mammals. Sleep in water while in motion (cetaceans, fur seals) is one strategy. At these times sleep develops unihemispherically, and it is USWS that allows motion (muscle thermogenesis and postural thermoregulation) and asymmetrical eye opening (monitoring of the environment). The second strategy of sleep in water is to become apneac diving for sleep (bilateral SWS and REM) to depth or under ice (true seals and walruses), which would be the only way to survive in freezing seas as well as an efficient retreat from potential predators. At the same time, the neurophysiological mechanisms underlying the described aquatic mammal sleep phenomenology are largely unknown.

Oleg Lyamin

See also: entries related to Evolution of Sleep

References

Castellini, M. A., Milsom, W. K., Berger, R. J., et al. (1994). Patterns of respiration and heart rate during wakefulness and sleep in elephant seal pups. *American Journal of Physiology, 266,* R863–R869.

Goley, P. D. (1999). Behavioral aspects of sleep in pacific white-sided dolphins (Lagenorhynchus obliquidens, Gill 1865). *Marine Mammal Science, 15,* 1054–1064.

Lilly, J. C. (1964). Animals in aquatic environments: Adaptations of mammals to the ocean. In D. B. Dill (Ed.), *Handbook of physiology—environment* (pp. 741–747). Washington, DC: American Physiology Society.

Lyamin, O., Kosenko, P., Lapierre, J., et al. (2008c). Study of sleep in a walrus. *Sleep, 31,* A24.

Lyamin, O. I., Lapierre, J. L., Kosenko, O. P., et al. (2008b). EEG asymmetry and spectral power in the fur seal. *Journal of Sleep Research, 17,* 154–165.

Lyamin, O. I., Manger, P. R., Ridgway, S. H., et al. (2008a). Cetacean sleep: An unusual form of mammalian sleep. *Neuroscience and Biobehavioral Review, 32,* 1451–1484.

Lyamin, O. I., & Mukhametov, L. M. (1998). Organization of sleep in the northern fur seal. In V. E. Sokolov, A. A. Aristov, & T. U. Lisitzina (Eds.), *The northern fur seal: Systematic, morphology, ecology, behavior* (pp. 280–302), Moscow: Nauka.

Lyamin, O. I., Mukhametov, L. M., & Siegel, J. M. (2004). Association between EEG asymmetry and eye state in Cetaceans and Pinnipeds. *Italian Archives of Biology, 142,* 557–568.

Lyamin, O. I., Oleksenko, A. I., & Polyakova, I. G. (1993). Sleep in the harp seal (*Pagophilus groenladnica*). Peculiarities of sleep in pups during the first month of their lives. *Journal of Sleep Research, 2,* 163–169.

Lyamin, O. I., Pryaslova, J., Kosenko, P. O., et al. (2007). Behavioral aspects of sleep in bottlenose dolphin mothers and their calves. *Physiology and Behavior, 92,* 725–733.

Lyamin, O. I., Pryaslova, J., Lance, V., et al. (2005). Animal behaviour: Continuous activity in cetaceans after birth. *Nature, 435,* 1177.

Lyamin, O. I., Shpak, O. V., Nazarenko, E. A., et al. (2002). Muscle jerks during behavioral sleep in a beluga whale (Delphinapterus leucas L.). *Physiology and Behavior, 76,* 265–270.

Mukhametov, L. M. (1984). Sleep in marine mammals. *Experimental Brain Research, 8,* 227–238.

Mukhametov, L. M., & Polyakova, I. G. (1981). EEG investigation of sleep in porpoises (*Phocoena phocoena*). *Journal of High Nerve Activity, 31,* 333–339.

Mukhametov, L. M., Supin, A., & Polyakova, I. G. (1977). Interhemispheric asymmetry of the electroencephalographic sleep pattern in dolphins. *Brain Research, 134,* 581–584.

Mukhametov, L. M., Supin, A., & Polyakova, I. G. (1984). Sleep in Caspian seals (Phoca caspica). *Journal of High Nerve Activity, 34,* 259–264.

Pryaslova, J. P., Lyamin, O. I., & Siegel, J. M., et al. (2009). Behavioral sleep in the walrus. *Behavioral Brain Research, 19,* 80–87.

Sleep in Children with Cancer

Sleep is a fundamental biological process necessary for life and well-being that is woven into the fabric of our lives. Cancer disrupts this process. Cancer occurs in about 15 per 100,000 children (Reis et al., 2005). The most common childhood cancers are leukemia and brain tumors, accounting for 27 and 22 percent of all childhood cancers. At present the overall survival rate for all childhood malignancies is 79 percent, which has led to a large population of children and young adults who are cancer survivors. However, neurosurgery and the toxic therapies used to successfully treat cancer result in a great deal of collateral damage, which together are termed late effects, present in up to 75 percent of childhood cancer survivors. Sleep problems are one of the least well-recognized late effects of cancer treatment.

The unique causes of sleep problems seen in children with cancer relate to:

1. Central nervous system (CNS) injury caused by brain tumors, neurosurgical procedures, or cranial radiation therapy (CRT). Injury to the medulla oblongata may damage the respiratory control center and lead to sleep disordered breathing. Injury to the hypothalamus, thalamus, and brain stem may result in excessive daytime sleepiness (EDS). Brain trauma resulting in seizures may lead to sleep fragmentation causing EDS and unusual nocturnal awakenings.

2. Side effects of chemotherapy—dexamethasone in adolescent and young adults—often leads to insomnia; in preadolescents dexamethasone may result in EDS (Hinds et al., 2007).

3. Fatigue is almost universal in adults and children with cancer (Ancoli-Israel, Moore, & Jones, 2001). Fatigue often leads to daytime napping and decreased daytime activity, which in turn may disrupt the circadian sleep/wake rhythm causing both insomnia and EDS.

4. Radiation therapy—radiation hypersomnia is seen in 60 percent of children treated with >2400 cGray of CRT and typically appears 3 to 14 days after treatment. Though usually transient, increase in total sleep time and persistent EDS are described in some

Table 6: Children with Cancer Seen in Sleep Clinic

Children with cancer seen in sleep clinic 1994–2009	Total # N =	EDS/long sleepers	Apnea	Insomnia	Circadian	Parasomnia
Total	70% of total	42/70 (60%)	28/70 (40%)	17/70 (24%)	3/70 (4%)	6/70 (9%)
Tumors of central nervous system	48					
Hypothalamus/brainstem	35 %	28/35 (80%)	16/35 (46%)	5/35 (14%)	2/35 (6%)	2/35 (6%)
Posterior fossa	7	6	2	2	0	1
Cortex	6	4	2	1	0	2
Leukemia/other blood	18 %	4/18 (22%)	6/18 (33%)	7/18 (39%)	1/18 (6%)	1/18 (6%)
Other solid tumors	4	0	2	2	0	0

Table 7: Treatments of Sleep Problems in Children with Cancer (children may have more than one problem)

Sleep problems	#	Treatments
Parasomnia $N = 6$		Anticonvulsants—3
Seizures	3	Clonazepam—1
Confusional arousals	2	Sleep extension/ sleep hygiene—1
Sleep eating	1	Topiramate
Sleep disordered breathing $N = 28$		
OSA $N = 20$	1	Tracheotomy
	8	CPAP/BIPAP
	4	T&A
	7	No treatment (AI < 5)
CSA $N = 6$	1	BIPAP + rate + O_2
	1	Tracheotomy + ventilator
	1	Diaphramatic pacers
	2	No treatment
	1	Anticonvulsants
	2	Oxygen
Hypoxia $N = 2$		
EDS/long sleeper $N = 42$	42	Sleep hygiene and extension
	17	Methylphenidate
	6	Modafanil
	4	Amphetamine salts
	4	Declined stimulants
	1	Treatment of drug abuse
	1	CPAP
	1	anticonvulsants
Insomnia $N = 17$		
	9	Sleep hygiene and sleep restriction
	3	Pain control
	3	Sedative hypnotics
	2	Melatonin
Circadian rhythm $N = 3$		
Blindness	1	Melatonin + sleep hygiene
DSPS	1	Melatonin + sleep hygiene
Irregular sleep/wake	1	Sleep hygiene

T&A—tonsillectomy and adenoidectomy; OSA—obstructive sleep apnea; CSA—central sleep apnea; CPAP—continuous positive airway pressure; BIPAP—bilevel positive airway pressure; AI—apnea index; DSPS—delayed sleep-phase syndrome

individuals, though the mechanism is not understood.

5. Pain is common in children with cancer and often leads to sleep disruption.

6. Stress, anxiety, depression, posttraumatic stress disorder are all commonly described in children with cancer (Langeveld et al., 2004) and sleep problems, particularly

insomnia, nightmares, and EDS may be secondary symptoms of these conditions.

7. Twenty-seven percent of cancer survivors have severe or life-threatening medical late effects, and 45 percent will have some chronic medical problems as a direct result of their cancer treatment (Oeffinger et al., 2006). Endocrine deficiencies of thyroid, cortisol, growth hormone, and vasopressin are common after CRT and may impact on sleep. Cardiorespiratory, gastrointestinal, neurological, and musculoskeletal later effects are all common after cancer treatment and all may affect sleep (see Table 6).

The largest review of sleep problems in children with cancer is a 15-year retrospective case series of children referred for a comprehensive sleep evaluation (Rosen & Brand, 2010). Though there is obvious referral bias in this population, it does allow for the characterization of the sleep problems in children with cancer. The sleep problems and types of cancers are described in the first table; the treatment is described in the second table. Sixty-eight percent of the children with cancer referred for sleep evaluation had brain tumors. Tumors involving the thalamus, hypothalamus, and brain stem accounted for 50 percent of the referrals, though this group of tumors comprises only 15 percent of all pediatric malignancies. The most common sleep problems found in these children with cancer were EDS/long sleepers seen in 60 percent of the children and sleep apnea in 40 percent. Both of these problems were successfully treated once they were recognized (see Table 7).

The sleep problems of children with cancer span the full spectrum of clinical sleep disorders (EDS, insomnia, sleep disordered breathing, parasomnias, and circadian-rhythm disorders) and are often present in combinations. Children with cancers involving the CNS, particularly brain stem, thalamus, and hypothalamus were the most frequently referred for sleep evaluation and the most commonly seen sleep problems were EDS and sleep disordered breathing. The unusual distribution of the types of cancers and types of sleep problems seen in this referral population may be the result of two factors. Children with cancer are likely to have the same background prevalence of the common sleep disorders seen in any child; and CNS-directed therapies affecting areas of the brain most important in sleep/wake regulation, the brain stem, thalamus, and hypothalamus are more likely to lead to EDS, obstructive sleep apnea, and central sleep apnea.

Gerald Rosen

See also: entries related to Sleep and Development; entries related to Sleep Disorders

References

Ancoli-Israel, A., Moore, P., & Jones, V. (2001). The relationship between fatigue and sleep in cancer patients: A review. *European Journal of Cancer, 10,* 245–255.

Hinds, P., Hockenberry, M., Gattuso, J., et al. (2007). Dexamethasone alters sleep and fatigue in pediatric patients with acute lymphoblastic leukemia. *Cancer, 110,* 2321–2330.

Langeveld, N., Grootenhuis, M., Voute, P., et al. (2004). Posttraumatic stress symptoms in adult survivors of childhood cancer. *Pediatric Blood Cancer, 42,* 604–610.

Oeffinger, K., Mertens, A., Sklar, C., et al. (2006). Chronic health conditions in adult survivors of childhood cancer. *New England Journal of Medicine, 355*(15), 1572–1582.

Reis, L., Eisner, M., Kosary, C., et al. (2005). *SEER cancer statistics review, 1975–2002.* Bethesda, MD: National Cancer Institute.

Rosen, G., & Brand, S. (2010). Sleep in children with cancer: Case review of 70 children evaluated in a comprehensive pediatric sleep center. Support Care Cancer, DOI 10.1007/s00520-010-0921.

Sleep in Disorders of Consciousness

While it is well known that abnormalities of sleep are extremely common in critically ill patients (for review see Parthasarathy & Tobin, 2004); mechanisms are still poorly understood and fine-grained analyses are missing (for review see Cologan et al., 2010). In brain-injured patients (BIPs) about half of total sleep time occurs during the daytime, and circadian rhythmicity is markedly diminished or even lost. In addition to sleep, the biological clock regulates several physiological, behavioral, and biochemical rhythms. However, polygraphic recordings are needed to reliably measure sleep quantity, quality, as well as circadian regulation in BIPs. Patients exhibit more frequent arousals and awakenings than normal, and decreases in REM and slow-wave sleep are common (e.g., Freedman, Gazendam, Levan, Pack, & Schwab, 2001). Note that the degree of sleep fragmentation is at least equivalent to that seen in patients with obstructive sleep apnoea. However, causes for sleep problems in BIPs are generally unknown although severity of the underlying disease is likely to be an important factor. Further factors contributing to sleep abnormalities in BIPs include acute illness, pain, discomfort, and increased alertness induced by continuous exposure to light. This is probably especially critical for BIPs, as sleep deprivation is known to have major and devastating impacts on immune functioning. And probably most alarming, sleep disruptions can induce sympathetic activation and elevation of blood pressure, which can contribute to the patient's morbidity.

In summary, little is known about the sleep experienced by BIPs and careful examination of sleep in disorders of consciousness, including circadian regulation is warranted. Guidelines on how to improve sleep in these patients are thus needed (e.g., curtailing unnecessary visits by hospital personnel during habitual sleep times or reduce noise and introduce ambient light levels), might support better recovery and might intercept complications that are related to weakened immune system functioning due to insufficient amounts of restful sleep.

Additionally, EEG patterns resembling sleep have been considered as favorable prognostic markers for long (e.g., Bergamasco, Bergamini, Doriguzzi, & Fabiani, 1968) and it has been reported that sleep patterns continue to improve during rehabilitation together with the recovery of cognitive functions (Ron, Algom, Hary, & Cohen, 1980). In a study by Evans and Bartlett (1995), it was shown that sleep-like traces with K-complexes in response to stimulation are indicative of a good outcome, whereas traces with no spontaneous arousal activity were indicative of death or vegetative state. A more recent study by Valente and colleagues (2002) compared the predictivity of different levels of sleep–wake organization with other possible prognostic indexes such as neuroradiological findings, age, or Glasgow coma scale scores. In this study based on 24 hours of polysomnographic recordings, the authors report that the presence of organized sleep patterns is highly predictive for good outcome. Especially NREM-sleep elements such as K-complexes and sleep spindles as well as REM-sleep elements alternating with NREM-sleep elements were related to good recovery.

It is concluded that polysomnography might carry considerable information about the ability of BIPs to recover by reflecting the residual integrity of the central nervous system and functionality of the brain (for review see Cologan et al., 2010). Yet the major challenge when studying sleep in critically ill patients remains; that is, scoring sleep in extremely altered and slowed EEG traces.

Manuel Schabus

References

Bergamasco, B., Bergamini, L., Doriguzzi, T., & Fabiani, D. (1968). EEG sleep patterns as a prognostic criterion in post-traumatic coma. *Electroencephalography & Clinical Neurophysiology, 24*(4), 374–377.

Cologan, V., Schabus, M., Ledoux, D., Moonen, G., Maquet, P., & Laureys, S. (2010). Sleep in disorders of consciousness. *Sleep Medicine Reviews, 14*(2), 97–105.

Evans, B.M., & Bartlett, J.R. (1995). Prediction of outcome in severe head injury based on recognition of sleep related activity in the polygraphic electroencephalogram. *Journal of Neurology, Neurosurgery, and Psychiatry, 59*(1), 17–25.

Freedman, N.S., Gazendam, J., Levan, L., Pack, A.I., & Schwab, R.J. (2001). Abnormal sleep/wake cycles and the effect of environmental noise on sleep disruption in the intensive care unit. *American Journal of Respiratory and Critical Care Medicine, 163*(2), 451–457.

Parthasarathy, S., & Tobin, M.J. (2004). Sleep in the intensive care unit. *Intensive Care Medicine, 30*(2), 197–206.

Ron, S., Algom, D., Hary, D., & Cohen, M. (1980). Time-related changes in the distribution of sleep stages in brain injured patients. *Electroencephalography & Clinical Neurophysiology, 48*(4), 432–441.

Valente, M., Placidi, F., Oliveira, A.J., Bigagli, A., Morghen, I., Proietti, R., et al. (2002). Sleep organization pattern as a prognostic marker at the subacute stage of post-traumatic coma. *Clinical Neurophysiology, 113*(11), 1798–1805.

Sleep in Insects

The origins and functions of sleep are ongoing biological mysteries. Did the first primitive organisms that occupied and then emerged onto land from the primordium of ancient oceans sleep? Did dinosaurs sleep? And if these organisms did sleep, what function, if any, did sleep serve in the survival of species? One approach to answering these questions may be to examine living organisms with ancient origins that have changed little from their ancient fossil ancestors. Mammalian species, most often the subject of modern sleep studies, emerged relatively recently in the fossil record, between 100 and 74 million years ago (Bininda-Emonds et al., 2007). On the other hand, a living, diverse group of organisms with ancient origins is insects. Insects first appeared in the fossil record approximately 400 million years ago, and modern insect orders, many of which have changed little from their early ancestors, have a fossil record extending to approximately 250 million years ago (Grimaldi & Engel, 2005). Thus, by studying insects, clues to the origins and function of sleep in living organisms could potentially be discovered.

The first issue in studying insect sleep is whether insects meet the behavioral criteria for sleep. The evidence strongly suggests that insects do, in fact, meet these criteria. The behavioral criteria include a species-specific posture, behavioral quiescence, elevated arousal thresholds, reversibility of quiescence with stimulation, and the homeostatic drive or rebound in sleep following deprivation. The first naturalistic observational studies of wasps, bees, flies, dragonflies, butterflies, and moths at the beginning of the 20th century are consistent with these well-established behavioral criteria. Recent work in the cockroach has demonstrated that the metabolic response to sleep deprivation as well as the effects of sleep deprivation on longevity are similar to those in mammals, further strengthening the argument that quiescence in insects is, in fact, sleep, and that this quiescence is functionally similar to sleep in mammals (Stephenson, Chu, & Lee, 2007).

With the exception of an expanding literature in *Drosophila,* the number of systematic studies on insect sleep is relatively small. (For a full review of this literature see Hartse, 2010.) Although the electrophysiology of sleep is most often studied in mammals, the electrophysiology of insect sleep is virtually unknown with a few exceptions. In one of a series of detailed studies on the honey bee, performed by Kaiser and associates, the electrophysiology of optomotor interneurons displayed a circadian sensitivity to horizontal movement of a light stimulus (Kaiser & Steiner-Kaiser, 1983). This sensitivity increased during the day with locomotor activity and decreased at night with behavioral quiescence. The homeostatic response to sleep deprivation in the honey bee was further documented as were age-related changes in rest–activity cycles. Differences in honey bee castes have been associated with differences in the circadian rhythmicity of sleep. Finally, neuroanatomical plasticity in sensory processing centers in the insect brain, specifically the mushroom bodies, suggests that aging and social experience may affect the expression of sleep in insects.

The most detailed information on the physiology and neurochemistry of sleep has emerged from studies in *Drosophila,* the fruit fly. *Drosophila* has been proposed as a model organism for the study of sleep. This small organism presents several advantages in the study of basic sleep mechanisms, including (1) the similarities in genetic sequence to human disease genes; (2) the identification of well-studied mammalian neurotransmitter systems, with the exception of orexin/hypocretin; and (3) the small size, rapid reproductive cycle, and short life span that allow for rapid assessment of genetic and molecular manipulations. However, the question arises as to whether *Drosophila* meets the criteria for sleep and whether it can be used as a model for the broader study of sleep mechanisms.

The literature strongly supports similarities between behavioral sleep in *Drosophila* and mammalian sleep. *Drosophila* exhibits a species-specific posture during quiescence, elevated arousal thresholds, and a homeostatic response to quiescence deprivation. Furthermore, there are age-related declines in behavioral quiescence similar to those observed in mammals, and

A busy day in the flowers before the sun goes down. (Kristyna M. Hartse)

in both mammals and *Drosophila* there is a similar alerting response to drugs, including caffeine, modafinil, and methamphetamine. Likewise, there is a similar response of increasing quiescence following antihistamine administration in both mammals and *Drosophila*. Besides these findings, there are additional important similarities between mammalian sleep and *Drosophila* quiescence.

One important area in which it is unlikely that there will ever be convincing similarities between mammals and *Drosophila* is in the electrophysiology of sleep, due to the neuroanatomical dissimilarities in brain structure. There is, however, evidence to suggest an electrophysiological correlate of quiescence recorded from *Drosophila* mushroom bodies. During waking there are bursting local field potentials (LFPs) in the mushroom bodies, which diminish with behavioral sleep, although it is clear that the absence of a waveform during *Drosophila* behavioral sleep is not equivalent to the presence of, for example, slow waves and sleep spindles, during mammalian sleep.

The genetic identification of short-sleeping fly strains as well as the genetic identification of differences between male and female flies suggest possible applications to human sleep disorders. Furthermore, the effect of aging on the deterioration in human sleep quality has been well studied, and studies in *Drosophila* suggest that oxidative stress produces deterioration of sleep in aged flies. Another area of similarity between mammalian and *Drosophila* sleep is in the similarities of response to signaling pathways and neurotransmitters, including serotonin, dopamine, and GABA. There may be neurotransmitters unique to *Drosophila* and other invertebrates, such as octopamine, and neurotransmitters unique to mammals, such as orexin/hypocretin, which serve unique functions in each species.

The study of insects, and specifically *Drosophila*, provides a potentially unique portal into the genetic and neurochemical bases of the mysteries of sleep. Ideally, insect studies will ultimately have broader applicability to the understanding of human sleep disorders and consequently to the development of more effective, targeted treatments for these disorders.

Kristyna M. Hartse

See also: entries related to Evolution of Sleep

References

Bininda-Emonds, O.R.P., Cardillo, M., Jones, K.E., MacPhee, R.D.E., Beck, R.M.D., Grenyer, R., et al. (2007). The delayed rise of present-day mammals. *Nature, 446,* 507–512.

Grimaldi, D., & Engel, M. S. (2005). *Evolution of the insects*. Cambridge: Cambridge University Press.

Hartse, K. M. (2010). Sleep in insects. In P. McNamara, R. A. Barton, & C. L. Nunn (Eds.), *Evolution of sleep: Phylogenetic and functional perspectives* (pp. 34–55). Cambridge: Cambridge University Press.

Kaiser, W., & Steiner-Kaiser, J. (1983). Neuronal correlates of sleep, wakefulness, and arousal in a diurnal insect. *Nature, 301,* 707–709.

Stephenson, R., Chu, K.M., & Lee, J. (2007). Prolonged deprivation of sleep-like rest raises metabolic rate in the Pacific beetle cockroach, *Diploptera punctata* (Eschscholtz). *Journal of Experimental Biology, 210,* 2540–2547.

Sleep in Patients with Alzheimer's Disease

Alzheimer's disease (AD) is the most common form of dementia in the United States. Current estimates indicate that 5.1 million Americans are living with AD. The prevalence increases with age, with 60 percent of those more than the age of 85 years affected. It is estimated that by the year 2050, 11 to 16 million individuals will have AD (Plassman et al., 2007). Cross-sectional studies suggest that approximately 25 to 35 percent of individuals with AD have problems sleeping (Dauvilliers, 2007). Sleep disturbances in AD are complex. These patients are susceptible to all of the sleep problems related to aging, as well as to a progressive deterioration and decrease in the number of neurons in the suprachiasmatic nucleus (SCN), which is critical in the homeostatic maintenance of the circadian rhythm (Wu & Swaab, 2007). Common symptoms include night-time sleep fragmentation, increased sleep latency, decreased slow-wave sleep, and increased daytime napping.

The relationship between sleep pathology and the pathogenesis of AD may be even more complex. Amyloid-β (Aβ) accumulation in the brain extracellular space is considered to be a hallmark of AD, although the precise role of Aβ in pathogens is still not completely understood. In a transgenic mouse model, it has been shown that chronic sleep restriction significantly increased Aβ plaque formation while a dual orexin receptor antagonist decreased Aβ plaque formation. Thus, the sleep–wake cycle and orexin may play a role in the pathogenesis of AD (Kang et al., 2009). This relationship between sleep and the pathophysiology of AD may also be reflected in the observation that sleep disturbances should be considered as one of the core noncognitive symptoms of mild cognitive impairment, or MCI, a condition often thought to be a precursor to AD (Beaulieu-Bonneau & Hudon, 2009).

Sleep Architecture

Certain sleep changes in AD seem to represent an exaggeration of changes that appear with normal aging. AD patients spend an increased amount of time in the N1 stage of sleep with increased number and duration of awakenings, compared to age-matched non-AD controls (Prinz et al., 1982). With disease progression, it is also very difficult to separate EEG features of N2 sleep from N1 sleep. Sleep spindles and K-complexes are poorly formed. They are also of lower amplitude, shorter duration, and less numerous (Montplaisir, Petit, Lorrain, Gauthier, & Nielsen, 1995; Prinz et al., 1982) than is the case in normal aging. The proportion of NREM sleep increases with further disappearance of the true delta wave pattern of slow-wave sleep (Montplaisir et al., 1995; Prinz et al., 1982). The percentage of time spent in REM sleep, which remains stable with normal aging, is reduced in patients with AD. A decrease in the mean REM-sleep-episode duration and REM-sleep percentage has been attributed to degeneration of the nucleus basalis of Meynert. The nucleus normally exerts an inhibitory influence on the nucleus reticularis of the thalamus, the rhythm generator responsible for NREM sleep (Buzsaki et al., 1998). REM sleep also depends on the abundance and integrity of the cholinergic system. The cholinergic disturbance in AD is accompanied by worsening of REM sleep. In addition, many subcortical structures such as the basal forebrain, distal and superior raphe nucleus, and the reticular formation of the pons and medulla seem to be involved in the initiation of sleep and oscillation between REM and non-REM states. All of these structures may be affected by the degenerative changes that are part of AD. Their deterioration may account for the sleep architecture and rhythm changes in AD (Weldemichael & Grossberg, 2010). The impact on REM may also be reflected in the observation that REM sleep without atonia may be more common in AD, even though the behavioral correlate of REM sleep behavior disorder is relatively uncommon (Gagnon et al., 2006).

Circadian Rhythms

There is also a progressive deterioration of circadian rhythms with aging. These include changes manifested by reductions in sleep quality and impairment in cognitive performance (Yu et al., 2009). The changes in the sleep–wake cycle have been attributed to alterations in the SCN and melatonin secretion (Hu, Van Someren, Shea, & Scheer, 2009). Though not clear, genetic risk factors such as in AD patients who are negative for the *ApoE4* allele have also been implicated in the development of sleep problems (Craig, Hart, & Passmore, 2006).

Studies of circadian core body temperature rhythms in patients with probable AD have shown a reduction in endogenous circadian amplitude and a delay in endogenous circadian phase of core body temperature (Ancoli-Israel et al., 1997). AD patients, however, have shown only a slight decrease in endogenous circadian amplitude when compared to normal aging, so it is unclear whether this is simply an exaggeration of normal aging (Czeisler et al., 1992).

Impact of Commonly Used Medications in AD

Acetylcholinesterase inhibitors (ACHEIs) are a group of agents that have been FDA approved for the treatment of AD. The commonly used ACHEIs include donepezil, rivastigmine, and galantamine. These are of particular interest because of concern that the central cholinergic effect will have an impact on sleep and, in particular, REM sleep. Donepezil treatment appears to enhance REM sleep and reduce slow frequencies of REM-sleep EEG, suggesting a possible action on REM sleep-related cholinergic neurons in patients with AD. Furthermore, REM sleep alpha power may predict the cognitive response to donepezil (Moraes Wdos et al., 2006). Although some reviews suggest no particular impact of galantamine on REM sleep (Stahl, Markowitz, Papadopoulos, & Sadik, 2004), there are case reports of galantamine causing unusual nightmares (Iraqi & Hughes, 2009) and rivastigmine causing REM sleep behavior disorder (Yeh, Yeh, & Schenck, 2010). The impact of donepezil on REM sleep is not always clear (Cooke et al., 2006), but there are studies suggesting an increase in REM sleep with treatment by donepezil in healthy volunteers after a single dose (Kanbayashi et al., 2002). Donepezil may also reduce decline in recognition performance in individuals vulnerable to the effects of sleep deprivation (Chuah et al., 2009). Of additional note is that cholinergic activity follows a circadian pattern. As a consequence, improved function may be seen during the day, but at night, there is an increased risk of sleep disruption (Davis & Sadik, 2006).

Sanford Auerbach

See also: entries related to Sleep and the Brain

References

Ancoli-Israel, S., Klauber, M. R., Jones, D. W., Kripke, D. F., Martin, J., Mason, W., . . . Fell, R. (1997). Variations in circadian rhythms of activity, sleep, and light exposure related to dementia in nursing-home patients. *Sleep, 20*(1), 18–23.

Beaulieu-Bonneau, S., & Hudon, C. (2009). Sleep disturbances in older adults with mild cognitive impairment. *International Psychogeriatrics, 21*(4), 654–666.

Buzsaki, G., Bickford, R. G., Ponomareff, G., Thal, L. J., Mandel, R., & Gage, F. H. (1998). Nucleus basalis and thalamic control of neocortical activity in the freely moving rat. *Journal of Neuroscience, 8*(11), 4007–4026.

Chuah, L. Y., Chong, D. L., Chen, A. K., Rekshan, W. R., III, Tan, J. C., Zheng, H., & Chee, M. W. (2009). Donepezil improves episodic memory in young individuals vulnerable to the effects of sleep deprivation. *Sleep, 32*(8), 999–1010.

Cooke, J. R., Loredo, J. S., Liu, L., Marler, M., Corey-Bloom, J., Fiorentino, L., . . . Ancoli-Israel, S. (2006). Acetylcholinesterase inhibitors and sleep architecture in patients with Alzheimer's disease. *Drugs and Aging, 23*(6), 503–511.

Craig, D., Hart, D. J., & Passmore, A. P. (2006). Genetically increased risk of sleep disruption in Alzheimer's disease. *Sleep, 29*(8), 1003–1007.

Czeisler, C. A., Dumont, M., Duffy, J. F., Steinberg, J. D., Richardson, G. S., Brown, E. N., . . . Ronda, J. M. (1992). Association of sleep-wake habits in older people with changes in output of circadian pacemaker. *Lancet, 340*(8825), 933–936.

Dauvilliers, Y. (2007). Insomnia in patients with neurodegenerative conditions. *Sleep Medicine, 4*(Suppl. 4), S27-S34. (*Note*: This article reviews neurodegenerative disorders associated with dementing illnesses and characteristic sleep disturbances related to these conditions.)

Davis, B., & Sadik, K. (2006). Circadian cholinergic rhythms: Implications for cholinesterase inhibitor therapy. *Dementia and Geriatric Cognitive Disorders, 21*(2), 120–129.

Gagnon, J. F., Petit, D., Fantini, M. L., Rompre, S., Gauthier, S., Panisset, M., . . . Montplaisir, J. (2006). REM sleep behavior disorder and REM sleep without atonia in probable Alzheimer disease. *Sleep, 29*(10), 1321–1325.

Hu, K., Van Someren, E. J., Shea, S. A., & Scheer, F. A. (2009). Reduction of scale invariance of activity fluctuations with aging and Alzheimer's disease: Involvement of the circadian pacemaker. *Proceedings of the National Academy of Sciences of the United States of America, 106*(8), 2490–2494.

Iraqi, A., & Hughes, T. L. (2009). An unusual case of nightmares with Galantamine. *Journal of the American Geriatrics Society, 57*(3), 565.

Kanbayashi, T., Sugiyama, T., Aizawa, R., Saito, Y., Ogawa, Y., Kitajima, T., . . . Shimizu, T. (2002). Effects of donepezil (Aricept) on the rapid eye movement sleep of normal subjects. *Psychiatry and Clinical Neurosciences, 56*(3), 307–308.

Kang, J. E., Lim, M. M., Bateman, R. J., Lee, J. J., Smyth, L. P., Cirrito, J. R., . . . Holtzman, D. M. (2009). Amyloid-beta dynamics are regulated by orexin and the sleep-wake cycle. *Science, 326*(5955), 1005–1007.

Montplaisir, J., Petit, D., Lorrain, D., Gauthier, S., & Nielsen, T. (1995). Sleep in Alzheimer's disease: Further considerations on the role of brainstem and forebrain cholinergic populations in sleep-wake mechanisms. *Sleep, 18*(3), 145–148.

Moraes Wdos, S., Poyares, D. R., Guilleminault, C., Ramos, L. R., Bertolucci, P. H., & Tufik, S. (2006). The effect of donepezil on sleep and REM sleep EEG in patients with Alzheimer disease: A double-blind placebo-controlled study. *Sleep, 29*(2), 199–205.

Plassman, B. L., Langa, K. M., Fisher, G. G., Herringa, S. G., Weir, D. R., Ofstedal, M. B., . . . Wallace, R. B. (2007). Prevalence of dementia in the United States: The aging, demographics, and memory study. *Neuroepidemiology, 29*(1–2), 125–132.

Prinz, P. N., Peskind, E. R., Vitaliano, P. P., Raskind, M. A., Eisdorfer, C., Zemcuznikov, N., & Gerber, C. J. (1982). Changes in the sleep and waking EEGs of nondemented and demented elderly subjects. *Journal of the American Geriatrics Society, 30*(2), 86–93.

Stahl, S. M., Markowitz, J. S., Papadopoulos, G., & Sadik, K. (2004). Examination of nighttime sleep-related problems during double-blind, placebo-controlled trials of galantamine in patients with Alzheimer's disease. *Current Medical Research and Opinion, 20*(4), 517–524.

Weldemichael, D. A., & Grossberg, G. T. (2010). Circadian rhythm disturbances in patients with Alzheimer's disease: A review. *International Journal of Alzheimer's Disease,* Article ID 716453, 9 pages.

Wu, Y. H., & Swaab, D. F. (2007). Disturbance and strategies for reactivation of the circadian rhythm system in aging and Alzheimer's disease. *Sleep Medicine, 8*(6), 623–636.

Yeh, S. B., Yeh, P. Y., & Schenck, C. H. (2010). Rivastigmine-induced REM sleep behavior disorder (RBD) in a 88-year-old man with Alzheimer's disease. *Journal of Clinical Sleep Medicine, 6*(2), 192–195.

Yu, J. M., Tseng, I. J., Yuan, R. Y., Sheu, J. J., Liu, H. C., & Hu, C. J. (2009). Low sleep efficiency in patients with cognitive impairment. *Acta Neurologica Taiwanica, 18*(2), 91–97.

Sleep in Patients with Parkinson's Disease

Although Parkinson's disease (PD) is primarily thought of as a motor disorder (the shaking palsy), sleep problems of varying degrees and types occur in up to 74 to 98 percent of patients with PD. Sleep problems may even predict the onset of PD by some 5 to 10 years. Sleep problems, finally, may contribute to or exacerbate some of the mood and cognitive disorders seen in PD patients. Thus, PD might be better understood as both a motor and a sleep disorder. Although the kinds and severity of sleep problems vary tremendously in PD patients, virtually all of them manifest insomnia, excessive daytime sleepiness, intense dreams, and abnormal movements at night. Laboratory (polysomnographic and electroencephalographic or EEG) studies of sleep in PD patients who are not depressed and not demented show decreases in sleep efficiency, as well as increases in sleep fragmentation with multiple night-wakings. By contrast, in normal aging, sleep problems typically involve a reduction in slow-wave sleep duration and few if any abnormalities of REM sleep.

Why might PD be associated with sleep problems?

The neuropathology of PD is consistent with dysfunction of sleep mechanisms in PD patients. The classical sleep centers that control sleep onset and offset as well as sleep intensity are located in the brain stem and hypothalamus—both sites that are severely affected by PD. In addition, the primary pathology of PD involves loss of dopaminergic cells in the substantia nigra (SN) and in the ventral tegmental area. These two subcortical dopaminergic sites give rise to two projection systems important for arousal, motor, affective, and cognitive functioning. The nigrostriatal system, primarily implicated in motor functions, originates in the pars compacta of the SN and terminates in the striatum. The meso–limbic–cortical system originates in the ventral tegmental area (VTA) and terminates in the ventral striatum, limbic sites, amygdala, frontal lobes, and some other basal forebrain areas. Dopamine levels in the ventral striatum, frontal lobes, and hippocampus of PD patients are approximately 40 percent of normal. The termination sites of both the nigrostriatal and the meso–cortical dopamine systems are all important for sleep processes, particularly REM sleep. Disrupting these sites via reduced dopaminergic stimulation may also affect sleep.

In addition to the dopaminergic dysfunction associated with PD there is also Lewy body (LB) degeneration, and Alzheimer-type changes that have been noted in brain stem nuclei (including the noradrenergic locus coeruleus and the serotonergic dorsal raphe nucleus—two sites implicated in sleep and arousal mechanisms), limbic structures, cholinergic forebrain structures, and in the cerebral cortex. The cholinergic pathology in the basal forebrain structures and the LB-type degeneration in limbic and in the cerebral cortex are also likely contributors to sleep disorders, dementia of PD, and to affective dysfunction of PD.

In summary, there is no shortage of reasons to expect sleep dysfunction in PD patients. But we can cite further contributing factors as well: The classic motor problems of PD such as rigidity make it difficult to get comfortable or to turn over in bed. The medications used to treat motor symptoms of PD may have all kinds of contradictor effects on sleep: some may make the patient drowsy while others may over arouse the patient. Finally the anxiety and depression associated with PD may influence ability to fall asleep or to achieve restful sleep.

I now turn to a brief survey of major sleep disorders of PD.

Insomnia in PD

There are no good estimates of the number of PD patients who report insomnia. Insomnia refers to the inability to fall asleep or to stay asleep long enough to achieve restorative benefits of sleep. PD patients with insomnia lie awake at night, and when they finally fall asleep, they awaken a couple of hours later feeling unrefreshed. Polysomnographic and EEG studies of sleep in PD patients who are not depressed show decreases in deep sleep, too much light sleep (Stage II), as well as increases in sleep fragmentation and multiple night-wakings.

Excessive Daytime Sleepiness (EDS) in PD

EDS is found in as many as 50 percent of PD patients and serious fatigue in about 60 percent of patients. Periodic limb movements, obstructive sleep apnea, and depression may all contribute to sleep maintenance problems and EDS. In addition, parkinsonian medications themselves may contribute to the excessive sleepiness. There have been several reports arguing that use of dopamine agonists, pramipexole, and ropinirole is associated with sudden and irresistible sleep attacks during the day in some PD patients. But other studies have failed to find any association between agonists and EDS. Mood problems also seem to be related to ESD in PD patients. In some recent studies EDS was related primarily to anxiety levels rather than to depression, stress, stage of disease, neuropsychological dysfunction, or to medication-related factors. In sum, the causes of EDS in PD patients remain unclear, but dopaminergic medications and anxiety levels are likely to be important contributors.

Sleep Disorder Breathing and Sleep Apnea in PD

Apnea refers to episodes of cessation of breathing during sleep. Central sleep apnea refers to a problem in the brain stem centers that control respiration. Obstructive sleep apnea refers to blockage in the breathing passages (nose, throat, etc.). When the patient with sleep apnea attempts to enter deep sleep, he stops breathing and then this lack of oxygen prompts him to wake up briefly to get some air. The awakening may not be conscious as it is often very brief, but it may happen dozens of times each night so that the person's sleep is fragmented and filled only with light rather than deep restorative sleep. During the daytime, the individual feels overwhelming fatigue and a drive for sleep. Preliminary studies of sleep disordered breathing in PD populations suggests that more than half of PD patients suffer some degree of apnea with obstructive sleep apnea being the most commonly documented form.

Periodic Limb Movement Disorder and Restless Legs Syndrome (RLS)

Periodic limb movements during the night are quite common in the elderly, including PD patients. RLS, which is frequently associated with periodic limb movements, is frequently seen in the middle-aged population, in the elderly, and in PD patients. In both disorders, there is a sensation in the legs that causes the patient to move his or her extremities and may contribute to insomnia. The PD patient with RLS often feels an irresistible urge to move the legs around during the night to get comfortable.

REM Sleep Behavior Disorder (RBD)

This is the disorder that may herald the onset of PD by as much as 10 to 15 years. RBD involves the loss of the normal motor inhibition associated with REM sleep so that patients literally begin to act out their dreams. While estimates vary dramatically, it appears that approximately 50 percent of PD patients have partial or complete loss of muscle atonia during rapid eye movement (REM) sleep. It is particularly interesting that most of the dreams that RBD patients act out and report upon awakening are filled with aggression. Common themes are that the patient or his wife or bed partner is being attacked by intruders, etc., and the patient physically, and sometimes violently, defends against the attack. One recent study of dream content in RBD patients demonstrated that compared to controls, patients with RBD reported a very high degree of aggression in their dreams. Sixty-six percent of RBD dreams and only 15 percent of control dreams had at least one episode of aggression. The percentage of aggressive episodes to friendly interactions in dreams of RBD patients was twice that of controls (86% vs. 44%).

The dream-enactment episodes are so real for the patients that they often injure themselves during an episode. Indeed, injuries are reported by more than 75 percent of patients. Video-polysomnographic monitoring reveals that hallucinatory episodes typically occur during REM sleep.

Interestingly, varying degrees of RBD may be present for years before the motoric manifestations of PD develop. One study of PD patients with RBD investigators found that the nighttime dream-related en-actment behaviors developed an average of three years before the motoric disorder (parkinsonism) in about half of those who had both conditions.

Sleep and Hallucinations in PD

Vivid dreams in PD patients often predict daytime hallucinations. Many PD patients without overt RBD report episodes of hal-lucinations. Hallucinations are thought to be experienced by as many as 33 percent of PD patients during the course of their illness. They are generally thought to be a complication of dopaminergic pharma-cotherapy and when present limit drug therapy for motor disability. They are, fur-thermore, a significant risk factor for nurs-ing home placement. Hallucinations in PD patients tend to occur in the visual rather than auditory modality and are frequently associated with vivid dreams. Interest-ingly, sleep disturbance is more common in hallucinators than in nonhallucinators, and therefore sleep problems rather than the medications per se may be potent con-tributors to hallucinosis in PD patients.

Sleep and Depression in PD

Chronic depression is seen in approxi-mately 40 percent of PD patients but major depression in PD is unlike reactive forms of depression in that it is characterized by prominent anxiety and less proclivity to-ward self-punitive ideation. In other forms of major depression sleep dysfunction is a prominent and core symptom of the dis-ease. Typically the problem is reduced REM latency and nonrestorative sleep no matter how long one stays in bed or sleeps. Some of these same sleep-related phenom-ena occur in PD patients with depression, but there are few controlled studies that have identified special aspects of sleep dys-function in PD patients with depression.

Sleep and Cognitive Disorders of PD

It should be noted briefly that PD is also associated with cognitive deficits—especially in mid and later stages of the dis-ease. These deficits involve problems with memory, attention, and concentration. Be-cause sleep is known to be involved in consolidation of memory, it follows that disruption of sleep, as occurs in PD, may also contribute to cognitive disorders of PD—but this proposition has not been thoroughly tested as yet.

In summary, disturbances in sleep, with its related consequences for mood and mind, obviously cause problems and re-duce the quality of life for both the patient and for the caregiver. Furthermore, an un-derstanding of the causal relationships be-tween sleep and PD symptoms may lead to better treatment and to better quality of life for PD patients and their caregivers. In particular, if sleep dysfunction contrib-utes to the development of cognitive (e.g., dementia) and affective (e.g., depression) dysfunction in PD patients, then early and aggressive therapies to treat sleep disor-ders could delay the development of cog-nitive, mood, and dementing illnesses in this population.

Patrick McNamara

See also: entries related to Sleep and the Brain

Reference

Stacy, M. (2002). Sleep disorders in Parkinson's disease: Epidemiology and management. *Drugs Aging, 19*(10), 733–739.

Sleep in Patients with Wilson's Disease

Wilson's disease (WD) is an autosomal recessive inherited disorder of copper metabolism resulting in pathological accumulation of copper in many organs and tissues. The disease is caused by a deficiency of a copper-transporting P-type ATPase (Bull, Thomas, Rommens, Forbes, & Cox, 1993), encoded by mutation of the *ATP7B* gene on chromosome 13 (band q14.3). More than 500 different forms of mutation have been identified up to now. Copper accumulation results in a variety of symptoms ranging from neurological and/or psychiatric disturbances to acute or chronic liver disease. Two main clinical forms—hepatic and neurological—are usually distinguished. The latter—present in about 40 percent of those affected—include dysarthria, dyspraxia, ataxia, and extrapyramidal signs, mostly of the dystonic kind (Kitzberger, Madl, & Ferenci, 2005). Neuropsychiatric features include a cognitive decline together with personality changes, mood disorders; even schizophreniform disorders can accompany the clinical symptoms. Treatment with penicillamine, zinc, or trientine is lifelong (even in asymptomatic cases) for a good response. Most WD patients can resume a good quality of life.

Sleep complaints, relatively frequently accompanying the clinical features of WD, however, mostly go unrecognized with WD patients and their physicians paying no attention to them. The first to notice increased sleep problems in a significant cohort were Portala, Westermark, Ekselius, and Broman (2002). The authors examined a group of 24 WD patients in a questionnaire study, and found statistic differences from their reference group in quantitative sleep variables (difficulties falling asleep, greater number of awakenings per night, sleepiness during the day), in daytime functions (fatigue, taking naps), and in REM-sleep disturbances (sleep paralysis, cataplexy). A total of 42 percent of treated WD patients had sleep problems. The conclusion was that the sleep complaints can be explained by disturbances in monoaminergic neurons (REM-off neurons) at the brain stem level resulting in altered REM-sleep function. Enhancement by altered circadian functions, localized in suprachiasmatic nuclei, can be considered as well.

The high frequency of sleep comorbidity compared with the control group was corroborated in another study (Nevšímalová et al., in press). Its authors examined 55 patients with WD in a questionnaire study, and the results correlated with age- and sex-matched control subjects. The questions were centered on sleep habits and sleep disorder comorbidities. The patients, as well as the control group, were then asked to fill in the Epworth sleepiness scale measuring chronic sleepiness and a screening questionnaire for REM sleep behavior disorder (RBD). Twenty-four patients underwent a sleep study—nocturnal video-polysomnography, followed by daytime multiple sleep latency testing (MSLT).

According to the results, the values of daytime napping, excessive daytime sleepiness, cataplexy-like episodes, and poor nocturnal sleep were significantly higher. Elevated subjective sleepiness was found in almost one third of our WD questionnaire respondents, and MSLT revealed borderline or shortened mean sleep latency again in one third of the cohort. Although the changes were found more frequently in patients with the neurological than in the hepatic form, the difference was non-significant. There were also surprisingly many REM-sleep dissociation symptoms occurring in narcolepsy, particularly cataplexy-like episodes and vivid dreams, but neither nocturnal polysomnography nor MSLT confirmed any sleep-onset REM periods in the patients' records. Almost half the WD patients responded positively to five or more screening questions suggesting conceivable clinical symptoms of RBD, more frequently so patients treated with D-penicillamine. Horrible nightmares accompanied by screaming loud and even nocturnal injuries were among their complaints. However, signs of REM sleep without atonia, which is typical of RBD, appeared in several patients, but none reached the straightforward criteria of 20 percent of the REM record that is necessary for RBD diagnosis.

WD is supposed to be associated with a dopaminergic deficit (Barthel et al., 2003), which can explain at least some of the clinical symptoms. Therefore, impairment of basal ganglia at the nigrostriatal dopaminergic level, and dysfunction of monoaminergic neurons at the brain stem level help to account for the clinical variety of sleep disturbances.

In conclusion, WD patients often suffer from sleep disturbances, and the spectrum of the sleep/wake symptoms also includes altered REM-sleep-dissociated symptoms.

Soňa Nevšímalová

See also: entries related to Hormones in Sleep; entries related to Sleep and the Brain

References

Barthel, H., Hermann, W., Kluge, R., Hesse, S., Collingridge, D. R., Wagner, A., & Sabri, O. (2003). Concordant pre- and postsynaptic deficits of dopaminergic neurotransmission in neurologic Wilson disease. *American Journal of Neuroradiology, 24,* 234–238.

Bull, A. I., Thomas, G. R., Rommens, J. M., Forbes, J. R., & Cox, D. W. (1993). The Wilson disease gene is a putative copper transporting P-type ATPase similar to Menkes disease gene. *Nature Genetics, 5,* 327–337.

Kitzberger, R., Madl, C., & Ferenci, P. (2005). Wilson disease. *Metabolic Brain Disease, 20,* 295–302.

Nevšímalová, S., Buskova, J., Bruha, R., Kemlink, D., Sonka, K., Vitek, L., & Marecek, Z. (in press). Sleep disorders in Wilson's disease. *European Journal Neurology.*

Portala, K., Westermark, K., Ekselius, L., & Broman, J. E. (2002). Sleep in patients with treated Wilson's disease: A questionnaire study. *Nordic Journal of Psychiatry, 56,* 291–297.

Sleep, Inflammation, and Cardiovascular Disease

Although scientists noted a relationship between inflammation and cardiovascular disease (CVD) as early as the 1920s, it was not until decades later that researchers began to examine more direct linkages among disturbed sleep, inflammation, and CVD. Within the past 10 years there has been burgeoning interest in understanding the mechanistic processes of how inflammation mediates the relationship between disturbed sleep and CVD.

Cytokines regulate and mediate immune and other inflammatory-related responses. The functions of proinflammatory cytokines are diverse, including developing and proliferating immune cell subsets, activating adhesion molecules and blood coagulation pathways, supporting atherosclerotic processes, and altering neurochemical and neuroendocrine processes. While acutely heightened inflammation states are a natural and needed part of the body's immune response to infection and injury, such states can adversely affect sleep quality and duration. For example, interluekin-6 (IL-6) and tumor necrosis factor-alpha (TNF-α) are acutely elevated in response to bacterial infection and are associated with sickness behaviors, including fatigue and increased sleep duration.

Low-grade, chronic inflammation also brings adverse consequences to sleep that are unremitting and ultimately can further exacerbate disease. For example, heart failure is characterized by significant inflammation across an extensive spectrum of pathways, including immune cells, endothelial cells, cardiac cells, and the liver. Heart failure is also characterized by disturbed sleep, including sleep apnea. Currently investigators are examining the degree to which the chronic inflammation in heart failure is associated with ongoing sleep disturbances, and the potential for feedback loops of inflammatory processes that further exacerbate symptoms and functional capacity (Khayat, Patt, & Hayes, 2009).

Sleep apnea is a good example of how disturbed sleep can enhance inflammatory states and subsequently contribute to the development or exacerbation of CVD (Mills & Dimsdale, 2004). Circulating levels of IL-6 and TNF-α are elevated in individuals with obstructive sleep apnea (OSA) and are correlated with carotid intima–media thickness, suggesting that apnea-related systemic inflammation is associated with progression of atherosclerosis and increased risk of cardiovascular morbidity. The circulating soluble receptor 1 of TNF is also elevated in sleep apnea and associated with the number of arousals during the night, as well as associated with CVD incidence. One of the reasons that nighttime sleep disturbance may increase CVD risk is that although inflammation is increased throughout the night in response to apneic events, it can remain elevated throughout the next day (Mills, Natarajan, von Känel, Ancoli-Israel, & Dimsdale, 2009). When sleep apnea is successfully treated with continuous positive airway pressure, the inflammation associated with apneic events is reduced.

In addition to cytokines and their receptors, endothelin-1 (ET-1) has been associated with disturbed sleep and CVD. ET-1 is a potent vasoconstrictor and mediator of inflammation that is elicited from endothelial cells. The increase in blood pressure that acutely accompanies apneic events can also increase endothelial shear stress, which results in endothelial production of ET-1. In OSA patients, ET-1 is strongly related to degree of hypertension (Gjorup et al., 2007). The elevation of ET-1 in sleep apnea appears to be related to hypoxia, a state of inadequate oxygen saturation that results from repeated breath suspensions. Elevated ET-1 levels have been associated with greater sleep latency, greater rapid eye movement (REM) latency, and more slow-wave sleep in sleep apneics. Elevated levels of ET-1 may be a consequence rather than a determinant of sleep quality.

Although disease states provide settings where the association between inflammation and sleep can be more easily observed, such relationships can also be found in healthy individuals. Within normal physiological ranges, elevated circulating levels of IL-6 have been associated with decreased slow-wave sleep and increased REM sleep. Elevated levels of IL-6 appear to be associated with poor sleep quality; however, there is still no formal consensus on the relationship of IL-6 or any other inflammatory biomarker on sleep architecture in healthy individuals.

Sleep disruption in healthy individuals provides another setting for examining sleep and inflammation. Total or partial sleep deprivation can lead to significant short-term increases of daytime levels of IL-6, C-reactive protein, and TNF receptors. These findings beg the question of whether chronic insufficient sleep in healthy individuals contributes to low-grade inflammation and increased CVD risk. There is evidence to support such a position. Caregivers of Alzheimer's disease patients, who are at increased risk of CVD, show disrupted sleep as a result of their caregiving role, including greater amounts of time spent awake after initial sleep onset and lower overall sleep efficiency. These sleep disturbances are associated with elevated levels of IL-6 as well as the coagulation marker D-dimer (von Känel, Loredo, Ancoli-Israel, & Dimsdale, 2006), both important mediators of the inflammatory processes of CVD and both predict CVD outcomes.

In summary, inflammation may mediate the relationship between inadequate sleep and CVD risk. Studies of diseased populations generally demonstrate that elevated levels of inflammation are associated with more disturbed sleep, and worse cardiac prognosis. Although the data are less straightforward for healthy individuals, there is also evidence to suggest that over time insufficient sleep may contribute to low-grade inflammation and, ultimately, increase risk of cardiac events.

Jessica Ann Jiménez and Paul J. Mills

See also: entries related to Sleep and Health; entries related to Sleep Disorders

References

Gjorup, P. H., Sadauskiene, L., Wessels, J., Nyvad, O., Strunge, B., & Pedersen, E. B. (2007). Abnormally increased endothelin-1 in plasma during the night in obstructive sleep apnea: Relation to blood pressure and severity of disease. *American Jounral of Hypertension, 20*(1), 44–52.

Khayat, R., Patt, B., & Hayes, D. (2009). Obstructive sleep apnea: The new cardiovascular disease. Part I: Obstructive sleep apnea and the pathogenesis of vascular disease. *Heart Failure Reviews, 14*(3), 143–153.

Mills, P. J., & Dimsdale, J. E. (2004). Sleep apnea: A model for studying cytokines, sleep, and sleep disruption. *Brain, Behavior, and Immunity, 18*(4), 298–303.

Mills, P., Natarajan, L., von Känel, R., Ancoli-Israel, S., & Dimsdale, J. (2009). Diurnal variability of C-reactive protein in obstructive sleep apnea. *Sleep and Breathing, 13*(4), 415–420.

von Känel, R., Loredo, J., Ancoli-Israel, S., & Dimsdale, J. (2006). Association between sleep apnea severity and blood coagulability: Treatment effects of nasal continuous positive airway pressure. *Sleep and Breathing, 10*(3), 139–146.

Sleep Intensity and the Homeostatic Regulation of Sleep

The importance of the intensity dimension of sleep was first uncovered in experiments on effects of sleep deprivation. The most dramatic effect of sleep deprivation in every mammalian species studied thus far has been the phenomenon of compensatory rebound, or the increase over baseline of sleep times and intensity, where intensity is measured by higher arousal thresholds, enhanced slow-wave activity (SWA; particularly enhanced delta power when spectral EEG analysis is used), enhanced REM frequencies per unit time, and deeper and longer sleep cycles. After sleep deprivation, mammalian animals attempt to make up for lost sleep by enhancing the intensity and duration of subsequent sleep. During the wakefulness or deprivation period, neurochemicals are thought to accumulate in proportion to the length of the wake period. One such possible chemical is adenosine, which acts in a sleep center (possibly the basal forebrain) to inhibit arousal/increase sleepiness and then dissipates at a rate depending on sleep intensity until it returns to baseline during sleep. Birds too demonstrate a compensatory rebound after sleep deprivation, but the rebound involves increased overall sleep times and cycles rather than enhancements in SWA. Birds also appear to exhibit a special form of SWA and very little REM-like sleep. SWA in birds, however, does not appear to be homeostatically regulated. SWA in NREM sleep in pigeons does not decline in the course of the dark period, suggesting that SWA in these animals is not building up some chemical that is depleted during waking, such as adenosine build-up in mammals. Moreover, SWA does not appear to increase after sleep deprivation. Unlike mammals, sleep spindles are absent during NREM in birds. As in aquatic mammals, unilateral eye closure and unihemispheric slow-wave sleep (SWS) also occur in birds. In both mammalian and in avian species compensatory rebound involves a change in sleep-cycle lengths.

Borbely (1982) first formalized the insight that mammalian sleep involved a balance between sleep amount and sleep intensity and that sleep was therefore under homeostatic control. In his two-process model of sleep regulation a sleep need process (Process S) increases during waking (or sleep deprivation) and decreases during sleep. This part of the model indexes restorative aspects of sleep and explicitly predicts that sleep is required for some restorative process of the brain or the body or both. Process S is proposed to interact with input from the light-regulated circadian system (Process C) that is independent of sleep and wakefulness rhythms. SWA is taken as an indicator of the time course of Process S, because SWA is known to correlate with arousal thresholds and to markedly increase during the previous waking period and during the rebound period after sleep deprivation in all mammals studied. Once a threshold value of Process S is reached (i.e., once the appropriate amount and intensity of SWS is reached), Process C will be activated. Simulations using the model's assumptions show that the homeostatic component of sleep falls in a sigmoidal manner during waking and rises in a saturating exponential manner during sleep.

The two-process model does not address homeostatic aspects of REM. REM, however, evidences rebound after sleep deprivation, but here the intensity component is likely to be some process associated with frequency (density) of REMs per unit time. In any case both REM and NREM are under homeostatic control and enhancements of sleep intensity over baseline addresses the homeostatic need for sleep. In short, these findings led to the assumption that *sleep intensity indexes functional need.*

Researchers have used a variety of measures to evaluate sleep intensity, including SWA, duration of Stages III and IV or SWS, sleep-cycle length, spindling activity, REM densities, and arousal thresholds. These measures of intensity, however, need to be evaluated (via both reliability analyses and via exhaustive review of the literature on each measure) for their power to index sleep intensity (Are they all measuring the same thing?) and then ranked in order of reliability. It may be that SWA and sleep-cycle lengths will rank first and second, as these are the measures that to date appear to best linked to restorative aspects of sleep.

Past comparative analyses of functional correlates of sleep quotas did not look at correlated evolution of sleep intensity with other ecological and life-history variables. Analyses using proxies for intensity (e.g., SWA, SWS, or sleep-cycle length) were necessarily limited because (1) no compilations of mean duration of SWS (Stage II and III NREM) were attempted; (2) the number of species with

values for sleep cycle were very low; and (3) no concerted attempts were made to collect new data that index intensity (e.g., SWA). Nor had previous analyses controlled for variables that are now known to alter intensity measures (torpor or hibernation).

Patrick McNamara

See also: entries related to Sleep Assessment

Reference

Borbely, A. A. (1982). A two process model of sleep regulation. *Human Neurobiology, 1,* 195–204.

Sleep, Memory, and Dreams

Memory

Memory consolidation is the process whereby recently acquired information is converted to a more permanent, long-term state, less vulnerable to disruption or loss. This dynamic process takes place over a period of days, weeks, months, and even years. There are now understood to be at least two different memory systems, declarative and nondeclarative, that are relatively independent of each other.

Declarative material is easily accessible to verbal description. The individual is aware of the information that is to be learned and aware that it can be accessed from memory store when desired. Declarative memory is further divided into semantic and episodic categories. Semantic memories comprise our factual knowledge of the world. Thus most of us know that Paris is the capital of France. However, memory of when we acquired this information is likely not available. Episodic memories include the information of interest as well as the contextual location of acquisition in time and place. Being able to recall what you ate for lunch as well as the fine details of who you were with and where you ate, is an example of an episodic memory.

Nondeclarative memories are not easily accessible to verbal description. Usually, learning does not occur at the conscious level. Assessment that nondeclarative memories exist can best be done by observing behavior. If someone says that they have learned to skate, the best indication that they have done so is to give a skating demonstration. There are several subtypes of nondeclarative memory. They include procedural memory (skills and habits), priming, and simple classical conditioning (which include emotional responses and skeletal musculature responses) (Maquet, Smith, & Stickgold, 2003).

Sleep States

The states of sleep in humans are conventionally divided into two separate categories, rapid eye movement sleep (REM) and nonrapid eye movement sleep (NREM). NREM sleep is further subdivided into three categories. Stage 1 is a light stage of sleep, typically seen at sleep onset with an electrical brain wave (EEG) frequency of 7 to 9 Hz. It typically does not last more than a few minutes before giving way to Stage 2 sleep. This stage has a slower EEG frequency of 5 to 7 Hz (often called theta waves), as well as special intermittent features including the spindle (12 to 16 Hz) and the K-complex. About 50 percent of the night is spent in this stage of sleep.

The third type of NREM sleep consists of large amplitude delta waves (1 to 4 Hz). This type of sleep, often called slow-wave sleep (SWS), is most prominent in the first third of the night and is minimal or absent in the last third of the night. There is reduced muscle tension in the large skeletal muscle groups during NREM sleep, but some tension remains and movement is possible. There are no eye movements during NREM sleep. During REM sleep, the EEG frequency is 7 to 10 Hz. There are phasic conjugate rapid movements of the eyes while the large skeletal muscles are completely immobilized and movement is not possible.

Throughout the night of sleep there is a 90-minute ultradian rhythm. Healthy young individuals begin the night with a few minutes of Stage 1, which then gives way to Stage 2, which is then followed by SWS. SWS is followed by a return to Stage 2 sleep and then a period of REM sleep occurs. The time for this cycle to complete is approximately 90 minutes. The individual then repeats the cycle by going from REM sleep to Stage 2, SWS, and then REM again. As the night continues, the amount of SWS diminishes and the amount of REM sleep increases. By the last third of the night, only Stage 2 and REM sleep occur.

Sleep States and Memory Consolidation

Three main approaches have been used to examine the relationship between sleep states and memory processes. One method involved observing the changes in sleep EEG following task acquisition compared with baseline and control values.

More recently, brain-imaging techniques have been used to observe changes in neural activity during postlearning sleep. A second approach has been to examine performance of participants exposed to postlearning sleep deprivation and compare their performance with those allowed normal postacquisition sleep. More recently, a day–night design has been used to avoid possible stress confounds. Participants either learn a task in the morning and are tested 12 hours later with no intervening sleep or learn the task in the evening and are tested 12 hours later in the morning. For this group, a normal night of sleep is included in the 12-hour time span. The third approach has been to present various kinds of sensory stimulation during postlearning sleep to artificially enhance memory consolidation. These methods have all provided evidence for a close relationship between sleep states and memory consolidation (Maquet et al., 2003; Smith, 2010).

Emotional Memory

Generally, emotionally charged memories are better consolidated after REM sleep than after NREM sleep. However, while emotionally positive material is vulnerable to REM-sleep loss, emotionally negative material is not. A brain-imaging study suggests that the negatively charged material can be consolidated by an alternate neural route if necessary. The results indicate an alternate system for memorizing extremely important survival information in case sleep becomes impossible for the organism following a traumatic natural event.

Declarative Memory and Sleep

Declarative memory consolidation has been reportedly enhanced by SWS, particularly episodic memory. Memory for such tasks as paired associate words, prose passages, landscapes, object locations, faces, and navigation within virtual or natural environments was superior following SWS. Several studies enhanced memory by artificially increasing postlearning SWS activity. Some studies have reported that Stage 2 sleep is also important, with most observing a postlearning increase in Stage 2 spindle activity. REM sleep was also reportedly involved in a small number of declarative learning studies. An imaging study suggests that SWS aids consolidation of semantic memories as well.

Nondeclarative Memory and Sleep

Skills and habits refer to learning that includes such activities as novel perceptual, motor, and cognitive tasks. Acquisition of a visual texture discrimination task required both SWS and REM sleep. Efficient consolidation of motor tasks, such as the finger-tapping sequence task and visuomotor tasks, like the rotary pursuit task, appear to involve Stage 2 sleep, although REM sleep has also been implicated. The type of sleep involved appears to depend on the initial skill level of the participant. In the rotary pursuit task, participants with low initial skill levels showed postlearning increases in REM sleep, while participants with high initial skill levels showed postlearning increases in Stage 2 sleep parameters. It has been suggested that individuals were using one of two overlapping consolidation systems. Those that found the task to be novel and were required to come up with a new cognitive strategy showed increases in REM-sleep parameters (such as minutes of REM sleep, density of actual REMs). Those that found the task to be similar to other activities that they already had learned, showed increases in Stage 2 sleep parameters (such as minutes of Stage 2, density, and average size of sleep spindles). This idea is consistent with the finding that cognitively more complex tasks, novel to the learner, require REM sleep for most efficient memory consolidation (Smith, Aubrey, & Peters, 2004).

Dreams and Sleep States

A dream can be defined as mental activity reported on awakening from a sleep state. Traditionally, dreams were considered to occur primarily during REM sleep. More recently, it has become clear that mentation can be reported from NREM awakenings as well, although the probability of obtaining a report (approximately 50%) is less likely than from REM sleep (80% to 90%). REM reports may be more salient as well. It is generally agreed that sleep mentation reports reflect the ongoing life of the dreamer.

Since children are learning a multitude of things from a very young age, it might be expected that their dreams would reflect this activity during postlearning sleep. However, the dreams of young children are less well developed than those of adults. Firstly, sleep states do not seem as closely related to memory consolidation in young children compared to adults. While

declarative tasks appear to be enhanced by postlearning sleep, it does not seem as vital for procedural tasks.

The recall rate for children is much lower than for young adults. For example, children age 9 to 11 have a recall rate of 20 to 30 percent from REM awakenings and only 6 percent from NREM awakenings. Dream reports are less mature in children and appear to mirror cognitive development. No dreams have been collected in a formal experimental paradigm following successful acquisition of a task in young children. However, given that the dreams are quite immature at young ages, while ability to learn many tasks is possible, it would seem unlikely that dreams are necessary for learning (Domhoff, 2010).

Dream Content Following Task Acquisition

There are not many studies that have examined the dream content of post-training sleep. Most studies examined the dreams in post-training REM sleep or looked at the mentation at sleep onset.

Several studies asked subjects to play the Tetris computer game, where shapes fall down the screen and must be manipulated to fit into a structure. Participants awakened just after sleep onset reported seeing the pieces falling. Similar results were obtained using a downhill skiing simulator (Alpine Racer). There was little evidence of episodic replay mentation from either task. Subjects did not recall the room, the experimenter, or other facets of the lab. Since one group in the first experiment was amnesic (temporal lobe damage), yet still experienced postgame Tetris piece mentation, it was concluded that the mentation was from a semantic rather than an episodic source. This idea was consistent with the results of another study reporting only 1 to 2 percent of dreams actually replayed waking experience.

For REM-sleep mentation, one study examined the dreams of individuals habituated to functioning with inverted prisms on. While there were few direct incorporations of this experience there was indirect metaphorical content. For example, "I wanted to know what it was. Then I looked at a word, but it was upside down." The dreams usually reflected increases in visual and motor difficulties. In another study, participants were exposed to second language learning. All students were in a French immersion environment for several weeks. Learning progress was correlated with increased time in REM sleep. For dream content, the more progress the student made, the shorter was the latency to French incorporations and communications. Students making minimal progress did not report any French incorporations in their dreams.

In a memory-enhancement study, participants were trained in a cognitive procedural task. A clicking sound was present in the background during acquisition and acted as the conditioned stimulus (CS). During the postlearning sleep night, they were subjected to the CS via mini-earphone. The clicks were triggered by maximum deflection of actual rapid eye movements during REM sleep. Test subjects were 23 percent better than controls. The clicks were believed to have acted as reminders to remember to process the recently acquired task. In a second study, using the same experimental paradigm, subjects were exposed to another cognitive procedural task (mirror trace). Participants had to draw pencil lines inside the margins of complex figures by watching their hand in the mirror. Dream length was found to be significantly longer for the test group compared to control groups, although time spent in REM sleep was equal for all groups. It was considered possible that the dreams were more intense for the test group. The most popular dream metaphor was reference to driving cars and trying to stay on the road. Dreams generally reflected the problem of staying on a road or path. There was virtually no episodic replay observed (Smith, 2010).

In summary, sleep mentation appears to reflect memory consolidation activity in certain situations. Present evidence does not provide support for the idea that sleep mentation aids memory consolidation.

Carlyle Smith

See also: Sleep and Mild Cognitive Impairment

References

Domhoff, G. W. (2010). Dream content is continuous with waking thought, based on preoccupations, concerns, and interests. *Sleep Medicine Clinics, 5,* 203–215.

Maquet, P., Smith, C., & Stickgold, R. (2003). *Sleep and brain plasticity*. Oxford: Oxford University Press.

Smith, C. T. (2010). Sleep states, memory processing and dreams. *Sleep Medicine Clinics, 5,* 217–228.

Smith, C. T., Aubrey, J. B., & Peters, K. R. (2004). Different roles for REM and Stage 2 sleep in motor learning: A proposed model. *Psychologica Belgica, 44,* 81–104.

Sleep, Nightmares, and Psychiatry

Sleep and circadian rhythms are strongly related to physical and mental health. Sleep disturbances and circadian changes affect body functions as well as mood and cognitions. Sleep abnormalities are very common in psychiatric disorders, in particular, in mood disorders and anxiety disorders. This is because hormonal changes in body and monoaminergic dysregulations in the central nervous system are described both in sleep disorders and in mood/anxiety disorders. Thus, sleep disturbances and dreaming disorders are one of the central issues of depression and anxiety disorders.

Insomnia is common among typical depressed patients. On the other hand, hypersomnia often occurs in atypical depressive patients, bipolar depressed patients, and adolescent depressives. Depressed patients often report difficulty in falling sleep, maintenance problems of sleep, and early awaking, named as initial, middle, and terminal insomnia, respectively. Sleep disturbances may have prognostic significance in predicting suicide among patients with mood disorders. Among objective markers of sleep abnormalities in depression, reduced REM-sleep latency was identified as an objective indicator of depressive disorder and an inverse correlate of its severity. Reduced REM latency has proved to be one of the robust and specific features of sleep in depressed patients. Other reported abnormalities in REM sleep include a prolonged duration of the first REM period, an increased density of eye movements, and an increased REM percentage of total sleep time. More interestingly, reduced REM-sleep latency was identified as an objective indicator of depressive disorder and an inverse correlate of its severity. Reduced REM latency has proved to be one of the specific features of sleep in depressed patients. Other reported abnormalities in REM sleep include a prolonged duration of the first REM period, an increased density of eye movements, and an increased REM percentage of total sleep time. Slow-wave sleep time is also reduced in depressed patients than healthy subjects. Among endogenous depressive symptoms, terminal insomnia, pervasive anhedonia, unreactive mood, and appetite loss are reported to be related to short REM latency in depressed patients.

Anxiety is commonly related to sleep disturbances. Sleep panic attacks are frequent in patients with panic disorder. Approximately one third of patients with panic disorder reports recurrent sleep panic. Interestingly, recurrent sleep panic is correlated with suicidality and depression among panic disordered patients. Posttraumatic stress disorder and other anxiety disorders are also associated with sleep-pattern changes.

Nightmares are long frightening dreams involving threats to survival or security, from which the sleeper awakens, and should be distinguished from sleep terrors, narcolepsy, sleep panic attacks, and other awakenings. Nightmares typically occur later in the night during REM sleep and produce vivid dream imagery, complete awakenings, autonomic arousal, and detailed recall of the event and may cause psychological distress and social or occupational dysfunction.

Recurrent nightmares may be associated with a high comorbidity of mood and anxiety disorder, in particular in young adults and adults. Frequent nightmares and terminal insomnia are common in melancholic depression.

The association of dream disturbances with ?ashbacks related to the trauma suggests that nightmares appear to be an effective coping mechanism in trauma victims. A relationship between dream anxiety and dissociative experiences and the causal role of childhood traumatic events may play a role in this relationship.

Nightmare disorder seems to be associated with self-mutilation, suicidal behavior, and borderline personality. It may be reasonable to attribute a role to nightmares as an adaptive coping strategy in dissociative disorders and borderline personality disorder. The dreams reduce the intensity of the emotional distress by juxtaposing the current trauma with various other events in the person's life, making connections to other similar or not-so-similar events. When trauma is dreamt about, it is no longer uniquely distressing; it gradually becomes part of a fabric or network. Thus, dreaming has an adaptive function and nightmares are common following a trauma. Thus, we suggest that nightmares are useful dreams to cope with the conflicts of traumatic events, if they are worked on appropriately in therapy.

Sleep-related violence is also a popular topic. It has forensic importance as well as clinical interest. Violent behavior during sleep includes a broad range of behaviors: self-mutilation, sexual assault, murder attempt, murder, and suicide and can be directed to other subjects, to objects, or to self. Smoking, caffeine, and alcohol intake increase it. Several disorders may be responsible for causing nocturnal violence: sleepwalking, sleep terrors, REM sleep behavior disorder, nocturnal psychogenic dissociative disorders, nocturnal seizures, obstructive sleep apnea, and periodic limb movement disorder.

Mehmed Y. Agargun

See also: entries related to Sleep and Health

Sleep Pattern and Its Determining Factors in University Students

Sleep patterns of university students are likely to become delayed and irregular. A considerable number of students meet the diagnostic criteria for delayed sleep-phase syndrome (DSPS), which is characterized by delayed habitual sleep–wake time relative to desired and socially acceptable time (Hazama, Inoue, Kojima, Ueta, & Nakagome, 2008). Because the sleep phase is prone to delay with advancing age during adolescence, the remarkable phenomenon of sleep-phase delay in university students could reflect the maturational process of biological rhythms. However, a longer delay in the sleep pattern is observed among university students than among nonuniversity students of the same age, such as workers. Since the sleep–wake phase of students is dramatically delayed shortly after they enter the university, we believe that milder regulation of schedules and restrictions by the university than those by high school might contribute to the delayed sleep patterns.

Similar to other cohorts, the amount of nocturnal sleep in university students has decreased by more than an hour in the last few decades. Steptoe, Peacey, and Wardle (2006) surveyed the sleep pattern of university students in 24 countries and showed that 21 percent of the students were considered short sleepers with less than seven hours of nocturnal sleep (Steptoe et al., 2006). They also suggested a relationship between short sleep and poor health. A survey conducted on a large population of university students revealed that more than 60 percent of the study population had poor sleep quality, which was measured using the Pittsburgh Sleep Quality Index (Lund, Reider, Whiting, & Prichard, 2010). As expected, the inadequate sleep time and irregular/delayed sleep pattern was likely to be related to poor sleep quality. In addition, their poor sleep quality also led to various daytime malfunctions such as increased depression-like symptoms and irritability, disturbed concentration, and daytime sleepiness, all of which possibly lead to students dozing off while attending classes or driving. The deterioration of academic performance, that is, low grade point average (GPA), is also related to the students' poor sleep habits. Many studies have suggested that inadequate sleep causes a decrease in cognitive performance such as the learning–memory process, which is essential for maintaining good academic performance (Curcio, Ferrara, & De Gennaro, 2006). It is speculated that the decrease in cognitive performance and the dozing off during classes due to inadequate night sleep lead to a low GPA. Moreover, interestingly, some studies have suggested that among university students, the sleep phase,

rather than the total sleep duration, has a stronger effect on their academic performance. A delayed bed off time, in particular, showed a strong association with poor academic performance (Eliasson, Lettieri, & Eliasson, 2010), and therefore, low GPA could be a result of absence from morning classes, which is attributable to the delayed sleep phase.

Factors influencing the sleep pattern of university students have been discussed in many studies. These studies showed that students' sleep patterns vary depending on their nationality, academic year, and their resident status, that is, whether they lived with or without their family. University students in Asian countries (Steptoe et al., 2006) and senior students (Asaoka, Fukuda, & Yamazaki, 2004; Hazama et al., 2008) have specifically been reported with poor sleep habits. A study using sleep logs showed that students who lived alone had a more delayed sleep phase on weekdays than those who lived with their families (Asaoka et al., 2004). In this study, there was no difference between these two groups in terms of the sleep phase on weekends, and the students living with their family had a longer commuting time than those living alone. Thus, existence of familial time cue and longer commuting time for the students who live with their family might be responsible for the early sleep phase in this group of students.

Daily activities such as watching television (TV), surfing the Internet, playing videogames, attending classes, and working part-time are also known determinants of sleep pattern. Many studies have suggested a relationship between the sleep pattern and these activities, especially during the night.

However, the extent to which each activity affects sleep patterns remains unknown. A study that investigated this issue in Japanese students through a time-use survey (Asaoka et al., 2010) showed that the influence of the daily activities on the students' sleep patterns differed between the students living alone and those living with their families. Among the students living alone, interpersonal communication late at night was most prominently associated with delayed bedtime. In addition, their sleep patterns seemed to change depending on the whether or not they had a class the next morning. On the other hand, students who lived with their family did not show change in their sleep patterns irrespective of their class schedules, and their sleep pattern was affected mainly by indoor activities such as watching TV and surfing the Internet. Although the differences between the two groups might partially depend on the existence/absence of familial time cue, further study is required to clarify the underlying cause of this phenomenon.

A good sleep pattern is an important factor for university students to maintain not only good health but also a good academic life, and hence, it is essential that their bedtime is not delayed. Previous studies have suggested that restricting the use of visual media and socializing activities at night could be effective in preventing the sleep-phase delay. Moreover, a revision of university schedules, such as the intensive morning schedules, may help in maintaining early bedtime, especially for the students living alone. However, most studies exploring the relationship between students' sleep pattern and the determinant factors were conducted by using cross-sectional questionnaires. Therefore, the causal relationships between the previously mentioned variables and students' sleep patterns are still unclear, despite the various studies. An intervention study was recently carried out, in which the duration of watching TV was restricted to 30 minutes or less per day for the university students (Asaoka, Fukuda, Tsutsui, & Yamazaki, 2007). The results showed that they went to bed 26 minutes earlier than their usual bedtime and increased their total nocturnal sleep time by 69 minutes; however, their morning physical activity declined after the intervention. This finding suggests that watching TV may be one of the important factors for delayed bedtime, but it may also play a role as a social time cue for maintaining regular sleep patterns, which help in maintaining their circadian rhythm. Future studies should be conducted to confirm whether restriction of other nocturnal activities such as surfing the Internet is helpful in both increasing students' sleep duration and preventing a delay in their bedtime.

Apart from the restrictions on nocturnal activities, education on good sleep habits is also essential to improve students' sleep habits. A previous study reported that a sleep education program that included sleep-hygiene guidelines, stimulus-control instructions, and information about caffeine products improved the sleep quality of the study participants (Brown, Buboltz, & Soper, 2006). Concurring with the phenomenon that sleep-deprived subjects cannot comprehend a decrease in the quality and quantity of their daily tasks, most university students with poor sleep habits are unaware of the fact that their poor academic performance is a result of their disturbed sleep patterns. In addition, a certain proportion of university students adopt irrational countermeasures for their deficient nocturnal sleep. For example, students try to compensate their sleep deficit by taking long daytime naps and/or prolonging their nocturnal sleep until the afternoon on weekends. Such behavior can disturb their sleep–wake rhythms, and possibly result in circadian-rhythm sleep disorders, especially DSPS. Therefore, sleep education that includes rational knowledge and the effects of sleep on the academic life and health of university students would be desirable.

Shoichi Asaoka and Yuichi Inoue

See also: entries related to Sleep and Development

References

Asaoka, S., Fukuda, K., Tsutsui, Y., & Yamazaki, K. (2007). Does television viewing cause delayed and/or irregular sleep-wake patterns? *Sleep and Biological Rhythms, 5*, 23–27.

Asaoka, S., Fukuda, K., & Yamazaki, K. (2004). Effects of sleep-wake pattern and residential status on psychological distress in university students. *Sleep and Biological Rhythms, 2*, 192–198.

Asaoka, S., Komada, Y., Fukuda, K., Sugiura, T., Inoue, Y., & Yamazaki, K. (2010). Exploring the daily activities associated with delayed bedtime of Japanese university students. *The Tohoku Journal of Experimental Medicine, 221*, 245–249.

Brown, F.C., Buboltz, W.C., Jr., & Soper, B. (2006). Development and evaluation of the Sleep Treatment and Education Program for Students (STEPS). *The Journal of American College Health, 54*, 231–237.

Curcio, G., Ferrara, M., & De Gennaro, L. (2006). Sleep loss, learning capacity and academic performance. *Sleep Medicine Reviews, 10*, 323–337.

Eliasson, A.H., Lettieri, C.J., & Eliasson, A.H. (2010). Early to bed, early to rise! Sleep habits and academic performance in college students. *Sleep and Breathing, 14*, 71–75.

Hazama, G.I., Inoue, Y., Kojima, K., Ueta, T., & Nakagome, K. (2008). The prevalence of probable delayed-sleep-phase syndrome in students from junior high school to university in Tottori, Japan. *The Tohoku Journal of Experimental Medicine, 216*, 95–98.

Lund, H.G., Reider, B.D., Whiting, A.B., & Prichard, J.R. (2010). Sleep patterns and predictors of disturbed sleep in a large population of college students. *Journal of Adolescent Health, 46*, 124–132.

Steptoe, A., Peacey, V., & Wardle, J. (2006). Sleep duration and health in young adults. *Archives of Internal Medicine, 166*, 1689–1692.

Sleep Patterns in Patients with Acute Coronary Syndromes

Sleep is essential for several restorative, metabolic, and immunologic functions. Restful sleep requires a normal sleep macro- and micro-architecture. There is plentiful scientific evidence to support the fact that sleep disruption leads to undesirable consequences (Banks & Dinger, 2007), especially for critically ill patients. Sleep disruption with acute quantitative or qualitative sleep deprivation, which has been studied mainly in healthy subjects, may impair physiological functions important for recovery, including tissue repair, overall cellular immune function (Oztürk et al., 1999), endocrine and metabolic functions (Spiegel, Leproult, & Van Cauter,

1999), and energy balance (Scrimshaw et al., 1966). In addition it can induce sympathetic activation and elevation of blood pressure (Leung & Bradley, 2001), which may contribute to patient morbidity. It is not difficult to imagine that an individual who has already become ill and requires hospitalization, such as a patient with acute coronary syndrome, should be more vulnerable to medical problems when sleep is disrupted. Research into the role of sleep and the effects of sleep deprivation in critically ill patients has been limited by confounding factors that make it difficult to quantify and isolate the effects of sleep on clinical recovery.

Sleep disruption in the intensive care unit (ICU), including the coronary care unit (CCU), is a well-recognized phenomenon that can have important adverse consequences for the critically ill patient. Patients experience severe alterations of sleep, with sleep loss, sleep fragmentation, and sleep–wake cycle disorganization. Many factors may contribute to these abnormalities, including environmental factors such as noise, patient care activities, disturbed light–dark cycle, medications (sedatives and inotropes), therapeutic and diagnostic procedures, and mechanical ventilation (Hardin, 2009); however, the contribution of each factor is not clear. The severity of the underlying disease is likely to be an important factor and needs to be determined.

Sleep can be assessed in terms of quantity (total sleep time and time spent in each sleep stage), quality (fragmentation due to micro-arousals, sleep-stage changes, wake after sleep onset, EEG sleep patterns), and distribution over the 24-hour cycle. Methods used to assess sleep include bedside inspection, patient's perception, polysomnography (PSG), and actigraphy. Attended overnight PSG remains the gold standard for sleep evaluation, but entails several technical difficulties and limitations when performed in the ICU environment, especially in patients recovering from critical illness. There are a number of studies evaluating sleep in critically ill patients, some involving polysomnographic recordings over 24 hours (Cooper et al., 2000; Freedman et al., 2001; Gabor et al., 2003), others with polysomnographic recordings during nighttime alone (Aaron et al., 1996; Broughton & Baron, 1978; Richards, Anderson, Chesson, & Nagel, 2002), and studies without polysomnographic recordings (Olson et al., 2001; Nelson et al., 2001). Investigators differ in their conclusions as to whether critically ill patients are sleep deprived, reporting large variations in total sleep time among patients in the ICU. Some studies found that critically ill patients have a normal or near normal total sleep time (Cooper et al., 2000; Freedman et al., 2001), while other investigators found a decrease in total sleep time (Gabor et al., 2003). The different findings among these studies may be due to different populations with different underlying medical and surgical problems, small groups of patients, or interference with the natural environment or routine treatment in ICU.

The quality and distribution of sleep over 24 hours are also affected, even in ICU hospitalized patients who have normal total sleep time. About half of total sleep time occurs in the daytime and the circadian rhythm is markedly impaired (Cooper et al., 2000; Gabor et al., 2003).

Critically ill patients exhibit more frequent arousals and awakenings than normal. The degree of sleep fragmentation is at least equivalent to that seen in patients with obstructive sleep apnea (Guilleminault et al., 1988). Additionally, an impairment in the distribution of sleep stages has been recognized. Critically ill patients spent less of their sleep time in rapid eye movement (REM) sleep or in Stages 3 and 4, known as slow-wave (SWS) or deep sleep, which is considered the most restorative type of sleep (Cooper et al., 2000; Freedman et al., 2001). Factors disturbing sleep, such as noise, may result in electroencephalographic arousals and awakenings, which may not only affect sleep microarchitecture but prevent the normal progress into deeper sleep stages (Carskadon & Dement, 2005). This disturbed sleep pattern may take several days to normalize after discharge from the ICU.

There is little knowledge about sleep quality impairment in patients admitted to the CCU with acute coronary syndromes (ACS). Early studies of patients in coronary care after acute myocardial infarction (MI), 30 years ago, had already recognized disturbed sleep architecture but suggested increased total sleep time (TST; Broughton & Baron, 1978; Dohno et al., 1979). Broughton et al., reported findings in 12 patients after an acute MI who underwent overnight PSGs in the ICU and thereafter in the ward, comparing them to matched controls (Broughton & Baron, 1978). The results were similar to other ICU patients, with increased wakefulness, more arousals and sleep-stage shifts, a low percentage of REM sleep, and an absence of the usual circadian variation in heart rate. There

were no sudden changes in sleep architecture after transfer to the general ward. However, the contributions of noise, patient-care activities, and disturbances of the light–dark exposure to sleep disruption in the CCU and general ward were not addressed specifically. Sleep abnormalities improved gradually over time with transfer to the hospital ward, even though normal sleep patterns were not restored in patients with acute MI until nine days after discharge from the ICU. The altered sleep patterns were largely attributed to the infarction itself. However, subsequent anginal attacks peaked at day 4 to day 5 and occurred more often during REM sleep. Similar results were obtained by Dohno et al. (1979), who observed sleep disruptions regardless of type of unit, length of hospitalization, gender, or medications in coronary patients in an open-ward CCU and in a semiprivate telemetry unit (Dohno et al., 1979). Moreover, they found that patients in the greater severity-of-illness group, as judged by a cardiologist, had more nocturnal awakenings and more sleep-stage changes, consistent with greater sleep fragmentation, than a comparable group with lesser severity of illness, indicating that severity of illness may turn out to be a very important cause of sleep disturbance in ICU patients.

In a more recent study, Ahmed BaHammam evaluated the sleep quality of 20 patients with acute MI within three days of the acute event and six months later, in the sleep disorder center, outside the CCU environment (BaHammam, 2006). Despite controlling for common sleep-disrupting environmental factors, patients with AMI had altered sleep architecture. Arousal index, spontaneous arousals, stage shifts, REM latency, and wake time were significantly greater, while TST, sleep efficiency, and (REM) sleep were significantly less during the acute event compared with six months later, findings that are in accordance with previous studies. The authors concluded that factors other than the CCU environment, patient care activities, mechanical ventilation, and medications are involved in sleep disruption, such as the underlying infarction itself. However, this study did not objectively assess the possible influence of circadian-rhythm disturbances, while the patients studied were heterogeneous with respect to concomitant sleep disorders, such as sleep-breathing disorders, restless legs syndrome (RLS), and periodic limb movement disorder (PLMD). The most recent study from our group assessed 22 patients with first ever ACS, who were not on sedation or inotropes, with attended overnight PSG in the sleep disorders unit within three days of the ACS and one and six months later (Schiza et al., 2010). This was the first study objectively controlled for circadian-rhythm disturbances and selected patients without concomitant diseases that could affect sleep architecture, such as RLS, PLMD, and current smoking. In accordance with the BaHammam study, TST, sleep efficiency, SWS, and REM sleep were significantly reduced and a significant impairment in sleep micro-architecture was noted due to an increased arousal index, during the acute event. Sleep architecture was improved one month later, while six months after the acute event sleep duration as well as sleep stages were within the normal ranges.

The findings of the previously mentioned studies highlight the major contribution of the illness severity and associated physiological and inflammatory changes to alterations in sleep architecture and deserve further research. The expression of many cytokines is unregulated in healing myocardial infarcts (Frangogiannis & Entman, 2005), with inflammatory cytokines having both somnogenic and sleep-inhibitory effects, and it has been reported to influence sleep and sleep depth (Krueger et al., 1995). It is known that proinflammatory cytokines, such as interleukin-1 (IL-1), IL-6, and tumor necrosis factor-alpha, are released after MI (Deten & Zimmer, 2002; Francis et al., 2004). It is worth noting that a recent study demonstrated that MI in rats is associated with the release of factors that provoke the inflammation of tissues, including the brain, and specifically the regions that control sleep, notably the REM-sleep phase (Bah et al., 2010). The authors reported decreased REM-sleep time, comparable with what has been observed in patients after MI (BaHammam, 2006; Dohno et al., 1979; Leung & Bradley, 2001; Schiza et al., 2010), which could be associated with a reduced number of brain stem neurons. However, the mechanisms by which brain stem neurons are lost after MI are unclear and need further investigation. One possibility is that proinflammatory cytokines could be involved in the decreased post-MI duration of REM sleep reported here, through apoptosis in the cholinergic neurons in the brain stem, which control REM sleep. This study indicates that the damaging effects of MI are apparently not confined to the heart, but also affect the brain. Furthermore, it might provide useful data related to the association between cardiac pathophysiology and sleep alterations in such patients.

It seems likely that sleep is important to the recovery process as an integral homeostatic mechanism. Indeed, it is well known that sleep plays a crucial role in postinfarction remission. Quality rather than quantity of sleep should be our primary target in the management of sleep disruption in ACS. Any preventive, pharmacological, or behavioral treatment is certainly a pathway that should be considered. However, research into the effects of protocols that enhance the quantity and quality of sleep during recovery from critical illness or injury are lacking. It remains to be determined whether improving sleep will have an impact on ACS.

In conclusion, sleep in patients with ACS poses unique challenges for patients, clinicians, and researchers. These patients experience severe sleep alterations, with reductions in several sleep stages, marked sleep fragmentation, and circadian-rhythm disorganization. The impact of these acute sleep alterations on the health of ICU patients remains unknown. These effects may delay recovery and decrease the chances for a positive outcome, but it remains to be determined if improving sleep will have an impact on patients with ACS.

Sophia E. Schiza

See also: entries related to Sleep Disorders

References

Aaron, J.N., Carlisle, C.C., Carskadon, M.A., Meyer, T.J., et al. (1996). Environmental noise as a cause of sleep disruption in an intermediate respiratory care unit. *Sleep, 19,* 707–710.

Bah, T.M., Laplante, F., Wann, B.P., Sullivan, R., et al. (2010). Paradoxical sleep insomnia and decreased cholinergic neurons after myocardial infarction in rats. *Sleep, 1*(33), 1703–1710.

BaHammam, A. (2006). Sleep quality of patients with acute myocardial infarction outside the CCU environment: A preliminary study. *Medical Science Monitor, 12,* 168–172.

Banks, S., & Dinger, D.F. (2007). Behavioral and physiological consequences of sleep restriction. *Journal of Clinical Sleep Medicine, 3,* 519–528.

Broughton, R., & Baron, R. (1978). Sleep patterns in the intensive care unit and on the ward after acute myocardial infarction. *Electroencephalography and Clinical Neurophysiology, 45,* 348–360.

Carskadon, M.A., & Dement, W.C. (2005). Normal human sleep: An overview. In M. Kryger, T. Roth, & W.C. Dement (Eds.), *Principles and practice of sleep medicine* (pp. 13–23). Philadelphia, PA: WB Saunders.

Cooper, A.B., Thornley, K.S., Young, G.B., Slutsky, A.S., et al. (2000). Sleep in critically ill patients requiring mechanical ventilation. *Chest, 117,* 809–818.

Deten, A., & Zimmer, H.-G. (2002). Heart function and cytokine expression is similar in mice and rats after myocardial infarction but differences occur in TNFalpha expression. *Pflugers Archives, 445,* 289–296.

Dohno, S., Paskewitz, D.A., Lynch, J.J., Kenneth, S., et al. (1979). Some aspects of sleep disturbance in coronary patients. *Perceptual and Motor Skills, 48,* 199–205.

Francis, J., Chu, Y., Johnson, A.K., Weiss, R.M., et al. (2004). Acute myocardial infarction induces hypothalamic cytokine synthesis. *American Journal of Physiology Heart and Circulatory Physiology, 286,* H2264–H2271.

Frangogiannis, N.G., & Entman, M.L. (2005). Chemokines in myocardial ischemia. *Trends in Cardiovascular Medicine, 15,* 163–169.

Freedman, N.S., Gazendam, J., Levan, L., Pack, A.I., et al. (2001). Abnormal sleep/wake cycles and the effect of environmental noise on sleep disruption in the intensive care unit. *American Journal of Respiratory and Critical Care Medicine, 163,* 451–457.

Gabor, J.Y., Cooper, A.B., Crombach, S.A., Lee, B., et al. (2003). Contribution of the intensive care unit environment to sleep disruption in mechanically ventilated patients and healthy subjects. *American Journal of Respiratory and Critical Care Medicine, 167,* 708–715.

Guilleminault, C., Partinen, M., Quera-Salva, M.A., Hyes, B., et al. (1988). Determinants of daytime sleepiness in obstructive sleep apnea. *Chest, 94,* 32–37.

Hardin, K.A. (2009). Sleep in the ICU: Potential mechanisms and clinical implications. *Chest, 136,* 284–294.

Krueger, J.M., Takahashi, S., Kapas, L., Bredow, S., et al. (1995). Cytokines in sleep regulation. *Advances in Neuroimmunology, 5,* 171–188.

Leung, R.S., & Bradley, T.D. (2001). Sleep apnea and cardiovascular disease. *American Journal of Respiratory and Critical Care Medicine, 164,* 2147–2165.

Nelson, J.E., Meier, D.E., Oei, E.J., Nierman, D.M., et al. (2001). Self-reported symptoms experience of critically ill cancer patients receiving intensive care. *Critical Care Medicine, 29,* 277–282.

Olson, D.M., Borel, C.O., Laskowitz, D.T., Moore, D.T., et al. (2001). Quiet time: A nursing intervention to promote sleep in neurocritical care units. *American Journal of Critical Care, 10,* 74–78.

Oztürk, L., Pelin, Z., Karadeniz, D., Kaynak, H., et al. (1999). Effects of 48 hours sleep deprivation on human immune profile. *Sleep Research Online, 2,* 107–111.

Richards, K.C., Anderson, W.M., Chesson, A.L., & Nagel, C.L. (2002). Sleep related breathing disorders in patients who are critically ill. *Journal of Cardiovascular Nursing, 17,* 42–55.

Schiza, S.E., Simantirakis, E., Bouloukaki, I, Mermigkis, C., et al. (2010). Sleep patterns in patients with acute coronary syndromes. *Sleep Medicine, 11,* 149–153.

Scrimshaw, N.S., Habicht, J.-P., Pellet, P., Piche, M.L., et al. (1966). Effects of sleep deprivation and reversal of diurnal activity on protein metabolism of young men. *American Journal of Clinical Nutrition, 19,* 313–319.

Spiegel, K., Leproult, R., & Van Cauter, D. (1999). Impact of sleep dept on metabolic and endocrine function. *Lancet, 354,* 1435–1439.

Sleep, Plasticity, and Metaplasticity

Throughout a lifetime of experience, our knowledge base and skills continue to evolve in a dynamic and flexible way. Fundamentally, such information storage and memory is represented in the brain by the strength of the connections, or synapses, between neurons within neuronal circuits. When synapses are strengthened, communication is enhanced, and neural activity generates stronger responses in connected neurons; when synapses are weakened, the evoked responses in connected neurons are reduced. Plasticity is a term used to describe these changes in the strength of neural connections as a result of experience. Metaplasticity reflects the regulation of plasticity, or a shift in the capacity for a synapse to undergo future plasticity based on its recent history (Abraham, 2008).

A growing body of literature suggests that sleep may engage processes of plasticity. Plasticity is not a unitary phenomenon, taking many different forms and reflecting diverse molecular and cellular mechanisms. Similarly, sleep is not a homogenous state, encompassing distinct stages and a variety of electrophysiological processes. The complexity of these physiological processes suggest that there may be multiple mechanisms linking sleep and plasticity, potentially explaining the difficulty in establishing a unified conceptual framework to reconcile conflicting findings in the sleep and memory literature (Rauchs, Desgranges, Foret, & Eustache, 2005). In recent years, two dominant models in the field have emerged. The first model involves reactivation or replay during sleep of neuronal firing patterns experienced during recent wakefulness. For example, sequences of neuronal activity patterns recorded from different brain areas of rats while they are learning to navigate a maze show coordinated replay during subsequent slow-wave sleep (Ji & Wilson, 2007). Such reactivation or replay can promote a use-dependent strengthening of synaptic connections, enhancing recently acquired memories for facts, events, and skills. The second model is known as the synaptic homeostasis hypothesis (Tononi & Cirelli, 2003). This model suggests that wakefulness is associated with widespread increases in synaptic strength, which taxes finite space and energy resources in the brain. Sleep, and in particular slow-wave sleep, is proposed to cause a general downscaling, or weakening, of synaptic strength to restore synaptic balance while maintaining the relative connection strengths. In this model, the general weakening of connections during sleep reduces the background noise in neural activity, and improved

signal-to-noise ratio can have a benefit on memory recall. These models are not mutually exclusive, potentially reflecting simultaneous and complementary processes.

The relationship between metaplasticity and sleep has not been well studied, with only one recent study in humans (Cohen et al., 2010). That study used noninvasive brain stimulation to induce plasticity in the motor cortex, evidenced by the change in the size of evoked motor responses measured in the hand. Each participant had two plasticity-induction sessions spaced 12 hours apart, either over day or overnight. This study demonstrated that a night with sleep was associated with a twofold increase in the magnitude of the evoked motor response in the second session compared to the first. In contrast, in the over-day group, the degree of induced plasticity was the same for both sessions. In other words, a night with sleep enhanced the capacity for the brain to undergo subsequent plasticity when the same environmental exposure was repeated.

In conclusion, sleep appears to engage processes of plasticity to modify existing knowledge and skills, either through neuronal replay, general synaptic downscaling, or perhaps other mechanisms. In addition, sleep may engage processes of metaplasticity such that synapses may become more responsive to undergo future changes in response to a given stimulus, perhaps one mechanism in which sleep could promote the process of learning to learn. A greater understanding of how sleep engages the processes of plasticity and metaplasticity can have widespread applications from education and training to rehabilitation of patients after neurological injury. Future work should also target the role of the circadian timekeeping system or its interaction with sleep state to modulate plasticity.

Daniel Aaron Cohen

See also: Sleep, Memory, and Dreams

References

Abraham, W. C. (2008). Metaplasticity: Tuning synapses and networks for plasticity. *Nature Reviews Neuroscience, 9*(5), 387–399.

Cohen, D. A., Freitas, C., Tormos, J. M., Oberman, L., Eldaief, M., & Pascual-Leone, A. (2010). Enhancing plasticity through repeated rTMS sessions: The benefits of a night of sleep. *Clinical Neurophysiology, 121*(12), 2159–2164.

Ji, D., & Wilson, M. A. (2007). Coordinated memory replay in the visual cortex and hippocampus during sleep. *Nature Neuroscience, 10*(1), 100–107.

Rauchs, G., Desgranges, B., Foret, J., & Eustache, F. (2005). The relationships between memory systems and sleep stages. *Journal of Sleep Research, 14*(2), 123–140.

Tononi, G., & Cirelli, C. (2003). Sleep and synaptic homeostasis: A hypothesis. *Brain Research Bulletin, 62*(2), 143–150.

Sleep Problems among Veterans of Foreign Wars

People who witness or participate in combat are exposed to levels of violence and trauma the rest of us can only imagine. In wars past, very little help was available for the veteran who experienced postcombat mental and sleep problems. From a policy point of view, this past neglect of postcombat mental problems was unfortunate, as these sorts of problems eventually extract a cost to both military effectiveness and civilian economic performance due to the impaired functioning of affected individuals. We now have a name for one form of the array of postcombat mental problems that affect our veterans. That name of course is posttraumatic stress disorder, or PTSD. One of the core symptoms of PTSD is sleep disturbance.

PTSD is a major health concern for the Veterans Administration (VA) and the veterans it serves. A 2005 report from the VA's Office of the Inspector General noted that the number of veterans receiving compensation for PTSD between 1999 and 2004 grew to 215,871 cases (Department of Veterans Affairs [DVA], 2005). Review of state variances in VA disability compensation payments (DVA, 2005), and continued increases are likely to have occurred with the subsequent intensification of the wars in Iraq and Afghanistan. Rates of PTSD diagnoses are likely to dramatically increase due to the ongoing Iraq/Afghan wars and indeed due to wars around the world. Surveys show that at least 11 to 17 percent of combat veterans are at risk for mental disorders, including PTSD, in the three to four months after return from combat duty and probably for much longer periods of time after return. One such survey assessed 16,318 Afghan veterans and 222,620 Iraq veterans and found that 19.1 percent returnees from Iraq compared with 11.3 percent returnees from Afghanistan screened positive for mental health problems, including PTSD. Thirty-five percent of Iraq war veterans accessed mental health services in the year after returning home; 12 percent per year were diagnosed with a mental health problem. Roughly 20 percent of active and 42.4 percent of reserve component soldiers required mental health treatment. Of 103,788 operation enduring freedom veterans seen at VA health care facilities, 25,658 (25%) received psychiatric diagnoses, including PTSD; 56 percent of whom had two or more distinct mental health diagnoses. Overall, 31 percent received mental health and/or psychosocial diagnoses. In a later study, Seal et al. (2007) found that among 750 Iraq and Afghanistan veterans who were referred to a VA medical center and five associated community clinics, 338 underwent postdeployment screening with 233 (69%) screening positive for mental health problems.

New treatment approaches are desperately needed to meet the mental health needs of the veteran population. Studies of sleep contributions to PTSD symptoms hold promise for developing better diagnostic techniques for PTSD and for developing innovative treatment approaches to PTSD and other mental health disorders of returning vets. Identifying specific effects of sleep disturbance on PTSD symptoms in the home environment should be considered as well since nightmares are more likely to occur in the home environment than in the sleep lab. Investigators should seek to clarify the role of sleep dysregulation in production of PTSD symptomology and thus allow for better and more targeted therapeutic interventions for PTSD. REM sleep-related measures such as REM-sleep density and REM-sleep dreams and nightmares are significant predictors of suicidal ideation in patients with trauma and in depressed individuals. Some individuals with sleep problems and with PTSD are at greater risk for suicidal ideation. If a clinician monitored such REM sleep and

dream-related indicators in individuals at risk for suicide, he or she could potentially identify early warning signs of new ideation around suicide and could therefore act to prevent a new suicide attempt. Individuals who have served their country in combat deserve to have their sleep problems seriously and conscientiously addressed by the health care system whose mission it is to serve veterans.

Patrick McNamara

See also: entries related to PTSD and Dreams/Sleep

References

Department of Veterans Affairs (DVA). (2005) Report no. 05–00765–137. Washington, DC: VA Office of Inspector General.

Seal, K. H., Bertenthal, D., Maguen, S., Gima, K., Chu, A., & Marmar, C. R. (2008). Administration postdeployment mental health screening of veterans returning from Iraq and Afghanistan. *American Journal of Public Health, 108*(4), 40–47.

Seal, K. H., Bertenthal, D., Miner, C. R., Sen, S., & Marmar, C. R. (2007). Bringing the war back home: Mental health disorders among 103,788 US veterans returning from Iraq and Afghanistan seen at Department of Veterans Affair facilities. *Archives of Internal Medicine, 167*(5), 476–482.

Sleep, Psychiatric Disorders, and the Transdiagnostic Perspective

It is unequivocally the case that sleep disturbance commonly co-occurs with psychiatric disorders. Insomnia, the most common sleep disturbance, is an ongoing difficulty initiating sleep, maintaining sleep, waking up too early, or experiencing chronically nonrestorative sleep. Insomnia is listed as a symptom in the current definition of many psychiatric disorders and there are many other disorders where insomnia is not listed as a formal symptom but insomnia is a known common feature. The goal of this article is to address two questions that arise from recognizing the comorbidity between insomnia and psychiatric disorders: (1) is insomnia an epiphenomenon or a mechanism and (2) is insomnia transdiagnostic?

Is Insomnia an Epiphenomenon or a Mechanism?

A widely held assumption is that insomnia is secondary to, or an epiphenomenon of, the so-called primary psychiatric disorder. However, evidence has accumulated to indicate that insomnia is not an epiphenomenon, but is often a key mechanism contributing to the multifactorial causation of psychiatric disorders. Specifically, insomnia is a risk factor for, and can contribute to, the development and/or maintenance of psychiatric disorders. Second, there is substantial evidence that insomnia impairs quality of life and incurs great personal costs due to economic and social disability. Third, evidence from the sleep-deprivation literature indicates that one of the strongest adverse effects of sleep deprivation is increased negative mood. Finally, studies have shown adverse effects of sleep deprivation on cognitive functioning, which may impair problem-solving ability. Moreover, it seems likely that there is a bidirectional sleep and mood relationship whereby an escalating cycle of disturbance in mood and symptoms during the

day interferes with nighttime sleep, which in turn contributes to mood regulation difficulty and symptoms on the subsequent day (Harvey, 2008).

Is Insomnia Transdiagnostic?

There has been a resurgence of interest in explicitly identifying and studying the common, or transdiagnostic, processes across psychiatric disorders. This is in contrast to the disorder focused approach often taken in which classification systems and research programs tend to specialize in one disorder, seeking to systematically illuminate that one disorder's cause, maintenance, and treatment. We propose that consideration be given to insomnia as a transdiagnostic process on the basis of (1) the high rates of co-occurrence between insomnia and psychiatric disorders, (2) the evidence across a range of disorders that the insomnia is not an epiphenomenon but contributes to onset, relapse, and maintenance, and (3) the transdiagnostic applicability of the bidirectional sleep and mood framework.

The advantages of explicitly recognizing insomnia as a transdiagnostic process are threefold. First, the results of the National Comorbidity Survey make a strong case for the relative rarity of pure cases. The majority of the lifetime disorders are comorbid disorders. A transdiagnostic perspective argues that perhaps disorders co-occur because they share common mechanisms (e.g., insomnia). Second, if some psychiatric disorders are similar with respect to the processes that maintain them, then advances made in the context of one disorder will be more rapidly tested for their application to other disorders. Third, a transdiagnostic approach might lead to the specification of a single treatment or treatment components that are effective across a wide range of disorders (Harvey, 2008).

Treatment Implications

Is it possible to develop one transdiagnostic treatment protocol that effectively treats insomnia in all psychiatric disorders? This is important, as developing and disseminating transdiagnostic treatment protocols would have massive public health implications by reducing the heavy burden on clinicians, who must already learn multiple treatment protocols that often share many common theoretical underpinnings and interventions. Also, given the association between poor sleep and impaired quality of life, it is possible that improving sleep improves the functioning of individuals with a range of psychiatric disorders. Finally, if insomnia and the symptoms/processes of psychiatric disorders are mutually maintaining, then does a transdiagnostic treatment also reduce symptoms and processes associated with the comorbid psychiatric disorder? One landmark study suggests the answer to the latter question is a resounding yes! Depression outcomes were substantially improved by administering the frontline treatment for insomnia, namely cognitive-behavioral therapy for insomnia (Manber et al., 2008).

Jennifer C. Kanady and
Allison G. Harvey

See also: entries related to Sleep Disorders

References

Harvey, A.G. (2008). Insomnia, psychiatric disorders, and the transdiagnostic perspective. *Current Directions in Psychological Science, 17,* 299–303.

Manber, R., Edinger, J., Gress J., San Peddro-Salcedo, M., Kuo, T., & Kalista, T. (2008). Cognitive behavioral therapy for insomnia enhances depression outcome in patients with comorbid major depressive disorder and insomnia. *Sleep, 31,* 489–495.

Sleep Quality: A Behavioral Genetic Perspective

Sleep quality refers to a collection of measurements of sleep including sleep latency (the time in minutes taken to get to sleep), sleep duration, sleep efficiency (time in bed divided by total sleep time), number of disturbances from sleep such as awakenings due to bad dreams or poor comfort, and the daytime effects of a poor night's sleep, among others. Subjective sleep quality is often assessed by self-report questionnaires and has widely been assessed by the Pittsburgh Sleep Quality Index (PSQI: Buysse, Reynolds, Monk, Berman, & Kupfer, 1989). The PSQI taps into seven components of sleep that can be combined to yield an overall measure of sleep quality. Sleep quality varies between individuals and this variation is accounted for by a combination of genetic and environmental influences. Behavioral genetic studies using twins provide a useful tool for assessing the relative contribution of genes and environments to any trait under study. By comparing the similarity within monozygotic twins (who share 100% of their genes) to the similarity within dizygotic twins (who share on average 50% of their segregating genes) on a trait, twin studies allow us to determine the relative contribution of additive genetic (the extent to which genes add up to influence behavior), shared environmental (environments that act to make twins within a pair similar), and nonshared environmental (environments that contribute to twin dissimilarity) influences on a trait. Using this technique, genetic influences have been found to account for around 33 to 44 percent of the variance in subjective sleep quality (Heath, Kendler, Eaves, & Martin, 1990; Partinen, Kaprio, Koskenvuo, Putoken, & Langinvainio, 1983). These heritability estimates can be directly compared to those of other phenotypes such as IQ—the heritability of which has been estimated to be between 50 and 90 percent. The remaining source of variance in sleep quality is largely accounted for by the nonshared environment. Such environmental influences may include negative life events, family conflict, relationship issues, ill health, or unemployment—all of which are known to be associated with poor sleep quality.

Objective measures of sleep quality can also be obtained using polysomnography. The latency, duration, and nightly patterns of the four sleep stages, as well as rapid eye movement sleep (REM), may give an indication of sleep quality. Using a twin design, Linkowski (1999) observed that genetic influences accounted for around 50 percent of the variation in Stages 2, 4, and delta sleep, although evidence for genetic effects on REM sleep was inconclusive. While this does not directly inform us about quality of sleep, it demonstrates that sleep patterns are significantly under genetic control, and that regularity in sleep stages may be important for good sleep quality.

Recent work has aimed to further understand the individual components of sleep quality. Barclay and colleagues (2010) examined the extent to which genes and environments account for the individual components of sleep quality, the phenotypic associations between them, and the overlap in the genetic and environmental influences accounting for the associations. Genetic influences accounted for between 30 and 47 percent of variance in the individual components, although there was no evidence for genetic effects on sleep duration. It is likely that since sleep length is largely under voluntary control, environmental influences contribute a greater extent. Consequently the effect of genes is attenuated by social pressures to stay out late at night coupled with the need to arise early in the morning—thus reducing one's sleep length. The individual components of sleep quality were largely correlated, which demonstrates that each of these aspects of sleep contribute to an underlying construct. Furthermore, genetic overlap between the components was substantial, which suggests that similar genes may be responsible for different aspects of sleep quality. Behavioral genetic studies assessing the genetic overlap between traits may help to guide molecular genetics. Knowledge of the genes influencing one aspect of sleep may be useful for identifying genes associated with correlated symptoms. Future studies aimed at identifying specific gene variants implicated in different aspects of sleep are necessary to further understand the complex processes underlying sleep quality.

Nicola L. Barclay

See also: entries related to Genetics of Sleep

References

Barclay, N.L., Eley, T.C., Buysse, D.J., Rijsdijk, F.V., & Gregory, A.M. (2010). Genetic and environmental influences on different components of the "Pittsburgh Sleep Quality Index" and their overlap. *Sleep, 33,* 659–668.

Buysse, D.J., Reynolds, C.F., Monk, T.H., Berman, S.R., & Kupfer, D.J. (1989). The Pittsburgh Sleep Quality Index: A new instrument for psychiatric practice and research. *Psychiatry Research, 28,* 192–213.

Heath, A.C., Kendler, K.S., Eaves, L.J., & Martin, N.G. (1990). Evidence for genetic influences on sleep disturbance and sleep pattern in twins. *Sleep, 13,* 318–335.

Linkowski, O. (1999). EEG sleep patterns in twins. *Journal of Sleep Research, 8,* 11–13.

Partinen, M., Kaprio, J., Koskenvuo, M., Putoken, P., & Langinvainio, H. (1983). Genetic and environmental determination of human sleep. *Sleep, 6,* 179–185.

Sleep-Related Hallucinations and Ghost Tales

Though there are many ghost stories in various cultures around the world, the pathogenesis of a few types remains to be figured out. One is the hypnagogic hallucination, usually observed in narcolepsy, when experienced by normal people without other diagnostic criteria. The other is highway hypnosis, in which fear is a component. Highway hypnosis is illustrated by tales such as "The Vanishing Hitchhiker" in the United States and "The Ghost Getting into the Taxi" in Japan (Furuya et al., 2009; Kon-no, 1975). Recently, we suggested the possibility that the vivid visual hallucinations seen in progressive posterior cortical atrophy (PCA) share a similar mechanism with some of the ghost tales experienced by normal people (Furuya, Ikezoe, Ohyagi, Miyoshi, & Fujii, 2006). Furthermore, reports of REM sleep behavior disorder or somnambulism (sleepwalking) (RBDS) are becoming more common (Stores, 2007).

Based on several review papers (Fuyuya et al., 2006; Stores, 2007), we developed diagnostic criteria consisting of central and core features to classify the ghost tales as far as possible into the four types described in Table 8.

Classification of Four Types of Hallucination

Hypnagogic Hallucination–Like Ghost Tales (HyH)

This type of hallucination is in principle the hypnagogic hallucination that occurs in narcolepsy patients. The ghost image is not vivid but often rather vague, and it is sometimes accompanied by a cenesthopathy such as an incubus/succubus, a sense of being touched. The ghost sometimes speaks, makes a noise, or shakes the bed or room, and on rare occasions, converses with the sleeper.

Highway Hypnosis–Like Ghost Tales (HHy)

Highway hypnosis (white-line fever or the vanishing hitchhiker) has been defined as a tendency to become drowsy and suddenly

Table 8: Major Criteria for Classification of Ghost Tales of Normal People. (Three core features are sufficient for a definite diagnosis, two for a probable diagnosis, and one for a possible diagnosis.)

1. **Hypnagogic hallucination–like ghost tales (HyH)**

    Central features (essential for a diagnosis of HyH): HyH appears while the experiencer is sleeping or when they are waking from sleep.

    Core features:
    a. The image of the ghost is clear or vague but not very vivid.
    b. It sometimes accompanied by cenesthopathy such as an incubus/succubus, a feeling of being touched or a feeling of breathed on.
    c. The ghost sometimes speaks, makes a noise, or converses with the experiencer.

    Differential diagnosis: narcolepsy, schizophrenia

2. **Highway hypnosis–like ghost tales (HHy)**

    Central features (essential for a diagnosis of HHy): HHy is a tendency to become drowsy and suddenly fall asleep, sometimes into the REM stage, when driving an automobile. In HHy, the conscious and subconscious minds appear to concentrate on different things. Thus, this hallucination appears while the experiencer does not recognize the change of consciousness level.

    Core features:
    a. The sleep- or trance-like state can occur with the driver (experiencer) sitting in an upright position and staring ahead.
    b. The image of ghost is usually clear but sometimes vague.
    c. The ghost sometimes speaks or has a conversation with the experiencer.

    Differential diagnosis: complex partial seizure, temporal lobe epilepsy

3. **REM sleep behavior disorder or somnambulism-like ghost tales (RBDS)**

    Central features (essential for a diagnosis of RBDS): In REM sleep behavior disorder, the loss of motor inhibition leads to a wide spectrum of behaviors during sleep. In the case of somnambulism, it is usually defined by or involves the person performing normal actions as if awake. Thus, RBDS is closely related to sleep.

    Core features:
    a. The experiencer of RBD often has a dream at the same time, which convinces him/her that the events were real.
    b. The experiencer notices an abnormality in the bedroom or the experiencer himself or a bed partner after awakening, when the RBD is accompanied by somnambulism.
    c. The image of ghost is not as clear as it is in HHy because it is a part of dream.

    Differential diagnosis: early stage of dementia with Lewy bodies (DLB, parkinsonism), drug abuse (including alcoholism), malingering disorder

4. **Vivid hallucination–like ghost tales (VH)**

    Central features (essential for a diagnosis of VH): VH is similar to the hallucination occurred in a patient with DLB or Charles-Bonnet syndrome (CBD). The ghost appears without any relation to sleep.

(Continued)

Table 8: Major Criteria for Classification of Ghost Tales of Normal People. (Three core features are sufficient for a definite diagnosis, two for a probable diagnosis, and one for a possible diagnosis.) *(Continued)*

Core features:
  a. The image of the ghost is clear or vivid.
  b. Hallucinations are purely visual (i.e., the ghost never talks or tries to touch the experiencer.)
  c. The ghost vanishes into air when the experiencer tries to touch it or throw something at the ghost.
Differential diagnosis: early stage DLB (parkinsonism), CBD, drug abuser (including alcoholism), schizophrenia

fall asleep, sometimes into the REM stage, while driving an automobile (Furuya et al., 2009). Theoretically, highway hypnosis is a kind of mental state that also occurs when a person concentrates on a simple mechanical task, so it may happen relatively frequently and in common situations; for example, workers performing simple repetitive tasks while deprived of sleep and walkers concentrating on the road at night using the faint light of a lantern may experience highway hypnosis. Thus, this type of hallucination seems to be unrelated to sleep at first, and the hallucinator does not recognize the change in his or her consciousness level. The image of the ghost is usually clear but sometimes vague.

REM Sleep Behavior Disorder or Somnambulism-Like Ghost Tales (RBDS)

In REM sleep behavior disorder, the loss of motor inhibition leads to a wide spectrum of behaviors during sleep. Somnambulism is usually defined by or involves the person performing normal actions as if awake (walking, opening/closing a door or window, and other acts) (Stores, 2007). The sleeper thinks that someone or something

like a ghost or monstrous creature has entered in the bedroom and done something. Thus, RBDS is closely related to sleep.

Vivid Hallucination-Like Ghost Tales (VH)

Vivid hallucination is similar to the hallucinations that occur in patients with dementia with Lewy bodies, some types of PCA, and Charles-Bonnet syndrome (Furuya et al., 2006; Stores, 2007). The ghost appears without any relationship to sleep at first and is a purely visual hallucination.

Classification and Analysis of Ghost Tales

We analyzed 183 reliable ghost tales collected by Japanese folklorists from 1900 to 1970 (Kon-no, 1975; Yanagita, 2006) and found that 66.1 percent of the tales of ghosts could be classified into the four types listed (see Table 8) (Furuya et al., 2009); 32.2 percent were sleep related (HyH and RBDS), and 35.0 percent were not sleep related (HHy and VH) (Furuya et al., 2009).

Conclusion

We propose the possibility that almost two thirds of ghost tales may be classified into one of four types of hallucinations experienced by normal people, which means that most of them are attributable to the same mechanisms as neurophysiological and neurodegenerative or psychological disorders.

Akihiro Watanabe and Hirokazu Furuya

See also: entries related to Sleep Disorders

References

Furuya, H., Ikezoe, K., Ohyagi, Y., Miyoshi, T., & Fujii, N. (2006). A case of progressive posterior cortical atrophy (PCA) with vivid hallucination: Are some ghost tales vivid hallucinations in normal people? *Journal of Neurology, Neurosurgery, and Psychiatry, 77,* 424–425.

Furuya, H., Ikezoe, K., Shigeto, H., et al. (2009). Sleep- and non-sleep-related hallucinations—Relationship to ghost tales and their classifications. *Dreaming, 19,* 232–238.

Kon-no, E. (1975). *Nihon Kaidan Syu [Ghosts tales in Japan]* (1st ed.). Tokyo, Japan: Syakaishisou-sya (in Japanese).

Stores, G. (2007). Clinical diagnosis and misdiagnosis of sleep disorders. *Journal of Neurology, Neurosurgery, and Psychiatry, 78,* 1293–1297.

Yanagita, K. (2006). *Toh-no Monogatari [The "Toh-no" Folktales]* (8th ed.). Tokyo, Japan: Kadokawa-Shoten (in Japanese).

Ghost of Oyuki (artist unknown, but presented as a work of Maruyama Ōkyo, 1733–1795; Japanese artist) (Hanging scroll picture: ink and colors on paper). Note the vague image of the lower part of the body, corresponding to the hypnagogic hallucination-like ghost (HyH; Table). (Extended loan to the University of California, Berkeley Art Museum from a private collection)

Sleep-Related Mental Activities in Insomnia: Role and Assessment

Insomnia is a widespread complaint affecting about 10 percent of the general population on a chronic basis. Insomnia is commonly explained by a hyperarousal state, present at bedtime, which could be cognitive as well as physiological, that interferes with normal sleep. Frequently, sleep habits and mental activities are modified following a night where insomnia is experienced to try to cope with the situation. Therefore, as time passes, sleep habits, environment (such as a bedroom or bedtime), and even mental activities become, by association, stimuli related to sleep disturbance and produce an insomnia state via a learning process (Morin, 1993). Sleep-related mental activities such as faulty beliefs, worry, attribution, attentional bias, sleep perception, and expectation play an important mediating role in perpetuating and exacerbating insomnia (Harvey, Tang, & Browning, 2005; Morin, 1993). To date, it is acknowledged that mental activities might contribute to cognitive arousal at bedtime (Harvey et al., 2005). For instance, some insomnia sufferers tend to have unrealistic expectations about their sleep requirements and worry excessively when such requirements are not met. Others fear the potential consequences of insomnia on their daytime functioning and tend to selectively channel their attention toward any evidence of such consequences. Some also evaluate quality of their sleep upon awakening in the morning and will modify their daily functioning according to their first sleep perception. However, such faulty expectations, perceptions, and excessive worry are producing emotional distress and heightening arousal, and will in turn feed the vicious cycle of insomnia.

A growing number of researchers and clinicians are recognizing the potential role of sleep-disruptive cognitions in insomnia and are thus incorporating cognitive therapy as a therapeutic component of psychological interventions for insomnia. Some clinical trials have shown that these therapeutic targets, including faulty beliefs and attitudes about sleep, are responsive to treatment and may actually play an important mediating role in reducing insomnia symptoms and in maintaining sleep improvements over time (Edinger, Wohlgemuth, Radtke, Marsh, & Quillian, 2001). To be able to assess these thoughts and beliefs related to insomnia, specific inventories or questionnaires are needed. Such inventories will help in evaluating patients' responses to insomnia treatment, which is of great clinical value. One of the first questionnaires related to thoughts in the context of insomnia was developed in 1993 and is called *Dysfunctional Beliefs and Attitudes about Sleep* questionnaire (Morin, 1993). It comprises 36 items evaluating five dimensions of beliefs. Later, several shorter versions of this questionnaire were developed, the most recent being the DBAS-16 (Morin, Vallieres, & Ivers, 2007). The DBAS-30 is also translated into several languages and is widely used around the world. This questionnaire, which possesses adequate psychometric properties, is an essential tool in evaluating beliefs and thoughts pertaining to insomnia. Other questionnaires targeting cognitive process at bedtime or cognitive arousal have also been developed. To name only a couple there are the presleep arousal scale (Nicassio, Mendlowitz, Fussell, & Petras, 1985) and Glasgow Content of Thoughts Inventory (Harvey & Espie, 2004).

In summary, the role mental activities play in insomnia is well acknowledged although not yet clearly understood and demonstrated. Sleep-related mental activities include cognitions such as sleep perception, attentional bias, worry, and specific faulty beliefs about sleep. Moreover, given the importance attributed to cognitive process, it would be warranted to evaluate the unique contribution of cognitive intervention alone to insomnia as it has not yet been assessed. Finally, a theoretical model that includes the full range of potentially involved cognitive processes is warranted to provide a global view of mental activities in insomnia.

Annie Vallières

See also: entries related to Sleep Disorders

References

Edinger, J.D., Wohlgemuth, W.K., Radtke, R.A., Marsh, G.R., & Quillian, R.E. (2001). Does cognitive-behavioral insomnia therapy alter dysfunctional beliefs about sleep? *Sleep, 24,* 591–599.

Harvey, A.G., Tang, N.K., & Browning, L. (2005). Cognitive approaches to insomnia. *Clinical Psychology Review, 25,* 593–611.

Harvey, K.J., & Espie, C.A. (2004). Development and preliminary validation of the Glasgow Content of Thoughts Inventory (GCTI): A new measure for the assessment of pre-sleep cognitive activity. *British Journal of Clinical Psychology, 43,* 409–420.

Morin, C.M. (1993). *Insomnia: Psychological assessment and management.* New York: The Guilford Press.

Morin, C.M., Vallieres, A., & Ivers, H. (2007). Dysfunctional beliefs and attitudes about sleep (DBAS): Validation of a brief version (DBAS-16). *Sleep, 30,* 1547–1554.

Nicassio, P.M., Mendlowitz, D.R., Fussell, J.J., & Petras, L. (1985). The phenomenology of the pre-sleep state: The development of the pre-sleep arousal scale. *Behaviour Research and Therapy, 23,* 263–271.

Sleep Spindles

Sleep stages are defined according to arbitrary criteria based on the occurrence and amount of specific phasic activities. During NREM sleep, brain activity is organized by spontaneous coalescent cerebral rhythms: spindles, delta, and slow oscillations. On EEG recordings, spindles appear as waxing-and-waning oscillations at a frequency of about 11 to 15 Hz and a duration of more than 500 milliseconds. Spindles are prominent during N2 sleep and are progressively replaced during deeper stages by low-frequency high-amplitude (slow and delta) waves. Besides, spindles are grouped by the slow oscillation. Spindles are suppressed during surface negative half-waves of the slow oscillation (down state), but increased during positive half-waves (up state).

The thalamus is a central structure for the generation of spindles. Within the thalamus, pacemakers of spindle oscillations are located in thalamic reticular neurons. This assumption is supported by the finding that spindles are preserved within the reticular thalamus disconnected from the remaining thalamus and cerebral cortex. Although spindles can be generated within the thalamus in the absence of the cerebral cortex, the neocortex is essential for the induction, synchronization, and termination of spindles. In the intact brain, spindles are produced through thalamo–cortico–thalamic loops (cf. Steriade & McCarley, 2005). In humans, EEG recordings have characterized spindle oscillations in terms of scalp topography. Although they are detectable on all EEG scalp derivations, spindles are most prominent over centro–parietal areas with a frequency above 13 Hz (De Gennaro & Ferrara, 2003). A second cluster of spindles is visible over frontal areas, with a frequency of about 12 Hz. From this topographical segregation the hypothesis emerged that two types of spindles are produced by distinct biological mechanisms. In addition this is in line with the finding that both spindle subtypes are differentially modulated by age, circadian and homeostatic factors, menstrual cycle, pregnancy, and drugs (De Gennaro & Ferrara, 2003).

EEG/fMRI studies of human sleep also support the existence of two spindle types (Schabus et al., 2007). In particular these data revealed that—besides *increased* brain responses in the lateral and posterior aspects of the thalamus, as well as in paralimbic (anterior cingulate cortex, insula) and neocortical areas—the fast spindle type is associated with increased hemodynamic activity in hippocampal and sensorimotor regions. This finding also indicated a possible differential functional significance of these two spindle types, with the fast spindle being more closely associated with cognitive functioning (e.g., Morin et al., 2008). Yet more research is needed to unravel the functional significance of these two spindle types.

In general spindles are of interest for cognition research as they have been directly related to the repeated activation of thalamo–cortical or hippocampo–cortical networks after learning. Specifically,

in rats, hippocampal ripples were found to occur in temporal proximity to cortical sleep spindles, indicating an information transfer between the hippocampus and neocortex (Siapas & Wilson, 1998). This neuronal replay in turn has been suggested as the basis for reorganization and consolidation of memories (Buzsaki, 1996; Steriade, 1999). Gais and colleagues were then the first to demonstrate that sleep spindle density is also related to declarative learning in humans (Gais, Mölle, Helms, & Born, 2002). Interestingly, it has also been postulated that an individual's learning potential might be well reflected in sleep spindle activity (cf. Schabus et al., 2006).

Manuel Schabus

See also: entries related to Sleep Assessment

References

Buzsaki, G. (1996). The hippocampo-neocortical dialogue. *Cerebral Cortex, 6*(2), 81–92.

De Gennaro, L., & Ferrara, M. (2003). Sleep spindles: An overview. *Sleep Medicine Reviews, 7*(5), 423–440.

Gais, S., Mölle, M., Helms, K., & Born, J. (2002). Learning-dependent increases in sleep spindle density. *Journal of Neuroscience, 22*(15), 6830–6834.

Morin, A., Doyon, J., Dostie, V., Barakat, M., Hadj Tahar, A., Korman, M., et al. (2008). Motor sequence learning increases sleep spindles and fast frequencies in post-training sleep. *Sleep, 31*(8), 1149–1156.

Schabus, M., Dang-Vu, T.T., Albouy, G., Balteau, E., Boly, M., Carrier, J., et al. (2007). Hemodynamic cerebral correlates of sleep spindles during human non-rapid eye movement sleep. *Proceedings of the National Academy of Sciences USA, 104*(32), 13164–13169.

Schabus, M., Hodlmoser, K., Gruber, G., Sauter, C., Anderer, P., Klosch, G., et al. (2006).

Sleep spindle-related activity in the human EEG and its relation to general cognitive and learning abilities. *European Journal of Neuroscience, 23*(7), 1738–1746.

Siapas, A. G., & Wilson, M. A. (1998). Coordinated interactions between hippocampal ripples and cortical spindles during slow-wave sleep. *Neuron, 21*(5), 1123–1128.

Steriade, M. (1999). Coherent oscillations and short-term plasticity in corticothalamic networks. *Trends in Neurosciences, 22*(8), 337–345.

Steriade, M. & McCarley, R. W. (2005). *Brain control of wakefulness and sleep.* New York: Springer.

Sleep Talking

In sleep talking (somniloquy), the essential feature is talking, with varying degrees of comprehensibility, during sleep (*International Classification of Sleep Disorders* [ICSD-2], 2005). It can occur in both REM and non-REM sleep at any time during the night (Rechtschaffen, Goodenough, & Shapiro, 1962). Sleep talking is highly prevalent, occurring in childhood always or often in 4 to 14 percent and now and then in 22 to 60 percent, and as adults in 1 to 5 percent and in 20 to 45 percent, respectively (Hublin & Kaprio, 2003). The true prevalence is not easy to estimate because subjects as a rule do not remember or are not aware of their sleep talking. There is no clear gender difference in childhood sleep talking, but in adults it may be more common in males (Hublin, Kaprio, Partinen, & Koskenvuo, 1998).

The occurrence of childhood and adult sleep talking are highly correlated: about 80 percent of adults with sleep talking have done so as a child (Hublin et al., 1998).

There are three patterns in occurrence. The first and largest subgroup (about two thirds of childhood sleep talkers) is formed by real childhood sleep talkers; that is, those who do so as adults quite rarely or not at all. In the second subgroup are those that talked in their sleep frequently as children and continued to do so quite frequently as adults. These persons can be called persistent sleep talkers, and this subgroup forms about one fifth of those who talked in their sleep as children. The third and the smallest group (less than one tenth of adult sleep talkers) is formed by those adults who started to talk in their sleep as adults; that is, adult-onset sleep talking (Hublin et al., 1998).

Genetic effects play a role in sleep talking (Hublin & Kaprio, 2003). In a twin study, the proband-wise concordance rate for childhood sleep talking was 0.53 in the monozygotic (MZ) pairs, and 0.36 in the dizygotic (DZ) pairs. For adults, the proband-wise concordance rate was 0.23 for the MZ pairs and 0.14 for the DZ pairs. The proportion of total phenotypic variance in liability to sleep talking attributed to genetic influences in childhood sleep talking was 54 percent in males and 51 percent in females, and for adults it was 37 percent among males and 48 percent among females (Hublin et al., 1998).

Traditionally sleep talking has been classified as one of the parasomnias, which are undesirable physical events or experiences during the entry to sleep, within sleep, or during arousals from sleep, reflecting central nervous system activation (ICSD-2, 2005). Now it is considered more as a sleep-related symptom that lies on the border between normal and abnormal sleep. It is common that parasomnias co-occur (Hublin, Kaprio, Partinen, & Koskenvuo, 2001). In childhood, the correlations were highest in sleep talking for co-occurrence with sleepwalking ($r = 0.73$), nightmares (0.50), and bruxism (0.43). The results are similar in co-occurrence as adults, although the correlations are somewhat lower (0.56, 0.43, and 0.39, respectively). In MZ twins the co-occurrence of sleepwalking and sleep talking is clearly higher (0.31) compared to DZ twins (0.05). The correlations are substantial (>0.15 in MZ pairs) in three combinations: sleep talking–sleepwalking, sleep talking–bruxism, and sleep talking–nightmares.

Sleep talking is usually benign but chronic cases in adults may relate to psychopathology (Rechtschaffen et al., 1962). In adults, psychiatric comorbidity is about twice as common in those with frequent sleep talking (highest in those with adult-onset sleep talking, odds ratio 3.8), compared to those with infrequent or no sleep talking, but most cases of sleep talking are not associated with serious psychopathology (Hublin et al., 1998).

In conclusion, sleep talking is common but little studied, reflecting the fact that it is usually a harmless phenomenon. However, if it is frequent or loud it can be disturbing, and sometimes the content can cause problems in intimate relationships.

Christer Hublin

See also: entries related to Parasomnias

References

Hublin, C., & Kaprio, J. (2003). Genetic aspects and genetic epidemiology of parasomnias. *Sleep Medicine Reviews, 7,* 413–421.

Hublin, C., Kaprio, J., Partinen, M., & Koskenvuo, M. (1998). Sleeptalking in twins: Epidemiology and psychiatric co-morbidity. *Behavior Genetics, 28,* 289–298.

Hublin, C., Kaprio, J., Partinen, M., & Koskenvuo, M. (2001). Parasomnias: Co-occurrence and genetics. *Psychiatric Genetics, 11,* 65–70.

International Classification of Sleep Disorders: Diagnostic and Coding Manual (ICSD-2) (2nd ed.). (2005). Chicago: American Academy of Sleep Medicine.

Rechtschaffen, A., Goodenough, D. R., & Shapiro, A. (1962). Patterns of sleeptalking. *Archives of General Psychiatry, 7,* 418–426.

Sleep Variables and Handedness: Methodological Issues and State of the Field

There are several issues that make it difficult to determine if sleep variables might vary as a function of hand use preference (handedness). Nevertheless, because individual variations in handedness may reflect individual variations in functional and structural brain organization, it is worthwhile to examine the sleep of different handedness groups. Ultimately, such investigations could help to shed light on neurophysiological processes that occur during sleep, as well as on the functions of sleep in general.

One issue that makes it difficult to determine handedness–sleep relationships involves the very definition of handedness. Traditionally, handedness has been divided into left- versus right-handers, with performance on one (e.g., writing hand) or multiple test items (e.g., drawing, using a knife, etc.) indicating handedness. Thus, the direction of hand preference—right versus left (regardless of whether one strongly prefers to use one vs. the other hand)—is the important measure. However, other work suggests that how strongly one prefers to use one hand (e.g., always one vs. the other hand, sometimes one vs. the other, or no preference) across a variety of test items is also, or in some cases more, important to investigate. Thus, in these latter investigations, degree of hand preference—consistent versus inconsistent (e.g., regardless of direction; that is, regardless of left vs. right hand)—is the means by which handedness is categorized. Still other studies examine handedness by categorizing across both degree and direction, comparing consistently left, consistently right, and inconsistent-handers.

Unfortunately, investigations of handedness–sleep relationships have not been consistent in their division of the handedness groups; it is therefore difficult to synthesize the body of literature into a coherent whole. Given the inconsistent classification of the handedness groups across studies, in the present article consistent-left-handers and inconsistent-handers are collapsed into a non-right-handed (NRH) group that is compared to right-handers (RH). It is hoped that what may be lost in lack of precision will be gained in coherence.

A second issue that makes it difficult to determine handedness–sleep relationships involves the methodology used to collect and define sleep variables. For example, while some studies examined the sleep of different handedness groups in a sleep laboratory, others examined equally important home sleep. Some studies focused on sleep-quantity measures, such as sleep length, while others focused on issues of sleep quality, such as insomnia-related measures. Some work objectively recorded sleep, while some focused on self-reported, subjective measures of sleep variables. Any attempt at synthesis of the literature must take this methodological variation into account; as will be seen, methodology can interact with both the measure examined and with the handedness groups tested, resulting in complex relationships between these variables.

Given the methodological challenges outlined earlier, why would one bother to suspect that individual differences in hand preference might indicate individual differences in sleep measures? First, NRH versus RH differ neuroanatomically. For example, NRH compared to RH have a larger corpus callosum, that part of the brain responsible for connecting the two cerebral hemispheres (e.g., Denenberg, Kertesz, & Cowell, 1991; Witelson & Goldsmith, 1991). NRH also have decreased neuroanatomical asymmetries; for example, in language-related areas (e.g., Propper et al., 2010). In addition to differences in structural organization, NRH versus RH differ in the functional organization of the brain, with reversed or bilateral lateralization of cerebral functions in NRH (Hellige, 1993). For example, NRH is associated with increased incidence of right hemisphere or bilateral language processing (e.g., Knecht et al., 2000), as well as with atypical neuroanatomic asymmetries in language areas (e.g., Propper et al., 2010). To the extent sleep recruits the same neuroanatomical substrates that differ between NRH and RH, the handedness groups will differ in their sleep. Comparisons between handedness groups can therefore inform us about the neuroanatomical structures involved in, and functional organization of the brain during, sleep.

In fact, despite the infancy of the field, there are demonstrated differences in sleep variables between handedness groups. For example, sleep quality may differ as a function of handedness, especially in studies examining self-report measures, or that look at pathologies associated with sleep. For example, NRH self-report greater symptoms of insomnia (Coren & Searlman, 1987; Hicks, DeHaro, Inman, & Hicks, 1999), including greater difficulty falling asleep, more middle-of-the-night awakenings, and greater difficulty falling back to sleep, compared to RH. In laboratory examinations, NRH also suffer from more severe sleep apnea compared to RH (Hoffstein, Chan, & Slutsky, 1993). The NRH have a higher incidence of enuresis (Ferrara et al., 2001) as well. However, in the only studies explicitly attempting to disentangle the contribution of direction versus degree of hand preference to sleep using objective at-home sleep monitoring, RH and left-handers, compared to inconsistent-handers, demonstrated longer time to fall asleep and an increased amount of time spent awake during the night (Propper, Christman, & Olejarz, 2007; Propper, Lawton, Przyborski, & Christman, 2004), the opposite of what would have been expected based on the self-report literature, suggesting an effect of methods of sleep assessment on sleep variables, and the possibility that degree, rather than direction, of hand preference may be an important mediator of handedness–sleep relationships. To further confound the

issue, several other investigations have reported no handedness differences in sleep quality (e.g., Porac & Searleman, 2006; Violani, De Gennaro, & Solano, 1988).

Other measures of sleep also demonstrate handedness effects, although again, these effects vary as a function of methodology. For example, self-reports indicate decreased sleep, and possibly decreased sleep needs, in NRH compared to RH (Hicks, Pellegrini, & Hawkins, 1979; Propper, 2000). At least partly consistent with the self-report literature, Kilgore, Lipizzi, Grugle, Killgore, and Balkin (2009) reported increased sleep duration, and better sleep, in RH compared to NRH, in a sleep laboratory, but not in at-home measures. However, Lehnkering Strauss, Wegner, and Siegmund (2006) reported actigraph-measured sleep-duration differences between the handedness groups, with NRH having a longer sleep duration compared to RH. Finally, sleep diary (Violani et al., 1988) and home monitoring (Propper et al., 2004, 2007) showed no handedness differences in sleep length.

Differences between handedness groups in sleep-duration variability as measured by sleep-duration deviation from a standard norm have also been reported, although again the direction of this difference has been conflicting. Hicks and colleagues (1979), using a questionnaire, reported greater deviation from a standard norm in the inconsistent-handers versus consistent-handers, while Violani and colleagues (1988), using a sleep diary, reported the opposite. Propper and colleagues (2004) found no handedness effects on this measure examining objectively recorded home sleep.

Very few other studies have gone beyond description of sleep duration or quality as a function of handedness. Those that have, have found a relationship between handedness and sleep architecture, or between handedness and other physiological components of sleep. For example, Propper et al. (2004, 2007) found differences in sleep architecture among consistently left-, consistently right-, and inconsistently handed individuals in objective home sleep. Left-handers spent the most time (M = 76%) in nonrapid eye movement (NREM) sleep, inconsistent-handers spent the second most time (M = 72%) in NREM, and RH the least amount of time in NREM (M = 62%). The opposite pattern was obtained for rapid eye movement (REM) sleep: left-handers spent the least amount of time in REM (M = 20%), inconsistent-handers the second most amount of time in REM (M = 24%), and right-handers the most (M = 31%). The number of discrete REM episodes, however, showed a different story, with inconsistent-handers having the most REM episodes (M = 4.7), left-handers the second most (M = 3.8), and right-handers the least (M = 3.2).

The handedness groups also differ in sleep-related physiological measures. Nielsen, Abel, Lorrain, and Montplaisir (1990) reported increased electroencephalographic coherence in NRH versus RH during wake, Stage 2, and REM sleep. Murri and colleagues (1984) found differences between NRH and RH in REM-sleep EEG asymmetry as measured by EEG power. Finally, Serafetinides (1991) reported differences in EEG amplitude as a function of both handedness and sleep time (first four hours vs. last four hours of sleep), with NRH demonstrating no change in amplitude as a function of sleep time, and RH demonstrating decreased amplitude during the last four hours of sleep in both the left and right hemisphere.

There are several points to be taken from the previously mentioned review. First, the method of sleep monitoring is an important variable to consider in examinations of handedness–sleep relationships. For example, self-report measures may not actually measure sleep, but rather some other cognitive process involved in the *perception* of sleep. The bulk of the literature indicates that it is in *the self-perception* of sleep in which the handedness groups differ. Specifically, it is interesting to note that the *perception of sleep quality and duration,* measured via self-report, does vary as a function of hand preference, with NRH believing they need less, receive less, and have poorer, sleep. It is not clear, on the other hand, if *objective* measures of sleep quality (other than examination of sleep-associated pathological conditions) or sleep duration show differences between handedness groups. Second, although sleep-duration measure results are conflicting, and vary as a function of methodology, laboratory measures clearly indicate differences between the handedness groups in sleep architecture and neurophysiology. The results of these studies suggest that during sleep, patterns of interhemispheric communication vary as a function of hand preference. It is likely that these individual differences in handedness effects reflect the differences in brain organization between NRH and RH; specifically, larger corpus callosum in the NRH may result in increased interhemispheric communication during sleep. Such findings suggest that sleep itself involves alterations in interhemispheric communication, possibly as a function of sleep stage. Third, given the overall paucity of studies examining sleep–handedness relationships, clearly more research is needed to disentangle the effects of the latter variable on the former.

Ruth E. Propper

See also: entries related to Sleep and the Brain

References

Coren, S., & Searleman, A. (1987). Left sidedness and sleep difficulty: The Alinormal Syndrome. *Brain and Cognition, 6,* 184–192.

Denenberg, V. H., Kertesz, A., & Cowell, P. E. (1991). A factor analysis of the human's corpus callosum. *Brain Research, 548,* 126–132.

Ferrara, P., Ruggiero, A., Diocialuti, L., Paolini Paoletti, F., Chiozza, M. L., & Calone, P. (2001). Primary Nocturnal Enuresis and left-handedness. *Scandinavian Journal of Urology and Nephrology, 35,* 184–185.

Hellige, J. B. (1993). *Hemispheric asymmetry: What's right and what's left.* Cambridge, MA: Harvard University Press.

Hicks, R. A., DeHaro, D., Inman, G., & Hicks, G. J. (1999). Consistency of hand use and sleep problems. *Perceptual and Motor Skills, 89,* 49–56.

Hicks, R. A., Pellegrini, R. J., & Hawkins, J. (1979). Handedness and sleep. *Cortex, 15,* 327–229.

Hoffstein, V., Chan, C. K., & Slutsky, A. S. (1993). Handedness and sleep apnea. *Chest, 103,* 1860–1862.

Kilgore, W. D., Lipizzi, E. L., Grugle, N. L., Killgore, D. B., & Balkin, T. J. (2009). Handedness correlates with actigraphically measured sleep in a controlled environment. *Perceptual and Motor Skills, 109,* 395–400.

Knecht, S., Dräger, B., Deppe, M., Bobe, L., Lohmann, H., Flöel, A. R., . . . Henningsen, H. (2000). Handedness and hemispheric language dominance in healthy humans. *Brain, 123,* 2512–2518.

Lehnkering, H., Strauss, A., Wegner, B., & Siegmund, R. (2006). Actigraphic investigations on the activity-rest behavior of right- and left-handed students. *International Chronobiology, 23,* 593–605.

Murri, L., Stefanini, A., Bonanni, E., Cei, G., Navona, C., & Denoth, F. (1984). Hemispheric EEG differences during REM sleep in dextrals and sinistrals. *Research Communications in Psychology: Psychiatric Behavior, 9,* 109–120.

Nielsen, T., Abel, A., Lorrain, D., & Montplaisir, J. (1990). Interhemispheric EEG coherence during sleep and wakefulness in left-and right-handed subjects. *Brain and Cognition, 14,* 113–125.

Porac, C., & Searleman, A. (2006). The relationship between hand consistency, health, and accidents in a sample of adults over the age of 65 years. *Laterality, 11,* 405–414.

Propper, R. E. (2000, June). *Perceived sleep needs and feelings of alertness: Handedness and familial sinistrality effects.* Poster presented at the American Psychological Society, Miami, Florida.

Propper, R. E. (2004). Handedness differences in self-assessment of sleep quantity: Nonright versus strong-right-handers. *Sleep and Biological Rhythms, 2,* 99–101

Propper, R. E., Christman, S. D., & Olejarz, S. (2007). Home-recorded sleep architecture as a function of handedness II: Consistent right-versus consistent left-handers. *Journal of Nervous and Mental Disease, 195,* 689–692.

Propper, R. E., Lawton, N., Przyborski, M., & Christman, S. D. (2004). An assessment of sleep architecture as a function of degree of handedness in college women using a home sleep monitor. *Brain and Cognition, 54,* 186–197.

Propper, R. E., O'Donnell, L. E., Whalen, W., Tie, Y., Norton, I. H., Suarez, R. O., . . . & Golby, A. J. (2010). A combined fMRI and DTI examination of functional language lateralization and arcuate fasciculus structure: Effects of degree versus direction of hand preference. *Brain and Cognition, 73*, 85–92.

Serafetinides, E. A. (1991). Cerebral dominance and sleep: A comparison according to handedness and time of sleep. *International Journal of Neuroscience, 61*, 91–92.

Violani, C., De Gennaro, L., & Solano, L. (1988). Hemispheric differentiation and dream recall: Subjective estimates of sleep and dreams in different handedness groups. *International Journal of Neuroscience, 39*, 9–14.

Witelson, S. F., & Goldsmith, C. H. (1991). The relationship of hand preference to anatomy of the corpus callosum in men. *Brain Research, 545*, 175–182.

Sleepiness and Driving

Anecdotally, motor vehicle accidents due to sleepiness have been reported since 1929 (Kennedy, 1929). Epidemiological studies indicate that sleep-related crashes represent up to 20 percent of all traffic accidents in industrial societies (Connor et al., 2002). In the United States, Israel, Germany, and Sweden, sleep-related vehicle accidents account for many accidents on nonurban roads and cause greater driver mortality and morbidity than other types of accidents because of the greater speed on impact (Akerstedt et al., 1994a; Langlois, Smolensky, His, & Weir, 1986).

Numerous studies have demonstrated that the underlying causes of excessive sleepiness include reduced or fragmented sleep, circadian variations in alertness, drugs that act on the central nervous system (CNS), and diseases that affect the CNS (Roehrs, Carskadon, Dement, & Roth, 2005). In the general population, insufficient sleep due to reduced time in bed at night is the most common cause of excessive sleepiness (Drake et al., 2010).

The proportion of accidents related to specific sleep disorders is not known. One study indicates an accident rate of 13 per million kilometers for those with a sleep disorder, compared to 0.8 for a control group (Horstmann et al., 2000). There is evidence that those with obstructive sleep apnoea hypopnea syndrome (OSAHS) have up to seven times greater risk of crashes compared to those without OSA (Terán-Santos, Jiménez-Gómez, & Cordero-Guevara, 1999).

The majority of sleep-related crashes are not in people with predisposing conditions but in drivers, largely young males, who are sleep deprived and who fall asleep while driving at night. There are clear effects of time of day on motor vehicle accidents, with peaks in the early morning and midafternoon (Akerstedt et al., 1994b; Langlois et al., 1986). Research has shown that sleep restriction for 24 hours impairs driver performance to the same extent as alcohol intoxication (Dawson & Reid, 1997).

Estimates of the proportion of accidents attributable to sleep vary widely: 1 to 3 percent in the United States and 10 percent in France. In the United Kingdom, approximately 300 people are killed on the roads per year due to a driver falling asleep at the wheel. In the United States, an estimated 1,202 people were killed annually as a result of sleepiness, drowsiness, and fatigue driving in 2009.

Many sleep-related vehicle accidents occur while drivers are at work (Leger, 1988)—for example, driving company cars or lorries (Maycock, 1996). The Department of Motor Transportation in the United States now considers that there is a high likelihood that every lorry will be involved in at least one sleep-related crash during the lifetime of the vehicle (Knipling &Wang, 1994). Around 40 percent of sleep-related crashes involve commercial vehicles. This type of accident is most frequent on highways/motorways and similar roads. In the United Kingdom, fatal road accidents involving lorries, per 100 million vehicle kilometers, is almost double that for cars (averaging 2.1 vs. 1.1 over the past five years). A survey in the United Kingdom found that 29 percent of 4,600 respondents admitted to having felt close to falling asleep at the wheel in the previous year, and 17.9 percent had accidents during the previous three years. Of these, and for those accidents on motorways, 15 percent were sleep-related vehicle accidents (Knipling & Wang, 1994).

Most drivers causing sleep-related vehicle accidents usually deny having fallen asleep. The evidence pointing to the accident being related to sleep has to come from other sources. There are different possible reasons for this denial—such as loss of insurance indemnity and fear of prosecution. The law puts the responsibility on the driver not to drive if sleepy. The U.K. Road Traffic Act 1988 (as amended) states that a driver must not drive without due care and attention. Section 3(1) of the Health and Safety at Work etc Act 1974 (HSW Act) makes clear that employers (and self-employed people) have duties to those other than their employees, and can be criminally liable for breaching the legislation. Additionally, organizations may be prosecuted under the Corporate Manslaughter and Corporate Homicide Act 2007 in the event of a fatality due to a gross failing in their management of health and safety. It is therefore important for employers to meet their legal duties to the public, while protecting the health and safety of its drivers and ensuring the need to improve public safety.

STATS 19, the United Kingdom's national database for road accidents, does not normally record causal factors. Even when these (or contributory) factors are assigned, they are often assigned incorrectly (Horne & Reyner, 1999). For example, many sleep-related vehicle accidents, whether these involve cars, lorries, or other vehicles, are simply attributed to driver inattention. This general situation regarding unreliable national statistics on sleep-related vehicle accidents is typical for most other Western countries (Akerstedt et al., 1994a,b).

Another reason for drivers to deny having fallen asleep may be that the driver genuinely had no recollection of actually having fallen asleep. Sleep laboratory studies show that people who fall asleep typically deny having been asleep if awoken within a minute or two (Bonnet & Moore, 1982). It has been shown that two to four minutes of sleep had to elapse before >50 percent of people acknowledged that they were asleep (Gastaut & Broughton, 1965). Drivers may be aware of precursory feelings of sleepiness, although they may not acknowledge having fallen asleep and may not even remember this after the accident (Horne & Reyner, 1999).

OSAHS is the best studied cause of sleepiness and its effects on driving performance. One study estimated that up to 15 percent of lorry drivers may have sleep apnoea and sleepiness (Howard et al., 2004). In the United Kingdom, there are approximately 500,000 drivers and that would equate to around 75,000 with OSAHS.

U.K. Driver and Vehicle Licensing Agency (DVLA) guidelines recommend that, for group-2 LGV/PCV license holders: For patients diagnosed with OSAHS "Driving must cease until satisfactory control of symptoms has been attained with ongoing compliance with treatment, confirmed by consultant/specialist opinion (i.e., can restart driving commercial vehicles). Regular, normally annual, licensing review [is] required." This means that the DVLA does permit drivers with OSA to get back to driving once their symptoms are controlled. Across the United Kingdom, this is commonly within 14 days of starting continuous positive airway pressure (CPAP) therapy (CPAP delivers air to the airways to keep them open). Therefore, commercial drivers should neither fear the necessary tests for OSAHS, nor that the DVLA will revoke their licenses, provided they are compliant with the effective therapy (Banerjee, 2011).

Sleep-related motor vehicle accidents can be reduced through a greater awareness by drivers and employers of the danger of driving while sleepy, and that such driving behavior is unacceptable. The risk of motor vehicle accidents among people with OSA can be reduced by its clinical diagnosis and treatment with CPAP. More research into the awareness of sleepiness among drivers and the subsequent risk of a motor vehicle accident is necessary, matched by an increase in public awareness of the risks of driving while sleepy.

Sopna Choudhury, Ajit Thomas, Shahrad Taheri, and Dev Banerjee

See also: Primary Disorders of Hypersomnolence and Dreams; entries related to Sleep Disorders

Note

Both Dr. Shahrad Taheri and Dr. Sopna Choudhury are funded by the National Institute for Health Research (NIHR) through the Collaborations for Leadership in Applied Health Research and Care for Birmingham and Black Country (CLAHRC-BBC) programme. The views expressed in this publication are not necessarily those of the NIHR, the Department of Health, NHS South Birmingham, University of Birmingham, or the CLAHRC-BBC Theme 8 Management/Steering Group.

References

Akerstedt, T., Czeisler, C. A., Dinges, D., et al. (1994a). Accidents and sleepiness: A consensus statement. *Journal of Sleep Research, 4,* 195.

Akerstedt, T., Kecklund, G., Zulley, J., Cronlein, T., Hell, W., & Langwieder, K. (1994b). Fatal highway accidents mainly caused by falling asleep. In T. Akerstedt & G. Kecklund (Eds.), *Work hours, sleepiness and accidents* (Stress Research Report No 248, Section of Stress Research, p. 104). Stockholm: Karolinska Institute.

Banerjee, D. (2011). Sleep, work and health; Part 2 obstructive sleep apnoea and the work place—The impact on road safety. *Occupational Health at Work, 7*(6), 16–18.

Bonnet, M.H., & Moore, S.E. (1982). The threshold of sleep: Perception of sleep as a function of time asleep and auditory threshold. *Sleep, 5,* 267–276.

Connor, J. R., Norton, J., Ameratunga, S., Robinson, E., Civil, I., Dunn, R., . . . Jackson, R. (2002). Driver sleepiness and risk of serious injury to car occupants: Population-based case-control study. *British Medical Journal, 324*(7346), 1125–1128.

Dawson, D., & Reid, K. (1997). Fatigue, alcohol and performance impairment. *Nature, 388,* 235.

Drake, C., Roehrs, T., Breslau, N., Johnson, E., Jefferson, C., Scofield, H., & Roth, T. (2010, June 1). The 10-year risk of verified motor vehicle crashes in relation to physiologic sleepiness. *Sleep, 3*(6), 745–752.

Gastaut, H., & Broughton, R. (1965). A clinical and polygraphic study of episodic phenomena during sleep. In J Wortis (Ed.), *Recent advances in biological psychology* (pp. 197–223). New York: Plenum Press.

Horne, J., & Reyner, L. (1999). Vehicle accidents related to sleep: A review. *Occupational and Environmental Medicine, 56,* 289–294.

Horstmann, S., Hess, C. W., & Bassetti, C., et al. (2000). Sleepiness related accidents in sleep apnoea patients. *Sleep, 23,* 383–389.

Howard, M. E., Desai, A. V., Grunstein, R. R., et al. (2004). Sleepiness, sleep-disordered breathing, and accident risk factors in commercial vehicle drivers. *American Journal of Respiratory and Critical Care Medicine, 170*(9), 1014–1021.

Kennedy, A. M. (1929). A note of narcolepsy. *British Medical Journal, 1,* 1112–1113.

Knipling, R. R., & Wang, J-S. (1994). *Crashes and fatalities related to driver drowsiness/fatigue* (research note). Washington, DC: Office of Crash Avoidance Research, U.S. Department of Transportation.

Langlois, P. H., Smolensky, M. H., His, B. P., & Weir, F. W. (1986). Temporal patterns of reported single-vehicle car and truck accidents in Texas USA during 1980–1983. *Chronobiology International, 2,* 131–146.

Leger, D. (1988). The cost of sleep-related accidents: A report for the National Commission on Sleep Disorders Research. *Sleep, 17,* 84–93.

Maycock, G. (1996). Sleepiness and driving: The experience of UK car drivers. *Journal of Sleep Research, 5,* 229–237.

Roehrs, T., Carskadon, M., Dement, W., & Roth, T. (2005). Daytime sleepiness and alertness. In M. H. Kryger, T. Roth, & W. C. Dement (Eds.), *Principles and practice of sleep medicine* (4th ed., pp. 39–50). Philadelphia: Elsevier.

Terán-Santos, J., Jiménez-Gómez, A., & Cordero-Guevara, J. (1999). The association between sleep apnea and the risk of traffic accidents. *New England Journal of Medicine, 340,* 847–851.

Sleeping and Dreaming Patterns in the Context of Attachment Relationships

McNamara and colleagues (McNamara, 1996; Zborowski & McNamara, 1998) theorized that REM sleep and dreams evolved (in part) to promote and facilitate attachment bonds. This theory stemmed from a line of evidence highlighting REM-sleep correlates, including amygdala and limbic system activation, increased levels of oxytocin, vasopressin, arginine vasotocin, testosterone (in men), other reproductive and caregiving neurochemicals, and sexual arousal. In addition, infants who sleep separated from their primary caregivers are more likely to be classified as insecurely attached, and insecure infants experience more night awakenings and sleep disorders. McNamara (2004) proposed that REM sleep is a viable candidate for a physiological mechanism through which humans can consolidate and integrate attachment experiences. Recent research on adult attachment has shown that anxious attachment contributes to decreased Stages 3–4 sleep in depressed women (Troxel, Cyranowski, Hall, Frank, & Buysse, 2007) and poorer sleep quality in the elderly (Verdecias et al., 2009). Anxious attachment is also associated with α-EEG anomalies (Sloan, Maunder, Hunter, & Moldofsky, 2007).

Extending this work into the realm of dream research, McNamara, Andresen, Clark, Zborowski, and Duffy (2001) found that anxious-attached individuals recalled more dreams than their secure counterparts. In addition, their dreams were longer and contained more high-intensity central images. The authors proposed that dreaming exists in part to promote relational strategies and processes, and therefore anxious-attached individuals would dream more frequently due to their hyperactivating attachment patterns.

Avihou (2006; unpublished dissertation) documented associations between dream content and attachment styles. Anxious-attached individuals dreamt of themselves as weak, helpless, or unloved, while avoidant-attached individuals dreamt of themselves as distant, uncooperative, emotionally unexpressive, or angry. Mikulincer, Shaver, Sapir-Lavid, and Avihou-Kanza (2009) separately reported findings from the same sample, coding a subset of distress dreams using three attachment-specific behavioral tendencies: (1) support seeking, (2) support availability, and (3) distress relief. Anxious-attachment scores correlated negatively with support availability and distress relief, while avoidant-attachment scores correlated negatively with support seeking and support availability.

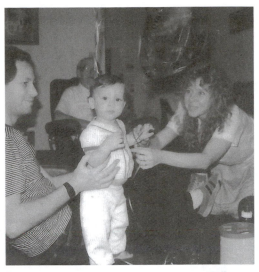

Secure base support for exploration. (Photo provided by Dylan Selterman)

Selterman and Drigotas (2009) examined the dreams of individuals in committed dating relationships. Anxious- and avoidant-attachment scores both uniquely predicted stress, conflict, and anxiety levels in dreams that contained romantic partners. The effects were stronger for avoidant attachment. Anxious attachment also correlated with feelings of jealousy, and avoidant attachment correlated with anger and less affection in dreams containing romantic partners.

An important point to note is that (nearly) all the effects listed earlier remained significant when statistically controlling for general, nonattachment distress (anxiety, depression), as well as other social/emotional/personality variables. This demonstrates the unique contribution of attachment to sleeping and dreaming processes over and above other psychological variables. Another consistent trend in this literature is the strong association between anxious attachment and sleep patterns, while avoidant attachment appears largely absent. However, effects between avoidant attachment and dream content are just as strong as effects for anxious attachment (if not more so). Future research should probe deeper into this discrepancy. Researchers should also examine how sleep and dream patterns impact relationship functioning and maintenance. Perhaps dream sharing/disclosure with attachment figures exists as a form of secure base support seeking, or as an intimacy-building activity.

Dylan Selterman

References

McNamara, P. (1996). REM sleep: A social bonding mechanism. *New Ideas in Psychology, 14*(1), 35–46.

McNamara, P. (2004). *An evolutionary psychology of sleep and dreams*. Westport, CT: Praeger.

McNamara, P., Andresen, J., Clark, J., Zborowski, M., & Duffy, C. A. (2001). Impact of attachment styles on dream recall and dream content: A test of the attachment hypothesis of REM sleep. *Journal of Sleep Research, 10*(2), 117–127.

Mikulincer, M., Shaver, P. R., Sapir-Lavid, Y., & Avihou-Kanza, N. (2009). What's inside the minds of securely and insecurely attached people? The secure-base script and its associations with attachment-style dimensions. *Journal of Personality and Social Psychology, 97*(4), 615–633.

Selterman, D., & Drigotas, S. (2009). Attachment styles and emotional content, stress, and conflict in dreams of romantic partners. *Dreaming, 19*(3), 135–151.

Sloan, E. P., Maunder, R. G., Hunter, J. J., & Moldofsky, H. (2007). Insecure attachment is associated with the α-EEG anomaly during sleep. *BioPsychoSocial Medicine, 1*(20), 1–6.

Veredecias, N. R., Jean-Louis, G., Zizi, F., Casimir, G. J., & Browne, R. C. (2009). Attachment styles and sleep measures in a community-based sample of older adults. *Sleep Medicine, 10*, 664–667.

Troxel, W. M., Cyranowski, J. M., Hall, M., Frank, E., & Buysse, D. J. (2007). Attachment anxiety, relationship context, and sleep in women with recurrent major depression. *Psychosomatic Medicine, 69*(7), 692–699.

Zborowski, M. J., & McNamara, P. (1998). Attachment hypothesis of REM sleep: Toward an integration of psychoanalysis, neuroscience, and evolutionary psychology and the implications for psychopathology research. *Psychoanalytic Psychology, 15*(1), 115–140.

Social Network Analysis of Dream Content

In a social network, people are represented by points, and if two people have a certain relationship, for example, are friends, their corresponding points are connected by a line. Although social networks have complex and individualistic structures, they tend to have some simple properties in common, such as short paths between points. In a dream social network, points represent characters in the dreams of an individual and a line connecting two points indicates that the corresponding characters were in a dream together. A dream social network shows how the dreamer's memory for people is organized in the dreaming brain.

Social interactions are a large part of the contents of dreams. During rapid eye movement (REM) sleep, when most dreams occur, a component of the brain involved in processing social interactions, the amygdala, is more active than during waking life. More social interactions occur during an interval of REM sleep than in an equal interval of waking life (McNamara, McLaren, Smith, Brown, & Stickgold, 2005). In any one, dream characters may seem to appear in a haphazard way, but over many dreams a systematic structure emerges.

The dream social network for Arlie, a middle-aged woman, is shown in the dream social network image. An isolated point corresponds to a character in a dream with no other character present except the dreamer. Islands of points connected to each other but not connected to the rest of the network represent characters appearing in a dream with each other, but not appearing in any other dream. A network constructed from the first few dreams of a series would consist mostly of islands. After many dreams, most points become connected in a large subnetwork, called the giant component. Because the dreamer is in every dream, illustrating her would clutter the network, so she is not represented. An exception is made when the dreamer is present in a metamorphosed form, as in a dream in which a woman dreamt she was a little boy. Metamorphosed forms of the dreamer are represented by points.

Dream reports of Arlie and many other people are available on the DreamBank Web site (Schneider & Domhoff, 2011). To construct the network one needs a reliable way to determine who is present in a dream. There is no way to learn who a dreamer is dreaming about by examining brain waves or other external measures; one must consider what the dreamer says. In a classic work, Calvin S. Hall and Robert Van De Castle developed a system for coding contents of dream reports (Hall & Van de Castle, 1966). The system gives simple rules for determining when to code a character of a dream. For example, the first rule that leads to a character being coded is "The character is described as being physically present in the dream."

With the system, a character need not be present in the dream to be coded. For example, if a belonging of a person is present in the dream, the person is coded as a character of the dream. The system was modified for the purpose of constructing networks, so a character is coded as present in a dream if the character interacted, or could have interacted, with another character or with the dreamer (Schweickert, 2007). Characters include people and person-like entities such as mythological figures and talking animals.

Social networks of characters in dreams have some of the same properties as social networks of people in waking life. A well-known property of a friendship network is a *short average path length,* sometimes dubbed six degrees of separation: Between two arbitrarily chosen people one can usually find a short path of friends and acquaintances. A network formed by connecting points together at random also tends to have short average path length. Perhaps surprisingly, the average path length in a typical waking-life social network is approximately the same as that of a random network with the same number of points and lines. Another property of waking-life social networks is *high clustering*: If A is a friend of B and B is a friend of C, then A and C tend to be friends of each other. In a random network, clustering is low; A and C are joined by a line with the same probability whether or not A and C are both joined to B by lines. The two properties of short average path length and high clustering do not ordinarily occur in the same network. Networks with both properties are special, and are called *small world networks.*

Many, but not all, dream social networks are small world networks. For the network in the dream social network image, the average path length is short, near that of a comparable random network. But its clustering is high, far greater than that of a comparable random network. This network is a small world network.

A dream social network that is not a small world network is that of the engine man, given this name because of the prevalence of locomotives in his dreams. The network has many sequences where A is in a dream with B, and B is in a dream with C, but A and C are not in a dream together. Triangles tend not to be completed and the clustering is near that of a comparable random network. The average path length is short, a little larger than that of a comparable random network.

Another property of social networks has to do with the number of points a given point is connected to. The number of points connected by a line to a given point is the *degree* of the given point. Many quantities in nature follow a normal distribution, with middle values the most common and high and low values uncommon. Degrees in social networks do not follow a normal distribution. The lowest values are the most common and the highest values the least common. The probability distribution of degrees is a Zipf distribution, sometimes called a power law. The higher a degree the less likely it is to occur; the probability a degree is k is inversely proportional to k. A few points, hubs, are highly connected

to other points. One consequence is that a short path between two points can usually be formed by starting at one point, going to a hub, and then proceeding to the other point. Degrees in both waking life and dream social networks typically have Zipf degree distributions.

One might think that a dream social network is simply a copy of the dreamer's waking-life social network, and thus they have properties in common. But this cannot be the explanation. Characters in dream social networks include celebrities and cartoon characters, not people the dreamer interacts with while awake. Sometimes one character metamorphoses into another, not an event of waking life. A poignant demonstration that dream- and waking-life social networks differ is that the person occurring most often in the dreams of Merri is her sister, but her sister was killed in an accident three years before Merri began her dream journal.

A more likely explanation of the common properties of dream- and waking-life social networks is that the dreamer's associative memory has the properties of short pathways, high clustering, and a Zipf degree distribution. Human semantic networks, such as a network made from the thesaurus, have these properties (Steyvers & Tenenbaum, 2005). Characters in dreams correspond to concepts of people and the concepts include mythological figures, talking animals, cartoon characters, and so on. Characters occur in a dream together when they are associated somehow in the dreamer's memory. One piece of evidence for this is that when an entity metamorphoses into another entity, the entities tend to be conceptually close.

People metamorphose into other people more often than into animals, and more often into animals than into objects (Schweickert & Xi, 2009). Deceased people and those who have moved away continue to appear if they are associated with people currently in the dreamer's waking-life social network. In REM sleep the dreamer follows associative pathways, and the structure of these pathways becomes visible in the dream social network.

One of many open questions is why some dream social networks have high clustering and some do not. To answer such questions we will need more information about the daily lives of dreamers, to compare dream- and waking-life social networks. Sleep is known to be important for memory consolidation, and it is likely that the contents of dreams are manifestations of some kind of memory processing during sleep. Observing how dream social networks change over periods of time may shed light on this processing.

Richard Schweickert

References

Hall, C. S., & Van de Castle, R. (1966). *The content analysis of dreams.* New York: Appleton-Century-Crofts.

McNamara, P., McLaren, D., Smith, D., Brown, A., & Stickgold, R. (2005). A "Jekyll and Hyde" within: Aggressive versus friendly interactions in REM and non-REM dreams. *Psychological Science, 16,* 130–136.

Schneider, A., & Domhoff, G. W. (2011). DreamBank. Retrieved from http://www.dreambank.net/

Schweickert, R. (2007). Properties of the organization of memory for people: Evidence from dream reports. *Psychonomic Bulletin & Review, 14,* 270–276.

Schweickert, R., & Xi, Z. (2009). Metamorphosed characters in dreams: Constraints of conceptual structure and amount of theory of mind. *Cognitive Science, 34,* 665–684.

Steyvers, M., & Tenenbaum, J. B. (2005). The large-scale structure of semantic networks: Statistical analysis and a model of semantic growth. *Cognitive Science, 29,* 41–78.

Watts, D. J. (2003). *Six degrees: The science of a connected age.* New York: W.W. Norton.

Sound-Work: The Neglected Sense in Working with Dream Images

Sound Awareness

Sound is the most direct, immediate, efficient, and effective way to perceive and transform that which vibrates with, without, and within us. The word sound, let us recall, also means *healthy, well, wholesome, robust,* and is often used to imply *vigor, strength, sensitivity, energy, sturdy, intact, whole*.

While sound—the audible aspect of vibration—accompanies all movement and serves to orient us, and much more, we tend to take it for granted in our lives, and certainly in our dreamwork. We generally take image as primary—but, let us not overlook that as vibration, sound is there from the beginning (notice the role of sound in creation myths from around the globe), and comes with each and every encounter.

All meetings involve, reflect, and produce new sounds. At the most basic physical level, sound travels in waves that affect and have an effect on the bodies they touch, generating further vibrations. We respond when touched.

Sound has a double effect, literally it *dissolves* (releases, breaks, cleanses, opens) and it *coagulates* (shapes, limits, organizes, creates)—structuring new and constantly changing forms. Brought into being by movement, sound also brings forth new movements.

While much therapeutic and spiritual work is being done with sound (music, toning, singing), surprisingly little attention has been given to linking sound-work to images from our dreams (and lives). Here, a case is made for developing an awareness founded on hearing, emitting, and listening experiences. Whether or not we are aware of sound—or participate consciously in it as a specific *sense*—it is constantly giving form to invisible and unknown aspects of our lives.

The potential of this proposal is revealed in what happens to the life of a person that explores and discovers him—or herself by working with vocal awareness, mindfulness, and practice. This proposal wants to incite interest and practice with the outer and inner sounds that come along with the images in our dreams (and lives).

Vocal Sound Awareness

It is not difficult to hide from our sounds. Actually hearing the sounds we emit tends to be disconcerting; it makes evident the scopes and limitations of our defense mechanisms. Listening to the sounds that we emit frequently has the effect of deconstructing the mind's belief systems, making automatic (unconscious) somatic, emotional, mental, and spiritual phenomena instantly more apparent.

Automatic aspects of our being appear in the sounds that we unexpectedly and involuntarily find ourselves emitting, often revealing something essential to the emotional—*inner*—sense of what we are saying. For those interested in unconscious manifestations and synchronicities, our voice offers vast and multifaced mirrors to help us recognize all sorts of unconscious phenomena. Becoming sensitive to the sounds in our voice can guide us in refining how we perceive and react reflexively, in how we think, feel, see, and take ourselves into the world.

All the more influential when unnoticed, sounds can dominate our relationships with others. We have only to note carefully what we communicate and convey with the *tone, speed, volume, intention, attitude, energy, sense,* and *direction* of what we say. Independently of the meanings we attach to words, sounds touch us directly and often more deeply. How something is said usually carries much more meaning than what is actually said. And it seems evident that we frequently react and respond more to the tone and rhythm of what is said than to the content itself.

The challenge is to develop a heightened awareness of the medium we call *sound*: around (outside) us, and within us.

Sound-Work and Dreams

Outer and inner happenings meet in our dream images, triggering vibrations at all levels of our being. This proposal involves resonating with the images that affect, as much as reflect, our different realities. The notion of *resonance* implies that vibrating with something triggers movements to differentiate, and invites us to enter a metaphorical experience, relevant to multiple levels of our inner and outer reality.

Like life itself, dreams present us with scenarios, which at any given moment conceal as much as they reveal. A dream scene is a place in which something is constellated; different aspects are highlighted as they come together to form a momentary whole. Scenes in dreams offer specifically different perspectives that somehow draw our attention to at least one nodal moment in the dream sequence, in which a certain tension—or dissonance—signals that something vital is at stake.

Dreams can be imagined as invitations to discover perspectives that may be new and different, and even alien to those of the ego; this is why our approach to dreams should not be *ego-syntonic*. My proposal is to use sound as a means to access, reveal, and connect with the dream experience beyond the ego's control. *Sound-work* implies nurturing a palpable relationship with the invisible.

Describing a sound without having heard it is like describing an image without having seen it. We must literally emit a sound to actually hear and listen to it. Let us give importance to the sounds that come to being through our mouths.

That the sounds in a dream image are sometimes not easily recognized does not mean that they are not present in the telling (and reliving) of the dramatic scenes in the image, and in the experience of the tension within the images themselves. This tension is made palpable and brought even more into life with sound awareness.

Most significant is that sound is a simple, basic, obvious, and immediate way for generating images. New images inevitably appear and transform with sound, revealing the primary, intimate, dynamic, and transformative relationship between sound and image.

Sound-Work and Imagination

Neither images, nor our phenomenological experience of them are in themselves perceptions. Rather, they are the result of an imaginal activity that affects and challenges us to question our perceptions. In the first paragraph of his book *Air and Dreams*, Gaston Bachelard writes: "The imagination . . . deforms what we perceive; it is, above all, the faculty that frees us from immediate images and changes them. If there is no change . . . there is no imagination; there is no imaginative act."

Dream images are not meant to be taken literally, concretely, objectively, nor to be translated into the language of the ego's well-rehearsed day-world perspectives (usually designed, as we know, to avoid fears of some kind of pain or discomfort)—nor to be converted, through interpretations, into something other than what they simply are—very precise experiences.

While taking the literalness away from words and content both awakens and weakens our defenses, it also allows the person to focus with increasing concentration on listening for the intention and emotional *tone* and *sense* of what is being expressed through the sound.

In themselves, images manifest, involve, express, and contain sound. Particular scenes are breeding grounds for new images to gestate and take form. *Sound-work* activates and releases this inherent potential in dreams.

As living metaphors, dream scenarios are a medium for presenting the dreamer with what is called for to bring new movement to his or her life. *Sound-work* facilitates this; certain moments in some images are setups for *sound experiences*.

Sound-work frees us of literal perspectives and personal needs for concluding and resolving things; it opens new ways of imagining, and allows the dream images to reveal aspects and perspectives alien to the ego's natural tendencies and inclinations. The sounds implicit to particular scenes in the dream—and the sounds we emit while resonating with its images—are our *prima materia*.

More than wanting to be understood, images that come back in dreams—and stay with us—beg to be reexperienced. *Sound-work* inevitably makes this happen, consistently dissolving our *identifications, attachments,* and *interpretations,* which usually translate into the *meanings* that we give to our dreams. At the same time, vital issues take on new forms: something unexpected coagulates. As the alchemists practiced and proclaimed for centuries: *dissolve that which is coagulated and coagulate that which is dissolved.*

Experiencing dream images through sound-work leaves multiple impressions in its wake, making it very difficult for all those involved to find themselves in a situation similar to the sound experience with the dream without reacting and responding in surprisingly creative and constructive ways.

This particular *sound-work* proposal encompasses: (1) Going beyond the literal, as most of us only sporadically notice sound in our dreams. (2) Recognizing and exploring the sounds that correspond with specific actions in our dream image sequences, and the resonance of this in our present-day lives. (3) Working with *how* we tell the dream to others. (4) Giving vocal form to the emotions awakened by our attending to the images presented by the dream.

In addition, it is critically important to work consistently to recognize and put all sorts of judgments and prejudices to one side, and to remember that the goal is not a cathartic experience. Instead, this proposal aims at connecting and relating ever more deeply to the issues that call attention to themselves in and through our dreams.

Through *sound-work,* the inner sense of things becomes more palpable and consciously experienced, allowing the person to be constructively transformed by taking into account concerns that go beyond his or her ego's reach. Emitting sound generates different kinds of inner movements. Sound forces us to breath, to *take in,* and to *release*—it involves our physical, emotional, mental, and spiritual bodies in a wide range of dynamics and processes.

While we may not notice the sounds that invariably accompany our dreams, it is virtually impossible to listen to the sounds we emit without indelibly altering our experience of the initial images, and generating new images. Trying to emit the sounds that we hear in our dreams—or in our working with them—inevitably makes us experience something essential to the sound, and to our lives.

People sometimes hesitate in consciously emitting the sounds that appear in (and with) the images in their dreams.

As if there were a kind of knowing that to emit the sound is to experience it. Not allowing the sound to take actual form is to somehow deny a highly dynamic aspect of it. The more willing a person is to allow the sounds that emerge from deeply within to appear and take form, the deeper the transformative experience.

The Imagination Is Vivified by Sound-Work

The call is to allow dream images to become deeply rich day-world experiences. More than an idea about something, *sound-work* is in itself an *experience*.

This proposal, therefore, is an invitation to allow *sound-work* to convert certain scenarios in our dreams into present-day lived experiences: relevant to ongoing cycles of transformation, to our creativity, and to fundamental well-being in our everyday lives.

Source of Inspiration: Alfred Wolfsohn (1896–1962)

A medic during the World War I, Alfred Wolfsohn was a man haunted by nightmares and auditory hallucinations, certainly influenced by his terrible memories of carrying wounded men, howling with pain, away from combat zones on his stretcher.

With no anesthesia to diminish their suffering, we can only imagine the sounds that emerged from the agony of those desperate men. Long after the war, these primitive piercing sounds continued to haunt Wolfsohn, not letting him be. Until the day when what we could only call desperation, led him to allow the sounds that he could not stop from hearing inside himself to emerge from the depths of his being and take form as *sound*.

The exercise took him beyond the reach of his ego's limits and control, and through a series of vivid experiences of sensations, emotions, feelings, thoughts, memories, associations, and unexpected new images, which in the end freed him of his inner torment.

Whether wittingly or instinctively, Wolfsohn had discovered that sustaining a focused vocal sound long enough, led beyond cathartic moments—and beyond all that we think and feel that we know of our cry (be it one of joy, of lament, of complaint, of desire)—brings more than relief to a condition: it actually transforms it.

Alfred Wolfsohn was transformed, and discovered the power that comes with allowing the dissonant, uncomfortable, possibly horrible sounds that unexpectedly emerge from the depths of our souls to guide us into fundamental shifts in our relationship with ourselves and with the world around us.

This vocal *sound-work* proposal honors Alfred Wolfsohn and attempts to further his insights with practice.

Sven Doehner

See also: entries related to Dream Content

References

Bachelard, G. (1999). *Water and dreams: An essay on the imagination of matter* (3rd ed.) (Trans. E. R. Farrell). Bachelard Translation Series. Dallas, TX: The Dallas Institute of Humanities and Culture.

Hillman, J. (1979). *The dream and the underworld*. New York: HarperPerennial.

Ihde, D. (2007). *Listening and voice, phenomenologies of sound.* Albany: State University of New York Press.

Space in Dreams

Space is generally regarded as an expanse measurable in terms of known dimensions: height, width, depth, and time, absolutely or relatively. While dreaming, the dreamer produces visual abstractions in space. Primarily thought-like, experiences in dreams might be accompanied by visual abstractions in space, of which the dreamer might or might not be aware; there might be an imaginary sphere of the body that provides an orientation to space; the symmetry of spatial experiences while awake might be contracted, expanded, or transformed while dreaming.

From the theoretical perspective of quantum physics, Bohm (Briggs & Peat, 1987) proposed that space, time, and matter are abstractions that unfold from the implicate order—a vast, boundless energy space—and surface, become explicit, in the explicate order. In accordance with Bohm, Ullman (1987) suggested that dreams vacillate between the two orders and therefore might present spatial and temporal content regarded as unusual to the dreamer.

Snyder and Gackenbach (1991) discussed spatially oriented body movement, a function of the vestibular system and the essential role of space in dreams. They referred to the intense activation of vestibular nuclei in the brain stem during rapid eye movement (REM) dreaming as well as the likelihood of the predominance of vestibular-bound imagery and movement patterns during dreaming.

During any stage of sleep, activation of the parietal lobe might indicate the presence of spatial experience. In a study of several hundred neurological and neurosurgical patients, Solms (1995) observed that patients experiencing disturbances in waking visual–spatial abilities as well as a complete loss of dreaming had brain damage located in the parietal region. During REM sleep, positron emission tomography (PET) and statistical parametric mapping indicated activation of the right inferior parietal lobe (Maquet et al., 1996). A PET scan study indicated some activation in the parietal cortex during REM sleep (Maquet, 2000). Based on the presence of positive electroencephalograph (EEG) brain potentials, the brain's parietal–occipital area became active immediately following REM sleep (Ogawa, Nittono, & Hori, 2002).

Brenneis (1970), Foulkes, Pivik, Steadman, Spear, and Symonds (1967), and Trosman, Rechtschaffen, Offenkrantz, and Wolpert (1960) have all researched the subject of spatial experiences in dreams. Brenneis (1970) studied the dreams of 183 male and female college students. From a spatial perspective, he concluded that males had a tendency to structure the space in their dreams in terms of *extension* and *separateness* from others and females in terms of *closeness* and *intimacy*. Erikson (1954) believed there were aspects of dreams that could be arranged in a configuration and manifest in one dream or a series of dreams. He identified *spatial* as one of seven possible *manifest configurations,* along with *verbal, sensory, temporal, somatic, interpersonal,* and *affective.* Erikson characterized the spatial aspect of dreams according to *spatial extension* and *motion*. When analyzing Freud's Irma dream, Erikson interpreted festivity in the dream as a reflection of affect, and he associated *festivity affect* with spaciousness, a spatial variable. He interpreted urgency in a dream as a reflection of affect, and he associated *urgency affect* with constriction, a spatial variable.

Foulkes et al. (1967) categorized *spatial* and *temporal* experience together as a dimension of dreams. After independent raters reviewed the dreams of 32 boys, the researchers reported that the spatial and temporal dimension was identified in 76 percent of dreams. Trosman et al. (1960) considered spatiality in dreams in terms of spatial expanse. The researchers assessed the dreams of two participants over a period of 34 nights in a sleep lab after recording an average of four or five dreams per night from each participant. Each dream was assessed on the basis of 12 dimensions: *spatial expanse, hedonic tone, excitation, activity, observer–participant, interpersonal involvement, clarity, thematic coherence, plausibility, elaboration, resolution,* and *success* (p. 603). Defined in terms of geographical space, spatial expanse was rated as low when the space was considered constricted and as high when the space was considered expansive. Trosman et al. (1960) reported a high positive correlation between spatial expanse and the dimensions of *excitation,* referring to degree or charge of emotional expression; *activity,* referring to amount of kinetic activity; *interpersonal involvement,* referring to degree of emotionally charged interaction; *clarity,* referring to vividness and lack of ambiguity; and *elaboration,* referring to the quality and diversity of dream content.

Brenneis (1970), Foulkes et al. (1967), and Trosman et al. (1960) have all researched the subject of spatial experiences in dreams and have reported that dreamers experience space, although the researchers themselves, not the dreamers, made this determination and described the experiences.

Tyburczy (2008) requested 28 dreamers to recall and describe spatial experiences in their dreams in their own words as well as by selecting and using spatial terms from 22 *spatial parameter, spatial experiential,* and *spatial view descriptor* categories contained in a content validated instrument, *Spatial Questionnaire Selections 2* (see Table 9).

The dreamers were also requested to select terms from emotions categories contained in *Emotions Questionnaire Selections* that was adapted from Goleman's (1995, p. 289) research on emotions to recall and describe emotional experiences in their dreams. Spatial parameter categories include *density, depth, dimension in space, direction, distance, energy, height, position in space, shape, spatially unusual or bizarre, time,* and *width.* Spatial experiential categories include *controlled in space, supported in space, contained in space, free of gravity in space, grounded in space, motion in space,* and *precarious position in space.* Emotions categories include *anger, sadness, fear, enjoyment, love, surprise,* and *disgust.* Response percentages for all research questions indicated that participants described experiences in dreams in terms of the spatial parameter categories of density (48.5%),, distance (48%), and position in space (48%), and in terms of enjoyment (46.4%) from the emotions categories. Significant relationships

Table 9: Spatial Questionnaire Selections 2

Area: spatial parameters

Spatial parameter categories (bold); terms (not bold)

Density: cramped; cluttered; compacted; compressed; crowded; crushed; dense; full; heavy; open; packed; spacious; thick; uncluttered; vacant; voluminous

Depth: abyss; bottomless; deep; downward; fathom; shallow; steep

Dimension in space: inner space; outer space

Direction: across; backward; down; east; forward; north; northeast; northwest; parallel; perpendicular; sideways; south; southeast; southwest; up; upward; west

Distance: away; close; distant; extension; far; gap; long; near; nearby; space; span

Energy: electrical; gaseous; solid

Height: apex; ceiling; elevation; heavenward; high; lifted; lofty; low; peak; pinnacle; short; summit; tall; top; upward; vast; vertical; zenith

Position in space: above; adjacent; behind; below; beneath; beside; extended; in; in front of; in the back; in the front; laterally; level with; location; lower; out; over; parallel with; point; positioned; prone; traversal; under; underneath

Shape: circle; crescent; ellipse; parallelogram; polygon; quadrilateral; rectangle; rhombus; sphere; spiral; square; star; trapezoid; triangle

Size: big; breadth; huge; immense; large; microscopic; minute; small; vast; voluminous

Spatially unusual or bizarre: channels switching; metamorphosis; superimposition; transfiguration; transformation

Time: accelerated; back; delayed; eternal; fast forward; forward; future; infinity; interval; past; present; rewind; timeless

Width: expanse; horizontal; narrow; wide

Area: spatial/experiential

Spatial/experiential categories (bold); terms (not bold)

Controlled in space: confined; constricted; harnessed; held down; impacted; manipulated; pinned down; pressured; smothered; suffocated; surrounded; trapped

Supported in space: boosted; carried; elevated; extended; held up; hovering; lifted

Contained in space: bound; closed-in; cramped; crowded; embodied; enclosed; entombed; encapsulated; immersed; in; sheltered

Free of gravity in space: boundless; floating; flying; weightless

Grounded in space: grounded; rooted; secured

Motion in space: ascend; bouncing; bounding; descend; elevated; falling; flung; glide; out of control; plummeted; propelled; pulled; pushed; raised; released; rising; rotating; sinking; soaring; spinning; spiraling; swaying; swinging; swooping; thrown; thrust; transported; trapped; turning; unleashed; wedged

Precarious position in space: bottomless; claustrophobic; cornered; dangled; frozen; hanging; paralyzed; perched; plummeted; suspended; tottering; unbalanced

Area: spatial view descriptors

Spatial view categories (bold); terms (not bold)

Obstructed/unobstructed: close; clear; cluttered; constricted; crowded; endless; expansive; far; horizon; near; opaque

Illumination: bright; dark; dim; light; well lit

Note: Developed by Susan M. Tyburczy, 2007–2008.

at the .01 level occurred between terms in categories reported in dreams, such as direction and time, dimension in space and spatially unusual or bizarre, size and time, supported in space and contained in space, energy and precarious position in space, and depth and sadness.

In response to specific interview questions, 27 of 28 dreamers reported experiencing space on their own, 21 with other people, 8 with living things, 20 with objects, and 18 with a visual–perceptual view. While experiencing space on their own, participants most frequently reported density (82.1%) and position in space (82.1%) from the spatial parameters category, motion in space (71.4%) from the spatial/experiential category, and enjoyment (75%) and fear (75%) from the emotions category. While sharing space with other people in recalled dreams, participants most frequently reported distance (75%) from spatial parameters, contained in space (46.4%), controlled in space (46.4%), and motion in space (46.4%) from spatial/experiential, and fear (60.7%) and love (60.7%) from emotions. While sharing space with living things other than people in their dreams, participants most frequently recalled and reported experiencing distance (75%) from spatial parameters, controlled in space (17.9%), and contained in space (17.9%) from spatial/experiential, and surprise (21.4%) from emotions in recalled dreams. While sharing space with objects in their recalled dreams, participants most frequently recalled density (64.3%) from spatial parameters, contained in space (39.3%) from spatial/experiential, and enjoyment (53.6%) from emotions.

Sixteen participants reported observing themselves as observers in their own dreams from 33 different positions in space grouped by the researcher into position headings, including above, adjacent, below, level with, and multipositions.

Future research topics considering human experiences with space in dreams might include spatial experiences in precognitive, lucid, or telepathic dreams or nightmares, spatially bizarre aspects of dreams, or the phenomenon of dreamers observing themselves as observers from spatial perspectives. The relationship between space and time in dreams is also a potential research topic. The roles that spatial experiences in dreams play in problem solving or memory-consolidation processes might be explored. Further neurological studies concerning the dreaming brain while experiencing space in specific situations are also suggested for future research.

Susan M. Tyburczy

References

Brenneis, C.B. (1970). Male and female ego modalities in manifest dream content. *Journal Abnormal Psychology, 76,* 434–442.

Briggs, J., & Peat, F.D. (1987). Interview, David Bohm. *Omni, 9,* 68–76.

Erikson, E. (1954). The dream specimen of psychoanalysis. *J Am Psychoanal Assoc,* 2–5.

Erikson, E. (1979). The dream specimen of psychoanalysis. In R.P. Knight & C.R. Friedman (Eds.), *Psychoanalytic psychiatry and psychology: Clinical and theoretical papers* (pp. 131–173). New York: International University Press.

Foulkes, D., Pivik, T., Steadman, H.S., Spear, P.S., & Symonds, J.D. (1967). Dreams of the male child: An EEG study. *Journal of Abnormal Psychology, 72,* 457–467.

Goleman, D. (1995). *Emotional intelligence.* New York: Bantam Books.

Maquet, P. (2000). Functional neuroimaging of normal human sleep by positron emission tomography. *Journal of Sleep Research, 9,* 207–231.

Maquet, P., Peters, J.M., Aerts, J., Delfiore, G., DeGueldre, C., Luxen, A., & Franck, G. (1996). Functional neuroanatomy of human rapid-eye-movement sleep and dreaming. *Nature, 383,* 163–166.

Ogawa, K., Nittono, H., & Hori, T. (2002). Brain potentials associated with the onset and offset of rapid eye movement (REM) during REM sleep. *Psychiatry and Clinical Neurosciences, 56,* 259–260.

Snyder, T.J., & Gackenbach, J. (1991). Vestibular involvement in the neurocognition of lucid dreaming. In J. Gackenbach & A. Sheikh (Eds.), *Dream images: A call to mental arms* (pp. 55–78). Amityville, NY: Baywood.

Solms, M. (1995). New findings on the neurological organization of dreaming: Implications for psychoanalysis. *Psychoanalytic Quarterly, 64,* 43–67.

Trosman, H., Rechtschaffen, A., Offenkrantz, W., & Wolpert, E. (1960). Studies in psychophysiology of dreams. *Archives of General Psychiatry, 55,* 602–607.

Tyburczy, S.M. (2008). *Recall of space in dream reports and exploring dreaming from a spatial perspective.* PhD diss., Saybrook Graduate School and Research Center, ProQuest (AAT 3379048).

Ullman, M. (1987). Wholeness and dreaming. In B.J. Hiley & F. D Peat (Eds.), *Quantum implications: Essays in honor of David Bohm* (pp. 386–395). New York: Routledge & Kegan Paul.

Sports and Dreaming

The continuity hypothesis in dream research suggests that the dream content reflects waking experiences (Schredl, 2003).

One study, for example, demonstrated that the amount of time spent in different waking activities (e.g., car driving) is related to the occurrence of the corresponding activity in dreams; that is, the continuity hypothesis is largely supported by studies investigating different types of waking-life experiences, for example, divorce, stress, life events, on dream content (for an overview see Schredl, 2003). For the topic of sports, several pilot studies (for an overview see Erlacher & Schredl, 2004) and single case studies (e.g., Domhoff, 1996) in athletes indicate that the continuity is also present for athletic activities—that is that frequent practicing during the day is reflected in the heightened occurrence of sport dreams. Up to now, only three studies (Erlacher & Schredl, 2004, 2010a; Schredl & Erlacher, 2008) investigated the relationship between daytime sport activities and dreams in a systematic way.

In the first study, Erlacher and Schredl (2004) demonstrated in a dream-diary study that sport students dream more often about sports (active participation and general sport themes) than do psychology students, reflecting sport students' engagement in sport activities and sport theory. In the second study, Schredl and Erlacher (2008) showed that the percentage of sport dreams for sport students was directly related to the amount of time spent with waking sport activities. As the group factor was still significant after controlling for amount of practicing sport, it was hypothesized that sport students talk and think about sports more often and may be more emotionally involved in sports than psychology students. In a large sample of German athletes ($N = 632$; study 3), the frequency of sports dreams was very high, almost 90 percent of the athletes reported this kind of dream (Erlacher & Schredl, 2010a). Within the athletes the frequency of sport dreams was associated with dream-recall frequency (entered as a control variable into the analysis), the number of practice hours per week, and the number of competitions/games during the last 12 months. This finding indicates that the continuity not only reflects the amount of time spent with the particular activity during the day but also might reflect worries and stress about performing experienced by the athletes.

To summarize, sport is reflected in the dreams of persons actively engaged in this waking-life activity. In the context of completion, it would be very interesting to study whether dreams reflect worries or even sport-related nightmares might have an effect on the athletes' performance. As there is evidence from case reports and a pilot study that athletes can train their sport within lucid dreams (Erlacher & Schredl, 2010b), it would be very promising to train athletes using lucid-dreaming techniques to increase their performance.

Michael Schredl and
Daniel Erlacher

References

Domhoff, G.W. (1996). *Finding meaning in dreams: A quantitative approach*. New York: Plenum Press.

Erlacher, D., & Schredl, M. (2004). Dreams reflecting waking sport activities: A comparison of sport and psychology students. *International Journal of Sport Psychology, 35,* 301–308.

Erlacher, D., & Schredl, M. (2010a). Frequency of sport dreams in athletes. *International Journal of Dream Research, 3,* 91–94.

Erlacher, D., & Schredl, M. (2010b). Practicing a motor task in a lucid dream enhances subsequent performance: A pilot study. *Sport Psychologist, 24,* 157–167.

Schredl, M. (2003). Continuity between waking and dreaming: A proposal for a mathematical model. *Sleep and Hypnosis, 5,* 38–52.

Schredl, M., & Erlacher, D. (2008). Relationship between waking sport activities, reading and dream content in sport and psychology students. *Journal of Psychology, 142,* 267–275.

Stage behind the Eyes— Theater and Dreams

Since the dawn of the Western drama in ancient Greece, dreams have featured frequently in and been used as inspiration for plays and other dramatic performance pieces. In this entry, I will touch on some examples and discuss why the relationship between dreams and theater seems so natural. I will end with a suggestion for further exploration of dream material in dramatic writing and performance.

Dreams have found their way into storytelling from earliest times. From Gilgamesh's dream of a great axe to Jacob's stairway to heaven dream in the Bible and the dreams of Agamemnon and Penelope in Homer's *Iliad* and *Odyssey,* dreams have always served to highlight important moments in narratives—the prophetic, the fantastic, the seemingly prosaic.

The first clear instance of a dream appearing in a theater piece is Atossa's dream in Aeschylus' *The Persians* (first performed in 472 BCE). Since that time theatrical storytellers have frequently used dreams as plot points, framing devices, and stylistic models. Dreams and dream references appear more than 200 times in works by Shakespeare, most significantly perhaps in *Richard III* and *A Midsummer Night's Dream*. They appear in the works of other dramatists as various as Calderon (*Life Is a Dream*), Strindberg (*A Dream Play*), and J. B. Priestley (the "Time Plays").

One reason for the connection between dreams and theater is that in both we readily accept that anything is possible. In dreams as in plays the prophetic and the magical, no matter how outlandish or absurd, can seem true and real, and the commonplace significant.

Another reason for the connection is that in both the theater of sleep (Almansi & Béguin, 2009) and the playhouse we can experience an intensity of emotion that in our waking lives we would try to avoid as embarrassing or outrageous. No performer wants to portray a character who is *slightly* homicidal, a *tiny* bit in love; dramatic characters tend to feel strongly and behave boldly, often irrationally. Hence powerful dream stories can serve as excellent models for drama. As Jon Lipsky (2009) writes in his wonderful book on group dream enactment, *Dreaming Together,* "We experience in sleep the passions of a Cyrano, of a Hedda Gabler, of a Richard III. We become a thief, a movie star, a randy lover" (p. 14). The continuing success of the theater confirms our urgent desire to experience the full range of emotions that life has to offer, and dream material can give us the dramatic license to incarnate those emotions on stage and examine them.

As in so many areas of dramaturgy, Shakespeare realized the usefulness of dreams as drama more fully than anyone.

In *Richard III* (the play in which the word dream appears most often—26 times), Clarence recounts a harrowing dream of drowning, which becomes a metaphor for his guilt and a premonition of his actual fate. Brakenbury, listening to the description, is terrified, as Shakespeare means us to be as we empathize with Clarence's dire and emotion-filled predicament. Other dreams are woven contrapuntally through the drama as enticements to action or inaction, as punishments and rewards, reminding us of the ever-present interplay of opposites and contradictions in our lives.

In *A Midsummer Night's Dream,* the emphasis is on the comical, sexual, and transformative qualities of dreams and the emotions they provoke. The play can be seen as a series of dreams within dreams, into which we are invited to enter willingly and from which, having learned something about ourselves, we awaken changed. Bottom's famous dream of becoming a donkey turns out to be partly real, as does Hermia's about a serpent, with its implications of sexuality, temptation, and danger. In fact all the lovers' actions are laced with images of good and bad dreams which unleash emotions and behavior that would otherwise be prohibited. Even Titania, Queen of the Fairies, is herself bewitched by the dream image of falling in love with an ass (Bottom as donkey). The play's ending leaves the characters finally awake and the audience with the wistful feeling of loss that so often follows a wonderful dream.

Playwrights have often appropriated the elasticity of time and space that we feel in dreams. J. B. Priestley (1937) wrote his *Time and the Conways* to explore the ideas of circular or serial time as put forth by amateur dream researcher J. W. Dunne (1927) in his essay *An Experiment with Time*, which argues that precognitive images in dreams suggest that time is not linear. Priestley believed in Dunne's conclusions and saw great dramatic possibilities in them. Presenting the Conway family, happy and unified after World War I but torn apart on the eve of World War II, Priestley manages to combine with great force and emotion the family's story, the politics and social milieu of England between the wars, and his ideas about time. As in dreams, images in his drama both embody meaning and obscure it, causing us to consider the more closely what we have seen.

August Strindberg's (1919) theatrical explorations are described in his preface to *A Dream Play*, where he writes that he "sought to imitate the disjointed yet seemingly logical shape of a dream. Everything can happen, everything is possible and probable. Time and space do not exist; the imagination spins, weaving. . .a mixture of memories, experiences, free associations, absurdities and improvisations. The characters split, double, multiply, evaporate, condense, dissolve and merge. But one consciousness rules them all: the dreamer's; for him there are no secrets, no inconsistencies, no scruples and no laws."

The dreamlike weaving together of disparate images that Strindberg mentions can be a source of inspiration to the performer working to build authentic character and narrative. Theater artists know that, like dreams, the best dramatic creations affect the viewer on many levels, as much intuitively as consciously. And using strong images mined from one's own subconscious can help break through barriers of performance anxiety to enhance the truthful enactment of strong emotional states. Performers can consciously draw on and effectively embody the vivid scenes and feelings revealed in dreams, combining them with other story elements to great effect.

It is important to touch on the question of how to distinguish between dramatically useful dream material and that which seems only the meaningless flotsam and jetsam of our ever-crowded minds. The answers are certainly as varied and layered as the people and dramatic pieces that attempt to incorporate dream imagery, and it would be useless to try to lay down strict rules. However, there are solid principles that can act as guides.

In my own work as a theater director, I have often used dream material in company-devised work. In doing so I have been careful first to define a clear theme for the piece and then to choose or reject dream images or sequences based on how well they develop that theme. In *What Dreams May Come*, a piece inspired by the book *Nightmares* by neuropsychologist Patrick McNamara (2008), a company of 10 university acting students were asked to do dream journaling over the course of several weeks and were then taken through a series of exercises designed to capture nightmare images, narrative sequences, and dialogue generated by their own subconscious minds on the theme "Face Your Fears." Young actors usually respond immediately to the idea of dream enactment because it gives them license to explore and to play. In this case, scores of dream fragments were written down, recorded, or worked out in movement. Many of these, however, were ultimately rejected as being either too obscure or too obvious. The weaving together of the remaining elements with video, sound, and group movement resulted in sequences that brought to coherent life on stage the universal and often enigmatic qualities of nightmares and powerfully illustrated the theme.

There are other examples too numerous to mention here, but before closing I can suggest an area of potential study that might combine scientific and performance research. Brain-imaging techniques such as functional magnetic resonance imaging have advanced in recent years to allow researchers to see emotional responses in the brain. Perhaps it will be possible in the future to observe more closely a dreamer's emotional responses during sleep and to compare them with the subject's memories of the dream. The conjunctions and disjunctions in these two narratives could be put into theatrical form to explore the relation of truth and fiction or the idea of multiple realities.

Given the variety of the treatment of dreams in the history of theater, it is safe to say that we have not yet exhausted the fruitfulness of studying the interrelation of these two modes of self-knowledge.

Robert Shampain

References

Almansi, G., & Béguin, C. (2009). *Theatre of sleep* (online Creative Commons Copyright). Retrieved from http://www.archive.org/stream/TheatreOfSleep/theatre_of_sleep_01.txt

Dunne, J. W. (1927). *An experiment with time*. London: Faber & Faber.

Lipsky, J. (2009). *Dreaming together*. Burdett, NY: Larson Publications.

McNamara, P. (2008). *Nightmares: The science and solution of those frightening visions during sleep*. Westport, CT: Praeger Perspectives.

Priestley, J. B. (1937). *Time and the Conways*. New York: Harper Brothers.

Strindberg, A. (1919). *A dream play*. University of California Press.

Stages of Sleep and Associated Waveforms

We are living in a rhythmic environment. Temperature and daylight vary with the seasons and with it vegetation and nature changes, as does the behavior of animals, humans, yet all living organisms. In short, to be successful in the course of evolution and everyday-life behavior of any creature must oscillate with the cadences of its environment. The most striking and obvious periodic behavior is the alternation between waking and sleeping behavior. The electrical rhythms generated by the massed firing of neuronal tissue in the brain characterize these two distinct states and are recorded by EEG, first described in 1929 by the Austrian psychiatrist Hans Berger. In general, high-frequency, low-amplitude rhythms are associated with alertness and waking or the dreaming stages of sleep. Low-frequency, high-amplitude oscillations on the other hand are associated with nondreaming sleep stages and with the pathological state of coma.

The rhythms are categorized by their frequency range each named after a Greek letter. The sequence of these Greek letters is not logical and can only be understood in historical terms. The frequencies of the potentials recorded from the scalp of normal humans typically vary from 0.5 to 50 Hz, and the amplitudes typically lie between 10 and 50 μV.

Since even the earliest empirical findings in EEG research the *alpha (α) rhythm* (8–13 Hz) has presented itself as the most dominant brain oscillations in the human EEG. The α-rhythm does tend to increase in amplitude during rest and relaxation and is relatively absent during intellectual functioning (for review see Klimesch, 1999). Thus, a strong α-rhythm can generally be observed in relaxed individuals who are awake with their eyes closed. Sensory stimulation or strain during the recording usually causes significant reduction of the α-rhythm and replacement with lower voltage, faster frequencies. The finding that alpha desynchronizes or becomes suppressed during mental activity was already described in the late 1920s by Berger (1929).

Alpha often has a mean frequency centering around 10 Hz with the maximum voltage over the parieto–occipital electrodes. However, evidence provided by Klimesch (1999) indicates that within the 8- to 13-Hz alpha range, different frequency bands should be differenced; lower alpha (6–10 Hz) reflecting attentional processes and upper alpha (10–12 Hz) reflecting the processing of sensory-semantic information. The α-rhythm is thought to be generated in thalamo–cortical feedback loops as discussed in detail by Lopes da Silva (1999).

Beta (β) waves (>14 Hz) occur in all individuals, are usually of low amplitude, and are normally distributed maximally over frontal and central regions. Generally spoken, beta rhythms signal an activated cortex. *Delta ( ) activity* (0.5–4 Hz) is normally not prevalent in the awake adult, but is a prominent feature of sleep and becomes increasingly dominant during the progress from light to deep stages. Delta waves have the largest amplitudes, normally between 20 and 200 μV. Electroencephalographic activity between 4 and 7 Hz or *theta (θ) activity* is seen in normal drowsiness and sleep, and during wakefulness in young children. Theta is also present in normal waking adults and has been related to the encoding of new information (cf. Klimesch, 1999).

Stages of Sleep

According to the new sleep classification from the American Academy of Sleep Medicine (AASM) (Iber, Ancoli-Israel, Chesson, & Quan, 2007) waking (W) is associated with trains of sinusoidal 8 to 13 Hz activity (predominantly over occipital brain areas). Light sleep (N1) is associated with low amplitude, predominantly 4 to 7 Hz activity and sharply contoured vertex waves (with duration <0.5 seconds). Deep sleep (N2) is characterized by K-complexes (well-delineated negative sharp waves immediately followed by a positive component, >0.5 seconds in duration) and sleep spindles (12–15 Hz waxing and waning oscillatory bursts). Last but not least, rapid eye movement sleep (R) is reflected by low-amplitude, mixed-frequency EEG, sawtooth waves (trains of sharply contoured 2–6 Hz waves), low chin EMG, and rapid eye movements in the electrooculogram.

Manuel Schabus

See also: entries related to Sleep Assessment

References

Berger, H. (1929). Über das Elektroenkephalogramm des Menschen. *Archives Psychiatriaca Nervenkraus, 87,* 527–570.

Iber, C., Ancoli-Israel, S., Chesson, A., & Quan, S. F. (2007). *The AASM manual for the scoring of sleep and associated events: Rules terminology and technical specifications.* Westchester, IL: American Academy of Sleep Medicine.

Klimesch, W. (1999). EEG alpha and theta oscillations reflect cognitive and memory performance: A review and analysis. *Brain Research Reviews, 29,* 169–195.

Lopes da Silva, F. H. (1999). Dynamics of EEGs as signals of neuronal populations: Models and theoretical considerations. In E. Niedermeyer & F. Lopes da Silva (Eds.), *Electroencephalography: Basic principles, clinical applications, and related fields* (pp. 149–173). Baltimore, MD: Williams & Wilkins.

Structural Analysis of Dream Narratives

A structural and functional approach to the analysis of everyday personal narratives was first proposed by Labov and Waletzky (1967). They defined narratives as "one method of recapitulating past experience by matching a verbal sequence of clauses to the sequence of events that actually occurred" (Labov & Waletzky, 1967, p. 20). They also suggested that narratives follow a distinctive sequencing schema, resulting in a fixed temporal order of six narrative units: (1) abstract, (2) orientation, (3) complication, (4) evaluation, (5) resolution, and (6) coda.

Dream narratives are a type of personal narrative, and it has been shown that orally elicited dream recall follows a similar temporal-linear, organized, structural schema to that of narratives of everyday personal events (Cariola, 2008). The temporal sequence of dream narratives is based on five narrative units, including (1) topic introduction, (2) orientation, (3) complication, (4) evaluation, and (5) coda.

The topic introduction unit represents a conversation turn sequence in which the topic of dreams may be introduced through sharing one's own dream memory in a social situation or in the form of a question directed at the conversational partner; for example, "What did you dream last night?" The topic introduction is also often reintroduced at the beginning of the orientation unit; for example, *in my dream*. Orientation units can be differentiated between real-life orientations and dream content orientations. Real-life orientations assume a causal and temporal boundary function with the narrator typically disclosing a personal event that is associated as a possible trigger for the dream event; for example, "One day I think. . .it leads from. . .I let my dog out in the garden once when she was younger. She was a rescue dog and I had to have a lot of control over her because she was very scared of people and she'd bite them." Real-life orientations also represent a bridge between an actual self-awareness of a waking conscious state and a self-awareness of a narrative conscious state. Dream content orientations introduce the dream event in the form of spatial contextual information, thus creating a virtual spatiotemporal frame in which the actions of the characters are situated; for example, "But that same night when I went to sleep I had a dream about me and my dog. . . uh. . .taking my dog to an island very strange on a boat."

The complication unit communicates the actions and encountered problems of the virtual protagonist. It can also be differentiated between simple and developing complications. Simple complications draw on a solitary complication event; for example, "I was at my parents' house and my teeth started crumbling. And then they just started falling out and crumbling. Then I remember looking into the mirror and trying to smile and seeing lots of gaps," whereas a developing complication conveys a complication that develops throughout the narrative in thematically and causally linked event.

The complication unit is followed by the evaluation unit that conveys, implicitly or explicitly, the narrator's personal attitude, feelings, and phenomenological point of view about the dream event; for example, "It was a bit weird." The evaluation unit may also function as a preclosing sequence that coincides with the coda unit; for example, "That is sort of the dream I can only remember. It seems quite short although in your mind you. . .it felt for ages. But that's pretty much the dream I had."

The coda unit represents the closing sequence of the narrative, most typically in the form of a closing statement of the moment of awakening "and then I woke up" or the recall of the dream; for example, "I cannot remember anything more." The coda unit may also coincide with the resolution unit (Labov, 1997).

Empirical research has not yet assessed the structural and functional framework of pleasant dreams and nightmares, for which "nightmares laden with tension and conflicts may or may not propose a resolution unit, whereas positive dreams may or may not imply a conflict, arousing positive emotions and therefore not calling for a resolution unit" (Cariola, 2008, p. 17). Habermas, Meier, and Mukhtar (2009) have, however, identified linguistic and structural differences in adults' and children's emotionally positive and negative personal narratives; for example, fear narratives reflected the lowest frequency of complication units as compared with other types of negative narratives, whereas happy and sad narratives reflected a sudden closing sequence in the form of a complication unit without the use of a following successive resolution unit.

Consequently, future research might investigate qualitatively and quantitatively the structural and functional framework of pleasant dreams and nightmares and thus establish a comprehensive linguistic and structural model of dream narratives.

Laura Annamaria Cariola

See also: entries related to Dream Content

References

Cariola, L. A. (2008). A structural and functional analysis of dream narratives. *Dreaming, 18,* 16–26.

Habermas, T., Meier, M., & Mukhtar, B. (2009). Are specific emotions narrated differently? *Emotion, 9,* 751–762.

Labov, W. (1997). Some further steps in narrative analysis. *Journal of Narrative and Life History, 7,* 395–415.

Labov, W., & Waletzky, J. (1967). Narrative analysis: Oral versions of personal experience: Essays on the verbal and visual arts. In June Helm (Ed.), *American Ethnological Society* (pp. 12–44). Seattle: University of Washington Press.

Toolan, M. (2005). *Narrative: A critical linguistic introduction.* New York: Routledge.

Subjective Experience across States of Sleep and Wakefulness

Historically, dreaming has been viewed as a state of consciousness largely disparate from that of waking cognition. Due to their apparently bizarre nature, dreams were once ascribed to external origins, as supernatural omens or messages from the gods. In the early 1900s, Freud translated this otherworldly view of dreams as messages into psychological terms, popularizing the notion that dreams originate from repressed wishes in an unconscious portion of the mind that is inaccessible to our waking thoughts. As this specific view of dreaming fell out of favor, more modern neuroscience-based approaches continued to emphasize dreaming as a neurophysiological state best viewed as distinct from all other forms of cognition. Following the first all-night electrophysiological studies of the sleeping brain in the 1950s, the discovery of rapid eye movement sleep (REM) provided an attractive candidate for a brain-state correlate of dream experience. At the time, dreams were thought to be confined exclusively to REM sleep (Dement & Kleitman, 1957). The activation–synthesis hypothesis of Hobson and McCarley (1977) built on this notion of REM as the neural substrate for dreaming, linking proposed features of dreaming (such as bizarreness, intense emotionality, and hallucination) to the elevated acetylcholine levels, brain stem activity, and desynchronized EEG that characterizes the REM state. However, subsequent research revealed that to the contrary, dream experiences often occur outside of REM (Foulkes, 1967), including during the deepest stages of slow-wave sleep. The REM state is consistently associated with high rates of dream recall (with participants recalling dreaming about 80% of the time when awakened from REM sleep), and dreams during REM tend to be particularly complex and emotional. However, dreaming is reported approximately 50 percent of the time from non-REM sleep as well, and cognition during these sleep stages can at times be as bizarre, vivid, and story-like as REM dreaming, particularly late in the night. These observations suggest that the generation of hallucinatory imagery and thought during sleep in general must be explained by mechanisms that are common to all stages of sleep.

In fact, recent evidence suggests that dreaming is best viewed as a part of a continuum of spontaneously generated cognition that occurs in all states of sleep, and which shares meaningful features with waking thought and imagery during periods of rest, when attention to sensory input is reduced. Research on the default mode of cognition during resting wakefulness has been particularly helpful in understanding the neural basis of daydreaming (Andrews-Hanna, Reidler, Huang, & Buckner, 2010), and how the study of waking cognition may inform our understanding of sleep and dreaming states (Wamsley & Stickgold, 2010). The term default network refers to a collection of brain regions that are particularly active during resting wakefulness (including medial temporal, medial prefrontal, midline, and parietal regions). This rest–activity network has been linked to the processing of memory, theory of mind, and preparation for future experience, reminding the neuroscience community that in rest, as in sleep, the brain continues to process information and to generate conscious experience. This network pattern during quiet wakefulness may provide a partial explanation for the construction of daydreaming, with one recent study reporting that individuals who experience more daydream-like thoughts of the past and future during a resting condition exhibit increased functional connectivity between components of the default network (Andrews-Hanna et al., 2010). Thus, this activity pattern appears to support the generation of spontaneous thought and imagery during wakefulness. Tellingly, similar patterns of brain activity are present throughout sleep, as medial temporal and midline frontal regions remain relatively active during both REM and NREM stages. As sleep and default-mode cognition also share electrophysiological and neurochemical features thought to support the generation of mental imagery, this thriving line of research in the cognitive neurosciences provides a promising window into mechanisms that may support dream experience.

Certainly, there are meaningful distinctions to be made between various states of sleep and wakefulness in terms of the form that subjective experience takes. That dreaming is more prevalent and more emotional in REM than in NREM sleep, for example, may yet prove to be instructive in linking particular qualities of dream experience to patterns of neural activity in the REM state. Yet at the same time, to understand dreaming, we must first understand the general mechanisms that produce spontaneous mental imagery in any state of consciousness. To date, a strong focus on interstate variations in cognition may have hindered progress in understanding these more basic neural correlates of off-line cognition. Following recent work on the default mode of brain function, future research could profitably explore neural mechanisms of off-line cognition common to REM sleep, NREM sleep, and wakefulness. In particular, the engagement of memory systems during quiet resting and during sleep states, both of which are associated with the reactivation of recent memory traces, suggests a common function for dream experience and waking cognition in the processing of new memories (Wamsley & Stickgold, 2010).

Erin J. Wamsley

See also: Sleep and Mild Cognitive Impairment

References

Andrews-Hanna, J.R., Reidler, J.S., Huang, C., & Buckner, R.L. (2010). Evidence for the default network's role in spontaneous cognition. *Journal of Neurophysiology, 104*(1), 322–335.

Dement, W., & Kleitman, N. (1957). The relation of eye movements during sleep to dream activity: An objective method for the study of dreaming. *Journal of Experimental Psychology, 53*(5), 339–346.

Foulkes, D. (1967). Nonrapid eye movement mentation. *Experimental Neurology* (Suppl. 4), 28–38.

Hobson, J. A., & McCarley, R. W. (1977). The brain as a dream state generator: An activation-synthesis hypothesis of the dream process. *American Journal of Psychiatry, 134*(12), 1335–1348.

Wamsley, E. J., & Stickgold, R. (2010). Dreaming and offline memory processing. *Current Biology, 20*(23), R1010–R1013.

Sumerian Dream Beliefs

Sumerian civilization was the first to develop writing and the first from which literary texts remain, dating back to the late third millennium BCE. Some of these texts contain accounts of dreams, especially of royal figures. The Sumerians made a distinction between clear dreams, which come only to people who have observed the proper ritual preparations, and obscure or symbolic dreams, which come to everyone else and require professional interpretation. A ruler who wished to obtain guidance from dreams would go to a special incubation hut made of reeds to sleep. The walls of the hut were permeable, so as to receive dream messages from the gods. The earliest Sumerian flood hero, Ziusudra, enters such a reed hut for incubation. Ziusudra is a model of piety: "humbly obedient, reverent, attending daily, constantly, bringing forth all kinds of dreams, uttering the name of heaven and earth" (Kramer, 1958, p. 29). His reward is a dream from his god, Enki, warning him of the coming flood. Similarly, in the *Epic of Gilgamesh,* the bull–man Enkidu has a pair of dreams that clearly foretell his death, and no further interpretation is necessary (Speiser, 1958, pp. 58–59).

The second type of dream is described in a text as "a closed archive basket of the gods" (Noegel, 2001, p. 47). This links the idea of interpretation with the act of reading a cuneiform tablet, as archival documents were stored in baskets. Literacy was very limited in Sumer; only a special class of scribes drawn mostly from the upper classes received training in the difficult cuneiform script. In later times, a special class of specialist priests and priestesses called *shailu,* or questioners, were called on to interpret dreams by asking specific questions of the dreamer from long lists of dream symbols and their correspondences provided on archival tablets. The correspondences included many mechanisms for dream insight on which we still rely today: analogy, punning references, free association, and inversion. Their goal was to solve the dream, image by image, almost as if it were a cryptic equation with but a single solution, and Noegel (2001, p. 53) comments that "in this sense dream interpretation in Mesopotamia represents less a preoccupation with ambiguity than an attempt at rendering ambiguity into a projected and authoritative reality."

The earliest of the Sumerian dream texts, and evidently the earliest recorded dream in history, is the dream of Dumuzi of Uruk. Not only is the dream text itself included but also its interpretation, by Dumuzi's sister Geshtin-anna. Her role as a professional dream interpreter indicates that as early as the middle of the third millennium BCE dreams—especially those of monarchs— were taken seriously and acted on. She interprets the symbols in Dumuzi's dream, on a one-for-one basis, as representing a danger to her brother, and urges him to flee. Bendt Alster (1972, p. 43), who published the first critical edition of this text, has provided ample evidence that the text of Dumuzi's dream has a formulaic quality that derives from poetic rather than oneirocritic demands.

Such one-for-one interpretations are common in later dream-interpretation texts. In the Babylonian *Epic of Gilgamesh,* there is another example of dream interpretation by a female figure. Gilgamesh, the young king of Uruk, has angered the elders of the town. They complain to the gods, who create Enkidu, a wild man who combines human and bull characteristics. As Enkidu approaches Uruk, Gilgamesh has two significant dreams that he brings to his mother, the goddess Nin-sun, Lady Wild-Cow, for interpretation. She interprets the symbols of the dream on a one-for-one basis, indicating the coming of a companion (Speiser, 1958, p. 46).

Similarly when the historical governor of the city of Lagash, Gudea, was perplexed by a dream, he brought it to a priestess of the goddess Nanshe, a daughter of Enki. Speaking as the goddess, the priestess interpreted the dream, using the same image-for-image method, indicating that Gudea should build a temple to his god Ningishzida, the consort of Geshtin-anna (Kramer, 1963, p. 138). Gudea's statues commemorate both the dream and the resulting construction project.

Curtiss R. Hoffman

See also: entries related to History of Dreams/ Sleep

References

Alster, B. (1972). Dumuzi's dream: Aspects of oral poetry in a Sumerian myth. In *Mesopotamia: Copenhagen studies in Assyriology, 1.* Copenhagen, Denmark: Akademisk Forlag.

Kramer, S. N. (1958). A Sumerian myth. In J. B. Pritchard (Ed.), *The ancient Near East: An anthology of texts and pictures* (Vol. 1, pp. 28–30). Princeton, NJ: Princeton University Press.

Kramer, S. N. (1963). *The Sumerians: Their history, culture, and character.* Chicago: University of Chicago Press.

Noegel, S. (2001). Dreams and dream interpreters in Mesopotamia and in the Hebrew bible (Old Testament). In K. Bulkeley (Ed.), *Dreams* (pp. 45–72). New York: Palgrave.

Speiser, E. A. (1958). Akkadian myths and epics. In J. B. Pritchard (Ed.), *The ancient Near East: An anthology of texts and pictures* (Vol. 1, pp. 31–86). Princeton, NJ: Princeton University Press.

Survivors of the Holocaust and Rwandan Genocide: Dream Accounts

Trauma experienced by genocide survivors is extreme to a level almost beyond comprehension. Many survivors witnessed the brutal murders of family and friends. Often their communities have been destroyed, and many have suffered physically from their ordeals. They are left with the feeling that the world failed them. Life for them will never again be the same. The dreams of genocide survivors provide a glimpse into significant posttraumatic stress disorder. These dreams frequently include seeing or receiving messages from deceased family members or reliving the horror through nightmares.

During the Holocaust, dreams of food were quite common. As prisoners were given barely enough food to survive, their bodies diseased and emaciated, food often became the main theme of their dreams. While some might consider these to be wish-fulfillment dreams, perhaps another purpose of these dreams was the mind's final attempt to fool the body a short while longer as a means of survival. Some Holocaust survivors described dreams that helped them to survive. In one example, a survivor heard his deceased father telling him to run. He awoke from his dream and escaped from the concentration camp with other boys after the watchman had fallen asleep, thereby avoiding the gas chamber. Another man who had decided to commit suicide dreamed of his mother telling him that he must live because there was no one else left in the family to tell their story.

In the years following the Holocaust, guilt became a common theme among survivors. In order to avoid death in the camps, one often had to choose his or her own best interests over that of fellow prisoners. Stealing bread or taking someone else's shoes was often a necessity to avoid death, the cost of which was looking back years later with painful regret. After liberation, the minds of survivors were free to begin contemplating the events they had lived through and all that they had lost. Nightmares of being back in the camps were very common among survivors in the years and decades following liberation.

The 1994 genocide against Tutsi in Rwanda was much different than the Holocaust as the killings took place over a period of only about 100 days. Survivors did not live in concentration camps for weeks or months on end as they did in the Holocaust. However, most of them personally witnessed the gruesome deaths of their families. Jean Nepomuscene Sibomana lost his family in the genocide. He watched as his mother and sister were hacked to death with machetes. His father and three brothers were also killed, leaving him as the only surviving member of his family. He survived alone in the wilderness for 103 days at the age of 10 before being found by Rwandan Patriotic Front soldiers. He told of one of his post-genocide dreams in which he was standing in the halls of the United Nations, pleading for someone to listen and come save his people. No one would listen. His dream was quite literal in his desire to share his story with the world. One of the themes of some dreams of genocide survivors is their desire to try and tell the world, or to make the world a better place.

Many people who were not targeted in genocides, but who were witnesses in some regard, also experience nightmares. A reporter during the genocide in Rwanda has since spoken of dreams of corpses and road blocks, which go along with his feelings of failure to be able to help the people at the time. Similar dreams have been experienced by people who were not targeted by the Nazis during the Holocaust. Fear prevented people from intervention, and that fear combined with guilt manifested itself in the dreams of these people.

The magnitude of genocide is such that the effects of it are multigenerational. It may take several more years to understand the extent of this fact with the Rwandan genocide as most of the survivors are still young adults. The Holocaust provides more historical evidence of the effects of it on second-generation and even third-generation survivors. The children of Holocaust survivors grew up often knowing little about their parents' ordeals and family history, leaving many with unanswered questions. Second-generation survivors also dealt with feelings of shame over their parents' lack of social and language skills in their adopted countries. Dream reports from second-generation survivors often include Nazis, swastikas, cattle cars, and other symbols commonly associated with the Holocaust.

David L. Kahn

References

Frankl, V. E. (1984). *Man's search for meaning: An introduction to logotherapy* (3rd ed.). New York: Simon & Schuster.

Ilani, O. (2008, January 5). *What did concentration camp inmates dream about?* Retrieved from http://www.haaretz.com/hasen/spages/979811.html

Ilani, O. (2008, May 2). *My mother came to tell me I had to remain among the living.* Retrieved from http://www.haaretz.com/hasen/spages/979526.html

Ilibagiza, I. (2007). *Left to tell: Discovering God amidst the Rwandan Holocaust.* New York: Hay House.

Papirblat, S. (2006, April 25). Holocaust effects: Son of *Holocaust survivor still carries scars; will next generation be different?* Retrieved from ynetnews.com

Rusesabagina, P., & Zoellner, T. (2006). *An ordinary man.* New York: Penguin Group.

Sebarenzi, J. (2009). *God sleeps in Rwanda.* New York: Atria Books, a Division of Simon & Shuster.

Weiss, I., & Kosino, B. (1998). Czechoslovakia, 1923. In A. Brostoff & S. Chamovitz (Eds.), *Flares of memory: Stories of childhood during the Holocaust* (pp. 198–224). New York: Oxford University Press.

Synesthesia

Synesthesia is a neurological blending of sensory experiences in unusual ways, such that a person might see pain or taste a sound. Intrigued by the not possible nature of it, also characteristic of many dreams, an independent dream researcher collected reports of synesthetes' dreams and dreamers' experiences of synesthesia. She suggests the two fields of study might have insights to offer each other, particularly about metaphor and psi.

In synesthesia, when a person perceives a stimulus, another specific sensation occurs at the same time. The musical note B might come with a taste like almonds. Or temperature may come with sound. Or pain with color. Or (in the standard notation for connecting an *inducer* with its synesthetic *correlate*), emotion → smell.

At least 63 such combinations have been observed (Day, 2010). Color is by far the most common correlate. Estimates of synesthesia's prevalence vary widely, but some researchers speculate that basic forms of syn, too, might be universal.

Some forms are *intramodal* (e.g., a visual inducer linked with a visual correlate), some are *intermodal* or *cross-dimensional* (two different sensory channels, such as touch → taste), and some are *conceptual*— one of the most common being a sense that days of the week or months of the year are arrayed spatially around the person. Combinations can be more complex, such as [pain → color, motion, location], and many synesthetes have more than one type. All combinations are one-way streets from inducer to correlate.

Synesthesia is instantaneous, an inseparable part of the experiencer's reality, although it can fade if a person stops paying attention to it. Most synesthesia has its

In *Zig Zag*, Carol Steen has realistically depicted her synesthetic experience of color and form constants that coupled with the sensations of an acupuncture session. she writes. "I watched the visions come once all the needles were in place. I saw swirling greens, and this amazing zig zag . . . What I paint is realistic. It's considered abstract by those who cannot see what I see, and accurate in feeling and gesture by those who [have similar synesthetic correlates]." (Carol Steen)

origins in early childhood, but it can also result from brain injury, the use of hallucinogenic drugs, or epileptic seizure. Studies have established that syn is not just vivid imagination or learned associations. Brain imaging shows perception activates more areas in synesthetes than nonsynesthetes, and psychological tests find that individual synesthetes' responses to a stimulus are consistent over long periods, unlike those of nonsynesthetes.

Yet syn experiences are highly individualistic. Responses can be brief and simple,

such as those of Des Hegarty. In a post to The Synesthesia List (May 18, 2004), a private e-mail community, he said, "As I relax in meditation or about to drop into sleep, if I am disturbed by a noise, it stimulates my visual senses and produces a short burst of what could best be described as TV snow."

At the other end are the long, elaborate experiences of the late Shawn Allen O'Neal, an artist, musician, and sound designer. His synesthesia was strongest in the hypnogogic state and did not require an external stimulus (personal communication, June 8, 2003):

A typical specific instance might involve a self-generating saxophone solo, which appears as a silvery, mercurial, highly reflective, morphing and vibrating orb which may leave an intermittent "trail" of its various forms as it (and I with it) accelerates, swooping and zooming forward in space. "Chords" of neon "worms" may chase and writhe around this form. "Beneath" this might be a rhythm section of percussion, marimbas, basses, etc., where each note "appears" in space as part of a "geodesic series" or fabric of spinning, multi-colored triangular panels, flocking, re-arranging and bursting forward like a scintillating reptilian skin, the faceted note-shapes with the most emphasis always glinting perfectly with the most light. (And yes, this is all without the aid of psychedelic drugs.)

Experiences can differ between waking and dreaming. For O'Neal (who went by his initials, Sao, in some online forums), the synesthesia so abundant as he fell asleep nearly disappeared in his dreams. On a few occasions, the syn in author Pat

Duffy's (2001) dreams has been of a different type than the grapheme → color correspondences in her waking life. In a Biology 202 paper online, Bryn Mawr College student Sadie White (2002), a nonsynesthete, wrote:

> I was staring, entranced, at a delicate white flower. It was like nothing I had seen or experienced in my waking life, because the pristine, thinly-veined petals were such an exquisite color that it manifested itself upon my dreaming brain as a color and a sound. The white song was a single note—like a distant choir lifting its voice in concerted wonder.

Wide-ranging individuality is something synesthesia and dreams have in common. So is the strong sense that the experience is real; is full of nuance and often difficult to describe; and has strong emotional involvement. ("Synesthetes often gush over trivial tasks such as remembering a name or phone number, calling it 'gorgeous' or 'delightful,' whereas mismatched perceptions—such as seeing a letter printed in the wrong color ink—can be like fingernails on a blackboard," say neurologist Richard Cytowic and neuroscientist David Eagleman [2009, p. 54].) For these reasons, perhaps, both dreams and syn are sources of creative material for much artistic expression (e.g., by synesthetes Vladimir Nabokov, Wassily Kandinsky, David Hockney, and Alexander Scriabin), or simply interesting enough to inspire great efforts at precise expression.

The creativity of syn and dreams overlapped in a life-guiding way for G. Roger Davis. A dream recounted in the journal *Dreaming* (Knudson, 2001) inspired Davis in his career as a composer and music professor. In it, the motion of trees *is* music:

> The trees were all blowing. The wind was blowing, and some were blowing that way and some were blowing this way. And it was a counterpoint of trees . . . Then gradually they all started to line up toward this climax, and I realized then in that dream how to write a climax in music. . . .

Unlike the musical compositions and other expressions it may inspire, though, synesthesia does not generate integrated perceptions. In that sense, it is also unlike dreams, many of which are full of distinct characters, landscapes, and objects (all considered to be *imagery*) and extensive narratives. Instead, syn generates generic tastes, sounds, and shapes—blobs, triangles, lines, spirals, and other geometric *form constants.*

Yet there is some overlap here with dream studies. In the hypnopompic state between dreaming and awakening, George Gillespie (1997) observes lattices. Ed Kellogg (1999) perceives basic forms in lucid dreams when he resists the human tendency to identify things. Dale Graff (2004) has found form constants to be integral to dreams:

> In the mid-1970s, I began incubating dreams that hopefully would reveal something basic about the nature of dream imagery and how [dreams] were constructed.

In time, the dreams presented *only* honeycombs, grids, lines (vertical, angled, horizontal), spirals and whirling white area globs! . . .At. . . times the dynamic forms merge to create recognizable shapes, as if a subconscious process was occurring that selected, fragment by fragment, what was required to build up the image.

Graff is a physicist and former director of the federal government's remote viewing research, Project Stargate. He says remote viewing perceptions, too, come through as form constants.

Cytowic and Eagleman (2009) have noted that unusual experiences such as déjà vu, clairvoyance, and a sense of portentousness seem somewhat common among synesthetes, and at least seven synesthetes among the small sample Sturzenacker contacted reported psi experiences—several of them attesting they have them often.

If researchers can discover how perceptions are tied together in synesthesia, they will have contributed to solving the larger *binding problem*. Very small regions of the brain specialize in analyzing different aspects of an object or scene, from the shape of a pen to its color to its orientation to how light changes at its edges. The question is how the brain puts all that data together into an integrated perception so a person can accurately reach for the pen and pick it up without a moment's hesitation.

Several theories exist (Ramachandran & Hubbard, 2003). From prenatal development into early childhood, humans have an overabundance of connections among various brain regions. Around age three, the number becomes drastically reduced, or *pruned*. A dominant theory is that synesthesia is a greater-than-usual cross-activation of different regions that results from an absence or inadequacy of pruning. A variation is that neurotransmitters do the cross-activating. Another theory is that some inhibitory mechanism might be missing, and that synesthesia involves unusual feedback or feed-forward along the brain's nerve pathways. As a group, syn investigators acknowledge that their research has focused almost exclusively on color-involved synesthesia, particularly the grapheme → color type, and that their theories cannot yet account for learning (of, e.g., the days of the week).

Given the importance of metaphor to dream interpretation, one of the most intriguing ideas about synesthesia is that it has played a role in binding meanings as well—that it, is the source of metaphor, and from that, language. Eric Odgaard and Lawrence Marks (2004) say it is important to distinguish between the vivid concurrents of strong synesthesia, which is rare, and the everyday weak synesthesia that they liken to metaphor. A 1929 experiment asked people to match each of two made-up words, bouba and kiki, with one of two pictures. Across cultures, they overwhelmingly matched the first to an amoeba-like shape and the second to a jagged, pointy one. Cytowic and Eagleman (2009) extend the case that metaphor arises from physical experience rather than being derived from abstract language. They propose a cognitive continuum: perceptual similarities → synesthetic equivalences → metaphoric identities → abstract language.

Shawn O'Neal (2003) posted this description of what happens once he tunes into the flow of synesthetic sensations in the hypnogogic state. Could it be an actual experience of moving along the continuum from synesthesia to metaphor?

I am able to look back and see that not only have larger patterns been created by whatever I am watching and listening to close up—but these larger patterns continue to evolve, or branch off and reconnect, so that the whole composition may fill enormous panoramic volumes of space, sometimes creating landscapes or architecture and sometimes simply accelerating nonobjectively into a void. Complete, coherent scenes may form and break up again in perfect synchronicity to the sounds, and often these scenes will suddenly, momentarily, poignantly reflect the sort of actual, natural scenes one might be reminded of by ordinary listening (such as "this reminds me of being on the ocean" or "in a valley of aspen trees at twilight" or "in a particular room"). Here too, the lapse of being aware that I am reminded of something and perceiving the manifestation of the thing I am reminded of is startlingly instantaneous.

What might researchers in the two fields, dreaming and synesthesia, be able to learn from focusing closely on how the abundant, mostly visual metaphors observed in dreaming are created?

Gloria Sturzenacker

References

Cytowic, R. E., & Eagleman, D. M. (2009). *Wednesday is indigo blue: Discovering the brain of synesthesia*. Cambridge, MA: The MIT Press.

Day, S. (2010). Types of synesthesia. *Synesthesia*. Retrieved from http://home.comcast.net/~sean.day/html/types.html

Duffy, P. L. (2001). *Blue cats and chartreuse kittens: How synesthetes color their worlds*. New York: Times Books.

Gillespie, G. (1997). Hypnopompic imagery and visual dream experience. *Dreaming, 7*(3).

Kellogg III, E. W. (1999, October 7–9). Lucid dreaming and the phenomenological *epoché*. Presented at the Society for Phenomenology and the Human Sciences Conference, Eugene, Oregon. (Abstract available at http://dreamtalk.hypermart.net/2001/abstracts/2001_kellogg_01.htm)

Knudson, R. (2001). Significant dreams: Bizarre or beautiful? *Dreaming, 11*(4).

Odgaard, E. C., & Marks, L. E. (2004). Developmental constraints on theories of synesthesia. In L. C. Robertson & N. Sagiv (Eds.), *Synesthesia: Perspectives from cognitive neuroscience*. New York: Oxford University Press.

Ramachandran, V. S., & Hubbard, E. M. (2003, May). Hearing colors, tasting shapes. *Scientific American, 288*(5), 52–59.

White, S. (2002). Synesthesia, report for Biology 202 course at Bryn Mawr College. Retrieved from http://serendip.brynmawr.edu/bb/neuro/neuro01/web1/White.html

T

Tarotpy Method

Pioneered during the early 1980s by Lauren Z. Schneider, MA, MFT, Tarotpy® is an innovative approach to dreamwork and depth psychotherapy. Evolved over 25 years, Tarotpy combines psychotherapeutic methods, dreamwork, hypnotherapy, family systems, semiotics, and Eye Movement Desensitization and Reprocessing (EMDR) with metaphysical tools.

Tarotpy uses the rich symbolic imagery of tarot, dream cards, and other image systems to actively engage unconscious and intuitive processes. These archetypal images arise from the same psychic pool as dreams. Tarotpy enhances dreamwork by bringing further insight to a specific night dream or stimulating imagination otherwise blocked in some clients. Often, a Tarotpy session is followed by reports of more vivid dreaming.

As with dreamwork, the core principle of Tarotpy is profound respect for the inherent wisdom, creativity, and wholeness of the psyche.

The client is instructed to select the deck, number of cards, formation, and name of each placement, creating a layout. The client thus lays the unconscious on the table, participating in a dreamlike consciousness with eyes wide open. Approached without preconceived ideas and with a respectful desire to discover their intelligence, the images create a bridge for unconscious material and intuition to flow between client and therapist.

While Tarotpy functions as a projective tool for assessment and exploration, a wealth of documented cases offers empirical evidence of an unconscious mastermind at play in the random selection of cards and images. The process appears more intentional than random in bringing information vital to emotional, physical, and spiritual growth into consciousness.

First Case

Sue was a young 21 year old, struggling to take her first steps toward financial and emotional independence. After two Tarotpy sessions, she shared a nightmare: "I'm in my room and there are ghosts. I crawl terrified to my parents' room. I have no voice to call out. I'm scared to enter, but break through the fear and go in. They wonder what's wrong with me. Finally I cry out, 'There are ghosts in my room!' Then I'm holding a large cell phone with letters on the screen that spell 'Tarotpy'."

The phone image suggested that Tarotpy might offer further guidance into the dream. I invited Sue to turn her attention inward and ask her unconscious: "How many cards do I need to see?" The number four came immediately into her mind. She selected a deck from the 30 plus decks in my office and randomly chose four cards, assigning each placement a special significance, specifically fight, doubt, courage, and strength.

Sue stared at the first card: The image of the dark-haired woman closely resembled Sue, and the ghostlike hands pulling the woman's hair matched the ghost image in her dream.

I asked about the card's explicit label, guilt; Sue said she felt guilty all the time. I reflected that children often take on the guilt of their parents' unresolved issues. As the child of an alcoholic, Sue was trying to directly voice these family ghosts.

The second card, entitled reception, is the archetype of the mother; the third, creative, that of the father. The images in Sue's layout constellated the images in her dream. She was powerfully affected.

"Amazing," Sue responded. "Tarotpy is helping me communicate with my intuitive self." As the dream phone indicated, Tarotpy tapped into her cellular connection.

Sue next focused on the placement she had named strength. Reflecting on the dream, Sue recognized two acts of strength: going into her parents' room and finding her

voice. The phrase *letting go* and the image of water dropping from a leaf prompted a visceral sense of peace and calmness.

Tarotpy opens a door beyond our personal, material, or rationalistic orientation and enters the realm of the dream where events are not linear and causal, but rather multilayered and simultaneous, where the ordinary and extraordinary merge. The meaningful connection between the card images and the client's dream has a powerful impact, spontaneously evoking new perceptions on emotional cognitive and embodied levels.

Second Case

Mary came in greatly depleted and desperate. She explained that she took care of her mother, who was in her early 90s. Mary felt that since childhood she had had to parent her mother. She was also taking care of her husband, who had become ill three years ago. Mary was the sole bread winner. I suggested that Tarotpy might offer insight into what she deemed a hopeless trap.

 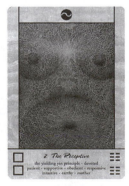  

OSHO Zen Tarot: The Transcendental Game of Zen, (c) OSHO International Foundation. www.osho.com/copyright / *Tao Oracle: An Illuminated New Approach to the I Ching*, Ma Deva Padma (c) 2002, www.thetaooracle.com, www.embraceart.com)

Even the first step of choosing from a variety of decks proved significant: Mary was exercising choice at a time when she felt she had none.

Contemplating the random selection of cards, Mary focused on a card depicting a dragon.

When asked what the dragon image evoked, Mary softened and said: "My animals."

"What do you get from your relationship with your animals?" I asked.

"Unconditional love," she said.

She relaxed and became fully present. I was impressed by this significant shift.

"Oh," she suddenly remembered, "I had a dream last night. In my backyard, there was a green creature. It was part snake, part alligator—Oh! It was a dragon and I was feeding it."

"You dreamed of a dragon?" I asked as we both stared awestruck at the card.

The dragon symbol is rarely found in tarot; against the odds Mary selected the image from her dream.

I inquired how she might feed her inner dragon.

"With my creativity," she responded.

I pointed out that dragon is a symbol for creativity throughout Eastern culture. The synchronicity between her dream and the dragon image dramatically shifted her perspective; she accessed that unconditionally loving and creative part in herself and felt renewed optimism.

Tarotpy's integrative method can accelerate the course of discovery, awareness, and transformation, reducing what may take months or years of treatment to a few sessions. Through actively engaging with imagery, a client can transform entrenched unconscious patterns and have more conscious choice over attitudes and behavior.

The synchronicity between dreams and images creates awe-inspiring moments that prompt healing of the mind, body, and spirit and reconnect us with our inner capacity for self-awareness and wholeness.

Lauren Schneider

References

Padma, D. (1994) *Osho zen tarot*. New York: St. Martin's Press.

Waldherr, K. (1997). *Lover's path tarot*. Stamford, CT: U.S. Games Systems.

Tau Protein and Sleep–Wake Cycle

Tau is a neuronal microtubule-associated protein implicated in microtubules

SEVEN OF STAVES

(Kris Waldherr)

stabilization, axonal establishment, and elongation during neuronal morphogenesis (Avila, Lucas, Perez, & Hernandez, 2004). Tau knockout animals, although phenotypically normal, have shown a significant delay in the axonal extension of hippocampal neurons and lag in stage development (Dawson et al., 2001), which may affect both neural coordination and synaptic efficiency in local- and long-range circuits. This hypothesis has been recently supported by *in vivo* electrophysiological studies that found a role of tau in hippocampal theta rhythm generation and formation of functional circuits between the frontal cortex and other brain regions through gamma oscillations (Cantero et al., 2010).

Sleep and resting represent global states whose control mechanisms are manifested at every level of biological organization, from genes to neural circuits and cerebral systems. Regulation of the sleep–wake cycle involves coordinated activity between the suprachiasmatic nucleus and diencephalic structures, as well as in regions of the basal forebrain and brain stem. The integrity of this complex circuitry requires stable and plastic properties of the neuronal cytoskeleton, which is assisted by tau during the early postnatal period. *In vivo* electrophysiological experiments performed in tau knockout mice have confirmed the role of tau protein in sleep–wake organization and underlying electrophysiology (Cantero et al., 2011). Tau-deficient animals show abnormalities of sleep–wake cycle characterized by increased wakefulness duration and decreased nonrapid eye movement (NREM) sleep time, a higher number of state transitions between NREM and wake, and shortened sleep bouts. Altered sleep structure in tau knockout mice is accompanied by a decline in delta power together with an enhanced spectral density of sleep spindles during NREM sleep. REM sleep, however, seems to be unaltered by the lack of tau.

The mechanistic role of tau protein in the sleep–wake cycle is supported by different lines of evidence. Tau interacts with the neural membrane through its amino-terminal projection domain. And slow-wave activity (<4 Hz) results from membrane hyperpolarization associated with slow oscillations in membrane potential of cortical and thalamocortical neurons. Therefore, the absence of tau may alter intrinsic membrane properties affecting, in turn, the emergence of slow-wave activity during NREM sleep. Subtle disruptions in neuronal microtubule dynamics in response to the absence of tau may have important consequences on circadian activity patterns. Indeed, microtubules have demonstrated modulation of the sensitivity states of different melatonin receptors (Jarzynka et al., 2009), which may impact on the regulation of the sleep–wake cycle. Consequently, tau, through its role in microtubule assembly, might contribute to the integrity of melatonin-regulated physiological processes affecting the sleep–wake circadian rhythm.

Overall, tau protein has an effect on mechanisms of control and maintenance of sleep–wake states and the underlying brain oscillatory patterns. Given that Alzheimer's disease represents one of the most prevalent tauopathies often associated with sleep disorders, relationships between microtubule dynamics and sleep–wake cycle may shed light on cellular disease processes involved in this prevalent neurodegenerative condition.

Jose L. Cantero, Eva
Hita-Yañez, and Jesus Avila

See also: entries related to Genetics of Sleep

References

Avila, J., Lucas, J. J., Perez, M., & Hernandez, F. (2004). Role of tau protein in both physiological and pathological conditions. *Physiological Reviews, 84,* 361–384.

Cantero, J. L., Hita-Yañez, E., Moreno-Lopez, B., Portillo, F., Rubio, A., & Avila, J. (2010). Tau protein role in sleep-wake cycle. *Journal of Alzheimer's Disease, 21,* 411–421.

Cantero, J. L., Moreno-Lopez, B., Portillo, F., Rubio, A., Hita-Yañez, E., & Avila, J. (2011). Role of tau protein on neocortical and hippocampal oscillatory patterns. *Hippocampus, 21*(8), 827–834.

Dawson, H. N., Ferreira, A., Eyster, M. V., Ghoshal, N., Binder, L. I., & Vitek, M. P. (2001). Inhibition of neuronal maturation in primary hippocampal neurons from tau-deficient mice. *Journal of Cell Science, 114,* 1179–1187.

Jarzynka, M. J., Passey, D. K., Johnson, D. A., Konduru, N. V., Fitz, N. F., Radio, N. M., . . . Witt-Enderby, P. A. (2009). Microtubules modulate melatonin receptors involved in phase-shifting circadian activity rhythms: *In vitro* and *in vivo* evidence. *Journal of Pineal Research, 46,* 161–171.

Teaching Courses on Dreams

People teach about dreams in many contexts and venues. Here we will treat mainly courses in colleges and universities. This is not intended to slight the importance of dream instruction occurring in the larger community: in homes, schools, free-standing institutes, and by solo practitioners. In fact, dream instruction inside and outside of academia is complementary—the former hewing more rigorously to scientific procedures and other discipline-appropriate standards, and the latter exploring uncharted territory often in a bolder fashion.

Two ways in which courses on dreams are distinctive are, first, in that the subject matter is inherently multidisciplinary (although individual courses are usually lodged in just one academic area); and, second, in that dream courses often will have a substantial experiential component, with students' own dreams as course content. Both of these distinguishing features are problematic in certain ways: Instructors educated in one discipline may not be conversant with the range of academic fields and perspectives with important things to say about dreams. And working with students' dreams may open the door to emotional vulnerabilities that call for careful consideration and handling.

Dreams may be approached through perspectives and methods of the sciences, social sciences, humanities, and arts—separately and in concert.

Sciences and Social Sciences

Dreaming processes draw on biological and psychological domains. Dream content lends itself to understandings of personal meanings and collective social concerns, via qualitative analyses of individual dreams and quantitative analyses of patterns in multiple dreams. Biological, psychological, and social approaches can use both observational and experimental procedures.

Examples of dream-related offerings in psychology include G. William Domhoff's course at the University of California at Santa Cruz, and Tracy Kahan's at Santa Clara University. Domhoff's emphasis is on dream content analysis, Kahan's on dreaming and sleeping processes. (It is noteworthy, however, that each covers such topics as how dreams have been viewed historically, clinical theory and applications, and dreams in society—that is, both instructors expand course topics to reflect the multidisciplinary quality of dream studies mentioned previously.) Don Middendorf at Evergreen State College teaches another worthy course on dream psychology. Laurel McCabe's course at Sonoma State University takes a depth psychology tack in exploring the uses of dreams in clinical work and psychological/spiritual growth. Other courses on dreams with a clinical focus include those by Deirdre Barrett at Harvard and Clara Hill at the University of Maryland.

Dream practices are studied in cultural context by anthropologists, whose findings and teachings provide a different, and valuable, perspective on dreams—that they are lodged firmly in systems of meaning, social organization, and control inherent in all societies. Contemporary dream offerings in anthropology include courses by Roger Lohmann at Trent University, Toronto; Jeannelle Marie Mageo at Washington State University; Mary Dombeck at the University of Rochester (School of Nursing); Iain Edgar, at Durham University, England; Robin Sheriff at the University of New Hampshire; and Charles Stewart, at University College, London.

While there are few, if any, dream courses lodged in other social sciences—economics, sociology, and political science—dreams in principle (in their contents, and how people interact concerning dreams) reflect social dynamics as well as the personal concerns of the dreamer. Dreams therefore illuminate society's myriad effects on the psyche of the individual. Waking political attitudes, for example, are related to both dream content and attitudes about dreams. Social scientists can draw on the accumulated body of dream knowledge in teaching about the connections between outer societal patterns and inner dream echoes.

Humanities and Arts

Writing

The ability to recall one's dreams, to articulate them in words, pictures and other creative productions, and to respond similarly to others' dreams, is a basic academic skill. This is especially true in terms of both compositional and creative writing. Dreams are the core proto-narrative. When recalled upon waking they can be written, and their content written about. An attention to dreams in courses on writing can shatter writer's block. College courses on writing that treat dreams as a central motif include Bernard Welt's at the Corcoran College of Art and Design and Jason Tugaw's at Queens College of the City University of New York (both of which make extensive use of blogs to foster student and student–instructor interaction). Other notable courses that have used dreams as a tool for writing instruction are Barbara Bishop's Freshman composition course at Marymount College in California, and Betsy Davids's course "Writing and Reading the Dream" at the California College of the Arts. Dreams and digital video are explored by Ruth Lingford at Harvard's Department of Visual and Environmental Studies. Allucquere Rosanne Stone studies and teaches surrealism through dreams at the University of Texas.

Philosophy and Religion

Aspects of dreams reflect basic philosophical and religious questions. Dreams and their interpretations can comment on both specific religious and nondoctrinal spiritual concerns. Class discussions in almost any dream course inevitably get around to questions about the difference between reality and illusion, how we can know that what we believe is true, the ultimate nature of the human mind, why is there evil, and whether God exists, among other existential matters. Thoughtful models for courses on religious and spiritual dimensions of dreams include those by Christopher Dreisbach at St. Mary's College of Maryland; Eleanor Rosch at University of California, Berkeley; Kimberley Patton at Harvard Divinity School; and Patricia M. Davis at the Graduate Theological Seminary. Kelly Bulkeley has written and taught widely on philosophical and religious dimensions of dreams, among many other dream topics. Instructors could provide themselves a sound, wide-ranging, multidisciplinary background education in dreams with Bulkeley's writings alone.

General Humanities, Film Studies, and the New Media

The mission of the humanities in all its fields is to ponder what is distinctively human, and how that complexity of being is manifested in literature, art, drama, dance, and in the historical unfolding of human activity. While humanities courses focused centrally on dreams are few, an exemplary offering is Bernard Welt's at the Corcoran College of Art and Design.

Film studies is a division of the humanities, and there are such close affinities between film and dreams that film deserves specific mention. Both dreams and films are story-like, primarily visual experiences with other sensory, emotional, and cognitive content. One is generally lost in a dream—not realizing it was only a dream until awakening. Similarly, one can be (and ideally is) lost; that is, swept up—in the experience of watching a film. Films both express and reflect dream content and process, and dreams may incorporate film imagery. There are many courses about films, but at this point courses explicitly treating the dream–film nexus are rare, despite an impressive literature on dream–film parallels.

Related to film, electronic media of all kinds have created new abilities to recreate, communicate, and comment on dreams and dream-related ideas. Educators are on the cusp of being able to create and transfer electronically versions of dream experiences that are remarkably faithful to the dreamer's original experience. Also, dreams may be discussed online by groups of persons not physically proximate. (Whether this is entirely a desirable practice is debatable, since face-to-face contact with its direct communication of tone and nuance is missing.)

The reviews by Welt of dreams in connection with perspectives and resources in general humanities (and in film) in

Dreaming in the Classroom, referenced later, provide the aspirant instructor with a rich array of materials on which to draw. Welt discusses how an understanding of dreams is informed by the humanities, and how, reciprocally, a dream perspective enhances our appreciation of literature, poetry, and the visual and performing arts.

Dream Course Topics

Course content will vary with the particular discipline, departmental home and the education and goals of the instructor. However, topics likely to be covered to varying degrees, whatever the disciplinary foundation, include: (1) common questions, conceptions, and misconceptions about dreams; (2) how dreams have been viewed and used historically in different cultures (including our own culture and time); (3) processes of sleeping and dreaming underlying dream generation; (4) dream recall and processing, using dream journals, systems of dream analysis, and discussion groups: (5) research findings on dreaming process and dream content; (6) dreams as reflected in (and inspiring) literature, art, drama, dance, and film; (7) religious and spiritual dreams; (8) lucid and paranormal dreams; and (9) dream interpretation, and applications of dreams in psychotherapy, counseling, and personal growth.

Dream courses generally are characterized by high student enthusiasm and interest. In particular, the dreams of the students infuse dream study with personal meaning, and spur deep interest in the course. Keeping journals of their dreams, sharing them in class dream-discussion groups, and analyzing themes in remembered dreams as term paper topics are ways to connect the course to students' personal dreams.

At first glance it would seem obvious that students' dreams should be included in the course in important, even central, ways. Instructors must decide how to weave students' dreams into course activities and assignments. I (King) allotted up to 40 percent or so of my semester-long dream psychology course to dream-discussion groups, to decidedly positive effect. However, there are important ethical (and at times even clinical) questions concerning the personal exposure and vulnerability that can ensue if students are routinely expected to share, and process, their dreams in the class. Students may not have bargained for this when they enrolled. Some (although a small minority) may find the quasi-clinical nature of attending to their dreams disturbing. Instructors should be sensitive to this and should consider such procedures as screening ahead of time, obtaining informed consent, protecting the anonymity of students' dreams (perhaps by foregoing or diminishing in importance dream-discussion groups), and so on. One useful approach is to have students work with their own dreams individually but not in discussion groups. Another is to aggregate students' dreams and analyze them quantitatively, but not interpret individual dreams.

There is a robust and creative array of dream-educative activities outside colleges and universities. Some primary and secondary school teachers employ dreams as a subject. Alternative, free-standing institutes with a major focus on dreams, workshops for professionals, community dream-discussion groups, and solo practitioners are often in the vanguard of theoretical innovation and creative pedagogy. In fact, academia historically has been somewhat timid in embracing dreams as a legitimate topic, and alternatives have sprung up to fill the void. Examples of, but by no means all, worthy courses and programs of study (and persons centrally involved) include Pacifica Graduate Institute (Stephen Aisenstet), the Haden Institute (Bob Haden), Saybrook Graduate School and Research Center (Stanley Krippner), Ecole Internationale de Reves (Nicole Gratton), and the Institute for Dream Studies (Justina Lasley).

There are also innovative courses lodged in conventional universities (e.g., John F. Kennedy university, Sonoma State University), and innovative practitioner/teachers who teach both within and outside academia, such as Jeremy Taylor, Alan Siegel, and Robert Bosnak.

The International Association for the Study of Dreams (IASD) holds an annual major conference and several regional conferences each year, as well as offering Internet-based continuing education. IASD's conference offerings are particularly valuable in that they feature the latest research findings, workshop, and other advances.

Future development of dream teaching will likely involve innovations in teaching dream interpretation, the use of digital electronic media, and increasing interdisciplinary integration. Woven through many, if not most courses is an attention to dream interpretation as an important topic and activity. Students want to understand the meaning and significance of their own dreams! Interpretive theories, procedures, and skills take center stage. Therefore the epistemology of dream interpretation is very important, and dream courses that include dream interpretation need to treat these matters carefully, and not assume that fidelity to particular theories of meaning and procedures insures accurate interpretations or adequate education. The loci of dream meanings—whether teased from the dream itself or brought to the dream from waking perspectives and needs, and the role of bodily processes in creating meaning are two important epistemological matters to be considered.

Similarly, as electronic media grow in sophistication, representations of dreams are becoming communicable in ways increasingly faithful to the dream experience itself. This may enhance dream sharing and the social deliberation about dream meanings. However, electronic communication is not face-to-face sharing, and something important may be lost as communication shifts from the latter to the former.

Interdisciplinary ways of teaching about dreams are likely to continue the progression from separate courses in different fields to multiple fields represented in the same course, and, therefore, to a truer integration of theory and method.

Prospective teachers can draw on the programs, scholars, and teachers noted in this discussion, and the rich array of textual materials on dreams, to design their own courses. Of course an understanding of the literature on dreams in one's field and a broader familiarity with material in other areas besides one's own is essential.

Philip H. King

Reference

King, P., Bulkeley, K., & Welt, B. (2011). *Dreaming in the classroom: Practices, methods and resources in dream education*. Albany: State University of New York Press.

Teaching Dreams via Dream Lab

Dream lab is an experiential pedagogic exercise developed to promote student knowledge of dream theories, physiology, and phenomenology (Bryson, Kinsey, Mastin, & Bryson, 2009; Bryson, Mastin, Pilgreen, & Bryson, 2008). Two versions of dream lab have been created thus far. The first is applicable to introductory level psychology as a means of enhancing student knowledge during the brief coverage of dreams in that course (Bryson et al., 2009). This version is aimed at introducing the topic of dreams with emphasis on breadth. The second version is designed to be utilized in an upper-level undergraduate course specific to the topic of sleep and dreaming (Bryson et al., 2008). The upper-level version is geared toward providing more depth and covers a broader range of theories.

Literature specific to dream education has been quite limited. This is not unexpected given that most teaching activities are based on well-established general methods and the empirical validation and publication of such activities is commonly not required prior to implementation. Further, there are relatively few offerings of courses or activities that are central to the topic of dreams despite being applicable to a broad range of academic disciplines (Bryson, 2010). Nonetheless, there are available works that describe dream-specific pedagogic activities. Frank and Trunnell (1978) and Ullman (1994) provided descriptions of teaching dream-specific materials to clinicians in training. Krippner, Gabel,

Green, and Rubien (1994) also described techniques for teaching dreamwork in community programs. In the past decade, efforts to promote the development of education specific to dreams have been pursued (Bryson, 2002, 2003; Bryson et al., 2008, 2009). This began with a description of an advanced undergraduate sleep and dreaming course that utilized the dream lab exercise (Bryson, 2002). Dream lab was also applied to an online version of this course and designed to reach a larger student population (Bryson, 2003). The specific techniques and pedagogic efficacy were established for the introductory psychology version (Bryson et al., 2009) and the upper-level advanced course (Bryson et al., 2008). Both versions are currently available to instructors.

Future research and development is encouraged in several areas. This includes the development of dream-specific coursework, supplemental materials and activities, community education, and online resources (Bryson, 2010). Efforts should also be made to explore new and innovative ways to address the study of dreams to all levels of higher education and in both the academic and clinical learning environments.

Jeff Bryson

References

Bryson, W. J. (2002). New curriculum benefits undergraduate psychology students. *Sleep Review, 3,* 10–12.

Bryson, W. J. (2003). Learning on the web. *Sleep Review, 4,* 10–14.

Bryson, W. J. (2010). Educational opportunities in the study of dreams and dreaming. In D. M. Montez (Ed.), *Psychiatric research trends: Dreams and geriatric psychiatry* (pp. 145–50). New York: Nova Science Publishers.

Bryson, W. J., Kinsey, C., Mastin, D. F., & Bryson, T. L. (2009). Dream lab for introductory psychology. *North American Journal of Psychology, 11,* 353–360.

Bryson, W. J., Mastin, D. F., Pilgreen, K. L., & Bryson, T. L. (2008). Dream lab: An experiential pedagogic approach to dream theories and characteristics. *Dreaming, 18,* 122–126.

Frank, A., & Trunnell, E. E. (1978). Conscious dream synthesis as a method of learning about dreaming: A pedagogic experiment. *Psychoanalytic Quarterly, 47,* 103–112.

Krippner, S., Gabel, S., Green, J., & Rubien, R. (1994). Community applications of an experiential group approach to teaching dreamwork. *Dreaming, 4,* 215–222.

Ullman, M. (1994). The experiential dream group: Its application in the training of therapists. *Dreaming, 4,* 223–239.

Television Consumption and Dreaming

Media such as television, movies, video and computer games, and Internet play a major role in the lives of U.S. children with an estimated duration of several hours per day. The question whether television viewing or playing computer games, especially those of violent and aggressive content, has negative effects on children's psyche might be answered by studying children's sleep patterns and dreaming in relation to media consumption. Fisher and Wilson (1987), for example, reported that a considerable amount of parents attributed the occurrence of nightmares to scary television programs. Children themselves also reported that scary dreams are triggered by something they had recently seen on television (Muris, Merckelbach, Gadet, & Moulaert, 2000). However, very few studies investigated the effect of media on dreams directly. A high rate of television-related nightmares occurring weekly in children was reported by two studies: 8.8 percent (Owens et al., 1999) and about 10 percent in children with the age mean of about 13 years (Van den Bulck, 2004). The frequency of television-related nightmares correlated weak but significant with the amount of television watching ($r = .20$; $N = 391$; Viemerö & Paajanen, 1992). Since nightmares are a common experience reported by children, it is not clear whether nightmare frequency is affected by television viewing or media use in general or whether the nightmares simply take up the media content. Reviewing the literature on children's nightmares, Schredl and Pallmer (1997) found that nightmare content varied over time with prominent dreams of the boogey man in the 1920s; ghosts, devils, or witches in the 1950s/1960s; and television or movie figures in the 1990s. This suggests that fairy tales, cinema, and television affect dream content. Unfortunately, precise prevalence data on nightmare frequency over this time span have not been collected to test the effect of modern media on nightmare frequency in children.

David Foulkes carried out several studies to investigate the effect of a single film (aggressive Western vs. neutral film) on dream content in children (Foulkes, 1979). The findings did not show a marked impact of the films on dreams in children, and research in adults has also shown that the effect of experimental stress on dream content is often very small; in contrast to the effect of real stress. Schredl, Blomeyer, and

Görlinger (2000) reported a nonsignificant correlation between the amount of television viewing and nightmare frequency in school-aged children (age range 7 to 11 years). In a second study (Schredl, Anders, Hellriegel, & Rehm, 2008), 252 school children (age 9 to 13 years) completed a questionnaire about media use and nightmares. The findings indicate that interindividual differences in nightmare frequency were not explained by interindividual differences in television viewing. In addition, no effect of the television films the evening before completing the questionnaire on the dreams the subsequent night could be demonstrated.

To summarize, whereas research demonstrated an effect of media on dream content, the question of possible negative effects of television consumption on dreams cannot yet be answered. Future studies might implement a longitudinal study design eliciting the media-use habits and the occurrence of nightmares by using diaries which include self-rating scales for the children as well as information obtained by parents.

Michael Schredl

References

Fisher, B. E., & Wilson, A. E. (1987). Selected sleep disturbances in school children reported by parents: Prevalence, interrelationships, behavioral correlates and parental attributions. *Perceptual and Motor Skills, 64,* 1147–1157.

Foulkes, D. (1979). Home and laboratory dreams: Four empirical studies and conceptual reevaluation. *Sleep, 2,* 233–251.

Muris, P., Merckelbach, H., Gadet, B., & Moulaert, V. (2000). Fears, worries, and scary dreams in 4- to 12-year-old children: Their content, developmental pattern, and origins. *Journal of Clinical Child Psychology, 29,* 43–52.

Owens, J., Maxim, R., McGuinn, M., Nobile, C., Msall, M., & Alario, A. (1999). Television-viewing habits and sleep disturbances in school children. *Pediatrics, 104*(3), e27.

Schredl, M., Anders, A., Hellriegel, S., & Rehm, A. (2008). Television viewing, computer game playing and nightmares in school children. *Dreaming, 18,* 69–76.

Schredl, M., Blomeyer, D., & Görlinger, M. (2000). Nightmares in children: Influencing factors. *Somnologie, 4,* 145–149.

Schredl, M., & Pallmer, R. (1997). Alpträume bei Kindern. *Praxis der Kinderpsychologie und Kinderpsychiatrie, 46,* 36–56.

Van den Bulck, J. (2004). Media use and dreaming: The relationship among television viewing, computer game play, and nightmares or pleasant dreams. *Dreaming, 14,* 43–49.

Viemerö, V., & Paajanen, S. (1992). The role of fantasies and dreams in the television viewing-aggression relationship. *Aggressive Behavior, 18,* 109–116.

Theoretical Models and Neural Basis

Anecdotal reports on scientific discovery, inventive originality, and artistic productivity suggest that creativity can be triggered or enhanced by sleeping and dreaming. Several studies confirm these anecdotes, showing that sleep promotes creative problem solving compared to wakefulness. For example, when subjects performed a cognitive task that could be solved much faster through applying a hidden rule, after a night of sleep more than twice as many subjects gained insight into the hidden rule as compared to a control group that stayed awake (Wagner, Gais, Haider, Verleger, & Born, 2004). Similarly, subjects benefited in a creativity task from an afternoon nap, including REM sleep, but not the same time staying awake (Cai, Mednick, Harrison, Kanady, & Mednick, 2009).

Creativity, defined as the ability to produce work that is both novel and appropriate, comes in many different forms; however, two phenomena might be interpreted as paradigmatic: insight and original productivity; for example, divergent thinking. The phenomenon of insight is illustrated by one well-known theoretical approach: According to the stage model, creative insights may be described by a process consisting of several stages. In the preparation stage the problem solver has to acquire relevant knowledge and explore the problem's dimensions. Despite efforts to solve the problem, at some point an impasse is reached and further attempts stuck at a futile point in the problem space, hence the problem is laid aside. An incubation phase follows, in which no further conscious work is applied to the problem, until in an illumination stage a creative solution pops up in the problem solver's mind. In the final verification stage this creative idea has to be rationally verified as a solution to the problem at hand, further elaborated and then applied. However, the stage model does not state what exactly happens in the incubation phase, which processes might facilitate the illumination, and how noninsight forms of creativity might be explained.

Psychoanalytical models of creativity emphasize the primary process concept, which denotes free-associative, dreamlike thinking compared to the more rational and analytical secondary process thinking. Cognitive models propose that a state of defocused attention facilitates creativity—creative individuals seem to have less narrowly focused attention than uncreative

ones, which leads to unorthodox connections of remote ideas that might eventually lead to creative cognitions. In a similar vein, creative individuals are proposed to have relatively flat association hierarchies, which accounts for the ability to make remote associations, whereas uncreative individuals are proposed to have relatively steep association hierarchies.

Physiological models emphasize the level of cortical arousal as an important variable influencing creativity: Both a lower level of cortical arousal—particularly in the prefrontal cortex—and a higher variability in cortical arousal levels are expected in creative compared to uncreative individuals, depending on specific phases of the creative process (Martindale, 1999). In addition, low levels of norepinephrine are proposed to facilitate creativity, shifting the brain toward intrinsic neuronal activation with an increase in the size of distributed concept representations and co-activation across modular networks (Heilman, Nadeau, & Beversdorf, 2003).

On the empirical side, data on the neural correlates of creativity are quite inconclusive. The prefrontal cortex seems to be of special importance; however, there is evidence for both prefrontal activation and prefrontal deactivation facilitating creativity—maybe again depending on the specific phase of the creative process. Brain areas showing selective activation for insight events are—besides the prefrontal cortex—the visual cortices, the hippocampus, and in particular the anterior cingulated cortex, which is thought to be involved in breaking the impasse that marks the critical step of insight into a problem (Dietrich & Kanso, 2010).

On a closer look, both theoretical models and empirical neuroscience of creativity suggest that sleep is an ideal state for creative incubation: Primary process thinking is explicitly conceptualized as dreamlike, and the hyperassociative nature of dreams can be considered as a prime example of a flat associative hierarchy. Defocused attention is a phenomenal feature of most dreams, physiologically probably caused by prefrontal cortex deactivation. The sleep cycle provides the brain with extremely alternating arousal levels, and the chaotic activation of the cortex in REM sleep through brain stem regions in absence of external sense data leads to a much more radical renunciation from unsuccessful problem-solving attempts, leading to co-activations of cognitive data that are highly remote in waking life. These co-activations, woven into a dream narrative in a self-organizing manner, repeatedly receive further innervations by the brain stem, leading to bizarre sequences of loosely associated dream topics that might eventually activate particular problem-relevant cognitions or creative cognitions in general (Hobson & Wohl, 2005). In addition in REM sleep, which is characterized by low levels of norepinephrine, visual cortices, the hippocampus, and the anterior cingulate cortex all have been shown to be strongly activated, potentially facilitating insight events. In conclusion, the phenomenological and neural correlates of sleeping and dreaming provide ideal conditions for the genesis of creative ideas and insights.

Martin Dresler

See also: entries related to REM Sleep

References

Cai, D. J., Mednick, S. A., Harrison, E. M., Kanady, J. C., & Mednick, S. C. (2009). REM, not incubation, improves creativity by priming associative networks. *Proceedings of the National Academy of Sciences, 106,* 10130–10134.

Dietrich, A., & Kanso, R. (2010). A Review of EEG, ERP, and neuroimaging studies of creativity and insight. *Psychological Bulletin, 136,* 822–848.

Heilman, K. M., Nadeau, S. E., & Beversdorf, D. O. (2003). Creative innovation: Possible brain mechanisms. *Neurocase, 9,* 369–379.

Hobson, J. A., & Wohl, H. (2005). *From angels to neurones: Art and the new science of dreaming.* Fidenza: Mattioli.

Martindale, C. (1999). Biological bases of creativity. In R. J. Sternberg (Ed.), *Handbook of creativity* (pp. 137–152). Cambridge: Cambridge University Press.

Wagner, U., Gais, S., Haider, H., Verleger, R., & Born, J. (2004). Sleep inspires insight. *Nature, 427,* 352–355.

Theory of Mind and Dreaming

Theory of mind is the ability to attribute mental states to other individuals by observing their body language or facial expressions. For instance, if one sees a person standing in front of the refrigerator gazing in, they might assume that the person wants something to eat. Using theory of mind, people can ascribe such intentions, needs, and desires to others without speaking. This mind reading begins to develop in humans between ages three and four and exists in other higher primates to promote complex social interaction by allowing one to anticipate the needs and behaviors of others, establish trust, and promote cooperation.

In 1992 di Pellegrino and colleagues discovered a cluster of cells in the premotor cortex of primates that reacted when a monkey performed an action or when it watched another perform the same action. In humans these mirror neurons reflect sensations and emotions that are then attributed to the mind of the other even when the individual does not see the task performed entirely. Because the individual feels the experience as though it is their own, they can often accurately infer the intentions of the other.

People report being aware of other characters having thoughts and feelings about them in their dreams, showing that theory of mind is maintained in the dream state despite changes in chemistry and activation patterns in the brain during sleep (Kahn & Hobson, 2005). The areas of the brain associated with theory of mind are activated during REM sleep, when the most dreams containing aggressive social interactions are produced. Accordingly, dreams containing theory of mind occur most frequently during REM sleep and are characterized by greater numbers of dreamer-initiated aggressive interactions than NREM dreams. Instances of theory of mind in REM dreams are largely associated with dreamer-initiated aggressive interactions with familiar male characters (McNamara, McLaren, Kowalczyk, & Pace-Schott, 2007), and the mental state is more often attributed to the dreamer than to the other characters (Schweickert & Xi, 2010). Metamorphoses of dream characters have no systematic relation to frequency of theory of mind. Characters and dreamers may morph into other forms or characters within dreams, but their original

mental state often remains from the first form (Schweickert & Xi, 2010).

False belief is a component of theory of mind in which the individual is aware that perception of the truth is based on personal experience and therefore other individuals may hold different beliefs based on their own experiences. False belief marks a universal milestone in mental human development that transcends language and culture (Ang & Pridmore, 2009). Some young children, autistic adults, and people with intellectual disabilities are unable to conceptualize individual experiences or use theory of mind to attribute mental states. Dodd, Hare, and Hendy (2008) reported that adults with intellectual disabilities have difficulty accurately conceptualizing dreams as an individual experience that cannot be witnessed by others, and found that the ability to accurately conceptualize them increased with receptive language ability.

As with all studies of dream content, studies on theory of mind in dreaming are limited by the use of dream reports to elicit a memory of the dream after the dreamer has woken up. This can be problematic, as dreamers may not fully remember their dreams and vary in their level of detail on recall. Future studies would benefit from exploring the function of theory of mind in dreaming and to see how it effects social interactions in the daytime.

Deirdre T. McLaren

References

Ang, G. K., & Pridmore, S. (2009). Theory of mind and psychiatry: An introduction. *Australas Psychiatry, 17*(2), 117–122.

di Pellegrino, G., Fadiga, L., Fogassi, L., Gallese, V., & Rizzolatti, G. (1992).

Understanding motor events: A neurophysiological study. *Experimental Brain Research, 91*(1), 176–180.

Dodd, A., Hare, D. J., & Hendy, S. (2008). The conceptualisation of dreams by adults with intellectual disabilities: Relationship with theory of mind abilities and verbal ability. *Journal of Intellectual Disability Research, 52*(Pt 4), 337–347.

Kahn, D., & Hobson, A. (2005). Theory of mind in dreaming: Awareness of feelings and thoughts of others in dreams. *Dreaming, 15*(1), 48–57.

McNamara, P., McLaren, D., Kowalczyk, S., & Pace-Schott, E. F. (2007). "Theory of mind" in REM and NREM dreams. In D. Barrett & P. McNamara (Eds.), *The new science of dreaming: Volume I: Biological Aspects* (pp. 117–132). Westport, CT: Praeger Perspectives.

Schweickert, R., & Xi, Z. (2010). Metamorphosed characters in dreams: Constraints of conceptual structure and amount of theory of mind. *Cognitive Science, 34,* 665–684.

Threat Simulation Theory

Why does the human brain produce dream experiences? According to the threat simulation theory (TST) (Revonsuo, 2000a, 2000b), dreaming evolved because it can simulate threatening events without any actual danger being involved and thus safely prepare the individual for potential future threats. Threat simulation dreams *rehearse the threat perception and threat-avoidance skills* that were critical to the survival of ancestral humans in their environment. Dreaming was selected for during human evolution and became a universal feature of the human mind. We still have it with us, although we no longer live in the ancestral environment where primordial threats to survival were abundant.

TST assumes that *dreaming is specialized in the simulation of threatening events,* especially the kinds of dangers that our ancestors faced. Empirical studies on the frequency and content of threatening events in dreams lend support to this idea (Valli & Revonsuo, 2009). Threatening events are frequent in dreams: 60 to 70 percent of the dreams of young adults involve some kind of threat. Threatening dream events are more frequent and more dangerous than the threats encountered by the same persons in their real life (Valli, Strandholm, Sillanmäki, & Revonsuo, 2008). Dream dangers are almost always directly targeted at the dreamer who tries to escape, defend, or otherwise survive the threat. Furthermore, male strangers and wild animals are the typical enemies in our dreams, as they were in the ancestral environment. Our earliest dreams in childhood are predominantly threat simulations. Out of 84 earliest remembered dreams in childhood, 35 percent were threat simulations where an enemy directly attacked or chased the dreamer. Overall, 60 percent depicted some kind of threatening situation (Bulkeley, Broughton, Sanchez, & Stiller, 2005). Nightmares and recurrent dreams have also been found to include threatening events in more than 60 percent of the reports, the majority simulating extremely dangerous events. In most dream samples, negative emotions and aggressive interactions occur much more frequently than positive emotions and friendly interactions do. By contrast, dreams seldom include modern everyday cognitive activities, such as reading, writing, or working with the computer.

Thus, dreams selectively include many elements that support threat simulation, but exclude some other elements prominent in our modern waking lives.

TST predicts that *real dangers encountered in the waking world activate the threat simulation system.* The strongest evidence for this idea comes from the effects of traumatic experiences on dreaming. Traumatic experiences increase threat simulation rates dramatically and posttraumatic nightmares can simulate the traumatizing events for months or years after the original trauma (for a review, see Revonsuo, 2000b). In a study directly testing this idea (Valli et al., 2005), children living in a peaceful country were found to have a relatively low frequency of threat simulation dreams (38% of dreams) By contrast, children living in war-like conditions had the highest frequency of threat simulation dreams ever observed in any population: as much as 80 percent of their dreams included some kind of threat. According to TST, dangerous real events strongly activate the threat simulation system, because then the dream simulations will automatically prepare the person to encounter and survive similar life-threatening situations in the future.

TST has been criticized by pointing out that not all dreams include threat simulations and that there are also highly positive dreams. TST does not rule out the possibility that the simulation of nonthreatening events (e.g., social interactions) is an additional function of dreaming, or the possibility that although dreaming has a function (the capacity to simulate threats), not every single dream necessarily has to manifest this function. Some empirical results do not entirely support TST (Valli & Revonsuo, 2009). More than one third of threat simulations in dreams remain incomplete because they are disrupted by awakening or discontinuity. Nightmares and recurrent dreams often contain fantastic threats not corresponding to reality, such as vampires and werewolves. However, such monsters are even more frightening than realistic enemies, and may simply render the rehearsal of threat-avoidance skills more efficient. The greatest weakness of TST is that so far there is no direct evidence that dreaming about threatening events would actually enhance threat-avoidance performance when the corresponding threat needs to be dealt with in reality. It is difficult to design empirical studies that would directly test this central idea of TST.

In conclusion, by appealing to the one simple theoretical idea of threat simulation as the original biological function of dreaming, TST predicts and explains a wide variety of common dream phenomena: nightmares, bad dreams, the observed biases toward negative rather than positive dream contents, the dominance of current concerns in dreams, and the powerful effects of stress and trauma on dreams. Furthermore, many sleep disorders with intense negative mental content can be interpreted as involving the overactivation of the threat simulation system.

TST has gained empirical support for its predictions, but further studies are required. Dream samples from hunter–gatherer populations should be collected to test the hypothesis that threat simulation works best in the natural environment that it originally evolved to simulate. Studies utilizing virtual threats in immersive video games might be used to trigger threat simulation dreams experimentally and then measuring their effects on performance in corresponding threatening situations in the video game world. There are thus multiple ways to continue testing the plausibility and the predictive and explanatory power of this new theory of the function of dreaming.

Antti Revonsuo

See also: entries related to Dream Theories

References

Bulkeley, K., Broughton, B., Sanchez, A., & Stiller, J. (2005). Earliest remembered dreams. *Dreaming, 15,* 205–222.

Revonsuo, A. (2000a). Did ancestral humans dream for their lives? *Behavioral and Brain Sciences, 23,* 1063–1082.

Revonsuo, A. (2000b). The reinterpretation of dreams: An evolutionary hypothesis of the function of dreaming. *Behavioral and Brain Sciences, 23,* 877–901.

Valli, K., & Revonsuo, A. (2009). The threat simulation theory in the light of recent empirical evidence—A review. *The American Journal of Psychology, 122,* 17–38.

Valli, K., Revonsuo, A., Pälkäs, O., Ismail, K.H., Ali, K.J., & Punamäki, R.L. (2005). The threat simulation theory of the evolutionary function of dreaming: Evidence from dreams of traumatized children. *Consciousness and Cognition, 14,* 188–218.

Valli, K., Strandholm, T., Sillanmäki, L., & Revonsuo, A. (2008). Dreams are more negative than real life—Implications for the function of dreaming. *Cognition and Emotion, 22,* 833–861.

Traditional Korean Dreams

So-called dog dreams reflect a Korean's everyday feelings and thoughts, imaginings, and experiences. So-called true dreams can reflect the same, but more importantly are clairvoyant and precognitive. They are of a quality that speaks to the heart and cannot be forgotten.

In traditional Korea, clairvoyant and precognitive dreams have played a vital role in the individual's and family's life at every level of society, including in the royal family and in affairs of the national government. Dreams have affected choices made at every stage of the course of national history.

Before the advent of communication systems such as the telephone or radio or the newspaper, true dreams provided a window to the future. During the time when communication was done by smoke signals and waving flags from mountain tops or with the help of couriers on horseback, often only dreams could inform people about news elsewhere or about news concerning themselves. Yet a dream of good fortune was not to be shared until after noonday, and not with anybody, for it could be stolen by the hearer. Dreams, however, could be sold, for example, for a fine piece of cloth. A person was not to be woken in sleep for fear that his dreaming spirit would stay in the dream world.

At isolated villages, virtuous women who prayed to the mountain spirit or Buddha before a bowl of clear spring water every morning, and disciplined men who performed ancestral rites, and or studied Confucian, Taoist, or Buddhist classics and, or meditated, for instance, developed clear minds, free of triviality that allowed the radar of their consciousness open to receive extrasensory dreams. Ancestors commonly appeared in dreams to offer advice in times of trouble. Women especially would wait for an auspicious dream in answer to their prayers; for instance, for a son. They believed that certain dreams told the truth, and were ready to remember and dwell on unusual dreams, and then share them with people whom they were close to.

Today, too, a Korean can experience dream prophecies from womb to tomb, from the birth of a child to the complaint of a spirit from the grave. We can journey through life on an ordinary Korean's dreams, as gleaned from more than a thousand collected mainly from my students at *Hankuk* University of Foreign Studies in Seoul in the 1980s and 1990s. They were asked to interview their parents and grandparents, particularly their grandmothers, and record, "My dreams that came true." This resulted in a collection of dreams, including of women and men who grew up in the early part of the 20th century, and had a traditional rural, as opposed to a modern urban, mind-set.

Chronologically, for dreams typically Korean, categories are ordered as follows (1) marriage dreams; (2) birth, including conception dreams; (3) scholar, including examination dreams; (4) good fortune, including lottery dreams; (5) ill fortune, including accident dreams; (6) death dreams; and (7) ancestor grave dreams.

Special dream categories include: (1) ginseng picker dreams; (2) shaman dreams; (3) monk and nun dreams; (4) admiral or general dreams; and (5) king dreams.

The method of interpretation includes the recognition of traditional village-life symbols, also *yin/yang* contrasts, especially for conception dreams, and straightforward evidence from the dream story. Dream-symbol books are popular and give formulas for various situations in dreams, but can be inaccurate without elaboration by an interpreter. Family members, neighbors, elders, shamans, fortune-tellers, and monks can help interpret dreams. Sometimes an artist was contracted to paint a remarkable dream, such as An Kyôn's painting for Prince Anp'yông, *Dream Journey to the Peach Blossom Land* (1447 CE), and especially, a conception dream, so it would not be forgotten.

Once an event is foreseen in a dream, the dreamer takes steps to prepare for its arrival. For example, if a person dreamt of a dragon coming into her classroom, she might prepare for marriage. If a person dreamt of a mountain ginseng, he might pray and prepare to set out for the intended location pointed out in the dream. Or if a person dreamt of an ink brush, he might study harder to pass the national exam in Seoul and set out on time.

Jeremy Seligson

See also: entries related to Cross-Cultural Dreams

References

Sources for Korean dreams abound in Korean dream dictionaries, newspaper archives, and court records. However, in English, aside from a few scholarly articles, dream examples can be found in the following resources.

Ilyeon. (2006). *Samguk Yusa* (Trans. Kim Dal-Yong as *Overlooked historical records of the Three Korean Kingdoms*. Jimoondang: Seoul, Korea).

Nanjung Ilgi. (1980). *War diary of Admiral Yi Sun-sin* (Trans. Taehung Ha, Ed. Powkey Sohn). Seoul: Yonsei University Press.

Seligson, F.J. (1989). *Oriental birth dreams.* Hollym: Seoul.

Seligson, F.J. (in press). *Traditional Korean dreams.*

Traffic Noise and Autonomic Arousals during Sleep

Transient excitations of the central and the autonomic nervous system occur frequently and spontaneously (without obvious reason) during normal sleep. Corresponding alterations are also evoked by acoustic stimuli. Studies on transportation noise were scarcely done, although they are highly relevant for residents near airports, in busy streets, and along railway tracks, who are permanently exposed to traffic noises during day and night.

Transportation noise is a major cause of extrinsic sleep disturbances with aftereffects on mood, performance, and health. As traffic volume increases further, traffic must—to avoid complete gridlocks—invade the night hours

Autonomic arousals are the first in a cascade of reactions or even the only response to noise. They encompass increases of ventilation, of systolic and diastolic blood pressure, and of peripheral resistance but are most often indicated by alterations of heart rate (HR).

The cardiac arousals described here were ascertained in a study where 24 persons were, during a total of more than 300 nights, exposed to various transportation noises with maximum levels ranging from 45 to 77 dBA (decibels). Sleep depth and HR were ascertained with polysomnography and electrocardiography, respectively.

The major influence on the extent and the pattern of the cardiac arousals is traced back to awakening. Without awakenings, the alterations are biphasic with an acceleration followed by a deceleration below baseline and then a slow increase back to prestimulus levels. The initial acceleration corresponds to a vagal inhibition, and the consecutive deceleration to an increase of the vagal tone accompanied by an inhibition of the sympathetic excitation.

While gender has no influence, the momentary sleep stage is most decisive. The lowest maximum HR elevations and the longest latencies occur during slow-wave sleep (SWS), the highest maxima and the shortest latencies in REM sleep.

Another major impact arises from the acoustical parameters. The influence of the traffic mode concerned the latency rather than the maximum that occurred earliest for railway noise and latest for aircraft noise. The most likely cause for this is probably the rate of rise.

The increase of sound-pressure levels per time unit that corresponds with the speed of the vehicle clearly determines the HR response. Faster increases in noise levels cause steeper HR accelerations with earlier and higher maxima and with steeper decelerations. This is most likely related to adaptation processes. The latter start immediately after stimulus onset and thus are the more effective while the slower the noise levels increase, thus preventing abrupt and excessive HR accelerations. This explains why aircraft noise with its characteristically slowly increasing noise levels causes only slow and moderate HR increases.

In case of awakenings, the HR elevation is—due to an increasing sympathetic tone—monophasic, reaching a maximum of about 30 bpm (beats per minute) after about 30 seconds followed by a slow decrease, where the baseline is not regained within a minute after stimulus onset.

This response is again not influenced by gender but significantly by the momentary sleep stage. The greatest and the smallest HR elevation occurred with awakenings from SWS and REM sleep, respectively. This corresponds to the extent of excitation that is largest and lowest for awakenings from SWS and REM sleep, respectively.

These responses are—in contrast to the biphasic response in the absence of awakening—scarcely influenced by the acoustic parameters. This concerns the traffic mode, the maximum noise level, and even the increase of the noise level. This leads to the conclusion that while the noise triggers the awakening response, only the latter determines, via strong sympathetic excitations, the extent and the pattern of the HR response. This assumption is supported by the fact that only the duration of awakening affects the extent of the response significantly. The amplitude of HR elevations and the latency to the maximum HR increase significantly with awakening duration.

There is no indication of habituation irrespective of whether these cardiac arousals are accompanied by awakenings or not. The extents of the biphasic as well as of the monophasic response instead marginally increase over the course of the night thus indicating a lack of habituation or even a sensitization as also the probability of awakenings increase slowly during the night.

These reactions are assumed to bear a pathogenic potential for the genesis of cardiovascular diseases as they do not habituate and do not correspond to any energetic need of the sleeping body. The validity of this conclusion remains open as similar alterations occur spontaneously (i.e., without external noise stimulation) and frequently during each night. The number of spontaneous arousals decreases, however, in favor of evoked arousals, meaning that noises cause a redistribution of cardiac arousal.

Barbara Griefahn and Mathias Basner

See also: Increasing Sleep Complaints; entries related to Sleep Disorders

Transcendent Dreams

Systematic classificatory methods (cf. Busink & Kuiken, 1996) have repeatedly identified three types of impactful dreams: nightmares, existential dreams, and transcendent dreams. Of these, transcendent dreams distinctively involve ecstasy and awe, magical success, vigorous activity, extraordinary sources of light, shifts in perspective, and moderately intense affect during the dream ending. Transcendent dreams are distinguishable from other impactful dream types—and from ordinary dreams—not by any single feature (e.g., ecstasy) but rather by a coherent profile of features involving feelings and emotions, motives and goals, sensory phenomena, movement characteristics, and dream endings. Like nightmares and existential dreams, transcendent dreams include visual discontinuities (e.g., explicit looking, sudden shifts in location); relatively intense affect, especially during dream endings; and compelling imagery that seems real to the dreamer even after awakening. However, despite such evidence of their shared intensity, their effects on waking thoughts and feelings differ. Transcendent dreams are distinctively followed by a shift toward previously ignored spiritual possibilities. That is, after awakening—and often for hours, days, or weeks—transcendent dreamers report that their dream continues to offer a renewal of spiritual potential, a sense of liberation from life's tangles and hindrances, and feelings of revitalization (Kuiken, Lee, Eng, & Singh, 2006).

These reported dream effects suggest that transcendent dreaming *per se* brings about shifts in spiritual potential, perhaps through the transformations of feeling, action, and self-reflection that occur within the dream. This suggestion is supported by evidence that transcendent dream narratives involve (1) unusual—even magical—abilities (e.g., miraculous healing); (2) actions that are emotionally uplifting (i.e., energetic and lively, although graceful and balanced); and (3) unusual sources of light, often with numinous qualities. There is also an element of heightened self-awareness in transcendent dreams. That is, transcendent dreamers (1) become aware of themselves as if from the outside; (2) identify themselves with two separate and autonomous agents (e.g., an observed self and an observing self); and (3) sometimes experience explicit lucidity (i.e., awareness of dreaming while dreaming). So, preternatural possibilities that transcend the natural world are evident within these dream narratives, often accompanied by forms of self-reflection that transcend the single-minded world of the dream.

However, even though both transcendent dreams and existential dreams involve altered forms of self reflection, the spiritual potential of transcendent dreams emerges independently of self-perceptual depth. Existential dreams are more likely than transcendent dreams to precipitate self-perceptual depth, while transcendent dreams are more likely than existential dreams to prompt shifts in perceived spiritual potential. However, sometimes a darker emotional moment precedes the concluding ecstasy of transcendent dreams, suggesting that the conclusion of the dream most powerfully determines its effect. The following example of a transcendent dream involves characteristically magical events and a clear transition through such a dark moment to exhilarating dream lucidity:

> I saw a few beautiful birds; they were flying around my house [and] then went down in my background. They were so beautiful that I want[ed] to touch them. Suddenly, one of them [was dead] because of me. I [was] very sad, so I tried to find out [whether] that was caused by me or not. Then, I came to a monk and ask[ed] him that. He told me just one sentence: "Don't worry, maybe you are dreaming." I woke up after he told me that.

This dream contains figures (the birds, the monk) that have a mysterious, even numinous, presence. Following awakening, reflection on these figures—and possibly the monk's gift of lucidity—is accompanied by reported rapture.

The features of transcendent dreams are reminiscent of theories of archetypal dreams that emphasize improbable or impossible events, heightened affect, and mythological parallels. However, equating transcendent with archetypal dreams is problematic. One reason is that the specification of mythological parallels is difficult to accomplish systematically. Another is that the term archetypal carries the connotations of some questionable aspects of Jungian evolutionary theory rather than directly reflecting these dreams' phenomenology. The term transcendent somewhat more aptly reflects dream elements that lie beyond material space–time referents (e.g., magical accomplishments), while remaining open to their here-and-now spiritual connotations. Perhaps like art, transcendent dreams gesture toward, without capturing, something more; they move the dreamer *toward* understanding of a timeless and spaceless   more-than-can-be-understood. The prototypically sublime moment for the Romantic poet was the daunting—but somehow enthralling—encounter with nature. There may be an echo of such moments in transcendent dreams.

Donald Kuiken

References

Busink, R., & Kuiken, D. (1996). Identifying types of impactful dreams: A replication. *Dreaming, 6,* 97–119.

Kuiken, D., Lee, M.N., Eng, T.C., & Singh, T. (2006). The influence of impactful dreams on self-perceptual depth and spiritual transformation. *Dreaming, 16,* 258–279.

Trauma Treatment and Dreams

There is a striking paradox in the large body of literature about the treatment of trauma. On the one hand, DSM-IV lists as a diagnostic criterion for posttraumatic stress disorder (PTSD) "The traumatic event is persistently reexperienced in [among other ways] recurrent distressing dreams of the event." On the other hand, there is very little in the trauma treatment literature that focuses directly on the dreams or nightmares, or discusses how to use or even understand them in the recovery process. If mentioned at all, nightmares are usually merely listed along with other symptoms of unresolved trauma. Often the reduction of frequency and intensity of nightmares is identified as an indication of recovery. Sometimes suggestions are offered about drugs that might be administered to reduce nightmares. But rarely is the dream or nightmare considered an important psychological experience in and of itself, full of meaning and potential for the trauma victim and the clinician. One result of this paradox is that clinicians working with trauma victims are rarely receiving training or even information about how to deal with their clients' dreams. And this is despite the fact that virtually every one of them is working with people who are experiencing dreams and especially nightmares associated with their trauma experience.

A number of recent publications about trauma treatment, doubtless used in the training of many clinicians, are especially egregious in their lack of discussion of dreams and nightmares. One influential example is by Briere and Scott (2006). These publications either fail to mention dreams or nightmares except as symptoms, or merely say that a reduction of nightmares is a sign of recovery.

There is one type of work with dreams, however, that does appear in the mainstream trauma treatment literature: imagery rehearsal therapy (IRT). This involves rescripting the nightmare while awake, by rewriting the ending, changing or bringing in new characters, or substituting less-troubling themes. While this is not a new idea (people working with dreams commonly have the dreamer manipulate the dream in various ways), its introduction into the trauma treatment literature is due almost exclusively to Barry Krakow and his colleagues (e.g., Moore & Krakow, 2007).

Foa, Keene, Friedman, and Chohen (2009) and several others discuss Krakow's work in some detail, concluding that IRT is quite successful in reducing nightmares in individuals with PTSD. One entire book (Davis, 2009) focuses on nightmares, providing a good overview of IRT and step-by-step procedures for organizing therapy sessions.

However, only a few treatment-focused publications place serious emphasis on the nightmare as a potentially important experience, the content of which may provide meaning for the dreamer. For example, Krippner and Paulson (2007), focusing on Iraq combat veterans, discuss dreams and nightmares throughout their book. They say, "Several useful approaches for dealing with nightmares have been developed over the years (e.g., desensitization, ventilating, expressive arts therapy, sandplay, confrontation during the nightmare, altering the dream scenario . . .), although most mental health professionals are unaware of them and prescribe medication instead" (Krippner & Paulson, 2007, p. 16).

Two publications take a really focused look at the dreams and nightmares of trauma victims. One is Barrett's (1996 [2001]) group of edited essays on dreams about childhood, war, natural disaster, and other trauma. The other is Bulkeley's (2003) book, in which he states, "Dreams following a crisis do not aim simply at making the person 'normal' again, with no other goal than restoring the emotional status quo ante—rather they aim at the development of a whole new understanding of self and world that is slowly created out of the broken ruins of the dreamer's pre-trauma self" (Bulkeley, 2003, p. 200). Direct attention to dreams and nightmares, with their special lens on the complex and evolving world of the trauma victim, can actually speed up this process.

Johanna King

References

Barrett, D. (Ed.). (1996 [2001]). Trauma and dreams. Cambridge, MA: Harvard University Press.

Briere, J. N., & Scott, C. (2006). Principles of trauma therapy: A guide to symptoms, evaluation, and treatment. Thousand Oaks, CA: Sage Publications.

Bulkeley, K. (2003). Dreams of healing: Transforming nightmares into visions of hope. New York: Paulist Press.

Davis, J. (Ed.). (2009). Treating post-trauma nightmares: A cognitive behavioral approach. New York: Springer Publishing Company.

Foa, E., Keene, T., Friedman, M., & Chohen, J. (Eds.). (2009). Effective treatments for PTSD (2nd ed.). New York: Guilford Press.

Krippner, S., & Paulson, D. S. (2007). Haunted by combat: Understanding PTSD in war veterans including women, reservists, and those coming back from Iraq. Westport, CT: Praeger Security International.

Moore, B. A., & Krakow, B. (2007). Imagery rehearsal therapy for acute posttraumatic nightmares among combat soldiers in Iraq [Research Letter]. American Journal of Psychiatry, 164(4), 683–684.

Types of Consciousness in Dreams

The psychological types that Jung identified, in his landmark 1921 publication (Jung, 1971), as the basic constituents of human cognition, consist of two attitudes, introversion and extraversion, capable of being deployed through four functions of consciousness: thinking, feeling, sensation, and intuition. Eight types of consciousness result: introverted and extraverted thinking; introverted and extraverted feeling; introverted and extraverted sensation; and introverted and extraverted intuition. These are pairs of function–attitudes so opposed in aim (in the case of the introverted member of each pair, toward the self, and in the case of the extraverted member toward the object) that they result in different experiences for the people using them, experiences that shape their ideas of what experience itself is (Shapiro & Alexander, 1975). When such consciousnesses appear together in dreams, they are often depicted as different kinds of people. People who appear unusually similar, however, are often of the same psychological type.

Example

A man just out of college came to psychotherapy to work on his problems with his mother. She frequently appeared in his dreams. In his childhood, he had strongly identified with her against his father. During leisure time she and he had loved to find things to do as intuitively as possible, based on what they could envision or know was likely to be fun in the moment, while his father insisted upon systematically planning the family's free-time activities. Then, father had seemed to make play work. Now, however, the young man found himself often in conflict with his mother. She would become enraged at his intuitive plans, particularly if they didn't include her. He would defend himself by becoming accusatory and "bitchy."

This man dreamed that he was taking his mother and another woman to their seats in a theater. The other woman, a movie actress known for never letting anyone bully her, was telling his mother off. This provoked his mother to retaliate verbally.

He decided upon waking that the women were similar in putting no effort at all into the search for seats. That made him realize that they had a different aim from his own, which was mainly to find a place in the theater where they could comfortably focus on the entertainment. The women put that second to asserting and justifying themselves.

Thinking about the characters in type terms helped the dreamer to appreciate its meaning. That he was drawn to the large, highly social theater, suggested that he was strongly extraverted. He must be highly intuitive, though, because he had envisioned the good performance that would take place without any knowledge of what it would actually be. He experienced the women's need to assert their egos as distracting, and their lack of attention to getting seated as burdensome. He woke with the thought, "They are not like me, and I shouldn't be trying to do things I like with them." He concluded that they were using their intuition in very different ways from his own.

Within his therapy, the dreamer began to think it better not to engage in quarrel with his mother, because it was causing him to draw upon a part of himself (the movie star) that was more narcissistic, more rageful, and more bitchy than his mother had ever been, and similarly blind to what it takes to get along in this world. This side of himself was trying to challenge his mother's effect on his personality hysterically, at the further expense of his actual nature.

This is an example of seeing in a dream a type of consciousness that the dreamer may be using inappropriately. That the consciousness appears in a negative guise helps the dreamer to affirm the type of consciousness that is actually a better fit. Much study of the nature of the types would be necessary to enable the dream interpreter to master type diagnosis (Haas, McAlpine, & Hartzler, 2001), but often that is not necessary. The dreamer can figure out that a particular type of mind-set is not a good fit and that another one is far more natural, if the therapist simply invites the client to contemplate his or her own dream.

John Eliott Beebe

References

Haas, L., McAlpine, R. W., & Hartzler, M. T. (2001). *Journey of understanding: MBTI interpretation using the eight Jungian functions.* Palo Alto, CA: Consulting Psychologists Press.

Jung, C. G. (1971). *Psychological types* (Trans. R. F. C. Hull & H. G. Baynes). In *The collected works of C. G. Jung* (Vol. 6). Princeton, NJ: Princeton University Press.

Shapiro, K. J., & Alexander, I. E. (1975). *The experience of introversion: An integration of phenomenological, empirical, and Jungian approaches.* Durham, NC: Duke University Press.

U

Ullman Method of Group Dreamwork

A psychiatrist and psychoanalyst, Montague Ullman came to believe that people outside the mental health professions have the capacity to help each other understand their dreams, and he devoted the last three decades of his life (he died in 2008) largely to extending dreamwork beyond the consulting room.

Unfortunately, a great many people who believe they are using the Ullman method are mistaken. Groups that do not use Ullman's clearly delineated, four-stage structure may be missing out on the depth of what Ullman called the discovery factor and, more important, risking frequent breaches of the safety factor that the Ullman method is structured to provide.

Ullman and Zimmerman (1979) traced the evolution of his method to four sets of experiences in his life. In psychoanalytic private practice, he marveled at the creative individuality that his patients brought to dreaming, like artists whose intended audience is only themselves. His classical Freudian training seemed a poor fit for his patients' dreams, which seemed more intent on revealing than concealing truths about the dreamer, albeit in an unfamiliar language of visual metaphor. As a community psychiatrist in the 1960s, Ullman helped train paraprofessionals in providing preventive services. Ullman's encounters with dream telepathy as a sleep laboratory–based researcher during the same period deeply influenced him; he stated that the experience "profoundly influenced my notions about the dreaming state, the role it plays in our lives, and the connections we can sometimes make with others when we are in this state" (Ullman & Zimmerman, 1979, p. 10). And a year and a half spent teaching dreamwork to psychotherapists in Sweden in the mid-1970s allowed Ullman to develop the basics of his group approach. (There is now an extensive network of Ullman-method dream groups in Sweden.)

Ullman believed there is nothing esoteric about dreamwork; as a natural and universal phenomenon, dreams should be universally accessible. Contrary to Freud or Carl Jung, however, Ullman maintained that there is nothing universal about the symbolism in dreams. Dream metaphors are too dependent on the individual's specific, immediate concerns and lifetime of experiences to be universal, and can be translated only in that individual context. His method, he said, is open to all theoretical approaches but tied to none.

The uniqueness of each dreamer guides everything about the Ullman method. The process is meant to always be in the dreamer's control: the dreamer chooses whether to continue from one stage to the next; what group input to accept, reject, or simply ignore; and how much to reveal of him- or herself. The group follows the dreamer's lead. Although an Ullman-method group will generally have a leader, that person is a facilitator and equal participant.

These points make the Ullman method significantly different from therapy, which is a hierarchical arrangement in that the therapist takes more control of the process, assumes the role of expert, and uses the dream as she or he sees fit to further the therapy (Ullman, 1990).

Ullman and Zimmerman (1979) explained why a group is the optimal place to do dreamwork: Asleep, a dreamer is presented with an honest reflection of the self; upon awakening, the person has to begin balancing honesty with expediency. That need can cause the dreamer to resist the dream's message. "Others who are not personally involved in the dream can often 'read' our metaphors better than we can, simply because they do not have to deal with the consequences of their reading," he wrote (p. 13). And because the group does not force the dreamer to confront his resistances, enough trust can develop such that the dreamer lowers the resistances willingly and becomes open to discovery.

Ullman described the structure and skills of his dream-group method in several chapters of *Working with Dreams* (1979), coauthored by Nan Zimmerman, a layperson whose questions and critiques helped him clarify the process. By 1996, when Ullman first published *Appreciating Dreams,* his detailed handbook on group dreamwork, he had refined the structure further.

Stage 1 is the sharing of the dream. First, the dreamer tells the dream as fully as possible, including the emotions in it, without commenting further other than to identify any dream characters who exist in waking life.

Then the group asks clarifying, factual questions about the dream, such as "Were you your current age? You said you drove to town—what kind of vehicle?" This is the only time the group is allowed to ask such direct questions.

Stage 2 is the game. Those who misunderstand the Ullman method usually are under the impression that the attitude adopted in this stage—if this were my dream—defines the entire method. Ullman was crystal clear, though, that it applies only to this early stage. He even said while training group leaders that the game is the least important stage.

If this were my dream refers to the fact that group members now try to imagine what the dream would mean in their own life if they had had it themselves—first the feelings, then the images. In this stage only, they are allowed to project any idea that comes to them, no matter how crazy or specific to themselves it may seem—as long as it does not conflict with the dream text. This stage comes before further comment by the dreamer to avoid influence from the dreamer's potential resistances. Conversely, to avoid putting pressure on the dreamer to nod or agree or otherwise acknowledge their projections, group members do not make eye contact with the dreamer during the game.

The game creates a pool of ideas that the dreamer might not have thought of, and—because the projections are the group members' own issues, it lets the dreamer know, "We're all in this together. We all have 'stuff'."

Stage 3 comprises several substages. In the first, the dreamer responds (or not) to the group however she wants, and makes any other comments she wants. This is open ended. The group has no input during the dreamer's response, but they will benefit from discovering which of their projections were mere biases.

Then a dialogue begins, first with a search for context. Here the group assists the dreamer in recalling the waking context in which the dream occurred, by asking very open-ended questions. Ullman's style of questioning was extremely gentle. He might say—approximately—"When you consider the images in the dream and the feeling tone of the dream, and you think back on what was on your mind last night as you went to sleep, is there anything you would like to say about that?"

Next there is the playback. Someone from the group reads the dream back to the dreamer in the second person ("You've just come home. You walk into the kitchen."), stopping frequently to allow the dreamer to add any new ideas. Group members can ask questions here in the open ended, non-leading way to highlight any large differences between what the dreamer is saying now and what he said earlier, and to make sure all aspects of the dream have been touched on.

The work on the dream wraps up, for now, with orchestrating projections from the group about possible meaning links between dream and waking life. This time the group does not get to run wild with their imaginations—it is *not* their dream now, so "If this were my dream" does not apply. Instead, this time the group confines its comments to the dream itself and whatever else the dreamer has said during the process. This time, unlike in the game, the group addresses the dreamer directly—for example, "You mentioned that you'd been nervous about calling for that job. I think that is what the dead telephone line in your dream represents." Again the group's ideas may or may not resonate for the dreamer, who again has a chance to respond.

Stage 4 is the follow-up, and it occurs at the group's next meeting. The session starts by giving the same dreamer a chance to make any additional comments about his dream. A group member might offer a delayed orchestration.

Misinformation about the Ullman method has led many dreamworkers to conflate it with the method taught by the Rev. Jeremy Taylor, even speaking of the Ullman–Taylor method or the "If this were my dream" method. Indeed, the similarity in their two methods is the awareness of group members' projections encapsulated in that phrase. (Ullman referred to his method as experiential dreamwork; Taylor uses the term projective dreamwork.) As already mentioned, though, Ullman considered the stage 2 "If this were my dream" approach the least important part; the stage 3 orchestrating projections are *not* from the perspective of group members taking the dream on as their own; and projections are not allowed in stage 1 or some stage 3 substages. Ullman–Taylor method and the "If this were my dream" method are, at best, serious misnomers for the Ullman method.

The crucial difference between the Ullman and Taylor methods is in structure. Although Taylor's method has a structure of touch-in and centering moments surrounding the work with individual dreams, the actual dreamwork has no structure. Projections and questions are allowed to flow freely as group members think of them (and, according to Ullman, can channel the work away from the dreamer's areas of resistance and toward the group's biases). In his 1983 book *Dream Work*, Taylor wrote, "These verbal exchanges encourage full participation by each group member at every moment, while retaining the central importance of the dreamer's own tingles and responses" (p. 86).

Ullman found that those all-important tingles and responses—the fragile unfolding of the dream's meaning within the dreamer—can easily get lost if the group is involved every moment. In fact, between his 1979 and 1996 books, he made his structure more distinct, sorting stage 3 into substages and clarifying the orchestrated closure, because without those, "questions were put to the dreamer in too random and anarchic a way and, on occasion, the questioning would get out of hand in the group's eagerness to solve the mystery of the dream" (Ullman, 1996, p. xix). Being given a game-type projection one minute, asked a clarifying question the next, and offered an orchestrating projection right after that requires the dreamer to do a lot of mental gear-shifting, with results that can become superficial. Ullman's structure gives both the dreamer and the group members some breathing room— time to process, feel, watch, and consider how best to verbalize (or be reminded not to verbalize). Used without proper reflection, even "If this were my dream" may do little more than thinly veil a group member's conviction that he knows for sure what the dream means.

The boundaries between stages also help maintain appropriate boundaries between the other group members and the dreamer. Each stage ending is a natural opportunity for the dreamer to stop the process without fear of offending the group.

Ullman was clear that the group exists to serve the dreamer. Its members are midwives to the dream: "Just as most babies are born to physically healthy mothers, so most dreams occur under circumstances in which the dreamer is ready to be confronted by the information in that dream. The group members . . . ease into view the meanings and feelings embedded in the imagery. . . . midwives have nothing to do with the conception of the child nor do they have anything to do with its upbringing. Their task is to assist in the natural function of birth. . . . The midwife is maximally helpful and minimally intrusive" (Ullman, 1996, p. xix).

Ullman-method groups have been the focus of studies by Varida Kautner (working with the elderly), Teresa De-Cicco (with female graduate students), Linda Raab (with HIV-positive men), and John Herbert (in a computer-mediated format).

Directions for further research could include application to additional specialized populations; study of the handling of posttraumatic stress disorder within the Ullman-method format; comparisons of the efficacy of the Ullman method versus others; and a study of what factors might predict that a dreamworker would do best in one type of group over another.

Meanwhile, dreamworkers, researchers, and organizations need to portray the Ullman method accurately, for their own integrity, to give Montague Ullman his due, and so dreamers will be able to make informed choices about how they can best benefit from working in groups.

Gloria Sturzenacker

See also: entries related to Dreams and Therapy

References

Taylor, Jeremy. (1983). *Dream work: Techniques for discovering the creative power in dreams.* Boston: Paulist Press.

Ullman, M. (1990). Basic dream work: An objective comparison of dream groups and therapy. *Dream Network Journal of the Exploration of Dreams, 9*(1). Retrieved from http://www.siivola.org/monte/papers_grouped/uncopyrighted/Dreams/Basic_Dream_Work.htm

Ullman, M. (1996). *Appreciating dreams: A group approach.* Thousand Oaks, CA: Sage Publications.

Ullman, M., & Zimmerman, N. (1979). *Working with dreams.* New York: Delacorte Press/Elaine Friede.

The Unconscious and Dreams before Freud

It is commonly assumed that both dream studies and the concept of the unconscious mind began with the theories of Freud. However, a considerable number of prominent philosophers, psychologists, doctors, novelists, and other writers extensively explored dreaming as well as the unconscious long before Freud published *The Interpretation of Dreams* in 1899. In the 18th and 19th centuries, emerging ideas about the respective natures of dreaming and the unconscious mind frequently intersected with and mutually influenced each other.

The Philosophical Approach to Dreaming and the Unconscious

In the middle of the 18th century, the German philosopher Leibniz developed the first purely psychological explanation of the unconscious mind as a collection of minute perceptions (Rand, 2004, pp. 259–373). Biran, a French philosopher, modified and expanded on Leibniz's minute perceptions by introducing the idea of highly influential, nonconscious affective impressions. Anticipating Freud by nearly a century, Biran also incorporated into his theory of unconsciousness a model of dreaming in which repression plays a central role.

Ideas about dreaming and the unconscious would be abundantly explored during the Romantic era. The German philosopher von Schubert argued that dreams consisted of a hieroglyphic language of symbols, in which the repressed aspects of a person were often expressed (Ellenberger, 1970, pp. 203–206). The creative as well as the terrifying power of dreams was prominently featured in the works of most Romantic fiction writers (Ford, 1998, pp. 108–129). Several Romantic works, such as Coleridge's *Kubla Khan,* Shelley's *Frankenstein,* and De Quincey's *Confessions of an Opium-Eater,* were directly inspired by dreams or dreamlike visions.

The Experimental Approach to Dreaming and the Unconscious

The experimental approach to studying the unconscious was introduced around 1850 by the German psychologist Fechner (Ellenberger, 1970, pp. 312–313). Through various experiments, Fechner measured the relationships between the intensities of various stimulations and perceptions. At the same time that Fechner and others were devising ways to scientifically investigate the nature of the unconscious, a few researchers were developing methods for experimentally studying the phenomenon of dreams.

Through prolonged and rigorous observations of his dreams, the German psychologist Scherner developed a comprehensive system of symbolic dream interpretation (Ellenberger, 1970, pp. 303–308). The French physician Maury established the tradition of investigating the effect of various sensory stimulations on dreams. The Marquis Hervey St. Denys, a French sinologist, embarked on the most direct method of dream experimentation by becoming aware that he was dreaming (lucid dreaming), and conducting investigations while dreaming.

The Clinical Approach to Dreaming and the Unconscious

Throughout the 19th century, animal magnetists, later known as hypnotists, developed clinical techniques for engaging the unconscious minds of subjects in order to further the healing of a variety of physical and mental diseases. During the 1880s and 1890s, there was a dramatic upsurge in scientific interest in hypnosis, as well as other nonordinary states of consciousness, particularly mediumship and the phenomenon of multiple personalities (Gauld, 1995, pp. 297–318).

This golden age of the unconscious (Gauld, 1995, p. 412) represented the formative professional years of Freud. His development of psychoanalysis emerged out of a decade of research into the application of hypnosis to the medical condition hysteria (Ellenberger, 1970, pp. 431–450). His research was heavily influenced by many of his contemporaries, including Charcot, Bernheim, Breuer, and Janet, his main rival. Among other innovations, Freud introduced the talking cure as a substitute for hypnotic induction, and shifted the primary domain of clinical exploration from the hypnotic trance to dreams, thus inaugurating the clinical era of dream studies.

During this time period, psychical researchers, most notably Myers and Flournoy, developed extensive, highly influential psychological theories that attributed to the unconscious mind superior mental capacities such as genius and creative inspiration (Ellenberger, 1970, pp. 313–318). Mediumistic research also stimulated significant contributions to dream theory. Van Eeden devised a technique involving the mediumistic researcher learning to control one's dreams, and would later coin the phrase "lucid dreaming." Flournoy was a significant mentor of Jung, and many of the mature Jung's ideas about dreams and the unconscious can be found, in germinal form, in his early medical dissertation on Helene Preiswerk, his mediumistic cousin (Ellenberger, 1970, pp. 687–691).

Chris Olsen

References

Ellenberger, H. (1970). *The discovery of the unconscious: The history and evolution of dynamic psychiatry*. New York: Basic Books.

Ford, J. (1998). *Coleridge on dreaming: Romanticism, dreams and the medical imagination*. Cambridge: Cambridge University Press.

Gauld, A. (1995). A history of hypnotism. Cambridge: Cambridge University Press.

Rand, N. (2004). The hidden soul: The growth of the unconscious in philosophy, psychology, medicine, and literature, 1750–1900. *American Imago, 61*(3), 257–289.

Use of Noninvasive Techniques in the Study of Dreaming

Recently, noninvasive brain stimulation techniques, such as transcranial direct current stimulation (tDCs) and transcranial magnetic stimulation (TMS), have become widely available. Both of these methods hold considerable promise for studying the role of different cortical regions in dreaming through stimulation of these regions during sleep and then collecting subsequent dream reports on awakening.

Transcranial Direct Current Stimulation

Although it has been available since the early 1900s, it is only in the last few years that tDCs has been rediscovered and used increasingly as a means to modulate cortical excitability. Due to its ability to induce focal changes in cortical excitability, it has been argued that tDCs is able to demonstrate causality (Fregni et al., 2005). This sets it apart from neuroimaging and lesion techniques, which can only demonstrate general associations between specific behaviors and patterns of activity of specific brain regions. Thus, tDCs, as well as other noninvasive brain stimulation techniques, have made it possible to test novel hypotheses regarding brain function emerging from neuroimaging and lesion studies in humans and animals.

The modulation of cortical excitability from tDCs occurs when the brain is stimulated through the application of a weak but constant direct current (Zaghi et al., 2010). Attached to a battery-driven device, the two electrodes are placed at two separate cortical locations on the human scalp, one which emits a positive charge (referred to as the anode or positively charged electrode) and the other a negative charge (known as the cathode or negatively charged electrode). Thus, depending on where the anode and cathode electrodes are placed, the resulting direct current passes through the intervening brain structures and surrounding tissue as it travels from the anode to the cathode to complete an electrical circuit. Furthermore, the direction of the modulatory effects of tDCs depends on the electrode polarity. Studies targeting different cortical areas have demonstrated that in general, anodal stimulation typically increases local cortical excitability (excitatory effect), whereas cathodal stimulation typically decreases local cortical excitability (inhibitory effect; see Antal & Paulus, 2008; Zaghi et al., 2010). The technique itself is relatively simple to administer and sham stimulation can be applied reliably. Finally, depending on the intensity and duration of the given stimulation, these changes in cortical excitability have been shown to persist beyond the period of stimulation. As most studies employ tDCs protocols, which use a 1-mA stimulation intensity, it has been found that 1 mA of tDCs for at least three minutes is needed to induce aftereffects in cortical excitability.

Such stimulation, however, typically induces short-lasting aftereffects of up to one minute (Antal & Paulus, 2008). Although the exact mechanisms of action are as yet still unknown, it is purported to involve localized changes in ion concentrations and resting membrane potentials. Specifically, the DC current is thought to induce shifts in extracellular sodium and calcium ion concentrations of neuronal populations directly under the anode and cathode by modulating the activity of the respective sodium- and calcium-dependent ion channels. Furthermore, this shift in extracellular sodium and calcium ion concentrations results in changes in the resting membrane potential of these neuronal populations, resulting in neuronal depolarization in the case of anodal stimulation or hyperpolarization during cathodal stimulation (Antal & Paulus, 2008; Zaghi et al., 2010). While these initial shifts in excitability (excitation and inhibition) are most likely due to these DC-induced nonsynaptic changes, a combination of nonsynaptic and synaptic (neuroplastic) processes is purported to underlie any persisting effects. More specifically, current evidence suggests that a combination of glutamatergic mechanisms (NMDA receptor mediated) and membrane mechanisms (de- and hyperpolarization) is responsible for tDCs-elicited aftereffects (Antal & Paulus, 2008).

Previous studies have shown tDCs to be an effective means of altering cortical excitability. It has been successfully used in studies targeting the motor, somatosensory, prefrontal, and visual cortices, thus paving the way for extensive clinical trials and potential therapeutic applications (George et al., 2009). Moreover, tDCs appears to affect a range of higher-order cognitive processes in healthy individuals, with recent studies reporting changes in cognitive functioning following tDCs in nonclinical participants. Some of these functions include the perception of motion aftereffects, amplitude of motor-evoked potentials during motor imagery, beta and gamma EEG spectral power in response to elementary visual stimuli, perception of contrast sensitivity, use-dependent motor cortical plasticity, as well as implicit motor learning (see Nitsche et al., 2008; Zaghi et al., 2010). Some of these studies have found short-term impairments in cognitive performance following a single session of tDCs. Typically, these short-term effects last for anywhere up to 30 minutes poststimulation. For instance, it has been found that intermittent anodal bilateral stimulation of the lateral prefrontal cortex (F3 and F4) can cause impairments in working-memory performance compared to the sham condition. Also, cathodal stimulation over the somatosensory cortex has been found to impair tactile perception for up to seven minutes poststimulation. Additionally, cathodal stimulation over the left supramarginal gyrus (TP3) has been found to have a detrimental effect on auditory working memory. However, short-term improvements in cognitive functioning following a single tDCs session have also been shown. For example, in a group of healthy subjects one study found that anodal stimulation of the left prefrontal cortex improved implicit probabilistic classification learning in the last 5 minutes of the 10-minute stimulation period, while another study reported enhanced working memory following anodal stimulation to the left dorsolateral prefrontal cortex in healthy participants in the last 5 minutes of a 10-minute stimulation period. Finally, in healthy individuals, anodal stimulation of the left V5 (an extrastriate visual area) enhanced performance in a visuomotor coordination task (specifically, improved visual motion perception by decreasing motion aftereffect duration) for up to 15 minutes poststimulation. For recent reviews of such findings see Antal and Paulus (2008), Nitsche et al. (2008), and Zaghi et al. (2010).

In regard to sleep research, tDCs has been used twice to investigate sleep-dependent memory-consolidation processes. In one study, Marshall, Molle, Hallschmid, and Born (2004) reported improvements in declarative memory performance in healthy participants following intermittent anodal tDCs applied bilaterally to the dorsolateral prefrontal cortex (F3 and F4) during slow-wave NREM sleep. Specifically, in this double-blind study, participants demonstrated a significant improvement in the retention of word pairs, compared to wake and sham stimulation conditions. The observed aftereffect would be considered long lasting as participants received the stimulation, were woken only after the end of the first NREM–REM sleep cycle, and then after 20 minutes of being awake, completed the memory task (thus, approximately 60 to 90 minutes poststimulation). In another well-controlled study, Nitsche et al. (2010) investigated the effects of tDCs applied to the prefrontal cortex during REM sleep on the consolidation of a motor sequence learnt before sleeping. It was found that anodal tDCs stimulation of the prefrontal cortex (3 cm anterior to C3) during REM sleep increased REM density and the recall of the learned movement sequences when participants were tested immediately after stimulation.

To date, tDCs has been limited to studies of the aforementioned brain regions (prefrontal, somatosensory, motor, and visual cortex) and predominantly to periods of wakefulness, with only two studies (Marshall et al., 2004; Nitsche et al., 2010) applying tDCs during sleep.

Transcranial Magnetic Stimulation

TMS generates an electric current across the brain via electromagnetic induction. A plastic-enclosed coil of wire is held next to the skull and when activated, produces a magnetic field that passes through the skin and skull, inducing an electric stimulation at the cerebral cortex. TMS can be applied as a single or paired pulse or persistently by repetitive stimulation (rTMS). Single- or paired-pulse TMS causes neurons in the neocortex under the site of stimulation to depolarize and impairs cortical function due to increased noise or enhanced inhibition. rTMS produces longer-lasting effects, which persist past the initial period of stimulation. rTMS generally has inhibitory cortical effects if presented at low frequency (>1 Hz) and excitatory effects when presented at high frequencies (>5 Hz).

Although TMS studies have not yet directly examined dreaming, some have investigated hallucinations, sleep states, and consciousness. For instance, the results of a recent meta-analysis have supported the conclusion that low-frequency rTMS over the temporoparietal junction is effective in reducing auditory hallucinations in schizophrenia (see George et al., 2009). In regard to sleep, Massimini et al. (2010) found that from TMS of the right premotor cortex during short-wave sleep SWS produced very focal high-density multisite EEG activation patterns localized at the site of TMS stimulation. However, TMS applied during REM sleep triggered more widespread and differentiated cortical EEG activation patterns, similar to that found during wakefulness. Consistent with this result, Ferrarelli et al. (2010) administered TMS to a group of healthy individuals during wakefulness as well as during pharmacologically induced loss of consciousness. They found that compared to wakefulness, TMS applied during a loss of consciousness was characterized by short-lasting local activity that failed to propagate beyond the site of stimulation. Thus, such authors have concluded that the EEG responses observed during SWS and loss of consciousness reflect a breakdown in cortical effective connectivity and that the spread of cortical activity observed during REM sleep represents intact consciousness, possibly dream consciousness, which is disconnected from the outside world. No study to date has investigated the relationship between such cortical interconnectivity and dreaming.

Conclusions

Currently, no study has examined the effect of TMS or tDCs during sleep related to subsequent dream reporting. If TMS and tDCs can affect cognitive functioning in both waking and sleeping participants, as demonstrated by several previous studies, then it is not unreasonable to propose that cognitive effects may be observed when such stimulation is directed at brain regions implicated in the dream report process. The most suitable cortical targets for tDCs would therefore be the prefrontal and the PTO association cortex due to: (1) its accessibility with tDCs (compared to the brain stem, thalamus and anterior cingulate gyrus), and (2) the fact that these regions are implicated as key cortical regions in dream reporting as evidenced by neuroimaging and lesion studies.

*Antonia J. Jakobson, Paul B.
Fitzgerald, and Russell Conduit*

See also: entries related to Sleep and the Brain; entries related to Sleep Assessment

References

Antal, A., & Paulus, W. (2008). Transcranial direct current stimulation and visual perception. *Perception, 37,* 367–374.

Ferrarelli, F., et al. (2010). Breakdown in cortical effective connectivity during midazolam-induced loss of consciousness. *Proceedings of the National Academy of Science U.S.A., 107,* 2681–2686.

Fregni, F., et al. (2005). Anodal transcranial direct current stimulation of prefrontal cortex enhances working memory. *Experimental Brain Research, 166,* 23–30.

George, M. S., et al. (2009). Controversy: Repetitive transcranial magnetic stimulation or transcranial direct current stimulation shows efficacy in treating psychiatric diseases (depression, mania, schizophrenia, obsessive-compulsive disorder, panic, post-traumatic stress disorder). *Brain Stimulation, 2,* 14–21.

Marshall, L., Molle, M., Hallschmid, M., & Born, J. (2004). Transcranial direct current stimulation during sleep improves declarative memory. *The Journal of Neuroscience, 24,* 9985–9992.

Massimini, M., et al. (2010). Cortical reactivity and effective connectivity during REM sleep in humans. *Cognitive Neuroscience, 1,* 176–183.

Nitsche, M. A., et al. (2008). Transcranial direct current stimulation: State of the art 2008. *Brain Stimulation, 1,* 206–223.

Nitsche, M. A., et al. (2010). Contribution of the premotor cortex to consolidation of motor sequence learning in humans during sleep. *Journal of Neurophysiology, 104,* 2603–2614.

Zaghi, S., et al. (2010). Noninvasive brain stimulation with low-intensity electrical currents: Putative mechanisms of action for direct and alternating current stimulation. *The Neuroscientist, 16,* 285–307.

Using Dreams in Cognitive-Behavioral Therapy

Working with dreams is very unusual among psychotherapists practicing cognitive-behavioral therapy (CBT). Yet Aaron Beck, one of the main founders of cognitive therapy, advocated the use of dreams in a 1971 paper, asserting that the clients' idiosyncratic way of conceptualizing themselves and the outside world greatly influenced dream content. However, any reference to dreams disappeared from the subsequent writings of Beck and of his main followers. The reasons were, first, that dreams were closely associated with psychoanalysis, second that their experimental study was difficult and, third, that behavioral therapists, with whom Beck started a close relationship, were not interested in such material.

Only a very limited number of CBT therapists have been using dreams (see Rosner, Lyddon, & Freeman, 2004). For example, Arthur Freeman has been doing so and found that dream content can be subject to the same cognitive restructuring (change of viewpoint) as waking thoughts, and Barry Krakow has developed an efficient treatment for recurrent nightmares. The use of dreams in CBT can be generalized if therapists adopt a conception of dreaming radically different from those of psychoanalysts and an interpretation method compatible with the methodology and principles of CBT. As far as the conception of dreaming is concerned, Beck already stressed the continuity between dream content and mental representations in the waking. Montangero (2009) presented a cognitive conception in which dreams are the extreme form of thinking with relaxed control, on a continuum starting with spontaneous remembrances and anticipations. He explained the specifics of dream content by the deactivation of certain cognitive abilities (executive functions) and by the necessity of representing ideas in a concrete, at least partly visual, and economic way. According to him, dreams can express any topic of interest or concern for the dreamer, usually when it has been insufficiently processed in the daytime.

As far as dream interpretation is concerned, Montangero proposes a method according to which the therapist has no preconceived idea as to what the dream is about. The meaning of the dream (i.e., the relationship between the dream and concerns, topics of interest, and life episodes of the dreamer) is discovered thanks to the descriptions, memories, and personal ideas of the client related to the dream content. The work with the dream comprises three steps before the client finds an interpretation (which is the fourth step). First, the complete description of the dream immerses the client in the memory of the dream experience. Everything that was visualized and everything that was present without being visualized has to be mentioned, concerning the events or actions, the setting, the characters, and possible objects. The client is also asked whether s/he felt an emotion during the dream scene. The second step is the systematic search for memory sources. The client is asked what memory comes to his/her mind about each main element of the dream report. For instance, "What memory comes to your mind about elephants?" and not "about the small brown elephant of your dream." For each retrieved memory source, the client specifies its subjective meaning; that is, the ideas and emotions linked to that episode. Third, the client is asked to reformulate the dream report by replacing the words of the initial report by a personal definition of the element, or by its function, its encompassing category, or the subjective meaning of the memory source related to that content. This reformulation in general terms usually permits the client to discover relationships between the dream report and concerns, topics of interest, or life episodes.

Once these topics are discovered, the therapist can use them in various ways, for instance:

- Discuss the importance of this topic in the client's life.
- Draw the client's attention on the biased way of representing the topic, which is often particularly apparent in the dream representation.
- Ask the client whether there would be a more realistic and pleasant way to deal with the same situation.
- Underline any representation in the dream of the client's resources.

This kind of dreamwork yields complementary information about the client and provides concrete and metaphorical representations of his/her problems and strategies. Research on the impact of dreamwork in CBT is needed, and will be possible when a sufficient number of therapists use a similar method.

Jacques Montangero

See also: Cognitive Approach to Dreaming

References

Montangero, J. (2009). Using dreams in cognitive-behavioral therapy: Theory, method and examples. *Dreaming, 19,* 239–254.

Rosner, R.I., Lyddon, W.J., & Freeman, A. (Eds). (2004). *Cognitive therapy and dreams.* New York: Springer.

Video Game Play and Dreams

It is important to consider why video game play is relevant for understanding dreams. Several points can be made. First, Revonsuo (2009) argues that dreams are useful for understanding the binding problem in consciousness. He defines consciousness-related binding as the connection between our personal sense that our consciousness is unified and the underlying biological mechanisms. This is illustrated in the dream state with its inherent bizarre nature. While during waking these semantic neural networks are hidden, due to the domination of sensory stimuli, dream study allows for their unfettered examination. In other words, bizarreness in dreams illuminates semantic neuronal networks. One type of bizarreness happens due to a skip in the track of the semantic network but it does not go too far afield. Other types of bizarreness indicate major departures from a given network.

Thus, having a waking situation, namely video game play, where subjects are exposed for long periods of time to unusual or bizarre experiences, can help to further illuminate the nature of bizarreness in dreams. Such a situation is not easily created in a laboratory with a few hours of viewing or interacting with media. In fact, in a study of video game effects on various cognitive and perceptual tasks, Boot, Blakely, and Simons (2011) found that while nonplayers trained with up to 1,000 hours of play improved their performance, they did not reach the skill levels on the cognitive/perceptual tasks as expert players. Boot et al. (2011) estimated expert players came into the laboratory condition with tens of thousands of hours of video game play. One can make the case that high-end gamers bring to research a lifetime of neuronal network effects that may depart from ordinary conscious experiences including dreams.

The second reason why inquiry into video games is important for dream researchers deals with one potential evolutionary function of dreaming, threat simulation (Revonsuo, 2009). Practice dealing with threats in dreams has evolutionary functionality in that it would result in better performance in subsequent waking. Video gaming may reduce this dream function because this need is being addressed in another imaginal realm (i.e., during a video game). Thus, video gaming offers the potential to investigate this evolutionary function of dreams. Relatedly, threats in dreams are often nightmarish. Thus, the rehearsal of nightmares while awake as a technique to decrease their intensity and persistence can be argued is the essence of some video games.

The third reason that studying video gaming informs dream studies is the potential of video gaming to act as preparation or training for dreaming lucidly and commanding some control over the dream as it progresses. Practice in this technologically generated imaginal realm seems to be associated with consciousness emerging in dreams. Thus such inquiries inform not only the question of how to have a lucid dream but also the broader question of the nature of consciousness when it emerges in sleep. Likewise, gamers are well practiced and expect to be in command of threatening enemies in virtual worlds so that in the biologically virtual world of the dream this skill is quickly utilized. In other words, gamers show more dream control.

Finally, on a pragmatic level, video games offer an opportunity for sleep and dream researchers to manipulate presleep stimuli within closely controlled conditions. An easily controlled and impactful presleep event is the use of a film to investigate the nature of dream incorporation. Films have been used to investigate stress. The advantage of a film is it allows presleep controlled manipulation to investigate incorporation questions.

However, as our media landscape is changing, so too are our opportunities to use media to investigate issues of dream incorporation. The problem with film, television, or radio is that they are all unidirectionally presented, or pushed at the passive viewer. In our waking lives we are not passive viewers, but active participants. This active participatory element is captured in computer use and, especially, video game play.

It is important to keep in mind that due to the increasing gaming pervasiveness in North American society, 67 percent of homes report video game play (ESA, 2011), and the effects of such VR-type exposure on dreams is important in and of itself. Although video games are escapable, and dreams typically less so (an exception being lucid-control dreams), there are many parallels between them in the sense that video games offer experience in an alternative reality that is accessible by most people. Other alternative realities, such as those created in hypnosis, are less widely accessible. Video gaming provides experiences in deep absorption not normally available to those without access to experiences that can result in alternative realities. Supporting this conjecture is a recent study in our laboratory. We found that the degree of self-reported presence, sense of being there, in dreams versus in a video game was not different, belying the oft-cited assumption that dreams are the gold standard of presence.

As communication studies history has taught, the typical introduction of new media is accompanied by fearful reactions from the public and existing media. Thus negative findings such as modeling of aggression, the potential for addiction, and lack of physical activity are most often discussed. However, numerous positive consequences of video game play have also been found from practice in social realms to various improvements in cognitive skills. Our research effort has been the impact of video game play on nighttime dreams. That impact could have been positive or negative, but it appears to be associated with largely positive dream outcomes. Video game play may act as a type of meditative experience to the extent that it requires similar levels of attentional absorption. Video gaming enhances the experience of dream lucidity along the lines of meditators' experiences of lucidity. These findings can be interpreted equally in terms of a psychology of imaginative absorption.

The question posed in our laboratory is what are the effects on the biologically constructed alternative realities of dreams by immersion in the technologically constructed worlds experienced during video game play? Throughout these studies we generally defined the hard-core gamer as someone who:

1. Plays video games on average several times a week,
2. Has a typical playing session of more than 2 hours;
3. Played 50 or more video games over their lifetime; and
4. Has been playing video games since grade three or earlier.

The dream dimensions that we have examined thus far include lucid dreams, dreams where you know you are dreaming while the dream is ongoing; control dreams, where the dreamer has control over some aspects of the dream; bizarreness, the degree to which dreams are unusual or odd; and nightmares, dreams that are so frightening that they wake the sleeper.

Lucid and Control Dreams

In several studies we were able to show that high-end gamers had more lucid and control dreams than those who rarely game (Gackenbach & Kuruvilla, 2008). This dream information was initially based on retrospective reflections on dream history and more recently on dream reports from the previous night's sleep. The first of these last night dream studies (Gackenbach, 2009) was for data from subjects who reported normal sleep length where they felt rested. Of the 800 plus college student respondents, only 152 fit these criteria. In a factor analysis of these dreams with dream type, media use, and gamer-history information, lucid and control dreaming were associated with high-end gamer history and heavier media use the day before the dream. While video game play was the marker on this factor, all media use was associated with lucid and control dreams. This is important to note as while not everyone may be gaming, just about everyone is using various electronic media and thus engaged to some extent in virtual worlds.

However, the lucid-dream–gaming association is less robust than the control-dream–gaming link. When asked to provide lucid dreams there was no difference between high- and low-end gamers in their self-reported incidence. But control of dreams seems to emerge as superior in high-end gamers across data-collection methods. This difference was most recently illuminated in a study where gamers were compared to two other groups frequently engaging in absorbing activities, for example, prayer/meditation and control group. Those who pray/meditate a lot had the highest levels of lucidity but gamers were significantly higher on lucidity than any other absorbing activity group. However, when it came to dream control, it was gamers who reported significantly more than both of the other absorbing groups.

Why might we expect this parallel between video game play and lucid-control dreaming? There are several reasons. Video games are technologically constructed alternative realities while dream worlds are biologically constructed alternative realities. One could argue that there is simply a practice effect. If you are in an artificial reality for hours a day, is it any surprise that you recognize something similar when you are in another one at night? Video gaming has been associated with improved spatial skills as has lucid dreaming. A lack of proneness to motion sickness is needed to play a lot of these games and lucid dreamers have better vestibular systems; thus, they are not susceptible to motion sickness. Finally, the high attention and absorption reported by players and in research on gaming is reminiscent of the same qualities associated with meditation, a group that has been found to have very high levels of lucidity in sleep.

Dream Bizarreness

Based on dreams collected and analyzed in hour-long interviews with hard-core gamers, higher imaginal and dead characters were found in gamers' dreams than in the norms (Gackenbach et al., 2009). We pursued this bizarreness finding in gamers' dreams in two additional studies (Gackenbach, Kuruvilla, & Dopko, 2009). In the first of these two studies (Gackenbach et al., 2009) recent dreams were collected in an online questionnaire from college students. Various media-use information was also gathered. It was found that high-end gamers evidenced more bizarre dreams than low-end gamers in two of the three types of bizarreness categories.

In the second study a two-week online dream diary was gathered from preselected research participants who varied on the four game-play criteria mentioned earlier. This resulted in high- and low-end gamer groups. In addition to the online dream-diary study we also asked the research participants about features that were bizarre for the subjects themselves, as well as various media-use information. For those who fulfilled the criteria for the dream-diary component of the research project, we administered a verbal and figural creativity test. It was found that high-end gamers had more bizarre than nonbizarre dreams than low-end gamers of both the self-reported and judges'-reported types, while the opposite was the case for nonbizarre dream elements. It is important to point out that media use the day before was controlled, and therefore a straight incorporation of bizarre game or other media elements into the dream does not account for this finding. In terms of the creativity assessment, no significant difference for verbal test resulted but significant differences for the figural test favoring the high-end gamer group were identified. We concluded that bizarreness in gamers' dreams is at least associated with their creativity and with their history of media use in the form of gaming, but not associated with the day before media use.

Nightmares

Due to our findings in an interview study of high-end gamers (Gackenbach et al., 2009), we became curious about nightmares. Less misfortune and more intense aggression, when it happened but occurring less often, was found among these hard-core gamers. This combination of findings led us to wonder about gamers' nightmares. We explored this question with additional content analysis on larger samples of gamers' dreams (Gackenbach & Kuruvilla, 2008), replicating these aggression and misfortune findings. Thus three studies were undertaken to further examine these results. In all three studies threat simulation, as an explanation for the aggression and misfortune findings, was explored (Gackenbach & Kuruvilla, 2008).

Revonsuo (2009) argues that dreaming is an adaptive process with an evolutionary foundation. It allows us to simulate threatening situations in the safety of a virtual environment of dreams. This continued practice during dreaming would allow an individual to better prepare for these possibly dangerous instances, were they to arise in the waking world. Gackenbach and Kuruvilla (2008b) asked the question, might gamers' dreams be lower in threat simulation because they have already practiced these responses in their game play during the day? Revonsuo (2000) method of dream content analysis for threat simulation was used on these dreams experienced the night before filling out the questionnaire. In a factor analysis of media use (including gaming history), threat simulation content variables, and various self-report variables of dream content, we found that when high-end gamers reported playing a lot of games the day prior to a reported dream, there was no association to threat in their dreams nor were these dreams seen as nightmarish or scary by the gamers despite reporting that the dreams were violent. In contrast, the low-end gamers did not play games the day before the dream but did watch violent television shows or movies and had dreams that were not only high in threat simulation, but also in violence, nightmarishness, and scariness. Thus we concluded that gaming might be viewed as a protection against threat simulation in dreams.

When we examined the dreamers self-reported emotions during these two types of negative dreams, negative emotions (anxiety, frustration, and fear) were found to be higher in bad dreams for high-end gamers, while positive emotions (sexual arousal and happiness) were found to be greater in nightmares for high-end gamers. When these same dreams were analyzed for threat simulation as a function of gamer history, there was an interaction between dream type (nightmare × bad dream) and gamer group (high vs. low). The high-end gamers showed the expected less threat in nightmares but more in bad dreams while the low-end gamers evidenced less of a difference in threat between the two dream types.

This study was followed by one examining soldiers who play video games. In this case they were asked for a recent dream and a military dream. Information was also gathered on these military gamers' emotional reactivity and history of trauma, including military, which has been shown to be predictive of nightmares. When these predictive factors were controlled, frequent gaming was associated with significantly less threat in military dreams. Thus it may be that high-end gaming may act as an inoculation against the nightmare at least in situations where there is real-world threat, such as being deployed for war.

Conclusions and Implications

Three general dream types have been examined in our program looking at the relationship between video game play and dreams. A participant–observer gamer in our research program illuminates our major findings. When asked, he responded that yes his dreams were lucid and bizarre, and he sometimes has aggression in his dreams but rarely nightmares. Rather he pointed out that he was in the third person in his dreams:

> I've just noticed that sometimes I'm just there as a hovering spirit watching things go on and I don't really have a role . . . I don't even pop up in my dreams, it's just like I'm watching a movie . . . I feel emotion definitely regardless of whether or not I'm the person involved. (Jordan Olischefski; Gackenbach et al., 2009)

In this entry, we reviewed three major areas of inquiry into dreams of gamers: lucid/control dreams, bizarre dreams, and nightmares. We have found higher lucid/control dreams in gamers and wonder if this is indicative of improved metacognition in dreams. Increased bizarreness in gamers might imply that gamers are capable of improved novel adaptive responses as per the global workspace theory of consciousness or creativity. Finally, in terms of aggression/misfortune in dreams we found some association between gaming serving a threat simulation function in waking and potentially a protective function regarding nightmares, if not bad dreams. While not entirely clear, taken together it seems that a case can be made that video game play while awake may make positive contributions to dreaming and is reminiscent of meditators' dreams.

Jayne Gackenbach

See also: entries related to Dream Content

References

Boot, W. R., Blakely, D. P., & Simons, D. J. (2011). Do action video games improve perception and cognition? *Frontiers in Psychology, 2*, 226.

ESA (2011). http://www.theesa.com/Entertainment Software Association.

Gackenbach, J. I. (2008). Video game play and consciousness development: A transpersonal perspective. *Journal of Transpersonal Psychology, 40*(1), 60–87.

Gackenbach, J. I. (2009). Electronic media and lucid-control dreams: Morning after reports. *Dreaming, 19*(1), 1–6.

Gackenbach, J. I., Ellerman, E., & Hall, C. (2011). Video game play as nightmare protection: A preliminary inquiry on military gamers. *Dreaming: APA's Online First* (August 22, 2011).

Gackenbach, J. I., & Kuruvilla, B. (2008). The relationship between video game play and threat simulation dreams. *Dreaming, 18*(4), 236–256.

Gackenbach, J. I., Kuruvilla, B., & Dopko, R. (2009). Video game play and dream bizarreness. *Dreaming, 19*(4), 218–231.

Gackenbach, J. I., Matty, I., Kuruvilla, B., Samaha, A. N., Zederayko, A., Olischefski, J., & Von Stackelberg, H. (2009). Video game play: Waking and dreaming consciousness. In S. Krippner (Ed.), *Perchance to dream* (pp. 239–253). Hauppauge, NY: Nova Science Publishers.

Gackenbach, J. I., Rosie, M., Bown, J., & Sample, T. (2011). Dream incorporation of video game play as a function of interactivity and fidelity. *Dreaming, 21*(1), 32–50.

Revonsuo, A. (2000). *Behavioral and Brain Sciences, 23*(6), 887–901; discussion 904–1121. Review.

Revonsuo, A. (2009). *Inner presence: Consciousness as a biological phenomenon.* Cambridge, MA: MIT Press.

Visual Art and Dreams

Historically widespread concepts of the dream as sometimes prophetic and supernatural in origin lie behind the most obviously dream-related visual art, which depicts specific dreams of important spiritual and historic figures, often representing both dreamer and dream. Such artworks were initially generated and viewed in a context of understanding shared by patron, artist, and audience. In European Christian art, especially in medieval illuminated manuscripts and church sculpture, the Biblical dreams of Jacob, the Pharaoh, and the Three Magi are the most frequently represented, with some attention to dreams of saints in Renaissance paintings. Throughout the Buddhist diaspora, the dream of Maya, mother-to-be of the Buddha, has been the basic dream subject. In Islamic manuscript illuminations, the night visions of the Prophet epitomize the divine dream. South Asian art, especially in illustrated manuscript books, draws on the Hindu Puranas for dream stories. In Egyptian and Greco-Roman antiquity, iconic sculptural figures of gods and goddesses associated with dream incubation (such as Asklepios, Amphiarion, Isis, and Serapis) were installed at incubation sites.

Many tribal and indigenous cultures create visual mappings and artifacts referring to shamanic and initiatory journeys in dream and to dreams of special significance to the community or an individual. A useful gathering of such work, with brief commentary, is provided by David Coxhead and Susan Hiller in their general survey *Dreams: Visions of the Night* (1976), including examples from Iroquois, Chumash, Chippewa, and Navajo Native American tribes, shamanic traditions of northern Europe and Asia, aboriginals in Central Australia, and the Saora in Orissa, India.

The 19th and 20th centuries opened up a broader set of options for the visual arts to engage dreaming. Changes in the role of the artist and art patronage, associated with the rise of individualism and the bourgeoisie, enabled artists to explore dream experience from more personal and introspective perspectives. Romanticism, with its valorization of subjective experience; symbolism, with its interest in hidden meaning; modern abstraction, with its disorienting approaches to the material world; and especially surrealism, with its explicit focus on the dream, offered fertile ground for dream content. In recent years, a number of survey exhibitions with substantial catalogues in North America and Europe have mapped the territory, though further dream-specific studies would be helpful for every artist, movement, and period involved. Lynn Gamwell's landmark exhibition assembled a particularly comprehensive look at 20th-century art of the dream; her essay in the catalogue *Dreams 1900–2000: Science, Art, and the Unconscious Mind* (2000) addresses the influence of Freud on art, proposing that two major streams of 20-century art-making, the unconscious mind and art-about-art, would have been inconceivable without Freud's theories of the dream and the unconscious. Neuroscientist J. Allan Hobson and art historian Hellmut Wohl detail correlations between late 20th-century neuroscience of the dreaming brain and Western art 1780–1950 in *From Angels to Neurones: Art and the New Science of Dreaming* (2005). An exemplary in-depth study of a single work is Norman Gee's *Ernst: Piéta or Revolution by Night* (1986), which traces Max Ernst's deployment of Freud's dream theory both in process and in content.

Dream of the Magi, stone capital, Cathédrale Saint-Lazare, Autun, by Gislebertus (French, 12th century). (Giraudon/The Bridgeman Art Library International)

The later 20th century and early 21st century have again expanded the range of dream-related visual art. New art media and formats such as video and the artist book have proven especially receptive to dream content. In contemporary performance and installation art, the public or documented act of dreaming may be itself the artwork. Art-making practices such as collage have been developed as dreamwork methods, shifting perceptions of dream art from professional artists and passive viewers to a participatory workshop context with aims beyond the boundaries of traditional art worlds.

Studies of the functions of dreaming in creativity have particular relevance to visual art. In *The Committee of Sleep: How Artists, Scientists, and Athletes Use Dreams for Creative Problem-Solving— and How You Can Too* (2001), Deirdre Barrett opens with a chapter on painting and sculpture which interrogates with nuanced understanding a few dozen historical and contemporary examples, including Salvador Dalí, Frida Kahlo, and Jasper Johns.

With the possible exception of medieval European work, which has been well studied, the entire field is still wide open for dream-focused studies that integrate concepts of the dream, the science of dreaming, and dreamwork practices with visual art perspectives. Asian, Middle Eastern, and indigenous contexts especially need far more attention. Studies that include the voice of the artist on issues of origin and process in contemporary work could be facilitated by the backlog of artist interviews and statements gathered in periodicals such as *Dreamworks* in the 1980s and *DreamTime* since the 1990s.

Betsy Davids

References

Barrett, D. (2001). *The committee of sleep: How artists, scientists, and athletes use dreams for creative problem-solving—and how you can too*. New York: Crown Publishers.

Coxhead, D., & Hiller, S. (1976). *Dreams: Visions of the night*. New York: Crossroad.

Gamwell, L. (Ed.). (2000). *Dreams 1900–2000: Science, art, and the unconscious mind*. Ithaca, NY: Cornell University Press.

Gee, N. (1986). *Ernst: Piéta or revolution by night*. London: The Tate Gallery.

Hobson, A., & Wohl, H. (2005). *From angels to neurones: Art and the new science of dreaming*. Fidenza: Mattioli. (Originally published in 1885.)

White Noise and Sleep

College students require between eight and nine hours of sleep every night for peak performance during the day; however, research indicates that most only receive between seven and eight hours each night (Carskadon, 2002). In addition, Forquer and colleagues (2008) found that 33 percent of college students at North Central University, in Minneapolis, reported sleep latencies of more than 30 minutes and 43 percent reported waking more than once each night. Finally, a survey by the American College Health Association (2005) reported that college students rated sleep difficulties as the third-largest impediment to academic performance, behind stress and illness. Therefore, it was hypothesized that improving sleep in college students may be associated with complementary improvements in academic performance.

Several strategies have been shown to help college students sleep better at night, including maintaining a consistent sleep schedule, improving sleep hygiene, and the use of continuous white noise. Continuous white noise, sound that covers the entire range of human hearing from 20 to 20,000 Hz, has been shown to improve sleep in adults and small children, but had never been systematically examined in college students. Forquer and Johnson (2007) recruited four college students who reported waking more than once per night or taking longer than 30 minutes to fall asleep to participate in a study examining the efficacy of continuous white noise for reducing sleep difficulties in college students. These students were provided with a Tranquil Moments Plus white noise generator. Participants were instructed to use the white noise setting between 60 and 75 decibels and set to play continuously from bedtime to wake time. Participants kept sleep diaries throughout the course of the experiment in which they recorded their bedtime, sleep latency, number and length of night-wakings, and rise times. White noise generators were implemented according to a nonconcurrent multiple baseline across subjects design, which involved baselines of varying lengths and introduction of white noise at different points in time for each participant. All four participants reported decreases in both frequency of night-waking and sleep latency while using the white noise; however, some of their sleep difficulties returned to baseline levels following discontinuation of the sound. Attempts to link improved sleep using white noise to improved academic performance were largely unsuccessful due to the types of cognitive measures being utilized. The free association task employed was too easy, leading to potential ceiling effects. Finally, students reported that they were comfortable using white noise and would recommend it to other students experiencing sleep problems.

There are several possible explanations for the effectiveness of continuous white noise for reducing sleep difficulties, including decreased arousal through the process of habituation, masking extraneous noises that may interfere with sleep, the resetting of the biological clock so that it does not include frequent night-waking or long sleep latencies, and stimulus control. Stimulus control is the process by which white noise may come to act as a discriminative stimulus in the presence of which decreased arousal is reinforced by sleep causing sleep to occur more frequently in its presence. Additional research is needed with larger samples, possible group designs, and the use cognitive tasks that more closely resemble actual academic performance.

LeAnne M. Forquer

See also: Increasing Sleep Complaints

References

American College Health Association. (2005). The American College Health Association National College Health Assessment (ACHA-NCHA), Spring 2003 reference group report. *Journal of American College Health, 53,* 199–210.

Carskadon, M. A. (2002). *Adolescent sleep patterns: Biological, social, and psychological influences.* New York: Cambridge University Press.

Forquer, L. M., Camden, A. E., Gabriau, K. M., & Johnson, C. M. (2008). Sleep patterns of college students at a public university. *Journal of American College Health, 56,* 563–565.

Forquer, L. M., & Johnson, C. M. (2007). Continuous white noise to reduce sleep latency and night waking in college students. *Sleep and Hypnosis, 9,* 60–66.

Women's Dreams across the Life Cycle

The notion that dreams reflect the conception of the self, of its relation with others, and with the environment is well suited to explore changes in women's dreams parallel to developmental changes in waking life (Hall, 1953). While content analysis of long dream series suggests that few changes take place in a person's dreams throughout adulthood (Domhoff, 2003), cross-sectional studies of home-collected dreams found changes, starting in early adulthood.

A study by Brenneis (1975), taking into account psychosocial changes from early adulthood to the 70s, led me to explore dreams of different age groups. While no evidence of drastic changes was found in the dreams of women from their middle 20s to the 40s, the impact of developmental changes became noticeable by the middle 50s (Côté, Lortie-Lussier, Roy, & De Koninck, 1996). Inconsistent or marginally significant results of other studies, resulting from small samples or from differences in data collection, limit the generalization of their findings. More systematic and inclusive studies were in order to trace the ontogenetic evolution of dreams from adolescence up to old age. A large study of the dreams of Canadian women and men, Francophone and Anglophone, ranging in age from 12 to 80 years, was initiated in 2005 at the University of Ottawa by Joseph De Koninck.

Home dream reports have been collected since then in Ottawa, the National Capital of Canada. Participants were contacted in high schools, universities, workplaces, and community centers. The present sample includes 412 women, distributed in five age groups: 88 from 12 to 17, 81 from 18 to 24, 80 from 25 to 39, 82 from 40 to 64, 81 from 65 up. One or two dreams from different nights were collected with instructions to report as many details as possible. Two independent judges scored them with the Hall and Van De Castle categories. Data were submitted to statistical analyses, after controlling for length. Reporting of the results takes into account psychosocial changes characteristic of successive life stages.

Findings relative to adolescence support those of previous studies. Teenagers chat in their dreams. Highlights of their reports are activities and friendly interactions, generally in the company of girls. But the reporting is factual and lacks emotion. Of all age groups they are the most successful. They portray themselves as victims of aggressions, physical or verbal. Their dreams reveal little about the age-related task of finding one's self through relationships with parents and other adults.

Young adults (18 to 24), mostly university students, have longer dreams than adolescents, with characters most often females. Friendly and aggressive interactions are more frequent than in the older groups. They are both aggressors and victims of aggressions. Sadness and anger are distinctive dream features. Success and failure are less frequent than in the other adult groups. Overall dreams reflect tense relationships with friends. Concerns about finding meaningful relationships find their way in dreams.

The dreams of the 25 to 39 group are as lengthy as those of the younger adults, with a marked decrease in the number of characters, male and female, and in the frequency of aggressions. Dreamers entertain more friendly interactions with familiar characters than any other group, suggesting intimacy, accentuated by interior settings. Emotions are similar to the younger women's. The high incidence of failure is a unique characteristic, while success is only occasional. Continuity with waking is reflected in concerns central to that period, including marriage or partnership, work and children. The conception of the self is one of inward reflection.

In the middle adulthood group, aged 40 to 64, dreams are shorter than the younger groups', contain fewer characters of either sex and less friendly and aggressive interactions, consistent with previous studies. Three components emerge: the dreamers are significantly more often aggressors, more successful, and angrier than any other group. It could reflect the independence and assertiveness women gain as they reach middle adulthood, in line with theories of female aging. It could refer to decreasing happiness, due to unmet expectations during this period, which coincides with pre- and post-menopause.

Findings about the oldest group are consistent with most studies devoted to this period. This is valid for the length of dreams, decreased number of characters, familiar and females, friendly and aggressive interactions, and total of emotions. Two results stand out: the sharp increase in outdoor settings and the prevalence of sadness, at variance with other studies. The salience of sadness may reflect a sense of loss, an interpretation that theories about old age would support.

This overview of age-related changes in dreams is but a summary of the issues relating to the inner life of women, during transitions from the security of one period to the unknown perspectives of the following one. Completing the normative study should provide answers.

Monique Lortie-Lussier

References

Brenneis, C.B. (1975). Developmental aspects of aging. A comparative study of dreams. *Archives of General Psychiatry, 32,* 429–434.

Côté, L., Lortie-Lussier, M., Roy, M.J., & De Koninck, J. (1996). Continuity and change: The dreams of women throughout adulthood. *Dreaming, 6,* 187–192.

Domhoff, G.W. (2003). *The scientific study of dreams: Neural networks, cognitive development, and content analysis.* Washington, DC: American Psychological Association.

Hall, C.S. (1953). A cognitive theory of dreams. *Journal of General Psychology, 49,* 273–283.

Neugarten, B.J. (1979). Time, age and the life cycle. *American Journal of Psychiatry, 136,* 887–894.

Yawning

The yawn is a stereotyped and often repetitive motor act characterized by gaping of the mouth accompanied by a long inspiration of breath, a brief acme, and then a short expiration of breath. Stretching and yawning simultaneously is known as pandiculation. It is not merely a simple opening of the mouth but a complex coordinated movement bringing together a flexion followed by an extension of the neck, a wide dilatation of the pharyngolarynx with strong stretching of the diaphragm and antigravity muscles.

Ethologists agree that almost all vertebrates yawn. Yawning is morphologically similar in reptiles, birds, mammals, and fish. These behaviors may be ancestral vestiges maintained throughout evolution, with little variation (phylogenetic old origins). Correlatively, yawning can be visualized as early as 12 weeks during the period of fetal development.

Systematic and coordinated pandiculations occur in a similar pattern and form across all animals, and consistently occur during behaviors associated with cyclic life rhythms: sleep arousal, feeding, and reproduction. Yawning appears as one undirected response to an inner stimulation, underlying the homeostasis of these three behaviors.

Species that sleep 8 to 12 hours and alternate between active and inactive periods (e.g., predatory carnivores and primates) yawn much more frequently (following a circadian rhythm) than herbivores. In humans, daily frequency of yawning varies between 5 and 15 times per day. The diurnal distribution of yawning frequency is illustrated by higher frequency upon waking and before sleep.

A good number of clinical and pharmacological data indicate that yawning involves a group of oxytocinergic neurons originating in the paraventricular nucleus of the hypothalamus (PVN), and projecting to extrahypothalamic brain areas (e.g., hippocampus, medulla oblongata, and spinal cord). The PVN is an integration center between the central and peripheral autonomic nervous systems. It is involved in a number of functions ranging from feeding and metabolic balance to sexual behavior and yawning. Activation of these neurons by dopamine and its agonists, excitatory amino acids (N-methyl-D-aspartic acid), oxytocin itself, or by electrical stimulation leads to yawning; conversely their inhibition by gamma-aminobutyric acid and its agonists or by opioid peptides and opiate-like drugs inhibit both yawning and sexual response. Other compounds modulate yawning by activating central oxytocinergic neurons: sexual hormones, serotonin, hypocretin, and endogenous peptides (adrenocorticotropin-melanocyte-stimulating hormone). Oxytocin activates cholinergic neurotransmission in the hippocampus and the reticular formation of the brainstem. Acetylcholine induces yawning via the muscarinic receptors of effectors from which the respiratory neurons in the medulla; the motor nuclei of the 5th, 7th, 9th, 10th, and 12th cranial nerves; the phrenic nerves (C1–C4); and the motor supply to the intercostal muscles.

Contagiousness of Yawning

It seems that hominids have the unique capacity to be receptive to the contagiousness of yawning. In humans, echokinesis only occurs in situations of minimal mental stimulation (public transport, waiting); people are not susceptible to this phenomenon during prolonged intellectual effort. Yawning appears to trigger a sort of social coordination function and reflects the capacity to unconsciously and automatically be influenced by the behavior of others. Autistic individuals who are characterized by impaired mental state attribution do not show contagious yawning. All these data support the hypothesis that contagious yawning shares the neural networks implicated in self-recognition and mental state attribution; it may therefore be that yawning is involved in empathy.

Excessive yawning is a source of embarrassment in social circles. There are multiple causes of excessive yawning, that is, a cluster of 10 to 50 yawns, many times a day. Of short duration, they may predict a vasovagal reaction or neurovegetative disorders (dyspepsia, migraine-like syndromes). All insults to the intracranial central nervous system or the hypothalamo–hypophyseal region may be involved: tumors with intracranial hypertension, infections, temporal epilepsy, strokes, etc. Actually, iatrogenic pathology (serotoninergic agents, apomorphine, acetylcholinesterase inhibitors, opiate withdrawal) is the most frequent explanation of pathologic cases.

Yawning does not accelerate blood flow. This blood-flow theory argued that yawning improved the oxygenation of the brain, in response to cerebral anemia. The inaccuracy of this hypothesis was formally invalidated by Provine, Tate, and Geldmacher (1987). In his studies, he has demonstrated that breathing neither pure O_2 nor gases high in CO_2 had any significant effect on yawning, although both increased breathing rate. In a second study, he has found that exercise sufficient to double breathing rate had no effect on yawning.

Although the available data are far from providing a complete and generally accepted account of the physiological function of yawning, progress has been made in ruling out previously held hypotheses.

Conclusion

Yawning and pandiculation are transitional behaviors, universal among vertebrates, closer to an emotional stereotypy than a reflex. Phylogenetically ancient and ontogenetically primitive, they may provide some evolutionary advantage. They seem to exteriorize homeostatic processes of systems controlling wakefulness, satiety, and sexuality in the diencephalon.

Olivier Nils Walusinski

See also: Fetal Sleep

References

Barbizet, J. (1958). Yawning. *Journal of Neurology, Neurosurgery, and Psychiatry, 21*(3), 203–209.

Collins, G. T., & Eguibar, J. R. (2010). Neurophamacology of yawning. *Frontiers of Neurology and Neuroscience, 28,* 90–106.

Deputte, B. L. (1974). Revue sur le comportement de bâillement chez les vertébrés. *Bulletin interne Société Française pour l'étude du comportement animal, 1,* 26–35.

Guggisberg, A. G., Mathis, J., Schnider, A., & Hess, C. W. (2010). Why do we yawn? *Neuroscience and Biobehavioral Reviews, 34,* 1267–1276.

Nahab, F. B. (2010). Exploring yawning with neuroimaging. *Frontiers of Neurology and Neuroscience, 28,* 128–133.

Platek, S. M., Mohamed, F. B., & Gallup, G. G., Jr. (2005). Contagious yawning and the brain. *Cognitive Brain Research, 23,* 448–452.

Provine, R. R., Tate, B. C., & Geldmacher, L. L. (1987). Yawning: No effect of 3–5% CO_2, 100% O_2, and exercise. *Behavioral and Neural Biology, 48*(3), 382–393.

Appendix:
Additional Resources on Sleep

A list of publications on the practice and treatment parameters on all the major sleep disorders can be found at http://www.aasmnet.org/practiceguidelines.aspx.

Reference Resources on Sleep Medicine Topics

American Electroencephalographic Society guidelines for standard electrode position nomenclature. (1991). *Journal of Clinical Neurophysiology, 8*(2), 200–202.

American Psychiatric Association. (2000). *Diagnostic and statistical manual of mental disorders* (4th ed.). Washington, D.C.: Author.

Beck, A., Steer, R. A., & Brown, G. K. (1996). *Beck depression inventory ®—II.* San Antonio, TX: The Psychological Corporation.

Boeve, B. F., Silber, M. H., Ferman, T. J., Lucas, J. A., & Parisi, J. E. (2001). Association of REM sleep behavior disorder and neurodegenerative disease may reflect an underlying synucleinopathy. *Movement Disorders, 16*(4), 622–630.

Bonnet, M. H. (2000). Sleep deprivation. In M. H. Kryger, T. Roth, & W. C. Dement (Eds.), *Principles and practice of sleep medicine* (3rd ed., pp. 53–71). Philadelphia: Elsevier Saunders.

Borbély, A. A., & Wirz-Justice, A. (1982). Sleep, sleep deprivation and depression, a hypothesis derived from model of sleep regulation. *Human Neurobiology, 1,* 205–210.

Brabbins, C. J., Dewey, M. E., Copeland, J.R.M., Davidson, I. A., McWilliam, C., Saunders, P., et al. (1993). Insomnia in the elderly: Prevalence, gender differences and relationships with morbidity and mortality. *International Journal of Geriatric Psychiatry, 8,* 473–480.

Braun, A. R., Balkin, T. J., Wesenstein, N. J., Varga, M., Baldwin, P., Selbie, S., et al. (1997). Regional cerebral blood flow throughout the sleep–wake cyclc. *Brain, 120,* 1173–1197.

Carskadon, M., & Dement, W. C. (2000). Normal human sleep: An overview. In M. H. Kryger, T. Roth, & W. C. Dement (Eds.), *Principles and practice of sleep medicine* (3rd ed., pp. 15–25). Philadelphia: Elsevier Saunders.

Chaudhuri, K. R., Pal, S., DiMarco, A., Whately-Smith, C., Bridgman, K., Mathew, R., et al. (2002). The Parkinson's disease sleep scale: A new instrument for assessing sleep and nocturnal disability in Parkinson's disease. *Journal of Neurology, Neurosurgery & Psychiatry, 73*(6), 629–635.

Corsi-Cabrera, M., Miro, E., del Rio Portilla, Y., Perez-Garci, E., Villanueva, Y., &

Guevara, M.A. (2003). Rapid eye movement sleep dreaming is characterized by uncoupled EEG activity between frontal and perceptual cortical regions. *Brain and Cognition, 51*(3), 337–345.

Dew, M.A., Hoch, C.C., Buysse, D.J., Monk, T.H., Begley, A.E., Houck, P.R., et al. (2003). Healthy older adults' sleep predicts all-cause mortality at 4 to 19 years of follow-up. *Psychosomatic Medicine, 65*(1), 63–73.

First, M.B, Spitzer, R.L., Gibbon, M., & Williams, J.B.W. (2002). *Structured clinical interview for DSM–IV–TR axis I disorders, research version, patient edn (SCID–I/P)*. New York: Biometrics Research, New York State Psychiatric Institute.

Germain, A., & Nielsen, T. (2003). Impact of imagery rehearsal treatment on distressing dreams, psychological distress, and sleep parameters in nightmare patients. *Behavioral Sleep Medicine, 1,* 140–154.

Hamilton, M. (1960). A rating scale for depression. *Journal of Neurology, Neurosurgery, and Psychiatry, 23,* 56–62.

Iber, C. (Ed.), Ancoli-Israel, I., Chesson, Jr., A., & Quan, S. (2007). *The AASM manual for the scoring of sleep and associated events: Rules, terminology and technical specification* (1st ed.). Westchester, IL: American Academy of Sleep Medicine.

Jafari, B., & Mohsenin, V. (2010). Polysomnography. *Clinics in Chest Medicine, 31*(2), 287–297.

Javaheri, S. (2010). Central sleep apnea. *Clinics in Chest Medicine, 31*(2), 235–248.

Johns, M.W. (1991). A new method for measuring daytime sleepiness: The Epworth sleepiness scale. *Sleep, 14*(6), 540–545.

Kapur, V.K. (2010). Obstructive sleep apnea: Diagnosis, epidemiology, and economics. *Respiratory Care, 55*(9), 1155–1167.

Kripke, D.F. (2003). Sleep and mortality. *Psychosomatic Medicine, 65*(1), 74.

Monk, T.H., Reynolds, C.F., Kupfer, D.J., Buysse, D.J., Coble, P.A., Hayes, A.J.,

et al. (1994). The Pittsburgh Sleep Diary. *Journal of Sleep Research, 3*(2), 111–120.

Montplaisir, J., Nicolas, A., Godbout, R., & Walters, A. (2000). Restless leg syndrome and periodic limb movement disorders. In M.H. Kryger, T. Roth, & W.C. Dement (Eds.), *Principles and practice of sleep medicine* (3rd ed., pp. 742–752). Philadelphia: Elsevier Saunders.

Natarajan, R. (2010). Review of periodic limb movement and restless legs syndrome. *Journal of Postgraduate Medicine, 56*(2), 157–162.

National Sleep Disorders Research Plan. (2003). Washington, D.C.: U.S. Department of Health and Human Services.

Nofzinger, E.A., Mintun, M.A., Wiseman, M.B., Kupfer, D.J., & Moore, R.Y. (1997). Forebrain activation in REM sleep: An FDG PET study. *Brain Research, 770,* 192–201.

Pack, A.I., & Pien, G.W. (2011). Update on sleep and its disorders. *Annual Review of Medicine, 62,* 447–460.

Rechtschaffen, A., & Kales, A. (1968). *A manual of standardized terminology, techniques and scoring system for sleep stages of human subjects.* Washington, DC: U.S. Department of Health, Education, and Welfare Public Health Service–NIH/NIND.

Schenck, C.H., & Mahowald, M.W. (2000). Parasomnias: Managing bizarre sleep-related behavior disorders. *Postgraduate Medicine, 107*(3), 145–156.

Wechsler, D. (1987). *WAIS-R manual.* New York: The Psychological Corporation.

Wechsler, D. (1997). *Wechsler adult intelligence scale (WAIS) III Manual.* New York: The Psychological Corporation.

Social Psychology of Dreaming

Adolphs, R. (2009). The social brain: Neural basis of social knowledge. *Annual Review of Psychology, 60,* 693–716.

Antrobus, J.S. (1983). REM and NREM sleep reports: Comparison of word frequencies by cognitive classes. *Psychophysiology, 20,* 562–568.

Barrett, D., & McNamara, P. (Eds.). (2007). *The new science of dreaming* (3 vol.). Westport, CT: Praeger Perspectives.

Belicki, K. (1986). Recalling dreams: An examination of daily variation and individual differences. In J. Gackenbach (Ed.), *Sleep and dreams: A sourcebook* (pp. 187–206). New York: Garland.

Blagrove, M., Farmer, L., & Williams, E. (2004). The relationship of nightmare frequency and nightmare distress to well-being. *Journal of Sleep Research, 13,* 129–136.

Born, J., & Wagner, U. (2004). Memory consolidation during sleep: Role of cortisol feedback. *Annals of the New York Academy of Sciences, 1032,* 198–201.

Braun, A. R., Balkin, T. J., Wesenten, N. J., Carson, R. E., Varga, M., Baldwin, P., et al. (1997). Regional cerebral blood flow throughout the sleep-wake cycle: An H2(15) O PET study. *Brain, 120*(7), 1173–1197.

Brenner, L. A., Vanderploeg, R. D., & Terrio, H. (2009). Assessment and diagnosis of mild traumatic brain injury, posttraumatic stress disorder, and other polytrauma conditions: Burden of adversity hypothesis. *Rehabilitation Psychology, 54*(3), 239–246.

Brown, R. J., & Donderi, D. C. (1986). Dream content and self-reported well-being among recurrent dreamers, past recurrent dreamers, and nonrecurrent dreamers. *Journal of Personality and Social Psychology, 50,* 612–623.

Dang–Vu, T. T., Desseilles, M., Petit, D., Mazza, S., Montplaisir, J., & Maquet, P. (2007). Neuroimaging in sleep medicine. *Sleep Medicine, 8*(4), 349–372.

Domhoff, G. W. (1996). *Finding meaning in dreams: A quantitative approach.* New York: Plenum Press.

Domhoff, G. W. (2003). *The scientific study of dreams: Neural networks, cognitive development, and content analysis.* Washington, D.C.: American Psychological Association.

Domhoff, G. W. (2005). The content of dreams: Methodologic and theoretical implications. In M. H. Kryger, T. Roth, & W. C. Dement (Eds.), *Principles and practice of sleep medicine* (4th ed., pp. 522–534). Philadelphia: Elsevier Saunders.

Fantini, M. L., Corona, A., Clerici, S., & Ferini–Strambi, L. (2005). Aggressive dream content without daytime aggressiveness in REM sleep behavior disorder. *Neurology, 65*(7), 1010–1015.

Goodenough, D. R. (1991). Dream recall: History and current status of the field. In S. J. Ellman & J. S. Antrobus (Eds.), *The mind in sleep: Psychology and psychophysiology* (2nd ed., pp. 143–171). New York: John Wiley and Sons.

Gregor, T. (2001). Content analysis of Mehinaku dreams. In K. Bulkeley (Ed.), *Dreams: A reader on the religious, cultural and psychological dimensions of dreaming* (pp. 133–166). New York: Palgrave.

Gregor, T. A. (1981). "Far far away my shadow wandered. . ." The dream theories of the Mehinaku Indians of Brazil. *American Ethnologist, 8,* 709–720.

Hall, C. (1963). Strangers in dreams: An empirical confirmation of the Oedipus complex. *Journal of Personality, 31,* 336–345.

Hall, C. S., & Van de Castle, R. (1966). *The content analysis of dreams.* New York: Appleton-Century-Crofts.

Hobson, J. A. (2007). Wake up or dream on? Six questions for Turnbull and Solms. *Cortex, 43*(8), 1113–1115 (discussion, 1116–1121).

Hobson, J. A., & Pace-Schott, E. F. (2002). The cognitive neuroscience of sleep: Neuronal systems, consciousness and learning. *Nature Reviews Neuroscience, 3*(9), 679–693.

Hobson, A. J., Pace-Schott, E. F., Stickgold, R., & Kahn, D. (1998). To dream or not to dream? Relevant data from new neuroimaging and electrophysiological studies. *Current Opinion in Neurobiology, 8,* 239–244.

Hu, P., Stylos-Allan, M., & Walker, M. P. (2006). Sleep facilitates consolidation of emotionally arousing declarative memory. *Psychological Science, 10,* 891–898.

Kahn, D., Stickgold, R., Pace-Schott, E.F., & Hobson, J.A. (2000). Dreaming and waking consciousness: A character recognition study. *Journal of Sleep Research, 9,* 317–325.

Kramer, M. (1993). The selective mood regulatory function of dreaming: An update and revision. In A. Moffit, M. Kramer, & R. Hoffman (Eds.), *The functions of dreaming* (pp. 139–195). Albany: State University of New York Press.

Kramer, M. (2000). The variety of dream experience: Expanding our ways of working with dreams. *Journal of the American Academy of Psychoanalysis, 28,* 727–729.

Kuiken, D., & Sikora, S. (1993). The impact of dreams on waking thoughts and feelings. In A. Moffitt, M. Kramer, & R. Hoffman (Eds.), *The functions of dreaming* (pp. 419–476). Albany: State University of New York Press.

Maquet, P., & Franck, G. (1997). REM sleep and amygdala. *Molecular Psychiatry, 2*(3), 195–196.

Maquet, P., Peters, J.M., Aerts, J., Delfiore, G., Degueldre, C., Luxen, A., & Franck, G. (1996). Functional neuroanatomy of human rapid-eye-movement sleep and dreaming. *Nature, 383,* 163–166.

McNamara, P. (2004). *An evolutionary psychology of sleep and dreams.* Westport, CT: Praeger/Greenwood Press.

McNamara, P., Auerbach, S., Johnson, P., Harris, E., & Doros, G. (2010). Impact of REM sleep on distortions of self concept, mood and memory in depressed/anxious participants. *Journal of Affective Disorders, 122*(3), 198–207.

McNamara, P., McLaren, D., Kowalczyk, S., & Pace-Schott, E. (2007). "Theory of Mind" in REM and NREM dreams. In D. Barrett & P. McNamara (Eds.), *The new science of dreaming: Volume I: Biological aspects* (pp. 201–220). Westport, CT: Praeger Perspectives.

McNamara, P., McLaren, D., Smith, D., Brown, A., & Stickgold, R. (2005). A "Jekyll and Hyde" within: Aggressive versus friendly social interactions in REM and NREM dreams. *Psychological Science, 16*(2), 130–136.

Nielsen, T.A., Kuiken, D., Hoffman, R., & Moffitt, A. (2001). REM and NREM sleep mentation differences: A questions of story structure? *Sleep and Hypnosis, 3*(1), 9–17.

Nishida, M., Pearsall, J., Buckner, R.L., & Walker, M.P. (2009). REM sleep, prefrontal theta, and the consolidation of human emotional memory. *Cerebral Cortex, 19*(5), 1158–1166.

Nofzinger, E.A., Mintun, M.A., Wiseman, M.B., Kupfer, D.J., & Moore, R.Y. (1997). Forebrain activation in REM sleep: An FDG PET study. *Brain Research, 770,* 192–201.

Ochsner, K.N. (2004). Current directions in social cognitive neuroscience. *Current Opinion in Nuerobiology, 14*(2), 254–258.

Perez–Garci, E., del Rio Portilla, Y., Guevara, M.A., Arce, C., & Corsi-Cabrera, M. (2001). Paradoxical sleep is characterized by uncoupled gamma activity between frontal and perceptual cortical regions. *Sleep, 24,* 118–126.

Plihal, W., & Born, J. (1997). Effects of early and late nocturnal sleep on declarative and procedural memory. *Journal of Cognitive Neuroscience, 9*(4), 534–547.

Revonsuo, A. (2000). The reinterpretation of dreams: An evolutionary hypothesis of the function of dreaming. *Behavioral Brain Science, 23*(6), 877–901.

Schneider, A., & Domhoff, G.W. (1996). DreamSat. Retrieved from http://www.dreamresearch.net/

Schneider, A., & Domhoff, G.W. (1999). DreamBank. Retrieved from www.dreambank.net

Scheinder, D., & Sharp, L. (1969). *The dream life of a primitive people.* Ann Arbor, MI: University Microfilms.

Schonbar, R. A. (1961). Temporal and emotional factors in the selective recall of dreams. *Journal of Consulting Psychology, 25,* 67–73.

Schredl, M., & Engelhardt, H. (2001). Dreaming and psychopathology: Dream recall and dream content of psychiatric inpatients. *Sleep and Hypnosis, 3,* 44–54.

Smith, C. (1995). Sleep states and memory processes. *Behavioural Brain Research, 69*(1–2), 137–145.

Smith, M. R., Antrobus, J. S., Gordon, E., Tucker, M. A., Hirota, Y., Wamsley, E. J., et al. (2004). Motivation and affect in REM sleep and the mentation reporting process. *Consciousness and Cognition, 13,* 501–511.

Stacy, M. (2002). Sleep disorders in Parkinson's disease: Epidemiology and management. *Drugs Aging, 19*(10), 733–739.

Stefanakis, H. (1995). Speaking of dreams: A social constructionist account of dream sharing. *Dreaming, 5,* 95–104.

Stepansky, R., Holzinger, B., Schmeiser-Rieder, A., Saletu, B., Kunze, M., & Zeitlhofer, J. (1998). Austrian dream behavior: Results of a representative population survey. *Dreaming, 8,* 23–30.

Stickgold, R. (1998). Sleep: Off-line memory reprocessing. *Trends in Cognitive Neurosciences, 2*(12), 485–492.

Stickgold, R., Scott, L., Fosse, R., & Hobson, J. A. (2001). Brain-mind states: I. Longitudinal field study of wake-sleep factors influencing mentation report length. *Sleep, 24*(2), 171–179.

Strauch, I., & Meier, B. (1996). *In search of dreams: Results of experimental dream research.* Albany: State University of New York Press.

Tedlock, B. (1992). *Dreaming: Anthropological and psychological interpretations.* Santa Fe, NM: School of America Research Press.

Vann, B., & Alperstein, N. (2000). Dream sharing as social interaction. *Dreaming, 10,* 111–120.

Vertes, R. P., & Eastman, K. E. (2000). The case against memory consolidation in REM sleep. *Behavioral Brain Science, 23*(6), 867–876.

Wagner, U., Gais, S., & Born, J. (2001). Emotional memory formation is enhanced across sleep intervals with high amounts of rapid eye movement sleep. *Learning and Memory, 8*(2), 112–129.

Walker, M. P., Brakefield, T., Hobson, J. A., & Stickgold, R. (2003). Dissociable stages of human memory consolidation and reconsolidation. *Nature, 425*(6958), 616–620.

Walker, M. P., Brakefield, T., Morgan, A., Hobson, J. A., & Stickgold, R. (2002). Practice with sleep makes perfect: Sleep-dependent motor skill learning. *Neuron, 35,* 205–211.

Walker, M. P., & Stickgold, R. (2006). Sleep, memory and plasticity. *Annual Review of Psychology, 10,* 139–166.

Wetter, T. C., Brunner, H., Hogl, B., Yassouridis, A., Trenkwalder, C., & Friess, E. (2001). Increased alpha activity in REM sleep in de novo patients with Parkinson's disease. *Movement Disorders, 16*(5), 928–933.

Wilson, M. A., & McNaughton, B. L. (1994). Reactivation of hippocampal ensemble memories during sleep. *Science, 265,* 676–679.

Zadra, A., Desjardins, S., & Marcotte, E. (2006). Evolutionary functions of dreams: A test of the threat simulation theory in recurrent dreams. *Consciousness and Cognition, 15,* 450–463.

Zadra, A., & Donderi, D. C. (2000). Threat perceptions and avoidance in recurrent dreams. *Behavioral and Brain Sciences, 23,* 1017–1018.

Phylogeny of Sleep

Abouheif, E. (1999). A method for testing the assumption of phylogenetic independence in comparative data. *Evolutionary Ecology Research, 1,* 895–909.

Achermann, P., & Borbély, A. A. (2003). Mathematical models of sleep regulation. *Frontiers in Bioscience, 1*(8), S683–S693.

Achermann, P., Dijk, D. J., Brunner, D. P., & Borbely, A. A. (1993). A model of human sleep homeostasis based on EEG slow-wave activity: Quantitative comparison of data and simulations. *Brain Research Bulletin, 31*, 97–113.

Ackerly, D. D., & Donoghue, M. J. (1998). Leaf size, sapling allometry, and Corner's rules: Phylogeny and correlated evolution in maples (Acer). *American Naturalist, 152*, 767–798.

Allison, T., & Cicchetti, D. V. (1976). Sleep in mammals: Ecological and constitutional correlates. *Science, 194*, 732–734.

Baron, G., Stephan, H., & Frahm, H. D. (1996). *Comparative neurobiology in Chiroptera: Vol. 1. Macromorphology, brain structures, tables and atlases.* Basel, Switzerland: Birkhauser Verlag.

Barton, R. A. (1998). Visual specialization and brain evolution in primates. *Proceedings of the Royal Society of London—Series B, 265*(1409), 1933–1937.

Barton, R. A. (1999). The evolutionary ecology of the primate brain. In P. Lee (Ed.), *Comparative primate socioecology* (pp. 167–194). New York: Cambridge University Press.

Barton, R. A., Aggleton, J. P., & Grenyer, R. (2003). Evolutionary coherence of the mammalian amygdala. *Proceedings of the Royal Society of London, 270*(1514), 539–543.

Barton, R. A., & Harvey, P. H. (2000). Mosaic evolution of brain structures in mammals. *Nature, 405*, 1055–1058.

Bininda-Emonds, O. R., Jeffery, J. E., & Richardson, M. K. (2003). Inverting the hourglass: Quantitative evidence against the phylotypic stage in vertebrate development. *Proceedings of the Royal Society of London—Series B, 270*(1513), 341–346.

Borbély, A. A. (1980). Sleep: Circadian rhythm versus recovery process. In M. Koukkou, D. Lehmann, & J. Angst (Eds.), *Functional states of the brain: Their determinants* (pp. 151–161). Amsterdam: Elsevier.

Borbély, A. A. (1982). A two process model of sleep regulation. *Human Neurobiology, 1*, 195–204.

Brooks, D. R., & McLennan, D. A. (1991). *Phylogeny, ecology, and behavior: A research program in comparative biology.* Chicago: University of Chicago Press.

Bryant, P. A., Trinder, J., & Curtis, N. (2004). Sick and tired: Does sleep have a vital role in the immune system? *Nature Reviews Immunology, 4*(6), 457–467.

Capellini, I., Barton, R. A., Preston, B., McNamara, P., & Nunn, C. L. (2008). Phylogenetic analysis of the ecology and evolution of mammalian sleep. *Evolution, 62*(7), 1764–1776.

Capellini, I., McNamara, P., Preston, B. T., Nunn, C. L., & Barton, R. A. (2009). Does sleep play a role in memory consolidation? A comparative test. *PLoS ONE, 4*(2), e4609.

Capellini, I., Nunn, C. L., McNamara, P., Preston, B. T., & Barton, R. A. (2008). Energetic constraints, not predation, influence the evolution of sleep patterning in mammals. *Functional Ecology, 22*(5), 847–853.

Clutton-Brock, T. (1991). *The evolution of parental care.* Princeton, NJ: Princeton University Press.

Cohen, J. (1998). *Statistical power analysis for the behavioural sciences.* Hillsdale, NJ: Erlbaum Associates.

Crile, G., & Quiring, D. P. (1940). A record of the body weights and certain organ and gland weights of 3690 animals. *Ohio Journal of Science, 40*, 219–259.

Desseilles, M., Vu, T. D., Laureys, S., Peigneux, P., Degueldre, C., Phillips, C., & Maquet, P. (2006). A prominent role for amygdaloid complexes in the Variability in Heart Rate (VHR) during Rapid Eye Movement (REM) sleep relative to wakefulness. *NeuroImage, 32*(3), 1008–1115.

Everson, C., & Toth, L. (2000). Systemic bacterial invasion induced by sleep deprivation. *American Journal of Physiology—Regulatory, Integrative and Comparative Physiology, 278*(4), R905–R916.

Felsenstein, J. (1985). Phylogenies and the comparative method. *American Naturalist, 125*, 1–15.

Finlay, B.L., & Darlington, R.B. (1995). Linked regularities in the development and evolution of mammalian brains. *Science, 268*(5217), 1578–1584.

Freckleton, R.P., Harvey, P.H., & Pagel, M. (2002). Phylogenetic analysis and comparative data: A test and review evidence. *American Naturalist, 160*(6), 712–726.

Garland, T., Dickerman, A.W., Janis, C.M., & Jones, J.A. (1993). Phylogenetic analysis of covariance by computer simulation. *Systematic Biology, 42*, 18–32.

Garland, T., Harvey, P.H., & Ives, A.R. (1992). Procedures for the analysis of comparative data using phylogenetically independent contrasts. *Systematic Biology, 4*, 18–32.

Gauthier-Clerc, M., Tamisier, A., & Cezilly, F. (1998). Sleep-vigilance trade-off in green-winged teals (Anas crecca crecca). *Canadian Journal of Zoology, 76*, 2214–2218.

Grenyer, R., & Purvis, A. (2003). A composite species-level phylogeny of the "Insectivora" (Mammalia, Liptyphyla Haeckel 1866). *Journal of Zoology, 260*, 245–257.

Grimm, V., & Railsback, S.F. (2005). *Individual-based modeling and ecology*. Princeton, NJ: Princeton University Press.

Grimm, V., Revilla, E., Berger, U., Jeltsch, F., Mooij, W.M., Railsback, S.F., et al. (2005). Pattern-oriented modelling of agent–based complex systems: Lessons from ecology. *Science, 310*, 987–991.

Hart, B.L. (1990). Behavioral adaptations to pathogens and parasites: Five strategies. *Neuroscience Biobehavioral Reviews, 14*, 273–294.

Harvey, P.H., & Pagel, M.D. (1991). *The comparative method in evolutionary biology*. New York: Oxford University Press.

Harvey, P.H., & Rambaut, A. (1998). Phylogenetic extinction rates and comparative methodology. *Proceedings of the Royal Society of London—Series B, 265*, 1691–1696.

Hill, R.A., & Lee, P.C. (1998). Predation risk as an influence on group size in crecopithecoid primates: Implications for social structure. *Journal of Zoology, 245*, 447–456.

Huelsenbeck, J.P., & Rannala, B. (1997). Phylogenetic methods come of age: Testing hypotheses in an evolutionary context. *Science, 276*, 227–232.

Huelsenbeck, J.P., Rannala, B., & Masly, J.P. (2000). Accommodating phylogenetic uncertainty in evolutionary studies. *Science, 288*(5475), 2349–2350.

Huelsenbeck, J.P., Ronquist, F., Nielsen, R., & Bollback, J.P. (2001). Evolution: Bayesian inference of phylogeny and its impact on evolutionary biology. *Science, 294*(5550), 2310–2314.

Kavaliers, M., & Colwell, D.D. (1995). Reduced spatial learning in mice infected with the nematode, Heligmosomoides polygyrus. *Parasitology, 110*, 591–597.

Kreuger, J.M., & Fang, J. (2000). Host defense. In M.H. Kryger, T. Roth, & W.C. Dement (Eds.), *Principles and practice of sleep medicine* (3rd ed., pp. 255–265). Philadelphia: Elsevier Saunders.

LeDoux, J.E. (2000). Emotion circuits in the brain. *Annual Reviews in Neuroscience, 23*, 155–184.

Lesku, J.A., Rattenborg, N.C., & Amlaner, C.J., Jr. (2006). The evolution of sleep: A phylogenetic approach. In T. Lee-Chiong (Ed.), *Sleep: A comprehensive handbook* (pp. 49–61). Indianapolis, IN: John Wiley & Sons.

Maddison, W.P., & Maddison, D.R. (1992). *MacClade analysis of phylogeny and character evolution*. Sunderland, MA: Sinauer Associates.

Maddison, W.P., & Maddison, D.R. (2006). *Mesquite: A modular system for evolutionary analysis.* Retrieved from http://mesquiteproject.org

Maddison, W.P., & Slatkin, M. (1991). Null models for the number of evolutionary steps in character of a phylogenetic tree. *Evolution, 45,* 1184–1197.

Maquet, P. (1999). Brain mechanisms of sleep: Contribution of neuroimaging techniques. *Journal of Psychopharmocology, 13,* S25–S28.

Maquet, P., & Franck, G. (1997). REM sleep and amygdala. *Molecular Psychiatry, 2*(3), 195–196.

Maquet, P., Smith, C., & Stickgold, R. (2003). *Sleep and plasticity.* New York: Oxford University Press.

Martins, E.P., & Garland, T. (1991). Phylogenetic analyses of the correlated evolution of continuous characters: A simulation study. *Evolution, 45,* 534–557.

Martins, E.P., & Hansen, T.F. (1996). The statistical analysis of interspecific variation: A review and evaluation of phylogenetic comparative methods. In E.P. Martins (Ed.), *Phylogenies and the comparative method in animal behavior* (pp. 22–75). New York: Oxford University Press.

McNamara, P. (2004). *An evolutionary psychology of sleep and dreams.* Westport, CT: Praeger.

McNamara, P., Capellini, I., Harris, E., Nunn, C.L., Barton, R.A., & Preston, B. (2008). The phylogeny of sleep database: A new resource for sleep scientists. *The Open Sleep Journal, 1,* 11–14.

McNamara, P., Nunn, C.L., & Barton, R.A. (Eds.). (2010). *Evolution of sleep: Phylogenetic and functional perspectives.* New York: Cambridge University Press.

Mitchell, M., & Taylor, C.E. (1999). Evolutionary computation: An overview. *Annual Review of Ecology and Systematics, 20,* 593–616.

Murphy, W.J., Eizirik, E., Johnson, W.E., Zhang, Y.P., Ryderk, O.A., & O'Brien, S.J. (2001). Molecular phylogenetics and the origins of placental mammals. *Nature, 409*(6820), 614–618.

Nunn, C.L. (1999). *A comparative study of primate socioecology and intersexual conflict.* Durham, NC: Duke University Press.

Nunn, C.L. (2002). A comparative study of leukocyte counts and disease risk in primates. *Evolution, 56,* 177–190.

Nunn, C.L. (2002). Spleen size, disease risk and sexual selection: A comparative study in primates. *Evolutionary Ecology Research, 4,* 91–107.

Nunn, C.L. (2003). Sociality and disease risk: A comparative study of leukocyte counts in primates. In P.L. Tyack (Ed.), *Animal social complexity* (pp. 26–31). Cambridge, MA: Harvard University Press.

Nunn, C.L., Altizer, S., Jones, K.E., & Sechrest, W. (2003). Comparative tests of parasite species richness in primates. *American Naturalist, 162,* 597–614.

Nunn, C.L., & Barton, R.A. (2001). Comparative methods for studying primate adaptation and allometry. *Evolutionary Anthropology, 10,* 81–98.

Nunn, C.L., Gittleman, J.L., & Antonovics, J. (2000). Promiscuity and the primate immune system. *Science, 290,* 1168–1170.

Nunn, C.L., Gittleman, J.L., & Antonovics, J. (2003). A comparative study of white blood cell counts and disease risk in carnivores. *Proceedings of the Royal Society London, Series B, 270,* 347–356.

Nunn, C.L., & van Schaik, C.P. (2000). Intersexual conflict and ecological factors in primate social evolution. In C. Janson (Ed.), *Infanticide by males and its implications* (pp. 388–419). Cambridge, MA: Cambridge University Press.

Omland, K.E. (1997). Correlated rates of molecular and morphological evolution. *Evolution, 5,* 1381–1393.

Pagel, M. (1994). Detecting correlated evolution on phylogenies: A general method for the comparative analysis of discrete characters. *Proceedings of the Royal Society of London, Series B, 255*, 37–45.

Pagel, M. (1997). Inferring evolutionary processes from phylogenies. *Zoologica Scripta, 26*, 331–348.

Pagel, M. (1999). Inferring the historical patterns of biological evolution. *Nature, 401*, 877–884.

Petraitis, P.S., Dunham, A.E., & Niewiarowski, P.H. (1996). Inferring multiple causality: The limitations of path analysis. *Functional Ecology, 10*, 421–431.

Preston, B.T., Capellini, I., McNamara, P., Barton, R.A., & Nunn, C.L. (2009). Parasite resistance and the adaptive significance of sleep. *BMC Evolutionary Biology, 9, 7*.

Purvis, A., & Rambaut, A. (1994). Comparative analysis by independent contrasts (CAIC) (2nd ed.). Oxford: University of Oxford Press.

Purvis, A., & Rambaut, A. (1995). Comparative analysis by dependant contrast (CAIC): An apple Macintosh application for analyzing comparative data. *Computer Applications in Bioscience, 11*, 247–251.

Rattenborg, N.C., Amlaner, C.J., & Lima, S.L. (2000). Behavioral, neurophysiological and evolutionary perspectives on unihemispheric sleep. *Neuroscience Biobehavioral Reviews, 24*(8), 817–842.

Rechtschaffen, A., & Bergmann, B.M. (2001). Letter: In response to Everson and Toth. *American Journal of Physiology, 280*, R602–R603.

Rice, W.R. (1989). Analyzing tables of statistical tests. *Evolution, 1*(43), 223–225.

Rice, W.R., & Gaines, S.D. (1994). Heads I win, tails you lose: Testing directional alternative hypotheses in ecological and evolutionary research. *Trends in Ecology and Evolution, 9*, 235–237.

Ridley, M. (1986). The number of males in a primate troop. *Animal Behavior, 34*, 1848–1858.

Sanderson, M.J., Purvis, A., & Henze, C. (1998). Phylogenetic supertrees: Assembling the trees of life. *Trends in Ecology and Evolution, 13*, 105–109.

Sibley, C.G., & Ahlquist, J.E. (1990). *Phylogeny and classification of birds: A study in molecular evolution.* New Haven, CT: Yale University Press.

Siegel, J. (2002). *The neural control of sleep and waking.* New York: Springer Verlag.

Stahl, W.R. (1965). Organ weights in primates and other mammals. *Science, 150*, 1039–1042.

Stearns, S.C. (1992). *The evolutions of life histories.* New York: Oxford University Press.

Stephan, H., Baron, G., & Frahm, H. (1991). *Comparative brain research in mammals: Vol. 2. Insectivores.* New York: Springer.

Stephan, H., Frahm, H., & Baron, G. (1981). New and revised data on volumes of brain structures in insectivores and primates. *Folia Primatology, 35*, 1–29.

Steriade, M. (2006). Brian electrical activity and sensory processing during waking and sleep states. In M.H. Kryger, T. Roth, & W.C. Dement (Eds.), *Principles and practice of sleep medicine* (4th ed., pp. 101–119). Philadelphia: Elsevier Saunders.

Strecker, R.E., Basheer, R., McKenna, J.T., & McCarley, R.W. (2006). Another chapter in the adenosine story. *Sleep, 29*(4), 426–428.

Takahashi, J.S. (1999). Narcolepsy genes wake up the sleep field. *Science, 285*(5436), 2076–2077.

Tobler, I. (2006). Phylogeny of sleep regulation. In M.H. Kryger, T. Roth, & W.C. Dement (Eds.), *Principles and practice of sleep medicine* (4th ed., pp. 77–90). Philadelphia: Elsevier Saunders.

Whiting, B.A., & Barton, R.A. (2003). The evolution of the cortico–cerebellar complex in primates: Anatomical connections predict patterns of correlated evolution. *Journal of Human Evolution, 44*(1), 3–10.

Zepelin, H. (1989). Mammalian sleep. In W.C. Dement (Ed.), *Principles and practice of sleep medicine* (1st ed., pp. 30–48). Philadelphia: Elsevier Saunders.

Zepelin, H. (1994). Mammalian sleep. In W.C. Dement (Ed.), *Principles and practice of sleep medicine* (2nd ed., pp. 30–48). Philadelphia: Elsevier Saunders.

Sleep Spindles

Berner, I., Schabus, M., Wienerroither, T., & Klimesch, W. (2006). The significance of sigma neurofeedback training on sleep spindles and aspects of declarative memory. *Applied Psychophysiology and Biofeedback, 31*(2), 97–114.

Clemens, Z., Fabo, D., & Halasz, P. (2006). Twenty-four hours retention of visuospatial memory correlates with the number of parietal sleep spindles. *Neuroscience Letters, 403*(1–2), 52–56.

De Gennaro, L., & Ferrara, M. (2003). Sleep spindles: An overview. *Sleep Medicine Reviews, 7*(5), 423–440.

De Gennaro, L., Ferrara, M., & Bertini, M. (2000). Topographical distributions of spindles: Variations between and within NREm sleep cycles. *Sleep Research Online, 3*(4), 155–160.

Donnet, A., Farnarier, G., Gambarelli, D., Aguglia, U., & Regis, H. (1992). Sleep electroencephalogram at the early stage of Creutzfeldt-Jakob disease. *Clinical Electroencephalography, 23*(3), 118–125.

Gais, S., Molle, M., Helms, K., & Born, J. (2002). Learning-dependent increases in sleep spindle density. *Journal of Neuroscience, 22*(15), 6830–6834.

Happe, S., Ludemann, P., & Berger, K. (2002). The association between disease severity and sleep–related problems in patients with Parkinson's disease. *Neuropsychobiology, 46*(2), 90–96.

Maquet, P., Smith, C., & Stickgold, R. (2003). *Sleep and brain plasticity.* Oxford: Oxford University Press.

Montplaisir, J., Petit, D., Lorrain, D., Gauthier, S., & Nielsen, T. (1995). Sleep in Alzheimer's disease: Further considerations on the role of the brainstem and forebrain cholinergic populations in sleep-wake mechanisms. *Sleep, 18*(3), 145–148.

Nader, R.S., & Smith, C.T. (2001). The relationship between stage 2 sleep spindles and intelligence. *Sleep, 24*(Suppl.), A160.

Nader, R.S., & Smith, C.T. (2003). A role for stage 2 sleep in memory processing. In P. Maquet, C. Smith, & R. Stickgold (Eds.), *Sleep and brain plasticity* (pp. 87–98). New York: Oxford University Press.

Neal, H., & Keane, P.E. (1980). Electrically and chemically induced spindling and slow waves in the encéphale isolé rat: A possible role for dopamine in the regulation of electrocortical activity. *Electroencephal Clinical Neurophysiology, 38,* 318–326.

Petit, D., Gagnon, J.F., Fantini, M.L., Ferini-Strambi, L., & Montplaisir, J. (2004). Sleep and quantitative EEG in neurodegenerative disorders. *Journal of Psychosomatic Research, 56*(5), 487–496.

Puca, F.M., Bricolo, A., & Turella, G. (1973). Effect of L-dopa or amantadine therapy on sleep spindles in parkinsonism. *Electroencephalography and Clinical Neurophysiology, 35,* 327–330.

Schabus, M., Gruber, G., Parapatics, S., Sauter, C., Klosch, G., Anderer, P., et al. (2004). Sleep spindles and their significance for declarative memory consolidation. *Sleep, 27*(8), 1479–1485.

Schabus, M., Hodlmoser, K., Gruber, G., Sauter, C., Anderer, P., Klosch, G., et al. (2006). Sleep spindle-related activity in the human EEG and its relation to general cognitive and learning abilities. *European Journal of Neuroscience, 23*(7), 1738–1746.

Shinotoh, H., & Calne, D. (1995). The use of PET in Parkinson's disease. *Brain and Cognition, 28,* 297–310.

Siapas, A.G., & Wilson, M.A. (1998). Coordinated interactions between hippocampal ripples and cortical spindles during slow-wave sleep. *Neuron, 21*(5), 1123–1128.

Sirota, A., Csicsvari, J., Buhl, D., & Buzsaki, G. (2003). Communication between neocortex and hippocampus during sleep in rodents. *Proceedings of the National Academy of Sciences, USA, 100*(4), 2065–2069.

Soderling, T. R., & Derkach, V. A. (2000). Postsynaptic protein phosphorylation and LTP. *Trends in Neuroscience, 23*(2), 75–80.

Steriade, M. (1997). Synchronized activities of coupled oscillators in the cerebral cortex and thalamus at different levels of vigilance. *Cerebral Cortex, 7*, 583–604.

Steriade, M. (1999). Coherent oscillations and short-term plasticity in corticothalamic networks. *Trends in Neuroscience, 22*(8), 337–345.

Steriade, M., MacCormick, D. A., & Sejnowski, T. J. (1993). Thalamocortical oscillations in the sleeping and aroused brain. *Science, 262*, 679–685.

Stickgold, R. (1998). Sleep: Off-line memory reprocessing. *Trends in Cognitive Neurosciences, 2*(12), 485–492.

Resources on Comparative Sleep Patterns and Evolution of Sleep

Papers with Juvenile Sea Mammal Data

Castellini, M. A., Milsom, W. K., Berger, R. J., Costa, D. P., Jones, D. R., Castellini, J. M., et al. (1994). Patterns of respiration and heart-rate during wakefulness and sleep in elephant seal pups. *American Journal of Physiology, 266*(3 Pt 2), R863–R869.

Flanigan, W. F. (1974). Nocturnal behavior of captive small cetaceans, II: The beluga whale, *Delphinapterus leucas* [Abstract]. *Sleep Research, 3*, 85.

Flanigan, W. F. (1975). More nocturnal observations of captive small cetaceans, I: The killer whale, *Orcinus orca* [Abstract]. *Sleep Research, 4*, 139.

Goley, P. D. (1999). Behavioral aspects of sleep in Pacific white-sided dolphins (Lagenorhynchus obliquidens). *Marine Mammal Science, 15*(4), 1054–1064.

Lyamin, O. I. (1987). [The ontogenetic development of the interhemispheric asymmetry of the EEG during slow-wave sleep in northern fur seals] (in Russian). *Zh Vyssh Nerv Deiat Im I P Pavlova, 37*(1), 157–159.

Lyamin, O. I. (1993). Sleep in the harp seal (*Pagophilus groenlandica)*: Comparisons of sleep on land and in water. *Journal of Sleep Research, 2*, 170–174.

Lyamin, O. I., Mukhametov, L. M., Chetyrbok, I. S., & Vassiliev, A. V. (1994). Sleep and wakefulness in southern sea lions (Otari byronia). *Journal of Sleep Research, 3*(Suppl 1), 152.

Lyamin, O. I., Mukhametov, L. M., Chetyrbok, I. S., & Vassiliev, A. V. (2002). Sleep and wakefulness in the southern sea lion. *Behavioural Brain Research, 128*, 129–138.

Lyamin, O. I., Mukhametov, L. M., Siegel, J. M., Nazarenko, E. A., Polyakova, I. G., & Shpak, O. V. (2002A). Unihemispheric slow wave sleep and the state of the eyes in a white whale. *Behavioural Brain Research, 129*(1–2), 125–129.

Lyamin, O. I., Oleksenko, A. I., & Polyakova, I. G. (1989). [Sleep and wakefulness in pups of harp seal (Pagophylus groenlandica)] (in Russian). *Zh Vyssh Nerv Deiat Im I P Pavlova, 39*(6), 1061–1069.

Lyamin, O. I., Oleksenko, A. I., & Sevostiyanov, V. F. (2000). Behavioral sleep in captive sea otters. *Aquatic Mammals, 26*, 132–136.

Milsom, W., Castellin, M., Harris, M., Castellini, J., Jones, D., Berger, R., et al. (1996). Effects of hypoxia and hypercapnia on patterns of sleep-associated apnea in elephant seal pups. *American Journal of Physiology, 271*, R1017–R1024.

Mukhametov, L. M. (1987). Unihemispheric slow-wave sleep in the Amazonian dolphin, Inia geoffrensis. *Neuroscience Letters, 79*(1–2), 128–132.

Mukhametov, L. M., Lyamin, O. I., Chetyrbok, I. S., Vassilyev, A. A., & Diaz, R. P. (1992).

Sleep in an Amazonian manatee, Trichechus inunguis. *Experientia, 48*(4), 417–419.

Mukhametov, L.M., Lyamin, O.I., & Polyakova, I.G. (1984). [Sleep and wakefulness in northern fur seals (Callorhinus ursinus)] (in Russian). *Zh Vyssh Nerv Deiat Im I P Pavlova, 34*(3), 465–471.

Mukhametov, L.M., Supin, A., & Poliakova, I.G. (1984). [The sleep in Caspian seals (Phoca caspica)] (in Russian). *Zh Vyssh Nerv Deiat Im I P Pavlova, 34*(2), 259–264.

Ridgway, S.H., Harrison, R.J., & Joyce, P.L. (1975). Sleep and cardiac rhythm in the gray seal. *Science, 187*(4176), 553–555.

Papers with Adult Sea Mammal Data

Lyamin, O.I. (1987). [The ontogenetic development of the interhemispheric asymmetry of the EEG during slow-wave sleep in northern fur seals] (in Russian). *Zh Vyssh Nerv Deiat Im I P Pavlova, 37*(1), 157–159.

Lyamin, O.I., & Chetyrbok, I.S. (1992). Unilateral EEG activation during sleep in the Cape fur seal, Arctocephalus pusillus. *Neuroscience Letters, 143*(1–2), 263–266.

Lyamin, O.I., Mukhametov, L.M., & Polyakova, I.G. (1986). [Peculiarities of sleep in water in northern fur seals] (in Russian). *Zh Vyssh Nerv Deiat Im I P Pavlova, 36*(6), 1039–1044.

Lyamin, O.I., Mukhametov, L.M., & Siegel, J.M. (2004). Relationship between sleep and eye state in cetaceans and pinnipeds. *Archives of Italian Biology, 142,* 557–568.

Lyamin, O.I., Shpak, O.V., Nazarenko, E.A., & Mukhametov, L.M. (2002). Muscle jerks during behavioral sleep in a beluga whale (Delphinapterus leucas L.). *Physiology & Behavior, 76*(2), 265–270.

Mukhametov, L.M., & Lyamin, O.I. (1994). Rest and active states in bottlenose dolphins (*Tursiops truncates*) [Abstract]. *Journal of Sleep Research, 3,* 174.

Mukhametov, L.M., Lyamin, O.I., & Polyakova, I.G. (1984). [Sleep and wakefulness in northern fur seals (Callorhinus ursinus)] (in Russian). *Zh Vyssh Nerv Deiat Im I P Pavlova, 34*(3), 465–471.

Mukhametov, L.M., Lyamin, O.I., & Polyakova, I.G. (1985). Interhemispheric asynchrony of the sleep EEG in northern fur seals. *Experientia, 41*(8), 1034–1035.

Mukhametov, L.M., & Polyakova, I.G. (1981). [EEG investigation of the sleep in porpoises (Phocoena phocoena)] (in Russian). *Zh Vyssh Nerv Deiat Im I P Pavlova, 31*(2), 333–339.

Mukhametov, L.M., & Supin, A. (1975). [EEG study of different behavioral states of freely moving dolphin (Tursiops truncates)] (in Russian). *Zh Vyssh Nerv Deiat Im I P Pavlova, 25*(2), 396–401.

Mukhametov, L.M., Supin, A.Y., & Polyakova, I.G. (1977). Interhemispheric asymmetry of the electroencephalographic sleep patterns in dolphins. *Brain Research, 134*(3), 581–584.

Mukhametov, L.M., Supin, A., & Poliakova, I.G. (1984). [The sleep in Caspian seals (Phoca caspica)] (in Russian). *Zh Vyssh Nerv Deiat Im I P Pavlova, 34*(2), 259–264.

Pilleri, G. (1979). The blind Indus dolphin (Plantanista indi). *Endeavour, 3,* 48–56.

Shurley, J.T., Serafetinides, E.A., Brooks, R.E., Elsner, R., & Kenney, D.W. (1969). Sleep in Cetaceans: I. The pilot whale, Globicephala scammoni [Abstract]. *Psychophysiology, 6,* 230.

Avian Sleep Reference List

Ainley, D.G. (1978). Activity patterns and social behavior of on–breeding Adélie penguins. *Condor, 80,* 138–146.

Amlaner, C.J., & Ball, N.J. (1987). A synthesis of sleep in wild birds. *Behaviours, 87,* 85–119.

Amlaner, C.J., & McFarland, D.J. (1981). Sleep in herring gulls (Larus argentatus). *Animal Behaviour, 29*(2), 551–556.

Ashkenazie, S., & Safriel, U.N. (1979). Breeding cycle and behavior of the semi-palmated sandpiper at Barrow, Alaska. *Auk, 96,* 56–67.

Ashmole, N.P. (1963). The biology of the wide awake or sooty tern *Sternal fuscata* on Ascension Island. *Ibis, 103,* 297–364.

Austin, G.T. (1976). Behavioral adaptations of the verdin to the desert. *Auk, 93,* 245–262.

Ayala-Guerrero, F. (1989). Sleep patterns in the parakeet Melopsittacus undulatus. *Physiology & Behavior, 46*(5), 787–791.

Ayala-Guerrero, F., Mexican, G., & Ramos, J.I. (2003). Sleep characteristics in the turkey Meleagris gallopavo. *Physiology & Behavior, 78*(3), 435–440.

Ayala-Guerrero, F., & Perez, M.C., & Calderon, A. (1988). Sleep patterns in the bird *Aratinga canicularis. Physiology & Behavior, 43*(5), 585–589.

Ayala-Guerrero, F., & Vasconcelos-Duenas, I. (1988). Sleep in the dove Zenaida asiatica. *Behavioral and Neurological Biology, 49*(2), 133–138.

Balda, R.P., Morrison, M.L., & Bement, T.R. (1977). Roosting behavior of the piñon jay in autumn and winter. *Auk, 94,* 494–504.

Ball, N.J., Amlaner, C.J., Shaffery, J.P., & Opp, M.R. (1988). Asynchronus eye–closure and unihemispheric quiet sleep of birds. In W.P. Koella, F. Obal, H. Schulz, & P. Visser (Eds.), *Sleep '86* (pp. 151–153). New York: Gustav Fischer.

Ball, N.J., Shaffery, J.P., Opp, M.R., Carter, R.L., & Amlaner, C.J. (1985). Asynchronous eye–closure of birds [Abstract]. *Sleep Research, 15,* 87.

Ball, N.J., Weaver, G.E., & Amlaner, C.J. (1986). The incidence of hemispheric sleep in birds [Abstract]. *Sleep Research, 15,* 58.

Bartholomew, G.A., & Dawson, W.R. (1979). Thermoregulatory behavior during incubation in Heermann's gulls. *Physiological Zoology, 52,* 422–437.

Berger, R.J., & Phillips, N.H. (1994). Constant light suppresses sleep and circadian rhythms in pigeons without consequent sleep rebound in darkness. *American Journal of Physiology—Regulatory, Integrative and Comparative Physiology, 267,* 945–952.

Berger, R.J., Walker, J.M., & Scott, T.D. (1970). Characteristics of sleep in the burrowing owl and tree shrew [Abstract]. *Psychophysiology, 7,* 303.

Berger, R.J., Walker, J.M., & Scott, T.D. (1972). Sleep in the burrowing owl (Speotyto cunicularia hypugaea). *Behavioral Biology, 7*(2), 183–194.

Boerema, A. S, Riedstra, B., & Strijkstra, A.M. (2003). Decrease in monocular sleep after sleep deprivation in the domestic chicken. *Behaviour, 140,* 1415–1420.

Brown, C.R. (1980). Sleeping behavior of purple martins. *Condor, 82*(2), 170–175.

Buchet, C., Dewasmes, G., & Le Maho, Y. (1986). An electrophysiological and behavioral study of sleep in emperor penguins under natural ambient conditions. *Physiology & Behavior, 38*(3), 331–335.

Burish, M.J., Kueh, H.Y., & Wang, S.S.–H. (2004). Brain architecture and social complexity in modern and ancient birds. *Brain, Behavior, & Evolution, 63,* 107–124.

Calder, W.A. (1975). Daylength and the hummingbirds use of time. *Auk, 92,* 81–97.

Campbell, S.S. & Tobler, I. (1984). Animal sleep: A review of sleep duration across phylogeny. *Neuroscience & Biobehavioral Reviews, 8,* 269–300.

Carpenter, F.L. (1974). Torpor in an Andean hummingbird: Its ecological significance. *Science, 183*(4124), 545–547.

Catling, P.M. (1972). A behavioral attitude of saw–wheat and boreal owls. *Auk, 89,* 194–196.

Corner, M.A. (1977). Sleep and the beginnings of behavior in the animal kingdom—Studies of ultradian motility cycles in early life. *Progress in Neurobiology, 8*(4), 279–295.

Corner, M. A., van Wingerden, C., & Bakhuis, W. L. (1973). Spontaneous motility bursts during sleep in the chick, as related to phasic "paradoxical" cerebral bioelectric activity. *Brain Research, 50,* 200–204.

Dario, A., Lopes, P., Freitas, G. C., Paschoalini, M. A., & Neto, J. M. (1996). Electrographic patters of postprandial sleep after food deprivation or intraventricular adrenaline injections in pigeons. *Brain Research Bulletin, 39,* 249–254.

Derksen, D. V. (1977). A quantitative analysis of the incubation behavior of the Adélie penguin. *Auk, 94,* 552–566.

Dewasmes, G., Buchet, C., Geloen, A., & Le Maho, Y. (1989). Sleep changes in emperor penguins during fasting. *American Journal of Physiology—Regulatory, Integrative and Comparative Physiology, 256*(2 Pt 2), 476–480.

Dewasmes, G., Cohen-Adad, F., Koubi, H., & Le Maho, Y. (1984). Sleep changes in long-term fasting geese in relation to lipid and protein metabolism. *American Journal of Physiology, 247*(4 Pt 2), R663–R671.

Dewasmes, G., Cohen-Ada, F., Koubi, H., & Le Maho, Y. (1985). Polygraphic and behavioral study of sleep in geese: Existence of nuchal atonia during paradoxical sleep. *Physiology & Behavior, 35*(1), 67–73.

Dewasmes, G., Cote, S. D., Le Maho, Y., Groscolas, R., Robin, J. P., Vardon, G., et al., (2001). Effects of weather on activity and sleep in brooding king penguins (Aptenodytes patagoincus). *Polar Biology, 24*(7), 508–511.

Dewasmes, G., & Loos, N. (2002). Diurnal sleep depth changes in the king penguin (Aptenodytes patagoincus). *Polar Biology, 25*(11), 865–867.

Dewasmes, G., & Telliez, F. (2000). Tactile arousal threshold of sleeping king penguins in a breeding colony. *Journal of Sleep Research, 9*(3), 255–259.

Dominguez, J. (2003). Sleeping and vigilance in black–tailed godwit. *Journal of Ethology, 21,* 57–60.

Fetterolf, P. M. (1979). Nocturnal behavior of ring-billed gulls during the early incubation period. *Canadian Journal of Zoology, 57,* 1190–1195.

Fuchs, T., Haney, A., Jechura, T. J., Moore, F. R., & Bingman, V. P. (in press). Daytime naps in night–migrating birds: Behavioural adaptation to seasonal sleep deprivation in the Swainson's thrush, *Catharus ustulatus. Animal Behaviour.*

Fuchs, T., Siegel, J. J., Burgdorf, J., & Bingman, V. P. (2006). A selective serotonin reuptake inhibitor reduces REM sleep in the homing pigeon. *Physiology & Behavior, 87,* 575–581.

Graf, R., Heller, H. C., Sakaguchi, S., & Krishna, S. (1987). Influence of spinal and hypothalamic warming on metabolism and sleep in pigeons. *American Journal of Physiology—Regulatory, Integrative and Comparative Physiology, 225,* 661–667.

Greenberg, R., Kelty, M., & Dewan, E. (1969). Sleep patterns in the newly hatched chick [Abstract]. *Psychophysiology, 6,* 226–227.

Hamerstrom, F., & Janick, K. (1973). Diurnal sleep rhythm of a young barred owl. *Auk, 90,* 899–900.

Hayward, J. L., Jr., Gillett, W. H., Amlaner, C. J., Jr., & Stout, J. F. (1977). Predation on gulls by bald eagles in Washington. *Auk, 94,* 375.

Hecht, J. (2004). Amazing talent of the bird that doesn't sleep. *New Scientist, 183*(7), 10.

Hishikawa, Y., Cramer, H., & Kuhlo, W. (1969). Natural and melatonin-induced sleep in young chickens—A behavioral and behavioral and electrographic study. *Experimental Brain Research, 7*(1), 84–94.

Iwaniuk, A. N., Dean, K. M., & Nelson, J. E. (2005). Interspecific allometry of the brain and brain regions in parrots (Psittaciformes): Comparisons with other birds and primates. *Brain, Behavior and Evolution, 65,* 40–59.

Iwaniuk, A. N., & Hurd, P. L. (2005). The evolution of cerebrotypes in birds. *Brain, Behavior and Evolution, 65,* 215–230.

Kacelink, A. (1979). The foraging efficiency of great tits (*Parus major* L.) in relation to light intensity. *Animal Behaviour, 27*, 237–241.

Karmanova, I. G., & Churnosov, E. V. (1972). Electrophysiological investigation of natural sleep and wakefulness in tortoises and chickens. *Journal of Evolutionary Biochemistry and Physiology, 8*, 47–53.

Karmanova, I. G., & Churnosov, E. V. (1974). [An electrophysiologic study of the diurnal rhythm of sleep and wakefulness in owls] (in Russian). *Zh Evol Biokim Fiziol, 10*(1), 48–57.

Karmanova, I. G., Khomutetskaya, D. E., & Churnosov, E. V. (1970). Peculiarities of the paradoxical stage of sleep in hens. *Journal of Evolutionary Biochemistry and Physiology*, 252–259.

Karplus, M. (1952). Bird activity in the continuous daylight of arctic summer. *Ecology, 33*(1), 129–134.

Key, B. J., & Marley, E. (1962). The effect of the sympathomimetic amines on behaviour and electrocortical activity of the chicken. *Electrocenphalography & Clinical Neurophysiology, 14*, 90–105.

Khomutetskiaia, O. E. (1983). [Electrical activity of different formations of the forebrain in the hen during sleep and wakefulness] (in Russian). *Zh Evol Biokhim Fiziol, 19*(2), 175–179.

Klein, M., Michel, F., & Jouvet, M. (1963). Etude polygraphique du sommeil chez les Oiseaux [Polygraphic study of sleep in birds]. *C R Seances Soc Biol Fil, 158*, 99–103.

Kovacs, S. A., Wilson, G. C., & Kovach, J. K. (1981). Normal EEG of the restrained twenty-four-hour-old Japanese quail (Coturnix coturnix japonica). *Poultry Science, 60*(1), 243–249.

Lefebvre, L., Reader, S. M., & Sol, D. (2004). Brains, innovations and evolution in birds and primates. *Brain, Behavior and Evolution, 63*, 233–246.

Lesku, J. A., Rattenborg, N. C., & Amlaner, C. J., Jr. (2006). The evolution of sleep: A phylogenetic approach. In T. Lee-Chiong (Ed.), *Sleep: A comprehensive handbook* (pp. 49–61). Hoboken, NJ: John Wiley & Sons.

Lima, S. L., Rattenborg, N. C., Lesku, J. A., & Amlaner, C. J. (2005). Sleeping under risk of predation. *Animal Behaviour, 70*, 723–736.

Margoliash, D. (2005). Song learning and sleep. *Nature Neurosience, 8*(5), 546–548.

Marshall, A. J. (1938). Bird and animal activity in the Arctic. *The Journal of Animal Ecology, 7*(2), 248–250.

Mascetti, G. G., Bobbo, D., Rugger, M., & Vallortigara, G. (2004). Monocular sleep in male domestic chicks. *Beahvioural Brain Research, 153*, 447–452.

Mascetti, G. G., Rugger, M., & Vallortigara, G. (1999). Visual lateralization and monocular sleep in the domestic chick. *Cognitive Brain Research, 7*, 451–463.

Mascetti, G. G., & Vallortigara, G. (2001). Why do birds sleep with one eye open? Light exposure of the chick embryo as a determinant of monocular sleep. *Current Biology, 11*, 971–974.

McFarland, D. J. (1977). Decision making in animals. *Nature, 269*, 15–21.

Mexicano, G., Huitron-Resendiz, S., & Avala-Guerrero, F. (1992). Effect of 5-hydroxytryptophan [5–HTP] on sleep in parachlorophenylalanine (PCPA) pretreated birds. *Proceedings of the Western Pharmacology Society, 35*, 17–20.

Monnier, M. (1980). Comparative electrophysiology of sleep in some vertebrates. *Experientia, 36*(1), 16–19.

Ookawa, T. (1967). Electrocencephalographic study of the chicken telencephalon in wakefulness, sleep and anesthesia. *Acta Scholae Med Gifu, 15*, 76–85.

Ookawa, T. (1972). Avian wakefulness and sleep on the basis of recent electroencephalographic observations. *Poultry Science, 51*, 1565–1574.

Ookawa, T., & Gotoh, J. (1964). Electroencephalographic study of chickens: Periodic recurrence of low voltage and fast waves during behavioral sleep. *Poultry Science, 43,* 1603–1604.

Ookawa, T., & Gotoh, J. (1965). Electroencephalogram of the chicken record from the skull under various conditions. *Journal of Comparative Neurology, 141,* 1–14.

Ookawa, T., & Kadono, H. (1968). Electroencephalogram of the Japanese quail (Coturnix coturnix japonica) during non–anesthetized and anesthetized periods. *Poultry Science, 47*(1), 320–325.

Ookawa, T., & Takagi, K. (1968). Electroencephalograms of free behavioral chicks at various developmental ages. *Japanese Journal of Physiology, 18,* 87–99.

Opp, M.R., & Ball, N.J. (1985). Bioenergetic consequences of sleep based on time budgets for free–ranging glaugous–winged gulls. *Sleep Research, 14,* 21.

Paredes, S.D., Pilar Terron, M., Cubero, J., Valero, V., Barriga, C., Reiter, R.J., et al. (2006). Comparative study of the activity/rest rhythms in young and old ring-dove (Streptopelia risoria): Correlation with serum levels of melatonin and serotonin. *Chronobiology International, 23*(4), 779–793.

Peters, J., Vonderahe, A., & Schmid, D. (1965). Onset of cerebral electricalactivity associated with behavioral sleep and attention in the developing chick. *Journal of Experimental Zoology, 160,* 255–262.

Phillips, N.H., & Berger, R.J. (1992). Melatonin infusions restore sleep suppressed by continuous bright light in pigeons. *Neuroscience Letters, 145*(2), 217–220.

Rashotte, M.E., Pastukhov, I.F., Poliakov, E.L., & Henderson, R.P. (1998). Vigilance states and body temperature during circadian cycle in fed and fasted pigeons (Columba livia). *American Journal of Physiology— Regulatory, Integrative and Comparative Physiology, 275,* 1690–1702.

Rattenborg, N.C. (1999). Half-awake to the risk of predation. *Nature, 397,* 397–398.

Rattenborg, N.C. (2000). Behavioral, neurophysiological and evolutionary perspectives on unihemispheric sleep. *Neuroscience & Biobehavioral Reviews, 24,* 817–842.

Rattenborg, N.C. (2000). Unihemispheric slow-wavesleep and predator detection in the pigeon (Columbia livia) [Abstract]. *Sleep, 23*(Suppl. 1), A43–A44.

Rattenborg, N.C. (2001). Unilateral eye closure and interhemipsheric EEG asymmetry during sleep in the pigeon (Columba livia). *Brain, Behavoir & Evolution, 58*(6), 323–332.

Rattenborg, N.C. (2006). Do birds sleep in flight? *Naturwissenschaften, 93,* 413–425.

Rattenborg, N.C., & Amlaner, C.J. (2002). Phylogeny of sleep. In T.L. Lee-Chiong Jr., M.J. Sateia, & M.A. Carskadon (Eds.), *Sleep medicine* (pp. 7–22). Philadelphia: Hangley & Belfus.

Rattenborg, N.C., Amlaner, C.J., & Lima, S.L. (1999). Period amplitude analysis of avian unihemispheric quiet sleep [Abstract]. *Sleep, 22*(1), S73.

Rattenborg, N.C., Lima, S.L., & Amlaner, C.J. (1999). Facultative control of avian unihemispheric sleep under the risk of predation. *Behavioural Brain Research, 105*(2), 163–172.

Rattenborg, N.C., Mandt, B.H., Obermeyer, W.H., Winsauer, P.J., Huber, R., Wikelski, M., & Benca, R.M. (2004). Migratory sleeplessness in the white-crowned sparrow (Zonotrichia leucophrys gambelii). *PLoS Biology, 2*(7), 924–936.

Rattenborg, N.C., Mandt, B., Uttech, R., Newman, S.M., Jones, S., Wikelski, M., . . . Benca, R.M. (2003). Migratory sleeplessness in the white-crowned sparrow (Zonotrichia leucophrys gambelii) [Abstract]. *Sleep, 26*(Suppl.), A117.

Rattenborg, N.C., Obermeyer, W.H., Vacha, E., & Benca, R.M. (2005). Acute effects of light and darkness on sleep in the pigeon

(Columba livia). *Physiology & Behavior, 84*(4), 635–640.

Reiner, A., Yamamoto, K., & Karten, H.J. (2005). Organization and evolution of the avian forebrain. *The Anatomical Record, Part A, 287A,* 1080–1102.

Rojas–Ramirez, J.S., & Tauber, E.S. (1970). Paradoxical sleep in two species of avian predator (Falconiformes). *Science, 167*(926), 1754–1755.

Schadé, J.P., Corner, M.A., & Peters, J.J. (1965). Some aspects of the electro-ontogenesis of sleep patterns. In K. Akert, C. Bally, & J.P. Schadé (Eds.), *Progress in brain research* (Vol. 18, pp. 70–78). Amsterdam: Elsevier.

Schaub, R., & Prinzinger, R. (1999). Long-term telemetry of heart rates and energy metabolic rate during thye diurnal cycle in normothermic torpid African blue-naped mousebirds (Urocolius macrourus). *Comparative Biochemistry and Physiology Part A: Molecular & Integrative Physiology, 124*(4), 439–445.

Schibata, M., & Kadono, H. (1970). Effects of urethane on electrocorticogram in the chicken. *Poultry Science, 49,* 1484–1491.

Schlehuber, C.J., Flaming, D.G., Lange, G.D., & Spooner, C.E. (1974). Paradoxical sleep in the chick (Gallus domesticus). *Behavioral Biology, 11,* 537–546.

Schmidt, D.F., Ball, N.J., & Amalaner, C.J. (1990). The characteristics and quantities of sleep in the Zebra finch (genus Taenopygia). *Sleep Research, 19,* 111.

Shaffery, J.P., Amalaner, C.J., Ball, N.J., & Opp, M.R. (1985). Ecological and behavioral correlates of sleep in free-ranging birds. *Sleep Research, 14,* 103.

Shaffery, J.P., Buchanan, G., Schmidt, D., & Ball, N.J. (1989). Sleep in the 1-day old mallard. *Sleep Research, 18,* 106.

Silva, E.E., Estable, C., & Segundo, J.P. (1959). Further observations on animal hypnosis. *Comparative Biochemistry and Physiology Part A: Molecular & Integrative Physiology, 97,* 167–177.

Stahel, C.D., Megirian, D., & Nicol, S.C. (1984). Sleep and metabolic rate in the little penguin, Eudyptula minor. *Journal of Comparative Physiology–B, 154,* 487–494.

Sugihara, K., & Gotoh, J. (1973). Depth-electroencephalograms of chickens in wakefulness and sleep. *Japanese Journal of Physiology, 23*(4), 371–379.

Susic, V.T., & Kovacevic, R.M. (1973). Sleep patterns in the owl Strix Aluco. *Physiology & Behavior, 11,* 313–317.

Szymcazk, J.T. (1985). Sleep pattern in the starling (Sturnus vulgaris). *Acta physiologica Polonicaonica, 36*(5–6), 323–331.

Szymcazk, J.T. (1986). Daily distribution of sleep states in the jackdaw, Corvus monedula. *Chronobiologia, 13*(3), 227–235.

Szymcazk, J.T. (1986). Daily rhythm of sleep-wakefulness in the starling, Sturnus vulgaris. *Acta Physiologica Polonica, 37,* 199–206.

Szymcazk, J.T. (1986). Sleep pattern in the rook, Coruvs frugilegus. *Acta Physiologica Polonicaonica, 37*(4–5), 191–198.

Szymcazk, J.T. (1987). Daily distribution of sleep states in the rook, Corvus frugilegus. *Journal of Comparative Physiology A, 161,* 321–322.

Szymcazk, J.T. (1987). Distribution of sleep and wakefulness in 24-h light-dark cycles in the juvenile and adult magpie, Pica pica. *Chronobiologia, 14*(3), 277–287.

Szymczak, J.T. (1989). Influence of environmental temperature and photoperiod on temporal structure of sleep in corvids. *Acta Neurobiologiae Experimentalis, 49,* 359–366.

Szymcazk, J.T., Helb, H.W., & Kaiser, W. (1993). Electrophysiological and behavioral correlates of sleep in the blackbird (Turdus merula). *Physiology & Behavior, 53*(6), 1201–1210.

Szymczak, J.T., Kaiser, W., Helb, H.W., & Beszczynska, B. (1996). A study of sleep in the European blackbird. *Physiology & Behavior, 60*(4), 1115–1120.

Szymcazk, J.T., & Narebski, J. (1988). Daily sleep pattern of the chaffinch, *Fringilla coelebs,* in two different seasons. *Journal of Interdisciplinary Cycle Research, 19,* 305–311.

Tamisier, A. (1973). Etho-ecological studies of Teal wintering in the Camargue (Thone Delta, France). *Wildfowl, 25,* 123–133.

Tamisier, A. (1982). Rythmes nycthemeraux des Sarcelles l'hiver pendant 1 eur hivernarge en camargue. *Alauda (Revue Internationale d'Ornithologie), 40,* 235–256.

Tehsin, R.H. (1988). Inducing sleep in birds. *Journal of the Bombay Natural History Society, 85*(2), 435–436.

Tobler, I., & Borbely, A.A. (1988). Sleep and EEG spectra in the pigeon (Columbia livia) under baseline conditions and after sleep deprivation. *Journal of Comparative Physiology A, 163,* 729–738.

Tradardi, V. (1966). Sleep in the pigeon. *Archives Italiennes de Biologie, 104*(4), 516–521.

Tymicz, J., Narebski, J., & Jurkowlaniec, E. (1975). Circadian sleep-wakefulness rhythm of the starling. *Sleep Research, 4,* 146.

Tymicz, J., Narebski, J., Pazur, W., & Strawinski, S. (1975). Circadian sleep-wakefulness rhythm of the chaffinch (*Fringilla coelebs*). In W.P. Koella (Ed.), *Sleep, Proceedings of the Second European Congress on Sleep Research, Rome* (pp. 285–287). Basel: Karger.

Underwood, H., Steele, C.T., & Zivkovic, B. (2001). Circadian organization and the role of the pineal in birds. *Micro Research & Technology, 53,* 48–62.

Van Luijtelaar, E.L.J.M., van der Grinten, C.P.M., Blokhuis, H.J., & Coenen, A.L. (1987). Sleep in the domestic hen (Gullus domesticus). *Physiology & Behavior, 41,* 409–414.

Van Twyver, H., & Allison, T. (1972). A polygraphic and behavioral study of sleep in the pigeon (Columbia livia). *Experimental Neurology, 35,* 138–153.

Vasconcelos–Duenas, I., & Ayala-Gerrero, F. (1983). Filogenia del sueño: Las aves. *Bol Estud Med Biol, Mex (Supplemento), 32,* 83–90.

Vasconcelos–Duenas, I., & Guerrero, F.A. (1983). Effect of PCPA on sleep in parakeets (Aratinga canicularis). *Proceedings of the Western Pharmacological Society, 26,* 365–368.

Verbeek, N.A.M. (1972). Daily and annual time budget of the yellow–billed magpie. *Auk, 89,* 567–582.

Walker, J.M., & Berger, R.J. (1972). Sleep in the domestic pigeon (Columba livia). *Behavioral Biology, 7*(2), 195–203.

Walker, J.M., Walker, L.E., Palca, J.W., & Berger, R.J. (1980). Nightly torpor in the ringed neck dove: An extension of SWS. *Sleep Research, 9,* 112.

Walker, L.E., Walker, J.M., & Berger, R.J. (1983). A continuum of sleep torpor in fasting doves. *Science, 122,* 194–195.

Walusinski, O. (2006). Le baillement: Naissance, vie et senescence. *Psychologie & Neuropsychiatrie du Vieillissement, 4*(1), 39–46.

Wambebe, C. (1986). Influence of some dopaminoceptor agents on nitrazempam–induced sleep in the domestic fowl (Gallus domesticus) and rats. *Japanese Journal of Pharmacology, 40,* 357–365.

Yamada, H., Oshima, I., Sato, K., & Ebihara, S. (1988). Loss of the circadian rhythms of locomotor activity, food intake, and plasma melatonin concentration induced by constant bright light in the pigeon (Columba livia). *Journal of Comparative Physiology–A, 163,* 459–463.

Yekimova, I.V., & Pastukhov, I. (1992). The GABAergic midbrain system is involved in the control of sleep and temperature homeostasis in pigeons. *Doklady Biological Sciences, 387,* 485–487.

Zepelin, H., Zammit, G.K., McDonald, C.S., Chopp, M., Wanzie, F.J., & Comas, M.G. (1982). Sleep in the domestic duck. *Sleep Research, 11,* 90.

Phylogeny of Sleep Data

Adams, P., & Barratt, E. (1974). Nocturnal sleep in squirrel monkeys. *Electroencephalography & Clinical Neurophysiology, 36,* 201–204.

Affani, J. (1972). Observations on the sleep of some South American marsupials and edenates. *Perspectives in Brain Science, 1,* 21–23.

Affanni, J.M., Cervino, C.O., & Marcos, H.J.A. (2001). Absence of penile erections during paradoxical sleep: Peculiar penile events during wakefulness and slow wave sleep in the armadillo. *Journal of Sleep Research, 10,* 219–228.

Alfoldi, P., Tobler, I., & Borbely, A.A. (1990). Sleep regulation in rats during early development. *American Journal of Physiology— Regulatory, Integrative and Comparative Physiology, 258*(3 Pt 2), R634–R644.

Allison, T., Gerber, S.D., Breedlove, S.M., & Dryden, G.L. (1977). A behavioral and polygraphic study of sleep in the shrews Suncus murinus, Blarina brevicauda, and Cryptotis parva. *Behavioral Biology, 20*(3), 354–366.

Allison, T., & Van Twyver, H. (1970). Sleep in the moles, Scalopus aquaticus and Condylura cristata. *Experimental Neurology, 27*(3), 564–578.

Allison, T., Van Twyver, H., & Goff, W.R. (1972). Electrophysiological studies of the echidna, Tachyglossus aculeatus, I: Waking and sleep. *Comparative Biochemistry and Physiology Part A: Molecular & Integrative Physiology, 110,* 145–184.

Ambrosini, M.V., Gambelunghe, C., Mariucci, G., Bruschelli, G., Adami, M., & Guiditta, A. (1994). Sleep-wake variables and EEG power spectra in Mongolian gerbils and Wistar rats. *Physiology & Behavior, 56*(5), 963–968.

Aristakesian, E.A. (1997). Comparative neurophysiological analysis of the waking-sleeping cycle during the early postnatal ontogeny in rats and guinea pigs. *Journal of Evolutionary Biochemistry and Physiology, 33*(6), 545–550.

Astic, L., & Royet, J.P. (1974). Sommeil chez la rat-kangourou, *Porours apicalis.* Etude chez l'adulte et chez le jeune un mois avant la sortie definitive du marsupium. Effects du sevrage. *Electroencephalography and Clinical Neurophysiology, 37*(5), 483–489.

Astic, L., Saucier, D., & Megirian, D. (1979). Sleep circadian rhythm in rat kangaroo (Potorous apicalis): Effect of food distribution. *Physiology & Behavior, 22*(3), 441–446.

Ayala-Guerrero, F., Vargas-Reyna, L., Ramos, J.I., & Mexicano, G. (1998). Sleep patterns of the volcano mouse (Neotomodon alstoni alstoni). *Physiology & Behavior, 64*(4), 577–580.

Balzamo, E. (1973). Etude des etats de vigilance chez *Papio cynocephalus* adulte. *C R Seances Soc Biol,* 167, 1168–1172.

Balzamo, E., & Bert, J. (1975). Sleep in *Papio anubis:* Its organization and lateral geniculate spikes [Abstract]. *Sleep Research, 4,* 138.

Balzamo, E., Bradley, R.J., & Rhodes, J.M. (1972). Sleep ontogeny in the chimpanzee: From two months to forty-one months. *Electroencephalography and Clinical Neurophysiology, 33,* 47–60.

Balzamo, E., Van Beers, P., & Lagarde, D. (1998). Scoring of sleep and wakefulness by behavioral analysis from video recordings in rhesus monkeys: Comparison with conventional EEG analysis. *Electroencephalography and Clinical Neurophysiology, 106,* 206–212.

Balzamo, E., Vuillon-Cacciuttolo, G., & Bert, J. (1978A). Cercopithecus aethiops: EEG et organization des etats de vigiliance. *Wake Sleep, 2,* 223–230.

Balzamo, E., Vuillon-Cacciuttolo, G., Petter, J., & Bert, J. (1978B). Etats de vigilance chez deux Lemuridae: Rhythmes EEG et organization obtenus par telemesure. *Wake Sleep, 2,* 237–245.

Barre, V., & Petter-Rousseaux, A. (1988). Seasonal variations in sleep-wake cycle in Microcebus murinus. *Primates, 19*(2), 53–64.

Batini, C., Radulovacki, M., Kado, R.T., & Adey, W.R. (1967). Effect of interhemispheric transection on the EEG patterns in sleep and wakefulness in monkeys. *Electroencephalography and Clinical Neurophysiology, 22*, 101–112.

Baumgardner, D.J., Ward, S.E., & Dewsbury, D.A. (1980). Diurnal patterning of eight activities in 14 species of muroid rodents. *Animal Learning & Behavior, 8*, 322–330.

Bell, F.R., & Itabisashi, T. (1973). The electroencephalogram of sheep and goats with special reference to rumination. *Physiology & Behavior, 11*, 503–514.

Berger, R.J., & Walker, J.M. (1972). A polygraphic study of sleep in the tree shrew (Tupaia glis). *Brain, Behavior and Evolution, 5*(1), 54–69.

Bert, J. (1970). Adaptation du sommeil aux conditions experimentales d'enregistrement chez deux Cercopithecinae (Papio papio et Macaca radiata). *Proceeding of 3rd Int Congr Primat, 2*, 49–53.

Bert, J. (1973). Similitudes et differences du sommeil chez deux babouins, *Papio hamadryas* et *Papio papio*. *Electroencephalography and Clinical Neurophysiology, 35*(2), 209–212.

Bert, J., Balzamo, E., Chase, M., & Pegram, V. (1975). The sleep of the baboon, Papio papio, under natural conditions and in the laboratory. *Electroencephalography and Clinical Neurophysiology, 39*, 657–662.

Bert, J., & Collomb, H. (1966). L'electroencephalogramme du sommeil nocturne chez le babouin. Etude par telemetrie. *J Physiol (Parris), 58*, 285–301.

Bert, J., Collomb, H., & Martino, A. (1967). L'electroencephalogramme du sommeil d'un prosimien. Sa place dans l'organisation du sommeil chez les primates. *Electroencephalography and Clinical Neurophysiology, 23*, 342–350.

Bert, J., Kripke, D.F., & Rhodes, J. (1970). Electroencephalogram of the mature chimpanzee: Twenty-four hour recordings. *Electroencephalography and Clinical Neurophysiology, 28*, 32–40.

Bert, J., & Pegram, V. (1969). L'electroencephalogramme du sommeil chez les Cercopithecinae: *Erythrocebus patas* et *Cerpothiecus aethiops sabaeus*. *Folia Primatol, 11*, 151–159.

Bert, J., Pegram, V., & Balzano, E. (1972). Comparison du sommeil de deux macaques (*Macaca radiata* et *Macaca mulatta*). *Folia Primal, 17*, 202–208.

Bert, J., Pegram, V., Rhodes, J.M., Balzano, E., & Naquet, R. (1970). A comparative sleep study of two cercopithecinae. *Electroencephalography and Clinical Neurophysiology, 28*(1), 32–40.

Breton, P., Gourmelon, P., & Court, L. (1986). New findings on sleep stage organization in squirrel monkeys. *Electroencephalography and Clinical Neurophysiology, 40*(6), 563–567.

Campbell, S.S., & Tobler, I. (1984). Animal sleep: A review of sleep duration across phylogeny. *Neuroscience & Biobehavioral Reviews, 8*, 269–300.

Carskadon, M.A., & Dement, W.C. (2006). Normal human sleep: An overview. In M.H. Kryger, T. Roth, & W.C. Dement (Eds.), *Principles and practice of sleep medicine* (4th ed., pp. 13–23). Philadelphia: WB Saunders.

Castellini, M.A., Milsom, W.K., Berger, R.J., Costa, D.P., Jones, D.R., Castellini, J.M., . . . Harris, E. (1994). Patterns of respiration and heart-rate during wakefulness and sleep in elephant seal pups. *American Journal of Physiology, 266*(3 Pt 2), R863–R869.

Chepkasov, I.E. (1980). Daily rhythm of sleep and wakefulness in the Arctic ground squirrel Citellus parryi during the summer season. *Zh Evol Biokim Fiziol, 17*, 77–80.

Cicala, G.A., Albert, I.B., & Ulmer, F.A., Jr. (1970). Sleep and other behaviors of the red kangaroo (*Megaleia rufa*). *Animal Behavior, 18,* 787–790.

Copley, M., Jennings, D., & Mitler, M. (1976). A study of continuous forty-eight hour Sleep-waking recordings in five dogs [Abstract]. *Sleep Research, 5,* 94.

Crofts, H. S., Wilson, S., Muggleton, N. G., Nutt, D. J., Scott, E. A., & Pearce, P. C. (2001). Investigation of the sleep electrocorticogram of the common marmoset (Callithrix jacchus) using radiotelemetry. *Clinical Neurophysiology, 112*(12), 2265–2273.

Crowcroft, P. (1954). The daily cycle of activity in British Shrews. *Proceedings of the Zoological Society of London, 123,* 715–729.

Crowley, T. J., Kripke, D. F., Halberg, F., Pegram, G. V., & Schildkraut, J. J. (1972). Circadian rhythms of *Macaca mulatta*: Sleep, EEG, body and eye movement, and temperature. *Primates, 13,* 149–168.

Dallaire, A., & Ruckebusch, Y. (1974). Rest-activity cycle and sleep patterns in captive foxes (Vulpes Vulpes). *Experientia, 30,* 59–60.

Dallaire, A., & Ruckebusch, Y. (1974). Sleep and wakefulness in the housed pony under different dietary conditions. *Canadian Journal of Comparative Medicine, 38,* 65–71.

Dallaire, A., & Ruckebusch, Y. (1974). Sleep patterns in the pony with observations on partial perceptual deprivation. *Physiology & Behavior, 12*(5), 789–796.

Deboer, T., Franken, P., & Tobler, I. (1994). Sleep and cortical temperature in the Djungarian hamster under baseline conditions and after sleep deprivation. *Journal of Comparative Physiology A, 174*(2), 145–155.

Deboer, T., & Tobler, I. (1996). Shortening of the photoperiod affects sleep distribution, EEG and cortical temperature in the Djungarian hamster. *Journal of Comparative Physiology A, 179*(4), 483–492.

Deboer, T., Vyazovskiy, V. V., & Tobler, I. (2000). Long photoperiod restores the 24-h rhythm of sleep and EEG slow–wave activity in the Djungarian hamster (Phodopus sungorus). *Journal of Biological Rhythms, 15*(5), 429–436.

Dijk, D. J., & Daan, S. (1989). Sleep EEG spectral analysis in a diurnal rodent: Eutamias sibiricus. *Journal of Comparative Physiology A, 165,* 205–215.

Elgar, M. A., Pagel, M. D., & Harvey, P. H. (1988). Sleep in mammals. *Animal Behavior, 36*(Pt 5), 1407–1419.

Estep, D., Canney, E. L., Cochran, C. C., & Hunter, J. L. (1978). Components of activity and sleep in two species of chipmunks: Tamias striatus amd Eutomias dorsalis. *Bulletin of the Psychonomic Society, 12,* 341–343.

Fischer, R. B., & Meunier, G. F. (1980). Effects of enclosure size on activity and sleep of a hystricomorph rodent (Octodon degus). *Bulletin of the Psychonomic Society, 16*(4), 273–275.

Flanigan, W. F. (1975). More nocturnal observations of captive small cetaceans, I: The killer whale, *Orcinus orca* [Abstract]. *Sleep Research, 4,* 139.

Flanigan, W. F. (1974). Nocturnal behavior of captive small cetaceans, II: The beluga whale, *Delphinapterus leucas* [Abstract]. *Sleep Research, 3,* 85.

Folk, G. E., Jr. (1964). Daily physiological rhythms of carnivores exposed to extreme changes in artic daylight. *Fed Proc, 23,* 1221–1228.

Folk, M. A. (1963). The daily distribution of sleep and wakefulness in the arctic ground squirrel. *Journal of Mammalogy, 44,* 575–577.

Fourre, A. M., Rodriquez, F. L., & Vincent, J. D. (1974). Etude polygraphique de la veille et du sommeil chez le herisson (*Erinaceus europaeus L.*). *C R Soc Biol Fil (Paris), 168,* 959–964.

Fragaszy, D. M. (1990). Early behavioral development in capuchins (cebus). *Folia Primatologica, 54*(3–4), 119–128.

Freemon, F. R., McNew, J. J., & Adey, W. R. (1971). Chimpanzee sleep stages.

Electroencephalography and Clinical Neurophysiology, 31, 485–489.

Friedmann, J., Estep, D., Huntley, A., et al. (1975). On the validity of using laboratory mice versus wild mice for Sleep Research [Abstract]. *Sleep Research, 4,* 142.

Galvao de Moura Filho, A. G., Huggins, S. E., & Lines, S. G. (1983). Sleep and waking in the three-toed sloth, Bradypus tridactylus. *Comparative Biochemistry and Physiology Part A: Molecular & Integrative Physiology, 76*(2), 345–355.

Godfrey, G. K. (1955). A field study of the activity of the mole (Talpa europaea). *Ecology, 36,* 678–685.

Gonzalez, F. F., Zaplana, J., Ruiz de Elvira, C., & Delgado, J. M. (1979). Nocturnal and diurnal sleep in Macaca sylvana. *Electroencephalography and Clinical Neurophysiology, 46*(1), 13–28.

Guitterres-Rivas, E. (1980). El ciclo vigilia-sueno del gato I. Estudio con diferentes condiciones de experiementacion. *Arch Neurobiol (Madr), 43,* 185–200.

Hartmann, E., Bernstein, J., & Wilson, C. (1968). Sleep and dreaming in the elephant [Abstract]. *Psychophysiology, 4,* 389.

Haskell, E. H., Walker, J. M., & Berger, R. J. (1979). Effects of cold stress on sleep of an hibernator, the golden–mantled ground squirrel (C. lateralis). *Physiology & Behavior 23*(6), 1119–1121.

Hofer, M. A. (1976). The organization of sleep and wakefulness after maternal separation in young rats. *Developmental Psychobiology, 9*(2), 189–205.

Hunter, J. D., & Milson, W. K. (1998). Cortical activation states in sleep and anesthesia, I: Cardio-respiratory effects. *Respiratory Physiology, 112*(1), 71–81.

Immelman, K., & Gebbing, H. (1962). Schlaf bei Giraffiden. *Z Tierpsychol, 19,* 84–92.

Jha, S. K., Coleman, T., & Frnak, M. G. (2006). Sleep and sleep regulation in the ferret (Mustela putorius furo). *Behavioural Brain Research, 172,* 106–113.

Jouvet–Mounier, D., & Astic, L. (1966). Etude du sommeil chez le cobaye adulte et nouveau-ne. *C R Soc Biol Fil (Paris), 160,* 1453–1457.

Kaemingk, K., & Reite, M. (1987). Social environment and nocturnal sleep: Studies in peer-reared monkeys. *Sleep, 10,* 542–550.

Kantha, S. S., & Suzuki, J. (2006). Sleep quantitation in common marmoset, cotton top tamarin and squirrel monkey by non-invasive actigraphy. *Comparative Biochemistry & Physiology, Part A, 144,* 203–210.

Karmanova, I. G., Maksimuk, F. M., Murav'eva, L. N., Pastukhov, Y. F., & Sazonov, V. S. (1979). [Specific features of the cycle "wakefulness–sleep" in the arctic lemming Dicrostonyx torquats] (in Russian). *Zh Evol Biokim Fiziol, 15,* 190–195.

Kas, M. J., & Edgar, D. M. (1998). Crepuscular rhythms of EEG sleep-wake in a hystricomorph rodent, Octodon degus. *Journal of Biological Rhythms, 13*(1), 9–17.

Kastaniotis, C., & Kaplan, P. (1976). Sleep and wakefulness in the Mongolian gerbil Meriones unguiculalus [Abstract]. *Sleep Research, 5,* 96.

Kilduff, T. S., & Dube, M. G. (1976). Sleep characteristics of the cotton rat (Sigmodon hispidus) [Abstract]. *Sleep Research, 5,* 97.

Kiyono, S. (1975). Sleep studies in gunn rats [Abstact]. *Sleep Research, 4,* 227.

Klemm, W. R. (1966). Sleep and paradoxical sleep in ruminants. *Proceedings of the Society for Experimental Biology and Medicine, 121,* 635–638.

Kripke, D. F., Reite, M. L., Pegram, M. L., Peram, G. V., et al. (1968). Nocturnal sleep in rhesus monkeys. *Electroencephalography and Clinical Neurophysiology, 24*(6), 582–586.

Kurt, F. (1960). Le sommeil es elephants. *Mammalia, 24,* 259–272.

Leinonen, L., & Stenberg, D. (1986). Sleep in Macaca arctoides and the effects of prazosin. *Physiology & Behavior, 37*(2), 199–202.

LoPresti, R.W., & McGinty, D.J. (1970). Sleep in the phalanger (Trichosurusvulpecula): An Australian marsupial [Abstract]. *Psychophysiology, 7,* 304.

Lucas, E.A. (1979). Effects of a short light–dark cycle on the sleep-wake patterns of the cat. *Sleep, 1*(3), 299–317.

Lucas, E.A., Powell, E.W., & Murphree, O.D. (1977). Baseline sleep-wake patterns in the pointer dog. *Physiology & Behavior, 19,* 285–291.

Lucas, E.A., & Sterman, M.B. (1974). The polycyclic sleep–wake cycle in the cat: Effects produced by sensorimotor rhythm conditioning. *Experimental Neurology, 42,* 347–368.

Lyamin, O.I. (1987). [The ontogenetic development of the interhemispheric asymmetry of the EEG during slow-wave sleep in northern fur seals] (in Russian). *Zh Vyssh Nerv Deiat Im I P Pavlova, 37*(1), 157–159.

Lyamin, O.I. (1993). Sleep in the harp seal (*Pagophilus groenlandica*). Comparisons of sleep on land and in water. *Journal of Sleep Research, 2,* 170–174.

Lyamin, O.I., & Chetyrbok, I.S. (1992). Unilateral EEG activation during sleep in the Cape fur seal, Arctocephalus pusillus. *Neuroscience Letters, 143*(1–2), 263–266.

Lyamin, O.I., Mukhametov, L.M., Chetyrbok, I.S., & Vassiliev, A.V. (1994). Sleep and wakefulness in southern sea lions (Otari byronia). *Journal of Sleep Research, 3*(Suppl 1), 152.

Lyamin, O.I., Mukhametov, L.M., Chetyrbok, I.S., & Vassiliev, A.V. (2002). Sleep and wakefulness in the southern sea lion. *Behavioural Brain Research, 128,* 129–138.

Lyamin, O.I., Mukhametov, L.M., & Polyakova, I.G. (1986). [Peculiarities of sleep in water in northern fur seals] (in Russian). *Zh Vyssh Nerv Deiat Im I P Pavlova, 36*(6), 1039–1044.

Lyamin, O.I., Mukhametov, L.M., & Siegel, J.M. (2004). Relationship between sleep and eye state in cetaceans and pinnipeds. *Comparative Biochemistry and Physiology Part A: Molecular & Integrative Physiology, 142,* 557–568.

Lyamin, O.I., Mukhametov, L.M., Siegel, J.M., Nazarenko, E.A., Polyakova, I.G., & Shpak, O.V. (2002). Unihemispheric slow wave sleep and the state of the eyes in a white whale. *Behavioural Brain Research, 129*(1–2), 125–129.

Lyamin, O.I., Oleksenko, A.I., & Polyakova, I.G. (1989). [Sleep and wakefulness in pups of harp seal (Pagophylus groenlandica)] (in Russian). *Zh Vyssh Nerv Deiat Im I P Pavlova, 39*(6), 1061–1069.

Lyamin, O.I., Oleksenko, A.I., & Sevostiyanov, V.F. (2000). Behavioral sleep in captive sea otters. *Aquatic Mammals, 26,* 132–136.

Lyamin, O.I., Shpak, O.V., Nazarenko, E.A., & Mukhametov, L.M. (2002). Muscle jerks during behavioral sleep in a beluga whale (Delphinapterus leucas L.). *Physiology & Behavior, 76*(2), 265–270.

Marks, G.A., & Shaffery, J.P. (1996). A preliminary study of sleep in the ferret, Mustela putorius furo: A carnivore with an extremely high proportion of REM sleep. *Sleep, 19*(2), 83–93.

McNew, J.J., Burson, R.D., Hoshizaki, T., & Adey, W.R. (1972). Sleep-wake cycle of an unrestrained isolated chimpanzee under entrained and free running conditions. *Aerospace Medicine, 43,* 155–161.

McNew, J.J., Howe, R.C., & Adey, W.R. (1971). The sleep cycle and subcortical-cortical EEG relations to the unrestrained chimpanzee. *Electroencephalography and Clinical Neurophysiology, 30*(6), 489–503.

Meddis, R. (1983). The evolution of sleep. In A. Mayes (Ed.), *Sleep mechanisms and functions in humans and animals: An evolutionary perspective B* (pp. 57–106). Berkshire, UK: Van Nostrand Reindhold.

Mendelson, W.B. (1982). The octagon degu: A diurnal small mammal for sleep studies [Abstract]. *Sleep Research, 11,* 89.

Miller, V. M., & South, F. E. (1981). Entry into hibernation in M. flaviventris: Sleep and behavioral thermoregulation. *Physiology & Behavior, 27*(6), 989–993.

Milsom, W., Castellin, M., Harris, M., Castellini, J., Jones, D., Berger, R., . . . Costa, D. (1996). Effects of hypoxia and hypercapnia on patterns of sleep-associated apnea in elephant seal pups. *American Journal of Physiology, 271,* R1017–R1024.

Mistlberger, R. E., Bergmann, B. M., Waldenar, W., & Rechtschaffen, A. (1983). Recovery sleep following sleep deprivation in intact and suprachiasmatic nuclei-lesioned rats. *Sleep, 6,* 217–233.

Mukhametov, L. M. (1987). Unihemispheric slow-wave sleep in the Amazonian dolphin, Inia geoffrensis. *Neuroscience Letters, 79*(1–2), 128–132.

Mukhametov, L. M., Lyamin, O. I., Chetyrbok, I. S., Vassilyev, A. A., & Diaz, R. P. (1992). Sleep in an Amazonian manatee, Trichechus inunguis. *Experientia, 48*(4), 417–419.

Mukhametov, L. M., Lyamin, O. I., & Polyakova, I. G. (1984). [Sleep and wakefulness in northern fur seals (Callorhinus ursinus)] (in Russian). *Zh Vyssh Nerv Deiat Im I P Pavlova, 34*(3), 465–471.

Mukhametov, L. M., Lyamin, O. I., & Polyakova, I. G. (1985). Interhemispheric asynchrony of the sleep EEG in northern fur seals. *Experientia, 41*(8), 1034–1035.

Mukhametov, L. M., & Supin, A. (1975). [EEG study of different behavioral states of freely moving dolphin (Tursiops truncates)] (in Russian). *Zh Vyssh Nerv Deiat Im I P Pavlova, 25*(2), 396–401.

Mukhametov, L. M., Supin, A. Y., & Polyakova, I. G. (1977). Interhemispheric asymmetry of the electroencephalographic sleep patterns in dolphins. *Brain Research, 134*(3), 581–584.

Mukhametov, L. M., Supin, A., & Poliakova, I. G. (1984). [The sleep in Caspian seals (Phoca caspica)] (in Russian). *Zh Vyssh Nerv Deiat Im I P Pavlova, 34*(2), 259–264.

Nicol, S. C., Andersen, N. A., Phillips, N. H., & Berger, R. J. (2000). The echidna manifests typical characteristics of rapid eye movement sleep. *Neuroscience Letters, 283*(1), 49–52.

Nishino, S., Riehl, J., Hong, J., Kwan, M., Reid, M., & Mignot, E. (2000). Is narcolepsy a REM sleep disorder? Analysis of sleep abnormalities in narcoleptic dobermans. *Neuroscience Research, 38,* 437–446.

Noser, R., Gygax, L., & Tobler, I. (2003). Sleep and social status in captive gelada baboons (Theropithecus gelada). *Behavioural Brain Research, 147*(1–2), 9–15.

Palchykova, S., Deboer, T., & Tobler, I. (2002). Selective sleep deprivation after daily torpor in the Djungarian hamster. *Journal of Sleep Research, 11,* 313–319.

Pegram, V., Bert, J., & Naquet, R. (1969). The ontogeny of EEG sleep patterns in the baboon [Abstract]. *Psychophysiology, 6,* 228.

Pellet, J., & Beraud, C. (1967). The circadian sleep-wakefulness organization of the guinea pig (Cavia porcellus). *Physiology & Behavior, 2,* 131–137.

Perachio, A. A. (1970). Sleep in the nocturnal primate, Aotus trivirgatus. *Proccedings of the 3rd Internaltional Congress in Primatology, 2,* 54–60.

Pilleri, G. (1979). The blind Indus dolphin (Plantanista indi). *Endeavour, 3,* 48–56.

Pivik, R. T., Bylsma, F. W., & Cooper, P. (1986). Sleep-wakefulness rhythms in the rabbit. *Behavioral and Neural Biology, 45*(3), 275–286.

Prudom, A. E., & Klemm, W. R. (1973). Electrographic correlates of sleep behavior in a primitive mammal, the Armadillo *Dasypus novemcinctus. Physiology & Behavior, 10,* 275–282.

Reite, M. L., Rhodes, J. M., Kavan, E., & Adey, W. R. (1965). Normal sleep patterns in Macaque monkey. *Archives of Neurology, 12,* 133–144.

Reite, M., & Short, R. (1985). Behavior and physiology in young bonnet monkeys.

Developmental Psychobiology, 19(6), 567–579.

Reite, M., Stynes, A.J., Vaughn, L., Pauley, J.D., & Short, R.A. (1976). Sleep in infant monkeys: Normal values and behavioral correlates. *Physiology & Behavior, 16,* 245–251.

Richardson, G.S., Moore-Ede, M.C., Czeisler, C.A., & Dement, W.C. (1985). Circadian rhythms of sleep and wakefulness in mice: Analysis using long-term automated recording of sleep. *American Journal of Physiology—Regulatory, Integrative and Comparative Physiology, 248*(3 Pt 2), R320–R330.

Ridgway, S.H., Harrison, R.J., & Joyce, P.L. (1975). Sleep and cardiac rhythm in the gray seal. *Science, 187*(4176), 553–555.

Robert, S., & Dallaire, A. (1986). Polygraphic analysis of the sleep-wake states and the REM sleep periodicity in domesticated pigs (Sus scrofa). *Physiology & Behavior, 37*(2), 289–293.

Robinson, E.L., Hsieh, J.K., & Fuller, C.A. (2003). A primate model of sleep regulation [Abstract]. *Sleep, 26*(Suppl.), A391.

Ruckebusch, Y. (1962). [Post-natal development of sleep in ruminants]. *C R Seances Soc Biol Fil, 156,* 1869–1873.

Ruckebusch, Y. (1963). Etude EEG et comportementale des alternantes veille-sommeil chez l'ane. *C R Seances Soc Biol Fil, 157,* 840–844.

Ruckebusch, Y. (1972). The relevance of drowsiness in the circadian cycle of farm animals. *Animal Behavior, 20*(4), 637–643.

Ruckebusch, Y., Barbey, P., & Guillemot, P. (1970). Les etats de sommeil chez le Cheval (Equus caballus). *C R Seances Soc Biol Fil, 31,* 658–665.

Ruckebusch, Y., & Bell, F.R. (1970). Etude polygraphique et comportementale es etats dev veille et de sommeil chez la vache (Bos taurus). *Ann Rech Vet, 1,* 41–62.

Sato, T., & Kawamura, H. (1984). Effects of bilateral suprachiasmatic nucleus lesions on the circadian rhythms in a diurnal rodent, the Siberian chipmunk (Eutamias sibiricus). *Journal of Comparative Physiology, A, 155,* 745–752.

Sazonov, V.S. (1981). Influence of the low environmental temperatures on wakefulness-sleep periodicity in the lemming. *Journal of Evolutionary Biochemistry and Physiology, 17*(4), 259–262.

Shurley, J.T., Serafetinides, E.A., Brooks, R.E., Elsner, R., & Kenney, D.W. (1969). Sleep in Cetaceans: I. The pilot whale, Globicephala scammoni [Abstract]. *Psychophysiology, 6,* 230.

Siegel, J.M., Manger, P.R., Nienhuis, R., Fahringer, H.M., Shalita, T., & Pettigrew, J.D. (1999). Sleep in the platypus. *Neuroscience, 91*(1), 391–400.

Snyder, F. (1974). Sleep-waking patterns of hydracoidea [Abstract]. *Sleep Research, 3,* 87.

Snyder, F., Bugbee, N., & Douthitt, T.C. (1971). Telemetric studies of 24-hour sleep-waking patterns in some primitive mammals [Abstract]. *Psychophysiology, 9*(1), 122.

Spies, H.G., Whitmayer, D.I., & Sawyer, C.H. (1970). Patterns of spontaneous and induced paradoxical sleep in intact and hypophysectomized rabbits. *Brain Research, 18,* 155–164.

Sterman, M.B., Knauss, T., Lehmann, D., & Clemente, C.D. (1965). Circadian sleep and waking patterns in the laboratory cat. *Electroencephalography & Clinical Neurophysiology, 19,* 509–517.

Strijkstra, A.M., & Daan, S. (1997). Ambient temperature during torpor affects NREM sleep EEG during arousal episodes in hibernating European ground squirrels. *Neuroscience Letters, 221*(2–3), 177–180.

Strijkstra, A.M., & Daan, S. (1998). Dissimilarity of slow-wave activity enhancement by torpor and sleep deprivation in a hibernator. *American Journal of Physiology—Regulatory, Integrative and Comparative Physiology, 275*(4 Pt 2), R1110–R1117.

Sunquist, M., & Montgomery, G. (1973). Activity patterns and rates of movement of two-toed and three-toed sloths, Choloepus hoffmani and Bradypus infuscatus. *Journal of Mammalogy, 54,* 946–954.

Susic, V., & Masirevic, G. (1986). Sleep patterns in the Mongolian gerbil (Meriones unguilculatus). *Physiology & Behavior, 37,* 257–261.

Swett, C. (1969). Daytime sleep patterns in free-ranging Rhesus Monkeys [Abstract]. *Psychophysiology, 6,* 227.

Takahashi, Y., Hoinhara, S., Nakamura, Y., & Takahashi, K. (1981). A model of human sleep-related growth hormone secretion in dogs: Effects of 3, 6, and 12 hours of wakefulness on plasma growth hormone, cortisol, and sleep stages. *Endocrinology, 109*(1), 262–272.

Tang, X., & Sanford, L. D. (2002). Telemetric recording of sleep and home cage activity in mice. *Sleep, 25*(6), 691–699.

Tauber, E. S., Michel, F., & Roffwarg, H. P. (1968). Preliminary note on the sleep and waking cycle in the desert hedgehog (Paraechinus hypomalas) [Abstract]. *Psychophysiology, 5,* 201.

Tenaza, R., Ross, B. A., Tanticharoenyos, P., & Berkson, G. (1969). Individual behaviour and activity rhythms of captive slow lorises (Nycticebus coucang). *Animal Behavior, 17,* 664–669.

Tobler, I. (1992). Behavioral sleep in the Asian elephant in captivity. *Sleep, 15*(1), 1–12.

Tobler, I., & Deboer, T. (2001). Sleep in the blind mole rat Spalax ehrenbergi. *Sleep, 24*(2), 147–154.

Tobler, I., Franken, P., & Scherschlicht, R. (1990). Sleep and EEG spectra in the rabbit under baseline conditions and following sleep deprivation. *Physiology & Behavior, 48,* 121–129.

Tobler, I., & Jaggi, K. (1987). Sleep and EEG spectra in the Syrian hamster (Mesocricetus auratus) under baseline conditions and following sleep deprivation. *Journal of Comparative Physiology A, 161*(3), 449–459.

Tobler, I., & Schwierin, B. (1996). Behavioural sleep in the giraffe (Giraffa camelopardalis) in a zoological garden. *Journal of Sleep Research, 5*(1), 21–32.

Toutain, P. L., & Ruckebusch, Y. (1975). Arousal as a cyclic phenomenon during sleep and hibernation in the hedgehog (Erinaceus europaeus). *Experientia, 31,* 312–314.

Ursin, R. (1968). The 2 stages of slow-wave sleep in the cat and their relation to REM sleep. *Brain Research, 11,* 347–356.

Valatx, J. L., & Bugat, R. (1974). [Genetic factors as determinants of the waking-sleep cycle in the mouse (author's transl)]. *Brain Research, 69*(2), 315–330.

Van Twyver, H. (1969). Sleep patterns in five rodent species. *Physiology & Behavior, 4,* 901–905.

Van Twyver, H., & Allison, T. (1970). Sleep in the opossum Didelphis marsupialis. *Electroencephalography and Clinical Neurophysiology, 29*(2), 181–189.

Van Twyver, H., & Allison, T. (1974). Sleep in the armadillo Dasypus novemcinctus at moderate and low ambient temperatures. *Brain, Behavior and Evolution, 9*(2), 107–120.

Walker, J. M., Glotzbach, S. F., Berger, R. J., & Heller, H. C. (1977). Sleep and hibernation in ground squirrels (Citellus spp): Electrophysiological observations. *American Journal of Physiology—Regulatory, Integrative and Comparative Physiology, 233*(5), R213–R221.

Walker, J. M., Walker, L. E., Harris, D. V., & Berger, R. J. (1983). Cessation of thermoregulation during REM sleep in the pocket mouse. *American Journal of Physiology, 244*(1), R114–R118.

Wauquier, A., Verheyen, J. L., van den Broeck, W. A., & Janssen, P. A. (1979). Visual and computer-based analysis of 24 h sleepwaking patterns in the dog. *Electroencephalography and Clinical Neurophysiology, 46*(1), 33–48.

Weitzman, E. D., Kripke, D. F., Pollack, C., & Domingues, J. (1965). Cyclic activity in sleep of *Macaca mulatta. Archives of Neurology, 12*, 463–467.

Wexler, D.B., & Moore-Ede, M.C. (1985). Circadian sleep-wake cycle organization in squirrel monkeys. *American Journal of Physiology—Regulatory, Integrative and Comparative Physiology, 248*, R353–R362.

Zepelin, H. (1970). Sleep of the jaguar and the tapir: A prey–predator contrast [Abstract]. *Psychophysiology, 7*, 305–306.

Zepelin, H. (1989). Mammalian sleep. In M.H. Kryger, T. Roth, & W.C. Dement (Eds.), *Principles and practices of sleep medicine* (pp. 81–92). Philadelphia: Saunders.

Zepelin, H., & Rechtschaffen, A. (1974). Mammalian sleep, longevity, and energy metabolism. *Brain, Behavior and Evolution, 10*(6), 425–470.

Zolovick, A., Stern, W., Jalowiec, J., Panksepp, J., & Morgane, P. (1973). Sleep-waking patterns in cats: Effects of 6-hydroxydopamine given into the dorso-lateral pontine tegmentum [Abstract]. *Sleep Research, 2*, 74.

Mammal Articles with REM Density Data

Balzamo, E., Bradley, R.J., & Rhodes, J.M. (1972). Sleep ontogeny in the chimpanzee: From two months to forty-one months. *Electroencephalography and Clinical Neurophysiology, 33*, 47–60.

Bert, J., & Collomb, H. (1966). L'electroencephalogramme du sommeil nocturne chez le babouin. Etude par telemetrie. *J Physiol (Parris), 58*, 285–301.

Mammal Papers with Arousal Activity Data

Affanni, J.M., Cervino, C.O., & Marcos, H.J.A. (2001). Absence of penile erections during paradoxical sleep: Peculiar penile events during wakefulness and slow wave sleep in the armadillo. *Journal of Sleep Research, 10*, 219–228.

Allison, T., Van Twyver, H., & Goff, W.R. (1972). Electrophysiological studies of the echidna, Tachyglossus aculeatus, I: Waking and sleep. *Comparative Biochemistry and Physiology Part A: Molecular & Integrative Physiology, 110*, 145–184.

Berger, R.J., & Walker, J.M. (1972). A polygraphic study of sleep in the tree shrew (Tupaia glis). *Brain, Behavior and Evolution, 5*(1), 54–69.

Carskadon, M.A., & Dement, W.C. (2006). Normal human sleep: An overview. In M.H. Kryger, T. Roth, & W.C. Dement (Eds.), *Principles and practice of sleep medicine* (4th ed., pp. 13–23). Philadelphia: WB Saunders.

Dallaire, A., & Ruckebusch, Y. (1974). Sleep and wakefulness in the housed pony under different dietary conditions. *Canadian Journal of Comparative Medicine, 38*, 65–71.

Hunter, J.D., & Milson, W.K. (1998). Cortical activation states in sleep and anesthesia. I: Cardio-respiratory effects. *Respiratory Physiology, 112*(1), 71–81.

Immelman, K., & Gebbing, H. (1962). Schlaf bei Giraffiden. *Z Tierpsychol, 19*, 84–92.

Kaemingk, K., & Reite, M. (1987). Social environment and nocturnal sleep: Studies in peer-reared monkeys. *Sleep, 10*, 542–550.

Ridgway, S.H., Harrison, R.J., & Joyce, P.L. (1975). Sleep and cardiac rhythm in the gray seal. *Science, 187*(4176), 553–555.

Ruckebusch, Y. (1972). The relevance of drowsiness in the circadian cycle of farm animals. *Animal Behavior, 20*(4), 637–643.

Sazonov, V.S. (1981). Influence of the low environmental temperatures on wakefulness-sleep periodicity in the lemming. *Journal of Evolutionary Biochemistry and Physiology, 17*(4), 259–262.

Strijkstra, A.M., & Daan, S. (1997). Ambient temperature during torpor affects NREM sleep EEG during arousal episodes in hibernating European ground squirrels. *Neuroscience Letters, 221*(2–3), 177–180.

Tenaza, R., Ross, B.A., Tanticharoenyos, P., & Berkson, G. (1969). Individual behaviour and activity rhythms of captive slow lorises (Nycticebus coucang). *Animal Behavior, 17,* 664–669.

Van Twyver, H., & Allison, T. (1970). Sleep in the opossum Didelphis marsupialis. *Electroencephalography and Clinical Neurophysiology, 29*(2), 181–189.

Walker, J.M., Glotzbach, S.F., Berger, R.J., & Heller, H.C. (1977). Sleep and hibernation in ground squirrels (Citellus spp): Electrophysiological observations. *American Journal of Physiology—Regulatory, Integrative and Comparative Physiology, 233*(5), R213–R221.

Mammal Sleep Papers with Spindling Data

Adams, P., & Barratt, E. (1974). Nocturnal sleep in squirrel monkeys. *Electroencephalography & Clinical Neurophysiology, 36,* 201–204.

Affani, J. (1972). Observations on the sleep of some South American marsupials and edenates. *Perspect Brain Sci, 1,* 21–23.

Affanni, J.M., Cervino, C.O., & Marcos, H.J.A. (2001). Absence of penile erections during paradoxical sleep. Peculiar *Journal of Sleep Research.* Penile events during wakefulness and slow wave sleep in the armadillo, *10,* 219–228.

Allison, T., Gerber, S.D., Breedlove, S.M., & Dryden, G.L. (1977). A behavioral and polygraphic study of sleep in the shrews Suncus murinus, Blarina brevicauda, and Cryptotis parva. *Behavioral Biology, 20*(3), 354–366.

Allison, T., & Van Twyver, H. (1970). Sleep in the moles, Scalopus aquaticus and Condylura cristata. *Experimental Neurology, 27*(3), 564–578.

Allison, T., Van Twyver, H., & Goff, W.R. (1972). Electrophysiological studies of the echidna, Tachyglossus aculeatus, I: Waking and sleep. *Comparative Biochemistry and Physiology Part A: Molecular & Integrative Physiology, 110,* 145–184.

Ambrosini, M.V., Gambelunghe, C., Mariucci, G., Bruschelli, G., Adami, M., & Guiditta, A. (1994). Sleep-wake variables and EEG power spectra in Mongolian gerbils and Wistar rats. *Physiology & Behavior, 56*(5), 963–968.

Ayala-Guerrero, F., Vargas-Reyna, L., Ramos, J.I., & Mexicano, G. (1998). Sleep patterns of the volcano mouse (Neotomodon alstoni alstoni). *Physiology & Behavior, 64*(4), 577–580.

Balzamo, E. (1973). Etude des etats de vigilance chez *Papio cynocephalus* adulte. *C R Seances Soc Biol, 167,* 1168–1172.

Balzamo, E., & Bert, J. (1975). Sleep in *Papio* anubis: Its organization and lateral geniculate spikes [Abstract]. *Sleep Research, 4,* 138.

Balzamo, E., Bradley, R.J., & Rhodes, J.M. (1972). Sleep ontogeny in the chimpanzee: From two months to forty-one months. *Electroencephalography and Clinical Neurophysiology, 33,* 47–60.

Balzamo, E., Vuillon-Cacciuttolo, G., & Bert, J. (1978). Cercopithecus aethiops: EEG et organization des etats de vigiliance. *Wake Sleep, 2,* 223–230.

Balzamo, E., Vuillon-Cacciuttolo, G., Petter, J., & Bert, J. (1978). Etats de vigiliance chez deux Lemuridae: Rhythmes EEG et organization obtenus par telemesure. *Wake Sleep, 2,* 237–245.

Barre, V., & Petter-Rousseaux, A. (1988). Seasonal variations in sleep-wake cycle in Microcebus murinus. *Primates, 19*(2), 53–64.

Batini, C., Radulovacki, M., Kado, R.T., & Adey, W.R. (1967). Effect of interhemispheric transection on the EEG patterns in sleep and wakefulness in monkeys. *Electroencephalography and Clinical Neurophysiology, 22,* 101–112.

Bell, F.R., & Itabisashi, T. (1973). The electroencephalogram of sheep and goats with special reference to rumination. *Physiology & Behavior, 11,* 503–514.

Berger, R.J., & Walker, J.M. (1972). A polygraphic study of sleep in the tree shrew (Tupaia glis). *Brain, Behavior and Evolution, 5*(1), 54–69.

Bert, J., Balzamo, E., Chase, M., & Pegram, V. (1975). The sleep of the baboon, Papio papio, under natural conditions and in the laboratory. *Electroencephalography and Clinical Neurophysiology, 39,* 657–662.

Bert, J., Collomb, H., & Martino, A. (1967). L'electroencephalogramme du sommeil d'un prosimien. Sa place dans l'organisation du sommeil chez les primates. *Electroencephalography and Clinical Neurophysiology, 23,* 342–350.

Bert, J., Kripke, D.F., & Rhodes, J. (1970). Electroencephalogram of the mature chimpanzee: Twenty-four hour recordings. *Electroencephalography and Clinical Neurophysiology, 28,* 32–40.

Bert, J., & Pegram, V. (1969). L'electroencephalogramme du sommeil chez les Cercopithecinae: *Erythrocebus patas* et *Cerpothiecus aethiops sabaeus. Folia Primatol, 11,* 151–159.

Bert, J., Pegram, V., Rhodes, J.M., et al. (1970). A comparative sleep study of two cercopithecinae. *Electroencephalography and Clinical Neurophysiology, 28*(1), 32–40.

Breton, P., Gourmelon, P., & Court, L. (1986). New findings on sleep stage organization in squirrel monkeys. *Electroencephalography and Clinical Neurophysiology, 40*(6), 563–567.

Carskadon, M.A., & Dement, W.C. (2006). Normal human sleep: An overview. In M.H. Kryger, T. Roth, & W.C. Dement (Eds.), *Principles and practice of sleep medicine* (4th ed., pp. 13–23). Philadelphia: WB Saunders.

Crofts, H.S., Wilson, S., Muggleton, N.G., Nutt, D.J., Scott, E.A., & Pearce, P.C. (2001). Investigation of the sleep electrocorticogram of the common marmoset (Callithrix jacchus) using radiotelemetry. *Clinical Neurophysiology, 112*(12), 2265–2273.

Crowley, T.J., Kripke, D.F., Halberg, F., Pegram, G.V., & Schildkraut, J.J. (1972). Circadian rhythms of *Macaca mulatta*: Sleep, EEG, body and eye movement, and temperature. *Primates, 13,* 149–168.

Dallaire, A., & Ruckebusch, Y. (1974). Restactivity cycle and sleep patterns in captive foxes (Vulpes Vulpes). *Experientia, 30,* 59–60.

Dallaire, A., & Ruckebusch, Y. (1974). Sleep and wakefulness in the housed pony under different dietary conditions. *Canadian Journal of Comparative Medicine, 38,* 65–71.

Deboer, T., & Tobler, I. (1996). Shortening of the photoperiod affects sleep distribution, EEG and cortical temperature in the Djungarian hamster. *Journal of Comparative Physiology A, 179*(4), 483–492.

Galvao de Moura Filho, A.G., Huggins, S.E., & Lines, S.G. (1983). Sleep and waking in the three-toed sloth, Bradypus tridactylus. *Comparative Biochemistry and Physiology Part A: Molecular & Integrative Physiology, 76*(2), 345–355.

Gonzalez, F.F., Zaplana, J., Ruiz de Elvira, C., & Delgado, J.M. (1979). Nocturnal and diurnal sleep in Macaca sylvana. *Electroencephalography and Clinical Neurophysiology, 46*(1), 13–28.

Leinonen, L., & Stenberg, D. (1986). Sleep in Macaca arctoides and the effects of prazosin. *Physiology & Behavior, 37*(2), 199–202.

Lucas, E.A. (1979). Effects of a short lightdark cycle on the sleep-wake patterns of the cat. *Sleep, 1*(3), 299–317.

Lucas, E.A., Powell, E.W., & Murphree, O.D. (1977). Baseline sleep-wake patterns in the pointer dog. *Physiology & Behavior, 19,* 285–291.

Lucas, E.A., & Sterman, M.B. (1974). The polycyclic sleep-wake cycle in the cat: Effects produced by sensorimotor rhythm conditioning. *Experimental Neurology, 42,* 347–368.

Lyamin, O.I., & Chetyrbok, I.S. (1992). Unilateral EEG activation during sleep in the

Cape fur seal, Arctocephalus pusillus. *Neuroscience Letters, 143*(1–2), 263–266.

Lyamin, O. I., Mukhametov, L. M., Chetyrbok, I. S., & Vassiliev, A. V. (2002C). Sleep and wakefulness in the southern sea lion. *Behavioural Brain Research, 128*, 129–138.

Marks, G. A., & Shaffery, J. P. (1996). A preliminary study of sleep in the ferret, Mustela putorius furo: A carnivore with an extremely high proportion of REM sleep. *Sleep, 19*(2), 83–93.

McNew, J. J., Howe, R. C., & Adey, W. R. (1971). The sleep cycle and subcortical-cortical EEG relations to the unrestrained chimpanzee. *Electroencephalography and Clinical Neurophysiology, 30*(6), 489–503.

Nicol, S. C., Andersen, N. A., Phillips, N. H., & Berger, R. J. (2000). The echidna manifests typical characteristics of rapid eye movement sleep. *Neuroscience Letters, 283*(1), 49–52.

Nishino, S., Riehl, J., Hong, J., Kwan, M., Reid, M., & Mignot, E. (2000). Is narcolepsy a REM sleep disorder? Analysis of sleep abnormalities in narcoleptic dobermans. *Neuroscience Research, 38*, 437–446.

Pivik, R. T., Bylsma, F. W., & Cooper, P. (1986). Sleep-wakefulness rhythms in the rabbit. *Behavioral and Neural Biology, 45*(3), 275–286.

Prudom, A. E., & Klemm, W. R. (1973). Electrographic correlates of sleep behavior in a primitive mammal, the Armadillo *Dasypus novemcinctus*. *Physiology & Behavior, 10*, 275–282.

Reite, M. L., Rhodes, J. M., Kavan, E., & Adey, W. R. (1965). Normal sleep patterns in Macaque monkey. *Archives of Neurology, 12*, 133–144.

Reite, M., & Short, R. (1985). Behavior and physiology in young bonnet monkeys. *Developmental Psychobiology, 19*(6), 567–579.

Reite, M., Stynes, A. J., Vaughn, L., Pauley, J. D., & Short, R. A. (1976). Sleep in infant monkeys: Normal values and behavioral correlates. *Physiology & Behavior, 16*, 245–251.

Ruckebusch, Y., & Bell, F. R. (1970). Etude polygraphique et comportementale es etats dev veille et de sommeil chez la vache (Bos taurus). *Ann Rech Vet, 1*, 41–62.

Sterman, M. B., Knauss, T., Lehmann, D., & Clemente, C. D. (1965). Circadian sleep and waking patterns in the laboratory cat. *Electroencephalography & Clinical Neurophysiology, 19*, 509–517.

Sunquist, M., & Montgomery, G. (1973). Activity patterns and rates of movement of two-toed and three-toed sloths, Choloepus hoffmani and Bradypus infuscatus. *Journal of Mammalogy, 54*, 946–954.

Susic, V., & Masirevic, G. (1986). Sleep patterns in the Mongolian gerbil (Meriones unguilculatus). *Physiology & Behavior, 37*, 257–261.

Tobler, I., & Deboer, T. (2001). Sleep in the blind mole rat Spalax ehrenbergi. *Sleep, 24*(2), 147–154.

Toutain, P. L., & Ruckebusch, Y. (1975). Arousal as a cyclic phenomenon during sleep and hibernation in the hedgehog (Erinaceus europaeus). *Experientia, 31*, 312–314.

Ursin, R. (1968). The 2 stages of slow-wave sleep in the cat and their relation to REM sleep. *Brain Research, 11*, 347–356.

Valatx, J. L., & Bugat, R. (1974). [Genetic factors as determinants of the waking-sleep cycle in the mouse]. *Brain Research, 69*(2), 315–330.

Van Twyver, H., & Allison, T. (1970). Sleep in the opossum Didelphis marsupialis. *Electroencephalography and Clinical Neurophysiology, 29*(2), 181–189.

Van Twyver, H., & Allison, T. (1974). Sleep in the armadillo Dasypus novemcinctus at moderate and low ambient temperatures. *Brain, Behavior and Evolution, 9*(2), 107–120.

Walker, J. M., Glotzbach, S. F., Berger, R. J., & Heller, H. C. (1977). Sleep and hibernation in ground squirrels (Citellus spp):

Electrophysiological observations. *American Journal of Physiology—Regulatory, Integrative and Comparative Physiology, 233*(5), R213–R221.

Wauquier, A., Verheyen, J. L., van den Broeck, W. A., & Janssen, P. A. (1979). Visual and computer-based analysis of 24 h sleep-waking patterns in the dog. *Electroencephalography and Clinical Neurophysiology, 46*(1), 33–48.

Weitzman, E. D., Kripke, D. F., Pollack, C., & Domingues, J. (1965). Cyclic activity in sleep of *Macaca mulatta*. *Archives of Neurology, 12,* 463–467.

Zepelin, H. (1989). Mammalian sleep. In M. H. Kryger, T. Roth, & W. C. Dement (Eds.), *Principles and practices of sleep medicine* (pp. 81–92). Philadelphia: Saunders.

Mammal Papers with Duration of Stages 3 and 4 of NREM or Slow-Wave Activity

Adams, P., & Barratt, E. (1974). Nocturnal sleep in squirrel monkeys. *Electroencephalography & Clinical Neurophysiology, 36,* 201–204.

Balzamo, E. (1973). Etude des etats de vigilance chez *Papio cynocephalus* adulte. *C R Seances Soc Biol, 167,* 1168–1172.

Balzamo, E., & Bert, J. (1975). Sleep in *Papio* anubis: Its organization and lateral geniculate spikes [Abstract]. *Sleep Research, 4,* 138.

Balzamo, E., Bradley, R. J., & Rhodes, J. M. (1972). Sleep ontogeny in the chimpanzee: From two months to forty-one months. *Electroencephalography and Clinical Neurophysiology, 33,* 47–60.

Balzamo, E., Vuillon-Cacciuttolo, G., & Bert, J. (1978). Cercopithecus aethiops: EEG et organization des etats de vigiliance. *Wake Sleep, 2,* 223–230.

Balzamo, E., Vuillon-Cacciuttolo, G., Petter, J., & Bert, J. (1978). Etats de vigiliance chez deux Lemuridae: Rhythmes EEG et organization obtenus par telemesure. *Wake Sleep, 2,* 237–245.

Batini, C., Radulovacki, M., Kado, R. T., & Adey, W. R. (1967). Effect of interhemispheric transection on the EEG patterns in sleep and wakefulness in monkeys. *Electroencephalography and Clinical Neurophysiology, 22,* 101–112.

Berger, R. J., & Walker, J. M. (1972). A polygraphic study of sleep in the tree shrew (Tupaia glis). *Brain, Behavior and Evolution, 5*(1), 54–69.

Bert, J. (1970). Adaptation du sommeil aux conditions experimentales d'enregistrement chez deux Cercopithecinae (Papio papio et Macaca radiata). *Proceeding of the 3rd International Congress in Primatology, 2,* 49–53.

Bert, J. (1973). Similitudes et differences du sommeil chez deux babouins, *Papio hamadryas* et *Papio papio*. *Electroencephalography and Clinical Neurophysiology, 35*(2), 209–212.

Bert, J., Balzamo, E., Chase, M., & Pegram, V. (1975). The sleep of the baboon, Papio papio, under natural conditions and in the laboratory. *Electroencephalography and Clinical Neurophysiology, 39,* 657–662.

Bert, J., Collomb, H., & Martino, A. (1967). L'electroencephalogramme du sommeil d'un prosimien. Sa place dans l'organisation du sommeil chez les primates. *Electroencephalography and Clinical Neurophysiology, 23,* 342–350.

Bert, J., Kripke, D. F., & Rhodes, J. (1970). Electroencephalogram of the mature chimpanzee: Twenty-four hour recordings. *Electroencephalography and Clinical Neurophysiology, 28,* 32–40.

Bert, J., & Pegram, V. (1969). L'electroencephalogramme du sommeil chez les Cercopithecinae: *Erythrocebus patas* et *Cerpothiecus aethiops sabaeus*. *Folia Primatol, 11,* 151–159.

Bert, J., Pegram, V., & Balzano, E. (1972). Comparison du sommeil de deux macaques

(*Macaca radiata* et *Macaca mulatta*). *Folia Primal, 17,* 202–208.

Bert, J., Pegram, V., Rhodes, J.M., Balzano, E., & Naquet, R. (1970). A comparative sleep study of two cercopithecinae. *Electroencephalography and Clinical Neurophysiology, 28*(1), 32–40.

Breton, P., Gourmelon, P., & Court, L. (1986). New findings on sleep stage organization in squirrel monkeys. *Electroencephalography and Clinical Neurophysiology, 40*(6), 563–567.

Crofts, H.S., Wilson, S., Muggleton, N.G., Nutt, D.J., Scott, E.A., & Pearce, P.C. (2001). Investigation of the sleep electrocorticogram of the common marmoset (Callithrix jacchus) using radiotelemetry. *Clinical Neurophysiology, 112*(12), 2265–2273.

Crowley, T.J., Kripke, D.F., Halberg, F., Pegram, G.V., & Schildkraut, J.J. (1972). Circadian rhythms of *Macaca mulatta:* Sleep, EEG, body and eye movement, and temperature. *Primates, 13,* 149–168.

Freemon, F.R., McNew, J.J., & Adey, W.R. (1971). Chimpanzee sleep stages. *Electroencephalography and Clinical Neurophysiology, 31,* 485–489.

Galvao de Moura Filho, A.G., Huggins, S.E., & Lines, S.G. (1983). Sleep and waking in the three-toed sloth, Bradypus tridactylus. *Comparative Biochemistry and Physiology Part A: Molecular & Integrative Physiology, 76*(2), 345–355.

Hunter, J.D., & Milson, W.K. (1998). Cortical activation states in sleep and anesthesia. I: Cardio-respiratory effects. *Respiratory Physiology, 112*(1), 71–81.

Immelman, K., & Gebbing, H. (1962). Schlaf bei Giraffiden. *Z Tierpsychol, 19,* 84–92.

Kaemingk, K., & Reite, M. (1987). Social environment and nocturnal sleep: Studies in peer-reared monkeys. *Sleep, 10,* 542–550.

Karmanova, I.G., Maksimuk, F.M., Murav'eva, L.N., Pastukhov, Y.F., & Sazonov, V.S. (1979). [Specific features of the cycle "wakefulness-sleep" in the arctic lemming Dicrostonyx torquats] (in Russian). *Zh Evol Biokim Fiziol, 15,* 190–195.

Leinonen, L., & Stenberg, D. (1986). Sleep in Macaca arctoides and the effects of prazosin. *Physiology & Behavior, 37*(2), 199–202.

Lyamin, O.I., & Chetyrbok, I.S. (1992). Unilateral EEG activation during sleep in the Cape fur seal, Arctocephalus pusillus. *Neuroscience Letters, 143*(1–2), 263–266.

Lyamin, O.I., Mukhametov, L.M., Chetyrbok, I.S., & Vassiliev, A.V. (1994). Sleep and wakefulness in southern sea lions (Otari byronia). *Journal of Sleep Research, 3*(Suppl. 1), 152.

Lyamin, O.I., Mukhametov, L.M., Chetyrbok, I.S., & Vassiliev, A.V. (2002). Sleep and wakefulness in the southern sea lion. *Behavioural Brain Research, 128,* 129–138.

Lyamin, O.I., Oleksenko, A.I., & Sevostiyanov, V.F. (2000). Behavioral sleep in captive sea otters. *Aquatic Mammals, 26,* 132–136.

McNew, J.J., Howe, R.C., & Adey, W.R. (1971). The sleep cycle and subcortical-cortical EEG relations to the unrestrained chimpanzee. *Electroencephalography and Clinical Neurophysiology, 30*(6), 489–503.

Miller, V.M., & South, F.E. (1981). Entry into hibernation in M. flaviventris: Sleep and behavioral thermoregulation. *Physiology & Behavior, 27*(6), 989–993.

Mukhametov, L.M., Lyamin, O.I., & Polyakova, I.G. (1985). Interhemispheric asynchrony of the sleep EEG in northern fur seals. *Experientia, 41*(8), 1034–1035.

Mukhametov, L.M., Supin, A.Y., & Polyakova, I.G. (1977). Interhemispheric asymmetry of the electroencephalographic sleep patterns in dolphins. *Brain Research, 134*(3), 581–584.

Nicol, S.C., Andersen, N.A., Phillips, N.H., & Berger, R.J. (2000). The echidna manifests typical characteristics of rapid eye movement sleep. *Neuroscience Letters, 283*(1), 49–52.

Nishino, S., Riehl, J., Hong, J., Kwan, M., Reid, M., & Mignot, E. (2000). Is narcolepsy a REM sleep disorder? Analysis of sleep abnormalities in narcoleptic dobermans. *Neuroscience Research, 38,* 437–446.

Palchykova, S., Deboer, T., & Tobler, I. (2002). Selective sleep deprivation after daily torpor in the Djungarian hamster. *Journal of Sleep Research, 11,* 313–319.

Pivik, R. T., Bylsma, F. W., & Cooper, P. (1986). Sleep-wakefulness rhythms in the rabbit. *Behavioral and Neural Biology, 45*(3), 275–286.

Reite, M. L., Rhodes, J. M., Kavan, E., & Adey, W. R. (1965). Normal sleep patterns in Macaque monkey. *Archives of Neurology, 12,* 133–144.

Reite, M., Stynes, A. J., Vaughn, L., Pauley, J. D., & Short, R. A. (1976). Sleep in infant monkeys: Normal values and behavioral correlates. *Physiology & Behavior, 16,* 245–251.

Robinson, E. L., Hsieh, J. K., & Fuller, C. A. (2003). A primate model of sleep regulation [Abstract]. *Sleep, 26*(Suppl.), A391.

Sazonov, V. S. (1981). Influence of the low environmental temperatures on wakefulness-sleep periodicity in the lemming. *Journal of Evolutionary Biochemistry and Physiology, 17*(4), 259–262.

Siegel, J. M., Manger, P. R., Nienhuis, R., Fahringer, H. M., Shalita, T., & Pettigrew, J. D. (1999). Sleep in the platypus. *Neuroscience, 91*(1), 391–400.

Takahashi, Y., Hoinhara, S., Nakamura, Y., & Takahashi, K. (1981). A model of human sleep–related growth hormone secretion in dogs: Effects of 3, 6, and 12 hours of wakefulness on plasma growth hormone, cortisol, and sleep stages. *Endocrinology, 109*(1), 262–272.

Ursin, R. (1968). The 2 stages of slow-wave sleep in the cat and their relation to REM sleep. *Brain Research, 11,* 347–356.

Van Twyver, H., & Allison, T. (1974). Sleep in the armadillo Dasypus novemcinctus at moderate and low ambient temperatures. *Brain, Behavior and Evolution, 9*(2), 107–120.

Wauquier, A., Verheyen, J. L., van den Broeck, W. A., & Janssen, P. A. (1979). Visual and computer-based analysis of 24 h sleep-waking patterns in the dog. *Electroencephalography and Clinical Neurophysiology, 46*(1), 33–48.

Reptile Sleep

Andry, M. L., Luttges, M. W., & Gamow, I. (1971). Temperature effects on spontaneous and evoked neural activity in the garter snake. *Experimental Neurology, 31,* 32–44.

Ayala-Guerrero, F. (1985). Sleep in a chelonian reptile (*Kinosteron sp*). *Sleep Research, 14,* 83.

Ayala-Guerrero, F., Calderon, A., & Perez, M. (1988). Sleep patterns in a chelonian reptile (*Gopherus flavomarginatus*). *Physiology & Behavior, 44*(3), 333–337.

Ayala-Guerrero, F., & Huitronresendiz, S. (1991). Sleep patterns in the lizard *Ctenosaura-pectinata*. *Physiology & Behavior, 49*(6), 1305–1307.

Ayala-Guerrero, F., & Reyna, L. V. (1987). Sleep and wakefulness in the lizard *Ctenosaura similis*. *Estud Med Biol Mex, 35,* 25–33.

Barthelémy, L., Peyraud, C., Belaud, A., & Mabin, D. (1975). Etude electronencephalographique de l'anguille (*Anguilla Anguilla* L.). *J Physiol (Paris), 70,* 173–185.

Belekhova, M. G. (1979). Neurophysiology of the forebrain. In C. Gans, R. G. Northcut, & P. S. Ulinski (Eds.), *Biology of the reptilian* (Vol. 10, pp. 287–359). London: Academic Press.

Belekhova, M. G., & Zagorulko, T. M. (1964). Coreelations between background electrical activity, after-dicharge and EEG activation response to photic stimulation in tortoise brain (*Emys lutaria*). *Zhurnal Vysshei Nervoi Deyatel'nosti imeni I.P. Pawlova, 14*(6), T1028–T1032.

Burr, W., & Lange, H. (1973). Spontaneous brain activity in some species of amphybians and a reptile. *Electroencephal & Clinical Neurophysiology, 34,* 735–736.

Campbell, S. S., & Tobler, I. (1984). Animal sleep: A review of sleep duration across phylogeny. *Neuroscience & Biobehavioral Reviews, 8,* 269–300.

Carrascal, L. M., & Díaz, J. A. (1989). Thermal ecology and spatiotemporal distribution of the Mediterranean lizard (*Psammodromus algirus*). *Holarctic Ecology, 12,* 137–143.

Castilla, A. M., & Bauwens, D. (1991). Thermal biology, microhabitat selection and conservation of the insular lizard *Podarcis hispanica atrata. Oecologia, 85,* 366–374.

Del Corral, J. M., Miralles, A., Nicolau, M. C., Planas, B., & Rial, R. V. (1990). Stereotaxic atlas for the lizard *Gallotia galloti. Progress in Neurobiology, 34,* 185–196.

Desmond, A. (1985). *The hot blooded dinosaurs: A revolution in paleontology.* London: Blond and Briggs.

De Vera, L., & González, J. (1986). Effect of body temperature on the ventilatory responses in the lizard *Gallota galloti. Respiratory Physiology, 65,* 29–37.

De Vera, L., González, J., & Rial, R. V. (1994). Reptilian waking EEG: Slow waves, spindles and evoke potentials. *Electroencephal & Clinical Neurophysiology, 90,* 298–303.

Flanigan, W. F. (1973). Sleep and wakefulness in iguanid lizards, Ctenosaura pectinata and Iguana iguana. *Brain, Behavior and Evolution, 8,* 401–436.

Flanigan, W. F. (1974). Sleep and wakefulness in chelonian reptiles, II: The red-footed tortoise, *Geocheloe carbonaria. Comparative Biochemistry and Physiology Part A: Molecular & Integrative Physiology, 112,* 253–277.

Flanigan, W. F., Knight, C. P., Hartse, K. M., & Rechtschaffen, A. (1974). Sleep and wakefulness in chelonian reptiles, I: The box turtle, *Terrapene Carolina. Comparative Biochemistry and Physiology Part A: Molecular & Integrative Physiology, 12,* 227–252.

Flanigan, W. F., Wilcox, R. H., & Rechtshaffen, A. (1971). The EEG and arousal continuum of crocodilian, *Caiman scleops* [Abstract]. *Electroencephalography and Clinical Neurophysiology, 34*(5), 521–538.

Gamundí, A., Roca, C., Bernácer, R., Nicolau, M. C., & Rial, R. V. (1998). Behavioural sleep and environmental factors in reptiles (*Gallotia galloti*). *Journal of Physiology, 509,* 88.

Gaztelu, J. M., García-Austt, E., & Bullock. T. (1991). Electrocorticograms of hippocampal and dorsal cortex of two reptiles: Comparison with possible mammalian homologs. *Brain, Behavior and Evolution, 37,* 144–160.

Gómez, T., Bolaños, A., López-García, J. A., Nicolau, M. C., & Rial, R. V. (1990). A case report of spontaneous electrographic epilepsy in reptiles (*Gallotia galloti*). *Comparative Biochemistry and Physiology, Series C, 97*(2), 257–258.

Gónzalez, J., & Rial, R. V. (1977). Eletrofisiologa de la cortez teleceflica de reptile (*Lacerta galloti*): EEG y potenciales evocados. *Rev Esp Fisiol, 33,* 239–248.

Gónzalez, J., Vera, L. M., García-Cruz, C. M., & Rial, R. V. (1978). Efectos de la temperature en el electrencefalograma y los potenciales evocados dc los reptiles (*Lacerta galloti*). *Rev Esp Fisiol, 34,* 153–158.

Hartse, K. M., & Rechtschaffen, A. (1974). Effect of atropine sulfate on the sleep related EEG spike activity of the tortoise (*Geochelone carbonaria*). *Brain, Behavior and Evolution, 9,* 81–94.

Hartse, K. M., & Rechtschaffen, A. (1982). The effect of amphetamine, Nembutal, aplpha–metyl thyrosine and parachlororphenylalanine on sleep related spike activity of the tortoise (*Geochelone carbonaria*) and on the cat ventral hippocampus spike. *Brain, Behavior and Evolution, 21,* 199–222.

Hermann, H., Jouvet, M., & Klein, M. M. (1964). Analyse polygraphyque du sommeil de la tortue. *C R Acad Sc Paris, 258,* 2175–2178.

Huey, R. B. (1982). Temperature, physiology and the ecology of reptiles. In C. Gans & F. H. Pough (Eds.), *Biology of the reptilian, physiological ecology* (Physiology C, Vol. 12, pp. 25–91). London: Academic Press.

Hunsaker, D., & Lansing, R. V. (1962). Electronecephalographic studies of reptiles. *Journal of Experimental Zoology, 149,* 21–32.

Huntley, A., & Cohen, H. B. (1980). Further comments on "sleep" in the desert iguana (*Dipsosaurus dorsalis*). *Sleep Research, 9,* 111.

Huntley, A., Friedman, J. K., & Cohen, H. G. (1977). Sleep in an Iguanid lizard (*Dipsosaurus dorsalis*). *Sleep Research, 6,* 104.

Karmanova, I. G., & Churnosov, E. V. (1972). Electrophysiological studies on natural sleep and wakefulness in turtles and hens. *Neuroscience and Behavioral Physiology, 6,* 83–90.

Luttges, M. W., & Gamow, R. I. (1970). Garter snakes: Studies of spontaneous and evoked brain responses with electroencephalography. *Communications in Behavioral Biology, 5,* 115–130.

McDonald, H. S. (1976). Methods for the physiological study of reptiles. In C. Gans & W. R. Dawson (Eds.), *Biology of the reptilian* (Physiology A., Vol. 5, Ch. 2, pp. 19–126). London: Academic Press.

Medina, L., Smeets, W. J., Hoogland, P. V., & Puelles, L. (1993). Distribution of choline acetyltransferase immunoreactivity in the brain of the lizard *Gallotia galloti. Journal of Comparative Neurology, 331,* 261–285.

Meglasson, M. D., & Huggings, S. E. (1979). Sleep in a crocodilian (*Caiman sclerops*). *Comparative Biochemistry and Physiology, Series A, 63,* 561–567.

Parsons, L., & Huggins, S. E. (1965). A study of spontaneous electrical activity in the brain of *Caiman sclerops. Proceedings of the Society for Experimental Biology and Medicine, 119,* 397–400.

Parsons, L., & Huggins, S. E. (1965). Effects of temperature on electroencephalogram of the *Caiman. Proceedings of the Society for Experimental Biology and Medicine, 120,* 422–426.

Peyreton, J., & Dusan-Peyreton, D. (1967). Etude polygraphique du cycle vieille sommeil chez trios genres de reptiles. *C R Soc Biol (Paris), 163,* 181–186.

Powers, A. S., & Reiner, A. (1993). The distribution of cholinergic neurons in the central nervous system of turtles. *Brain, Behavior and Evolution, 41,* 326–345.

Rial, R. V., Almirall, H., Gamundí, A., & Nicolau, M. C. (1994). Delta EEG in active reptiles: A key in the evoltuin of waking and sleep states. *Journal of Sleep Research, 3*(1), 219.

Rial, R. V., & Gónzalez, J. (1978). Kindling effect in the reptilian brain: Motor and electrographic manifestations. *Epilepsia, 19,* 581–589.

Rial, R. V., Nicolau, M. C., Gamundí, A., Tomoner, G., & Akaârir, M. (1998). The problem of the amplitude in the reptilian EEG. *Journal of Sleep Research, 7*(2), 224.

Romo, R., Cepeda, C., & Velasco, M. (1978). Behavioral and electrophysiological patterns of wakefulness-sleep states in the lizard *Phrinosoma regali. Bol Estud Med Méx, 30,* 13–18.

Rose, B. (1981). Factors affecting the activity in *Saloporus virgatus. Ecology, 62*(3), 706–716.

Sato, M., Okano, Y., & Inoue, S. (1989). Polygraphic correlates of rest-activity behaviour in turtles. In J. Horne (Ed.), *Sleep: 88* (pp. 225–226). New York: Gustav Fischer Verlag.

Servit, Z., & Strejkova, A. (1972). Thalamocortical relations and the genesis of epileptic electrographic phenomena in the forebrain of the turtle. *Experimental Neurology, 35,* 50–60.

Susic, V. (1972). Eletrographic and behavioral correlations of the rest-activity cycle in the sea turtle *Carette caretta* L. (Chelonia). *Journal of Experimental Marine Biology and Ecology, 10,* 81–87.

Tauber, E. S., Roffwarg, H. P., & Weitzman, E. D. (1966). Eye movements and electroencephalogram activity during sleep in diurnal lizards. *Nature, 212,* 1612–1612.

Tauber, E. S., Rojas-Ramirez, J., & Hernandez Peón, R. (1968). Electrophysiological and behavioral correlates of wakefulness and sleep in the lizard (*Ctenosaura pectinata*). *Electroencephal & Clinical Neurophysiology, 24,* 424–433.

Van Twyver, H. (1973). Polygraphic studies of the American alligator. *Sleep Research, 2,* 87.

Vasilescu, E. (1970). Sleep and wakefulness in the tortoise (*Emys orbicularis*). *Rev Roum Biol Zool, 15*(3), 177–179.

Walker, J. M., & Berger, R. J. (1973). A polygraphic study of the tortoise (*Testudo denticulata*): Absence of electrophysiological signs of sleep. *Brain, Behavior and Evolution, 8,* 453–467.

Warner, B. F., & Huggins, S. E. (1978). An electroencephalographic study of sleep in young caimans in a colony. *Comparative Biochemistry and Physiology Part A: Molecular & Integrative Physiology, 59,* 139–144.

About the Editors

Deirdre Barrett, PhD, is a psychologist on the faculty of Harvard Medical. She is past president of both the International Association for the Study of Dreams and APA Division 30: The Society for Psychological Hypnosis. She has written four books, including *The Committee of Sleep* and *The Pregnant Man: Cases from a Hypnotherapist's Couch*. She is the editor of four additional books, including *The New Science of Dreaming* and *Trauma and Dreams*. She is editor-in-chief of IASD's journal, *Dreaming*. Dr. Barrett's commentary on dreams has been featured on *Good Morning America, The Today Show*, CNN, Fox, and The Discovery Channel. She has been interviewed for dream articles in the *Washington Post,* the *New York Times, Life, Time,* and *Newsweek*. Her own articles have appeared in *Psychology Today* and *Invention and Technology*. Dr. Barrett has lectured at Esalen, the Smithsonian, and at universities around the world.

Patrick McNamara, PhD, is associate professor of neurology at Boston University School of Medicine. He is the author of numerous publications on sleep and dreams. He has been particularly interested in using evolutionary approaches to understanding nature and functions of sleep and dreams.

List of Contributors

Vivien C. Abad, MD, MBA
Sleep Disorders Center
Palo Alto Medical Foundation
Sunnyvale, California

Emily Abrams, BA
Boston University School of Medicine
Department of Neurology
Boston, Massachusetts

Mehmed Y. Agargun, MD, Professor of Psychiatry
Yuzuncu Yil University
Kadikoy, Turkey

Hamdan Al-Jahdali, MD, FRCPC, FCCP
Associate Professor
Head of Pulmonary Division
Medical Director of Sleep disorders
Center
King Saud University for Health
Sciences
King Abdulaziz Medical City, Riyadh,
Saudi Arabia

Neil Michael Alperstein, PhD
Professor
Department of Communication
Loyola University, Maryland

John Antrobus, PhD
Emeritus Head, PhD Program in Cognitive Neuroscience
City University of New York

Marzieh Hosseini Araghi, BSc
Birmingham and Black Country National
Institute of Health Research (NIHR)
Collaborations for Leadership in Applied
Health Research and Care (CLAHRC)
Theme 8
Birmingham, United Kingdom

Teresa Arora, BSc
School of Clinical and Experimental
Medicine, College of Medical and Dental
Sciences, University of Birmingham, Birmingham, United Kingdom
and
Heartlands Biomedical Research Centre
(HBMRC), Heart of England Foundation
Trust, Birmingham, United Kingdom

Shoichi Asaoka, PhD
Department of Somnology, Tokyo
Medical University
Japan Somnology Center,
Neuropsychiatric Research Institute
Tokyo, Japan

Sheila McNellis Asato, MA
Certified Embodied Imagination Coach
Director of Monkey Bridge Arts
Faculty, Minnesota Center for the Book
Arts
Minneapolis, Minnesota

Mercedes Atienza, PhD
Laboratory of Functional Neuroscience
Department of Physiology, Anatomy, and
Cell Biology
University Pablo de Olavide, Seville,
Spain

Sanford Auerbach, MD
Associate Professor of Neurology, Psychiatry and Behavioral Neuroscience,
Boston University School of Medicine
Director, Sleep Disorders Center, Boston
Medical Center
Boston, Massachusetts

Jesus Avila, PhD
Institute of Molecular Biology "Severo
Ochoa"
Autonomous University of Madrid, Madrid, Spain

Dev Banerjee, MD, FRCP
Heartlands Biomedical Research Centre
(HBMRC), Heart of England Foundation
Trust, Birmingham, United Kingdom
Aston Brain Centre, Aston University,
Birmingham, United Kingdom

Nicola L. Barclay, PhD Student
Psychology Department
Goldsmiths
University of London, United Kingdom

Deirdre Barrett, PhD
Harvard Medical School/Cambridge
Health Alliance
Clinical Assistant Professor of Psychology in Psychiatry

Cambridge, Massachusetts

Jeremy Barris, PhD
Philosophy Department
Marshall University
Huntington, West Virginia

Radhika Basheer, PhD
Associate Professor
Department of Psychiatry
Harvard Medical School, Research
Health Scientist and
VA Boston Healthcare System
Cambridge, Massachusetts

Mathias Basner, MD, MSc
Unit for Experimental Psychiatry
Division of Sleep and Chronobiology
Department of Psychiatry
University of Pennsylvania School
of Medicine
Philadelphia, Pennsylvania

John Eliott Beebe, MD
Psychiatrist and Jungian Analyst
C.G. Jung Institute of San Francisco
Teaching Faculty
San Francisco, California

Francesca Bisulli, MD
Department of Neurological Sciences
University of Bologna
Bologna, Italy

Lia Rita Azeredo Bittencourt, MD, PhD
Division of Medicine and Biology
of Sleep
Department of Psychobiology
Universidade Federal de São
Paulo—UNIFESP
São Paulo, Brazil

Michael H. Bonnet, PhD
Professor of Neurology
Wright State University

Boonshoft School of Medicine
Dayton, Ohio

Steven David Brass, MD, MPH
Co-Director of Sleep Medicine
Assistant Clinical Professor in the
Department of NeurologyUniversity of
California Davis Health System
Sacramento, California

Daniel R. Bronson
Assistant Researcher
WebSciences International
Los Angeles, California

Jeff Bryson, MS, MA
PhD Candidate, Clinical Psychology
Fielding Graduate University
Santa Barbara, California
and
Adjunct Instructor
Department of Psychology, Jacksonville
State University, Jacksonville, Alabama

Rohit Budhiraja, MD
Pulmonary, Critical Care & Sleep
Physician
Director, Sleep Laboratory,
Southern Arizona VA HealthCare
System
Assistant Professor of Medicine,
University of Arizona,
Tucson, Arizona

Kelly Bulkeley, PhD
Visiting Scholar
The Graduate Theological Union
Berkeley, California

Melissa M. Burnham, PhD
Associate Professor
Department of Educational Psychology,
Counseling, and Human Development
University of Nevada, Reno
Reno, Nevada

Orfeu Marcello Buxton, PhD
Brigham and Women's Hospital
Harvard Medical School
Boston, Massachusetts

Edward Bruce Bynum, PhD, ABPP
Director of Behavioral Medicine
University of Massachusetts Health
Services
Amherst, Massachusetts

Ian G. Campbell, PhD
Department of Psychiatry and Behavioral
SciencesUniversity of California, Davis

Jose L. Cantero, PhD
Laboratory of Functional Neuroscience
Department of Physiology, Anatomy,
and Cell Biology
University Pablo de Olavide, Seville,
Spain

Michelle Cao, DO
Division of Sleep Medicine
Stanford University
Stanford, California

Isabella Capellini, PhD
Durham University, Durham, United
KingdomQueen's University, Belfast,
Ireland

Daniel P. Cardinali, MD
Chief Pulmonary & Sleep Medicine
Associate Professor of Medicine
Hospital Universitario Austral
Universidad Austral
Argentina

Laura Annamaria Cariola, PhD
Student
Department of Linguistics and English
Language
County South
Lancaster University
United Kingdom

Alison Cartwright, MSc, BSc
Birmingham and Black Country National
Institute of Health Research (NIHR) Col-
laborations for Leadership in Applied
Health Research and Care (CLAHRC)
Theme 8, Birmingham, United Kingdom

Michael H. Chase, PhD
President, WebSciences International
Los Angeles, California

Sopna Choudhury BSc
Birmingham and Black Country National
Institute of Health Research (NIHR) Col-
laborations for Leadership in Applied
Health Research and Care (CLAHRC)
Theme 8, Birmingham, UK
College of Medicine, College of Medical
and Dental Sciences, University of Bir-
mingham, Birmingham, United
Kingdom

Stephen D. Christman, PhD
Professor
University of Toledo
Psychology Department
Toledo, Ohio

Laurel Clark, DM, DD
Ordained minister in the Interfaith
Church of Metaphysics
Certified Psi Counselor
President of the School of Metaphysics,
Windyville, Missouri
On the Faculty of the College of Meta-
physics, Windyville, Missouri

Daniel Aaron Cohen, MD, MMSc
Assistant Professor in Neurology
Harvard Medical School
Neurologist, Department of Neurology
Beth Israel Deaconess Medical Center
Boston, Massachusetts

Russell Conduit, PhD
School of Psychology and Psychiatry
Monash University
Clayton, Victoria, Australia

Christine Elizabeth Cooper, PhD
Department of Environment and
Agriculture
Curtin University
Bentley, Western Australia

Michael Czisch, PhD
Max Planck Institute of Psychiatry
Munich, Germany

Barbara D'Amato, Psya.D, LP
Boston Graduate School of
Psychoanalysis
Brookline, Massachusetts
and
The Center for Modern Psychoanalytic
Studies
New York, New York

Heidi Danker-Hopfe
Competence Center of Sleep Medicine
and Sleep Research
Department of Psychiatry and
Psychotherapy
Charité—Universitaetsmedizin Berlin
Berlin, Germany

Subimal Datta, PhD
Professor of Psychiatry and Neurology
Boston University School of Medicine
Boston, Massachusetts

Betsy Davids, MA
Professor Emerita
California College of the Arts
San Francisco, California

Teresa L. DeCicco, PhD
Associate Professor
Department of Psychology

Trent University
Peterborough, Ontario

Luigi De Gennaro, PhD
Associate Professor, Department of Psychology, University of Rome "Sapienza"
Rome, Italy

Natale Gaspare De Santo
Italian Institute for Philosophical Studies

Rosa Maria De Santo
Dr. in Psychology, Specialist in Psychotherapy
Fellow of the Italian Institute for Philosophical Studies
Director Laboratory for Quality of Life
Dialysis Unit Neoren at Montesarchio
Naples, Italy

Gayle M. V. Delaney, PhD
Director of the Delaney & Flowers Center for the Study of Dreams, San Francisco, California
Founding President, International Association for the Study of Dreams (IASD)

Sven Doehner, PhD
Director of the Instituto de Psicología Profunda en México, A.C.

G. William Domhoff, PhD
Distinguished Research Professor in Psychology
Department of Psychology
University of California, Santa Cruz
Santa Cruz, California

Martin Dresler, PhD
Max Planck Institute of Psychiatry
Munich, Germany

Xavier Drouot, MD, PhD
Centre du Sommeil
Service de Physiologie—Explorations Fonctionnelles

APHP, GroupeHenri Mondor
Créteil, France
and
EA 4391
Excitabilité Nerveuse et Thérapeutique
Université Paris 12
Créteil, France

Markus Dworak, MD
Department of Psychiatry
Harvard Medical School and VA Boston Healthcare System
Boston, Massachusetts

Iain Ross Edgar, PhD
Senior Lecturer
Durham University
Anthropology Department
Durham, United Kingdom

Marcia Emery, PhD
Professor
Holos University, Bolivar, Missouri
Energy Medicine University, Sausalito, California

Daniel Erlacher, PhD
Institute of Sport and Sport Sciences
Heidelberg University
Heidelberg, Germany

Maria Livia Fantini, MD, MSc
Neurology Unit, Santa Croce Hospital, Mondovì, Italy, and
Sleep Disorder Center, Dept of Clinical Neurosciences, H San Raffaele Institute, Milan, Italy

Julio Fernández-Mendoza, PhD
Postdoctoral ScholarSleep Research and Treatment CenterDepartment of Psychiatry
Penn State College of Medicine-Hershey, Pennsylvania

Raffaele Ferri, MD
Department of Neurology
Director, Oasi Institute for Research on
Mental Retardation and Brain Aging
(IRCCS)
Troina, Italy

Gianluca Ficca, PhD
Associate Professor
Department of Psychology
University of Naples II
Caserta, Italy

Jill Fischer, MS, APRN, BC
Jungian Psychotherapist
Board certified, Advanced Psychiatric
Nurse Practitioner
Clinical Director of The Santa Barbara
Healing Sanctuary
Co-Founder of the International Society
for Embodied Imagination

**Paul B. Fitzgerald, MBBS, MPM, PhD,
FRANZCP**
Alfred Psychiatry Research Centre
The Alfred Hospital
Prahran, Victoria, Australia

Loma K. Flowers, MD
President of Equilibrium Dynamics and
Clinical Professor of Psychiatry at the
University of California, San Francisco,
(volunteer series)

Judith Ann Floyd, PhD RN FAAN
Professor
Wayne State University
Detroit, Michigan

LeAnne M. Forquer, PhD
Assistant Professor of Psychology
Pikeville College
Pikeville, Kentucky

Hirokazu Furuya, MD, PhD
Clinical Neurologist
Chief Scientist of Clinical Research
Center
National Ōmuta Hospital
Ōmuta, Fukuoka, Japan

Jayne Gackenbach, PhD
Department of Psychology, Grant
MacEwan University
Edmonton, Alberta, Canada

Lisa Gallicchio, PhD
Epidemiologist
The Prevention and Research Center
Mercy Medical Center
Baltimore, Maryland

Eugene Gendlin, PhD
Professor Emeritus
University of Chicago
Chicago, Illinois

Carla Gerona, PhD
Assistant Professor
Georgia Tech
Atlanta, Georgia

Lee T. Gettler, MA
PhD Candidate Northwestern University
Department of Anthropology,
Northwestern University, Evanston, Illinois
and
Mother-Baby Behavioral Sleep Labora-
tory, University of Notre Dame, Notre
Dame, Indiana

Katie Glaskin, PhD
Associate Professor
Anthropology & Sociology
School of Social & Cultural Studies
University of Western Australia
Crawley, Western Australia

Roger Godbout, PhD
Department of Psychiatry, Université de Montréal
and
Sleep Laboratory & Clinic, Hôpital Rivière-des-Prairies
Montréal, Québec, Canada

Julián Jesus González, PhD
Professor of Physiology
Departamento de Fisiología
Instituto de Tecnologías Biomédicas
Universidad de La Laguna
Tenerife, Spain

Claude Gottesmann, PhD
Université de Nice-Sophia Antipolis
Nice, France

Tzivia Gover, MFA
Holyoke Community College
Holyoke, Massachusetts

Nancy Grace, MA
Beverly, Massachusetts

Michael A. Grandner, PhD
Postdoctoral Fellow at the Center for Sleep and Respiratory Neurobiology
University of Pennsylvania
Philadelphia, Pennsylvania

Barbara Griefahn, MD, Univ-Prof
Institute for Occupational Physiology
Dortmund University
Dortmund, Germany

Dr. Fabian Guénolé
Practicien Hospitalier
Centre Hospitalier Universitaire de Caen
Caen, France
Institut National de la Santé et de Recherche Médicale

Unité 923
Neuroanatomie et fonctionnement de la mémoire humaine
Paris, France

Mark Hagen, MA
Director, International Institute for Dream Research
Hamilton, Ontario, Canada

Maurice E. Hamilton, MD
Rheumatologist
Los Altos, California

Ernest Hartmann, MD
Professor of Psychiatry, Tufts University School of Medicine
Director of the Sleep Disorders Center, Newton Wellesley Hospital (retired)
First Editor in Chief of *Dreaming*
Past President of IASD

Kristyna M. Hartse, PhD
Clinical Director
Sonno Sleep Centers of Texas and New Mexico
El Paso, Texas

Allison G. Harvey, PhD
Clinical Science DepartmentUniversity of California, Berkeley
Berkeley, California

Clara Hill, PhD
Professor, University of Maryland
Department of Psychology
College Park, Maryland

Eva Hita-Yañez, PhD Student
Laboratory of Functional Neuroscience
Department of Physiology, Anatomy, and Cell Biology
University Pablo de Olavide, Seville
Seville, Spain

J. Allan Hobson, MD
Professor of Psychiatry, Emeritus
Harvard Medical School
Boston, Massachusetts

Kerstin Hoedlmoser, PhD
University of Salzburg
Department of Psychology
Division of Physiological Psychology
Laboratory for "Sleep and Consciousness
Research"
Salzburg, Austria

Curtiss R. Hoffman, PhD
Professor
Department of Anthropology
Bridgewater State University, Bridgewater, Massachusetts

Douglas Hollan, PhD
Professor of Anthropology
University of California at Los Angeles
Los Angeles, California

Charles Chong-Hwa Hong, MD, PhD
Assistant Professor
Department of Psychiatry and Behavioral
Sciences
Johns Hopkins University School of
Medicine
Baltimore, Maryland

Caroline L. Horton, PhD
Department of Psychology
Leeds Metropolitan University
Leeds, United Kingdom

Robert J. Hoss, MS
Director of DreamScience Foundation
and Officer
Past President of the International Association for the Study of Dreams

Christer Hublin, MD, PhD
Assistant Chief Medical Officer
Finnish Institute of Occupational Health

Docent (Adjunct) Assistant Professor of
Neurology
Helsinki University
Helsinki, Finland

Victoria Hughes, BA
Founder, Director, Artist
The ArtRand Center for Applied Creative
Strategies
Certified Clinical Hypnotherapist
Santa Fe, New Mexico

Ryan Hurd, MA, BA
Certificate in Dream Studies
Independent Researcher
Dreamstudios.org

Tracy N. Iacovelli, BA
Graduate Assistant
Psychology Department
Montclair State University
Montclair, New Jersey

Yuichi Inoue, MD, PhD
Department of Somnology, Tokyo Medical University
Japan Somnology Center, Neuropsychiatric Research Institute
Tokyo, Japan

Lee Irwin, PhD
Professor
Religious Studies Department
College of Charleston
Charleston, South Carolina

Antonia J. Jakobson, B App Sc (Hons)
School of Psychology and Psychiatry
Monash University
Clayton, Victoria, Australia

James E. Jan, MD, FRCPI
Clinical Professor
Senior Research Scientist Emeritus
Diagnostic Neurophysiology

BC Children's Hospital
Vancouver, British Columbia, Canada

Jessica Ann Jiménez, MA
San Diego State University /University of
California, San Diego Joint Doctoral Pro-
gram in Public Health
San Diego, California

Patricia Lynn Johnson, BA
Department of Neurology
Boston University School of Medicine
Boston, Massachusetts

Katy Alicia Jones, PhD
Senior Research Fellow
Turning Point Alcohol and Drug Centre
Fitzroy Melbourne Victoria, Australia

Tracey Lea Kahan, PhD
Department of Psychology
Santa Clara University
Santa Clara, California

David Kahn, PhD
Harvard Medical School
Boston, Massachusetts

David L. Kahn
Independent Dream Researcher

Jennifer C. Kanady, BS
Clinical Science DepartmentUniversity of
California, Berkeley
Berkeley, California

J. Lee Kavanau, PhD
Department of Ecology and Evolutionary
Biology
University of California at Los Angeles
Los Angeles, California

Ian Keen, PhD
Visiting Fellow
School of Archaeology and Anthropology
College of Arts and Sciences

Australian National University
Canberra, Australia

David B. King, MSc
PhD Student, Health Psychology Program
Department of Psychology
University of British Columbia
Vancouver, British Columbia, Canada

Johanna King, PhD
Licensed Psychologist
Retired from clinical practice and teach-
ing at California State University, Chico
Chico, California

Philip H. King, PhD, MA
Professor of Quantitative Methods and
Psychology (Retired)
Hawaii Pacific University
Honolulu, Honolulu

Roger M. Knudson, PhD
Professor Emeritus
Department of Psychology
Miami University
Oxford, Ohio

Erin Koffel, MA
PhD Candidate
University of Iowa
Iowa City, Iowa

Waud H. Kracke, PhD
Department of Anthropology
University of Illinois, Chicago
Chicago, Illinois

Stanley C. Krippner, PhD
Saybrook University
San Francisco, California

Donald Kuiken, PhD
Professor
Department of Psychology
University of Alberta
Edmonton, Alberta, Canada

Robert G. Kunzendorf, PhD
Professor, Department of Psychology
University of Massachusetts, Lowell
Lowell, Massachusetts

Caroline Kussé
PhD Student in Neurosciences
Cyclotron Research Centre
University of Liège
Liège, Belgium

David C. Lahti, PhD
Department of Biology
Queens College
City University of New York
Flushing, New York

George Lakoff, SB
Goldman Distinguished Professor of cog-
nitive Science and Linguistics
University of California, Berkeley
Berkeley, California

Jaap Lancee
Utrecht University
Utrecht, Netherlands

Justina Lasley, MA
Institute for Dream Studies, Founder and
Director
International Association for the Study of
Dreams, past board member
Carl Jung Society—Atlanta, Georgia, and
Charleston, South Carolina

Glenda Lassi, PhD
Department of Neuroscience and Brain
Technologies
Italian Institute of Technology (IIT)
Genova, Italy

Christopher J. Lennings, PhD
LSC Psychology
Faculty of Health Science

University of Sydney
Sydney, Australia

Jenn Lewin, PhD
Boston University
Visiting Assistant Professor
Department of English and Writing
Program
Boston, Massachusetts

Shenghui Li, MD, PhD
School of Public Health
Shanghai Jiaotong University School of
Medicine
Shanghai, People's Republic of China

Ruth Lingford, MA
Professor of the Practice of Animation
Department of Visual and Environmental
Studies
Harvard University
Cambridge, Massachusetts

Roger Ivar Lohmann, PhD, MA
Associate Professor
Department of Anthropology
Trent University
Peterborough, Ontario, Canada

Monique Lortie-Lussier, PhD
Adjunct Professor
School of Psychology
University Of Ottawa

Brandon S. Lu, MD, MS
Division of Pulmonary and Critical Care
Medicine
California Pacific Medical Center
San Francisco, California

Oleg Lyamin, PhD
UCLA and VA GLAHS Sepulveda, CA,
USA
Utrish Dolphinarium Ltd., Moscow,
Russia

Severtsov Institute of Ecology and Evolution, Moscow, Russia

Tallulah Lyons, Med
Cancer Wellness, Integrative Oncology Center at Piedmont Hospital
Cancer Support Community-Atlanta
Integrative Oncology Center affiliated with Northside Hospital
Atlanta, Georgia

Alfio Maggiolini, PhD
Psychotherapist
Professor of Psychology of Adolescence
Department of Psychology
Milan University
Milan, Italy

Raffaele Manni, MD
Sleep Medicine and Epilepsy Unit
IRCCS "C. Mondino" National Institute of Neurology Foundation
Pavia, Italy

Pierre Maquet, Prof Dr MD
Research Director FNRS
Cyclotron Research Centre
University of Liège
Liège, Belgium

Cristina Marzano, PhD
Research Assistant
Department of Psychology
"Sapienza"—University of Rome
Rome, Italy

Laurel M. McCabe, PhD
President of the School of Metaphysics
Windyville, Missouri
Faculty of the College of Metaphysics
Ordained minister in the Interfaith Church of Metaphysics
Certified Psi Counselor

James J. McKenna, PhD
Department of Anthropology and Mother-Baby Behavioral Sleep Laboratory
University of Notre Dame
Notre Dame, Indiana

Deirdre T. McLaren, BA
Research Assistant II
Brigham and Women's Hospital
Department of Sleep Medicine
Boston, Massachusetts

Patrick McNamara, PhD
Director, Evolutionary Neurobehavior Laboratory
Associate Professor of Neurology and Psychiatry
Boston University School of Medicine and
VA Boston Healthcare System
Department of Neurology
Boston, Massachusetts

Peter Meerlo, PhD
Center for Behavior and NeurosciencesUniversity of GroningenThe Netherlands

Thomas Metzinger, Prof, Dr
Department of Philosophy
Johannes-Gutenberg University
Mainz, Germany

Emmanuel Mignot, MD, PhD
Craig Reynolds Professor of Sleep Medicine
Professor of Psychiatry and Behavioral Sciences
Stanford University Center For Narcolepsy
Palo Alto, California

Paul J. Mills, PhD
Department of Psychiatry
University of California, San Diego
San Diego, California

Jacques Montangero, PhD
Emeritus Professor
University of Geneva
Geneva, Switzerland

Jaime M. Monti, MD
Professor
Department of Pharmacology and
Therapeutics
School of Medicine Clinics Hospital
Montevideo, Uruguay

Peter Morgan, MD, PhD
Associate Professor
Yale University Department of Psychiatry
New Haven, Connecticut

Timothy Morgenthaler, MD
Division of Pulmonary and Critical Care
Medicine
Mayo Clinic, Rochester, Minnesota

Lana Nasser, MA
Jordan University
Amman, Jordan

Reverend Geoff Nelson, Dmin, Mdiv
Presbyterian Minister

Soňa Nevšímalová, MD, DSc
Professor of NeurologyDepartment of
Neurology
Charles University
1st Faculty of MedicinePrague, Czech
Republic

Tore Nielsen, PhD
Professor of Psychiatry, Université de
Montreal
and

Director, Dream & Nightmare
Laboratory, Hopital du Sacre-Coeur
Montreal, Quebec, Canada

Yuval Nir, PhD
Department of Psychiatry
University of Wisconsin
Madison, Wisconsin

Isabelle Noth, PD Dr. Habil
Theology Department
University of Zurich
Zurich, Switzerland

Charles Nunn, PhD
Department of Human Evolutionary
Biology
Harvard University
Cambridge, Massachusetts

Chris Olsen, MAT
Adjunct Faculty
Institute of Transpersonal Psychology
Palo Alto, CA

Edward Pace-Schott, PhD
University of Massachusetts,
Amherst
Psychology Department
Amherst, Massachusetts
and
Associate Research
Massachusetts General Hospital
Department of Psychiatry
Harvard Medical School
Cambridge, Massachusetts

James F. Pagel, MD, MS
Associate Clinical Professor of
Family Medicine
University of Colorado School of
Medicine, Southern Colorado Family
Medicine
Pueblo, Colorado

Director, Sleep Disorders Clinic of Southern Colorado, Parkview Medical Center
Pueblo, Colorado

Krijn Pansters, PhD
Universiteit van Tilburg
Faculteit Katholieke Theologie
Franciscaans Studiecentrum
Heidelberglaan 2
Utrecht, Netherlands

Stephen Bixby Parker, PhD
Alaska Medical Psychology (private practice)
Anchorage, Alaska

Kimberley C. Patton, PhD, AB AM
Professor of the Comparative and Historical Study of ReligionHarvard Divinity School
Cambridge, Massachusetts

Cynthia Pearson, BA
Member and former executive board member, of the International Association for the Study of Dreams
Chair, Long Term Journal Keeping panels, annual IASD conferences, 1998–2010
Founder, Dreamjournalist.com

Daniel Pérez-Chada, MD
DirectorDepartment of Teaching & ResearchFaculty of Medical Sciences-Pontificia Universidad Católica Argentina Professor EmeritusUniversidad de Buenos Aires
Buenos Aires, Argentina

Andrew J. K. Phillips, PhD
Division of Sleep Medicine
Brigham & Women's Hospital
Harvard Medical School
Cambridge, Massachusetts

Sylvie Poirier, PhD
Université Laval
Quebec, Canada

Ruth E. Propper, PhD
Associate Professor
Psychology Department
Montclair State University
Montclair, New Jersey

Carolyn Pytte, PhD
Queens College and The Graduate Center
Department of Psychology
City University of New York
Flushing, New York

Victoria Rabinowe, BA
Certified in DreamTending and Advanced DreamTending
Director of The DreamingArts Institute
Santa Fe, New Mexico

Alberto Raggi, MD
Department of Neurology
Oasi Institute for Research on Mental Retardation and Brain Aging (IRCCS)
Troina, Italy

Niels C. Rattenborg, PhD
Max Planck Institute for Ornithology—Seewiesen
Sleep & Flight Group
Seewiesen, Germany

Henry Reed, PhD
Professor of Transpersonal Studies
Atlantic University
Virginia Beach, Virginia

Antti Revonsuo, PhD
University of Skövde, Sweden and University of Turku, Finland
Turku, Finland

Rubén Victor Rial, PhD
Professor
Universitat de les Illes Balears
Palma de Mallorca, Illes Balears,
Spain

Jan Roberts, MA, MASc
Psychologist
Leumeah, Australia

Gerald Rosen, MD
Associate Professor
Department of Pediatrics
University of Minnesota School of
Medicine
Minneapolis, Minnesota

Carol S. Rupprecht, PhD
Professor of Comparative Literature
Emerita, Hamilton College
Clinton, New York

Richard A. Russo, MA
Associate Director of the Dream
Institute of Northern California
Berkeley, California

Meredith Sabini, PhD, MS
Founder-Director, The Dream
Institute of Northern California
Berkeley, California

Pradeep Sahota, MD
Professor and Chairman
Department of Neurology
University of Missouri, Columbia
Columbia, Missouri

Dr. Mohamed Omar Salem, MB ChB
Associate Professor
Department of Psychiatry
Faculty of Medicine
United Arab Emirates University
Al-Ain, United Arab Emirates

Esther Sammut, B App Sc, PGDip (Psych), M Psych (Clinical)
School of Psychology and Psychiatry
Monash University
Clayton, Victoria, Australia

Rogerio Santos-Silva, PhD
Division of Medicine and Biology
of Sleep
Department of Psychobiology
Universidade Federal de São
Paulo—UNIFESP
São Paulo, Brazil

Cornelia Sauter
Competence Center of Sleep Medicine
and Sleep Research
Department of Psychiatry and
Psychotherapy
Charité—Universitaetsmedizin Berlin
Berlin, Germany

Manuel Schabus, Priv Doz, Ass. Prof, Dr
University of Salzburg
Department of Psychology
Division of Physiological Psychology
Laboratory for "Sleep and Consciousness
Research"
Salzburg, Austria

Carlos Schenck, MD
Professor of Psychiatry, University of
Minnesota Medical School
Senior Staff Psychiatrist, Minnesota
Regional Sleep Disorders Center and
Hennepin County Medical Center
Minneapolis, Minnesota

Sophia E. Schiza, MD, PhD
Assistant Professor of Thoracic Medicine
Medical School
University of Crete
Crete, Greece

Lauren Schneider, MA, MFT
Director of the Institute of Dreams
and Tarotpy
Westlake Village, California

Michael Schredl, PhD
Head of Research, Sleep Laboratory,
Central Institute of Mental Health
Mannheim, Germany
and
Associate Professor, Department
of Social Sciences, University
of Mannheim
Mannheim, Germany

Hartmut Schulz, PhD
Free University Berlin
Retired Professor
Department of Educational Science and
Psychology
Berlin, Germany

Richard Schweickert, PhD
Professor
Department of Psychological Sciences
Purdue UniversityWest Lafayette,
Indiana

Jeffrey R. Schweitzer, MA
Department of Psychology
Miami University
Oxford, Ohio

Jeremy Seligson, JD
IASD Regional Representative for Asia
Research Fellow, Wongkwang Digital
University
Department of Yoga and Meditation

Dylan Selterman, MA
Doctoral Candidate, Psychology
Department
Stony Brook University
Stony Brook, New York

Anthony Shafton, AB, MA
Robert Shampain, BFA
non-degree graduate study in Directing,
Ericksonian Hypnotherapy Director
and
Lead Faculty Boston University Los Angeles Graduate Certificate Programs

Rishi Sharma, PhD
Postdoctoral Fellow
Harry S. Truman Memorial Veterans'
Hospital
University of Missouri, Columbia
Columbia, Missouri

Priyattam J. Shiromani, PhD
Professor and Senior Research Scientist
Ralph H. Johnson VA Medical Center
Medical University of South Carolina
Department of Psychiatry
Charleston, South Carolina

Tamar Shochat, DSc
Department of Nursing
Faculty of Social Welfare and Health
Sciences
University of Haifa
Haifa, Israel

Alan Siegel, PhD
Associate Clinical Professor
Department of Psychology
University of California, Berkeley
Berkeley, California

Wonjin Sim, PhD
Assistant Professor
Counseling Psychology Program
Chatham University
Pittsburgh, Pittsburgh

Carlyle Smith, PhD
Professor Emeritus, Trent University
Director of Trent Sleep Laboratories

Adjunct Professor Department of
Neuroscience, Queens University
Kingston, Ontario

Mark Solms, PhD
Chair of Neuropsychology
University of Cape Town
Cape Town, South Africa

Kristin Chase Spoon, MD
Center for Sleep Medicine
Mayo Clinic
Rochester, Minnesota

Victor I. Spoormaker, PhD
Max Planck Institute of Psychiatry
Munich, Germany

Karina Stavitsky, MA
Boston University
Department of Psychology
Boston, Massachusetts

Axel Steiger, MD
Professor
Max Planck Institute of Psychiatry
Department of Psychiatry
Munich, Germany

Charles Stewart, DPhil
Department of Anthropology
University College London
London, United Kingdom

Gloria Sturzenacker, MS
Editor and Writer
Member of the International Association
for the Study of Dreams

Kasia Szpakowska, PhD, FSA
Senior Lecturer in Egyptology, Department of History and ClassicsCentre for
Egyptology and Mediterranean Archaeology (CEMA)Swansea University
Wales, United Kingdom

Shahrad Taheri, MD, PhD, FRCP
School of Clinical and Experimental
Medicine, College of Medical and Dental
Sciences, University of Birmingham
Birmingham, United Kingdom
and
Heartlands Biomedical Research Centre
(HBMRC), Heart of England Foundation
Trust, Birmingham, United Kingdom
and
Birmingham and Black Country National
Institute of Health Research (NIHR) Collaborations for Leadership in Applied
Health Research and Care (CLAHRC),
Theme 8
Birmingham, United Kingdom

Leila Tarokh, PhD
E.P. Bradley Sleep Research Laboratory
Providence, Rhode Island
Department of Psychiatry and Human Behavior, Alpert Medical School of Brown
University Providence, Rhode Island
Institute of Pharmacology and Toxicology, University of Zurich
Zurich, Switzerland

Reverend Jeremy Taylor, D.Min.
Cofounder and Past President of the International Association for the Study of
Dreams, (IASD)
Founder-Director of the Marin Institute
for Projective Dream Work (MIPD)

Michele Terzaghi, MD
Sleep Medicine and Epilepsy Unit
IRCCS "C. Mondino" National Institute
of Neurology Foundation
Pavia, Italy

Mahesh M. Thakkar, PhD
Harry S. Truman Memorial Veterans'
Hospital and

Assistant Professor of Neurology
and Research Health Scientist
University of Missouri, Columbia
Columbia, Missouri

Ajit Thomas, MD, MRCP
Heartlands Biomedical Research Centre
(HBMRC), Heart of England Foundation
Trust, Birmingham, United Kingdom

Liat Tikotzky, PhD
Ben-Gurion University of the Negev
Beer-Sheva, Israel

Paolo Tinuper, MD
Department of Neurological Sciences
University of Bologna
Bologna, Italy

Irene Tobler, PhD
Institute of Pharmacology and Toxicolo-
gyUniversity of Zurich
Zurich, Switzerland

Lorenzo Tonetti, MS
University of Bologna
Department of Psychology
Bologna, Italy

Robert Tonkinson, PhD, FASSA
Emeritus Professor of Anthropology;
Hon. Sen. Research FellowEditor, *An-
thropological Forum*
Anthropology and Sociology
The University of Western Australia
Nedlands, Western Australia

Giulio Tononi, MD, PhD
Department of Psychiatry
University of Wisconsin
Madison, Wisconsin

Misa Tsuruta, MA
PhD Student
Department of Psychology

The New School for Social Research
New York, New York

Valter Tucci, PhD
Department of Neuroscience and Brain
Technologies
Italian Institute of Technology (IIT)
Genova, Italy

Sergio Tufik, MD, PhD
Division of Medicine and Biology of
Sleep
Department of Psychobiology
Universidade Federal de São
Paulo—UNIFESP
São Paulo, Brazil

Susan M. Tyburczy, PhD
Saybrook University
San Francisco, California

Annie Vallières, PhD
Professeure adjointe
Université Laval
Québec, Canada
Centre d'étude des troubles du sommeil
Centre de recherche Université Laval
Robert-Giffard,
Centre de recherche du Centre hospitalier
universitaire de Québec

Robert Van de Castle, PhD
Professor Emeritus, University of Vir-
ginia, Health Sciences Center
Past President and first recipient of the
Lifetime Achievement in Dreamwork
Award, Association for the Study of
Dreams

Jan Van den Bulck, PhD, DSc
Leuven School for Mass Communication
Research
Katholieke Universiteit
Leuven, Belgium

Alexandros N. Vgontzas, MD
Sleep Research and Treatment Center
Department of Psychiatry
Pennsylvania State University College of
Medicine
Hershey, Pennsylvania

Ursula Voss, PhD
Bonn University
Department of Psychology
Bonn, Germany

Olivier Nils Walusinski, MD
Family Physician
Private Practice
Brou, France

Erin J. Wamsley, PhD
Instructor
Harvard Medical School and Beth Israel
Deaconess Medical Center
Boston, Massachusetts

Jong Hwan Wang, MD, PhD
Department of Otolaryngology
Gimpo Woori Hospital,
Gimpo-si, Gyeonggi-do, South Korea

Akihiro Watanabe, MD
Clinical Neurologist
Department of Neurology

Neuro-Muscular Center
National Ōmuta Hospital
Ōmuta, Fukuoka, Japan

Nathaniel F. Watson, MD, MS
Associate Professor of Neurology
University of Washington
Co-director, UW Medicine Sleep Center
Seattle, Washington

Renate Wehrle, PhD, BSc
Psychologist
University Medical Center
RegensburgRegensburg, Germany

Bernard Welt, PhD
Professor, Arts and Humanities
The Corcoran College of
Art and Design
Washington, DC

Judith Lisa White, PhD
Clinical Psychologist and Certified
Embodied Imagination Therapist in
Private Practice
Los Angeles, California

Jennifer M. Windt, MA
Department of Philosophy
Johannes-Gutenberg University
Mainz, Germany

Ann Sayre Wiseman, MA
Independent Artist, Teacher, Art and
Dream Therapist

Carol M. Worthman, PhD
Professor
Department of Anthropology
Emory University
Atlanta, Georgia

Calvin Kai-Ching Yu, PhD
Associate Professor and Associate
Head of Counseling and Psychology
Department
Hong Kong Shue Yan University
Hong Kong, China

Index

Aboriginal Australia,: dreams and "the dreaming," **1–2,** 38, 155–56; significance of dreams in Western Australian Desert, **591–92**

Acetylcholine, 237, 413, 482, 489, 559, 746, 810

Achuar people (southeastern Ecuador), **3–4**

Acromegaly and obstructive sleep apnea, 469

Actigraphy sleep measurements, **4–6;** acute coronary syndrome study, 697; arthritis studies, 594; children daytime nap studies, 434; and chronotype assessment, 122; defined, 4; obesity studies, 620

Activation-synthesis hypothesis of dreaming, **7–9**

Active sleep, 267, 280, 495, 640, *See also* REM (rapid eye movement) sleep

Acute coronary syndromes, sleep patterns, **696–700**

Acute sleep deprivation, **9–11,** 485; arousal influences, 10–11; behavioral effects, 9–10; physiological influences, 11; recovery from, 11

Adams, Jenni, 392

Addictions and mood connection, 157–58

Addison's disease, 333

Adenosine, 132, 413, 540, 659, 686

Adenosine triphosphate (ATP), 96–97

ADHD. *See* Attention deficit/hyperactivity disorder (ADHD) in children

Adjustment disorders, 463

Adler, Shelley, 369

Adolescents and sleep, **660–61;** cell phone use, 411–12; changes in homeostatic bioregulatory mechanisms, 660; circadian rhythm shifts, 642–43; development, 642–43; dreams of, **13–14;** EEG and brain development, **15–16, 657–58;** effects on academic performance, 410, 642–43; eveningness, 122; influence on teen driving, 16; persistent sleep debt, 642, 644, 661; REM sleep vs. elderly persons, 21; and school schedules, 642; self-assessment tools of Circadian typology, **572–73;** and sleep cell phone use, **12–13;** television viewing, 411; video/computer game playing, 411. *See also* Teenagers and sleep disordered breathing

Adopted men's dreams, 17

Adopted women's dreams, **17–18**

Adult nightmare content, **461–62**

Aeneid (Virgil), 278